HAUNTED SKIES

VOLUME EIGHT

1980

JOHN HANSON & DAWN HOLLOWAY

With BRENDA BUTLER

HAUNTED SKIES VOLUME 8 1980

First paperback edition printed 2013 in the United Kingdom.

A catalogue record for this book is available from the British Library.

ISBN 978-0-9574944-1-1

Published by
Haunted Skies Publishing

For more copies of this book, please email: johndawn1@sky.com

Telephone: 0121 445 0340

Designed and typeset by Bob Tibbitts ~ (iSET)

Printed in Great Britain

FOREWORD
By Philip Mantle

WE have now reached volume number eight of this mammoth task undertaken by John and Dawn. Before I go any further I would like to take my hat off to both authors for the continuation of this top class work. To undertake what John and Dawn have set out to do could have been overwhelming to some authors, but they have diligently kept at it and, once again, they have produced an excellent publication and a significant contribution to both British and world ufology.

In this volume the authors have concentrated on just one year, that of 1980. It is a year I remember well myself, having only become interested in ufology in the late 1970s. In 1980 I was still learning the ropes of UFO research and investigation with colleagues at the Yorkshire UFO Society.

For many UFO researchers in Britain 1980 was the year that British ufology finally came of age. We have to remember that the modern UFO era began in June 1947 with the sighting by civilian pilot Kenneth Arnold, followed shortly in July of the same year by the alleged UFO crash near Roswell, New Mexico. In 1980 the Roswell case was just beginning to re-emerge but it was the USA that was the home of ufology and some of the most interesting cases as well.

All was to change in December 1980, with the alleged landing of a UFO in Rendlesham Forest, Suffolk.

The forest lay between the twin American air bases RAF Bentwaters and RAF Woodbridge. I'll not go into detail here of this case, as it is covered more than adequately by the authors within the pages of this book.

For British UFO researchers this case could equal anything that the Americans had, or anyone else for that matter.

Of course the UFO sceptics have an entirely different opinion, but irrespective of that, it was, to many, this incident which finally put UK ufology on the map. The late 1970s had seen some fascinating incidents. Many, if not all, have been covered in previous volumes by the authors, but 1980 saw an upward trend in UFO sightings around the UK which was to continue throughout the decade.

The year 1980 is also significant for me as well. I and my colleague, Mark Birdsall, investigated the alleged landing of a UFO near Normanton, in West Yorkshire. Again the authors cover this event in this book. It was the first such case I had ever been involved with and it is one that still resonates with me to this very day.

But 1980 was not all about the events in Rendlesham Forest. As you will see from the contents page of this book, UFO sightings came in from right across the UK. This year also saw the 'birth' of a new and controversial phenomenon that, at the time, was unique to the UK – 'crop circles' – now found just about all over the world. The debate on crop circles continues.

So was 1980 the year that British ufology finally came of age? For me personally it was, and having only just entered into ufology, I believe I could not have picked a better time. Read on and see if I am correct or not.

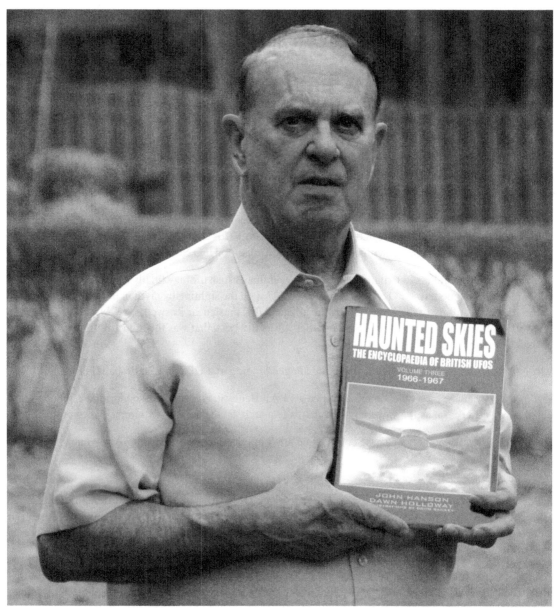

Colonel Charles Halt, Deputy Base Commander of Woodbridge in 1980, seen here recently displaying a copy of 'Haunted Skies'

INTRODUCTION

We will also examine, in our 8th Volume of *Haunted Skies,* the UFO events which occurred in 1980, including what is undoubtedly alleged to be one of the most important and controversial UFO incidents that has taken place on English soil, involving a sighting of a landed unidentified flying object and its alien occupants, witnessed by members of the USAF Airbase, stationed at RAF Woodbridge and Bentwaters, in Suffolk.

The events were important enough to be brought to the attention of The Lord Hill-Norton, to whom we wrote, wondering why such a prominent figure had taken an interest in a matter, which still attracts ridicule to this present day. In one of a number of letters sent to us he said:

> *"My position is and always has been that there are physical objects, almost certainly not man-made, regularly detected in Earth's atmosphere. I want to know what they are, who, or what is directing them, and what is their purpose."*

Courtesy of the Disclosure Project

Many people whom we came across over the intervening years felt frustrated with the *apparent* indifference adopted by the Ministry of Defence's 'flying saucer desk' who have always (irrespective of whatever decade) declined to be drawn into any discussion over sightings of UFOs brought to their attention.

They seek to convince us that the majority of UFO sightings can be explained and, as they are subsequently of no 'defence' significance, then they are of no interest. But common sense dictates the opposite.

What they are and where they come from, and what their agenda is, must be of interest to them – despite the official stance adopted towards enquires made to them by the public.

One of our greatest problems in creating an awareness of their existence, through the publication of *Haunted Skies,* is – because we have never had, and are unlikely to have, any interest from the BBC and national newspapers – who have consistently ignored us, despite having asked for some for the books!

At the time of beginning to prepare this Volume (in December, 2009) we learned of the closure of Air Desk 2a, at the MOD, as part of a cost-cutting exercise. This may give the impression UFOs are no longer of any importance to the authorities – highly unlikely, in our opinion, knowing the many occasions involving what appears to have been attempts to intercept UFOs by the RAF, and of the irrefutable evidence offered by so many people who have described seeing saucer-shaped, apparently structured, craft of unknown origin in our skies rather than a conventional aircraft.

Although three years have now passed following various 30th Anniversary 'celebrations' held in Rendlesham Forest, and organised lectures at Woodbridge, it is important to bear in mind that what was witnessed by the airmen in the forest during the end of December 1980 has its many parallels with other sightings we were to come across over the years.

A cursory search of the Internet for what many people believe to be the UK equivalent of the famous Roswell incident reveals a staggering number of web entries relating to the UFO incident, which took place in Rendlesham Forest, Suffolk, during December 1980, and still the subject of controversy.

Brenda Butler

We decided to invite Brenda Butler, a long-term friend, to be part of this Volume – an action made to recognize her boundless enthusiasm and dedication, not only towards documenting the UFO subject, but to her ongoing investigation into those events that, while although they took place now over 30 years ago, still continue to attract her attention – despite having suffered a stroke last year. She is a remarkable woman, to whom we pay tribute, and thank her for her assistance, over the years, in providing us with much material covering this period of UFO history.

If someone, new to the subject, conducted their examination of declassified documents, released through the medium of the Public Records Office, from the MOD, as being a cross-section of what is representative of reported UFO sightings, in order to form an opinion as to the existence of UFO phenomena, we would not be writing any of these books.

However, common sense dictates that they are of interest, and always have been. How can they not be? Our apparent inability to determine the nature of what UFOs represent, and where they come from, should not prevent us asking questions about something we deserve an answer to.

Calendar of UFO events – 1980

Chapter 1 – January 1980: UFO over Kent. Strange 'figure', Trowbridge. UFO over Surrey. UFO over Leicestershire. 'Flying Saucer' over Birmingham. UFOs over Kent. Close Encounter – Heald Moor, Lancashire. UFO over Farnborough, Hampshire. 'Strange lights' over Cambridgeshire. UFOs over Essex. UFO over London. Pulsating lights over Cambridgshire.

Chapter 2 – February 1980: UFOs over Suffolk. UFO over Suffolk. Triangular UFO over Dudley. UFO over Merseyside. UFO over Worcestershire. UFO over Bexleyheath, London. UFO display over Cambridgeshire. UFO over Merseyside. UFO over Peterborough. Rectangular UFO over Yorkshire.

Chapter 3 – March 1980: UFO over Bradford. UFO over Plymouth. Another UFO over Plymouth. UFO over Warwickshire. UFO over Frome. Strange 'figures', Merseyside. UFO over Halton, Cheshire. Brenda Butler. UFO over Tayside. UFO over Dundee.

Chapter 4 – April 1980: UFO tracked on radar. UFO activity increases. Pilot attacks UFO over Peruvian Capital. Another unwelcome visitor. UFO over Swindon.

Chapter 5 – May 1980: UFOs over the motorway. UFO display, Hartlepool. Close Encounters, Suffolk. UFO Exhibition, San Francisco.

Chapter 6 – June 1980: UFO over Avon and Essex. Authors' investigation into the Zygmund Jan Adamski death. Tiny 'beings' of West Malaysia. UFO over Suffolk. UFO over Somerset. Close Encounter, Torva, Cumbria. UFO over Devon. UFO over Pontefract. Close Encounter, Egham, Surrey. UFO over Kent. Russian spy radio recovered.

Chapter 7 – July 1980: UFO landing, Normanton, Yorkshire. Police sight UFOs over pylon. Mushroom-shaped UFOs over Cheshire. Close Encounter, Bramshott, Hampshire. 'Flying Saucer' over Birmingham. UFO formation over York. Triangular UFO over London. Green light over Salisbury.

Chapter 8 – August 1980: Open day for Sky Scan. Crop circles found, Westbury, Wiltshire. UFO under water, Lancashire. Cigar-shaped UFO over Essex. UFO Encounter, Herefordshire. UFO over Leominster. 'T'-shaped UFO, Devon. UFO over Hopton, Norfolk. UFOs over Mere. Encounter with UFO. UFO over Aveley. UFO over Todmorden. UFO over Kidderminster. UFO over Norfolk. UFOs over Derbyshire. UFO over Wigan. 'Flying Saucer' seen near Temple Meads, Bristol.

Chapter 9 – September 1980: UFO over West Sussex. Close Encounter at Great Yarmouth. UFO over Hawley Woods, Hampshire. UFO over Fife. UFO over Birmingham. Lights in the sky over

Worcestershire. UFOs over Tyneside. UFO over Lincolnshire. UFO Notts. and Essex. UFO over Dovercourt. UFO over West Yorkshire. UFO over Wolverhampton. UFO over Redditch. UFO over Studley. Encounter with UFO, Cheshire. UFOs over Devizes.

Chapter 10 – October 1980: Strange orange glow over East Lothian. 'Flying Saucer' over Anglesey. UFO over Emley Moor. UFO over Hampshire. UFO over Wiltshire. UFO over Criccieth. UFO over London. UFO over Anglesey.

Chapter 11 – November 1980: UFO over Accrington. UFO over Oxford. Close Encounter, Plymouth. UFO over Poole. UFO over Bodmin. Close Encounter, Plymouth. Explosions over London. 'Flying Saucers' over Suffolk. Bradford UFO. Close Encounter, Cumbria. UFO over Todmorden. UFO over Essex.

Chapter 12 – December 1980: UFO over Poole, Dorset. UFO over Basildon. UFO over Canvey Island. UFO over Parliament. Cosmos returns to Earth. UFO over RAF Alconbury. UFOs sighted over RAF Welford Airbase, Berkshire. Further UFO sightings at the base. Diamond UFO over RAF Coltishall. Previous sightings at the Base.

The Rendlesham Forest Incident includes – Did a UFO land in Suffolk? Lighthouse was the explanation. Gordon Creighton of *Flying Saucer Review*. How the public learned about the incident. Letter to the MOD – it was a lighthouse! Colonel Charles Halt. Exact dates confirmed. Brenda Butler – How it all began. UFO and its occupants sighted. Triangular craft seen over Woodbridge area, 1979. What are Triangular UFOs? Triangular UFO over Staffordshire. Diary of Brenda Butler. Close Encounter in the forest. Landing area pointed out. Airman Steve Roberts. February 1981 – A visit to see Squadron Leader Donald Moreland. Centenary House, Leeds – Lecture by Colonel Halt. John Burroughs. Jim Penniston. Philip Mantle Interview. Dennis Porley. Chris Arnold. Involvement of the Suffolk Police. David King. Suffolk Constabulary. Letter to Georgina Bruni. Police visit the forest again. Letter to Georgina Bruni. Followed by strange lights. UFO over Woodbridge Suffolk. Colonel Halt's narrative continues. Sgt James Penniston narrative continues. Triangular UFO over Leicestershire. The Object was tracked on radar. Steve Roberts. Air Traffic Controllers tracked down and interviewed. Larry Warren. UFO landing and occupants – 1969. *Daily Mail*, August 2011. *OMNI Magazine*. Brenda Butler. Colonel Halt's narrative continues. The landing sites. The route. John Burroughs. Film taken of the UFO encounter. Colonel Halt's narrative continues. Colonel Halt during interview with Robert Hastings. Unauthorised aircraft lands at RAF Woodbridge in 1980. Visit to see Colonel Halt. Bob Tibbitts, former head of Coventry UFO Research Group. Nick Pope comments on Georgina Bruni. The Lord Hill-Norton.

Witness time line: Meteor Display over Europe, 25th December 1980. UFO sighted over Airbase, 25th December 1980. Official response following debriefing. Anne Hopton-Scott. UFOs sighted over Ipswich. Strange lights seen over Airbase, 11pm, 26th December 1980. Strange lights seen, 11pm, 26th December 1980. Strange lights over the forest, 11pm, 26th December 1980. UFO seen and security alert, 26th December 1980. UFO seen over the forest. Marks found in forest. Alert at the Airbase, 27th December 1980. UFO seen over Woodbridge, 2.30am, 27th December 1980. Highpoint Prison placed on alert, 27th December 1980. Questions raised in the House, April 2001, Lord Steven Bassam. Silver missile seen in the forest, 27th December 1980. Bright 'light' seen over Rendlesham Forest, 11pm, 27th December 1980. Chuck Daldorf, 27th/28th December 1980. Rick Bobo interviewed by Georgina

Bruni. Interviews with Bill Ferris and Richard Kirk. 'Lights' seen over the Airbase, 28th December 1980. End of witness time line.

First World War UFO sighting, Suffolk. The Halt tape recording. Mike Sacks. RAF Neatishead. The faulty Radar tape. UFO display over RAF Neatishead. Nigel Kerr. Gary Baker. Visit to the MOD, 1983. Ralph Noyes. It was the Lighthouse! Chris Pennington – A Russian aircraft landed! It was a Russian Satellite. Apollo Command Module. Was it a UFO that crash-landed and needed repairs? Charles Affleck. Probe Group and their investigation. Colonel Halt interviewed by Brenda Butler. 1996, Robert Hastings and interference with Nuclear Missiles on Base. Project Moondust. Material recovered from the landing site. UFO Conference, Nebraska 1983. UFO filmed over Suffolk, 2000. UFO photographed over Suffolk, 2011. UFO Display over Suffolk, 2004. Fall of stones, and even an elephant! John Hanson and Dawn Holloway. Gordon Goodger. Don Ramkin. Orbs, Mists and Light Phenomena. Glowing object over Bentwaters – 1995.

The Investigation Continues

Additional information received from Matt Lyons of BUFORA. UFOs sighted over Rendlesham Forest 2013. Squadron Leader Donald Moreland. Previously unpublished information now shown. Colonel Halt addresses audience in 2012. Project Blue Book. MUFON Report on Travel Voucher – received from David MacDonald, Executive Director. 'Spinning top' UFO over the Forest, 27th December 1980. Mystery men now identified – 30 years later! Britain's Project Blue Book. Alien seen on the Airbase. Lieutenant Alan Brown. Transcript of interview held with Sgt Randy Smith. Control Tower, Bentwaters – 1983. Declassified Documents of interest. The Lighthouse was not the answer! Colonel Halt comments on the taped interview with Adrian Bustinza and Larry Warren 1984. Ray Bouche. Chuck De Caro. The Office of Special Investigations. Major O'Day denies any involvement by OSI and concludes it to be a hoax. Interview with Adrian Bustinza in 1987. Larry Fawcett interview. Colonel Williams denies knowledge. Sgt. Adrian Bustinza describes the alien machine. Steve Roberts. In June 2013 MOD declassified its UFO files. David and Linda Bryant of Spacerocks website, the couple photograph apparent humanoid image in the forest.

INDEX and CREDITS

Examining The Evidence

Strange light seen, December 26th 1980. Statements taken: John Burroughs, Jim Penniston. Jim said this at the National Press Club. Ted Conrad remarks on Penniston and Burroughs. Jim's Facebook entry response to Conrad. Deep Throat illustration as used in Sky Crash. Mike Sacks. Bob Tibbitts – Consultant for *Haunted Skies*, comments. David Bryant. Master Sergeant J.D. Chandler. Fred Buran. Monroe Ruby Nevels. Major Malcolm Zickler. Claim of piece of metal found at Rendlesham landing site. Examination of metallic debris found in Ohio USA. Metallic debris falls from UFO Ohio. Nathan's Metal. A visit to the Forest in August 2013. Landing at Midnight, Ipswich Fire Service. Georgina Bruni speaks at UFO Conference. 2002, Tim Egercic of the 81st Police Squadron. Gary Tomoyasu, Base Photographer. The Hull connection, December 1980. UFO sighted – Interference with Motor Vehicle. Billy Rhodes (Wedgner) UFO sighted over Hull. UFO over Hull – January 1987. Further Documents. Final, few words. Update on samples. VOLUME 9 1981-1986 – Peek into the future.

Haunted Skies Scrapbook

ACKNOWLEDGEMENTS

Gordon Creighton, formerly the editor of *FSR* (*Flying Saucer Review*), a distinguished diplomat, whose knowledge of UFOs was second to none. We felt privileged when he invited us to be consultants, following a visit to his house in Rickmansworth, Hertfordshire, to discuss the publication of *Haunted Skies*, and granted us permission to refer to some of the cases contained within *FSR*.

Sadly, Gordon passed away some years ago. We were honoured to attend his funeral and would also like to thank his son, Philip Creighton, for permission to refer to cases contained within the magazine.

Brenda Butler, now a good friend, from Leiston, Suffolk, who is considered a leading worldwide authority on the events that took place in Rendlesham Forest, in December 1980, and permission granted by Jenny Randles, for the use of any of her work, and various conversations held with Dot Street.

Brenda also allowed us access to an enormous wealth of tape-recorded interviews, photographs, personal diaries, and sighting reports, obtained while running the *East Anglian Paranormal Research Association*, with Ron West. We would also like to thank Colonel Charles Halt, Peter Robbins, for photos, Larry Warren for permission to use some of his photographs, Peter Parish for his sketches, Chris Pennington for his knowledge on the subject, Jim Penniston, John Burroughs, and Nick Pope for material regarding Georgina Bruni.

Margaret Ellen Fry (*now a firm friend*) – author/head of *The Welsh Federation of Independent Ufologists* and member of *Contact UK* – for her assistance, understanding, and the opportunity to share not only her many personal experiences but access to investigations into reported UFO activity, going back to the 1950s.

We would like to thank **Philip Mantle** for encouragement, assistance and submission of a Foreword. Philip has also supplied us with many rare photographs, relating to other researchers, including Mark and Graham Birdsall, and original case files relating to investigations carried out by the *Yorkshire UFO Society*. In particular we would like to thank Graham Birdsall for his permission to refer to his excellent investigation held into the curious case of Zygmund Adamski, who was found deceased in Todmorden coal yard, in 1980, and retired Police Officer, Alan Godfrey.

Daniel Goring, former editor of *Earth-link* magazine – a specialist in his own field, responsible for many investigations during the 1970s, around the London and Essex areas – for his assistance and allowing us to quote from specific sightings contained within the magazines. He has also put us in touch with many witnesses and UFO researchers, including Bill Eden, Phyllis Mooney and Edward Harris. Daniel has also provided us with a considerable number of previously unpublished sighting reports from around the mid to later part of the 20th Century, and should be praised for his commitment to recording for posterity, the events covered by his group.

Ivan W. Bunn of the *Lantern* magazine series – We would like to thank you for all your help in allowing us access to research and investigations into reported UFO activity, over the years.

Nicholas Maloret, of WATSUP – We would like to thank him for his continuing encouragement and permission to refer to a number of investigations conducted by him, and other members of the organisation.

Peter Tate, Bristol UFO Researcher – Thank you for your immense assistance and for providing us with various documents and sighting reports, researched by you over the years, including personal letters from Arthur Shuttlewood. A 'smashing' man (who is no longer with us) remembered for those scintillating conversations, held late in the evening, discussing UFOs in your own imitable style, interspersed with liberal doses of humour – a pleasure to have known.

Ian Myrzglod, of *Probe* – We would like to thank him for advice and assistance, and allowing us to refer to a number of UFO sightings investigated by his group. Also thanks to Marty Moffat, and others, for the loan of photographs.

Matt Lyons, head of BUFORA, for his continued support and encouragement with producing the *Haunted Skies* series of books. He is a credit to the organisation.

Omar Fowler – previously with SIGAP (*Surrey Investigation of Anomalous Phenomena*) – now PRA, Derby (*Phenomenon Research Association*) and consultant for *Flying Saucer Review* – for allowing us permission to refer to specific cases, over the years, and access to your synopsis, entitled *UFO Guardian of the Planet Earth*, which relates to many reports of UFO activity, catalogued by you.

Malcolm Robinson, SPI (*Scottish Phenomena Investigations*) for his assistance.

Tony Pace, previously head of UFO Investigations for BUFORA, for advice and encouragement over many years, and allowing us to include details from him and Roger Stanway's investigations into reported UFO activity over the Staffordshire area.

Bob Tibbitts of CUFORG (*Coventry UFO Research Group*) who has allowed us access to the Group's archives, and for personal letters and his typesetting and graphic design work.

Those delightful ladies – **Kathleen Smith** and **Pat Smith** – along with Pat's then husband, **Fred Smith**, previously members of the of the *Isle of Wight UFO Society*. They were responsible, together with **John Feakins** and **Rose & Leonard Cramp**, for producing over 80 early UFO magazines (*UFOLOG*) cataloguing UFO activity over the British Isles during the mid 20th Century. Thank you, Kath, for entrusting us with a staggering amount of personal letters and UFO files, collected by you and other members, which would have been lost from history if it had not been for your dedication in cataloguing such matters.

Sadly, Kath passed away a few years ago – now gone, but not forgotten.

We would like to commend **Paul & Denette France** for their help and encouragement. Sadly, Denette – who was responsible for assisting us with some of the early investigations, preparing various sketches and keeping us awake with her cackling laughter – died at the age of 50. She is sadly missed; a dynamic woman who loved life.

We would also like to thank **Wayne Mason, David Sankey, Steven Franklin, David Bryant, Jason Chapman**, and others, who have furnished us with illustrations for use in Volume 8.

We would also like to thank the many people whom we met in Rendlesham Forest, over the years, for the use of literally hundreds of anomalous photographs which, in the main, were taken by Brenda Butler, Peter Parish, Don Ramkin, David & Linda Bryant, and others from various groups and organisations.

Mason

Maude

Finally, special thanks to our much loved dog, Maude, who accompanied us. Sadly, she passed away on the 18th May 2009.

We would also like to say farewell to Mason – a lovely dog, owned by Brenda Butler.

Mason, who died at an early age, was a regular companion during those night-time walks through the forest. He had some very entertaining habits for those unwary visitors who met him for the first time. This included picking up a long branch, which was held between the jaws at a horizontal angle, and then running from one end to another of a queue of walkers, tapping them gently on the backs of their legs.

If we have forgotten anyone, we apologise and will include them in the credits for *Haunted Skies* Volume 9.

CHAPTER 1
JANUARY 1980

UFO over Kent

AT 8am on 1st January 1980, a gold crescent-shaped object was seen in the sky over Whitstable, Kent.

During the afternoon of the same date, Philip Stockdale – a schoolboy living in Barnehurst, Kent – contacted Margaret Fry, after sighting a blue ball-shaped object in the sky, which passed between the clouds before descending, apparently making an inspection of his garden and moving away. This UFO seems to have adopted the same mannerisms of the one involved in the Met-Police helicopter chase, the previous year, according to now retired Police Constable William Bishop, who (2012) still continues to try and find out further information, despite there being no official record of that matter.

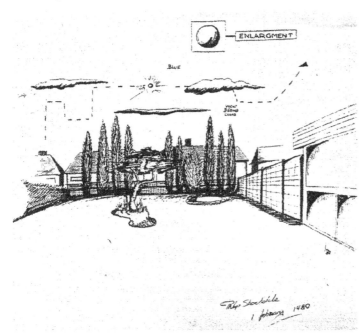

(Source: Valerie Martin)

At 1pm on 2nd January 1980, a red, domed, object was seen in the sky over Edgware, Middlesex. Unfortunately, this is the only information we have on the incident. At 7.54pm the same day, a fluorescent object was reported in the sky over Balsall Common, on the A452, close to the border with Birmingham. The witness told Margaret Westwood, of the Birmingham group, UFOSIS, that he watched it for about ten minutes and it was not an aircraft, or helicopter.

At 7.12pm on 4ᵗʰ January 1980, a saucer-shaped object was sighted over Haslington, Crewe.

At 11.30pm, an oblong object was sighted in the sky over Winsford, Cheshire. Just over a minute later, it vanished from view.

On the 2ⁿᵈ, 3ʳᵈ, 4ᵗʰ and 8ᵗʰ January 1980, a mysterious *'star-like object'* was seen in the sky over the Crayford, Barnehurst, and Dartford areas. Many people contacted the police and various authorities, wishing to identify the object, which was described as being far larger than any star. One of those witnesses was Margaret Fry, who has been a valuable source of assistance with regard to reported UFO activity over the years that we have known her. As we have said before, she is a credit to what UFO research is all about.

(Source: Margaret Fry)

Strange 'figure', Trowbridge

Mr Rodney James, aged 33 – a lecturer in painting and decorating at Trowbridge College, Wiltshire – was awoken at 5am on 5ᵗʰ January 1980, by a glowing *'figure'* inside his bedroom, who communicated the following conversation, telepathically:

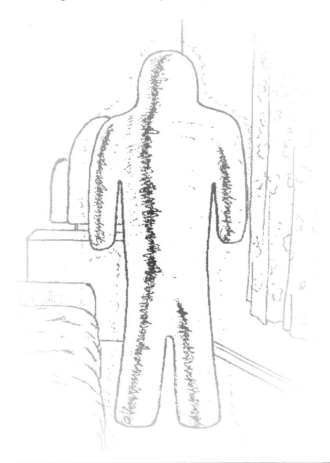

"When Homo sapiens were just developing, they explored this planet and some of their kind mated with the Earth people to form a very adaptable race. They knew this would take many Earth years, but the result would be a race of people who would colonize planets around theirs. They know that they are close to this because they have taken samples to these planets and they have survived for a few years. When there become too many people, they send one of their own to start conflict or disease to reduce the numbers, so the planet can support them. Their main problem, at the moment, is that the Earth is gradually splitting into two along the rift. Crescent-shaped craft are being used to fire missiles from each point into the ground, which turns into a liquid which solidifies; they hope this will prevent the split."

At this point the shimmering green-white light *'figure'* – likened to a 3D projection, some 7ft in height, with a lack of facial features, feet and hands, ending in stumps – faded, like a TV picture from the outside into the centre, and disappeared from view.

Mr James, who has told this extremely strange version of events which befell him, to many people, over the years – and accepted their sceptical response – was judged a genuine person by various UFO investigators that had met him on a number of occasions (some of whom we had spoken to) and saw no reason to suspect a hoax – although they did consider whether there was a likelihood that this 'experience' was as a result of a hypnopompic dream (a vivid dreamlike hallucination, which occurs as one is waking up) Mr James said:

> *"You must make of it as you will. I do not necessarily think that what I saw was an extraterrestrial being. I don't know what category to put it into."*

(Source: *Probe*, Ian Mrzyglod)

UFO over Surrey

At 7.30am on 5th January 1980, an oblong-shaped UFO was seen in the sky over St. Ann's, in Barking, Essex. Seconds later, it disappeared from view.

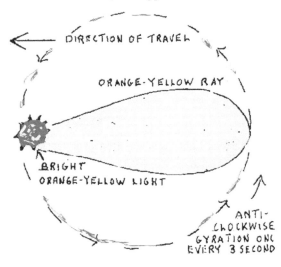

At 5pm, the same day, Richard Pywell – Physicist and member of the British Astronomical Association, from Ottershaw, Surrey – was about to start his car, when he saw a yellow *'light'* moving slowly across the sky, which was:

> *". . . five times the brightness of Venus, heading eastwards. Around it was a ray of rotating light, which increased in size as it came around to the rear. I saw a twin-engine 'Piper' aircraft, descending towards Fairoaks Aerodrome, and actually pass under the 'light'. I continued to watch the 'light' for five minutes or so, until it was lost from view in the distance."*

At 5.50pm, again on the same day, a white coloured UFO was reported in the sky over Upper Team, Stoke-on-Trent. **(Source: Personal interview/SIGAP/UFOSIS)**

At 8pm on 6th January 1980, a number of mysterious lights, resembling stars, were seen in the sky over Little Walden, Essex, for five minutes. It is believed that this was the same phenomena seen 30 minutes later – this time over Saffron Walden. **(Source: Dan Goring)**

UFO over Leicestershire

On 7th January 1980, Cameron Wyatt (12) from Willow Crescent, Market Harborough, Leicestershire, and Adrian Goldthorpe, were out playing, with two friends, at the bottom of the road, at 4.30pm, when they saw:

> *". . . a saucer-shaped object, with a round dome underneath showing five flashing lights following a tractor across a nearby field. The driver seemed unaware that there was a UFO behind him. A few seconds later it disappeared."*

The sighting came after a weekend of interrupted power supplies in the area – later explained away by the Electricity Board as a switch fault, which separated the grid at Wellingborough.

(Source: Crystal Hogben, *Magic Saucer/Marlborough Mail,* 10.1.80/Mr J Capewell, BUFORA)

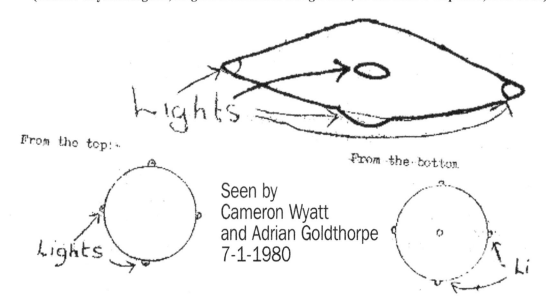

Seen by
Cameron Wyatt
and Adrian Goldthorpe
7-1-1980

At 7.45pm on 8th January 1980, another sighting of mysterious lights was reported over Gt. Warley, Brentwood, in Essex.

'Flying Saucer' over Birmingham

Schoolboys from Great Barr, Birmingham – Darren Sinar and Dean Basford – were out playing near Highfield Road, in early January 1980, when they saw:

> *". . . an object, which looked like a saucer, with another 'saucer' turned upside-down and placed on the top, moving up and down above us in the sky, showing flashing lights on its top, bottom, and along the sides."*

This was not the only UFO report in the area, according to the newspaper, who outlined the sighting of *'a long strip of light'* seen in the sky, three months ago, by Mrs Denise Kenny, who took some photographs of the object.

The whereabouts of Mrs Kenny, and those photos, allegedly being examined by a local UFO Society, remain unknown. **(Source: The *Sandwell Evening Mail,* 15.1.80)**

At 3am on 10th January 1980, a square-shaped UFO was seen moving through the sky over Bastable Avenue, Barking, in Essex. It was seen to hover in the sky for approximately 20 minutes, before moving away and out of sight.

SANDWELL EVENING MAIL 15 JAN 80

Close encounter of a

Wadelt — 14.1.80

flying kind

TWO Great Barr school-boys have had their own 'close encounter of the third kind" — when a "UF" hovered over them.

And the two youngsters have drawn almost identical pictures of the unidentified flying object which they say flew over Sandwell last night.

Darren Sinar, aged 11, and his friend Dean Basford, aged 11, both of Highfield Road, were playing near Dean's home when an object hovered above them in the sky.

"It loked like a saucer with another saucer turned upside down and placed on top of it," said Dean.

"Lights were flashing on on the top and bottom of it, and all along the sides. It hovered in the sky for about 15 minutes and kept moving up and down. We were petrified."

The two youngsters ran home where Dean's mother — who didn't believe them — asked them to draw what they had seen. She was surprised when both drew very similar pictures — although

the boys sat in different corners of the room.

"It was in the sky for some time. It obviously an aircraft or a helicopter," said Darren.

Three months ago, 31-year-old mother of five, Mrs. Denise Kenny, who also lives in Highfield Road, reported a strange light hovering in the sky. B43SA

She took photographs of it and these are now being investigated by a local UFO Spotting Society.

Mrs. Kenny said the object — which she described as a long strip of light — hovered for some minutes before disappearing.

Dean Basford

Daren Sinar with his "UFO" drawing.

UFOs over Kent

On 11th January 1980, Mrs 'Pixie' Revell from Whitstable, Kent, was driving home along Thanet Way, near the Long Reach roundabout, at 8.55pm, when she saw:

> "... two shafts of piercing light to my left, above which could be seen a number of small red lights in a square, about 200yds away, and 100ft off the ground.

Between the beams of light were what appeared to be criss-cross metal strips, like angle iron; I thought, at first, it might have been a helicopter in trouble, trying to land by the lights on the roundabout. I slowed down, thinking what idiot would try and land near the roundabout, but didn't stop. The next thing that happened was that I actually drove underneath whatever it was, as it landed on the ground over nearby ancient woodland. As I was on my way to pick up my husband, I didn't stop, but when I drove past the same place, ten minutes later, there was nothing to be seen. I felt traumatised, for some months, as a result of this incident."

Mrs Revell was later contacted by Mr Paul Rigden, who told her that his son, Jeremy (14) of Applegarth Caravan Park, Seasalter, and his friend, Trevor Mulford, had sighted:

MYSTERY CRAFT THAT BEAMED DOWN FROM SKY

18·1·80

A WHITSTABLE woman believes she may have seen an unidentified flying object on Friday night.

Mrs. Pixie Revell, of Grimthorpe Avenue, was driving along Thanet Way near the Long Reach roundabout when she saw two strong beams of light and three or four small ones in the sky.

"The craft looked as if it was trying to come into land, but I could not tell how far it was off the ground." said Mrs. Revell.

"I slowed down, but did not stop.

"I saw probes of angle iron coming from the craft and it was not a plane. I thought at first it was a helicopter or that someone was in trouble and trying to land by the lights of the roundabout, but when I came back ten minutes later everything had gone.

"I am a reasonably level-headed person and there was no noise at all coming from the craft."

Mrs. Revell said she saw the object at 8.55 p.m. and at the time there were no vehicles on the roundabout or in front on the road.

Mrs. Pixie Revell who thinks she saw a U.F.O. near the Long Reach roundabout. WC8840/14

We saw UFO as well say two schoolboys

25·1·80

Jeremy Rigden (left) and his friend Trevor Mulford draw their impression of the object they saw at Seasalter. WF9484/9

BEAMS OF LIGHT SPOTTED IN SKY

TWO Whitstable boys think they saw the unidentified flying object spotted by Mrs. Pixie Revell at Long Reach roundabout.

Jeremy Rigden (14) of Saddleton Road, and his friend Trevor Mulford (14), of Applegarth Caravan Park, Seasalter, said they saw two strong beams of light moving towards Thanet Way on the same Friday night that Mrs. Revell saw them.

After reading about the story in last week's Whitstable Times they realised they had probably seen the same thing.

"They were coming over the marshes towards Thanet Way and I was looking out to sea when I saw them," said Trevor.

"At first I thought it was an ordinary jet light but then we thought it was a spaceship and that was why we hid in the shed until it had passed over.

"I thought I saw a slight piece of iron coming at an angle out of its side."

After they had seen the object both boys told their fathers. At first Jeremy's father Paul disbelieved them, but when he read about Mrs. Revell's experience he rung her up to tell her of Jeremy's.

Both boys said there was

but I think they were scared this time because there was no noise but just these two lights coming from it."

"All the family like: science fiction and I really believe there must be some thing there."

Mrs. Valerie Martin, o Kingsdown Park, Whit stable, a member of the British U.F.O. Research Association, said she and Mrs. Revell rang Manston and were told it could have been a helicopter or Har rier jet.

"There was no sound a all according to the boy: and Mrs. Revell, so this seems very puzzling, but really do not know what i could have been." said Mrs

". . . two strong 'beams of light' moving towards Thanet Way, heading over the marshes",

. . . which they initially took to be an aircraft, until it passed overhead – allowing them to see what looked like

". . . a slight piece of iron projecting out of its side, at an angle".

Mrs Valerie Martin – a member of BUFORA – carried out an investigation into this matter and contacted RAF Manston, who suggested to her that it could have been a helicopter or 'Harrier' Jump Jet.

(Source: As above/Personal interview)

At 8.30pm on 11th January 1980, two mysterious white beams of light were seen in the sky over Seasalter, Kent.

This was followed by a sighting, at 8.55pm, of an object, described as showing red and white beams of light, over Whitstable, Kent. A short time later, a third sighting occurred over Mytchett, Surrey, at 9.35pm, when a red and white oblong object was seen in the sky – presumably the same UFO.   (**Source:** *FSR*)

At 8.12am on 12th January 1980, a crescent-shaped object was seen in the sky for five minutes over Cotheridge, in Worcestershire.   (**Source:** *Sky Scan*)

Close Encounter – Heald Moor, Lancashire

Ex Royal Marine William Clifford Barrett (59) of Dixon Street, Barrowford, Burnley, Lancashire – who had seen active service during the Second World War and had taken part in saving some of his comrades lives, while under fire – told of a UFO sighting that took place when employed as lorry driver, at 6.15am on 14th January 1980. However, prior to outlining that incident far more fully, it may be of some interest to tell of an earlier incident of some strangeness, which occurred three weeks previously, just before Christmas 1979, as the location was the same for both.

> *"At about 9.00am, I was crossing the bridge over the Burnley to Todmorden railway line when I noticed a jeep on the embankment, close to the railway line to my left. Puzzled, I continued on my journey. Seconds later, a police car pulled out of the lay-by and allowed me to pass him. As the Police car overtook me I flashed my lights at the vehicle, which came to a halt. Strangely, nobody got out. I stopped, got out of my vehicle, and walked over to the car and told the officer inside about the jeep. At this point I noticed some tyre tracks, presumably made by the jeep, which led from a farm above the railway line, and continued through two fields, before coming up against broken fences. Although I couldn't see the jeep at that point, I wondered if the marks had been made by the vehicle before ending up down the embankment. The policeman said to me 'My duty is done' and drove away."*

We concur with the observations made by BUFORA investigators – Jenny Randles and Peter Hough – that there is no evidence to link this matter with the UFO incident that was to take place, other than they occurred at exactly the same spot, which provides us with some suspicion, albeit tenuous, that there was a connection.

Returning to the event of the 14th January, William had been to Courtaulds Mill, at Hollingsworth, to pick up a large consignment of yarn. As he had to drop off a package in Todmorden, he made his way along the A646, heading south- east, towards Todmorden, on a dark cold morning, with lots of cloud about.

After driving over the railway bridge at Heald Moor, in his Ford Custom 10-ton vehicle, owned by Brookvale Mills, he approached the lay-by on his right, where he had encountered the police vehicle and jeep previously. He then became aware of a loud humming sound. Seconds later, the headlights of his vehicle picked-up a strange shape on the road ahead, described by him as a large, dark, metallic object, showing three red 'beams of light' projecting from the top onto the ground. He said:

> *"I recalled seeing several men moving around it, as if doing some type of task. I thought, at first, that they were workmen, using a machine to lay tar along the road. The machine they were using looked like a toast rack.*
>
> *As I came closer to the object, now crawling along the road, I realised it was a tortoise-shaped 'craft', with a curved pipe on top, which led into the thin air. I wondered if this*

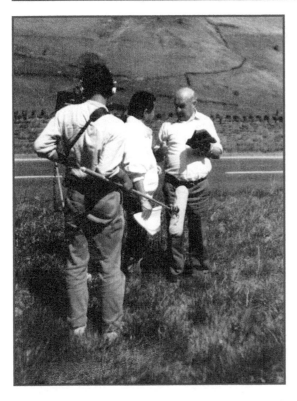

was some sort of refuelling operation, or that some secret weapon was being tested. I wasn't unduly worried because I saw two 'figures', who then moved from the side of it and appeared to be inspecting the red beam.

All I observed was their silhouettes in front of the light. One of the 'figures' wore a peaked cap and a dark two-piece uniform – the type a policeman, or military, would wear; his arms were at his side. The second 'figure' was wearing a one-piece suit, grey or silver in colour, and he was stooping down looking at the object, as if inspecting it for damage.

The lights were bright – like arc welders – flickering and rotating. They caused the silhouettes of the men to break up as they moved in front of them, not unlike a laser display casting a dim reflection on the bracken that glowed red."

Suddenly the lorry lost power to its lights. William 'felt black' and believed he may have lost consciousness, although the sound of the diesel engine was still being heard. The next thing he was aware of was 'coming to' and finding himself at some unspecified point along the road, approximately about a quarter of a mile away, before the village of Portsmouth – power having been restored to the lights.

William told Jenny and Peter that all he could think of was 'escape' and told of seeing some people and a van after passing Mons Mill, on the outskirts of Todmorden. (The scene of the Alan Godfrey encounter in June 1980)

"It was growing first light. I passed the clock face on Todmorden fire station but never noticed the time, because it's usually incorrect. I passed the Police Station but decided not to report what had taken place, feeling that they wouldn't have believed me. As I headed towards Oldham, I noticed my left leg was aching, but thought nothing of it.

When I reached my destination, at Oldham, another truck turned up, which I thought odd as it doesn't arrive till later.

I asked the driver for the time. He told me it was 9.10am, which shocked me, as I realised I couldn't recall what had happened in the two hours of missing time."

William arrived home in the evening, and went to bed early. As he undressed for bed, he noticed a strange bruise mark just behind the back of his left knee. It was about the size of a ten pence piece, and stood out from the skin about a 16th of an inch. It was very light blue in colour, showing an X-ray or star effect on the

Dear Sir,
11/8/1985

This as been my problem for the last five years. The story I am about to tell is true in every word, the reason for wanting to tell it is because I maybe holding back some vital information. The reason why I have kept it to myself is because I was afraid, not at the time, but afterwards I thought it was some thing "supernatural" I have been a some thing "supernatural" I have been a driver for the last forty years. I was stopped by a U.F.O. in the Todmorden valley at about 6.15 a.m. on the 14th Feb 1980. The only proof of this story is what was there. and what I saw, before I was frozen. that winter morning was fine, but was frozen. that winter morning was fine, but was no moon. or no east because there was no moon. or no east because there was just stars to be seen. My experience was just stars to be seen. My experience was between "Clivager and the railway bridge between "Clivager and Todmorden" when I turned that corner I said to myself. whats going on here, first the noise, looking straight ahead. of me 60 yards noise, looking straight ahead. of me 60 yards in front was this machine. which I thought was plumes underneath, of course they were in front was this machine. which I thought not. there were people, moving about infront of it. so I was quite relaxed thinking they were work men working on the road. But it have to be off the road.

①

belive it, it had taken me over three hours, a journey that only takes one hour. Now does one explain it. I dont smoke. and drink. I dont have black-outs or anything like that. or I would not be a driver. That night. when going to bed, had a look at my leg. God, what the hell is that. a bruise about as big as a ten pence piece. light blue in colour and standing up about ⅛ of an inch. thinking. how could these out of space people have done this to me. I was parked out of my cab. thats what I thought they have simple ways. for two years I said nothing to any one. not even my own doctor. thinking some one must listen to my story. decided to write to "Grenada Television" This is your night My wife said. That programe is for only civil rights. never mind. they were some very decent people. they sent me a lovely reply, stating that U.F.O. are a phenomena and very gratefull to them. and gave me your address. Sir a machine will self boosters is not. a phenomena. just one load of power. these space ships dont come down to earth with given el. but our defence. nothing living just with these our

③

ther I saw a pipe on the top. It must be something. if pipe. No. it could not be the pipe ends. As I got nearer the redness as gone, it's now white. there is two figures of people now silhouetted between the Machine and me. One stood straight up. the other with bent knees. I thought whats up with him, standing like that? little did I know it was a police man being lead into that space ship. because when I got parralel with the machine I looked back and saw the front of the people. the one stood straight was in uniform the other was light grey. the lights on a U.F.O. are not good because they are orks. My distance would be about 50 feet. looking straight to my front. What the hell, is happening I have no. lights. breaking. dead man out of gear. I have stopped. then my body jumped. the lights are on. I'm motoring going down the valley I did not see a vehicle or a person until I was going past "Morse Mill," passing the police station, thinking, shall I report it. No. I escaped so it does not matter. Any way what would they have said. Its coming light the clouds are breaking. On my journey to "Littom. my left leg is aching before at my destination I could not

②

the weakest part of man is the brain they put us to sleep, so simple. I think it is the fuel they use. When people have a nervous disability in hospital, the treatment. "electricity" is just through the brain very slow. so they go to sleep. Now when the lights went out on my lorry. some thing was taking the heat from the bulb elements. the power was being drawn to it. When I was parralel with the machine there were this rays being deflected slowly by some thing going round at the top of each one. my opinion is that this white heat treated underneath. goes up through the pipe on top. onto it's own body. then the boosters draw in the heat. I wish you success with the technology of these U.F.O. for the sake of mankind these vehicles would be very good. I think people could be put to sleep in hospital. with out anasthetic.

Yours faithfully

Mr. W. G. Bossatt

②

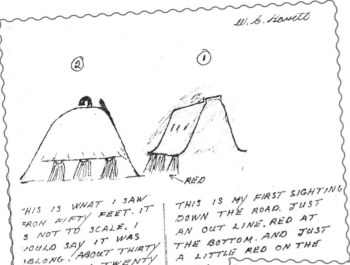

W. C. Howitt

② ①

← RED

THIS IS WHAT I SAW FROM FIFTY FEET. IT IS NOT TO SCALE. I WOULD SAY IT WAS ABLONG. ABOUT THIRTY FEET LONG. TWENTY FEET HIGH. THE WIDTH I DONT KNOW. THE RAYS ARE FROM UNDER A CANOPY. AT THE TOP OF THE RAYS WAS ARKS. THERE MUST BE HOLES IN THE BODY ABOVE THE ARKES. AS THE MACHINE WAS SILHOUETTED IN ITS OWN LIGHT. THERE WERE NO WINDOWS

THIS IS MY FIRST SIGHTING DOWN THE ROAD. JUST AN OUT LINE. RED AT THE BOTTOM. AND JUST A LITTLE RED ON THE BODY.

edge. Next morning, the bruise had disappeared.

Following his experience William attempted to contact various people, hoping that they may be persuaded to carry out some investigation into the matter, but was initially unsuccessful.

In 1981, he wrote to the *Sunday Mirror*, but never received any reply. Some months later, he wrote to *Granada TV*.

W. C. Howitt

HAT WINTER MORNING WAS FINE, BUT WAS OVERCAST ECAUSE THERE WAS NO MOON OR STARS TO BE SEEN. Y EXPERIENCE WAS JUST OVER THE BRIDGE THAT HE RAILWAY RUNS UNDERNEATH. BETWEEN 'CLIVAGER' ND 'PORTSNOUTH' VILLAGE. IN THE 'TODMODEN' VALLEY HEN TURNING THAT CORNER. THINKING. WHATS GOING N. FIRST THE BUZZING NOISE. LOOKING STRAIGHT HEAD. DOWN THE ROAD. AND A LITTLE TO THE RIGHT YBE 60yₐₑₛ THERE WAS A MACHINE. WITH PEOPLE NOOVING ABOUT IN THE RAYS. THINKING THEY WERE VORK MEN. THE RAYS WERE A KIND OF RED. I THOUGHT WAS FLAMES. GETTING NEARER I THOUGH ITS REFUELIN ECAUSE THERE WAS A PIPE ON THE TOP. THEN THE ED CHANGED TO WHITE. NOW. THERE WERE TWO IGURES OF PEOPLE SILHOUETTED BETWEEN THE NACHINE AND ME. ONE STOOD STRAIGHT. THE OTHER VITH BENT KNEES. GETTING PARALLEL. TO THE MACHINE WAS LOOKING STRAIGHT INTO THE RAYS. AND TURNED O LOOK BACK. ONE WAS A POLICE MAN. THE OTHER NAS LIGHT GRAY IN COLOUR. LOOKING STRAIGHT IHEAD. I SHOUTED OUT. MY LIGHTS ARE OUT. I JUST AW BLACK. I REMENBER STOPING. AND STARTING. AGAIN. UT THE TIME LOST. NO. !

THIS IS THE OLD ROAD. IS NOW A LAY BY.

SPACE SHIP

MY LORRY

STOP NO

PORTSMOUTH VILLAGE.

CLIVAGER → VILLAGE

⑤

In 2012, we contacted William and spoke to him at length about his experience. He told us that the strange mark is still there on the back of his leg, and that he regards what happened to him as the most incredible experience he has ever come across during his life.

At 5.30pm the same day, a circular object seen in the sky was reported over Fishponds, Bristol; five seconds later, it vanished from sight.

(Source: *UFO 1*)

At 8.15pm on 15th January 1980, a spinning red globe was seen in the sky over Bradley, North Yorkshire, according to Tony Dodd.

UFO over Farnborough, Hampshire

At 4am on 20th January 1980, milkman Fred Smith was 'on his round' through the streets of Cove, near Farnborough, when he paused to look up at the clear night sky – still dotted with a few stars, with the promise of a fine day – and noticed an illuminated object in the sky, approaching his position from the North. Thinking it was probably a high flying aircraft or satellite, he continued to observe – his curiosity now aroused – and checked his watch, which showed 4.07am.

> *"The 'light' had now increased in size and was beginning to take on a crescent shape, with a bluish haze around it.*
>
> *It didn't look man-made. I began to feel uneasy. By now there was no doubt it was crescent-shaped, with a bluish glow all around it, flying quite fast, at a high altitude, when I realised it was slowing down. Suddenly it came to a stop, hovering in the sky above Farnborough. I could feel the hairs on the back of my neck standing on end. After a short time, the 'craft' slowly turned around and accelerated away northwards, and was soon gone from sight."*

Fred tried to put it to the back of his mind and get on with his job, but fate was to decree this was not the only strange thing he was going to witness that early morning.

At 5.26am a Boeing 747 aircraft flew slowly through the sky overhead, followed by the appearance of the now familiar strange 'luminous craft' approaching across the sky from the North.

Fred said,

> ". . . *its crescent shape becoming visible, as it stopped overhead and began circling over Farnborough. I was spellbound. It was doing this sort of skidding motion – almost a sideways movement as it circled – then it flew inwards and stopped over Farnborough, again, completely silent for 6-7minutes.*"

Several minutes later, the silent glowing 'craft' turned again and accelerated away, northwards.

(Source: Omar Fowler, SIGAP/PRA)

Other sightings for this day included a report of a dome-shaped UFO, seen at 7.30pm over Chalford, in Surrey.

Strange Lights over Cambridgeshire

Harston Hill, Cambridgeshire the area where unusual lights were reported on January 21st, 1980

On 21st January 1980, some unusual 'lights' were reported in the sky over the village of Harston, Cambridgeshire.

On 23rd January 1980, a giant, red glowing, semicircular, object was seen by bus conductress Elaine Granger and her driver, Ron Andrews, hovering over Marshall Airport (now Cambridge Airport), making a low whirring noise. She had this to say:

> *"We were travelling back from the bus depot in a car. Just as we turned into the road to Teversham, we saw a big orange-shaped object, like a half-moon over the airfield. Ron stopped the car and we got out. We watched it hovering over the airport for about three minutes. It then began to glow red and started to move slowly, towards the direction of Cherry Hinton. We got into the car and went to Coldhams Lane, to see if we could see it, but it had gone. Suddenly, it appeared right in front of us .It was so low you could only see half of it above the rooftops of houses. It made a low whirring noise."*

Enquiries made with Marshall Airport revealed that it had closed at 6pm.

The *Cambridge News* (28.1.1980) told of having been contacted by James and Lynda Howarth of Station Road, Histon. The couple were reported to have confirmed the sighting made on the 23rd by Elaine Granger.

Mrs Howarth said,

> *"We watched a long glowing half moon shaped object for at least ten minutes, while we were driving along the A45 from Newmarket towards Histon. It seemed to be circling, and after quite a time flew away. We thought we had lost sight of it, but moments later it came back much closer than before. It was very large – much bigger than any aeroplane I had ever seen. We saw it clearly."*

Other witnesses included Spaldwick women – Mrs Irene Laurence and Mrs Mary Johnson – who were driving home from St. Ives, Cambridgeshire, on the same evening, along the A604, when they saw:

> *". . . a huge, orange coloured, half-moon shaped object, low on the horizon."*

The women did not take too much notice of what they had seen, until they read an account from Cambridge bus conductress – Elaine Granger.

(Source: Brenda Butler/*Hunts. Post,* 31.1.80 – 'Was the strange light a UFO?')

UFOs over Essex

Other reports included a spate of sightings from the Chelmsford area of Essex. These details were given to us from Peter Tate of UFO International. We are fairly sure that these took place in 1980, as opposed to 1979, judging by the date on the sighting report. Unfortunately they cannot be confirmed, as sadly Peter has passed away.

Oval-shaped object seen over London, at 7.15pm, on 23rd January 1980.

A red sphere seen over Kingswood. Bristol, at 11pm on 24th January 1980, for 3-5 minutes.

A round object seen over North Street, Barking, at 9.37pm on 24th January 1980, for 19 minutes.

At 10pm on the 24th of January 1980 a bright bullet shaped object showing what appeared to be five windows was seen in the sky over Woolwich by Mr & Mrs McQuilan. This was seen motionless in the sky for 30 minutes during which time a number of small blue lights were seen to moving in and out of it. It then headed off in a northerly direction before being lost from sight. Other sightings included:

A round object seen over Gt. Waltham, Chelmsford, at 10.40pm on 25th January 1980, for 3 minutes.

A saucer-shaped object seen over North Avenue, Chelmsford, on 26th January 1980, for 10 minutes.

Oval-shaped UFO over the A130, at Rettendon, Essex, on 26th January 1980, at 10.30pm, for 3 minutes.

A round object seen over Broomfield Road, Chelmsford, on 26th January, at 10.40pm, for 3 minutes.

A saucer-shaped object over Hilary Close, Chelmsford, on 26th January (time not given).

A saucer-shaped object over Park Way, Chelmsford, at 10.35pm on 26th January 1980, for 3 minutes.

A saucer-shaped object over Readers Corner, Chelmsford, at 10.50pm on 26th January 1980.

A cigar-shaped UFO over Hatfield Peverel, on 26th January 1980.

At 5.45pm on 27th January 1980, Linda Pilsworth and her friend, Samantha Benstead (12) reported having sighted:

> *". . . what looked like half a moon in the sky, hovering over Hale Street, Cambridge. It was glowing orange and every now and then flashed a green light. About 5 minutes later, we saw another one rising from behind houses, towards the direction of the airport."*

A round object was seen over Savernake Road, Chelmsford, on 27th January 1980, at 6.10pm.

UFO over London

At 6.45am on 29th January 1980, Mrs Ena B. Hosgood of Plumstead Corner, London SE18, went into the living room to pull back the curtains. She was surprised to see an object in the sky,

> *"resembling a beautiful sparkling eternity ring, showing brilliant white lights on the top and red at the bottom; the object was hovering right on the chimney stack of my next door neighbour's house. On further inspection I was able to make out that the lights on the bottom was a continuous line of red light. I watched if for about 8 minutes before it slowly moved away toward the direction of Woolwich, making a loud engine sound"*

After being contacted by Ena, Margaret Fry from Bexleyheath, made her way over to see her.

After interviewing her, the two women sat there, chatting and having a cup of tea, while looking out of the window, which faces tall iron railing, overlooking the clipped lawn of the nearby church. By now darkness had fallen.

Margaret Fry

Margaret Fry:

> *"From this position a small, elongated object, came moving through the air towards us, making a loud 'putting' noise; it cleared the iron railing. It stopped just inches from the dining room window. Here it fluttered so rapidly, we could make out that it had a bulging centre, with tapered end, and was about 2-3ft long. We watched in astonishment, wondering if the thing would crack the glass and come in. Soon the sound began to recede and the object then moved away."*

(Source: *Link to the Stars,* **Mary Ellen Fry)**

Pulsating lights over Cambridgeshire

At 6.20pm on 29th January 1980, a round object was seen in the sky over Gt. Leighs. At 7.30pm Harston resident – Mark Gordon – was walking over Newton Hill, Cambridgeshire. In an interview later conducted with Brenda Butler, he told her:

> *"I noticed two pulsating red, green and white lights, approximately five miles away in the sky. They were constantly darting about, changing direction, stopping, and hovering. Five minutes later, they vanished from view."*

(Source: Peter Tate, Brenda Butler & Ron West/*Hunts. Post,* **31.1.80)**

We also came across details published in *FSR,* Volume 32, in which it was alleged that a young girl at Coleshill, in Dorset, had watched a huge cigar-shaped craft gliding slowly above her house. According to her, it had four large, square portholes. On each porthole she was able to see a purple bearded humanoid, who stared out at her before the object moved silently away.

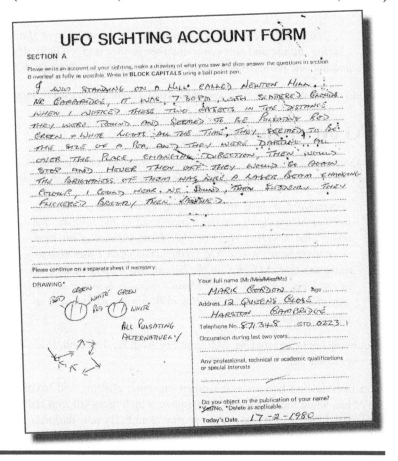

CHAPTER 2
FEBRUARY 1980

UFOs over Suffolk

RAF Woodbridge, now immortalized in UFO history as being the location of a number of mysterious events, which occurred in nearby Rendlesham Forest, Suffolk, during the end of December 1980, was also the scene of a UFO sighting during February 1980, according to retired Captain Lori Rehfeldt – then a Law Enforcement Officer, at RAF Bentwaters.

> *"I was on patrol with Airman Duffield, outside the Base, near RAF Woodbridge, at 3.00 am. – a place that literally 'scared the hell out of me', when we saw a strange 'light' in the sky moving up and down, left and right – a bit like an 'Etch o' Sketch board'. I contacted the Police Control room, at Bentwaters. They advised me to contact Woodbridge, which I did. They suggested we must have seen an aeroplane – an explanation I was not inclined to accept but decided to drop the matter, as some of the personnel had already began to refer to Rehfeldt's UFO."*

(Source: Richard Conway, BUFORA/Personal interview)

From our own visits to the area, we always found it to be a pleasant, warm, place by day but very eerie at night, when thick mists swirl around the forest tracks, blotting out sound – not forgetting the many anomalies captured on film and, occasionally, seen with the naked eye.

Captain Lori Rehfeldt

Even stranger were the falls of stones – which we witnessed personally, on a number of occasions, during 2002 onwards – incredible but true.

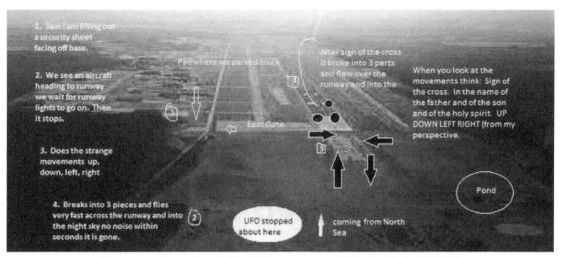

1. 3am I am filling out a security sheet facing off base.

2. We see an aircraft heading to runway we wait for runway lights to go on. Then it stops.

3. Does the strange movements up, down, left, right

4. Breaks into 3 pieces and flies very fast across the runway and into the night sky no noise within seconds it is gone.

Pad where we parked truck

East Gate

UFO stopped about here

After sign of the cross it broke into 3 parts and flew over the runway and into the

When you look at the movements think: Sign of the cross. In the name of the father and of the son and of the holy spirit. UP DOWN LEFT RIGHT (from my perspective.

Pond

coming from North Sea

Diagram superimposed on the Woodbridge runway, provided by Captain Lori Rehfeldt

UFO over Suffolk

Another sighting of something strange took place in the same year, according to Ernie Grainger and his wife, of Coronation Avenue, Hollesley, in Suffolk, who were in the back garden of the house, just as the ten o'clock news came on TV.

> *"A black triangular shaped 'craft' appeared in the sky, showing two red and one white light.*
> *It passed silently over our house and headed towards the Bentwaters Airbase. We think it was*
> *a USAF spy plane. We watched it for five minutes, until it became lost from sight."*

(Source: Ron West/Brenda Butler, East Anglian UFO & Paranormal Research Association)

Triangular UFO over Dudley

District Nurse – Sue Bowen, from *Meadow Lark* Public House, in Dudley, was driving home along Dibdale Road, during the very early 1980s, when she saw:

> *". . . a black, triangular shaped object, with an orange spotlight at each of the three angles.*
> *It was so low I felt physically sick and afraid. I tried to rationalise what it was. Suddenly, it*
> *shot off into the distance and was a speck of light in the sky – then gone."*

Sue gathered herself together and drove home, trembling with fear and tearful, after telling her husband what she had seen. **(Source: Personal letter)**

At 9am on 2nd February 1980, a silver-white metallic object was reported seen in the sky over Epsom Downs. Later the same day, at 1pm, an object resembling a *'cap'* was seen in the sky over Stone Cross, West Bromwich, by a number of people. A yellow light was seen moving through the sky over Dartford, Kent, at 10.45pm on 2nd February 1980.

UFO over Merseyside

Mrs Stella Edge from Hoylake, Wirral, Merseyside, was at home on 6th February 1980, when she heard a high-pitched sound resonating through the house. Despite a check of the electrical appliances within the house, and examination of the nearby street, the source of this noise could not be traced.

After a couple of hours, the sound began to recede, but returned to its original high-pitch during the evening meal – a matter brought to the attention of Stella, by her husband and daughter, who burst out laughing when somebody suggested, in conversation, that the noise sounded like a spaceship taking off. How ironic those words would turn out to be!

At 6.15am on 7th February 1980, an orange-yellow coloured *'ball of light'* was seen moving through the sky over Chertsey, in Surrey. Was there any connection with what was seen by Stella?

The following evening, Stella noticed an intense *'glare of light'* emanating from behind the drawn curtains. Wondering what was causing this *'glare'*, she pulled back the curtains and was confronted by the sight of:

> *". . . a brilliant white 'disc' of sharply defined light, surrounded by haze, motionless in the air, just above the gable end of a nearby house. After a few minutes it began to rise slowly upwards, out of the range of my vision. I rushed out into the street and, at first, couldn't see it – then, as my eyes adjusted to the darkness, I saw it almost resting on the rooftop of a house, a short distance down the street, accompanied by a tiny object that looked like a 'star'. I stood watching – now very frightened. All of a sudden, the 'star' shot away from the disc-shaped object and went out of sight. The 'disc' then tilted slightly and rushed away through the sky, in a blur of speed, towards the direction of the churchyard.*
>
> *The next morning, I telephoned the Police to report the matter."*

(Source: Personal interviews)

Hoylake
Wirral
Merseyside

2 DEC. REC'D

Dear Mr Bell.

As requested I am writing bout my sighting of a UFO. I can't be sure of the date, sometime early Jan. or Feb of this year, I do know it was a Thursday evening 7-0 to 7-30 pm. What I saw was a brilliant white disc shape object of light, No sound, No beam, and just below roof level. This seemed to be stationary over the end of the rear yard of my house. I saw the light through my closed curtains, and this caused me to move the curtain aside and look out. No movement or sound for some minutes then a very very slow move upwards. I went to the front of the house + into the street, the houses are terraced, no gardens. Looking up I didn't see anything at first, then almost resting on the rooftops 2 houses away

this same shape appeared, as I watched I realised that the tiny star like dot I hadn't thought connected with the shape in the rear yard, was still along side the shape. I was able to watch a few more minuets before any further movements from it, first to move was the tiny light very fast across the street and over the opposite roof tops, Once this had gone, the large disc still very bright, seemed to tilt slightly then moved off so fast it was unbelievable, this went down the street away from me and disappeared over roof tops, + near that surround our local church yard. Well I really was almost dazed by it all, such silent speed. My husband was asleep in bed, I told him as soon as the UFO disappeared, he was on night duty so I didn't want to wake him earlier, on my first sight. I can't explain what I saw, my daughter rang the local police next day, they had no calls other than hers, + I said no to there question as to weather I wanted there to call on me. I felt no fear or threat from the UFO. One other item

Yours most Sincerely
Stella Edge

may interest you, on the afternoon of the day before (Wednesday) my husband + I heard a strange high pitched sound, so much so that we thought of a new machine and checked both back + front of the house to see if any cars etc, or even a flock of birds was the cause of this sound. Anyway my daughter after our evening meal, sat with us watching early T.v. shows, when once again the sound returned, We said nothing, untill she herself brought our attention to it, then told her of our earlier hearing of it. It was low cloud all day Wednesday + my first explanation of this sound I described to my sister as "just like you hear on a film when a space ship is around". Little did I ever dream or think, that on the following day Thurs. I would see a UFO, but this time no sound at all. Finally I add this, I didn't dream it, or thought I'd seen it, It was there, and I'm not one of those highly imaginative women who have nothing better to do than suddenly start seeing optical illusions. *S wish*

UFO over Worcestershire

Simon Marshall – now a freelance photographer, working in the Redditch area – spoke to us about what he saw, during the early 1980s, while travelling to work, one morning, on his moped.

> *"I was aged 16, at the time, and heading towards the* Man on the Moon *Public House, Redditch Road, Kings Norton, on a cold and frosty morning. As I passed Wasthill Lane, on my left, I noticed, with shock, that I was being followed by this huge 'square of light', about 50ft away, on the left-hand side. Panicking, I opened up the throttle and tried to outrun whatever it was. Suddenly, it shot off across the sky and disappeared into the early morning darkness."*

(Source: Personal interview)

UFO over Bexleyheath London

On the 11th of February 1980, Margaret Fry her daughter Jacqueline Fowler and niece Julia Lewis were at the front of the house in Bexleyheath Kent when they noticed a bright star like object in the sky. It then began to expand and as it did so descended until it was approximately 200ft above their head. They were then surprised to see nine small lights moving in and out of the larger object as it moved overhead. The larger object described as being the size of an aircraft carrier, and apparently silver metallic in appearance maintained its position in the sky for about an hour before moving away.

At 4.15pm on 13th February 1980, three lights were seen in the sky over Beare Green, Surrey. According to the witnesses, they were constantly changing pattern as they flew over. **(Source: Mr M. Tyrell)**

UFO Display over Cambridgeshire

On 17th February 1980, Brenda Butler from Leiston, Suffolk, decided to visit Harston Hill, Cambridgeshire, after learning that a *BBC* film crew were on their way there, following further reports of UFOs brought to their attention.

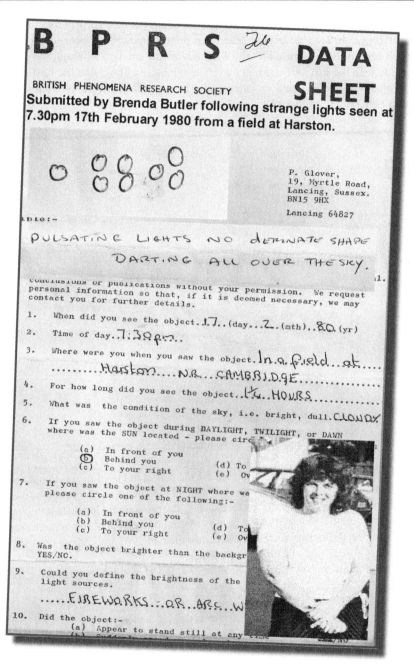

B P R S 26 DATA SHEET

BRITISH PHENOMENA RESEARCH SOCIETY
Submitted by Brenda Butler following strange lights seen at 7.30pm 17th February 1980 from a field at Harston.

P. Glover,
19, Myrtle Road,
Lancing, Sussex.
BN15 9HX

Lancing 64827

title:-

PULSATING LIGHTS NO DEFINATE SHAPE
DARTING ALL OVER THE SKY.

conclusions or publications without your permission. We request personal information so that, if it is deemed necessary, we may contact you for further details.

1. When did you see the object. 17. (day ...2. (mth) ..80. (yr)

2. Time of day. 7:30pm..

3. Where were you when you saw the object. In a field at Harston NR CAMBRIDGE

4. For how long did you see the object.. 1½ HOURS

5. What was the condition of the sky, i.e. bright, dull. CLOUDY

6. If you saw the object during DAYLIGHT, TWILIGHT, or DAWN where was the SUN located - please circ
   (a) In front of you
   (b) Behind you
   (c) To your right   (d) To
                              (e) Ov

7. If you saw the object at NIGHT where wa please circle one of the following:-
   (a) In front of you
   (b) Behind you
   (c) To your right   (d) To
                              (e) Ov

8. Was the object brighter than the backgr YES/NO.

9. Could you define the brightness of the light sources.
   .....FIREWORKS..OR..ARC..W

10. Did the object:-
    (a) Appear to stand still at any

"At 7.30 pm, a UFO was seen to materialise in the sky, and then descend to within a few feet off the ground, before slowly changing in colour to that of diffused orange, out of which emerged eight smaller luminous objects. These then began to dart about all over the place – 'as if playing a game of tag'. About an hour later a second UFO arrived and moved towards the first one – witnessed by many people, including the BBC film crew, who captured it on film."

We wrote to the *BBC* at Brentford, Middlesex, asking if we could obtain a copy of the film. They informed us that because of copyright laws governing television programmes, they were unable to sell, or loan, programmes which had not been released by the *BBC Worldwide* market, although were able to confirm, from enquiries made with the *BBC Archives,* at Caversham Park, Reading, that the East Anglia Television Magazine programme – *Weekend* – had included a short item, relating to investigations held into UFO activity, at Harston Hill, on 25th April 1980.

Information & Archives
Written Archives Centre

Tel : 0118 9469282
June 21st 2000

Dear Mr. Hanson,

Thank you for your letter of June 12th, which has been passed to me.

I have checked our programme indexes for the period in question and found that the East Anglian television magazine programme *Weekend* included a short item investigating UFOs at Harston on April 25th 1980. Unfortunately, the programme log does not give sufficient information to indicate whether or not any film of the supposed phenomenon was shown, when any such film may have been shot, nor the names of any camera crew involved.

I am sorry about this, but regional programmes tend not to be documented as fully as others.

Yours sincerely,

Jeff Walden
Senior Document Assistant.

Unfortunately, the 'Log' did not give sufficient information to indicate whether any film of the supposed phenomenon was shown, or the names of the camera crew involved.

In the middle of February 1980, the police, in March, Cambridgeshire, confirmed that they had received a number of calls regarding UFOs sighted over the town, described as looking like *'a massive ball of orange flame'* in the sky – apparently also seen by some of their own officers.

UFO over Peterborough

More than a dozen railway men, working at the town's locomotive yard, watched a strange object hovering and diving through the sky, over the Flag Grass Hill area. Driver – Stanley Bolton – was one of the witnesses.

> *"It was about 12.30am. The foreman had just sent me outside to do a job. You could hear a pin drop – it was that quiet. I then saw this really bright 'light', which turned orange as it moved over Creek Road. It looked like it was burning up – far too big to be a 'shooting star', or a plane. It was about a hundred times the size of a star."*

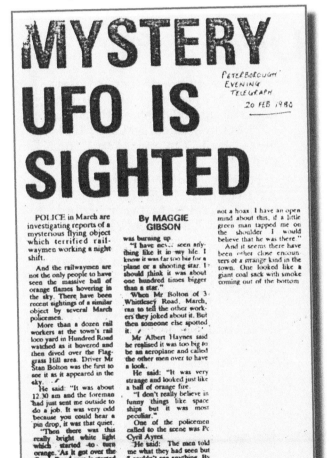

PETERBOROUGH EVENING TELEGRAPH 20 FEB 1980

When Mr Bolton told other workers about what he had seen, they laughed at him – until they saw the object themselves. By the time Police Constable Cyril Ayres arrived, in response to 999 calls made, there was nothing to be seen.

> *"The men told me what they had seen, but I couldn't see anything. By their attitude, I knew it was not a hoax. I have an open mind about this. If a 'little green man' tapped me on the shoulder, I would believe that he was there."*

(Source: Brenda Butler/DIGAP/
Peterborough Evening Telegraph,
20.2.80 –
'Mystery UFO is sighted'/
Personal interview)

At 8.45pm on 19th February 1980, a cluster of white and green lights were seen over Parson Drive, Cambridgeshire.

Rectangular UFO over Yorkshire

At 8pm on 25th February 1980, Halifax resident – James Carter – and three friends, saw:

> *". . . a rectangular object, showing a scarlet light",*

moving across the sky towards the direction of Mytholmroyd, for five minutes, before it moved behind a cloud and disappeared. A spokesman at Leeds /Bradford Airport suggested it was probably an airplane, or helicopter. **(Source**: *Daily Express*, **26.2.80** – 'Five see UFO')

This was followed by a sighting of a red *'ball of light'* seen rushing through the sky over Milton Keynes, at 7.40am, the following morning.

DAILY EXPRESS 26|2|80

Five see UFO 1980

FIVE people say they saw a UFO over Calderdale at about 8 pm yesterday.

Mr Jimmy Carter, aged 26, of Tennyson Street, Bradshaw, Halifax, said he and three friends saw a rectangular object in the sky above Bradshaw at 7.50 pm.

"It had a scarlet light and it was there for about five minutes," he said.

"It went behind a cloud and disappeared."

He said it was travelling towards Mytholmroyd.

Eleven-year-old Sam Holroyd, of Melrose Avenue, Lee Mount, Halifax, watched it for about eight minutes at 8 pm.

Sam, a pupil of Lee Mount Junior School, said the object hovered up and down in the sky.

"I'm fairly sure it was a UFO. I don't think I'm mistaken," he said.

Halifax Police Community Affairs Office Inspector Michael Danskin said he had received no reports of UFO sightings.

A spokesman in the operations office at Leeds/Bradford Airport said he had not heard of any UFO sightings yesterday.

"I've been in the business for 30 years and in my experience it is usually an aeroplane or helicopter," he said.

CHAPTER 3
MARCH 1980

UFO over Bradford

ON 2nd March 1980, Bradford resident – Lorna Mandell – was driving along Micklethwaite Lane, near Crossflatts, between 4-5pm, with her two children, when they saw a flashing red circular object, with a glowing red twinkling centre and shimmering edges, descending vertically through the sky, despite a strong wind blowing at the time. As it touched the ground, the light in the middle disappeared and the object was lost from view. **(Source: Graham Birdsall, Yorkshire UFO Society)**

UFO over Plymouth

Following information obtained relating to a radio broadcast, which took place between the Control Tower, at Plymouth Airport, and the pilot of an aircraft, about the sighting of a UFO in the sky, at 8.23pm on 6th March 1980, members of the Plymouth UFO Group, headed by Bob Boyd, visited the Airport and spoke to Richard Courtney – the civilian Flight Controller.

"I was looking towards the Caradon TV mast, when a 'bright light' shone through the clouds between the TV mast and Kit Hill. I radioed an incoming 8.45pm flight and advised him I was going off the air for a few minutes, to confirm a UFO. I made my way out of the flight tower. When I looked over into the sky where I had seen the UFO, there was nothing to be seen. By this time, the manager had joined me. Suddenly the 'light' came on again. The manager couldn't believe his eyes."

He said:

"'The hairs on the back of my neck were standing on end'.

The 'light' – now flashing on and off a brilliant diamond blue in colour, with a large area of diffused light around it – was above and shining through the clouds, at a height of two thousand feet. The glow from the object spread over a large area of the sky. You could make out clearly the disc in the centre. The 'light' then went out again; at this point I had to go back to the Control Tower and the 'light' was still there in the sky. I radioed the incoming aircraft

and asked him to confirm a visual on the UFO. He told me he could see the 'light' but was unable to assist further, as he was preparing for landing. At 8.31pm, the light disappeared for the last time."

(Source: Bob Boyd, Plymouth UFO Group – UFOs over Plymouth, File 8005)

Another UFO over Plymouth

Another spectacular sighting took place in the early part of this month, involving Plymouth town crier – Ken Headon – who had seen service in the Merchant Navy. Was there a connection with the previous sighting?

Ken was at home with his wife and children in their flat near the city centre, when his son called his father's attention to something strange in the sky. Ken looked through the window and saw a huge object, which appeared to be spinning rapidly, hovering in the sky over the Millbrook area.

Ken called his neighbours out to see the object, which gave off a bright glow and had a number of brightly coloured lights around its rim, flashing intermittently. The party of people watched the UFO for about 15mins, some 30° above the skyline, until it then flew away at high speed, seawards.

Bright glow appeared to be spinning rapidly

Bright multi-coloured lights flashing intermittantly

It should not come of any surprise to learn that Ken had also sighted other UFOs during his life; the first was at sea, during the Second World War, another took place in the late 1950s, when he and some workmen at Whitleigh sighted a spinning white disc, showing a dome on top. The object then flew off westwards, at tremendous speed. **(Source: Bob Boyd)**

At 5.15pm on 9th March 1980, a mysterious cluster of red flashing lights was seen in the sky over Baildon and Ilkley Moor, by a number of people, who contacted the Police, at Shipley, who in turn telephoned the Air Traffic Control, at Leeds/Bradford Airport, thinking it might have been a distress flare, but were told they had no knowledge. Coincidently, the Police themselves admitted their own officers had sighted the UFOs themselves, at an altitude of 6-700ft, north of Ilkley.

(Source: *Bradford Telegraph and Argus*, 12.3.80)

UFO over Warwickshire

Nicholas George – a subcontractor, from Stratford-upon-Avon – was driving home along the A422, just after 7pm on 11th March 1980, approaching the Temple Grafton turn-off, when he noticed a *'blob of light'*

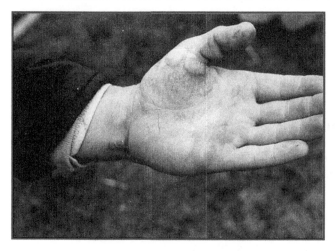

in the sky, towards the south-east, through the windscreen of his car. Feeling uneasy, he began to slow down, in order to obtain a closer look.

To his horror, a large brilliant cigar-shaped object appeared, with dark red patches on its curved end. He said:

"I took my left hand off the steering wheel and applied the brakes. This caused the vehicle to veer off the road and hit the kerb, coming to a stop. Very shaken, I got out of the car and lit up a cigarette, looking out over the open countryside for any sign of the object, at which point I noticed my left-hand felt tender and oddly dark in places. There was a circle of damaged skin, with a blue/purple narrow ring around its edge. The centre was made up of dead skin. Next to this was another large blister, filled with fluid."

Mr George contacted the Worcestershire-based UFO Group – *Sky Scan* – who tape-recorded an interview with him, in which he had the following to say:

"Only one hand was affected because I was smoking, at the time, with my right hand – the left thumb hooked under the wheel. The funny thing is that it didn't hurt like a normal burn. At the time it felt tender, but it was dark outside and I didn't pay much attention. When I arrived home after work, several hours later, my hand was sore. The blisters came later."

The Investigators – Tony Green, Derek Lawrence and Margaret Webb – confirmed the base of the thumb was swollen and red. There was a circle of damaged skin, approximately 1.5-2.0cm across, with a blue/ purple coloured narrow ring around its edge. The centre was made up of dead skin. Next to this was another large blister – 1.5cm filled with fluid. Under the metal expanding watch strap was a small blister and mark – still visible a week after the incident. Emphasising the professionalism of this select UFO group, (member's invitation only) was the decision to have the vehicle examined by a fully-qualified mechanic – then to contact the manufacturers of the windscreen, to ascertain whether a burst of microwave energy, striking the windscreen from a nearby microwave tower, could have explained away the incident. (This stretch of road was to be the subject of other sightings of UFOs over the years.)   **(Source: As above)**

The UFO activity over the Bradford area continued with a sighting, at 8.30pm on 13th March 1980, by a woman from Tyersal, Bradford, who reported having seen a brightly-lit glowing, revolving object, travelling swiftly across the sky, heading towards the direction of Leeds.

At 7.30pm on 17th March 1980, two unusual 'red lights' – one brighter than the other – were seen motionless in the sky over a densely populated area of Swindon. According to the woman concerned,

"The larger 'light' had a dome on top. It disappeared from sight first, followed by the other. Both were seen above rooftop level".

She then telephoned the police. She was later visited by members of the Swindon-based group SCUFORI, who interviewed her and speculated whether she may have mistaken a familiar object for something else.

(Source: *Skywatch Gazette*, No. 4, 1980/Aerial Phenomena Investigation)

Another UFO sighting took place, at 10.5pm, the same evening – this time over Kidderminster, when a white *'disc'* was seen moving at tremendous speed across the sky, by Mrs Dorothy Smith, shortly after having given birth to her daughter, Victoria.   **(Source: Crystal Hogben, *Magic Saucer,* Kidderminster)**

UFO over Frome

Thirty minutes later, at 10.35pm on 17th March 1980, Steven Dayman-Johns and his wife, Julie, were travelling back home to Frome, Somerset, in a 1973 Datsun Cherry car, along Ridgeway Lane – a narrow road (approximately one and-a-half miles long) – when Julie brought her husband's attention to a white object she saw move through one quarter of the car's windscreen, before coming to a halt in the sky.

Steven stopped the car and, after switching off the headlights, stood on the sill of the car and sighted the object in the sky – which had no definite outline but appeared to have a darker ring running around its top. After a few minutes, he got back into the car and continued on his journey, keeping the object under observation until it suddenly moved away, at a phenomenal speed, towards Wanstrow, emitting a faint light from its front and rear.

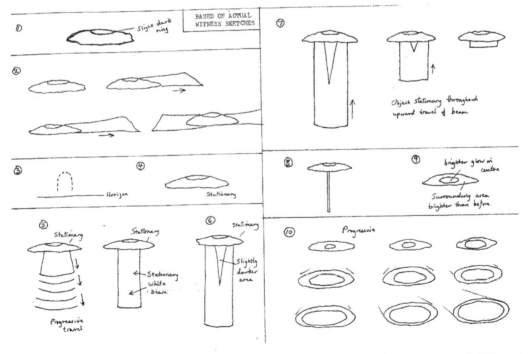

Steve decided to make his way to higher ground, and drove to the end of Ridgeway Lane to the T Junction, being overtaken by a motorcycle, who sounded his horn several times at them. They turned left at the junction and pulled into a lay-by, about 150yds from the junction. After getting out they looked across

The light/object as seen by Steven Dayman-Johns, who annotated this actual photograph

the sky but couldn't see the object, although they noticed a whitish glow on the horizon in the shape of an upturned letter 'U'. Their curiosity now aroused even further, they got back into the car and drove to where they had originally seen the object, along Ridgeway Lane.

Just before reaching the lay-by, they saw a bright vertical beam of light behind the trees, catching them in its brilliant glare. Once again, they made their way towards it, driving along Marston Lane and up and over Cheese Hill, where they caught sight of it, two to three fields away – a bright 'beam' projecting downwards from its centre, solid in appearance, rather than a beam of light. At this point, Julie began to feel frightened and refused to get out of the car. Steven observed that the top of the 'beam' had a 'V'-shaped darker area inside it.

A few minutes later, he decided to walk over and have a closer look, but Julie pleaded with him not to go. Getting back into the car, the couple drove along the road – still keeping an eye on the object, which was glowing brighter and apparently closer to where they were positioned. Stopping once again, he switched off the car headlights. Within seconds, the object dropped in height and approached them silently, at high speed, passing over their car (now the size of an outstretched hand at arm's length) some 50ft off the ground, before disappearing, finally, from view.

Despite a lengthy, detailed investigation into the matter, by members of SCUFORI – (Jan Wojtowigz, Raymond Smithers and Bob McGregor) – when a number of rational explanations were considered, currently it still remains unidentified. **(Source: Martin Shipp/*Probe Report*, Vol. 4, No. 2, October 1983)**

Strange 'figures', Merseyside

At 11.00pm on 17th March 1980, Margery Sherrard, her daughter, Deborah, and friend, Teresa Malvaney, were on their way to Knowsley, to drop off Teresa, after a keep fit class. As they drove along Holt Lane, Margery noticed a bright light descending through the sky, which they first took to be an aircraft on its way to Liverpool Airport, several miles to the south-west, described as being 'orange, with white lights; the other, a red diamond'. As they continued on their journey, they passed a 'strange figure' walking along the road, with long grey hair and thin face – about 50yrs of age.

After arriving at their destination, they made the return journey back along the same route, when they were forced to swerve to avoid striking the same man (a coincidence you may say) but as they reached Knowsley Lane, they encountered a third similar 'figure' walking along the middle of the road. At no time did either of these 'men' acknowledge the presence of the vehicle. **(Source: Brian Fishwick)**

UFO over Halton, Cheshire

In March 1980, George Hays from Halton, Cheshire, was on his way home, at 7.30pm, when he noticed a bright light in the sky. As he headed towards the Runcorn Bridge, the light extinguished but re-appeared some 200yds away. As he neared the bridge, the light seemed to be hovering above the railway bridge that runs alongside.

"The lights appeared to be on a dark triangle and were flashing blue/white at their extremities. In between these were smaller lights. Other cars moving in opposite directions slowed down, and my car radio suffered considerable interference until I reached the other side."

Brenda Butler

According to Brenda Butler, from Leiston, Suffolk – a veteran UFO Researcher, whose investigations into the UFO/Paranormal subject spanned over 25 years:

"1980 was a year of considerable UFO activity for me and my colleague, Dot Street, from BUFORA.

It started in March 1980, when a lady from Gorleston, near Yarmouth, Norfolk, telephoned me, reporting having seen a huge orange 'light' in the sky, heading towards the coast, which she believed came down somewhere near the sea.

The woman told me that she and her neighbours had gone outside, at 10.30pm, after the house lights had began to flash on and off. This was when they saw the UFO.

I also remember interviewing another woman in Gorleston, living on the Yarmouth Road. She saw this orange 'light' going across the sky. After having watched it, they went back inside the house. About an hour later, they were watching TV. A shadow went across the front room curtains. They opened the curtains and looked out and saw the figure of a man, wearing what looked like a helmet. Frightened, she sent her terrier dog outside but it ran back inside. Looking upwards, she was amazed to see the orange 'light' in the sky again. One of the young boys in the family told her he saw a man, dressed in a funny hat and black clothes, running out of the garden."

UFO over Tayside

At 4.45am on 30th March 1980, off duty Police Constable David Cathro, living on the Gowrie Park Housing Estate, was awoken by a metallic humming noise, which increased in sound.

"From my bedroom window that overlooks the Carse of Gowrie, I saw four 'dull glows' moving across the sky, about three quarters of a mile away, in a diamond formation, accompanied by the noise, which grew louder but changed its pitch. They then stopped and appeared to be over Star Inn Road. Suddenly, one of the 'lights' came away and slowly descended to the ground in the vicinity of Benvie, where I lost sight of the formation, although I could still hear the noise for a short time afterwards. I alerted the neighbours and we all stood outside watching. One of them produced a pair of binoculars. I looked through and saw an object, shaped like a rugby-ball, with a white top and glowing orange base.

I telephoned the police, at Forfar, and explained to them what I had seen. They checked with the Airport and told me there was nothing plotted on Radar for that area. Enquiries made, the following day, revealed the object had been hovering over a Compressor Plant, at Forfar."

At 4.50am, the same morning, off duty Police Constable Graham Irving and his wife, also living on the same estate, were awoken by a strange metallic humming noise and low frequency vibrations. Graham and his wife dashed to the window, which faces north-west over the Carse of Gowrie, and saw four dull orange lights travelling from right to left, north to north-west. The couple then went back to bed, as the lights and noise were beginning to fade.

Graham said:

"Suddenly the noise became loud again; once again, we went to the window and looked out. We saw four objects hovering approximately 1km away, to the north-west, in the Benvie area. After about five minutes one of the objects slowly descended towards the ground, until it was out of sight. After hovering for a long time, the other three lights departed northwards."

A subsequent search of the area by local police, who were contacted, revealed nothing untoward. A 132Kv Power line runs across the area to Benvie. It is said that similar noises were heard by two milk delivery boys in the Menziehill area of the City.

UFO over Dundee

We spoke to Mr Bert Perry about what he saw hovering in the sky, over Baldovie, near Dundee, at 5.00pm., towards the end of March 1980.

> *"I saw a silver 'ball of light' just hanging in the sky, with something projecting from underneath it, although, because of the distance involved, I couldn't make out what this actually was. I presumed, to begin with, that it was a weather balloon, or parachute. All of a sudden, it began to travel towards the North and then stopped for about twenty minutes, motionless in the sky, before once again moving towards the East, where it rose up and I lost sight of it. Although I managed to take a photograph of it, I was disappointed to discover the image was far too small to see anything worthwhile."*

(Source: Personal interviews/*BUFORA Journal***, Vol. 10, No. 2, April 1981/Steuart Campbell)**

A FASCINATING THEORY ON EXOLUTION

Did the Missing Link really come

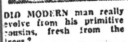

Daily Express 21.4.1980

from a flying saucer after all?

DID MODERN man really evolve from his primitive cousins, fresh from the trees?

Or should we be looking for an out-of-this-world link to explain the evolution from Ape Man to Advanced Technological Man?

There's a fascinating theory this week in a new and challenging book* by Maurice Chatelain, a space engineer who was one of the team which helped send America's Apollo spacecraft to the Moon.

His claim is simple, but arresting: That extraordinary visitors from a civilisation in deep space landed on Earth around 65,000 years ago and found it good.

Adapted

But they were not fully adapted to Earth's water, air and gravity. So, says Chatelain, they created a hybrid race by crossbreeding, with existing primitive proto-humans to produce a new race.

This would explain the rapid "evolutionary" advance from primitive "humans" with a brain capacity of 800 cubic centimetres to modern man, with one of twice as much.

Chatelain produces a mass of evidence, ranging from the ruins of Atlantis to the Pyramids of Egypt.

He cites such baffling riddles as the astounding maps copied in the sixteenth century, from much more ancient originals, by the Turkish admiral Piri Reis.

These showed, remarkably accurately, the Antarctic continent — which even in the sixteenth century was undiscovered, far less mapped.

Chatelain also tells of the Antithykera clock, discovered on the bed of the Mediterranean in 1900. About 2,000 years old, it was equipped almost unbelievably, with a differential gear mechanism. Used for calculating planetary movements, it was based on accurate calculations which were, necessarily, far, far older.

Chatelain's most startling arguments, however, revolve around the mathematical number he calls the Nineveh Constant—the basic number on which astronomical calculations can be made.

This immense figure, translated into our decimal system, works out at 195,955,200,003,909. It was found on tablets in the excavated ruins of the palace of the Assyrian King Assurbanipal, who reigned around 650 B.C.

Evidence

With astronomical evidence, Chatelain worked out that this great constant of the solar system could only have been computed 64,800 years ago and that it relied in part on the revolution periods of three planets—Uranus, Pluto, and Neptune — which are invisible to the naked eye.

Primitive man, with a 800cc brain, could not have computed it. So the answer, says Chatelain, is that he had help.

But who visited Earth? Now we're back to that old riddle, the Unidentified Flying Object. UFOs were seen and photographed from spacecraft Gemini 4 over Hawaii in June, 1965, says Chatelain.

And astronaut James Lovell photographed them from Gemini 7 on December 4, in the same year, looking like "gigantic mushrooms with their propulsion systems (Chatelain's words) clearly showing a glow on the underside. . . ."

Mysteries

Perhaps another world IS watching. Perhaps there HAS been a visit. Over the centuries, absurdities have steadily become genuine mysteries and then, sometimes, commonplace facts.

The questions Chatelain raises cannot easily be dismissed. There are still more things, though readers, in Heaven and Earth than are dreamed of in our philosophy.

* "Our Ancestors Came From Outer Space," published by Arthur Barker, price £5.95.

DOUGLAS ORGILL

CHAPTER 4
APRIL 1980

UFO tracked on Radar

URING the evening of 1st April 1980, the pilot of a civilian aircraft, en route from Nottingham to Bristol, sighted an object, likened to *'a car headlight, shining through the mist'*, moving through the sky, at about 40mph. Enquiries made, later, revealed the UFO had been tracked on radar by Birmingham Airport. **(Source: UFOSIS, Birmingham)**

UFO activity increases

At 1.30am on 5th April 1980, a flashing mass of what looked like *'white spikes'* was seen in the sky over Upper Dicker, Sussex. Later that evening, at 8.30pm, two objects, described as *'golden basket in shape'*, were seen in the sky over Looe Cornwall. **(Source: Mr D. Cutler)**

At 9pm on 7th April 1980, a white star-shaped object was seen over the M11 Motorway.

At 8.30pm on 8th April 1980, two UFOs – described as one being red in colour, the other white and spinning – were seen heading north-eastwards, across the Firth of Forth, and Dalgetty Bay, Fife. Was this the same UFO reported over Edinburgh, at 9.30pm on the same day, described as red and white 'lights' moving slowly through the sky?

At 10pm on 9th April, Dorothy Smith (mother-in-law of Shirley Smith) from Offmore Farm Estate, Kidderminster, was walking along the road, when she noticed a bank of coloured lights, forming the lower edge of a transparent circle in the sky, under a single bright light. **(Source: Crystal Hogben,** *Magic Saucer***)**

On the 10th April 1980, an unusual light was seen in the sky, said to be almost as bright as the Sun, throughout the North of England, early today. In Manchester, 40 people telephoned the police, saying they had seen flare flashes in the night sky. In Stockport, police, fire and ambulance men, were called to a field where it was said an object had landed, but nothing was found. Air traffic controllers at Manchester Airport said that the whole sky was brilliantly lit up for a few seconds. People from North Wales to the Scottish border contacted the police. An airport spokesman said the most likely explanation was that an unusually large piece of space debris had re-entered the atmosphere, causing the sky to flare up.

(Source: *Burton Daily Mail***, 10.4.1980 – 'Space Rubbish Lights Sky'**

We appreciate that the next incident falls out of the territorial jurisdiction of the UK but felt it was worthy of mention, as it involved an attack on a UFO by an air force jet fighter. Whether there was any connection with the UFOs seen around the UK leading up to and after the event is something we cannot answer

Pilot attacks UFO over Peruvian Capital

On the morning of 11th April 1980, an unusual object was detected close to Fuerza Aerea Peruana (FAP) base in La Joya, Arequipa, a thousand kilometres south of the city of Lima (Peruvian Capital). The object, like a balloon glowing in the Sun's reflection, was sighted hovering in the sky, by many people, approximately three miles away, and at an altitude of approximately 1,800ft altitude.

FAP directed Lieutenant Oscar Santa Maria Huerta, a pilot of the Peruvian Air Force to take-off in his Sukhoi 22 aircraft and take down the spherical glowing object, as it was without clearance in a restricted airspace. (One presumes that they may have thought this was a balloon).

Oscar complied and approached the object, which was hanging motionlessly about 600 meters above the ground, at 7.15am. After landing, the object reappeared and hovered in the sky above the base for two more hours. Lt. Santa María described the object as follows

> *"It was about 30ft in diameter. It was an enamelled, cream-coloured dome, with a wide, circular, metallic base. It had no engines, no exhausts, no windows, no wings or antennae. It lacked all the typical aircraft components, with no visible propulsion system."*

From left to right: Rodrigo Bravo Garrido, captain and pilot for the Aviation Army of Chile, Dr Anthony Choy, founder, OIFAA, Peruvian Air Force with Oscar Santa Maria Huerta, Commander, Peruvian Air Force (Ret.).

When within firing range, Oscar pulled the trigger, launching sixty-four 30mm. shells, some of which missed the target and went towards the ground, but the majority hit the object directly, without exploding or causing any harm. (Approximately 1,800 men at the base witnessed the event.)

The UFO then started to climb in height, and proceeded farther from the FAP. It made a sudden stop at 36,000 ft., forcing Lt. Santa Maria to veer aside since he was merely 1500 feet away.

The Lieutenant then decided to fly up higher, to approach it from above, having slightly below 100 rounds left. Just as he locked on to the target, ready to attack, the UFO performed a straight vertical ascent, evading the approach. He had the object locked for an attack for two more times subsequently, but just when he was about to hit the trigger, it moved away, always eluding his attempt. At this point, being nearly out of fuel, Santa María was forced to abandon his mission and withdraw. He was 84 kilometres from his base, and 22 minutes had passed since his initial contact with the object.

Following the declassification of documents by the U.S. Department of State, Oscar Santa Maria was subsequently interviewed by many researchers and reporters, over the years and became known worldwide through cable TV.

Three days later, on 14th April 1980, a circular UFO, showing a number of *'portholes'* along its length, spilling out yellow light, was seen travelling 30-40ft off the ground, over fields, on the outskirts of Grantham, Lincolnshire.   **(Source: Richard Thompson)**

Another Unwelcome visitor

In the spring of 1980, Hilary Porter – the Farnborough-based Vice chairwoman of BEAMS, who has spent now over 30 years researching the UFO/paranormal subject – was to find herself the subject of attention. It happened one evening, at about 7.30pm, just after she had put her daughter to bed. As she began to settle down in front of the TV and relax, nothing could have prepared her for what was about to transpire.

"All of a sudden my relaxation was shattered as I noticed someone there, outside, practically right up against my lounge window! My first fleeting thoughts were how they could have got in, as we have high wooden fencing and bushes three quarters of the way around, and link wire fence divided gardens on the other side. My thoughts then turned to calling the police. This intruder was of absolutely giant stature, which I judged to be no less than 6ft 7ins high – so tall, in fact, that 'he' was bending 'his' head down into the little fanlight window to peer into my room!

I looked on, startled, terrified and yet outraged at the cheek of whoever this might have been. As I stared, I could see that the uninvited visitor was dressed in black from head to foot, had a helmet-type of head covering, with something like a black visor on it (yet this helmet seemed to blend into the suit somehow) and 'he' was wearing what I assumed to be gauntlets.

Hilary Porter seen here with partner Ken Parsons. Hilary is Vice-chairman of the Farnborough UFO and paranormal research group – BEAMS

I froze to the spot, thinking to myself that either this is an extremely tall person, dressed in biker's gear, or as my heart told me, it's something not of this world. I thought, 'stay as calm as you can and observe as much as you can – it's important to your research'. At this point the visitor raised 'his' right hand. For some reason I did the same and raised my right hand, as if in reply. Next, this 'being' suddenly moved, but without walking . . . zooming backwards, a good 5ft and up to my garden wall. The 'figure' then moved up onto the garden steps, at least another 5ft to his left . . . again, without walking, as I didn't notice any legs and the movements were truly super-humanly fast.

Because of 'his' huge stature, 'he' blocked out most of the view of my neighbour's greenhouse and shed, and I noticed that, as 'he' stood there, the sunlight was making a sheen on 'his' suit, but I had never seen a material quite like 'he' was wearing before. Then the visitor quickly vanished right before my eyes – yet rather than frighten me off the whole subject of UFOs and aliens, this encounter served to strengthen my interest further."

Hilary and her partner, Ken Parsons, are a credit to what UFO research is all about. They are often forgotten people in this business, whose expertise in matters such as these are invaluable. We have always found them very helpful and willing to impart their information, rather than treat it as their own specific property. They are to be commended for their dedication and assisting others to come to terms with trauma that can sometimes follow such sightings.

This illustration shows a tall being sighted in Bradford, West Yorkshire, 1955 – similar in description to that which Hilary Porter had encountered in 1980

UFO over Swindon

On 29th April 1980, Mr Everett from Penhill, Swindon, had just left home, at 9.05pm, when he saw what appeared to be:

> "... two red lights in the sky over the Haydon area of Swindon. I stood and watched them for about five minutes, to ensure that they were not aircraft lights. They appeared to be circling. I made a visit to a local shop and when I returned about five minutes later, one of the lights had gone out. The remaining one appeared to circle the sky, once more – then it dropped down vertically and grew in size as it did so. The object increased its intensity and appeared to produce a dark vertical band in its centre, which split the light into two. It then vanished as if it had been switched off."

Mr Everett was not the only witness. His wife also confirmed having seen some of the phenomenon take place.

Bizarrely, according to investigators from SCUFORI, a well-known member of a UFO group had also seen the UFO, but was too frightened to fill in the sighting report!

(Source: Skywatch Aerial Phenomena Investigations Club, Swindon)

CHAPTER 5
MAY 1980

UFOs over the Motorway

GARETH Hughes – then a teacher from The Wirral, Merseyside – was driving home along the northbound carriageway of the M53 Motorway, at about 4am on 15th May 1980, and approaching junction 2, opposite Bidston Hill, when he noticed a bright light close to the ground, estimated to be 300ft away, and massive in size.

> *"It resembled two curved, black artillery shells, angled at 45° towards me, showing two beams of light projecting from the rear, which didn't go all the way to the ground but stopped in mid-air. I could see two pink-reddish jets of flame behind each 'shell' as I now continued on my journey."*

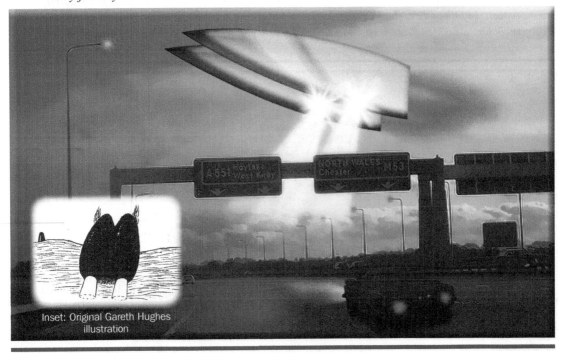

Inset: Original Gareth Hughes illustration

The following day he then telephoned the *Wallasey News* and spoke to them about the incident, following which he contacted Alan Bell at MIGAP (Merseyside Investigators into Aerial Phenomena).

(Sources: As above/Omar Fowler, PRA/*Flying Saucer Review*, Volume 27, No. 2, August 1981/ Alan Bell, MIGAP)

Cigar-shaped UFO over Suffolk

At 6.30pm the same day, Brian Murphy and his friend – Andrew Keen – were fishing off Orford Quay, Suffolk, when they saw a silver, cigar-shaped object, motionless in the sky.

> *"It moved away and then came back It was as bright as the sun, and kept flickering and making a buzzing noise. It was a clear night. I would say it was about the size of a football in the sky. We watched it for about an hour, and then it just vanished in front of our eyes."*

(Source: Brenda Butler/Ron West, EAPRA)

UFO display, Hartlepool

Neil Sutheran was taking the family dog for a walk along the beach, at Hartlepool, in company with his first wife, in May 1980, when he noticed eight coloured lights in the sky out to sea:

> *"They were initially stationary, but then started to move up and down erratically. We stood and watched them for about ten minutes, until they shot away at terrific speed, in a northerly direction along the coast. The manoeuvres they performed were like nothing I had ever seen before, moving up, down, and around, in fluidity – unlike any helicopter or aircraft. I recall a report, the following evening, in the* Hartlepool Mail, *stating that others had seen the 'lights', including a police officer, who had tried to chase them over Peterlee, County Durham."*

Author and journalist, Arthur Shuttlewood, who wrote 'The Warminster Mystery', which was published in 1967, seen here relaxing at home.

17 Portway,
Warminster,
21. 5. 80

Dear Ian, Julie & NUFOR(West) friends,

Thanks for your pleasant letter. I quite understand the situation regarding Harry.

Maybe the enclosed couple of lengthy articles, broken into chapters, will make a short series for your planned mag? I like the sound of 'Probe,' also...

The material is from my latest work, sent to W. H. Allen & Co. (London). It should appear in print either late this year, or early 1981. Therefore, it's exclusive to you & to 'Probe'! Okay?

Every good wish & regard. I hope to skywatch occasionally at Cradle on warm summer Saturdays, from 9.30 p.m. onward. God bless. Always,

Your old pal,
Arthur.

Close encounters, Suffolk

The A14 – a busy dual-carriageway, linking the Midlands with the East Coast – was to become a familiar journey during our visits to Leiston, over the years. Although we had never seen anything unusual ourselves along this particular route, we were to read about various encounters between motorists and mysterious 'globes of light' having taken place along this unlit stretch of road.

We contacted Marion from Framlingham, in Suffolk, after listening to a tape-recorded interview conducted with her, by Brenda Butler and Dot Street, following an extraordinary incident, which took place along the A14, on 29th May 1980.

Marion said:

> *"We were driving to Baldock, in Hertfordshire, in the family Mini. There were three of us in the car – my eldest daughter Sarah (driving), with my youngest daughter, Pandora (aged 11), in the back. We set off on the early evening. Right from the beginning we had problems with Pandora, who became quite emotional – for no apparent reason – followed by the sighting of dark red, flickering, lightning – something we had never seen before.*
>
> *As we approached Framlingham, we noticed a 'bright white light' in the sky just above the horizon that seemed to 'hang' in the sky, rather peculiarly, as it was still daylight.*
>
> *We stopped the car and got out, in order to satisfy our curiosity as to whether this 'light' was actually moving, or not.*
>
> *It wasn't moving. Now feeling a little uneasy, we recommenced our journey, agreeing that, if we saw a police car, or police officer, we would bring the matter to his attention.*
>
> *When near to Bury St. Edmunds, a curious thing happened. The 'light', still prominent in the sky, seemed to 'hop over' to a bank of built-up black cloud, and disappear – much to our relief.*
>
> *After leaving Bury St. Edmunds, we continued along the A14, when my eldest daughter, Sarah, drew my attention to the fact that the journey seemed a very queer one, as it appeared to be taking forever to complete, and that the local countryside – a familiar route of ours – did not look right.*
>
> *Suddenly, without any prior warning of unusual weather conditions, we entered what we took to be a patch of thick fog. Actually, it was more like dense smoke, alternating between thick patches, and swirling up from holes in the ground – the most remarkable thing I had ever seen in my life. By now, tensions inside the car were considerably heightened. Pandora, who had previously been asleep, was now wide awake.*
>
> *As we reduced speed, in order to cope with the hazardous driving conditions along this straight stretch of dual-carriageway, in complete contrast to what had been a clear, dry, evening, illuminated by a full moon, we noticed what at first we took to be the outlines of a number of heavy lorries, travelling towards the East, passing through this bank of 'fog'. In a way I find difficult to explain, there seemed to be something horribly wrong about this part of the journey, although I cannot put my finger on what it was that created so much fear*

with the appearance of these strange lorries. Pandora remarked that it was almost as if the lorries were driving themselves and that they had evil faces. Naturally, I dismissed this as an overactive imagination.

After arriving at the house in Baldock, we settled down for the night – the three of us sharing the same bedroom, trying to forget about all the problems we had encountered – when my eldest daughter suddenly jumped out of bed, at 12.45am, shouting to me that she had just seen a 'red light' flash across the sky. We all rushed to the window, but there was nothing to be seen. It was a brilliant moonlit night – just like daylight. We stood at the window for a little while, and then I told the two girls we were going into the garden.

Later, thinking about my actions, I was curious why I decided to go into the garden on my own, as I am a nervous person, but felt impelled to go there. I stood in the garden, when I was amazed to see the appearance of an object travelling from the left, behind some barns in the near distance.

It was enormous – the size of a house – totally silent, showing a number of curious red brick-shaped lights along its base and at the top.

I couldn't distinguish the outline of the object because of the dazzling white lights on its

B P R S 2266 **DATA**

SHEET

2301

BRITISH PHENOMENA RESEARCH SOCIETY

BRENDA BUTLER,
Elm Tree Farm,
Aldringham, Leiston,
Suffolk, IP16 4PU

LEISTON 830551.

P. Glover,
19, Myrtle Road,
Lancing, Sussex.
BN15 9HX

Lancing 64827

This questionnaire has been prepared so that you can give BPRS as much information as possible concerning the unidentified phenomenon that you have observed. Please try to answer as many questions as you can. The information that you give will be used for research purposes and will be regarded as confidential material. Your name will not be used in connection with any statements, conclusions or publications without your permission. We request personal information so that, if it is deemed necessary, we may contact you for further details.

1. When did you see the object **30.** (day. **5.** (mth). **80** (yr)

2. Time of day... **12.45. a.m**

3. Where were you when you saw the object **Standing in Garden, GOSMORE, HITCHIN**

4. For how long did you see the object... **Difficult to say — 2 - 3 minutes;**

5. What was the condition of the sky, i.e. bright, dull. **Bright. MOONLIGHT**

6. If you saw the object during DAYLIGHT, TWILIGHT, or DAWN where was the SUN located - please circle one of the following:

    (a) In front of you
    (b) Behind you   (d) To your left
    (c) To your right   (e) Overhead.

7. If you saw the object at NIGHT where was the MOON located - please circle one of the following:-

    (a) In front of you ✓
    (b) Behind you   (d) To your left.
    (c) To your right   (e) Overhead.

8. Was the object brighter than the background of the sky. YES/NO. **Object object was not but lights were**

9. Could you define the brightness of the object to any known light sources. **Dazzling white lights Bright red lights**

10. Did the object:-
    (a) Appear to stand still at any time

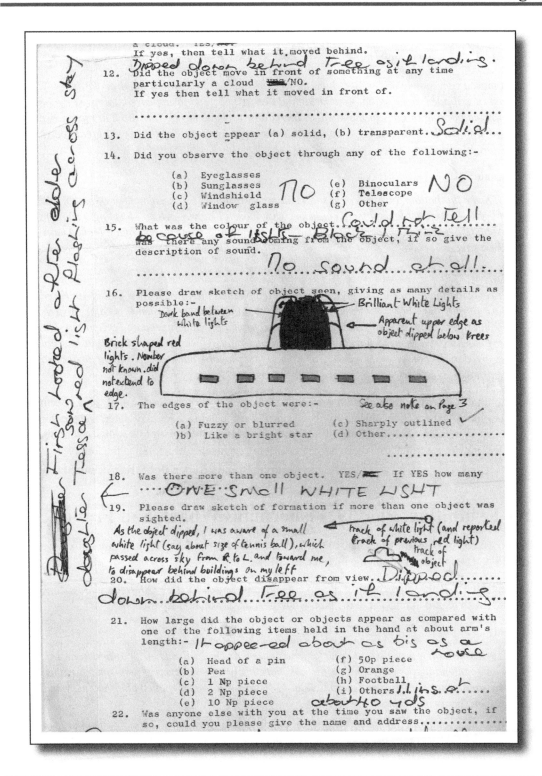

a cloud. YES/NO
If yes, then tell what it moved behind.

Dipped down behind Tree as it landing.

12. Did the object move in front of something at any time
particularly a cloud YES/NO.
If yes then tell what it moved in front of.

....

13. Did the object appear (a) solid, (b) transparent. *Solid*

14. Did you observe the object through any of the following:-

    (a) Eyeglasses
    (b) Sunglasses   (e) Binoculars *NO*
    (c) Windshield *no*   (f) Telescope
    (d) Window glass   (g) Other

15. What was the colour of the object. *Could not tell because of lights — Black. Then*
was there any sound coming from the object, if so give the
description of sound. *No sound at all.*

....

16. Please draw sketch of object seen, giving as many details as
possible:-
Dark band between white lights — *Brilliant White Lights*
Apparent upper edge as object dipped below trees
Brick shaped red lights. Number not known. did not extend to edge.

17. The edges of the object were:-   *See also note on Page 3*

    (a) Fuzzy or blurred   (c) Sharply outlined
)b) Like a bright star   (d) Other.............

....

18. Was there more than one object. YES/NO If YES how many
ONE small WHITE LIGHT

19. Please draw sketch of formation if more than one object was
sighted.
As the object dipped, I was aware of a small white light (say about size of tennis ball), which passed across sky from R. to L. and toward me, to disappear behind buildings on my left — *track of white light (and reported track of previous red light)* *track of object*

20. How did the object disappear from view. *Dipped down behind Tree as it landing.*

21. How large did the object or objects appear as compared with
one of the following items held in the hand at about arm's
length:- *It appeared about as big as a house*

    (a) Head of a pin   (f) 50p piece
    (b) Pea   (g) Orange
    (c) 1 Np piece   (h) Football
    (d) 2 Np piece   (i) Others *I.I. ins. at*
    (e) 10 Np piece   *about 40 yds*

22. Was anyone else with you at the time you saw the object, if
so, could you please give the name and address.............

First looked at like older one and looked red light flashing across sky

Dipped Tassoned

'body'. It then dipped downwards, the white lights appearing to squash down – as if they had been withdrawn, somehow – allowing me to see the outline of a 'flying saucer' shaped object, with a dome on its top.

It moved very slowly and went behind the bottom half of a tree, a few hundred yards away, and then dipped, once again, went straight down to earth and disappeared, followed by the frenzied barking of dogs in the locality. Incredibly, a 'white light' – identical to the one we had seen earlier that evening – appeared in the right-hand part of the sky, at great speed, before also disappearing."

Pandora said:

"It had a flat bottom. Inside I could see, running horizontally across, a number of red 'blocks of light'. In the top of the object I could see what looked like two 'pylons', forming a triangle – a bit like a heart in shape. When it tilted, this 'pylon thing' went shorter and it looked more like a saucer."

Marion:

"I reported the matter to the police and then telephoned the local United States Air Force Base (it may have been Mildenhall) and spoke to an officer there, when it became obvious the questions being asked of me were being read from a previously prepared pro forma. The next morning, we went to have a look around and realised whatever we had seen had not occurred at the bottom of the garden, as we had first thought, but over a cornfield, about two fields away, bordered by a group of electricity pylons."

Marion told us that following the UFO event, the family were to experience unusual things occurring at home. They included household objects going missing but reappearing, a few days later, and problems with the electrical system on the Austin Mini. From our conversations held with this well-spoken, intelligent woman, we saw no reason not to believe her version of the events that had befallen the family.

(Source: Brenda Butler/Dot Street/Personal interview)

USA Exhibition, Pier 39, Fishermans Wharf, San Francisco

Although we do not know the exact date of the Exhibition held at the above location, we think it was some time in 1980. (Despite searches on the internet, in 2012)

We are indebted to Peter Vines for his write-up contained in *Search West UFO Research Magazine*, No. 2, dated 1981, with regard to his visit to the pier, while presumably on holiday there.

Peter said:

"The Exhibition was organised by no lesser a figure than Dr. J. Allen Hynek. My first thoughts, prior to attending the pier, were that it was more likely to be a carnival atmosphere, rather than an attempt to treat it in a serious vein. My fears were soon dispelled after having found a superb array of exhibits.

There were copies of documents from the US Government, dispelling and endorsing the case for UFO investigation. Predictably, most of the material on show had been extracted from the files of Project Blue Book. I had the rare opportunity to listen to the tapes of the original

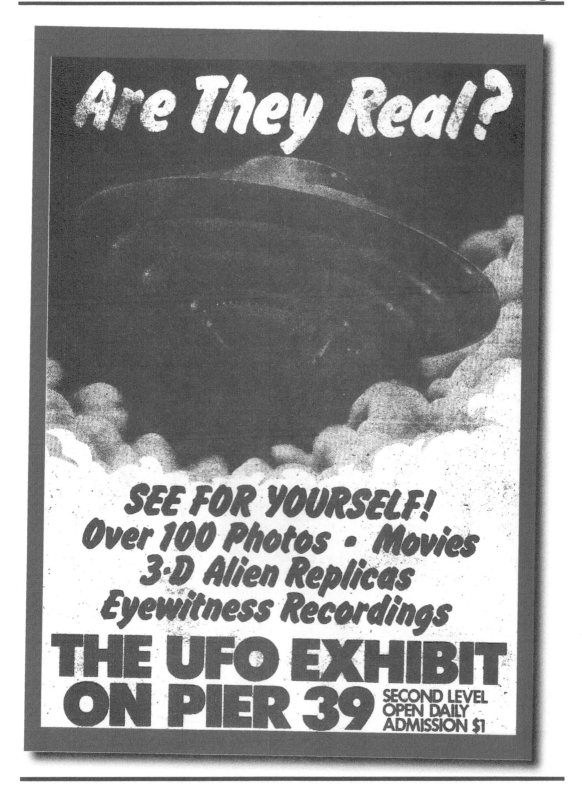

tape-recorded interview with Betty and Barney Hill, conducted while under hypnosis. This proved interesting and quite chilling. As they relived their experiences, it made me realise just how traumatic the encounter had been.

The exhibition also contained numerous cubicles, seating ten to twelve people in each. Inside the cubicles was a TV showing continuous video tapes of UFO films. The quality and origin of the films varied widely from 8mm home movies to astounding footage, taken by Gemini and Apollo astronauts. I was disappointed to notice that there wasn't one article of British origin. Warminster didn't even get a mention. I was surprised to see such a large attendance. I couldn't help thinking that the average American citizen takes a far stronger and more intelligent interest in the subject than his British counterpart. It's a great pity that we, in Britain, haven't more people like Dr. Hynek – people with the influence and finance to stage an exhibition of the calibre. Full marks Dr. Hynek."

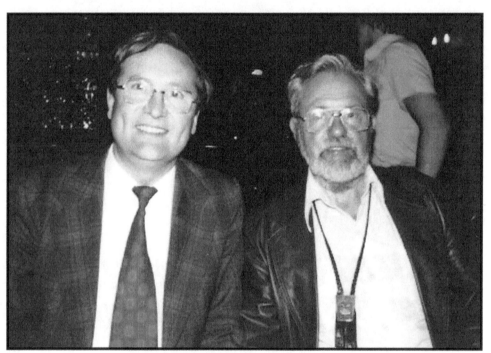

Martin Shipp on the left, and Dr. Allen Hynek on the right

CHAPTER 6
JUNE 1980

UFO over Avon and Essex

MR Peter Francombe was travelling along the Clevedon Road, through Tickenham Village, Avon, at 10.45pm on 3rd June 1980, with Barbara Shakespeare and her two young children, when he sighted a peculiar light in the sky and pulled in to take a closer look.

"It flashed brightly, approximately three times every couple of seconds, and then moved erratically across the sky, made a 90° turn to the north-west, and began to hover again. We continued on our journey and saw it, once again, before it disappeared from view into the clouds."

(Source: Brenda Butler/Ron West)

At 10.55pm on 5th June 1980, Peter Jones from Billericay, Essex, was driving along the A127 arterial road, towards Southend-on-Sea, and had just passed the turning for Orsett and Brentwood, when he saw:

". . . a vivid green, glowing light – the size of a bus, with brighter parts that looked like lights – heading at terrific speed across the sky, about a mile away, as it came over the top of my car. I thought it was going to crash. It then disappeared behind trees in the distance."

Five minutes later, Bill and Mavis Jones from Billericay, Essex, were travelling along the A127, towards Southend-on-Sea, at 11pm.

"As we passed the Brentwood turn-off, a vivid green cigar-shaped object, illuminated inside with a number of bright lights, shot across the top of our car – so close, we thought there was going to be a collision."

(Source: BUFORA/Mavis Jones/Brenda Butler/Ron West)

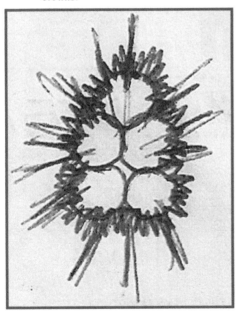

Peter Francombe's illustration of the light seen June 3rd, 1980

Sunday Mirror

22p   September 27, 1981   No. 958   ★

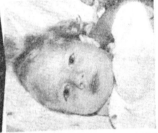

First picture of the White Cliffs baby
FULL STORY AND MORE PICTURES —PAGE 5

AMAZING UFO DEATH RIDDLE

Experts baffled by burns on man

Priscilla Presley's new life —CENTRE PAGES

MY LOVER AGED 22, BY OLIVIA NEWTON-JOHN —See Page 17

A MAN'S mysterious death is at the centre of one of the biggest UFO riddles in years.

His body was found with strange, unexplained burns in a town he had never visited before.

Experts believe that Polish-born Zygmunt Adamski, 56, could have died of fright.

And one of two policemen called to the scene is said to have told of seeing a

By JOHN SHEARD and STEWART BONNEY

flying saucer only hours before.

Extensive inquiries ordered by West Yorkshire coroner Mr James Turnbull failed to reveal any ordinary reasons for Mr Adamski's death.

And last week Mr Turnbull told us: "It is quite the most mysterious death I have investigated in 12 years as a coroner."

Mr Adamski, who lived quietly with his wife Lottie

in Thornfield Crescent, Tingley, near Leeds, was found on a pile of coal in a yard at Todmorden 30 miles away. He had been missing for five days.

There were burns on his scalp, neck and the back of his head from a corrosive substance that forensic experts could not identify.

Although they will not admit it publicly, West Yorkshire police are understood to have seriously considered the possibility that Mr Adamski's death was somehow linked with the UFO sighting.

Mr Turnbull said: "As a

Victim — Mr. Adamski with his wife Lottie

trained lawyer I have to rely on facts. Unfortunately we have not been able to uncover any facts which may have contributed to this death.

"I tend to believe that there may be some simple explanation.

"However, I do admit that the failure of forensic scientists to identify the corrosive substance which

caused Mr Adamski's burns could lend some weight to the UFO theory.

"As a coroner I cannot speculate. But I must admit that if I was walking over Ilkley Moor tomorrow and a UFO came down, I would not be surprised I might be terrified, but not surprised.

"I cannot believe that all the thousands of reports of this sort of phenomenon—covering almost every country in the world and going back through the ages—result from human error."

UFO investigators say

Continued on Page 2

Crunch day for Labour — Page 4

Suspicious death of Zygmund Jan Adamski –
Born 17-8-1923, died June 1980

Many of the readers will be all too familiar with the mysterious events that surround the discovery of the above named, who was found deceased at Tomlin's Coal Yard, at the side of Todmorden Railway Station, 30 miles away from where he lived, at 3.45pm on 6th June 1980 – and of the controversy surrounding his departure from the family home, a few days before the wedding of his god-daughter, on the 7th June.

RIDDLE OF POLICEMAN 'WHO SAW A UFO'

Trevor Parker who found the mystery body

From Page One

they interviewed the policeman who spoke of the sighting.

They say he agreed to undergo hypnosis and while in a trance he recalled seeing a flying saucer earlier on the day that Mr. Adamski was found.

West Yorkshire police would not allow us to interview the officer.

This is the unbelievable story uncovered by Sunday Mirror investigators.

Mr. Adamski vanished on June 11 last year after setting off on foot from his home to buy potatoes at a corner shop.

Pile of coal

Coal merchant's son Mr. Trevor Parker found his body in a hollow on top of the pile of coal in Todmorden, where Mr. Adamski had no known connections.

There was no indication as to how he got there.

His face, cheeks, forehead

Coroner James Turnbull

and clothes were NOT marked by the corrosive substance, suggesting that when the burns were inflicted the top half of his body was naked.

Mr. Adamski, who became a soldier and later a miner after fleeing Poland in the war, was found wearing a jacket but without a shirt.

His watch and wallet were missing but he had £5 in his pocket.

Consultant pathologist Dr Alan Edwards said death was caused by heart failure, possibly due to "a severe shock or fright".

Police probed Mr Adamski's background in an attempt to find clues to his death.

But they found that he drank little, did not gamble, and was unlikely to have enemies.

Coroner Mr Turnbull adjourned the inquest three times and appealed for anyone who could solve the riddle to come forward.

Then he recorded an open verdict.

Worldwide

Mr Turnbull told us: "An open verdict means that this case is still technically under investigation."

"It is an intractable mystery. The police, too, have not closed their file."

Mr Graham Birdsall, area co-ordinator for Contact International UK, the largest UFO study movement, said: "There is worldwide interest in this case. It is the biggest UFO story for many years.

"The fact that the police

have even considered the possibility of UFO involvement is unique."

Mr Birdsall and Mr Walter Reid, of the British UFO Research Association, confirmed that the PC involved underwent hypnosis.

"There is no obvious explanation why the body was there", said Mr Reid. "It would seem he was literally dropped there".

Mr Adamski's widow, who is confined to a wheelchair, said: "He was a good man with no enemies.

"He must have been kidnapped, by who or what and for what reason, I don't think I will ever know."

UFO enthusiasts' files list him as a CE-3—Close Encounter of the Third Kind.

New threat to Times

SUNDAY TIMES journalists turned up for work as

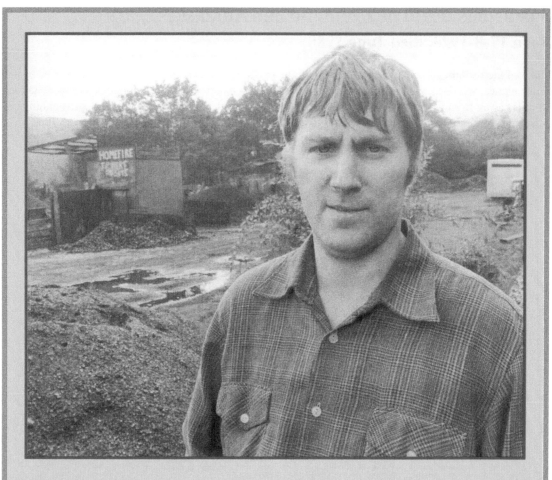

WE were able to track down an excellent 'period' photo of J. W. Parker's coal yard, from Mirror Pix©. This shows Trevor Parker posing at the yard – behind him can be seen the pyramidal heaps of coal beans in their separate bunkers. The photo was used in the newspapers at the time but didn't show any worthwhile detail. Over the years speculation continues, as to the cause of the demise of Mr. Adamski – incredibly it was even suggested he may have been struck by ball lightning, while out for a stroll!

Mr Adamski, who had lived in Tingley since 1960, married Leokadia Kowalska in 1951 – she was to sadly suffer from multiple sclerosis in later life. In 2004, Chris Zielinski contacted Nick Pope, wishing to get in touch with Alan Godfrey or anybody else that might have had special interest in the case, after explaining he had been the person who had identified the deceased at Hebden Bridge Mortuary. Nick advised him to obtain a copy of a video entitled "Death by Unnatural Causes", that had accompanied issue 18 of the "Unopened Files" published by Mark Birdsall of *Eye Spy Magazine*. This included an interview with Alan Godfrey. In 2012 we left telephone messages with Mark to contact us about the matter but received no reply.

His unusual death led to much Press speculation in the months that followed, including ridiculous suggestions made by journalists, John Sheard and Stewart Bonney, from the *Sunday Mirror* (27th September 1981) quote: 'UFO Death Riddle', who inferred that Mr Adamski's death was, in some way, connected with UFO activity – a hypothesis given further weight by the suggestion that the only way this man could have ended up on the coal pile was from having been put there from above!

Sensational claims like these, although initially raising the public's awareness about UFOs in general, ultimately create the opposite effect and do much harm, by bringing the subject into the realms of ridiculousness. Unfortunately, the myths surrounding this particular incident continue to flourish, despite it being patently clear that the death of this man was not caused through any alien interaction.

Anyone who bothers to examine the facts behind this case properly for themselves, rather than accepting, on face value, the astonishing, unsubstantiated, wild claims made by certain parties, who have deliberately attributed the death of this man to some form of alien interaction, to raise their own status within the community, will see for themselves that, while Mr Adamski died in mysterious circumstances, it was the hand of 'man' which was responsible. We felt it was important to bring to the readers' attention the 'real truths' behind a matter that still continues, to this present day, to be associated with UFO activity by the media.

One fairly recent example of this was a documentary, produced by *Fire Fly Productions*, shown on Channel 5, as one of a series on UFOs, presented on UK television, in 2008, entitled: 'Britain's Closest Encounters', at 8pm on the 23rd July. Despite sending them a full report appertaining to a reinvestigation into the case, carried out by David Sankey and ourselves, which showed there wasn't even a tenuous connection with reported UFO activity, they emailed us back saying that: *"It would not be doing the viewing figures any good by presenting the result of your investigations"*.

Sequence of Events

Chris Zielinski (long-time family friend)

> *"I was born in 1953. My dad Henryk lived up the road, at the time, and got to be friends with both of them (he died in June 1978) and they took me 'under their wing'. Sometimes I used to help 'Ziggie' repair his Datsun car, registered number AWX 82S. He treated me like a son and I treated him like a father. I always found him to be a quiet man but with a stubborn streak, very unassuming. He liked to keep in the background, rather than liking the limelight. He was not a great conversationalist, and was ill at ease with people – in short he was a shy man, that didn't like mixing with others.*
>
> *I remember a woman came to stay with the 'Adamski's', after having taken out a Court injunction against her husband, 'J' who she alleged had assaulted her. The couple later divorced and she went to live at Bradford. At the time, I was going out with her daughter *Stephanie, who, out of the blue, finished our relationship. Some months later, I was in the Polish Club, at Chapel Town, Leeds, when Stephanie came in and showed me an engagement*

---

*Authors enquiries with Leeds Registry Office, in 2012, revealed that no wedding took place on the 7th June 1980, involving anybody called Stephanie as we had hoped to obtain her current whereabouts. Following various telephone conversations with Chris in 2005, he agreed to meet us in Leeds, to discuss the matter further. Unfortunately, despite emails, telephone messages, and letters sent to his home address, we never heard anything more from him and have no idea of his current whereabouts.

Man's body found in old goods yard

12 JUN 1980

POLICE were today trying to identify the body of a man found in an old railway goods yard near the main Halifax-Manchester line at Todmorden.

The man, aged 50 to 60, is believed to have been of Polish or Ukrainian origin. He carried no papers to give police a lead to his identity.

His body was found by a coalman yesterday afternoon.

Photographs of the dead man were today being circulated in a bid to establish his identity.

Police do not suspect crime and a post-mortem has revealed that the man was a chronic bronchitis sufferer who had a severe chest deformity.

A CID spokesman in Halifax said the man died only a few hours before his body was discovered.

"There are no suspicious circumstances but we are anxious to trace the man's movements before his death and his identity." he said.

The man was 5ft 6in tall, of medium build and sallow complexion. His hair was dark and closely cropped.

He was wearing a brown John Collier jacket covering a white Aertex vest. He had brown trousers and shoes with blue patterned socks.

The goods yard near the main railway line where he was found is used as a coal depot by J. W. Parker, coal merchants, of Rochdale Road, Todmorden.

Mr Parker's son, Trevor, discovered the body when he went to make a pick-up at mid-afternoon yesterday.

ring, telling me she had decided to get married, and asked 'Ziggie' (her godfather), to give her away, as, she was unwilling to ask her real father 'J', because of the domestic situation which existed between her parents.

This decision was to cause much bitterness; 'J' had never forgiven 'Ziggie' and Lottie for looking after his wife, and was not very happy about 'Ziggie' giving her away. In the run-up to the wedding, 'Ziggie' became very agitated. He admitted to me he was extremely worried about making a speech in front of so many people. I told him not to worry and everything would be ok. He used to call around at my house, nearly every day before the wedding, complaining why it was that Stephanie's father couldn't give her away. I told him why, but he didn't seem to understand."

Jenny Randles

"Chris Zielinski, a long-standing and close friend of his, spoke of the last time he saw him alive on the Wednesday 4th June, 1980. They had a drink together, but Adamski went home to take care of Lottie. He appeared to be his usual self. Mr Zielinski describes the Adamski marriage as happy and regards it as unthinkable that Zygmund would have voluntarily left his wife. On Saturday 7th June, he was due to give his god-daughter away and looked forward to this. The 'Adamski's' also had staying with them Zygmund's cousin and son. On Friday 6th June, Zygmund and his cousin went to Leeds on a shopping trip. They returned from Leeds in the early afternoon. Zigumnd, Lottie, and the cousin and boy, ate lunch together. At 3.30pm Zygmund went to the local shop to buy some potatoes. After talking briefly to a neighbour, he strolled away and was never seen alive again."

Chris Zielinski

"On Friday 6th June, I saw 'Ziggie' at his house, when he received a telephone call from somebody. I don't know who it was but, a short time later, 'Ziggie' told me he was going to fetch a 20Kg. bag of potatoes. Why didn't he use his car? I said I would come with him. He told me he wanted to go on his own. After he failed to turn up, I went to see the relative 'J' concerned and found him in one hell of a state. He was sweating and said he didn't want to speak to the police. I explained they just wanted to interview him and eliminate him from their enquiries. He agreed to come with me to Bradford Police Station. I spoke to the officer on the desk. He didn't seem that interested and just took details down from me. The next time I saw him (Ziggie) was in the mortuary."

Mrs Adamski

*"I still cannot understand it; he had been in Leeds, shopping.
When he got home he remembered he had forgotten some
potatoes for tea. He said he was slipping out to get some.
I never saw him alive again", she said. "No-one seems to
know what happened and I can only think he was kidnapped,
or something,"*

We believe Mrs Adamski had her suspicions who was responsible for her
husband's abduction, but was too frightened to say anything.

Body of Mr Adamski found by Trevor Parker

*"I started work at 8.00am and left the coal yard unattended,
at about 11.00am, to visit other premises, but didn't return
until 3.45pm, when I discovered a man, lying face down,
approximately ten feet up the pile of anthracite beans (man-
made coal) with his head facing the top. I initially thought
it was a drunken man, sleeping off a bout of drink, and
contacted the ambulance station."*

Ambulance men arrived after 999 call made by Mr Parker

We learnt from a photograph taken of Mr Adamski, shortly after the body
was recovered, that he was found dressed in a string vest, no shirt, and a
brown 'John Collier' jacket, with trousers incorrectly buttoned – his watch
and wallet were later found to be missing. It is clear, from the amount of
coal residue on his face, that he was probably found by the ambulance men
lying face down (presumably turned over by them, during their examination,
and left on his back) which was the position the police found him in when
they arrived, a short time later, being greeted by one of the ambulance crew,
who said, *"You've got a murder on your hands."* Following their attendance,
the ambulance was moved between the bunkers – which consisted of three
wooden panels, some 5ft in height – so as to prevent travellers in passing
trains being able to view the deceased.

PC Alan Godfrey

PC Alan Godfrey:

*"He was lying on his back with
his eyes open, looking straight
up, no sign of rigor mortis. I
remember a theory, suggested
by the CID, who thought he
might have fell asleep under
a lorry, and the acid fell on
his neck, but this wasn't the
explanation, as I remember the
Pathologist telling me that it*

Riddle of coal yard death
– 5 SEP 1980
man

THE RIDDLE of a Polish
man found dead in a coal
yard in Todmorden is still
unsolved after more than 12
weeks of police inquiries.

Mr Zigmunt Jan Adamski,
aged 57, was found dead in the
former railway goods yard
near the main Halifax to
Manchester line on June 11.

He lived with his crippled
wife in Tingley, near Leeds,
before he disappeared.

Despite extensive police inquiries there has been no trace
of his whereabouts since his
mystery disappearance five
days before he was found dead.

Detective Inspector John
Boyle said at the resumed inquest into Mr Adamski's death
that burns on his head, which
appeared to have been caused
by a corrosive liquid, had been
examined by three top doctors.

It was not known whether
the injuries were self-inflicted
or caused by someone else.

Extensive police inquiries
had covered a wide area of
Yorkshire and Lancashire.

But Mr Adamski's widow,
Mrs Leokadia Adamski, said:
"I am not satisfied because I
do not know what happened to
my husband."

Calderdale coroner Mr
James Turnbull said he would
call further witnesses when the
inquest was re-opened at a date
to be fixed.

There were two other op-
tions open to him: To conclude
the inquest and record an open
verdict, or to adjourn the
proceedings in the hope that
police inquiries uncovered new
evidence.

Pathologist Dr Alan
Edwards told an earlier hearing that Mr Adamski died of a
heart attack.

But where he spent the last
few days of his life and why he
was in Todmorden remain a
mystery.

wasn't acid on his neck. He was certainly alive on the day he was found. It's a real mystery, although one thing I do know – it was nothing to do with any aliens . . . that's a load of rubbish!"

The police considered various theories as to how Mr Adamski had arrived at the side of the station. Had he caught the train from Leeds, to Todmorden and walked down into the coal yard of his own accord, or had he been moved to the coal yard by somebody (after death) and placed onto the pile of coal beans as some sort of 'statement' by his captors?

Mr Adamski was in the process of applying for retirement from Lofthouse Colliery Pit, due for closure in 1981, as he wanted to be able to look after his wife, Leokadia (Lottie) who suffered from Multiple Sclerosis? Could he have jumped from a bridge onto a passing coal lorry on its way to 'Parkers' coal yard, causing the injuries, and then been transferred onto the coal pile by an unsuspecting operator? We believe it is unlikely he caught a train to Todmorden coal yard. He certainly was not 'delivered' there by a coal lorry, as Mr Parker confirms no coal deliveries took place on that day, or the previous few days.

The manner of Mr Adamski's disappearance (seemingly out of character for a man, who would presumably have been looking forward to giving away his god-daughter, Stephanie) and the peculiar circumstances in which he was found, with injuries inflicted to the back of his neck, was the cause of much suspicion by the attending police officers. PC Alan Godfrey, who was one of those officers, still remains perplexed and commented to us: *"Why do the public and the media still insist on linking this incident with what happened to me?"* (See November 1980).

Somebody else who was to take a keen interest in this case was veteran UFO Investigator Philip Mantle, whose own father was a coal miner, at the same Colliery. *"There is no link between his death and UFOs. My father worked with him for years. The word at Lofthouse Pit was that his wife's relatives had 'done him in'. His wife had wanted to go back to Poland, but he never did. It's a bit of a coincidence that her relatives were here when he disappeared. I lived at Tingley for years where 'Adamski' lived, right next to the M62 Motorway. He went to the local shop (which I have been in) and never came back. If there was a UFO, don't you think someone else might have seen it?"*

Deceased taken to the Mortuary and Open Verdict

A photograph of the deceased, taken at the Mortuary, was obtained and shows Mr Adamski with hair cut short but not cropped; presumably, the hair was cut short before the post-mortem. There are traces of coal dust around both nostrils and what appears to be coal dust underneath the chin, consistent with the face and body. The same photo shows traces of coal dust leading downwards from under the chin at an oblique angle – an effect which one would expect to see on the skin outside the area of the shirt worn (if the victim had been wearing a shirt) with one vital difference – his shirt was never found.

Unfortunately, without being privy to the evidence submitted by the Forensic Scientist, who gave evidence at the Coroner's Inquest, any further comment would be pure speculation, although we understood the burns to his head were caused approximately two days previously (certainly not as many as five) occurring between eight and ten hours previously to the body being found, which would put it at around 7am on the 11th June 1980.

Post Mortem Photo

We were able to obtain a photograph taken of Mr Adamski's face at the Morgue which shows the injury to the neck. Contrary to the information contained in the *Weekend* Magazine dated the 30th March 1983 which says that the police claimed Mr Adamski was spotlessly clean as if he had stepped from a shower. This is incorrect although they gave the correct height (6ft) of the coal heap. The photograph shows coal dust below the left nostril and upper lip. We decided not to include the photo knowing that if this was published it would have been made available on the Internet and that while to our knowledge there are no living relatives in the UK, it didn't seem morally right to include it, although we have included the injury to the neck, as this is important evidence.

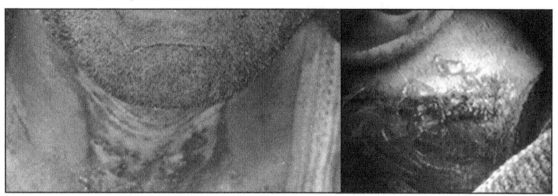

Acupuncturist involved prior to death

On 7th July 1980, the *Halifax Courier* ran a story about the case. *'The mystery of the last few days of a 57- year-old man's life before he was found dead at Todmorden deepened today, when police established he had visited Lancashire for medical treatment. It is now known that he visited an acupuncturist, in Nelson, on Friday, June 6th.*

Detective Inspector John Boyle of Halifax, who is leading the inquiry, said today that the Lancashire connection was the only new development and that Mr Adamski's whereabouts on the days leading up to his death remained a mystery.'

Coroner Mr James Turnbull

Coroner – Mr James Turnbull – was quoted, then, as saying:

> *"It is quite the most mysterious death I have investigated in 12 years as a coroner. As a trained lawyer, I have to rely on facts. Unfortunately, we have not been able to uncover any facts which may have contributed to this death. I tend to believe that there may be a simple explanation. However, I do admit that the failure of forensic scientists to identity the corrosive substance, which caused Mr Adamski's burns, could lend some weight to the UFO theory.*

> *As a coroner, I cannot speculate but I must admit that if I was walking over Ilkley Moor, tomorrow, and a UFO came down, I would not be surprised. I might be terrified but not surprised. I cannot believe that all the thousands of reports of this sort of phenomenon, covering almost every country in the world, and going back through the ages, result from human error."*

(Ironically, opinions expressed in this way were to be banned, following new guidelines for Coroners, laid out in Rule 36(2) The Coroners Rules, 1984).

We thought it extraordinary that a man in his position (a trained solicitor) could, contrary to his declaration as above, actually speculate on the cause of the death. Worse, he condemned (with others) this mystery to be forever connected (not even tenuously) with the nefarious notion the events that befell Mr Adamski were, in some way, connected with UFO activity.

UFO experts to probe man's death riddle

– 6 OCT 1981

UFO experts have decided to investigate the strange death of Polish-born miner Mr Zygmunt Adamski.

Mr Adamski's body was discovered on a coal tip at Todmorden goods yard a year last June and extensive police inquiries have failed to discover the events before his death.

He lived in Leeds and had been missing for five days before his body was found.

Now Mr Walter Reid, who lives in Leeds and two other UFO experts are to look into the circumstances of Mr Adamski's death.

Mr Reid, a member of the British UFO Research Association met Mr Graham Birdsall, of another UFO group, Contact UK, and Mr Nigel Mortimer, of National UFO Network.

"We decided there are definite grounds for a full major investigation into Mr Adamski's death," said Mr Reid.

Police officers investigated a possible UFO link with Mr Adamski's death but came across no concrete evidence.

The UFO link was put forward after several reports of strange sights in the sky around the time of Mr Adamski's death and later.

Mr Reid said there were many big questions left unanswered by the police investigation into the death of the miner, who lived at Tingley, near Leeds.

"Anyone who may be able to help us can contact me at home, 17, Lanshaw Terrace, Belle Isle, Leeds," said Mr Reid.

The police still have an open file on Mr Adamski and would welcome any information about the events leading to his death.

Five people have reported the sighting of a dark object with red and white flashing lights hovering 1,000 ft above Stoodley Pike.

Mr David Redman, a disc jockey at the Shoulder of Mutton, Blackshaw Head, saw the object as he was unloading his equipment at the pub on Sunday night.

He called the landlord, Mr Dennis Hunt, who came out with his bar staff, Mr Trevor Pool and his wife, Elaine, and a customer.

"Mr Redman called us out at 7.12 and when we went back in at 7.20 it was still there," said Mr Hunt.

Another UFO was seen over Queen's Road, Halifax, last Saturday.

Riddle of body in goods yard

Todmorden News & Advertiser 13.6.1980

MYSTERY surrounds the death of a man thought to be Polish or Ukrainian whose body was discovered on a coal heap in the Todmorden Railway Station goods yard.

Police were yesterday trying to discover the identity of the man who was described as having a shaven head, probably because of a skin complaint from which he suffered.

The man, thought to be of Polish or Ukrainian origin, was said to be between 50 and 60 years old, 5 feet 6 inches in height, medium build with dark hair and a sallow complexion.

His body was found on the coal heap at 4 pm on Wednesday when police immediately set about the task of identifying the man, who was not carrying any papers or other means of identification.

"We are requesting the co-operation of members of the public who might be able to help us find the identity of this man," said Police Community Affairs Officer Insp Trevor Greenwood.

The clothes on the body were a brown jacket with a "John Collier" label.

brown trousers, brown shoes and blue patterned socks.

"We are not applying any suspicious circumstances to this body yet," said Insp Greenwood. But investigations were being continued.

Inspector Greenwood thought the body had been on the heap for "one or two days at the most."

The Calderdale Coroner, Mr James

Turnbull, had been informed and a post mortem examination was being carried out yesterday morning, he said.

The goods yard near the main railway line where the man was found is used as a coal depot by J. W. Parker, coal merchants, of Rochdale Road, Todmorden.

Mrs Parker's son, Trevor, discovered the body when he went to make a pick up at mid afternoon yesterday.

West Yorkshire Police Press Office

West Yorkshire Police press liaison officer – Bob Baxter – who was contacted by Graham Birdsall, said:

"I found the press stories ridiculous. There were no sightings of UFOs reported to us. The corrosive marks could have been washed away by extensive rain that fell at the time; hence the reason why the forensic people could not identify them. In any case, the guy probably had medical treatment, for some of his hair had been shaved away, and also, the man, 'Adamski', did not die of fright – as some papers have reported."

Inquest deemed Open-verdict – Body released

Although an Open verdict was recorded (which means the case is still open and that the police have not closed their file) incredibly, the body of Mr Adamski was released by the Court on the 17th July 1980, which suggests this matter was no longer regarded as a suspicious death, because, if this had been the case, the body would not have been released at such an early time, given the suspicious circumstances that lay behind the recovery of the body and its attendant circumstances. Why was this course of action adopted, and on whose instructions, and why did the West Yorkshire CID allow this to take place, if the death was

IAR 767920

CERTIFIED COPY OF AN ENTRY

Pursuant to the Births and   Deaths Registration Act 1953

| **DEATH** | Entry No. 6 |

| Registration district | Todmorden | Administrative area | Metropolitan District of Calderdale |
| Sub-district | Todmorden | | |

1. Date and place of death — Dead body found on eleventh June 1980 at Todmorden Railway Station Coke Yard, Todmorden

2. Name and surname — Zygmund Jan ADAMSKI

3. Sex — Male

4. Maiden surname of woman who has married — ———

5. Date and place of birth — 17th August 1923 Masiechowice, Poland

6. Occupation and usual address — Coal Miner 2b, Thornfield Crescent, Tingley, near Wakefield

7.(a) Name and surname of informant — Certificate received from J.A. Turnbull Coroner for the Metropolitan District of Calderdale. Inquest held 25th September 1980

(b) Qualification

(c) Usual address

8. Cause of death —
Heart failure due to Ischaemic heart disease. Chronic bronchitis and emphysema

(Open Verdict)

9. I certify that the particulars given by me above are true to the best of my knowledge and belief

Signature of informant

10. Date of registration — Twenty seventh September 1980

11. Signature of registrar — Florence Dean Registrar

Certified to be a true copy of an entry in a register in my custody.

*Superintendent Registrar
*Registrar
*Strike out whichever does not apply

Date 10th January 2006

not as a result of an accident? We have our own thoughts on why this course of action was adopted, but no proof.

Graham Birdsall's investigation, conducted in 1981

Somebody else who took an active interest in this case was Graham Birdsall – then Co-ordinator / Investigator for Contact UK – who wrote to Coroner, Mr James Turnbull, on the 16th November 1981, on behalf of himself, Nigel Mortimer (NUFON), and BUFORA Representative – Walter Reid.

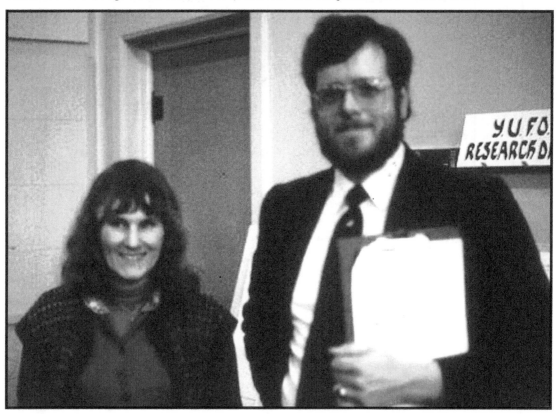

Jenny Randles and Graham Birsdsall. See end of this section for Graham Birdsall's Report.

"Further to our telephone conversation of November 9th, please find enclosed a series of questions, which have been agreed upon by the investigators researching the 'Adamski' case as being those which most need answering, in order for us to proceed further with the case. We fully appreciate the difficulties you may have in answering them all, in part, in full, or at all, but we do wish to convey to you our feelings on the matter; namely, all cooperation by the police officers involved in this case has now ceased, certain officers have been refused permission to look at the 'Adamski' file. The bottom line is that a cloak of secrecy has now enveloped the whole affair. The question must surely be, why?

In eleven years of researching phenomena, I have never known such secrecy, and the questions set out are plain enough. It is this type of questioning that seems to throw individuals into some type of fear, but we would ask, what on Earth is there to be frightened about? We do not for a moment believe, as some newspapers would have you believe, that Mr Adamski was abducted by some kind of craft – that is pure speculation put out by individuals, clawing for a story.

However, those stories have captured the imagination of people on both sides of the Atlantic, and it is now our duty to pour over the facts and present them in a manner which will end this speculation once and for all. I make no secret of the fact that we are looking to you to furbish us with those facts, but I will be surprised if you, yourself, do not come up against the same brick wall we have been knocking our heads against for the last two months. We greatly appreciate the cooperation you are giving, and trust that you will go some way to helping us report this case as factually as we can.

Looking forward to your reply,

Graham Birdsall"

Walter Reid also wrote to Mr Turnbull on the 5th October, presumably asking for further information, and received a letter from him on the 19th October 1980.

"Copies of depositions taken in Court are only available to 'properly interested persons', as specified by stature.

I am afraid that neither you nor your organisation fall within this category, and therefore, it will not be possible for me to supply a copy of the depositions to you; on the other hand, I do not wish to appear unhelpful and I would be perfectly prepared to disclose the details of the investigation made on my behalf to you at an interview, if this could conveniently be arranged.

J. A. Turnbull."

In a letter dated the 24th November 1981, Mr Turnbull wrote back to Graham Birdsall.

"Dear Mr Birdsall,

Re: Zygmunt Jan Adamski

Thank you for your letter of the 16th November.

I can but acknowledge at this stage, since providing replies to your questions will take a certain amount of research and time.

I will write to you again as a soon as possible.

Signed, J.A. Turnbull"

Lost days man saw acupuncturist

— 7 JUL 1980

THE MYSTERY of the last few days of a 57-year-old man's life before he was found dead at Todmorden deepened today when police established he had visited Lancashire for medical treatment

Polish-born Mr Zigmunt Jan Adamski left his home at Tingley, near Leeds, on Friday, June 6 to do some shopping. He never returned home.

It is now known that he visited an acupuncturist in Nelson later that day.

But his movements from then until the following Wednesday, June 11 — the day his body was found at a Todmorden coal yard — remain a mystery.

Detective Inspector John Boyle, of Halifax, who is leading the inquiry, said today that the Lancashire connection was the only new development and that Mr Adamski's whereabouts on the days leading up to his death remained a mystery.

"We would appeal for any information to help establish this man's movements between June 6 and 11," he said.

The Calderdale Coroner, Mr James Turnbull, has not ruled out the possibility of crime.

At an inquest, opened and adjourned in

Halifax last week, Mr Turnbull also appealed for witnesses who could help piece together the mystery of the last five days of his life.

Mr Adamski, a miner, of Thornfield Crescent, Tingley, was said at the inquest to be a quiet man with no enemies.

The inquest heard that the former prisoner-of-war, a coalface worker at Lofthouse Colliery, had been dead for between eight and ten hours before his body was discovered by a coalman at a merchant's depot near Todmorden Railway Station.

Dr Alan Edwards, a consultant pathologist, said the man had died of a heart attack with the poor condition of his lungs a contributory factor.

Mr Adamski was dressed as he had left home with the exception of his shirt — but a wallet and wristwatch were also missing.

Police are also baffled by scars on the back of the head and side of the neck.

It is thought the marks were caused by acid or scalding within just two days of Mr Adamski's death.

Meanwhile, Mr Adamski's invalid widow, Leokadia, has been granted permission for his body to be taken to Poland for burial.

The body will not be released, however, until police inquiries have advanced to their satisfaction.

Contact UK   I2, Miles Hill Street, LS7 2EQ   Contact UK
September '8I   0532 484345   Issue 9

- -

Editorial: 'The Adamski Case'

It is rather ironic that having experienced one of the most quietist periods of ufo activity in this region for many years, we should be at the heart of one of the most mysterious cases ever to hit these shores for decades. At least that is what some would have us believe. Having studied this case intensely over the past few days, I have to admit that there are facets which baffle me, the police, and others, notably Nigel Mortimer. Nigel, of Nufon, was of course the man who investigated the case, and as I write this newsletter to you, a meeting has been arranged between us, so we can glean all the facts surrounding the case, and perhaps reach agreement on one or two sticky points. However, as this newsletter is designed to keep you up to date on local ufo events, I am prepared to divulge information relating to the case which you may not have read in the press. Adamski was last seen alive at tea-time June 6th 1980 - and his body was not found until June IIth. The marks on his forehead, and down his cheeks were some sort of corrosive burn marks. These marks were there three days before the body was found. There were three faint scratch marks on the hands, but they would not have caused pain, they might have caused a tickling sensation. Adamski was a man of good character, but being an ex-Tole, occasionaly voiced strong political arguments towards and against the Soviet Union, however, the police have ruled out some sort of political revenge taken against him. The body was found on a coal tip, thirty foot up, yet Adamski was as clean as a man who had just taken a shower. The police came to the conclusion, and it is an incredible one, that the body had been lowered onto the top of the coal tip from above...from some sort of aircraft. You will have read reports that a policeman had seen a ufo in the vacinity at the time of Adamski's dissapearance,that man was P.C. Alan Godfrey, of Todmorden. What now transpires is that Jenny Randles has managed to put the man under post-hypnotic regression to reveal further details about the ufo, and if that is true, and I have no reason to doubt it, then West Yorkshire Police must have not only had to give permission, they must have really thought a ufo <u>might</u> have caused Adamski's death, as stated at the inquest. I will have more to say to you at our next meeting about this case, but one thing I am not prepared to say at this stage is that an encounter with a ufo caused the death of this man, for that would be foolish in the extreme. What I will say to you is this; there have been cases in the past which has resulted in one common feeling felt by the witness(es), that feeling is fear, a fear of the unknown. It is something I have experienced myself when alone at night I saw a ufo in the night sky, it was no different from other lights in the sky, nor was it doing anything unusual, it simply passed very high overhead. I had seen many such lights in the past, but why should this particular light give me the 'shakes'? I simply dont know, nor pretend to know, but what would a close encounter do to a mans nervous system, what would it do to a man like Adamski?, a man who had never even considered the possibility that they exist? I fear that if the story is true, then an encounter with a ufo or entities will have proved too much of a strain on his heart, it should not be forgotten that when police found Adamski, his face, stiff and deadly white, showed a look of sheer terror. The papers are full of this story at the moment, and the Sunday Mirror is taking a real interest in the case, my phone has hardly stopped ringing with various people wanting information, quotes, background material etc. The time to conduct a real investigation of this case will be when the 'hoo-haa' dies down, only then will we be able to disect each piece of information and draw conclusions. Having said that, there is no doubt we have a major case on our hands, and that interest in the ufo is once again on the rise. I would not be too surprised to see a few strangers at our next meeting.

(1)

On Saturday, September 19th, 1981, the Yorkshire Evening Post had as its main headline; "DID UFO KILL THIS MAN?". A sub-title read; "Police and experts probe amazing 'aliens' theory." It was a Y.E.P. exclusive by Tony Harney, and it included two photographs, one of the deceased, Mr Zygmunt Adamski, alongside his wife Lottie outside their home, and of a Mr Nigel Mortimer, underneath of which a caption read,"UFO expert".

Before giving a full transcript of the story, as it appeared in the Evening Post, one important fact should be entered. Nigel Mortimer had written to the co-author of this report some three weeks prior to the story emerging in the press, requesting information on how to become an investigator of UFO phenomena. That co-author, Graham W. Birdsall, the Co-ordinator/Investigator for Contact International (UK) for this region, was therefore somewhat sceptical about Mr Mortimer's credentials, particularly in view of the fact that in eleven years of research into the phenomena, he had never heard of the man up until September 1st 1981, when he had written to him in reply to the letter he recieved.

THE ARTICLE

"Police trying to solve one of West Yorkshire's most mysterious deaths today revealed they had considered the amazing theory that UFO's – unidentified flying objects – might have been involved.

The body of Yorkshire miner Mr Zygmunt Jan Adamski, 57, was found on a tip at Todmorden on June 11 last year – five days after he left his home 30 miles away in Thornfield Crescent, Tingley, Leeds, to buy potatoes from a shop 200 yards away.

The inquest decided Mr Adamski died from natural causes – but the mystery surrounding his death and the riddle of his five missing days have baffled police ever since.

Mr Adamski, a coal face worker, suffered from angina, according to his wife, Mrs Lottie Adamski, but this did not prevent him working down the pit.

An inquest was told exhaustion could have caused heart failure resulting in his death. But a leading pathologist also said he may have "died of fright."

Among the other puzzling aspects are:

Burns were found on Mr Adamski's neck and head – and forensic scientists have been unable to explain them;

Despite the most intensive inquires and widespread appeals no witness has come forward to say he or she saw Mr Adamski over the five days between his leaving home and his body being found. According to relatives he had never been to Todmorden in his life and did not know the area;

At the time of Mr Adamski's disappearance there were reports of UFO activity in the area where his body was found, including reports by the police.

A spokeswoman for West Yorkshire police said the file on the death of Mr Adamski was still open. "If further information comes to light we will pursue those lines of enquiry again," said the spokeswoman.

(2)

Now some of the countries top UFO experts - including Mr Nigel Mortimer of Otley - are investigating Mr Adamski's death.

One of the theories they are considering is that he was 'kidnapped' by aliens.

The description of the burn marks on Mr Adamski was given by consultant pathologist Dr. Alan Edwards at the inquest conducted by Calderdale Coroner Mr James Turnbull.

Dr. Edwards also referred to scratches on the palms of both hands and on each knee.

Dr. Edwards also said his death was caused by heart failure which could be related to a severe shock or fright.

Mr Turnbull recorded a verdict that Mr Adamski died from natural causes although he added that crime could not be ruled out and he appealed to the public to help piece together the missing days in the life of Mr Adamski.

Mrs Adamski is still mystified by what happened to her husband. "I still cannot understand it. He had been in Leeds shopping."

When he got home he remembered he had forgotten some potatoes for tea, he said he was slipping out to get some. I never saw him alive again," she said.

"No one seems to know what happened and I can only think he was kidnapped or something," said Mrs Adamski.

Top UFO experts feel Mrs Adamski is right and, amazingly, claim his kidnappers may not be from earth. Mr Mortimer, of Meagill Rise, Otley, a member of Northern UFO News said there were a reported and recorded number of sightings of what were thought to be UFO's in the Todmorden area at the time of Mr Adamski's death.

"One of these sightings was made by a local police officer and they are documented. I am investigating this case and as far as I can gather his disappearance and death are inexplicable.

"Had the unfortunate man been a victim of a mysterious UFO phenomenon?" asks Mr Mortimer. " (End of article).

(3)

Steps were taken to set-up a joint investigation into the mystery at once on my instigation, with Nigel Mortimer of Nufon, and Walter Reid of Bufora agreeing to the need to conduct such an exercise.

Obvious question marks hung like a giant cloud over the circumstances involving the mans disappearance and death, and our first task was to glean as much information on the mans background as possible.

Mr Adamski was a normal person, tee-total, and had no criminal record.

There was a suggestion made and put to the police that because he was a Polish exile and anti-communist some political motive might be behind his death, but the police ruled this out because in their words he was "not a political activist."

He was a smashing neighbour according to those who lived nearby.

The journalist who covered the story for the Evening Post, Tony Harney, told me that the marks found on the body were as follows;

Three scratch marks on each hand, but they were not even superficial. They might cause a tickle sensation, but no more, which would seem to rule out torture.

The burn marks on the head were corrosive, and unidentified. However, they had been on the body for some three days before the man died. Before Tony Harney concluded our conversation I asked him for the name of the police officer(s) who had alledgedly observed a UFO at the time of Adamski's dissapearence. **PC Godfrey's sighting was in November 1980**

He gave me the name of P.C. Alan Godfrey, of Todmorden police.

I had no records myself of any activity in or around that area for the period of June 6 to II, and it was a surprise that West Yorkshire police had not contacted me (as is the usual case), particularly in view of the fact that one of their own officers was involved.

The mystery deepened somewhat when it was learned that Alan Godfrey was one of the first officers on the scene once the body had been found, and that he himself had not only seen a UFO, but was undergoing hypnotic regression to reveal a close encounter experience which occured in November of that same year.

I kept our senior research officer Derek Mansell up to date with matters in a series of long and detailed phone conversations. It was important he suggested, that we attempt to answer the following questions;

Why did the West Yorkshire police allow a UFO group to put one of their own men under this treatment?

What is the character of the policeman like?

Who put him under hypnosis, and what of his character?

Derek also wanted to know if an excavator could have been used to dump the body on the tip?, and had the body now been buried, or still kept on ice? It was vital he said, that we obtain a copy of the coroners report, and the forensic data, in order to check the findings using our own experts.

(4)

Shortly after we began the investigation, Tony Harney came up with the revelation that Jenny Randles had been researching this case for some months, and that he believed she was about to publish a book on her findings.

As Nigel Mortimer was subscribed to the Northern UFO Network, it was suggested to him that he attempt to find out as much information as possible from them, but both he and Walter Reid of Bufora reported that no information was forthcoming.

Several pieces of news did appear in the newsletters sent out by the group, but a surprising phone call from Peter Warrington (Bufora) added to the mystery. Shortly before this call, the Sunday Mirror had printed a front page article which dealt with the Adamski case.

Peter Warrington was upset (to put it mildly), that the Sunday Mirror had got hold of the story, and why Nufon had not even been mentioned. He was angry that the story had mentioned a policeman, and denied that he had any knowledge of such a man undergoing post-hypnotic regression.

It transpired, after I let it be known to Peter the identity of the policeman, that he did now acknowledge the fact that Alan Godfrey was undergoing hypnotic regression, but that the Sunday Mirror were wrong to assume that this was in some way connected with the Adamski case. Peter requested that I make no attempt to contact this man as he was already on the carpet for revealing his experiences to the group without their prior permission.

Given that this was the truth, and I respect Peter Warrington as an author with highly held principles, I agreed not to interview Alan Godfrey.

However, Walter Reid of Bufora did speak to Godfrey before my conversation with Peter, and a transcript of that conversation reads as follows;

Mr Godfrey?," Yes, speaking," my name is Reid, I am a representative for the British UFO Research Association and I would like to ask you some questions, "certainly, go ahead." Firstly I would like to mention that I am researching the Adamski case and would like to ask you about your experience with regards to a UFO encounter. "Well, I can tell you that I did encounter something rather unusual, but I cannot remember what it was." Well did you see a UFO?, "Oh, God certainly I did, I was driving down a road and there was a green glow, I had never seen anything like it before, but it was weird." Did anyone else see anything?,"yes, I believe a few other officers saw some unusual objects and made a report, but I have never heard anything else about it." Could I send you an RI sighting report form, which I would like you to complete and send back to me? "Well, I'm afraid that I have had rather enough of forms, and my wife is rather upset by the whole thing, so I would prefer to leave it for now, if you dont mind." Yes, I will be in touch again and thank-you for your assistance.

Needless to say, the questions asked of Godfrey were totaly unsuitable, and it was at this stage that I doubted WR'sability to provide myself and Nigel Mortimer with accurate information, and the fact remained that I had agreed not to interview Godfrey myself. A poor state of affairs.

With the assistance of Data Research, the net was spread far and wide to record UFO activity on the days when Adamski dissapeared.

(5)

On June 4th 1980, Buenos Aries, Argentina, at 12.00 midnight local time, a large disc shaped object was seen moving very fast across the sky.

On June 7th, 1980, Nottingham, England, at 9.00pm, a large disc shaped object was seen hovering very low, it then flew along hedge tops as if looking for something. The object was some 70-80 feet in diameter. The witnesses, a family in a car, had stopped when they first saw the object. They got out to observe it, but were frightened out of their wits when it came towards them. A shadow of sorts enveloped their car as it passed overhead, to disappear.

There were two sightings in the United States, but these were on June 13 - 14, and eliminated from this enquiry.

The press meanwhile were heavily involved with the case, and before too long references were being made to the coincidence of the surname Adamski and that of his American "counterpart" in the fifties. These articles only served to create more distrust among senior officers of the West Yorkshire police, and those investigating the case.

Certain facts came to the surface as we treaded carefully amongst various people and evidence. Alan Godfrey had experienced a close encounter of the third kind, and he had revealed this in confidence to a friend who was a member of Kufora, the Manchester group. He had been "carpeted" by senior officers for not revealing facts about his experiences, and had in effect been told to speak to no-one.

Another member of the group, Mr Harry Harris, had offered his services to the widow of Mrs Adamski.

As the information began to come in, I contacted the press liason officer for West Yorkshire Met. Police, Bob Baxter to ask him for any comments. He found the press stories ridiculous and added; "There were no sightings of UFO's reported to us, the corrosive marks could have been washed away by extensive rain that fell at the time, hence the reason why the forensic people could not identify them. In any case, the guy probably had medical treatment, for some of his hair had been shaved away, and also, the man Adamski did not die of fright as some papers have reported."

There had been no mention of the fact that the hair or scalp of Adamski had been shaved in earlier reports, and if this was so, would not the police have located the person or persons who carried out any treatment?

As yet another meeting took place between Walter Reid, Nigel Mortimer and myself, it was Nigel's words that somewhat surprised me. He said that he first raised the mystery of Adamski's death and possible involvement of UFO's to try and involve more people locally in the subject. He had read articles in a Nufon newsletter which dealt with the case, and he had submitted these, along with several reported sightings in the area to the press.

More information concerning the finding of the body came to our notice, with yet more intriging facts.

Trevor Parker, a coal merchants son had found the body at 1.15pm, June 11, 1980. It had not been there the day before, nor had he seen it at 10.00am that very same morning it was discovered. There was no shirt on the body, his watch and wallet were missing, but there was £5 on him. It looked as if the body had been placed gently on the coal tip.

(6)

Even one of the police officers who surveyed the grim scene agreed with this opinion, going as far to say that only a helicopter could manage such a feat. The coal tip itself was smooth, there were no marks to suggest anyone had scaled it. The body was spotlessly clean, as if he "had just stepped from a shower."

Alan Godfrey it transpired, had had close encounters at the tender ages of seven and thirteen, had seen UFO's before Adamski's death in June.

We discovered that on November 28, 1980, he had a further encounter, and how, under hypnosis, he revealed how he sighted a craft, been taken aboard, and experimented on, although exact details still lay in the hands of Eufora. We also found through various contacts, that after the regression, entities appeared in his bedroom, and what is more his wife saw them and became very alarmed. We learned that the couple and their children were upset at this appearance.

Efforts were made to find out who conducted the regression, but these proved unsuccessful, however we did learn that Harry Harris took part.

Nigel Mortimer experienced a more surprising incident yet, one that we should mention.

A police officer of senior rank visited him at his home - the man denied that UFO's were involved, and demanded to know the name or names of police officers involved in the case who had seen UFO's ! Nigel got the impression that he was politly being told to forget this case.

We know that other officers had confided in Godfrey that they too had seen UFO's. We know that Godfrey felt he might in some way be connected with the death of Adamski, it was an uneasy feeling that he had.

Some fifteen months had elapsed since Adamski had died when we began our investigation, but we attempted to prick peoples memories by asking for any information relating to the case through a press circular, which appeared in several papers. Unfortunately we had no new information which we did not already have in our posession from those members of the public who responded to our appeal.

Research through old newspapers threw up more clues. On July 7th 1980, the Halifax Courier ran a story about the case, it began; "The mystery of the last few days of a 57 year old man's life before he was found dead at Todmorden deepened today when police established he had visited Lancashire for medical treatment. It is now known that he visited an acupuncturist in Nelson on Friday June 6. Detective Inspector John Boyle of Halifax, who is leading the inquiry, said today that the Lancashire connection was the only new development and that Mr Adamski's whereabouts on the days leading up to his death remained a mystery."

"Dr Alan Edwards, a consultant pathologist, said the man had died of a heart attack with the poor condition of his lungs a contributory factor

"Meanwhile, Mr Adamski's invalid widow, Leokadia, has been granted permission for his body to be taken to Poland for burial."

So, less than a month after the discovery of the body, and with so many questions left unanswered, without reaching the stage where an inquest has even begun to answer the mystery, the body is shipped out of the country. Quite extraordinary.

(7)

Other interesting facets surrounding the case, and not broadcast by the media were items like this, which appeared in the Halifax Courier on June 13th, 1980; "He" (Adamski) "had been seen in public houses in the Todmorden area, said Det. Chief Insp Baines."

And six days later, in the same paper, this appeared; "He had been missi from home for some time and had been seen wandering around the countrysi said a police spokesman."

On July 4th, 1980, another article in the same paper gave details which we had been crying out for, yet up till the time of our researching thes matters, had received no co-operation from various sources.

It began; "Mr Christopher John ZIELINSKI, of Leeds, said that before Mr Adamski's disappearence he had been told his application for early retirement from the pit had been rejected."

"He wanted to retire because he needed to look after his wife, who is an invalid," Mr Zielinski said. "He was very disappointed when he was told I would have to continue working."

Some would argue that this could be a reason for his leaving home, perhap depressed, but then another important fact emerged.

Mr Adamski was looking forward to giving away his god-daughter at a wedding two days after his disappearance, Polish relatives were staying with him at the time. He had never disappeared before. He was a quiet man with no enemies.

Significantly perhaps, we discovered that Trevor Parker had first visite the coal yard at 8.30am, not at 10.00am, and that he discovered the body at 4.00pm, not 1.15pm, as later reports indicated.

Great efforts were made to locate the acupuncturist in Nelson, Lancashire and although I travelled to the town, and found the address of such a practitioner, his secretary told me that the man Adamski was not a regular patient if he had visited her employer, as records that she kept would only give details of regular patients. If Adamski had seen him, no record of such a visit would have been made. A poor excuse if ever I heard one, but should there be a reason for not giving me information?

On October 19th, 1981, we received the following letter from the Coroner J.A. Turnbull, the man who conducted the inquest on Adamski. It was in reply to our request to see a copy of the report on the inquest.

Dear Sir,

> re: Zygmunt Jan Adamski, deceased.

Thank you for your letter of the 5th October.

Copies of depositions taken in my court are only available to "properly interested persons" as specified by statute. I am afraid that neither you nor your organisation fall within this category and therefore it will not be possible for me to supply a copy of the depositions to you.

On the other hand I do not wish to appear unhelpful and I would be perfectly prepared to disclose the details of the......(cont)

(2)

investigation made on my behalf to you at an interview if this could
be conveniently arranged."

It should be noted that Mr Harry Harris who looked after the affairs of
Mrs Adamski was a solicitor, and could therefore obtain depositions. My
understanding of the situation is that Mr Harris offered his services
free of charge, and spent a considerable amount of his own money not
only on this case, but on the Alan Godfrey episode as well.

Having taken due note of Mr Turnbull's offer of help, we compiled a list
of some 37 questions which we believed needed answering or clarifying,
on the Adamski case itself. These were dispatched on November 16th, 1981.

On November 24th, 1981, I received the following reply from the Coroner.

Dear Mr Birdsall,

     re: Zygmunt Jan Adamski, deceased.

     "Thank you for your letter of the 16th November. I can but acknowle-
dge it at this stage since providing replies to your questions will take
a certain amount of time. I will write to you again as soon as possible."

In the June 1981 issue of **Northern UFO News**, investigators Norman Collinson and Harry Harris gave brief details of the case, and also brief
details of Alan Godfreys close encounter.

They wrote; "Two seperate incidents are involved, which may or may not
have any connection."

Jenny Randles wrote; "Harry Harris, Mufora member and solicitor, investigated the case for us (and the mans widow) but no reason for disappearence
or motive for murder was found. The case is quite inexplicable."

She went on;"Alan D (Godfrey) was involved in the above case and very
puzzled by it. He of course saw no UFO correlation in it, having no interest in the subject."

The rest of the article dealt with Alan Godfrey, and the fascinating
encounter that he had with a UFO. It mentioned how, on November 28, 1980,
he was called to an estate in Todmorden to investigate a report that some
cows were roaming about. How, after two hours of fruitless searching, he
returned to the same area at 5.15am. How he came across an oval shaped
object in the road, with white lights pouring out from the top of the
object, and windows from the base. The lower half of the object rotated
clockwise, and it was some 20' across and 12' deep. The object was some
5' above the road surface and came within 2' of the tops of some street
lights in the road. Alan Godfrey was some 100' away from the object, and
at this stage sketched the object on a pad using a clipboard.

He noticed how his car headlamps reflected their beam of light off the
object, and how the trees adjacent trembled, (although there was no
breeze). He also saw that the ground directly beneath the object was dry,
yet heavy rain soaked other parts of the road. Both his UHF and VHF
channels were silent when he tried to radio his base, although he pointed
out that there are radio black spots in the area.

(9)

The article then continued; "There is now a dramatic continuity break.
He found himself further down the road past where the object itself had
been, looking back to find the object gone. He has no idea how he got
there or where the object went. His engine had been running all the time.
He then heard a distinct voice say to him..."You should not be seeing this.
It is not for your eyes D (Godfrey). You will forget it." He drove back,
but as he is not sure of the exact times involved, the length of time
lapse is unknown but was no more than minutes."

"Clearly this is a classic and investigation is still proceeding. We
envisage conducting a regression hypnosis experiment to see what might
emerge, but of course any such memory would be of a different order to his
conscious memory which is why the objective story is presented at this
stage for consideration."

In the October issue of the same newsletter Jenny Randles expressed
annoyance at the breaking of the Adamski case by the Sunday Mirror.

In it she wrote; "Whatever you may have seen from the media and their
sources (whoever they might be) are most patently not the true facts."
                                                        Circumstantial
She went on;"However, there is nothing but rather flimsy evidence to link
 his death with UFO's...despite what the media and spokesmen from UFO
organisations Bufora and Contact said in print. These people have not
(to our knowledge) had any contact with the case, other than what they
have read, and their comments (possibly misquoted) are certainly erron-
eous. It is ridiculous to suggest that ufologists are treating the strange
death of Mr Adamski as a CE3!"

She added that the mention of the fact that a police officer peripherally
involved had undergone hypnosis and recalled a UFO contact on the day of
Mr Adamskis death was a "total fabrication".

She concluded; "We are still trying to discover how the story "blew up"
like this, since there was no reaction to the Adamski death when it appeared locally at the time (although there was no UFO to link with it at that
moment of course). It seems that a misguided ufologist, perhaps having
read MUN or FSR or both, alerted the media for some reason. If so his
motives must be questioned for publicity of this nature is the very last
 hing we need. Certainly the media have had no access themselves to the
FSR or MUN article, have not discussed the matter with Mufora, nor the
policeman. Neither did the person who "leaked" this consider the anonymity
factor or consult with Mufora before taking his irresponsible action.
And the reprecussions are horrific. The police officer (whom his superiors
obviously have identified) is in serious trouble. So too is Mufora. The
official secrets act is being dangled. Harry Harris stands to lose a great
deal of money, and ufology valuable data, because all contact between the
witness and ourselves must now cease. This all stems from the foolhardy
relationship between a ufologist and the media. It is a very serious
warning to every single one of us."

(10)

Quite clearly, as the cat had been let out of the bag so to speak, our colleagues at Nufon, Nufora, Nufoin or whatever you like to call them, were upset. And understandably so.

There are one or two points which do need clearing up. Nigel Mortimer, who was described in the original Evening Post article as a "UFO expert", and who described himself as belonging to the Northern UFO News, was the misguided ufologist who passed on details to the press. That is their pigeon, and nobody else's. It is quite true that I spoke with a man from the Sunday Mirror, that was only to be expected as my phone number and work on the subject is well known around here. When Jenny Randles talks of a possible misquote, she is right. Not knowing the case inside out, I told this journalist that _if_ the story is true, then it would be the biggest UFO story to hit these shores for many a year. I also pointed out to all and sundry that for my part, the connection between the death of Adamski and UFO's from what I read in the Evening Post was speculation of the highest order.

The journalist who spoke with Mortimer and later to me, was the first person to mention anything about hypnotic regression, and if anyone got their wires crossed it was these two.

The fact remains that Nufon printed these articles, and that one of their own members leaked information to the press in order to arouse interest locally in the subject,for whatever reason Nigel Mortimer had, I would say that a question mark on printing the article at all must be raised with those powers that be that produce the newsletter.

I must point out, that this investigator adhered to the wishes of Peter Warrington not to question Alan Godfrey, but it would appear that the damage had already been done.

It came as quite a shock to read Godfrey's experience with the UFO, and results of his hypnotic regression in the Sunday Mirror some months after our enquiry began. It fell to Jenny Randles to offer an explanation in a newsletter article;

"Following comment in the October issue regarding the death of Mr Adamski and Alan D's (Godfrey's) contact experience (or alleged contact) five months later the matter has once more hit the headlines in the national press. Indeed as I write Mufora is having to battle off the press from all over the world, as we are still very unhappy about media coverage of this case. After readers inquires a few facts must be pointed out. In JUNE 1980 the Adamski disappearence and death received substantial local publicity. Nigel Watson and Paul Bennet have supplied information on UFO's cited by the media as having been in the vicinity between the 7th (when Adamski vanished) and the 11th (when his body was found) (June 7 – huge orange ball over Bradford; June 8 – similar objects over Todmorden & Halifax, and after this an apparent spate in South Bradford). From this it is hardly surprising that the "Adamski was killed by UFO's" rumour spread.

'Why the national press did not latch onto this is unknown. In November 1980 Alan D (Godfrey) had his experience and _this_ was featured in the local paper, including his real name. Mufora investigated this, and also the Adamski story, with preliminary conclusions as stated in FSR. There is nothing but speculation to link Adamski with UFO's, and nothing at all to link his death with Alans sighting. Because of the nature of the case when publishing in FSR a pseudonym was given to Alan D (Godfrey)...cont.

(7)

(although he had not requested this of us). In this way it was hoped to control the situation. The resultant publicity (which still seems baffling in light of the facts) led to the official ban on Alan D (Godfrey), and Bufora's regression hypnosis sessions stopped midtrack. The origin of the recent SUNDAY MIRROR "exclusive" on these sessions is not known, nor how they overcame the ban. Certainly Bufora has <u>not</u> cooperated, as a group, with the press, and we are trying hard to sort out what is occuring. Ufologists are advised not to accept what they read in the papers but await, when the time is right, for Bufora to follow the FSR article, "A Policeman's Lot" with the true facts, as they appear to stand. The situation remains highly confused, and I am as confused as most of you are."

Confused is the right word for it. And I was equally disturbed by the comings and goings of Walter Reid, who had a fixation about a cover-up on the part of Nufon. This Bufora investigator dispatched several letters containing wild accusations which cited Jenny Randles as architect of such a cover up, and without my knowledge. In fairness to her, she detailed all the evidence in a long and lengthy letter to Walter Reid, which I read. Having digested the letter and its content, it was quite clear that far from being obstructive on the matter, she had been as open as anyone. Yet Walter insisted on continuing this theme of a cover up in any report we compile. For this reason, and the fact that he decieved a number of people by claiming to be the Bufora co-ordinator here in Yorkshire and Northumberland when he was nothing of the sort I later learned, our relationship and co-operation on the case ceased forthwith.

Apologies for any such accusations which may or may not have included my name or Contact's were immediately sent to Jenny Randles. And I withdrew certain statements made to a journalist in Todmorden, which were based on what Walter Reid had in effect passed to me.

This report therefore, is intended to be an accurate account of events, and will obviously be up-dated in the future. Yet, one puzzling aspect still remains; why did Alan Godfrey reveal his experience to the Sunday Mirror, and why did Bufora allow them to view a recording of the regression?

My information is that the Sunday Mirror approached West Yorkshire police, and asked permission to print certain facets of his experience. But they did not reveal to the police the full extent of their inquiry, or what form it would take once printed. It came as a bombshell to senior officers, and caused "great embarrasment all round", they had "no knowledge at all" that the story would turn out the way it did. It would have "an effect on his police career," as the police are very concious of publicity.

All in all, a very serious situation, one that should never have arisen, and one which should concern each and everyone of us.

As this report deals in the main with the Adamski case, I would close by repeating much of what has been stated earlier, that circumstantial evidence alone cannot convince anyone that UFO's figured in this mans disappearence and death. Yet even as I write, news has reached me that two police officers now say that they saw UFO's on the day his body was found. It is hoped that further information will be forthcoming on this, and that the Coroner's answers to our questionaire will shortly reach us. But is to him, that I leave the last word. "As a trained lawyer I have to rely on facts. Unfortunately we have not been able to uncover any facts which may have contributed to this death. I tend to believe that there
cont

(12)

may be some simple explanation. However I do admit that the failure of forensic scientists to identify the corrosive substance which caused Mr Adamski's burns could lend some weight to the UFO theory. As a coroner I cannot speculate, but I must admit that if I was walking over Ilkley moor tommorow and a UFO came down I would not be surprised. I might be terrified, but not surprised.

"I cannot beleive that all the thousands of reports of sort of phenomenon - occuring in almost every country in the world and going back through the ages - result from human error.

"IT IS QUITE THE MOST MYSTERIOUS DEATH I HAVE INVESTIGATED IN I2 YEARS."

J.A. Turnbull.
H.M. CORONER.

Report dated: January 29th I982.

Author: Graham William Birdsall
Co-ordinator/Investigator
Contact International (UK)

On 11th February 1982, Graham received a letter from Mr Turnbull.

"Thank you for your further letter of the 9th February, the contents of which I carefully note.

I am afraid that my staff and I have been under very considerable pressure during the last few months, and research such as that invited by your letter of the 16th November has had to take second place. However, I am now in a position to deal more fully with your questionnaire, which is returned, together with the best answers available. I shall be glad to have a copy of your report, after which I will indicate whether there are any aspects which I would not wish to be made generally known.

Yours faithfully,

Signed, J.A. Turnbull"

Mr Turnbull eventually wrote back to Mr Birdsall with the following answers to thirty seven questions, as shown in documents obtained by David Sankey and the authors, quote:

Question: What was the height of the coal tip?

Answer: A maximum of 12ft. The deceased was found in a hollow, about 6ft up.

Question: What time was the body discovered?

Answer: Mr Trevor Parker discovered the body at 3.45pm.

Question: Did Mr Parker disturb the body?

Answer: No.

Question: Was the body face up?

Answer: Yes.

Question: Was the coal tip wet?

Answer: Yes.

Question: Was the body wet?

Answer: Yes.

Question: What marks (if any) were found on the coal tip?

Answer: None.

Question: Was a soil analysis made of the coal tip?

Answer: No.

Question: Were any corrosive materials kept on the site?

Answer: No.

Question: Where were the superficial cuts on the body located?

Answer: Palms of both hands, both knees, and side of right thigh.

Question: Was there a pattern to the cuts?

Answer: No.

Question: Was any clothing torn as a result of these cuts?

Answer: No.

Question: What form did the corrosive substance take (colour, odour etc)?

Answer: Not ascertainable.

Question: Where did the corrosive substance rest on 'Adamski'?

Answer: Top of the head towards back of the skull, down back of head, left ear and round towards the front of the neck, finishing at top of breast bone.

Question: Was the substance found solely on the body? The effect of the substance caused 'horrific scars'.

Answer: Yes.

Question:: When did the substance strike 'Adamski'?

Answer: A day or two before death.

Question: How deep did it penetrate the skin?

Answer: Full thickness burn tissue.

Question: 'Adamski's' head had been shaved. To what extent was the head shaved?

Answer: His hair was shorter when he left home.

Question: Who could have undertaken this task?

Answer: The head was actually shaved at post-mortem.

Question: Was any antiseptic ointment found around the shaved area?

Answer: 'Adamski' was clean-shaven and well-kept; his shirt was missing, along with other items, he had greasy ointment on burn areas.

Question: Did 'Adamski' have a great deal of money with him when he left home?

Answer: £20, maybe more.

Question: Was a check made with his Bank to see if any money had been withdrawn, during the five missing days?

Answer: Yes – Nothing withdrawn.

Question: Before 'Adamski' disappeared, he had been told that his application for retirement from Lofthouse Colliery had been rejected. Could this have been a major contributory factor to his leaving home?

Answer: Not substantiated.

Question: Did Mrs Adamski give evidence at the inquest?

Answer: Yes.

This next question is asked on the following grounds; Mr Adamski was in the same clothes as when he left home, five days earlier. These clothes were, according to reports, clean. Was the question ever raised on there being a possibility that he spent those missing days with a female companion, who tended his scald or burn marks – and washed his clothing?

Answer: Yes – not very likely.

Question: Was the Solicitor who represented Mrs Adamski a Mr Harry Harris?

Answer: Not represented at the Inquest – Approached by Harris, later.

Question: Were you aware that Mr Harris is connected with the Northern UFO Network? Detective Inspector John Boyle, of Halifax, who led the inquiry, is reported as saying that 'Adamski' visited an acupuncturist in Nelson, Lancashire, on the day he disappeared. Is this true or false?

Answer: Highly unlikely and certainly not established.

Question: Was it Mrs Adamski who told police her husband had never visited Todmorden before?

Answer: Yes.

Question: When was Mr Adamski reported missing?

Answer: 6th June, 1980.

Question: When was the post-mortem carried out and by whom?

Answer: Dr. A.T. Edwards, 11th June, 1980.

Question: Was there more than one post-mortem?

Answer: No.

Question: Who was the forensic scientist involved in trying to identify the corrosive substance, and what experience had he of this type of case?

Answer: Leslie Albert King, MSc. Ph.D.

Question: What were the conclusions of the pathologist and forensic scientist? Was a second opinion called for, or other expert help requested? *(Answer not given).*

Question: When was Mr Adamski's body shipped out to Poland – and who had to give permission for this?

Answer: 17.7.1980. HM Coroner.

Question: Would it be possible for this organisation to run its own tests on a piece of the substance found on 'Adamski'? (We would use the services of people whom I can only disclose their identities to you in confidence and by word of mouth – suffice to say they are the experts in chemical research).

Answer: No.

Dan Goring comments in *Earth-link*, 1982

Another person who became interested in the matter was Dan Goring, head of the Essex UFO Society. He wrote a lengthy article in his *Earth-link* Magazine, published in 1982 about the matter, and pointed out the number of errors made in the newspapers, in stark contrast to the version of events published in the June 1981 Northern UFO News, and October 1981, Northern Ufology.

Dan takes us through the chain of events beginning with the last journey undertaken by Mr Adamski, who went out to purchase some potatoes from the local corner shop and was never seen again, until found on the top of a pile of coal, some 30 miles away. According to the *The Sunday Mirror*, it was alleged that Consultant Pathologist – Dr. Alan Edwards – said death was caused by heart failure, possibly due to a severe shock or fright.

> *"Incredibly it was even suggested at the inquest that the only way the body could have got onto the top of the coal heap was by being dropped from the air. There was a busy railway line next to the coal bunker, yards away, and we know that the body of Mr Adamski wasn't there in the morning, as an inspection had been carried out by Mr Parker.* The Sunday Mirror *said Mr Adamski was found wearing a jacket, without a shirt, and missing his wallet and watch, although there was £5 in his pocket."*

Dan Goring

The same newspaper tells us that the Inquest into the death of this man was adjourned three times, and various appeals were made for people to come forward. The Coroner then recorded an open verdict, which technically means that it is still under investigation. *The Sunday Mirror* alleged that one of the two policemen, who arrived at the scene, recalled seeing a 'flying saucer' only hours before, and that as a result of this, the West Yorkshire Police seriously considered the possibility that Mr Adamski's death was somehow linked with the sighting! Mr Walter Reid, of BUFORA, was claimed to have told the Press that, *"It would seem he was literally dropped there".*

Of course, we know now that Alan Godfrey did not sight his UFO until November of that year – a space of some five months – which means that the newspaper article was written after the verdict was given by James Turnball, at the final Inquest in September. At the BUFORA lecture in London, on 3rd October 1983, Mr Lionel Beer expressed the opinion that the seemingly remarkable coincidence between the man's surname and that of George Adamski was just coincidence.

Investigation conducted by ourselves and David Sankey in 2005

In view of the Open Verdict recorded by the Coroner – Mr James Turnball – we decided to contact the West Yorkshire Police, under the Freedom of Information Act, in December, 2005, asking them if they

john dawn

Lelle Needed

From:	"HMC" <hmc@bradford.gov.uk>
To:	"john dawn" <johndawn@hansonholloway.fsnet.co.uk>
Sent:	28 December 2005 10:40
Subject:	RE: Zigmund Adamski - Application to Obtain Copy of Coroner's Inquest

The Inquisition comes within the documents only available to interested persons. I think the form you refer to is the After Inquest form submitted to the Registrar, upon which the Death Certificate would be based. Similarly this is not a public document, but the Death Certificate I believe is. Your enquiry should be addressed to the Registrar at Halifax for that purpose.

-----Original Message-----
From: john dawn [mailto:johndawn@hansonholloway.fsnet.co.uk]
Sent: 23 December 2005 15:48
To: Angela Plovie
Subject: Re: Zigmund Adamski - Application to Obtain Copy of Coroner's Inquest

Thanks, can you tell me whether as a member of the Public, I can obtain a copy of the Death certificate, relating to Mr Adamski, and also a copy of the Inquisition as lodged with the registrar of Births and deaths, please? which would have been submitted by Mr Turnbull within a few days of the initial inquest.

Look forward to hearing from you, have a Happy Christmas!

John Hanson.

----- Original Message -----
From: Angela Plovie
To: john dawn
Sent: Friday, December 23, 2005 12:04 PM
Subject: RE: Zigmund Adamski - Application to Obtain Copy of Coroner's Inquest

Further to the above matter, I understand that you have written to my predecessor also, who has discussed matters with me.

He has asked me to acknowledge your letter, which of course I do, and that he adopts the same stance as I.

-----Original Message-----
From: john dawn [mailto:johndawn@hansonholloway.fsnet.co.uk]
Sent: 22 December 2005 18:23
To: Angela Plovie
Subject: Re: Zigmund Adamski - Application to Obtain Copy of Coroner's Inquest

Ok Angela thank you very much for your kind advice,
I shall foward a letter on to the West Yorkshire Police
for the information of the Chief Constable.
asking him to consider re opening the case as I have
new information thats suggests the culprit was a local
man, in the meantime II reconstruct my own Inquest File!

Thanks you ,

28/12/2005

were willing to allow us access to any relevant Police documents pertaining to this incident still on file, taking into consideration the nature of information obtained from Chris Zielinski – a close family friend of 'Adamski' and his wife, who told us:

> *"I believe 'Adamski' was held against his will and that this unlawful detention ultimately led to his death."*

In an answer, dated 19th December 2005, an Officer advised us that although the verdict was an open one, all documentary evidence was lodged with the Coroner's Department, and we should approach them for information.

We emailed the Coroner's Court, at Bradford, and asked if we could have sight of the original Coroner's file on the death of Zygmund Adamski, explaining the reasons behind our request, but were advised by Angela Plovie, from that Department, 'this would not be possible, as you are not judged an interested party'.

Corporate Review Department
Information Management Section
PO Box 9
Laburnum Road
Wakefield
WF1 3QP

Tel: 01924 292486 / 292202 / 292719
Fax: 01924 292726
Email: foia@westyorkshire.pnn.police.uk
Website: www.westyorkshire.police.uk

Friday, 30 December 2005

Dear Mr Hanson,

FOI Reference No: 460/2005

Thank you for your email dated 14th December 2005 and received by my office on 16th December 2005. You have requested the following information under the terms of the Freedom of Information Act 2000:

It has been a widely held opinion by some people over the years that Zigmund Adamski. was found dead in mysterious circumstances on the 11th of June 1980, at Parkers Coalyard, Todmorden, was in some way connected with reports of UFO activity in the area, a hypothesis ,I find ridiculous. Can you tell me please whether it is possible to examine any documents relating to the Police investigation, and subsequent evidence tendered at three hearings at the Coroner Court presided by Mr. James Turnbull the then West Yorkshire Coroner, taking into consideration the verdict was left open, can the same be said for this investigation, is the 'File' currently held in an archive?

Your request will now be considered and you will receive a response within the statutory timescale of 20 working days as defined by the Act, subject to the information not being exempt or containing a reference to a third party. In some circumstances West Yorkshire Police may be unable to achieve this deadline. If this is likely you will be informed and given a revised time-scale at the earliest opportunity.

In exceptional circumstances, there may be a fee payable for the retrieval, collation and provision of the information you request. If this is the case you will be informed and the 20 working day timescale will be suspended until we receive payment from you. If you chose not to make a payment then your request will remain unanswered. Some requests may also require either full or partial transference to another public authority in order to answer your query in the fullest possible way. Again, you will be informed if this is the case.

Yours sincerely

Inspector
pp Steven Harding
Head of Information Management

Freedom of Information Project Officer
West Yorkshire Police
PO Box 9, Laburnum Road
Wakefield
WF1 3QP

Corporate Review

Tel: 01924 292719
Fax: 01924 292494
Email: jb46@westyorkshire.pnn.police.uk
Website: www.westyorkshire.police.uk

Your ref:
Our ref: FOI 460-2005

19 December 2005

Dear Mr Hanson

I refer to your recent email regarding our response to your FOI request.

Your question can be answered simply that the papers are with the Coroners Office, and even though the verdict was an "Open Verdict" that is where all the papers relating to this incident were forwarded.

As such they now fall under the remit of the Coroner. You must contact the Coroner as stated in my initial response to progress this matter further.

In addition, to confirm our response, all other papers, which the Police may have held, have been destroyed in accordance with our weeding policy.

Yours sincerely

We sent an email and also a letter to Mr James Turnbull, hoping he would be prepared to discuss the matter with us, knowing that, over the years, he had made himself available for interview with members of the Press and often appeared in documentaries made into the death of Mr Adamski. However, we never received any answer from him – a rather dissatisfactory state of affairs, if one accepts that in this day and age, especially with the aid of DNA, many 'cold cases' are now being opened and reinvestigated, especially when there is a suspect.

Taking into consideration the ambiguous and hardly the slightest association between UFOs and the death of Mr Adamski, it is not only the journalists and the media who should be blamed for this situation,

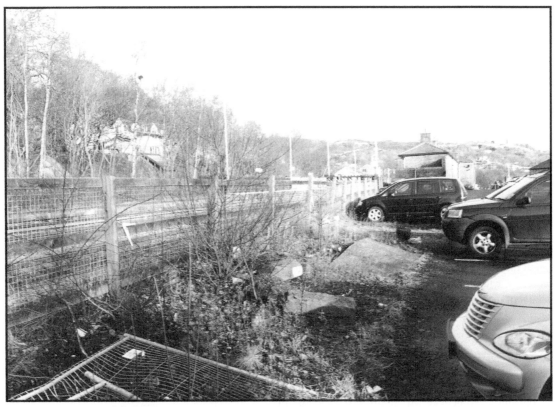

The scene next to the main railway line, near to where Mr Adamski's body had been found.

although it now seems counter-productive to identify other parties responsible for bringing this matter to the attention of the newspapers – now nearly 30 years later.

We believe Zygmund was kidnapped, or coerced, to keep away from the forthcoming wedding. (The 7th June 1980)

We know he was found with one day's stubble on his face, indicating wherever he had been for those missing 4-5 days, he had washed and shaved and his hair (shown short in the photo, taken after his death) had been cropped, prior to post-mortem.

Following our contact with Chris – then a close member of the family, whom Graham Birdsall had spoken to, many years previously – we discovered that a woman friend of Mrs Adamski's, had complained of being assaulted by her husband and that she had sought sanctuary with the couple, after taking out a Court injunction to stop him visiting the house, which may well corroborate rumours heard by Philip Mantle, at the time.

Chris:

> *"Mr Adamski had fallen out with a family member, just before the wedding, and I suspect this person (whose identity is known to us) locked him in a garden shed and that, while trying to escape, he came into contact with battery acid, or paint stripper, causing the corrosive*

type substance burns to the back of his neck, which remain unidentified, despite forensics analysis, made at the time, although there must have been far more information given to the Court by the Forensic Expert. "At the inquest I had the opportunity to cross-examine the man concerned, who told the Court he was sea fishing out at Blackpool, which I believe to be a lie, and feel, to this present day, he was involved in the disappearance of 'Ziggie', whose name has been besmirched in this stupid manner."

We wondered about the peculiar 'ring' mark or 'cup' marks found on the back of the head of the deceased. Could he have been administered treatment known as moxibustion, or moxa, which consists of placing a small glass, or bamboo jar, or cup, containing a cotton ball, soaked in alcohol, against the skin and igniting it – a treatment used for rheumatism, painful joints, sprains, paralysis and asthma.

Was this treatment used? Did it go wrong? Were ointments proscribed? Could this tie in with his shirt being missing? Who was the practitioner involved? Why were there three scratch marks on each hand of the victim not even superficial?

In a bid to locate the acupuncturist, Graham Birdsall travelled to Nelson on the 28th October 1981, and found the address of a practitioner, run by a Mr Hopkinson, who was out at the time. Graham spoke to his secretary, who told him that the man, 'Adamski', was not a regular patient, as her records kept, only gave details of regular patients. If 'Adamski' had seen him, "no record of such a visit would have been made".

Graham, rather puzzling to us, stated that he thought this was a rather poor excuse and wondered why there should be a reason for not giving him the information? Does this suggest that the source of this information was a trusted one and likely to yield results?

There is also talk of a man, known as Mr Mattram, from the Nelson area, who may have been practicing acupuncture. We believe Mr Adamski died whilst in the hands of his captors, after suffering from a heart attack, as was discovered following a post-mortem being conducted. We believe that someone 'out there' (whose identity is known to us) knows the answer. Will 'he' or 'they' finally have the courage to come forward and clear the name of this man? We doubt it, after so long.

Ironically, although an Open Verdict was recorded, which means the case is still open and the police have not closed their file, there appears to be nobody interested in wanting to reopen this case and finally remove this smear from Mr Adamski's hitherto good character. We will be sending a copy of this report to the West Yorkshire Police asking them if they would be prepared to at least examine the original file, at Coroners Department, but don't feel optimistic about the outcome.

The matter was even raised by Warminster based UFO author Arthur Shuttlewood, who mentioned it in one of his letters.

1

17 Portway,
Warminster,
Monday.

Dear San,
The young Kingston (Jamaica) student "contactee" story is being fully investigated by a UFO investigatory unit in the USA, but I feel sure that he will emerge as completely honest!
Yesterday's "Sunday Mirror" story rings genuinely to me; but strange that no-one spotted the coincidence of the name Adamski!! More than coincidence, I'd say...
Sorry if I offended you by my remarks about "giving up". I still take a passing interest in "another dimensional" framework, but have perforce given up sky-watching per se. Futile, as so much world-wide testimony floods in!
Warminster's true place in UFO lore will become more evident to all in years to come,

In 2006 we sent these details to *UFO Magazine* who published them.

Putting the record straight....

a re-investigation into classic UFO folklore

Time is the one element of our life that we have yet to control. In the sci-fi worlds of *Stargate*, *Star Trek* and *Doctor Who* it seems control of the flux may one day be possible. We know that space and gravity play a part in the workings of time and that keeping synchronous satellites in orbit needs time corrections from Earth as space does have an effect on the passage of time. Einstein tried to explain this but didn't fully understand it.

Neither do I.

What I do know is not only does time travel at different speeds the faster and further you venture, it also appears to speed up increasingly the older you get.

It seems like just a few years have passed since I sat at secondary school as a first-former, watching man land on the Moon and as far as pop music goes isn't Queen still No.1?

I'm sure you know where I'm coming from.

The incident that got me involved in the subject happened in 1980 towards the end of the year, October, but I don't remember the exact date.

1980 was a very significant year for UFO events in the United Kingdom: Rendlesham Forest, PC Alan Godfrey are two major events in the UFO calendar. Philip Mantle has reports of alien abduction in his book *'Without Consent'*, co-written by journalist Carl Nagatis, even the story of 'The Ilkley Moor Alien' featured in this particular year.

However there was one other story that captivated some of the UFO community within West Yorkshire and beyond (once the press got the story). It even spawned a comment from West Yorkshire Coroner, James Turnbull, who, when asked about possible UFO involvement (in the story you are about to read) replied, "If I was walking on Ilkley Moor and came across a flying saucer, I'd be shocked, but perhaps not surprised..." I quote from memory not verbatim, but it's pretty accurate.

The case I am referring to involved PC Alan Godfrey, a few weeks prior to his UFO sighting. Alan was a regular police constable and during his work on this particular day, he was called to attend the discovery of a body found in a coal yard in Todmorden. The body was that of a Polish miner who had ventured thirty miles from his home near Wakefield. The reason for this, we don't know, but the following article by John Hanson (himself a retired police officer) puts the events in perspective and removes any possible UFO involvement in the case.

Mysterious death of Zigmund Adamski.

a re- investigation by
***John Hanson, Dawn Holloway &
David Sankey***
© *2008*

Many of the readers will be all too familiar with the mysterious events that surround the discovery of the above named, who was found deceased at Tomlins Coal yard, at the side of Todmorden railway station, 30miles away from where he lived, at 3:45pm on the 6th of June, 1980, and of the controversy surrounding his departure from the family home,

a few days before the wedding of his goddaughter on the 7th of June.

His unusual death led to much newspaper speculation in the months that followed, including ridiculous suggestions made by journalists John Sheard and Stewart Bonney from the *Sunday Mirror* (27 Sept 1981, quote '*UFO Death Riddle*'), who inferred that Mr. Adamski's death was in some way connected with UFO activity, a hypothesis given further weight by the suggestion the only way this man could have ended up on the coal pile was from having been put there from above!

His peculiar disappearance, seemingly out of character for a man who would presumably have been looking forward to giving his goddaughter, Stephanie, away, and the circumstances in which it occurred, raised much suspicion by the investigating police officers, especially after the discovery of injuries inflicted to the back of the neck. One of those officers was PC Alan Godfrey, who we spoke to about the matter. He still remains unsatisfied that the real truths have never come out.

Enquiries made into this matter, now 26 years ago, by the author John Hanson and Doncaster-based UFO researcher, David Sankey, revealed some insight into the background of the deceased, who it was said by one source (known to the authors) that Adamski was not looking forward to giving his goddaughter away, as he felt this duty should have been carried out by somebody else within the family circle, with whom he was on

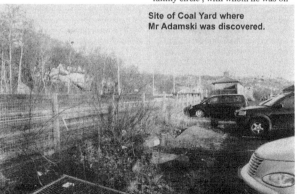

**Site of Coal Yard where
Mr Adamski was discovered.**

bad terms.

We felt it time to put the record straight with regard to the ridiculous, long-held speculation that this man's death had been brought about through alien interaction! Being literally frightened to death, according to one unsubstantiated source.

In view of the 'Open Verdict' recorded by the Coroner, Mr. James Turnball, I decided to contact the West Yorkshire Police under the Freedom of Information Act in December, 2005, and ask them if they were willing to allow me access to any relevant police documents pertaining to this incident still on file, taking into consideration the nature of information obtained recently from someone who was a close family friend of Adamski and his wife, who I consider to be a reliable source, which alleges Adamski was held against his will and that this unlawful detention ultimately led to his death.

In an answer dated the 19th of December, 2005, an officer advised me that although the verdict was an open verdict, all documentary evidence was lodged with the Coroner's department and I should approach them for information.

I emailed the Coroners Court at Bradford and asked if we could have sight of the original Coroner's file on the death of Zigmund Adamski, explaining the reasons behind our request, but were advised by Angela Plovie, from that department, this would not be possible as 'I was not judged an interested party'

I sent an email and also a letter to Mr. James Turnbull, hoping he would be prepared to discuss the matter with me, knowing over the years he had made himself available for interviews with members of the press and filmed documentaries made into the death of the Mr. Adamski, but I never received any acknowledgment. Could his attitude be governed by (alleged) previous remarks made by himself in the newspapers at the time? Quote: "The failure of the forensic scientists to identify the corrosive substance which caused Mr. Adamski's burns could lend some weight to the UFO

theory." Ironically, opinions expressed in this way were to be banned following new guidelines for Coroners laid out in Rule 36(2) The Coroners Rules 1984.

Having seen a photograph of Mr. Adamski taken shortly after the body was recovered (found dressed in a string vest, no shirt and a brown 'John Collier' jacket, with trousers incorrectly buttoned, his watch and wallet later found to be missing), it was clear from the amount of coal residue on his face that he was probably found by the ambulancemen lying face down, presumably turned over by them during their examination and then left on his back, which was the position that the police found him in when they arrived a short time later, being greeted by one of the ambulance crew who said, *'You've got a murder on your hands.'*

PC Alan Godfrey, first officer on the

Alan Godfrey

scene: "He was lying on his back with his eyes open, looking straight up, no sign of rigor mortis. I remember a theory suggested by the CID who thought he might have fell asleep under a lorry, and the acid fell on his neck, but this wasn't the explanation as I remember the pathologist telling me that it wasn't acid on his neck. He was certainly alive on the day he was found. It's a real mystery, although one thing I do know, it was nothing to do with any aliens. That's a load or rubbish."

According to Trevor Parker, who was in charge of the coal yard and to whom we spoke, he started work at 8am and left the coal yard unattended at about 11am to visit other premises, not returning till 4pm when he found the deceased lying face down, approximately ten feet up the pile of anthracite beans (man-made coal) with his head facing to the top of the heap.

So it would appear the man was taken there after 11am, as the bunker was in full view, during the presence of Mr. Parker, who initially thought when he saw him that this was a drunken man sleeping off a bout of drink, and contacted the ambulance station.

Following their attendance, the ambulance was moved between the bunker which consisted of three wooden panels 5 feet in height, so as to prevent passengers in passing trains being able to view the deceased.

The police considered various theories as to how Mr Adamski had arrived at the side of the station:

Had he arrived on a train from Leeds and walked down into the coal yard of his own accord?

Had he been taken to the coal yard by somebody and placed onto the pile of coal as some sort of 'statement' by his captors, taking into consideration, Mr Adamski was in the process of applying for retirement from Lofthouse Colliery Pit, due for closure in 1981, as he wanted to be able to look after his wife Leokadia(Lottie) who suffered from multiple sclerosis?

Could he have jumped from a bridge onto a passing coal lorry on its way to Parkers coal yard, causing the injuries and then been transferred onto the coal pile by an unsuspecting operator?

We believe it is unlikely he caught a train to Todmorden coal yard. He certainly wasn't 'delivered' there by a coal lorry - as Mr. Parker confirms, no coal deliveries took place on that day or the previous few days.

Another line of enquiry we looked at involved a telephone conversation, made to Mark Birdsall of *UFO Magazine*, with whom we spoke, stating Mr. Adamski had fallen out with a family member just before the wedding and that this person, whose identity is known, locked him in a garden shed and that while trying to escape, he came into contact with battery acid, causing the corrosive type substance burns to the back of his neck, which remain unidentified

4

despite forensic analysis made at the time, although there must have been far more information given to the Court by the forensic expert. Unfortunately, we are not privy to the evidence submitted by that official to the Coroners Inquest.

So any further comment would be pure speculation, although we were able to ascertain that the burns to his head had been caused two days previously (certainly not as many as five), occurring between 8 and ten hours previous to the body being found, which would put it at around 7am on the 11th of June, 1980.

We wondered about the peculiar ring mark or cup marks found on the back of the head of the deceased and pondered in line with other, previously unpublished, information whether there was any truth in the suggestion made by an unnamed police officer, who told a third party that Mr. Adamski had been receiving treatment from an unidentified acupuncturist in Nelson, Lancashire, who had administered treatment known as moxibustion or moxa, which consists of placing a small glass or bamboo jar or cup, containing a cotton ball soaked in alcohol, against the skin, and igniting it (a treatment used for rheumatism painful joints, sprains, paralysis, and asthma). *(A theory also considered by the late Graham Birdsall)*

Was this treatment used, did it go wrong, were ointments prescribed, could this tie in with his shirt being missing?

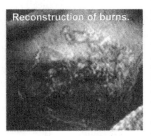
Reconstruction of burns.

This leaves us with the distinct possibility, bearing in mind the nature of conversations held with a person who declines to be named, that Mr. Adamski was the victim of a family feud, a theory backed up by comments made by Mrs. Adamski at the time, who was convinced her husband had been kidnapped.

We believe he was kidnapped, or coerced to keep away fromthe forthcoming wedding. We know he was found with one day's stubble on his face, indicating wherever he had been for those missing 4-5 days, he had washed and shaved and that his hair had been cropped.

We were also told that Mr. Adamski fell out with a member of the family whose wife sought sanctuary with the Adamskis and that an injunction was taken out against the person concerned to stop him visiting the house. If in fact this information was correct, it tells us much about why Mr Adamski went missing, especially because of his connection with the family, unfortunately without any proof we cannot make this public as it would, of course, leave us open to legal proceedings.

We have every reason to believe the offender(s) may still be out there, despite being interviewed, albeit briefly, by the West Yorkshire Police during their investigation into the matter, not that we necessarily infer Mr. Adamski was murdered. It is more likely he died whilst in the hands of his captors after suffering from a heart attack, as was discovered following a post mortem being conducted

Ironically, although an open verdict was recorded, which means the case is still open, and that the police have not closed their file, there appears to be nobody interested in wanting to reopen this case and finally remove this smear from Mr. Adamski's hitherto good character.

We believe that someone 'out there' knows the answer. Will they finally have the courage to come forward and clear the name of this man? We doubt it after so long.

*John Hanson, Dawn Holloway &
David Sankey*
© 2008

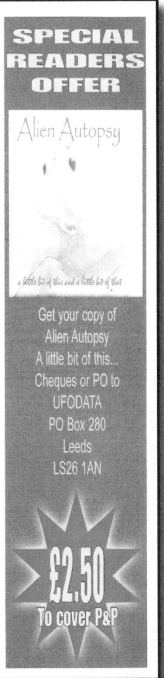

(Sources: *FSR*, Vol. 27, No. 2, 1981, Jenny Randles/Alan Godfrey/Harry Harris/
Norman Collinson/David Sankey)

Tiny 'beings' of West Malaysia

Although the next incident happened many miles away from the UK, it was so strange that we decided to include it, if only for its value, in contrasting it with similar sightings in the UK. Did it happen or was it a figment of imagination?

In June 1980, a number of manifestations occurred near a school in Lumut, West Malaysia. There were several witnesses to these events, which would, in the normal passage of time, have been dismissed as hoaxes, or hallucinations. Fortunately, in addition to the children, there were two teachers.

The incident was initially kept away from the public and media, following a meeting which took place at the school, when it was decided that details would be kept confidential. When news of the strange incidents leaked out, even journalists who went to the school were banned from interviewing the witnesses. It was only some months later, according to Dan Goring – head of the Essex-based UFO Group – that some details were obtained, following an investigation by Ahmad Jamaludin

At about 10.30am on 18th June 1980, two girls, aged 12, went to the back of the school to throw some rubbish away.

As they did so, they were astonished to see two strange small *'figures'*, described as very hairy, monkey like, about 2ins tall, less than 7ft away, in the grass. One of them was dressed in a white suit, with a white hat and white boots; the other, wearing all black. They were carrying what looked like a pack and a long weapon on their backs. Their feet did not appear to touch the ground. It was ascertained that several hours before this incident (presumably the previous afternoon) another schoolgirl was going to the toilet, when she encountered a large hairy monkey like creature. Suddenly the *'creature'* shrunk in size to just a few inches, at which point the girl fainted.

At about 12 noon the same day, after hearing of what had transpired, some of the students, accompanied by two teachers, conducted a search of the area. It is then alleged that three entities were seen carrying what appeared to be packs on their backs, and that after being lost from view, behind a rock, they took off in a small UFO.

(Source: *Malaysian UFO Bulletin,* **No. 3, October 1981/***Earth-link,* **March 1982)**

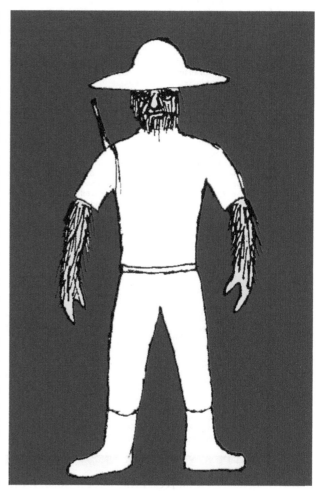

Two inches tall entity – based on witness sketch.

It was of interest to discover that Malaysia had also witnessed many other UFO sighting over the years. They included a strange encounter with a 3-inch-tall man-like creature sometime in 1975 or 1976 in Kuantan, Malaysia, which occurred about 9 miles from the town of Kuantan. It was also alleged that the small UFO which ferried the tiny entity is said to have landed in the Royal Malaysian Air Force Base there.

The sighting appeared on the front page of the *New Straits Times* published in Kuala Lumpur, Malaysia. The report entitled "Believe it or Not" omitted to mention any UFO. The witness Paul Lazario, aged nine, a pupil of the RMAF Primary School, said:

> *"I saw the creature two days ago near a drain at the RMAF field. It was stopping to drink water, I caught it but it escaped from my grip and ran into some undergrowth near the drain, it had two feelers on the head and held a steel-like rod in its hand. A pistol was hanging from its waist. It was brown in colour and looked like a man".*

Paul said he told his friends what he had seen and in the evening three of them went to the spot near the field. According to schoolboy, Neo Lee Ann, 12, all three saw the creature moving about on the area.

> *"When it saw us, it ran into the undergrowth and disappeared."*

A teacher of the school, Mr Yew Kim Guan, said when he heard the story he went to investigate.

> *"There was no sign of the creature in the area, but I saw a red Indian-like wigwam, beautifully weaved out of grass. It was partly crushed; I didn't know whether to believe their story"*

(Source: Ahmad Jamaludin, *Flying Saucer Review*, Vol. 26, No. 5, Jan. 1981 (UK)

Understanding the work carried out into these reports which stretched back many years, we felt it appropriate to outline some information about Mr Ahmad Jamaludin who is the author of *A Summary of Unidentified Flying Objects and Related Events in Malaysia* (1950-1980), which was published by the Center for UFO Studies, USA in 1981. An unusual finding of this study was that many Malaysian CE3

Mr Ahmad Jamaludin

cases featured encounters with tiny UFOs and tiny entities, measuring in the inches rather than the feet.

Since that time, Ahmad has continued to compile sighting reports from his region. The finding about small objects and entities still holds. He finds it frustrating that the local media tend to either ignore the UFO subject or not treat it seriously. The first Malaysian UFO Conference was held in Kuala Lumpur in December 1995. A UFO organisation was also formed: UFO Research in Asia (UFORIA), but it has unfortunately not endured.

Ahmad has continued to self-publish several UFO studies. The most recent includes *UFO Reports in Southeast Asia* (1800-1996) (January 1997), which contains 86 sighting abstracts from eight countries plus statistical analyses. *Search for a Common Denominator in UFO Manifestations and Seismic Events* (November 1997) investigates straight line and star-shaped alignments and postulates that UFOs and seismic events are triggered by a common external source. He has also written for popular UFO magazines (see *Alien Encounters,* October 1997). He is to be commended for his part played in recording such phenomena. **(Sources: WWW.2012)**

UFO over Suffolk

On 18th June 1980, Mr Andrews from Rainbow Close, Ipswich, was walking past Ipswich Hospital, at 10.30pm, when he saw:

> " . . . a long, narrow object, flying through the sky. It had five square windows on the side. One end was thicker than the other. I watched it for several minutes, until it was lost in the distance."

(Source: Brenda Butler/Ron West)

UFO over Somerset

On 21st June 1980, switchboard operator Alma Millard, from Horfield, Bristol, was out walking with friends, at Bossington, near Porlock, Somerset, when she noticed:

> ". . . what I first thought was a small cloud, breaking away from a much larger cloud – then I suddenly realised the small cloud was moving much faster than the large one, making a pulsating movement, which made me keep my eyes fixed on it. Inside the cloud was a rounded to oval outline, which was forcing the cloud forward slightly in a pointed movement. There was no sound. It came out of a large cloud from Porlock Hill, travelling into a large cloud over Selworthy Beacon. Unfortunately, I tried to get my friends to see it but the sighting was over. The object, although travelling fast, didn't appear out of the cloud it travelled into."

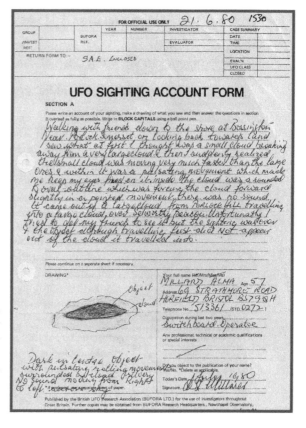

A sighting report was completed by Mrs Millard and sent to Ian Mrzyglod – an investigator for *Probe*, who then forwarded a copy on to Mr Terence Meaden – Director of the Tornado Research Organisation, in Trowbridge, asking for his opinion as to what he thought the phenomenon to be.

Mr Meaden:

> "The eyewitness of 21st June 1980 has given a clear description of what I recognise as an attempt by a cloud to form a funnel cloud vortex beneath it. The witness saw the initial stage

of development – a small pointed funnel, stationary and pulsating, beneath a larger cloud (cumulus, stratocumulus and cumulonimbus). If further development had occurred, a tornado like cloud would have appeared. Sometimes these even reach ground level. Occurrences were very common in June this year. I have funnel cloud reports for the following dates: 1st June, Southend – 9th June – May 24th June, Lincs. – 25th June, Brixham and Boscombe Down, in Wiltshire – 26th June, Ormskirk, and Goole. Also funnel clouds to ground level (i.e. tornadoes on June 5th, Nairn – June 23rd, Hull – 24th, Norwich – an explanation accepted by Mrs Millard for the cause of what she had seen."

Close Encounter – Torva, Cumbria

Mary Sinton – the owner of a successful bed and breakfast farm accommodation in the Cotswolds, spoke about an extraordinary sighting that happened in June 1980, while on a camping holiday in Torver, Cumbria.

"I was with my boyfriend, Paul, at the time, and returning back to the campsite in our Hillman Imp *car, along the A593, Ambleside to Coniston Road (Grid reference longitude 323, latitude 999/8, No. 7 English Lakes, South-East area). As we turned a bend in the road, close to the campsite, I was astonished to see nine tall 'figures', stood in a group of trees near the side of the road, caught in the glare of the spotlights fitted to the* Hillman Imp *I was travelling in.*

I estimated they were at least 7ft tall and identically dressed, wearing silver-white coloured helmets and body armour, carrying what looked like a rod, carried vertically in front of each of them – reminding me of a regiment of soldiers, stood to attention on the parade

ground. As we drove past, I left it for a few seconds and then shouted out, in great excitement, 'Did you see them, Paul?' One look at his face confirmed he had, although, oddly, he had only seen one 'figure'. When we arrived at the campsite, we felt very nervous and had trouble sleeping, wondering if anything else was going to happen.

The next morning, we discussed what had happened and wondered whether we should let the police know but, on reflection, thought they would never believe us."

We spoke to Paul, who confirmed the events given by his ex-girlfriend. He said:

"It was the most unusual thing I have ever seen in my life. It defies explanation."

(Source: Personal interview)

Our Volumes of *Haunted Skies* contain similar sightings of what appear to be robotic humanoids rather than living beings.

But who are we to judge?

It would be so easy if you weren't there to dismiss such sightings as a result of vivid imaginations, but if you were there how on earth do you come to terms, having seen something like this?

Also in the same month was a report of two illuminated objects, seen in a nearby field by a family returning home, one evening, along a 'B' class road, between Garboldisham and Kenninghall, Norfolk. The family stopped off at a nearby farmhouse to warn the occupants, but after receiving no answer from the house, continued on their journey. **(Source: Norfolk UFO Society)**

UFO over Devon

At 10.30pm on 24th June 1980, Tony Lloyd – then aged 17 – was at his home address, when a large 'flash of light' lit up the room.

> *"I shouted for my mother to come and have a look, and rushed outside, just in time to see a bright orange 'globe' hovering low down in the sky, over the sea, a few miles away – too large to be an aircraft, or flare. I telephoned the Coastguard.*
>
> *A few minutes later, a white 'light', or 'beam', shot out of the larger object and headed northward – then the orange 'globe' disappeared."*

Other witnesses were Police Constable John Daniel, and his friend – retired Metropolitan Police Commander, Ivor Thorning – who viewed the object through binoculars.

PC Daniel said:

> *"We watched it for five minutes before it began to fade away. It looked like a bright light, with a white circle underneath, hovering over the sea off the coast of Totnes, Devon. I have flown thousands of miles in helicopters and it was no helicopter we were watching."*

Mr Thorning said:

> *"Main light went out, leaving a 'lingering glow'"*

Another witness was Mrs Todd, of Southway, Plymouth, who saw flashing lights in the sky at about the same time, and called her daughter.

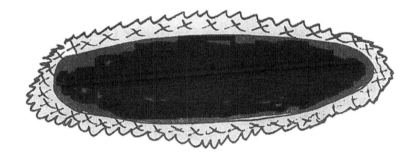

> *"We went outside and saw this cigar-shaped object, with flashing lights all around it, before extinguishing a minute later, allowing us to see a dark grey cigar shape – quite visible in the night sky, directly over Porsham Wood, about 500yds away from the house, before it slowly faded from view."*

Other reports described it as looking like a black sphere, with wings, hovering in the sky.

Another report from Mrs J. Hamar of Venton, just outside Plymouth, tells of a 'bright golden light' seen in the sky, at 10.30pm. Rushing outside, Mrs Hamar saw:

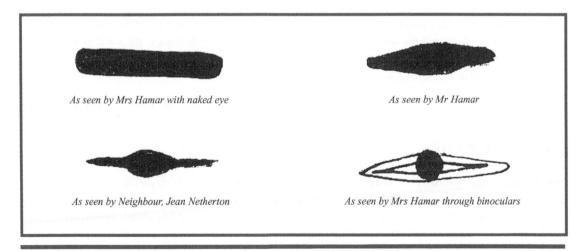

As seen by Mrs Hamar with naked eye

As seen by Mr Hamar

As seen by Neighbour, Jean Netherton

As seen by Mrs Hamar through binoculars

"... what looked like a bird or glider, motionless in the sky; I rushed to my neighbours and borrowed some binoculars, and on looking through them, saw what looked like a 'flying saucer'. I alerted other neighbours and we continued to watch it, although I didn't see it go."

Mrs Hamar said: *"No lights, apart from initial 'glow'"*

According to Bob Boyd, of the Plymouth-based UFO Group, the authorities and police were inundated with reports of UFOs from all over South Devon, including Ashburton, Brixham, Teignmouth and Newton Abbot – later explained by the police as being unusual cloud formations and lightning flashes, whilst the Brixham coastguard suggested it was a helicopter, using a powerful searchlight, which was reflecting off the clouds! **(Source: Bob Boyd, Plymouth UFO Group/Personal interviews)**

UFO over Pontefract

At 10.45pm, during June 1980, at Pontefract, West Yorkshire, following a report by a member of the public, a uniform police officer attended a Pontefract home, where he viewed for himself a UFO through binoculars. Eventually up to eight police officers (including some in plain clothes) arrived at the home to see the object, which was described as a spherical bright light, surrounded by a red glow, with blue and green lights. Checks with radar proved negative. **(Source: *Daily Mirror*)**

Close Encounter – Egham, Surrey

At 11.30pm on 24th June 1980, a 23 year-old man was walking along the Thames, heading back home, when he noticed what at first he took to be a meteorite trailing across the sky, heading east to west, with a small tail behind it.

"It then changed direction, heading north to south, going at an incredible speed, before slowing down and appearing to descend and land not far from where I was stood.

I ran up the hill, thinking an aircraft had crashed. As I reached the site my memory became clouded, but I do remember seeing four 5ft 7ins humanoids, moving very quickly around a landed object. My next memory was of standing with one leg on the tiles of the roof of the house next door and the other leg on the window ledge of my bedroom; the window was open. I don't remember exactly what happened, but later found strange marks on the back of my legs and at the base of my head."

(Source: WWW: UFO Organization.com)

UFO over Kent

Five days later, on 29th June 1980, Margaret and Ronald Fry – then living in Bexleyheath, Kent, were driving out of the Blackwall Tunnel, at 10.50pm., when they saw what looked like the Sun, slowly descending through the sky, except this object was between 4-8 times the size of the Sun! The couple turned off towards Woolwich, hoping to sight the UFO, but it had disappeared. **(Source: Personal interview)**

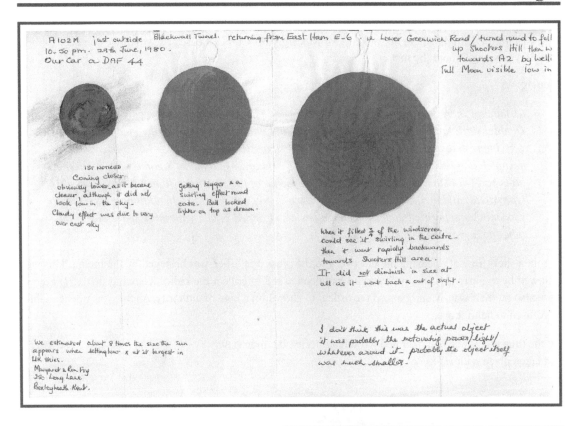

A102M just outside Blackwall Tunnel. returning from East Ham E-6 ia Lower Greenwich Road / turned round to fell
10.50 pm. 29th June, 1980. up Shooters Hill then w
Our Car a DAF 44 towards A2 by Welli
Full Moon visible low in

1ST NOTICED
Coming closer.
obviously lower as it became
cleaner, although it did not
look low in the sky.
Cloudy effect was due to vary
over east sky

getting bigger & a
swirling effect round
centre. Ball looked
lighter on top as drawn.

When it filled ¾ of the windscreen.
could see it swirling in the centre.
then it went rapidly backwards
towards Shooters Hill area.
It did not diminish in size at
all as it went back & out of sight.

I don't think this was the actual object
it was probably the motivating power/light/
whatever around it - probably the object itself
was much smaller.

We estimated about 8 times the size the sun
appears when setting low & at it largest in
UK skies.
Margaret & Ron Fry
250 Long Lane
Bexleyheath Kent.

Russian spy radio recovered

We conclude our chapter with something that has nothing to do with UFOs whatsoever, other than to set the record straight with regard to unsubstantiated rumours of a Russian connection with the events that took place in 1974, at the Berwyn Mountains.

In June 1980, Mr Goronwy Morris was ploughing his father's land on the Llanarmon to Maengwynedd Road, when he came across a polythene black sack, some eight inches from the surface. Inside was a metal box, with a key attached. Without realising the dangers of any possible explosive contained inside, he turned the key and to his surprise found a radio inside the box.

Goronwy told his father, Aubrey, what had taken

place, and showed him the radio. Aubrey then took the box to the County meeting of the Farmers' Union of Wales, held in Denbigh, where he spoke to Mr Meurig Vale, County Secretary, whom we contacted, albeit over 30 years later, about the matter!

Meurig:

> *"I thought there was a good story here and very keen to find out what was going on over Denbighshire land, without authority. I knew that once the story broke the media would be very interested, and took a photograph of the radio, which I was advised by a friend could despatch and receive messages outside the UK. There was no maker's name visible, but the bolts had USA stamped on them. Housed on the lid of the case were 40 metal cased, crystal type valves, all labelled with what appeared to be frequency details. In addition to this there was another separate frequency change device, wrapped in felt, with three spare electronic tubes an aerial and cranking handle."*

Within a short time of releasing the discovery to the press, the office was besieged by the media. This was followed by the arrival of the police, who had been asked to collect the radio. Knowing that a *HTV* crew were also on their way, Meurig asked the officer to show him a note of authority. As this was not available, he refused to hand it over.

By the time the police had obtained written authority, the interview had taken place with *HTV.*

Moscow and the Welsh connection

By IVOR WYNNE JONES

THE MERSEYSIDE and North Wales Connection has surfaced yet again in the murky world of espionage, following the startling information volunteered by KGB defector Stanislav Levchenko about the spy transmitter unearthed four years ago on a farm at Llanrhaeadr-ym-Mochnant in Clwyd.

Except for a brief letter from the Home Secretary to Mr Tom Ellis, then MP for Wrexham, saying the transmitter was of Soviet-bloc origin, the government has refused to discuss the incident.

Major Levchenko (42), now in hiding in the United States was more forthcoming in a dramatic two-way press conference with Lord Bethell, Euro MP for London North West, at the European Parliament in Strasbourg, recently.

He said his role was to pose as a journalist for the purpose of familiarising himself with Liverpool where, in a crisis, he would be responsible for reporting shipping movements, especially nuclear submarines.

He had been trained to return to Liverpool either by parachute or submarine, landing as near as possible to the city—probably in North Wales.

Asked how he would send his information to Russia he reminded his audience of the portable transmitter accidentally dug up in the area some years ago.

"That is our means of communication. In the GRU (Military Intelligence) one of the tests is to bury such things for future use, while stationed abroad with the Soviet Embassy, trade missions or pretending to be a journalist," he said.

When Mr Whitelaw wrote to Mr Ellis in March 1961 he said the transmitter, found nine months earlier, was an obsolete model of the 1960s.

Now it just so happens that the 1960s were a period of extraordinary Soviet interest in North Wales. In 1965 Alexander Soldatov, then Russian Ambassador to London, spent a holiday at the Imperial Hotel, Llandudno.

He was accompanied by his wife, Rufina, daughters Olga and Natalia, and a large personal staff who were by no means always in close attendance when the family went out and about in a single, though

very large car.

Where the surplus staff went while the Soldatovs spent their time at such attractions as the Royal Welch Fusiliers museum, at Caernarfon Castle, is now a matter for speculation.

In 1969 Igor Laptev, First Secretary at the Russian Embassy in London, turned up at Llandudno's North Western Hotel, accompanied by 30 of his staff.

Mr. Laptev returned to Llandudno in 1970, when he was accompanied by 42 of the embassy staff.

In February, 1971, six Russians, describing themselves as members of a trade mission, booked in at the Wynnstay Hotel, Llanrhaeadr-ym-Mochnant—one of the more sleepy corners of Clwyd.

During the evening three of the party walked out of the hotel with a parcel, and were away for about two hours before they returned without it. Next morning they all left although the embassy had booked their rooms for four nights.

MI5 identified Igor Laptev as a top Soviet spy in October, 1971, and he was expelled from Britain, along with 104 of his KGB colleagues.

Among the first to greet the expelled spies in Moscow was Alexander Soldatov, by then the Soviet Deputy Foreign Minis-

ter—the man who had opened up the Soviet path to North Wales.

It was in June, 1980, that Goronwy Morris (26), ploughed up the transmitter, in its locked container and waterproof covering, at Pen-y-Maen, Llanrhaeadr-ym-Mochnant.

That night it was taken to a meeting of the Denbigh branch of the NFU, where county secretary Meurig Voyle had the presence of mind to call in the press and have it photographed, before informing the police.

It was a sophisticated lightweight portable transmitter, capable of high-speed sending of a previously punched tape, with rapid and accurate change of 40 crystal-controlled frequencies. Some of the components had been manufactured in America.

There was no private or commercial use for which such equipment could be licensed in Britain, and it had been purpose-built to frustrate detection by direction-finding equipment.

Within hours of the spy transmitter being handed over to the police several unidentified Home Office officials descended on the farm with metal detectors and other equipment and a form for Goronwy Morris to sign, surrendering any right to what he had found.

Seven months later Mr. Voyle was tidying his desk in Denbigh when he chanced to find a tiny piece of micro-film which could only have fallen from the transmitter while it was in his office.

Mr Voyle obtained a print from the micro negative, to reveal pages of instructions in clumsy English, headed: "Transmitter handling and maintenance."

With an official blanket of silence, even to the extent of denying knowledge of the whereabouts of the transmitter, the mystery appeared insoluble—until Major Levchenko spoke out from his American hideout.

The Soviets have sentenced him to death in his absence from which one assumes his information to be valuable.

There no longer seems to be any reason why the British government should remain so secretive about the Llanrhaeadr-ym-Mochnant transmitter.

The NFU's Meurig Voyle. Inset: The Kremlin's Alexander Soldatov.

Meurig was very keen to find out more and contacted the police and the Home Office, but they declined to answer his questions. He then contacted two MPs – Mr Tom Ellis and Mr Geraint Morgan – asking them if they could assist. They wrote to the Mr William Whitelaw – the Home Secretary – who replied, telling them that he knew of the radio but could not give any more information, due to security issues.

Mr Ellis received a short letter from Mr Whitelaw, stating that the device was of foreign origin and was being examined by security service experts. *"Beyond that, I'm afraid I can't go."* Mr Ellis, felt *"there was something very 'fishy' about this"*.

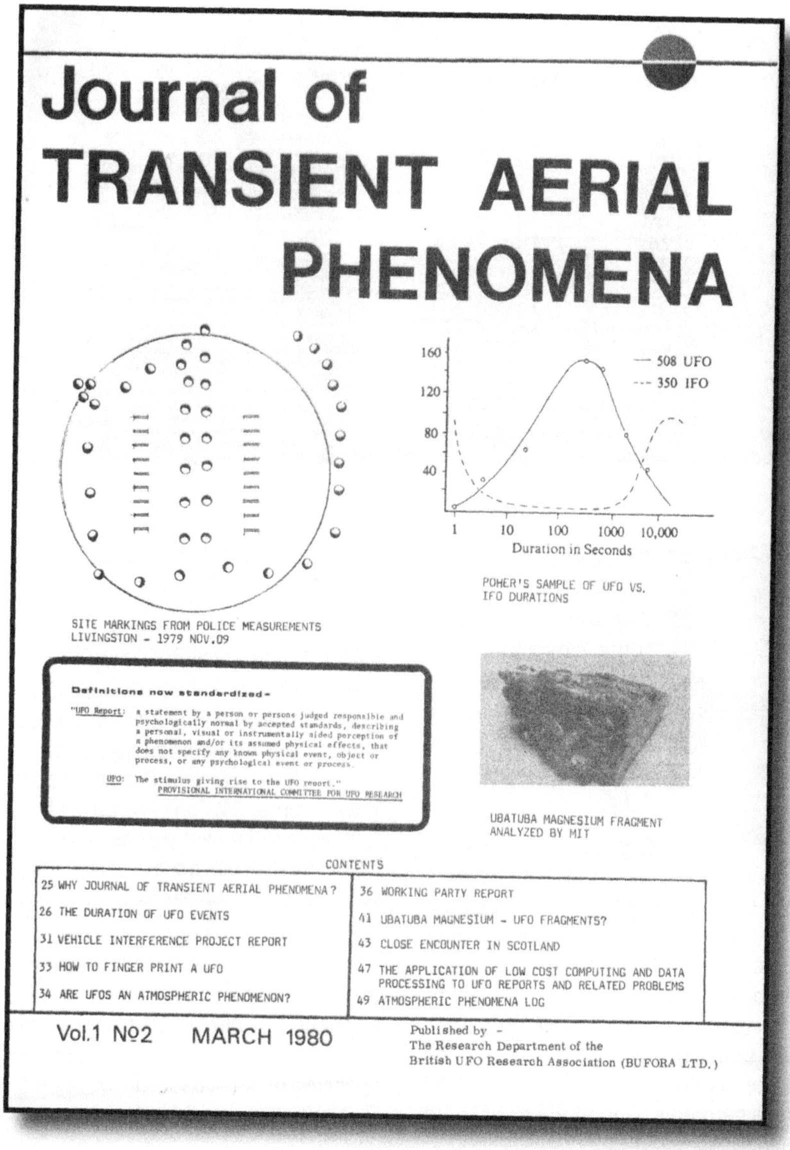

Journal of
TRANSIENT AERIAL
PHENOMENA

SITE MARKINGS FROM POLICE MEASUREMENTS
LIVINGSTON - 1979 NOV.09

POHER'S SAMPLE OF UFO VS. IFO DURATIONS

Definitions now standardized -

"UFO Report: a statement by a person or persons judged responsible and psychologically normal by accepted standards, describing a personal, visual or instrumentally aided perception of a phenomenon and/or its assumed physical effects, that does not specify any known physical event, object or process, or any psychological event or process.

UFO: The stimulus giving rise to the UFO report."
PROVISIONAL INTERNATIONAL COMMITTEE FOR UFO RESEARCH

UBATUBA MAGNESIUM FRAGMENT ANALYZED BY MIT

CONTENTS

Vol.1 №2 MARCH 1980

Published by -
The Research Department of the
British UFO Research Association (BUFORA LTD.)

Bob Tibbitts:

The next case from July, 1980 in Normanton, Yorkshire, contains some similarities to a case covered in the very first volume of *Haunted Skies* – that of Cathie Connolly, in 1940.

Eighteen-year-old, Cathie was out strolling down a country lane near Meriden, Coventry when, glancing past the gate to a field, she came across a landed craft which she first took to be a metallic building. A row of 'smoking chimneys' were in front of the object, along with a group of tall 'men' who appeared very unusual. They had tall foreheads and tanned complexions, strange eyes and all wore one-piece garments. One of the 'men' held a type of device in his hands which was pointed at Cathie.

As she continued to walk, she glanced around again, to find the strange structure had vanished!

What ensued was a series of events which spanned several years. On one occasion, one of these 'men' – who had cat-like features and blue tinged skin – calmed Cathie telepathically, with these words: *'We are not going to hurt you. We just want to know if you are pregnant'*. She was being held down on a surface inside what she took to be 'a spaceship', by a group of these odd-looking 'men'.

The Cathie Connolly case is an example of one of the earliest abduction or contactee cases to have happened in the UK that also involved possible genetic experimentation and time distortions. An overview of the case can be found in *Haunted Skies* Volume 1, 1940-1959.

CHAPTER 7
JULY 1980

A T 8.45pm on 2nd July 1980, Christine Harris of Baildon, Bradford, was amazed to see a silver and black metallic 'flying saucer' hovering in the sky, above Lister Mill, Manningham, Bradford, before heading off towards the direction of the city centre.

UFO landing – Normanton, Yorkshire

We contacted veteran UFO researcher/author, Philip Mantle – author of a number of books on the UFO subject – after learning of his and Mark Birdsall's investigation into a report of a landed UFO on 7th July 1980, at Normanton – then a large mining community, situated a few miles outside of the city of Wakefield, close to the M62 and M1 motorways – by local resident, Mrs Joyce Westerman.

Phil:

> *"There were seven witnesses, six of whom were the children of Mrs Westerman. One afternoon, on the weekend, Joyce was at home with the children outside the house, near the end of a cul-de-sac, behind some fields, containing electricity pylons, playing a ball game and enjoying the sun, when her 8-year-old daughter suddenly ran into the house, shouting and crying, and telling her mother to 'come quick, an aeroplane has just landed in the field'".*

Joyce ran outside and saw, just a matter of a few hundred yards away, in the fields adjacent to her house, an object on the ground, described as being dull grey in colour, and had the appearance of a Mexican hat. Around the object stood three very tall 'men', all of who appeared to be dressed in silver suits. These 'men' seemed to be pointing a dark instrument at the ground. The children and Mrs Westerman made their way over the field, towards this object, and stopped at a fence. The 'men' walked to the rear of the object and it rose vertically, stopped in mid-air, and then shot off at an angle at a high rate of speed. Needless to say, they were speechless.

Phil and Mark then interviewed the children who had seen the object land separately, and found their version of events was very consistent.

> *"The children had been playing ball behind the house where Mrs Westerman lived. 8-year-old Sandra told us how the ball they were playing with had been thrown up into the air as*

part of the game. As she went to catch the ball, she observed a strange object in the sky and shouted to the rest of the children to look, and pointed skyward. They all observed a silvery coloured object, disc-shaped, with a rim around the perimeter, at low level, just above the electricity pylons. It suddenly stopped in mid-air, a few hundred feet up, hovered for a few seconds, and then slowly landed in the field. Sandra immediately set off at this point to get her mother, leaving the other children, who ran towards the landed object, but stopped when they reached a fence which enclosed the field. From the rear of the landed object (perhaps as long as a large Volvo *car), emerged three very tall humanoids, carrying an object in their hand, resembling a torch – their heads and face being covered by some kind of 'visor', all-in-one silver suits, with no zippers, buttons or seams, and gloves or mittens, covering their hands, and wearing a wedged-shaped boot. None of these 'men' appeared to communicate with each other and their actions were slow and precise."*

It was at this point that Mrs Westerman and her daughter, Sandra, caught up with the other children. They continued to observe this strange spectacle, for about a minute or so. Suddenly, one of the humanoid figures looked up and noticed Mrs Westerman and the children all standing behind the fence. The three very tall 'men' quickly walked away behind the object and were never seen again.

A few seconds later, the object silently rose from the ground and stopped in mid-air, before moving off at an angle at high speed. All seven individuals were amazed by what they had just seen and Mrs Westerman – the only adult there – had to calm the children down. All seven witnesses hardly spoke about this incident

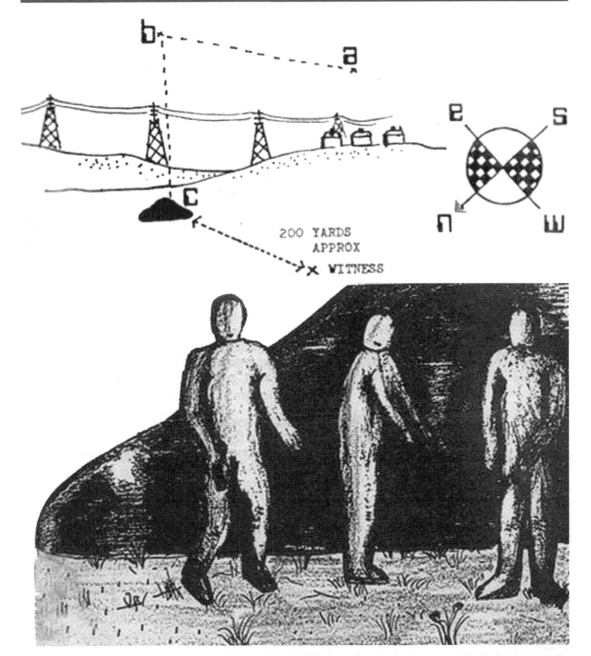

throughout the years, and had never told anyone outside of the family about it – until relating it to Philip and Mark Birdsall.

> *"All six children related similar accounts to us. There were minor discrepancies, but we expected to find that from different people and several years after it had happened. All of the children were of the opinion that the dark object the 'men' had in their hands, and were moving about, looked like a torch, but it had no light and gave off no sound. The 'uniforms'*

the men were wearing were metallic silver and creased when the men moved. The location of this event is interesting. The field lies at the end of the houses, which in turn forms part of a large housing estate. There are many electricity pylons in the field, making it very difficult for such things as helicopters to land."

At the interview, a young man by the name of Andrew Lewis was invited to attend by Mrs Westerman. He was a friend of the children, at the time, and although he did not observe anything unusual himself, he arrived shortly afterwards and confirmed how excited they all were. Another friend was Danny Shore. He was one of the seven original witnesses and 13 years old at the time. He estimated the whole incident lasted no more than between 5-10mins.

Phil and Mark were impressed by the credibility of the witnesses. At no time did they call the object a 'spaceship', or a 'flying saucer', and there was no way Mrs Westerman wanted any publicity – she would not even allow them to take her photograph.

Phil:

"Both Mark and I could find no reason for them to concoct such a story. Mrs Westerman did say that she was amazed that no-one else had seen the object. It was a sunny day and it flew at low level over the housing estate. So there you have it. This is the one UFO case that most impressed me above all others. Why? Well it's not just because I was involved in it, and it is not necessarily what the witnesses related to us. Instead it is the witnesses themselves. Normanton had a large miner's community. In fact, Mrs Westerman's husband worked at a local colliery. My late father worked down the mines all his life and I grew up with people very much like Mrs Westerman. Added to that, and despite our best efforts, neither Mark Birdsall nor I could find any rational explanation for this event. It either happened as they reported it to us, or they were lying and we could find no evidence of the latter."

(Source: As above/*Telegraph and Argus*, 23.11.92)

Author and researcher – Philip Mantle

Police sight UFOs over pylons

In early July 1980, Police Constable Stephen Howarth and Chris Fernhead, from Littleborough Police Station, were on their way to Todmorden. Prior to leaving the police station, the building had been experiencing a series of fluctuations in the electrical power supply. Enquiries with the Electricity Board had revealed no known faults to the power supply.

Image © Copyright Nigel Homer. This work is licensed under the Creative Commons Attribution-Share Alike 2.0 Generic Licence

The edge of Norland Moor, looking in the direction of the Ryburn Valley

As the officers drove along Norland Moor, between Littleborough and Todmorden, they saw a hat-shaped UFO beside two electricity pylons. The object appeared to be rotating and changing colour, from yellow to bluish-white, and then back again to yellow. The object slowly began to rise into the sky. At the same time the officers began to hear radio transmissions from the South Wales police, approximately 200 miles away, when normally the radio would only be 20-30 miles! The officers then observed a second object to the North that was identical to the first. Both objects began to rise into the sky and at 4.30am, they were out of sight as they moved off at speed to Denshaw.

(Source: *Yorkshire Evening Post,* 11.7.80)

Lay-by and pylons near to the Normanton By-pass.

At 2.30am on 12th July, a man living in County Durham reported having sighted an object hovering in the sky,

> ". . . making a low humming noise; it was a clear night, there was a half moon showing. I saw a brilliant white beam of light shining upwards from the UFO. I watched it for about eight minutes."

(Source: North-East Amateur UFO Society)

Mushroom-shaped UFOs over Cheshire

People living in Hazle Grove, Stockport, Cheshire, contacted the police after a spate of mushroom-shaped UFOs were sighted over the area, during July 1980. The officers were surprised to hear that the sightings had been occurring over the last six months, but were unable to offer any explanations.

One of the residents was Mr Ronald Gingell of Newlyn Close, Hazel Grove. He said:

> "It stayed in the sky for a few minutes, and all of the family, including my two sons, saw it. It was more or less cylindrical in shape, showing large red and white lights. I telephoned my brother at the airport; he confirmed there had been no flights in the area at the time."

Another witness was Robert Hulse of Buglawton, near Macclesfield.

> "My wife and I were driving home in separate cars that night. I saw white lights over Fools Nook, close to Jodrell Bank. We also saw a large red light hovering over the road, but it was a completely different shape."

Diana Shaw and her friend, Susan Edwards, were walking down Offerton Lane, when they told of seeing what looked like:

> ". . . a flying mushroom-shaped object in the sky, which was moving slowly. We laughed, at first, but then felt a little frightened."

Liz Bolton, from Middle Hillgate, was looking out for her children, when she saw them pointing upwards into the sky.

> "I looked and saw this large fluorescent object, mushroom in shape, spinning across the sky. It made a shushing noise and was flying low. It then disappeared from view behind an office block, and I grabbed the kids and ran home."

Close Encounter – Bramshott, Hampshire

At 8.30pm on 18th July 1980, six off duty nurses, living at Cox's and Bramley Cottages, in the bottom grounds of High Hurlands Nursing Home, Gentiles Lane, Bramshott Road, near to the village of Passfield, Hampshire, were disturbed by the sound of a strange humming noise.

Two of the nurses – Georgina and Elona – decided to take a look outside and then shouted for the others to join them. The group then watched, with disbelief, as a saucer-shaped object flashing with red and green lights began to slowly descend over the nearby apple trees, some 30ft off the ground.

One of the girls – Hazel – fetched a camera and took a photograph before it eventually disappeared, 15-20 minutes later.

At the top of the hill, nurses Diane Edworthy and Helen Monger were on duty when they heard the sound of someone moving about at the back of the building, followed by the dogs barking furiously, at 12.15am. (19.7.80)

Diane:

> *"A short time later, Helen told me she had seen a 'figure' by the back door, so I decided to ring the police from the first floor office at the left-hand side of the building, and ask them to attend, fearing we had prowlers. After making the 999 call, at 12.35am, I happened to glance up at the French windows that give access to an outside* balcony, 15-20 feet off the ground, and was astonished, but not frightened, to see a 'figure' in black, at least 6ft tall, peering through the window at me. He was covered in black and wearing a huge helmet over his head, preventing me from seeing if he had any neck, or face, and covered all over in what looked like a leather outfit, with fabric that glistened. By the time I had regained my senses he was gone, making a thudding noise as he left."*

*An up-to-date photo shows that the stairs have been removed)

Diane Edworthy describing the events that happened that night in July 1980

A few minutes later, she received a telephone call from the nurses at the bottom of the hill, about half a mile away, who told her that they had heard some strange noises, and wondered if there was a prowler about. Dianne told them she had already telephoned the police.

When the police arrived from Whitehill, they searched the area with a police dog, but found nothing. Diane formed the impression that they didn't believe them.

The next day she was told by the owners that they had found someone sleeping rough, which she believes was deliberately put forward to prevent any publicity getting out.

Diane:

> *"I don't know if any of the photos turned out but I heard that a naval officer, at Portsmouth, had seized the photos and illustrations, drawn up by the two girls. Oddly, I never saw Elona again from that date. A few weeks after the event a police officer brought an American around to the house, who told me he was from Cape Canaveral, and questioned me about what had occurred. Unfortunately, I began to receive a number of telephone calls from all sorts of people who wanted to see me, including cranks, so I had to put a stop to it, but I was intrigued to hear from a man, living in Headley Down, who told me about an identical 'figure' he saw 25years ago in the area."*

(Source: Personal interview/Omar Fowler, PRA)

'Flying Saucer' over Birmingham

George Morton from Stratford Road, Hall Green, Birmingham – an ex-Signalman with the RAF, during the Berlin Airlift of 1949 – presented to Prince Charles, in a ceremony held at Bushy Park, London, over 50 years later, described what it was he and his mother saw in July 1980. When we met him, some years ago now, he proudly showed us his fish '*Brownie*', whom he was very fond of. We never thought of asking him for a photograph of himself, because at that time we hadn't even produced *Haunted Skies* Volume 1. We found him a real gentleman and it was a privilege to talk to him about his life and UFO sighting.

George:

> *"At that time, my mother – Ada – was alive and used to sleep downstairs, in the front sitting room, due to ill health. At about midnight, I went over to the curtains and drew them back. I was stunned to see a grey, dome-shaped object, just like a 'flying saucer', with a blue/white field of, presumably, 'energy' surrounding it, covering the width of Pembroke Croft, which backs onto Robin Hood Cemetery. It looked to be only a few feet above the houses.*

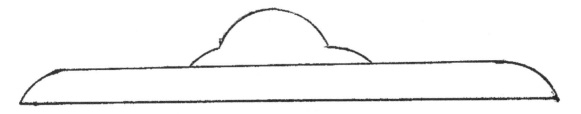

GEO. F. MORTON
1589 STRATFORD ROAD
HALL GREEN
BIRMINGHAM
B28 9JB
TEL NO: 0121 - 744 2966

31/12/99.

Dear John,
        Following our recent telephone chat, here are brief detail of my UFO siting.
Year..............1980.
UFO position.....Hovering over Robin Hood cemetry in Shirley.
Time.............Shortly after midnight.
Viewing position..My front loung window.
Witness..........My Mother.

Local newspaper report stated that Solihull Police station had been flooded with calls of the siting, and that local authoritie could not give any explanation.

                Truthfully,

                George Morton.

Excitedly, I shouted for my mother, who came over to have a look. Within a minute or so, it moved a fraction to the right and then headed off across the sky, towards Shirley, Solihull, very quickly. A few days later, I was looking through some newspapers, when I came across a report of a UFO seen over Shirley. So many people had seen it that the switchboard at the Police Station was jammed with callers."

(Source: Personal interview)

It is possible that one of these witnesses may have been Wendy Parker – a housewife, living near Baldwins Lane, Hall Green, near Shirley. She was getting ready for bed, in the summer of the same year, when her husband shouted her to look through the window.

> *"I looked out and saw an object, shaped like a 'disc' – similar in size to a full moon – burnt sienna in colour, moving from right to left over the horizon. Suddenly, it gave off a brilliant flash,*

flooding the house with light. I pulled the curtains, now scared. When I plucked up the courage to have a look, there was nothing to be seen.

I telephoned the police, at Shirley, reporting the matter. The officer there told me he hadn't received any other reports, but I later discovered, while reading the local newspaper, that a couple living in Knowle, Warwickshire, had sighted a luminous 'disc' flying over their house."

(Source: Personal interview)

UFO formation over York

In the same month (July) Mrs Yvonne Howard, and her husband, were driving home to York, after holding a 'disco' at Sutton-on-Derwent, at 2am, when they sighted a red flashing light in the sky. Within seconds there were two, three, and then six, of the objects moving in a cluster across the night sky.

Mrs Howard:

"They were travelling in a straight line, 500ft off the ground, about a mile away from us, and making a faint whirring noise. We gave chase and followed them to Acaster Malbis, but were unable to catch up, and lost sight of them."

(Source: Personal interview/*Yorkshire Post,* July 1980 – 'Couple in York UFO mystery')

Triangular UFO over London

David Cheesman from Lewisham, London, was at home one evening, with his brother, Michael, when they heard a cracking noise – like an aircraft, breaking the sound barrier – followed by a bright 'light', which struck the blinds on the window, scattering light into the bedroom.

"My brother went out to have a look and, upon his return, told me he had seen a pitch-black triangular object, displaying a light in each of its corners, moving slowly across the sky. What I can't understand is why I didn't go out and have a look for myself. I wasn't frightened at all, and the answer eludes me."

(Source: Personal interview)

Green Light over Salisbury

At 5pm in July 1980, housewife Karen Ward was sat in her front lounge at Wing Road, Bulford, Salisbury, Wiltshire, when she noticed a bright green 'ball' floating through the air, about 300yds away.

"I stood up and watched it for about fifteen seconds – then sat down, thinking I had seen things. When I looked back, it had gone. I told my husband, later, about it. He didn't disbelieve me. It was the size of a football, maybe a little larger, and shining – like the Sun – some 20ft off the ground."

(Source: Personal letter to BUFORA)

		YEAR	NUMBER	INVESTIGATOR	CASE SUMMARY	
GROUP	BUFO REF.				DATE	
INVEST REF:				EVALUATOR	TIME	
					LOCATION	
RETURN FORM TO:—					EVAL'N	
					UFO CLASS	
					CLOSED	

BRITISH UFO SOCIETY

Head Office: 47 Belsize Square
London N W 3

Tel UFO HOTLINE 01 794 3093

UFO SIGHTING ACCOUNT FORM

SECTION A

Please write an account of your sighting, make a drawing of what you saw and then answer the questions in section B overleaf as fully as possible. Write in **BLOCK CAPITALS** using a ball point pen.

AS I WAS SITTING IN MY FRONT ROOM I SAW A BRIGHT GREEN BALL ABOUT 300 YDS AWAY JUST FLOATING AND MOVING TO THE RIGHT. I WAS VERY CALM WHEN I SAW IT BUT ALSO AMAZED, I KNEW IT WAS NOT OF THIS WORLD OR ATALL NORMAL. I STOOD UP AND WATCHED IT FOR AT LEAST 15 SECONDS. I SAT DOWN BECAUSE I THOUGHT I WAS SEEING THINGS WHEN I STOOD BACK UP IT WAS GONE. I KNOW I SAW IT I TOLD MY HUSBAND LATER HE DOESN'T DISBELIEVE ME BUT ITS HARD TO REALLY UNDERSTAND. IT WAS THE SIZE OF A FOOTBALL MAYBE SLIGHTLY LARGER. IT WASN'T MUCH OF A SIGHTING OF A UFO BUT I KNOW THAT IT WAS SOMETHING NOT OF THIS WORLD. IT WAS A CLEAR DAY AND I'M SUPRISED THAT NO BODY ELSE SAW IT AS IT WAS A VERY BRIGHT GREEN AND VERY CLEAR.

Please continue on a separate sheet if necessary.

DRAWING*

THE UFO
THIS IS THE VIEW FROM MY FRONTROOM WINDOW I LIVE IN A FLAT. THE SECOND FLOOR

*If preferred, use a separate sheet of paper.

Your full name (Mr/Mrs/Miss/Ms)
KAREN WARD   Age 21
Address 8 WING ROAD - BULFORD
SALISBURY - WILTSHIRE

Telephone No. .... (STD ....)

Occupation during last two years DRIVER FOR ARMY & SALES REP

Any professional, technical or academic qualifications or special interests
I AM INTERESTED IN THE HILL CHALKINGS + UNUSAL HISTORICAL HAPPENINGS

Do you object to the publication of your name?
*YES/ *Delete as applicable.
NO.
Today's Date 4TH OCT 80
Signature K Ward

SALISBURY
WILTSHIRE
30TH SEP 1980

Dear Mr. Rogers

After reading your article in the AD News today I thought that you maybe interested in my UFO sighting I was sitting in my frontroom and I saw a green ball which was about the size of a football maybe a little larger floating across the road. It was bright green and shinning like the sun. It was about 20 feet off the ground and about 300 yards from my window. I watched it for about 15 seconds (at a guess). I had stood up when I saw it and I sat down for a second after seeing it and when I looked again it had gone. This happened about 2½ months ago and I'm

really pleased to beable to tell someone who is interested and knows about UFOs. I really thought that I was going a little wierd but I honestly did see it and this is definately not a made-up story.

I do hope to hear from you soon. Since this sighting I have become very interested in UFOs because I believe I've really seen one.

Yours sincerely
KWard.

MRS. KAREN WARD.

---

190 Rye Road,
Hoddesdon,
Hertfordshire, EN11 0JH.
Hoddesdon, 464405.
Monday Oct 3 1983.

MR K BEABEY,
Mr R SMITH.

Dear Sirs,

For many years, I have been an official member, of the British, U.F.O society. In the past, I have had the experience of, actually seeing, two U.F.O's, in different parts of our, beautiful country. The object, I shall always remember. I have to take my daughter into work, especially, on weekends, because my daughter, is a Nurse, and employed at a hospital, which on a Sunday, is very difficult to get to, especially when my daughter, is on the early turn. One Sunday Morning, after dropping my daughter, off at the hospital, myself and my wife, with me driving the car, came back home to Hoddesdon, along the A-10. When we actually noticed, there was something in the sky, travelling EAST, at a fair height. The object looked, like a large cigar shaped AIRSHIP, with a great big SQUARE BLACK box, at the end of the tail, of the airship. I said it looked like a AIRSHIP, but, it HAD No VISIBLE MEANS of Propulsion. But was TRAVELLING AT A FAIR SPEED, AND MAKING No Noise, AT ALL. When my wife at first, noticed this object. I immediately pulled up my car, to a full stop, in the Middle of the road, and watched this object, for about five Minutes, but because it was fairly early, in the Morning, there was no other traffic, on the road, except one, or two jogger, who also witnessed the event. I made enquiries at our local police station. rang around various airports, but there was No official, or unofficial, flights or aircraft at that time, of the Morning. The other incident which did occur I can assure you, happened at Kessingland Suffolk Not far away from Wood bridge Suffolk.

I am in the fortunate position, where I own a bungalow, at Kessingland Suffolk. At our property, we have got a fairly large telescope, and of course various binoculars. We rarely go to bed early, at Kessingland, and this particular night, we decided to go for a long walk, along the cliffs. At about 1.30 AM in the Morning. My dog whom we had with us, started barking, and whinning, and looking out to sea. There was four of us in my party plus there was quiet, a few people night looking, on the beach itself. The object we noticed at first seemed to be spinning, over the sea. A WHITE ROUND BRIGHT LIGHT, IT DISAPPEARED once, and it looked as though it actually went into the sea. We all watched this object, for around 15 minutes, quite amazed, at what it was doing, then it shot right up into the sky, turned and went west, it went very fast, and we watched it until it disappeared, like a meteorite...

CHAPTER 8
AUGUST 1980

Sky Scan Open Day

ON 9th August 1980, Sky Scan – the Worcestershire-based UFO Organisation – staged an exhibition of their work, during an Open Day for the public and fellow researchers – some of whom travelled from Crewe and Bristol, which included a film, entitled, 'The UFO Factor', produced by Chris Hardwicke that contained interviews with Arthur Shuttlewood – a copy of the film being sent to us, in 2009.

Scenes from the film 'The UFO Factor', produced by Chris Hardwicke, featuring an interview with Arthur Shuttlewood

Crop Circles found – Westbury, Wiltshire

Firmly believed, by some, to be the forerunner of the English crop circle phenomenon, attracting huge public interest during the 1980s, was the discovery of three circular depressions found in a cornfield belonging to Mr Scull – a local farmer – beneath the Westbury White Horse, Wiltshire, on or about the 12th or 13th August 1980 – matters that were brought to the attention of the *Wiltshire Times,* who erroneously presumed they were formed on or about that date, when, in fact, enquiries carried out by Ian Mrzyglod/Mike Seager, from 'Probe'/(NUFOR) South-west, ascertained the first (harvested on the 15th August 1980) had actually appeared in May 1980, with the second circle being found on the 3rd July 1980, and the third on the 21st July 1980.

Ian:

> *"The two depressions, neither exactly circular, were slightly different in size and had differences with regards to shape and 'bed'. The circular depression was designated as number one, this being measured as 58ft, 7ins along its largest diameter, while the number 2 measured 6ft 8ins in diameter. We found the second impression far greater interest than the first, as it was strange how something could flatten the corn totally, as depicted here on the left-hand side of the circle, with the right-hand side being very uneven, with a 'chunk' taken out at the 4 o'clock position and a 'dent' in the circle – almost duplicated in size, which consisted of unaffected corn, slightly bending in a clockwise manner but not flattened.*

> *The 'beds' of the 'nests' consisted of flattened corn, although in number 2 there were small patches where the corn was still standing at varying heights, between 1ft. 6ins and 3ft. 6ins. In general, the corn was totally flattened at ground level, creating a spiral effect in each circle that extended from the centre, in a clockwise direction. However, the centres of the two spirals were not in the actual centre of the depressions themselves.*

> *Close examination of the corn revealed no damage, burn mark, or holes, in the soil, indicating the corn was flattened by air pressure, or presume of a similar nature. There was no sign of any tracks in the field leading to, or from, the depressions, except for small tracks made by Mr Scull and ourselves. Samples of soil and corn were taken and submitted to Bristol University for analysis.*

> *A peculiar aspect of both depressions was the way in which the perimeter had been formed. There was not the slightest hint of tapering an effect a hovering helicopter would produce; in other words, the flattening effect did not gradually reduce outwards until the corn was left unaffected. In this instance, the corn was totally flattened to a level of 3ins. right to the perimeter, when it was then abruptly untouched."*

Enquiries with the Meteorological Office at RAF Lyneham, for weather conditions on that night, revealed heavy rain until midnight, caused by a warm front from the west – then light drizzle, with scattered fog patches for the rest of the night, with low cloud, with a base averaging between 100 and 200ft, 6-12 mph.

A spokesman, from RAF Lyneham, pointed out that: *"The weather was not responsible – I suggest you try elsewhere!"*. Enquiries with the police also met with negative results; however, the group learned of

an unidentified light source seen on the evening of the 13th August 1980. Whether the effects were caused by whirlwinds or lightning strikes, as some would have us believe, it is a question we cannot answer, although we have seen for ourselves the effects of wind damage on crops, which appears similar to man-made crop formations, as found in other parts of the UK.

A letter from Arthur Shuttlewood relating to the crop circle at Westbury in Wiltshire.

UFO under water, Lancashire

On 14th August 1980, Andrew Nightingale was walking towards Helmshore Bay, Lancashire, at 8.50pm, accompanied by his friend, looking for somewhere to fish, when they saw nine pulsating red lights, forming a circle under the water. Within ten minutes, the light had faded away.

(Source: Mr A. Bramhill, BUFORA)

Cigar-shaped UFO over Essex

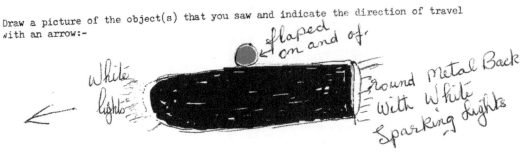

Draw a picture of the object(s) that you saw and indicate the direction of travel with an arrow:-

At 3.30am on 17th August 1980, Mrs Ethel Gatward of Tilbury, Essex, was finding it difficult to get to sleep when she noticed a white light in the clear sky. She got out of bed and went to the window, and

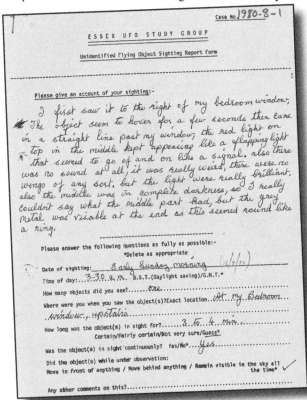

was astonished to see a cigar-shaped object moving slowly through the sky, towards the north-east direction, about 200ft off the ground, approximately 100yds away. In the middle of the object was a red flashing light.

She then opened the window and held it steady with her arms outside, over the ledge and continued to watch the object – now at roof top height a mere 50ft away. She then switched on the bedroom light and awoke her husband. He wasn't interested, and went back to sleep.

Ethel:

"I first saw it to the right of my bedroom window. The object seemed to hover, for a few seconds, and then came in a straight line past my window. The red light on top, in the middle, kept appearing like a flapping light that seemed to go on and off – like a signal. There was no sound, or wings, of any

20. London Rd. (85)
Tilbury.
Essex.
RM18-8DU.

18.8.80.

Dear Sir,

Would you be able to send the UFO Magazine to me for my daughter and I, us I saw saw a cigar shaped object with very bright lights at 3-30 Sunday morning, also in the middle was a Red orange flashing as I opened my bedroom window to get a better view of it there seemed to be a big ball of light in line with this object from where it came in, I should say it was about 200 feet up, but there wasn't any sound, and it went straight by our bedroom window

and I opened the window so I could hear anything but there was no sound from it at all, it seemed to glide by slowly, but when I woke up on the Sunday morning I felt very sick also when I tried to eat some bread I couldn't, but I felt better by dinner time, now I wonder, did I get any radium from it. if there is any money to send I will send P.O. for same,

Yours Truly,
Mrs. E. Gatward.

Draw a picture of the object(s) that you saw and indicate the direction of travel with an arrow:-

White lights   Red flaped on and of   too dark to see what this was. as this was in Darkness   Round Metal Back with White Sparking lights

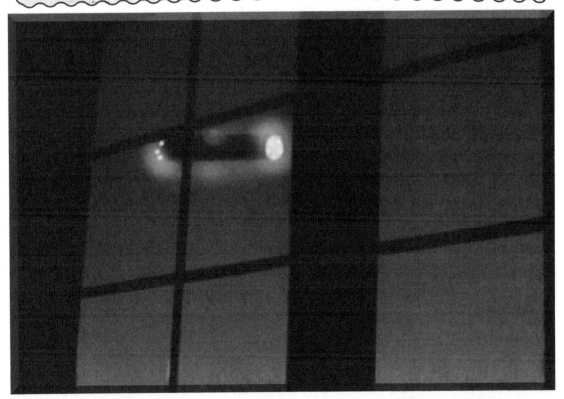

sort. The lights were brilliant; the middle was in complete darkness. There was grey metal visible at the end – this seemed like a ring. It was the shape of an elongated bullet, and about the size of a car. I could see light beams emitting from its nose and tail. There were no wings seen, or appendages, and it was totally silent."

After watching it move away and out of sight, she then went back to bed. When she awoke on the Sunday morning, she felt very sick, her arms were *'tingly'*, and she was unable to keep food down until later in the day. (It is speculated that the medical condition may well have been caused by her having had her arms out of the open window during the time of observation.) She also told of having experienced a roaring noise in her left ear, which lasted for about 30 minutes.

Carol Munday and Bill Eden – Investigators with the UFO Study Group – interviewed Mrs Gatward, when they established that prior to the sighting having taken place, Ethel had been out for the evening and had consumed one glass of sherry.

On the morning of the incident, she had been unable to sleep. At 3.29am, she noticed a white light in the sky in the north-east direction, at an estimated distance of 100 yards away. At first she thought it was an aircraft, heading towards her direction. She then noticed a red flashing, or flapping light, as it closed in on her position – now about 150 feet away, she realised this was no aircraft.   **(Source: As above)**

UFO Encounter, Herefordshire

Veteran Sports Reporter Jeremy Finney, from the *Hereford Times* – a 'down-to-earth' man, with no previous interest in UFOs – still wonders to this present day what exactly happened to him, on 18th August 1980, while travelling home from work.

> *"To be honest, it's not really a matter I like speaking about, as I can normally guess people's reaction when I tell them – apart from that, you don't expect 'down-to-earth' reporters, like myself, to have strange experiences.*

All I can tell you is that at 5.50pm, I was driving along the A49, past Dinmore Hill – a regular route home – when I saw this 'blazing ball of red light' fall from a spherical cloud, silently in an arc, over fields, about half-a-mile away, and disappear. I don't believe what I saw can be explained naturally, as I experienced a period of missing time, which I am unable to account for, but I prefer to leave things as they are."

HT. 29/8/80

Mystery blazing ball in sky sighted again

A MYSTERIOUS blazing ball which baffled sports reporter Jeremy Finney when he spotted it in the sky near Dinmore last week has been sighted again.

This time two Scotsmen working on contract in North Herefordshire claim to have been mystified by a blazing light in the sky over Pembridge.

John McKay and Rick Moises are constructing grain silos on Shobdon airfield and living in a caravan between Eardisland and Pembridge.

One night last week they watched what they describe as a "blazing barn" lighting up the sky about four miles west of Pembridge.

"It was about 11 p.m. and we were going to bed. I was standing in the doorway of the caravan just getting some fresh air. Suddenly I saw the blazing sight. I thought it was a barn on fire but suddenly it disappeared, then reappeared again.

"John was in bed but I got him up because I didn't want him thinking I was seeing things," said Mr Moises.

Mr McKay said they watched the spectacle for about six minutes before it once again suddenly disappeared from sight.

They said they had not told many people about their experience before hearing that there had been a similar sighting near Dinmore.

"When we heard that this other chap had seen something we decided to tell people about what had happened to us," explained Mr Moises.

Mr Finney, of Green Lane, Leominster,

spotted a blazing ball falling from a cloud at about 5.50 p.m. on August 18. Just hours later on the same stretch of the A49 two Leominster women claim they had a nightmare journey when they appeared to be transported back in time and to have no control over what they were doing.

Maureen Freeman and Carol Stringer, of Barons Cross, said that they had been captivated by the colour of the sky and then appeared to be "travelling along a track" for eight miles of the A49 between Wellington and Leominster.

0?   ...713 *(work)*
May 4, 2000.

Dear Mr Hanson,

Apologies for not replying sooner to your letter concerning the sighting of unidentified objects in the sky.

My experience of August 18, 1980, was that at about 5.50pm I was travelling alone along the A49 near Dinmore Hill when I saw, as I described at the time, a blazing ball of light falling from a cloud. As far as I remember it was spherical and red with an orange outer hue. It fell in an arc from the cloud to the ground – in fields – and then disappeared.

Dimensions were hard to judge and I would say that it was about half a mile away. I expected an explosion when it hit the ground but there was nothing and no signs that anything unusual had occurred.

I told colleagues at The Hereford Times but there were no accidents reported in that area.

I have kept an open mind on the subject of UFO and do not think that what I saw was a freak of nature. It was too clear at the time to be mistaken.

I later had a similar experience to that reported by two Leominster women at the time of my sighting.

Whether I was influenced in some way by their report I don't know, but I, too, appeared to be trapped in a time warp.

I think it was within a couple of years that I was on a bus trip to Manchester when I had the experience of being completely alone while taken along a tunnel which was continually closing in, bringing pressure on my head. This went of for some time while the tunnel became narrower and narrower in a sort of autumnal light before the pressure lifted, my head cleared, and I was sitting normally with the others again. I don't think I dreamt it as I had not been dozing off, but I didn't mention it to anyone else at the time.

The only other paranormal activity I can recall is seeing the ghost of my maternal grandmother when I was about 16 (I'm 57 now). We lived in an old three-storey house where my grandmother had died about seven years previously. I had a bedroom on the top floor and her ghost appeared through the wall one night. I leapt out of bed and the apparition left. Again, I don't think I was dreaming.

I'm sorry if these reports are a bit disjointed but hope they are some help to you.

Yours sincerely,

Jeremy Finney

Richard Birtle and companion!

On the 4th January 2013 we drove to Dinmore Hill. This locality is divided by the A49 – a fast-moving stretch of road, linking Leominster and nearby Wellington, in the county of Shropshire.

After discovering that a hexagonal-shaped object had been seen from Dinmore Hill, over the Clee Hill area, in March 2010, we visited the witness concerned – Richard Birtle – a successful farmer, living at the top of Dinmore Hill (private estate) with his wife, Mary, and friendly parrot.

Richard had this to say:

"The farm lies at a height of 752ft and lies next to a nearby microwave tower. We often see the RAF jets flying below us. On occasion they have circled us, disturbing the cattle. Recently I have seen what looks like a number of hexagonal rings, flashing red and green in colour, over the Clee Hill direction. Through binoculars the rings can be clearly seen.

I don't know what this phenomenon is, but it is apparently a regular feature to the landscape and can be seen at about 10pm some nights."

Richard also told of having witnessed what appears to have been a sonic boom, reported by many people living in the Shropshire/Herefordshire area, at 10.45pm, on 31st August 2012, caused by a meteor shower, when thousands of tiny particles of debris entered the Earth's atmosphere.

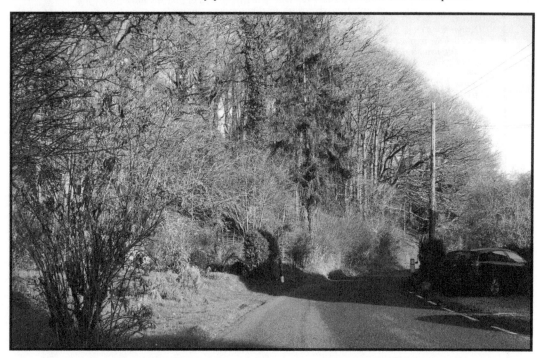

Dinmore Hill area . . . location of sightings in 1980 of a 'blazing ball of red light' and more recently, 'hexagonal rings, flashing red and green in colour, observed by Richard Birtle.

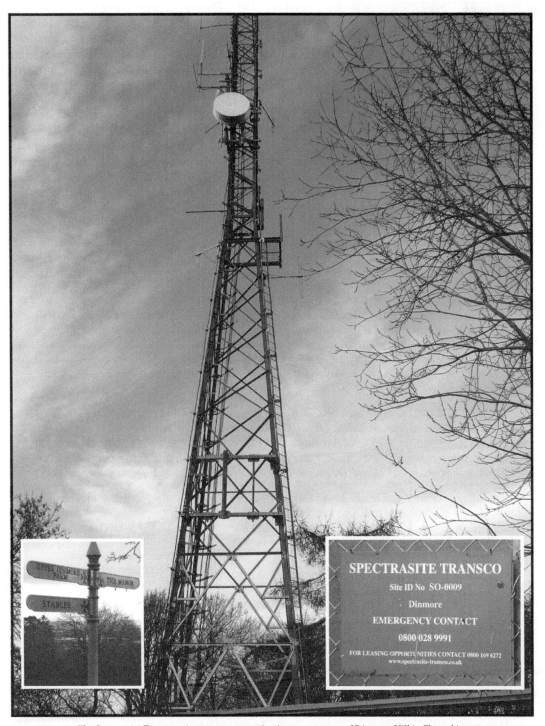

The Spectrasite Transco microwave communications tower atop of Dinmore Hill in Shropshire.

In November 2007 Jeremy Finney retired, after a 40-year association with the newspaper. To mark the end of Jeremy's 46-year career in journalism, he was presented with a variety of gifts by his colleagues at the *Hereford Times*. Editor – Liz Griffin – also presented a bouquet of flowers to his wife, Celia, who retired from her job as a hairdresser on the same day.

Richard Prime, who joined the *Hereford Times,* in 2003, as a writer and sub-editor, succeeded Jeremy as Sports Editor. We spoke to Jeremy who now spends much time on the golf course enjoying his retirement in 2007, hoping that he may be able to remember additional information about the mysterious encounter. While unable to help any further, he remains intrigued as to the nature of what took place now over 30 years ago.

UFO over Leominster

Margaret Freeman, now living in Powys (a nurse at the time) was with her friend – Carol – travelling towards Leominster, at 10pm on 18th August.

> *"As I turned onto the main Hereford to Leominster Road, after commenting on the reddish colour sky, we saw what looked like a railway carriage, with different coloured windows in front of us. My recollection of what took place next is somewhat vague, but it felt like I was floating. I remember a journey along an ancient lane, with a hedge on both sides. I saw a sign – a triangular one, with a circle in it – hanging out of the hedge. I then became aware of approaching a bend.*
>
> *Desperately, I tried to force the car around – acutely aware I was in no position to drive at all. Oddly, I saw no other vehicles. I heard Carol remarking we were in Leominster. Although I was coming around from whatever had ailed me, I still didn't feel right. My next memory was having a cup of tea with the nursing sister at the Hospital, and Carol pointing to her watch, telling me it was 10pm! This seemed impossible. It had been 10pm when we set out.*
>
> *I continued on my journey, dropping Carol off at her home. As she got out of the car, she asked, 'Are you going to tell John (my husband) what happened?' I replied, 'What on Earth are you on about?' Immediately I felt this terrible pain in my head and it all came rushing back to me."*

In 2012 during a review of the incident we were able to identify Carol Stringer as the other party concerned. We traced her son Jason who, at the time of the incident, was aged six – he had no problem remembering the incident.

> *"I remember my mother coming home and telling how they had been driving the car and ended up in a field in the middle of nowhere after seeing flashing lights."*

We then contacted Carol, and asked her about the incident involving herself and Margaret.

> *"My friend Margaret came from Cwmbran where she was living. We went to visit an auntie of mine living at Wellington. We left my auntie's house at 9pm after having tea and cake. Margaret was learning to drive so I was sat by the side of her in the front passenger seat, we drove past the church yard at Dinmore and then turned left when I noticed the sky was strong*

red and black. I remarked to Margaret about the sky but she didn't answer. We carried on driving towards Leominster. At some point I asked Margaret 'where are we' as we appeared lost. She never answered me. All of a sudden we found ourselves driving along a dirt track road, its edges were overgrown. I saw what I thought was an iron sign in the hedgerow, moving backwards and forwards, making a noise. Suddenly we were close to the cemetery at Leominster. Margaret said she was going to see a friend at the Priory Hospital. We arrived there at 10.30pm – which didn't make sense as the trip from Wellington to Leominster was normally half an hour – so where had we been for the missing time?"

Carol added:

"I had a friend who lived on a farm, at Aymestrey. She was out lambing at 4.30am, when a massive ball of blue and white light appeared, and came over the top of her and landed in the field. She put the sheep away and walked across the field to see where it had gone but there was nothing to be seen."

Telephone Classifieds – HEREFORD 69601   LEOMINSTER & BROMYARD NEWS, AUGUST 27, 1980   7

EXPERIENCE ON A49 LEAVES FRIENDS FRIGHTENED

Strange drive by two women took them back in time

Mrs Freeman (left) and Mrs Stringer on the main Leominster to Hereford road.

TWO Leominster women, who are now too frightened to drive along the A49 road at night, claim they were transported back in time when they drove from Wellington to Leominster late one evening recently.

Auxiliary nurse at Leominster's Old Priory Hospital, Maureen Freeman, claims she was "completely taken over" as she drove along the main road between Hereford and Leominster.

Mrs Freeman, a learner-driver, had been to Wellington with her friend Carol Stringer to visit Mrs Stringer's grandmother.

Both women are adamant that all they remember of the journey is getting into their car, then somehow travelling along a narrow brown track edged by bright green, slightly overgrown, hedges.

"It all started when we looked at the sky. It just

made you look at it. Although it was at night it was a pretty bright blue colour with a black band across the centre and orange lights hanging from it," said Mrs Freeman, of 18 Footway Croft.

SIGHTINGS

Their weird and worrying experience happened just hours after a large burning "red ball" is said to have emerged from a cloud in the Dinmore area.

This was spotted by sports reporter Jeremy Finney as he drove home from Hereford to Leominster at about 5.50 that evening.

"I was approaching the Old Comrade public house when this big red ball came out of a cloud. It went into a curve and appeared to end up in a field near Dinmore. It was like a burning ball, but it is difficult to say how big it was because I don't know how far away it was," he said.

Mr Finney thought he saw a man near the Old Comrade pointing at the sky. But no one at the public house had heard any tales of UFOs or strange sightings — even over the bar at the end of a good session.

The RAOC Depot at Moreton-on-Lugg said it had not held any exercises which could have resulted in such sightings.

Mrs Freeman and Mrs Stringer, of 36 Portna Way, claim they have no idea what caused them to imagine they were on an old track.

"All I know is that I was travelling along this track. I saw this very sharp bend coming up and must have braked. Then my friend and I seemed to come to. We were on the last bridge before you get into Leominster," said Mrs Freeman.

"I am really frightened about it. I don't remember driving along the road.

negotiating the other bridges or bends, or seeing any other traffic. We could have been killed," she added.

WATCHING

The close friends did not mention the experience, even to each other, until they started getting "piercing pains" in their temples sometime later that evening.

Mrs Freeman explained:

"We left Wellington at 10.10 p.m., then all this happened. But the strange thing is that even though we called at the Old Priory and stayed talking for some time, we still left the hospital at 10.30 p.m.

"There is no way I could have done that journey in less than 20 minutes and it seemed as if we were travelling along the track for hours and hours.

"It was after we got home that the pains started, and we began to talk about what

had happened. It was almost as if we had suddenly been released from something."

Mrs Freeman is now frightened to go to bed at night and is adamant that she will never drive along the A49 when it is dark again.

"I still feel now that someone is watching me. I shan't be happy until I know whether something awful happened on that road many years ago," said the worried mother-of-three.

Talented family plans concert

THE musical Byram-Wigfield family of Brimfield is once again planning to take to the stage to charm an audience with its talents.

Last year the family who

Youths to appeal against sentence

SOLICITORS gave notice at Leominster Magistrates' Court last Thursday that their clients would appeal against a detention sentence.

Nigel David Birch, aged 19, of Sheridan Road, Hereford, and Ian Smith, 17, of Rogers Avenue, Hunderton,

car without consent at Leominster on June 29.

Birch was fined £25, or seven days in a detention centre to run concurrently, for using a car without third party insurance, and disqualified from driving for 12 months.

He also admitted driving without a licence and was

Margaret Freeman

Over the years this stretch of road was to become the focus of other reports involving complaints from motorists of being paced by UFOs. It is of interest to note that the A49 road meets up with the A5 at Shrewsbury, which has been plagued with sightings of strange objects all the way up to the Welsh border with Chirk. The A5 runs for about 260 miles (including sections concurrent with other designations) from London, England to Holyhead, Wales. Through England, the road largely took over existing turnpike roads, which mainly followed the route of the Anglo-Saxon *Wæcelinga Stræt* (Watling Street), much of which had been historically the Roman road Iter II.route which later took the Anglo-Saxon name Watling Street.

'T'-shaped UFO

At 9pm on 20th August 1980, Ruth Sutherland – then aged 14 – was stood outside her house at Poundgate, Dartmoor, some four miles away from Newton Abbot, South Devon, talking to a friend, when they noticed a small, spinning, egg-shaped object, gold in colour, heading across the sky towards them, which slowed down and changed direction.

> *"Two huge objects appeared in the sky, side by side, filling up the sky – so big we could barely see the sky at the side of them. They were three-dimensional. We could see the nuts and bolts on the structure. One was saucer-shaped. Underneath it looked like this. The other resembled a gigantic 'T'-shaped object. As they came nearer we could see lights underneath, flashing in sequences. The object looked solid in appearance, as if constructed – so in the space of a few minutes we had seen three different types of UFOs."*

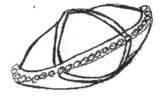

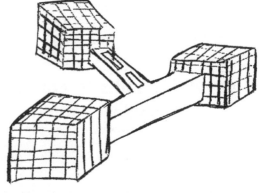

Handwritten letter (left columns)

Dear Mr. Hanson,

Thank you for your letter. How interesting & lovely that you should want to write to me. What site did you find my details on? You are the second person to contact me about this through the internet. The other person* (who lives locally & have become friends) may be of interest to you also, who has sighted huge UFO's. I have asked his permission to include their address & you may find what
* they would love to speak to you!

---

(3)

My incident was in Aug 1980 - about the 20th I believe. I was 14 & with a friend - outside our house. It wasn't light & wasn't dark (Dimpsy - this is known as in Devon). I lived at Postbridge then which was on Dartmoor (about 6 miles from where I live now)..

We noticed in the far distance - both facing a small egg shaped thing which was very golden in colour. This moved across the same way, coming towards us & then moving wither away — so moving further north then 'south'. As it wasn't dark, this object was very bright - like a golden egg. It swivelled as it moved, so spinning is a better description.

MOVING
[sketch of oval] then back across the same path

? In the space of a few minutes I witnessed 3 sightings. However it is Summer on Dartmoor - many others were to see unusual things in the sky. I can remember attending a meeting in a local farmhouse with others that had seen objects — there were others who couldn't believe. A spokesman of the UFO Society also came, & I can remember reading in loads of pages of questions about these, prior to this meeting. I feel I must state at the time I was 14 and had no concept of science fiction, Star Trek or anything similar. What was sinister - (the ...

---

(4)

he has experienced & his knowledge of considerable interest. He has a great deal of thoughts & knowledge. Andy also knows a man who is called Roy Dutton. He is an ex military man (I believe this is correct) who is a well respected and expert —who has been on tv etc. He is retired, but Andy could put you in touch with him. Mr. Dutton lives in Torquay I believe.

I was also going to write a book of people's experiences — but being a mum & working full time has prevented this. I always welcome people who wish to tell me what they have experienced.

Within moments, two huge objects seemed to appear, side by side filling up our sky. We could barely see any other sky, there two were huge. They were 3 Dimensional & we were able to view 'bolts' or trivets (see sketch).. The Saucer shape was classic & came from the north we believe, but they just seemed to 'appear'. As they came nearer, we had to look up wards & we could see underneath the craft. There were flashing lights, moving in sequences, & the construction seemed to be of the most solid construction — ie like a ship.

I hope these pictures make sense to you.

---

by the UFO' spokesman or 'men-in black' following us & possibly threatening us! I could never understand this - but apparently America & Russia were very interested in our sightings.

Anyhow

Hope this is of use to you. Many people believe that I'm not (full) kidding to say the experiences this. My friend's father (who was with me) was a milkman & it was him who had contacted the UFO society as he had heard of others sightings. August is a popular month for sighting.

Let me know when book is published.

Kind regards

Karen

UFO over Hopton, Norfolk

Just 45 minutes later, Mr Leslie Gary Frost – an Engineer by occupation, from Sidegate Road, Hopton, on the Norfolk coast – was helping his wife, Margaret, bring in the washing, as dusk fell, on a cloudless, moonlit night, when he was staggered to see two jet black massive structures, showing a pattern of red and white lights moving towards him, approximately 150ft above the ground.

"The top one was about 200ft off the ground. They appeared solid, rather than translucent. I stood there with my son, who had come out of the house, mesmerized by what we were seeing. The one reminded me of a huge manta ray, with three large red lights at its front, with two brilliant lights at the rear. It halted in mid-air, throwing a shadow over us, and then there was a terrific flash of light and a small triangular object appeared, which began to circle the sky, for ten minutes, over a nearby water tower."

Margaret:

"I went to fetch in the washing. Lots of lights came over, very slowly, from the back field. They looked like a formation of planes coming in, displaying red and white lights. One of the red ones shone brighter

than the others. They couldn't have been planes – they were moving too slowly and making a droning noise. My husband wanted to see more, so he and my son went to have a closer look. I went inside."

Anthony Mark Frost: (10)

"We went up the garden to get the washing in and Dad said, 'Look at that!' Me and mum looked and saw three red lights and two white lights. Me and Dad went to get a better view. There were two, because one broke off and it gave a flash and the big one went away, but the little one went around me and Dad. We then went inside the house, then we went down to Hopton to phone the police, and a police lady came and she asked me some questions – then I went to bed."

Mr Frost confirmed he was interviewed by a policewoman, who told him she would be sending a report to the MOD. After nothing else was heard, Mr Frost contacted Brenda Butler and Dot Street, who went to interview him; otherwise, we would have been none the wiser. After details had been given to the Press, Mr Frost was dismayed to find the published article failed to accurately reflect what had really happened and contacted the police at Lowestoft, when he was then advised his report had been passed to the MOD.

020880N | REF. | EVALUATOR | TIME | LOCATION | EVAL'N | UFO CLASS | CLOSED

RN FORM TO:–

UFO SIGHTING ACCOUNT FORM

SECTION A

Please write an account of your sighting, make a drawing of what you saw and then answer the questions in section B overleaf as fully as possible. Write in BLOCK CAPITALS using a ball point pen.

WENT TO FETCH WASHING IN ABOUT 9-45 OR 9-50 LOT OF LIGHTS COMING VERY SLOWLY OVER THE BACK FIELD MY HUSBAND AND SON WANTED TO SEE MORE CLEARLY, SO WENT UP THE FIELD, I WENT IN THE HOUSE. IT LOOKED LIKE A ~~FOR~~ FORMATION OF PLANES COMING. BUT TO SLOWLY. DROANING NOISE NOT QUITE LIKE A PLANE. THEY WERE RED AND WHITE LIGHTS IT MUST HAVE TURNED SLIGHTLY ONE OF THE RED LIGHT SHONE A LOT BIGGER AND BRIGHTER I WAS ONLY OUT FOR ABOUT 3-4 MINUTES

Please continue on a separate sheet if necessary.

DRAWING*

*If preferred, use a separate sheet of paper.

Your full name (~~Mr~~/Mrs/~~Miss~~/~~Ms~~) MARGARET FROST Age

Address 2-3 BRETT COTTAGES SIDE GATE RD HOPTON

Telephone No. – (STD)

Occupation during last two years HOUSE WIFE

Any professional, technical or academic qualifications or special interests NO

Do you object to the publication of your name? *Yes/~~No~~. *Delete as applicable.

Today's Date 23-8-80

Signature M. Frost

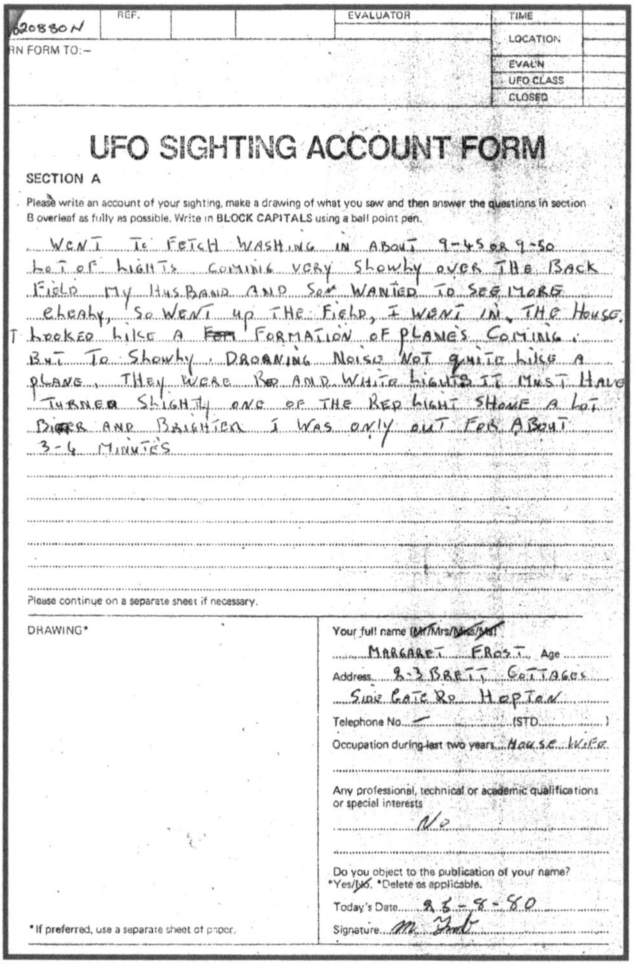

Mr Frost:

"I've often wondered if there was any connection with heavy interference to my television set, about a week before the UFO sighting took place. I knew it wasn't the TV, as a replacement set showed the same problem. Some time after the incident, I did receive a visit from two men, who told me they were from the University of Swindon, and very interested in looking at some scale models I had built of the UFOs I had seen. After taking a number of photographs of those models. they told me, in a very threatening manner, 'Leave it alone', which is exactly what I did until you contacted me."

It appears that no such place existed, which should not come of any surprise. What gives these nameless, unidentified, persons the right to threaten people like Mr Frost? We presume that they are fearful of reports such as this being brought to the attention of the public. **(Source: Brenda Butler/Dot Street/personal interview)**

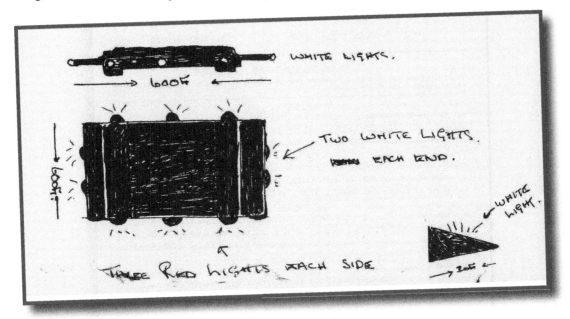

UFOs over Mere

On 25th August 1980, Mrs Esme Evans, from Warminster, was driving her Ford Cortina along the B3095, Mere to Warminster Road, at 10.45pm (OS map reference 345 North longitude, 825 West latitude) when she became aware of a strange noise and thought the car was about to break down. Worried, she increased speed, hoping to get to a telephone, by which time the noise was deafening.

> *"After about a mile and a half, the noise began to recede. I glanced across to my left and saw an enormous brilliant white light, which just 'switched off', revealing two yellow lights – like the shapes of cat's eyes, lower down, which then also faded from view."*

This and other cases including rare hand written letters from Arthur Shuttlewood were sent to us by Bristol UFO researcher Peter Tate who, prior to his death a few years ago, was a regular contributor towards the production of *Haunted Skies*. It seem appropriate to now include a colour photograph of Peter, who was very much an old English gentleman and was always keenly interested in the UFO subject – gone but certainly not forgotten.

**(Source: Peter Tate/Letter to Arthur Shuttlewood/
Personal interview)**

PROBE

M.A.U.F.O.G

UFO Research Organisation

16 Marigold Walk,
Ashton,
Bristol. BS3 2PD.

Tel. 0272 666270
646710

SR1.A.   UFO SIGHTING REPORT FORM: INITIAL STAGE
Please complete this form to the best of your knowledge, and if unsure on any particular
points, please state "Don't know".

WITNESS

Full name (Mr/Mrs/Miss/Ms)........ESME J. EVANS.......................... Age..38...

Address.....U, SHELLEY WAY, WARMINSTER WILTS................................

Current Occupation..HOUSEWIFE/COMPANY SECRETARY.. Telephone No.215476..(STD).2985.

LOCATION

Location of Witness.....MERE - WARMINSTER....(½ MILE FROM KINGSTON DEVERILL).

Day & Date of Sighting. MONDAY..AUGUST..25.1980. Time of Initial Sighting. 10:45..

Description of Weather Conditions.....VERY CLEAR FULL MOONLIT NIGHT..........

THE SIGHTING

No. of Objects.....3..... Colour..WHITE - YELLOW....... Shape..SEE DRAWING..

Sounds AH HUMMING WHIRRING.. Odours......NONE......... Estimated Speed. 50-60 MP.

Did the Object(s) appear solid?...YES...... Apparent Size..2FT / 1ft across

Describe the Movement of the Object(s)....................................

Estimated Distance....4 MILES.......... Estimated Angle of Elevation. VERTICAL HORIZON

Estimated Altitude at Beginning. ZERO. & at End. ZERO.. Brightness. BRILLANT........

Direction When First Seen......... Last Seen........ Duration of Sighting..........

Attention of the Witness Drawn to the Object Because..OF THE INITIAL NOISE.....

.... How Did the Sighting End?....SWITCHED OFF.............

Any Unusual Environmental Effects?......NO......................................

GENERAL

To Whom and When Was the Sighting Reported?..REPORTED TO ARTHUR SHUTTLEWOOD + POLICE

Was Anyone Else Present?.....NO........ Did They See It?....N/A.................

Have You Had Any Previous Sightings?....NO..... Were Any Photographs Taken?....NO....

DRAWING: (PLEASE MARK DIRECTION OF MOTION WITH ARROWS).
Colour if Possible.

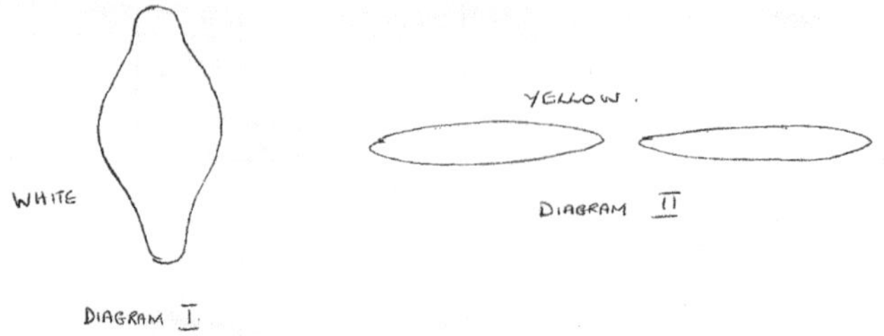

YELLOW.

WHITE

DIAGRAM II

DIAGRAM I

FIG.1   FIG 2.

Encounter with UFO

Two days later, on 27th August 1980, Gateshead waitress – Marjorie Stainthorpe – was driving towards Winlaton, at 3.00am, near Shibdon Bank, when she became aware of a blue and green coloured 'ball of light' following behind the vehicle. *"I was terrified. When I arrived home, I found myself shaking with fear. I don't know what it was, but it wasn't any aircraft."* Enquiries with the local coastguards revealed a blue/green 'flash of light' was sighted over Marsden Rock, on the same evening, which was explained away as a shooting star. **(Source: Personal interview)**

UFO over Aveley

We couldn't help but wonder if there was a connection with an incident, which occurred on 28th August 1980, involving Anthony Richard Constable – a cafe proprietor by employment – his wife, Josephine, sister, Carol Frisk, and the couple's two children – Dean (10), and Scott (8) – and what was encountered by John Day and his family, some six years previously, in 1974. (See *Haunted Skies* Volume 2)

Anthony was driving his Ford Escort along Aveley Road, heading towards Aveley, at about 8.30pm, on a warm and pleasant evening.

> *"We noticed two bright red lights, motionless in the sky, 30° above the eastern horizon, and decided to take a closer look, our curiosity aroused, and drove along Mill Road into Aveley High Street. At a point near the roundabout, we noticed the 'lights' were approximately 200yds away, over the Stifford Road, and drove cautiously along Stifford Road (now almost directly underneath the two red 'lights'). We discussed getting out but decided against it, feeling frightened."*

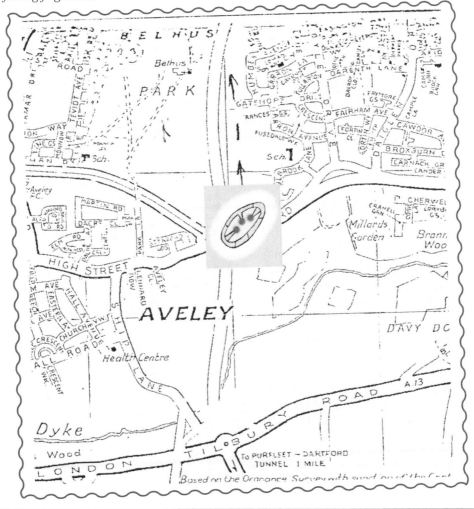

Interview Conducted 19th Sept 1980

UFO SIGHTING ACCOUNT FORM

SECTION A

Please write an account of your sighting, make a drawing of what you saw and then answer the questions in section B overleaf as fully as possible. Write in **BLOCK CAPITALS** using a ball point pen.

This event came to my attention via Maureen Hall.

The witnesses were out for an evening drive and heading South along the Aveley Rd. Whilst approaching the roundabout adjoining the roads (as shown on map) they noticed two bright reddish lights hovering over another road a few hundred feet away. Deciding to obtain a closer look the family drove to the roundabout and down Stifford Road and found themselves almost directly underneath the lights. There now appeared three stationary red lights spaced equally apart emanating from a large oval or round greyish body. Looking from the safety of their car (a Ford Escort) the family observed for 2-3 mins. they admitted that they were "scared to get out." They estimated the height at 4-500'. After driving up the road a little to turn the car the mass sped off very rapidly towards the North. Arriving home efforts were made to locate a source to which the case could be referred via Daily Mirror.

They sat there, watching the objects – now visible clearly as:

> *". . . three red lights, spaced equidistantly apart from each, together brighter than street lights, showing from the underside a large light grey oval to circular-shaped mass, estimated to be at a height of 4-500ft, its diameter equivalent to approximately three inches at arm's length".*

Anthony decided to approach the object from the opposite direction and, after turning the car, looked up and was astonished to see that it had vanished from sight.

(Source: Maureen Hall/Robert Easton, BUFORA/ Dan Goring, *Earth-link*)

UFO over Todmorden

At 12.30am on 29th August 1980, Hasan Dhaimash – a resident of Todmorden, Lancashire – was driving home, with some friends, when they saw a red *'light'*, heading eastwards across the sky, towards another similar object.

"They met up and began to make these up and down movements – as if communicating with each other in some way. After a few minutes, the second 'light' disappeared. The other then headed off along the way it had come. We heard a noise like the wind and decided to continue our journey, thinking that was the end of it, when, all of a sudden, some 'lights' appeared on the road in front of the car and disappeared from sight, leaving us all shaken."

(Source: Mr A. Bramhill, BUFORA)

UFO over Kidderminster

Kidderminster resident, Crystal Hogben, Editor of *Magic Saucer* – a magazine devoted to children's UFO sightings – was at her home address on 30th August 1980, when she received a knock on the door, at 9.30pm, by Keith Barker (13) who asked her to come outside, as it was National Sky watch night.

"I set off with Keith and a friend, Daren (8) on the way to a nearby farm, offering clear views of the sky, when Darren shouted, 'Look at that!' I looked out and saw a white 'light' in the sky, moving out from Cassiopeia. It seemed to divide into three lights moving across the sky in a great zigzag arc of movement, forming a triangle, before being lost from view."

UFO over Norfolk

Another strange encounter took place a few days later, towards the end of August 1980, according to the records kept by UFO/Paranormal historian Ivan W Bunn. Whom we had the pleasure of meeting some 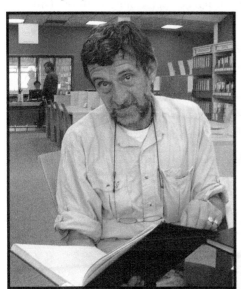 years ago involving Kim Sergeant, who was driving his girlfriend home, towards Blofield, on the A47 – not too many miles away from the scene of the previous UFO incident at Hopton, when they noticed a glowing red 'ball of light', hovering just above the sky line, which suddenly appeared to 'latch on' to their car. Much to the couple's consternation, the UFO continued to follow them.

"It reached the end of the road, just in front of us, and began to slowly descend. I stopped the car. To our further fright, it stopped motionless in the air and started to float towards us. I started up the car and raced away. To my relief, as we neared my girlfriend's house, it vanished behind some trees."

(Source: Borderline Science Investigation Group)

UFO/Paranormal historian Ivan W Bunn.

UFOs over Derbyshire

A report obtained from the archives of the now defunct Nottinghamshire UFO Investigation Society, run by Les Hall, Sydney Henley and Peter Ann, allows us a unique opportunity to examine for ourselves some spectacular events, which occurred during the early morning of 31st August 1980, involving a number of residents from various parts of the County, who contacted the authorities and newspapers after sighting an unidentified flying object moving across the sky.

It began at 12.20am. Two separate groups of people (some in a car, travelling back to their campsite, at Beresford Dale, Derbyshire) and the others (already on the campsite) noticed a number of *'lights'* moving towards their position from the south-east. As they moved closer they saw a large oval shape, carrying two broad *'beams of light'* at the front, with six smaller red lights below the base.

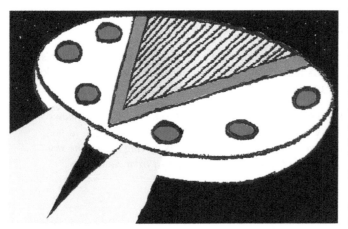

They stopped the car and got out, just in time to see it move away towards the North, making a faint buzzing or humming noise. At about the same time the other group, who were already on the campsite, sighted a square-shaped object in the sky, with rounded corners, showing two bright white lights – like those carried by a medium-sized aircraft. The object, flying straight and level across the sky, at an estimated altitude of 1,500-2,000ft, was in view for 6-7mins, as it headed away in a north-west direction, making a humming noise.

At 12.30am the same morning, a woman resident of Ashbourne was saying goodnight to a friend, when they saw a mass of flashing and pulsating red, blue, and green lights, approaching from the Ormston direction (south-east).

> *"It was larger than a four bedroom house and making a humming noise. As it passed overhead, calves in a nearby field scattered. Our dog rushed into the house, clearly distressed."*

At about the same time, over Chaddesdon, some 12 miles away from Ashbourne, a householder noticed a *'large bright star'* in the sky. Curious, she looked out and saw, with amazement:

> *". . . a large, dome-shaped object, covered with yellow/white lights, hovering above the rooftops of houses opposite, level with my position. It reminded me of a bright chandelier, and was about four times the size of a full moon. I watched, as it headed away westwards."*

At 12.35am a cluster of red, white, green and blue, lights (higher than the rest) were seen moving across the sky over the Nestles factory, in Ashbourne. As it approached closer, the witness received an impression of two fuselage and five or six portholes. It then banked a few degrees to the left, enabling the witnesses to see a distinct impression of a high tail fin and something apparently ducting from the bottom of the 'craft' – like steam, or vapour.

Was there a connection with what schoolboy Bill Dillon saw in 1957 while a pupil at Ramridge School in Bedfordshire? Full details of which have been previously outlined in *Haunted Skies* Volume 1.

1957

1980

1970's   2006

Bill Dillon, an intelligent man and competent artist, has been assisting the authors over the years with various snippets of information and welcome advice regarding the production of *Haunted Skies*. He is shown at the school on a photo taken in the 1970; and is and always has been adamant that what he saw in 1957 was no airship but a vessel constructed by alien hands, which appears to be the case, rather than any airship.

At 12.37am, on the 31st of August 1980 a local disc jockey and his wife were driving home through the outskirts of Mapleton, towards Mayfield, when they noticed a group of lights, surrounded by what appeared to be mist, heading in their direction.

> *"It looked like two car headlights, shining upwards, with a row of blue lights and a green light, with a yellow flashing light underneath. It was so low it narrowly missed colliding with the corner of a house before flying away, towards Dovedale, accompanied by a buzzing noise."*

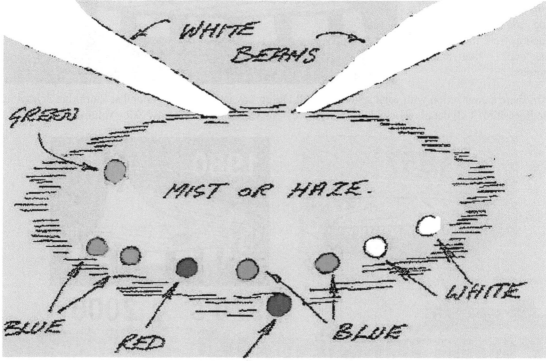

The Society was to receive yet another report for the same day – this time, from Shelton Lock, Derbyshire, when a silver upside-down saucer-shaped object, with a *'cup'* on top, rotating around a centre flashing light, was sighted hovering over power lines.

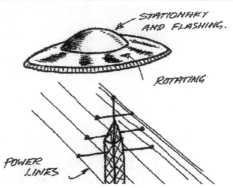

In 2010 we met up with Sydney Henley, of APRA Books, who described the sad circumstances of the death of Peter Ann and the removal of *"a mountain of sighting files, unceremoniously dumped on the floor of the living room by the relatives"* belonging to the club, the current whereabouts of which are not known.

(Source: Sydney Henley/Nottinghamshire UFO Investigation Society)

UFO over Wigan

"THE CURTAINS LIT UP FROM OUTSIDE. I THOUGHT THE CAR WAS ON FIRE."

WHAT was the strange flying object that appeared in the sky over Golborne at 2 a.m. on Sunday morning?

THIS was the opening line to an article which appeared in the *Leigh and District Journal*, September 1980, and it drew me like a moth to a flame.

After interviewing the newspaper's editor, I made appointments to see the three witnesses, all of whom had observed the same phenomenon from two different locations.

Golborne is a small mining town 10 miles west of Wigan. Like most of industrial Lancashire, the town is surrounded by acres of rough, rugged countryside. It was over some fields, on the Golborne boundary, that the "strange flying object" was observed.

by Peter Hough, Chairman of the Manchester UFO Research Association

Disturbed

I found Mrs Hollins, a woman in her mid-forties, independent and friendly. As we sat sipping tea, I switched on my cassette, and she told me what had happened during the early hours of August 31.

"At about two a.m. I was disturbed and noticed the curtains lit up from outside. Our car was parked on the front and I was sure it had caught fire.

"I opened the curtains and was relieved to see the car was all right, but at the same time startled to see this thing in the sky. At first I thought it might be a helicopter, so I went outside."

Mrs Hollins and her family live in a bungalow. Their front garden has an uninterrupted view over fields and woodland. It was mild that night and overcast, but around the hovering UFO, the sky glowed a curious bright red.

"Whatever it was, the thing certainly wasn't a helicopter. From where she stood it looked round, grey, with an outer black ring. On the front were three dark blue "nodules." Yellow and red flames

issued from its rear.

"As I watched, something, I'm not sure what exactly, lowered itself from beneath the thing into some trees, then slowly returned into the machine."

During this time the object had remained fixed in the sky. Now, at a terrific speed, it moved soundlessly towards her, then turned sharply north before quickly changing to a southerly direction. Then it was lost from sight.

"I wasn't a nervous person before the sighting," she said, "but that really shook me up."

Sparks

That same weekend, Elaine Morgan was closing her bedroom window just half a mile away when she called out to her mother. Something very odd hung in the sky! It was emitting sparks from beneath a rectangular object which was completely soundless. An orange mist clung to the rear, and the sky behind was bright orange.

"I was scared, and just wanted to turn my back on it," Elaine admitted. It was a long time before they were able to sleep.

A fruitless search was made of the area, and both Manchester International

The view from Mrs Hollins garden. The object hovered above the trees.

Sydney Henley

At 1.40am the same morning, Edna Proctor and her daughter, Edith, sighted what they thought was a helicopter hovering above a reservoir at Golborne, near Wigan, described as:

". . . an oval or rectangular object, surrounded by a sort of orange 'mist' at the rear, out of which came red sparks. Through the 'mist', a slowly pulsing red light was seen. On the side of the object was an orange 'patch', or window; at the end were two yellowish lights."

Another witness was Mrs Brenda Hollins – also from Golborne – who appears to have sighted the same object over the reservoir, although she did not see the windows or the lights on the object, probably due to the angle of observation. She said,

". . . the object lowered something into the reservoir and then raised it up, before shooting across the sky and disappearing from sight."

Jenny Randles and Peter Hough:

"The case took a mysterious turn when the main witness told Peter that a scientist with an American

accent working for Jodrell Bank Science Centre had called and advised her not to have anything to do with 'cranks' from the UFO field, but invited her to go to Jodrell to assist in further investigation. We were puzzled for many reasons – not least because we worked with Jodrell and knew their interest in UFOs was peripheral (there were even routine sightings received at their switchboard to me for follow-up, and still do decades later). Ultimately, the witness just stopped cooperating. She had agreed to meet us, but appeared to flee the house when Peter and I arrived, leaving the back door open and food cooking on the grill. Later she told me she was called away but now did not want to talk further. At a dead end, we wondered why this witness had suddenly become so uncooperative. I was never able to forget the Golborne case, because the following year there seemed to be a re-run in the Rossendale Valley, about 30 miles (50km) north-east of Wigan. This time there were four independent sets of witnesses".

(Source: Jenny Randles, Peter Hough *The Pennine UFO Mystery*/Jenny Randles *UFO Casebook* 'Objects In The Sky And Beams Behaving Badly', May 2011, WWW)

'Flying Saucer' seen near Temple Meads, Bristol

William McQuaid of Knowle, Bristol telephoned us in 2007 wishing to bring our attention to something that he witnessed around the 1980 period.

"At the time I was employed as a catering steward for British Rail. One morning we were on our way to Cardiff and had just left Temple Mead Station, Bristol. I happened to look out of the window and see a sight that shocked me to the core. A spinning silver saucer shaped object showing a completely smooth outer surface, with no sign of any rivets joins or windows, showing a dome at the top and bottom, hovering in the air about 6ft away from where I was. I estimated it was about 3ft in length and 2ft wide, my first thoughts were that it was radio controlled. There was a man asleep in a nearby carriage, but for some inexplicable reason, I didn't try and awake him".

CHAPTER 9
SEPTEMBER 1980

UFO over West Sussex

IN the early hours of 2nd September 1980, a family living in Crawley, West Sussex, were awoken by a noise that shook the house. When they rushed to the window they saw a round object, covered in lights, disappearing over nearby trees, making a low and high-pitched sound.

(Source: East Anglian UFO & Paranormal Research Association)

Close Encounter at Great Yarmouth

At 7.30pm. 2nd September 1980, Shirley Skinner, a housewife from South Town Road, Great Yarmouth, watched, with amazement, as an oblong-shaped object, with a glowing light in its centre, crossed the sky.

> *"I tried to settle down for the evening and started to watch the TV. At about 8pm, I glanced through the kitchen window and saw, with some fright, what looked like two shiny black pointed crash helmets, with red 'bands' sticking up, a few feet above the hedge. I wondered what on earth they were, but lacked the courage to go out and have a look. I shut the curtains. When I next looked out, they had gone."*

(Source: Brenda Butler & Ron West)

UFO SIGHTING ACCOUNT FORM — completed form showing a handwritten account, drawing of two figures with shiny black helmets and brilliant red visors above a hedge, and signed by Shirley Skinner, 123 Southtown Road, Gt Yarmouth, Norfolk. Today's Date 3-9-80.

UFO over Hawley Woods, Hants.

At about the same time, David Stephenson, from Farnborough, Hampshire, was out walking, near Hawley Woods, when he saw a large *'ball'* of green light, hovering over the nearby lake.

> *"All of a sudden, the water began to bubble and it shot off upwards into the sky."*

(Source: Crystal Hogben, *Magic Saucer*, Jan/Feb. 1981)

At 11.50pm., two oval-shaped objects were seen rapidly crossing over the sea, at Walton-on-the-Naze, Essex. This was followed by a report on the 4th September, when a group of people, out walking in the same locality, at 1.40 am., saw what at first they took to be the lights of a pier – until it projected a beam of light over the sea, stopped in mid air before changing course to the north-west, and then became soon lost from view.

UFO over Fife

At 00.35am., on the 6th September 1980, Christina Campbell and her daughter, Barbara, had just finished clearing up at the family-run public house, *The Commercial Inn,* at Colinsburgh, Fife, when they saw:

> *"a dull red colour cigar-shaped object in the sky, towards the direction of Anstruther, in the centre of which was a brilliant flashing light – like a flashgun going off".*

The object was then lost from sight behind buildings in the NNW direction, five minutes later. The matter was reported to RAF Leuchars, who could offer no explanation.

(Source: *BUFORA Journal,* Vol. 12, No. 2, April 1980)

UFO over Birmingham

Tony Caldicott, from Kings Norton, Birmingham, was out fishing at the side of the canal, at Parsons Lane, Kings Norton, at 4pm. 6th September, 1980, when:

> *"A man came up to me. He said, 'Have you ever seen a cloud like that?' I looked up and saw an object in the sky, which was bell shaped – then it changed to a 'cigar', or 'tube', in the sky – a process of behaviour it repeated seven times over in the 45 minutes period we watched it. I have to comment that when it was 'cigar' in shape, it tilted to an angle of 45 degrees, before moving higher in the sky. The man said it looked metallic, which wasn't my impression at all. It seemed more like a cloud in substance, but was no cloud."*

(Source: Personal interview)

Lights in the sky over Worcestershire

At 8.45pm. on the 7th September 1980, four boys out fishing, at Trimpley Reservoir, close to Habberley Valley, just outside Kidderminster, (a locality to be the source of a number of UFO reports over the years), sighted:

"three 'lights' in the sky – the first, moving in a straight line – the second, zig-zagging then two of them entered a cloud, leaving the third to carry on, which descended over nearby trees, about 200 yards away, surrounded by haze, before moving away out of sight".

(Source: Crystal Hogben, *Magic Saucer*)

UFOs over Tyneside

On 8th September, a triangular formation of *'three lights, with a red light inset'* was seen over Tyneside, by a number of residents, who contacted the police. Enquires made with RAF Acklington confirmed they had received other UFO reports, adding,

"We have no further information about this and, if we did, we would not be allowed to release the information."

Four days later, on the 12th September 1980, the *Eastern Daily Press* brought their readers' attention to a spate of UFO sightings, which had taken place over Kings Lynn and Cambridge.

UFO over Lincolnshire

At 10.10pm the same day Mr J. Eccles, from Kirton Lindsey, Gainsborough, Lincolnshire, was walking along the B1398, a few hundred yards from the village, when he noticed, *"A bright orange oblong-shaped object, motionless in the sky, 200 yards away, a few hundred feet off the ground"* A short time later, the object headed off south-east. **(Source: Richard Thompson)**

UFO over Nottinghamshire and Essex

At 4.35am on the 15th of September 1980, a resident of Mansfield Nott's got up and put the dog outside before beginning to prepare breakfast. Suddenly the animal rushed back into the house in an agitated condition. The man went outside into the back garden and saw a bright light high in the sky which was descending.

"I was stunned when the light stopped in mid air about 60ft above me, allowing me to see a saucer shaped craft about 60ft in diameter. It was about 12ft thick in the centre and had a green dome on top showing green portholes around its centre. The bottom 'ring' was spinning and throwing beams of light downwards. Suddenly a similar object shot down from the sky, and hovered for a few minutes before shooting away over the town. The other one stayed for about ten minutes making a high pitched whine, before also heading away in the same direction take by its companion."

(Source: Mr William Blythe)

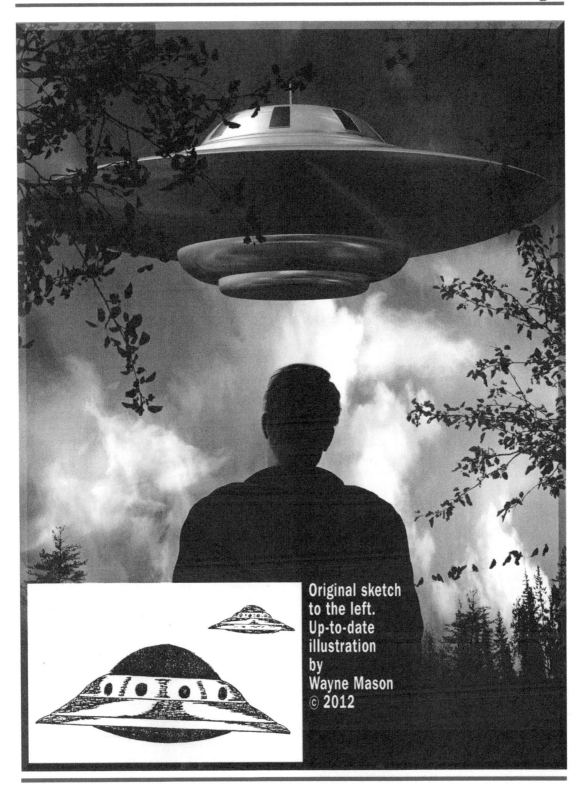

Original sketch
to the left.
Up-to-date
illustration
by
Wayne Mason
© 2012

UFO over Dovercourt

Just after 1pm., on the 15th of September 1980, Dovercourt, Essex, housewife – Jean Cook of Deans Close was hanging out her washing when her husband, Derek, a fireman by occupation directed her attention to something he could see in the sky.

"I saw a bright, round, silvery object – the shape of a children's swimming ring, gliding through the sky, about 200 feet above us. It had a small dome on top and, as it flew, it wobbled slightly, allowing view of a black underside, before it disappeared behind some trees."

Mr Cook said:

"It had no windows and it may have been my imagination but it seemed to be making a humming noise. It slowly glided away towards the direction of the hospital. My son Kevin was so convinced it had landed behind the hospital that he went over to have a look but found no sign of it."

Other witnesses were Jean's sister-in-law, Vivienne Cook and her children Alan (12) and Alison (9).

Mr Cook telephoned the Harwich police to report the matter. The MOD later confirmed they had received details of the incident and . . .

"that it would be investigated, especially if it appeared to have defence implications."

They then added:

"There was apparently a great deal of meteorite activity coming from what was known as the Perseid shower and this was likely to increase next year"

The incident was investigated by Bob Easton for BUFORA, and also Mr William Martindale of

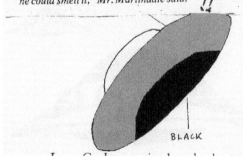

Humming UFO 16/9/80

FIVE Dovercourt people, including one of the town's firemen, saw what they believe was a UFO over the town yesterday.

"It was bright silver on top, black underneath and looked like a motor car hubcap in shape," said fireman Derek Cook, of Deans Close, Dovercourt.

Mr. Cook said he was in the garden when the object appeared to be spinning in the sky just after 1 p.m.

"It had no windows and it may have been my imagination, but it seemed to make a humming noise," said Mr. Cook.

It slowly glided off north eastwards in the direction of the hospital and Mr. Cook's 18-year-old son Kevin was so convinced it had landed behind the hospital that he drove off to look for it. But there was no sign of it.

Mrs. Jean Cook and sister-in-law, Mrs. Viv Cook, saw the UFO, and so did Viv's 12-year-old son Alan and daughter, Alison, nine.

Mr. Cook informed Harwich police, and today the Ministry of Defence in London said they expected reports would come in on the sighting. It would be investigated, especially if it appeared to have defence implications.

Meteorites

The M.o.D. spokesman said there was apparently a great deal of meteorite activity coming from what was known as the Percid Shower and this was likely to increase next year.

Mr. William Martindale of Needham Market, who has documented a number of UFO sightings in the past few years, said Mr. Cook's experience was typical of many along the East Anglian coast.

"One came so close to a Leiston man on the beach that he could smell it," Mr. Martindale said.

BLACK

Needham Market who had by then documented a number of UFO sightings around the Suffolk area. He said:

"Mr Cook's sighting was typical of many along the East Anglian coast"

(Source: *BUFORA Journal* 10, No. 2, April, 1981/Unknown newspaper 'Humming UFO 16.9.1980')

UFO over West Yorkshire

According to Gary Heseltine's excellent database PRUFOS (Police Reporting UFOs), we are told that on the late evening of the 15th of September 1980, two uniformed police officers were on duty in the vicinity of Wetherby, when they observed an object travelling silently across the sky at an altitude of 2,000 feet. They decided to follow the object in their police vehicle, and told of seeing it change direction and head towards York.

Alerted by the West Yorkshire Police two officers of the North Yorkshire Police, PC Roy Allen and PC Richard Gordon, parked up at the side of the road. PC Allen:

"We were waiting on the York bypass when suddenly we saw it. The light stopped moving and hovered in the sky for some time. Eventually it moved off in the direction of Hull."

Police made checks at a number of RAF bases but could not find a satisfactory answer. A senior officer at York said:

"There is nothing more we can do. It has been logged as a UFO."

Gary Heseltine:

"The above case is one of the first investigations carried out by Graham Birdsall and Mark Birdsall. They interviewed many of the people involved. A scientist later stated that the object seen was the planet Venus. In addition, a number of photographs were taken by a Scene of Crime Officer that appeared to support the Venus theory. However, I have examined the statements of several of the officers concerned and they are very specific about there being a definite change of direction over Wetherby. In addition, the altitude quoted by some of the officers is only 2,000 feet and the object was followed in a police vehicle for several miles."

(Source: *FSR* Volume 26, No 4. Nov 1980)

UFO over Wolverhampton

Pam Blakey – from Perton, near Wolverhampton, formerly employed as a secretary at RAF Cosford, Shropshire – described a nightmare journey whilst driving home, in September 1980, with her husband, one early morning, involving the appearance of a mysterious 'light' that appeared in the sky, which

". . . still 'sends shivers down my spine' to this present date.

We had been out visiting some friends and were returning home to Perton, just after 3am, when we saw what, at first, we took to be the headlight of a farm tractor, stationary, over a farmer's field.

As we continued on our journey through unlit countryside, with Peter driving, we noticed the 'light' was now following us. All of a sudden, the darkness was flooded with brilliant silver light, turning night into day. My first thoughts were that it was a police helicopter hovering over our car. Panicking, I shouted out to Peter to get us home as quickly as possible, realising that it was only a few feet above us.

As we entered Perton, driving along The Parkway, with this luminous object still behind us, I admit to being terrified. When we pulled up at the front of the house and dashed in, the 'ball of light' shot upwards into the sky. Thinking this was the end of it, I rushed upstairs to the bedroom window and looked out, where I saw the object – now triangular in shape, hovering over a small coppice, in Sedgewick Drive, before it once again shot upwards into the sky, where I never saw it again."

Pam told us, although she went to work a few hours after this incident, she was disinclined to bring the matter to anybody's attention – fearing nobody would believe her and that her position of employment may have been in jeopardy. She believes there was a link between the sighting of this unidentified object and a marked deterioration in her health, involving nosebleeds, persistent headaches, depression and the lack of co-ordination.

In addition to this, the couple reported a number of electrical malfunctions around the house, necessitating the replacement of some of the domestic appliances installed in the property.

Peter:

"We noticed something very unusual about the red 'Allegro' company car that was only twelve months old. When I examined the vehicle, the day after the incident, I found the red paint on the roof had turned to orange. Although I tried to cut the paintwork back to its original colour, it still showed orange. Shortly after this, the car was returned to the company."

(Source: Personal interview)

UFO over Surrey

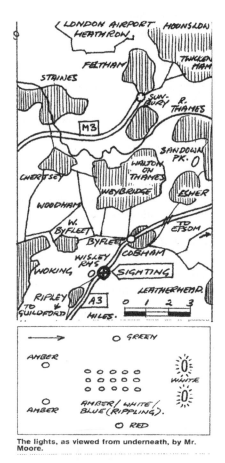

The lights, as viewed from underneath, by Mr. Moore.

On the 17th of September 1980, Civil Servant, Gary Moore – accompanied by his friend, Andrew Johnstone, an electrical fitter by trade – was driving home to Portsmouth, southwards, along the A3, after having just gone through the village of Cobham, at 12.30am. While descending a hill, with a good clear view of the open countryside, their attention was drawn to a 'bright light' in the distance, which, as they travelled closer, was seen as two lights, similar in appearance to two car headlights, approximately 200 feet off the ground, stationary in the sky. Gary decided to pull into a lay-by and get out of the car, curious as to what the lights could be –

"Suddenly, we were able to make out other lights on the 'craft', which consisted of a red light on the front left-hand side, and a green light on the right-hand side. In the centre section of the object appeared a flickering square of lights – something like three rows of five lights – glittering in amber, white, blue, sequence, as the lights rippled backwards and forwards. At the rear could be seen two amber lights, about the same width apart as the 'headlamps'. Whatever it was, it was massive."

After passing overhead the object, estimated to be at least 200 feet long, with its huge rectangular body – reminiscent of some majestic airborne oceanic liner, was soon lost from sight as it passed over a nearby hill.

(Source: Omar Fowler, PRA)

UFO over Redditch

On the 18th of September 1980, the West Mercia Police were called to the Church Hill area of Redditch, Worcestershire, after four schoolboys – Tim Belmont, Peter Bevington, Stuart Heath and Colin Humphries – contacted them, reporting having sighted a clover-shaped UFO, hovering about ten feet above a house in Sandhurst Close, at 9pm.

Tim was the first to see the object, which he took to be a bird – then realised it was stationary, with a red flashing light on each wing. Colin Humphries:

"I was out walking, with three other schoolboys, in the Church Hill area, on what was a stormy evening, with lightning flickering overhead. All of a sudden, we were shocked to see a cigar shaped 'thing', metallic in appearance, with red flashing lights along its 'wings', hovering about ten feet above a house in Sandhurst Close. Our excitement soon turned to fear, so one of us telephoned the police. By the time they arrived, the 'flying cigar', or

whatever it was, had moved away. The police told us it was probably lightning, following a heavy storm in the area."

**(Source: Derek Waugh, Redditch UFO Study and Investigation Group/*Redditch Indicator*, 26.9.80,
'Close Encounter with a 4ft UFO')**

At 1pm., Stanley Day – a resident of Studley – was at his home address, during the same day when he saw

"An object moving slowly over the Redditch Estates, showing two orange/red flashing lights, heading towards Birmingham."

(Source: Personal interview)

UFO over Studley

At 9pm the following day, September 19th 1980, Mrs Rina Oakes was returning home, driving past Coughton Court – a stately home, situated just off the Alcester Road, a few miles from Studley.

"It was pouring with rain at the time, but I noticed what looked like a 'cigar of light' stationary in the sky, over Coughton Court – then the windscreen wipers failed, but after I had driven a few hundred feet along the road, they came back on again. This was the first and last time they would ever let me down. Was there a connection with what I saw?"

(Source: Personal interview)

Coughton Court near Studley, West Midlands.

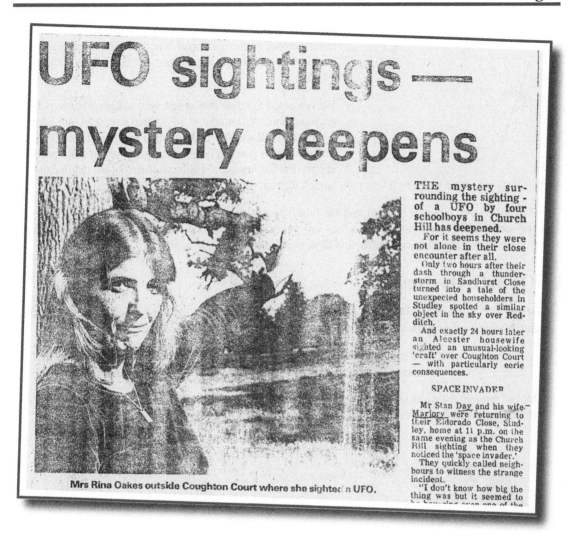

UFO sightings — mystery deepens

THE mystery surrounding the sighting of a UFO by four schoolboys in Church Hill has deepened.

For it seems they were not alone in their close encounter after all.

Only two hours after their dash through a thunderstorm in Sandhurst Close turned into a tale of the unexpected householders in Studley spotted a similar object in the sky over Redditch.

And exactly 24 hours later an Alcester housewife sighted an unusual-looking 'craft' over Coughton Court — with particularly eerie consequences.

SPACE INVADER

Mr Stan Day and his wife Marjory were returning to their Eldorado Close, Studley, home at 11 p.m. on the same evening as the Church Hill sighting when they noticed the 'space invader.'

They quickly called neighbours to witness the strange incident.

"I don't know how big the thing was but it seemed to ...

Mrs Rina Oakes outside Coughton Court where she sighted a UFO.

Encounter with UFO Cheshire

On the 21st of September, 1980, a motorist and his family were returning home along the A530, near Wimboldsley, when they saw what appeared to be two *'stars'* in the sky, followed by a heavy burst of static on the VHF radio, installed in the vehicle. Curious as to the source of these two *'stars'* in the sky, the driver stopped and got out of his vehicle. As he did so –

> *"the top 'star' dropped downwards and headed straight for me but stopped in mid air, about 500 yards away, approximately 200 feet off the ground, before taking off and meeting up with the second object. Both of them then sped across the sky, where they were soon lost from view."*

As a result of this incident being brought to the attention of Terry Cleaver and Mark Tyrell – UFO Investigators for the *Federation of UFO Research* ('FUFOR') – the two men subsequently published a

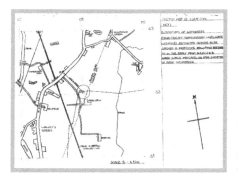

detailed report into the incident, which revealed the permanently fixed memory of the transceiver, tuned in to a two metre repeater station GB3M.N set, to receive at 145.650, had been altered to 145.525.

We contacted the man concerned, who asked us not to publish anything about this matter at all – when we asked him why, he declined to tell us. Whether this had anything to do with the family's earlier visit to a hospital is matter we can only speculate about – but while we are willing to withhold the man's details – we felt this was too important a matter not to publish.

Thirty minutes later, Graham Belcher and his family were driving home to Crewe, some 25 miles away from the scene of the first incident, when they saw two white rectangular shaped *'lights'* crossing the sky, over Connah's Quay, heading eastwards, and disappearing in a *'flash of light'*.

UFOs over Devizes

At 6.30am, 23rd September 1980, Julie Box, of Pans Lane, Devizes, Wiltshire, got up to see her soldier husband, Michael, off to work at the Queens Lancashire Regiment, Warminster, when he told her:

> *"I've just seen six UFOs, one behind the other, pass over the brow of a nearby hill (some 2-3 miles away), while looking through the kitchen window".*

Julie looked through the window and saw two objects, moving from left to right, flying across the clear blue sky, which inexplicably vanished from view, accompanied by heavy interference on the radio.

N.U.F.O.R. [SOUTHWEST].

M.A.U.F.O.G.

National U.F.O. Research

Main HQ, Brighton.

Tel, 0272   666270
         646710

16 Marigold Walk,
Ashton,
Bristol. BS3 2PD.

SR1.A.   UFO SIGHTING REPORT FORM: INITIAL STAGE

Please complete this form to the best of your knowledge, and if unsure on any
particular points, please state, "Don't know".

WITNESS

A) Full name(Mr/Mrs/Miss/Ms)...Michael...Bax............. Age.36.....
     Address. 28 Dragon Ave....... Current occupation...Soldier......
     .... Telephone No 214000 (STD)(WARM)
                        EX.2310

LOCALE

B) Location of witness(es)...Garden of Same House.........
     Day & Date of sighting..22.7.80...... Time of initial sighting.0640..
     Description of weather conditions.....Clear.............

THE SIGHTING

C) The object: Colour(s).Gold......... No of objects...Six...........
     Shape.............. Sound(s)...No...... Odours, if any...No...
     Did the object(s) appear solid?..Yes..... Estimated speed.Don't know
     Apparent size of object(s).small...... Brightness.Very....
     Describe the movement of the object(s).Single file formation....
     Estimated distance....½...1 mile... Estimated altitude.....at end......
     Estimated angle of elevation.Great.. Estimated duration of sighting.30 secs
     Direction of object(s) at beginning..S/E....., at end....S/E......
     Attention of the witness drawn to the object because...of the
     brightness of lights. How did the sighting end?...went to work
     Any unusual environmental effects?...No.................

GENERAL

D) To whom and when was it reported?......Press...Same morning by wife
     Was anyone else present?..Wife...... Did they see it?..Yes..........
     Have you had any previous sightings?..No... Did you photograph it?..No..

Please complete the reverse of this sheet by giving an account of the
incident and drawing a sketch of the object(s) and marking with arrows,
the direction of movement (if any).

SR1.B.   ACCOUNT OF THE INCIDENT (and any items not covered by previous questions).

Awoken at 6:30 a.m. By husband for work. Went down for coffee. He then said that he had seen 6 UFO'S through the back kitchen window. I was slightly annoyed as I thought he was taking the mickey. But after telling me a 2nd time I went to the window and after about 20 seconds saw to my astonishment 6 extremely bright objects which to myself swear they were alien. They moved from left to right, went behind the hill, and then just appeared from nowhere myself as soon as I saw them I knew that they were not aircraft or car lights, helicopters or anything of that description. more so in my mind because an airplane can not hover, a helicopter can but not to just disappear like a light being put out. I would argue this point with anyone. It was something I will never forget for the rest of my life.

DRAWING (PLEASE MARK DIRECTIION OF MOTION WITH ARROWS).
(Colour if possible).

[ ] If you do not wish your name to be published, mark 'X' in box.

This information is acurate to the best of my knowledge.

Signature...Julie D. Box......   Date..7-10-80..

SR1.B. ACCOUNT OF THE INCIDENT (and any items not covered by previous questions).

Radio turned itself on for a second or so and turned itself off again. Objects appeared moving from right to left as we looked at them appeared between five house lower and ?? of the objects lived and disappeared and reappeared again a few mins later often would ?? about twenty mins ?? I left my wife still watching them as I had to go to work.

DRAWING (PLEASE MARK DIRECTIION OF MOTION WITH ARROWS).
(Colour if possible).

If you do not wish your name to be published, mark 'X' in box.

This information is acurate to the best of my knowledge.

Signature....................... Date. 16 - 10 - 80

Six strange objects in Wilts sky

WERE THEY UFOs or not? That was the question a Devizes couple were asking themselves today.

Soldier Michael Box, 23, and his wife Julie, 20, were mystified by their sightings from the back garden of their home at Drake's Avenue, off Pans Lane, at 6.30 am.

"I was in bed when Michael excitedly called me down to see these strange objects in the sky above the brow of a hill on the sky-line," said Julie.

"We could see six round objects, gleaming as brightly as stars, above the hilltop. Then suddenly, three went out like a light, and the other three disappeared behind the hill before re-appearing from another direction — and suddenly vanishing."

Julie said, "I was only wearing my nightdress at the time—I was absolutely shivering, and Michael, who is in the Queen's Lancashire Regiment at the School of Infantry at Warminster, was late for work. We were absolutely fascinated."

Julie said the objects were silhouetted against a clear blue sky and were visible for about 10 minutes.

Later, she said, two helicopters appeared in the vicinity. "But the objects we saw certainly were not helicopters, or flares."

NEW South Wales statistics show that 75 per cent of adults who drowned in the state last year had been drinking beforehand. Ken Booth, Sports Minister, said today in Sydney.

TWO gunmen shot dead a part-time policeman in Northern Ireland late last night. Mr Ernest Johnston, 34, was ambushed outside his home near the border in County Fermanagh.

Inquiry starts

A PUBLIC inquiry into Bath City Council's refusal for a proposed change of use of 7 St James's Street from retail to either restaurant or residential started yesterday at the Guildhall.

Boxer: Slight improvement

BRITISH boxer Johnny Owen, who underwent brain

Car raided

THIRTEEN cassettes have been stolen from a car in Palmer Street, Frome. They belong to Mr Douglas Smith, of Stowey Street, Frome.

The couple contacted the *Bath and West Evening Chronicle,* who published their sighting on the 24th of September 1980.

After reading about the incident, Mike Seager and Terry Chivers, of *National UFO Research* organisation, conducted an investigation into the matter, when they established the weather had been cloudy, with a cloud base of 700 feet, visibility nine kilometres, in slight rain, rather than a blue sky and that a visit to the brow of the hill revealed no descent on the other side.

Enquires made with RAF Lyneham revealed there had been an Army Scout helicopter in the area concerned, at the time, which indicated the sighting report may have been unreliable, especially after they were unable to arrange a personal interview with the couple concerned. Was it a hoax, or were the 'Box's' warned not to become involved any further with the UFO organisation concerned?

We wrote a number of letters to Terry, then still a councillor, living in the Wiltshire area (2009) – asking if he would be prepared to speak to us with regard to his very active involvements in a number of UFO sightings and crop circles during the 1980's. We eventually spoke to him in 2011 about a number of investigations carried out by him and other members of *Probe.*

(Source: *Bath & West Evening Chronicle* 24.9.80 – 'Six strange objects in Wilt's sky' Mike Seager/Terry Chivers, National UFO Research)

2nd Psychics & Mystics Fayre & UFO Show
Alexandra Palace, 27-28 September 1980

were peering at the panels. It was reported that 9,000 attended this *Fayre*, although the first fayre earlier in the year had attracted some 14,000. Sales of literature from the *Bufora* stand were sufficient to cover costs, and the bonus was the resulting new members and additional people coming to the London lectures.

Gay Wilson, the organiser of this event, offered *Bufora* very favourable terms for participation. Since the Association needed to raise funds and publicise itself to a wider audience, it was agreed, as an experiment, to go ahead. It was recognised that the *Fayre* was a 'fringe' event, but equally *Bufora* was able to demonstrate that UFO research could be handled in a serious manner, as opposed to the para-religious and theosophical approaches adopted by the *Aetherius Society* and *Viewpoint Aquarius*, both of which were exhibitors.

Lionel Beer spent three weeks assembling and mounting photographs and associated material, together with the painstaking task of 'Letrasetting' captions and headings. The display included well-known photographs (some of which were of suspected fakes): UFOs on movie-film: historical phenomena and unusual man-made objects, all with appropriate captions. A poster showing humanoid types drew much attention and there was also a small, colourful selection of book covers. Without any modesty, it could be said that the displays attracted very considerable interest and on the Sunday afternoon, people up to three deep

The displays in a stand area of about 15ft. x 6ft. were set up in only 90 minutes prior to the formal opening of the *Fayre* at 11 am. This was done by Betty Wood, Arnold West, his daughter Averil and Lionel Beer. Wilf Grunau, *Bufora* Treasurer, provided a 40 minute talk on UFOs in the demonstration area of the *Fayre* during the Saturday lunch-hour. Other members who assisted in manning the stand included Pam Kennedy, Eve Demuth, John Shaw, Robert Morison, Mr & Mrs Leslie Bayer and their son Christopher. To sum up, this was a successful exercise in public relations for the Association and provided useful experience for those involved.

Anecdote

Gay Wilson orginally wrote to Lionel Beer on 10 July, soliciting *Bufora's* participation. And what happened on 10 July? This was the day the Great Hall burnt down! One might well ask, what price their psychics and mystics now? However, the event was subsequently transferred back to the Palm Court area at the western end of the site, which, together with the BBC transmitter at the eastern end, remained intact.

Burnett's Printing Works, Cyprus Rd, Burgess Hill, W Sussex. Tel B Hill 3126 (*STD*) 04446.

Lionel Beer – pictured here with Jon Downes (seated), who had previously published Volumes 1-6 of the 'Haunted Skies' series.

A letter penned by the late Arthur Shuttlewood in September, 1980, relating to crop circles and 'Probe' magazine.

CHAPTER 10
OCTOBER 1980

Strange orange glow over East Lothian

ON the 3rd of October 1980 Peter Douglas (11) and three friends were out playing on the Muirpark adventure playground near their homes in Tranent East Lothian. When at 7.15pm they saw an orange light covering about half of the sky towards the North West direction. It then vanished but reappeared a few minutes later as a fuzzy oval shape visible for a few seconds on each occasion it was seen.

(Source: BUFORA)

'Flying Saucer' over Anglesey

In October 1980, schoolboys – David Prytherch & Gerald Kellahan, from Syr Thomas Jones School, Amlwch, sighted:

> *"A brightly lit saucer shaped object, full of coloured lights, which made a swishing noise as passed overhead. It looked like a crab underneath, as it passed directly above our heads, at around 8.00 pm., before heading on towards Parys Mountain, joined, shortly afterwards, by a bigger version of the first."*

David's father, Ken Prytherch, Postmaster at Penysarn, described his son's agitated condition and that, after being told what happened, invited him to illustrate what he had seen – identical to that drawn by Gerald. Apparently, the boys weren't the only ones to sight the UFO. Members of the McGuire family, from Tyn Ffynnon, claimed to have seen 'lights' which seemed to land on the mountain, after darting about in the sky.

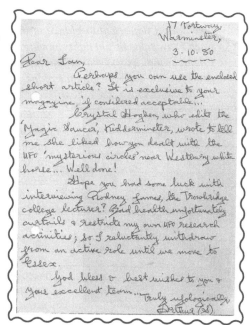

(Source: *The North Wales Chronicle*, **16.10.80 – 'UFO lands on Parys Mountain')**

UFO over Emley Moor

Russell Callaghan was working as a bus conductor, in Bradford, during October 1980.

> "We finished early on that day and had little time to spare, so we parked on Odsal Top, looking outwards over Emley Moor. It was about 3.45 pm. The sun had gone in. It wasn't quite dark. We were shocked to see a silver spinning 'disc' in the sky at about a thousand feet off the ground. Within eight seconds it had gone."

Russell one of the leading UFO Researchers in the country, was very much involved in *UFO Magazine* before its demise, after the death of Graham Birdsall.

UFO over Hampshire

On the 9th October 1980, Nurse Diane Edworthy, stationed at High Hurlands Hospital, Liphook, Hampshire, found herself once again witnessing another example of UFO behaviour – this time over the orchard, close to the main building.

> "*I was working with a girl, called Cathy, at about midnight. She drew my attention to an awful humming noise she could hear. I listened but couldn't hear anything at all. A short time later, I happened to glance through the window overlooking the rear of the building, when I saw some bright lights moving slowly across the sky, towards the front of the building. I thought that was very odd and, although I couldn't give any distance, they seemed close enough to be over the grounds of the Hospital, rather than higher up, if they had been high up, I wouldn't have seen them.*

Nurse Diane Edworthy

> *I alerted Cathy and we stood there, watching what looked like a huge star in the sky, as it changed colour from white to intense blue in an explosion of light. After twenty minutes, or so, it changed colour again from blue to red, green and orange, before going back to white again. At this point we had to get on with our duties, so it wasn't until 12.45am. We had another look and saw flashing lights coming from the 'Star'. We opened the window and saw it was now only a few hundred yards away from us, and about 20 feet off the ground, with lots of flashing red and green lights over the edge of the orchard. It stayed there for some time, spinning and throwing off lights, until at 3.30am. It and the 'Star' just disappeared.*"

This matter was originally reported to Hilary Porter a member of *The UFO Info Exchange Library* in Swindon, Wiltshire, as a result of a telephone call from the two nurses at High Hurlands Hospital, Liphook, Hampshire.

"The hospital sisters were so upset and distraught they actually couldn't speak much at first, but I managed to reassure them and told them to take as long as they wanted. Gradually they calmed down and started to relate what was going on – they said that for some months now there had been a UFO that flew over the hospital and hovered there for quite some time.

Apparently they had observed it's movements very well, and told me how the object always came from the Guildford direction then moved away southerly, towards the Portsmouth area. But they went on to say things have got very scary now; this craft seems to be getting bolder as time goes on, and is now landing in the old orchard within the grounds of the hospital, and a big, tall 'being' is often seen prowling the area following each landing. Staff coming off, or going on duty from the nurse's home are seeing this visitor popping up all over the place, and they are terrified. Not only that but this 'being' had taken to coming right up to the windows of the wards, where handicapped, sick children are being cared for, so they are having to put the blinds down as it's scaring the life out of these little ones.

The lights of this craft could be seen from a window in the staffing quarters, one of the nurses went just outside the door, armed with her camera, and took several pictures, but because it was very dark they didn't turn out. I was sympathetic and stunned by all the things these nurses had to tell me; then they asked me if I would go straight down to Liphook to investigate, but I explained that I had a small daughter to look after. I was on my own and couldn't leave her, as she too was handicapped"

Hilary was to then pass the matter on to Omar Fowler who conducted an investigation into the incidents concerned.

(Sources: Omar Fowler /SIGAP Journal *'Pegasus'*, November/December 1980.
FSR Volume 30, No. 6, 1985/Personal interview)

UFO over Wiltshire

At 12.15am on the 18th or 25th of October 1980, Andy James Siekera of Leaze Road, Melksham, Wiltshire was in the back garden feeding his rabbits when he noticed an object following an unusual course across the sky.

> *"It was moving at a fast speed in a series of up and down movements while maintaining the same course. Suddenly it gave of a blinding flash of light which hurt my eyes, concerned I ran back indoors".*

The sighting lasted approximately 25 seconds. The object was seen moving from a North to North-East direction, in a series of estimated 75° to 45° steps.

(Source: *Search West Magazine* No2)

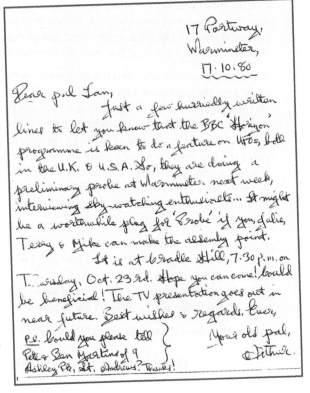

UFO over Criccieth

We spoke to retired police officer Kevin Babb, of the North Wales Constabulary who had himself investigated reports of strange objects seen in the sky while a serving officer at the time. One of them involved Julie Noutch, aged 18, who was a front seat passenger in a car being driven by her aunt, Phyllis Hughes along Tabor Road, near Pentrefelin close to Criccieth, at 7pm on 22nd October 1980.

> *"As we turned a right-hand bend, we noticed seven orange lights forming a circle in the sky, just above the horizon – presumably connected with the appearance of a moving green light, about a mile away. I asked my Aunt to stop, so we could have a closer look. She refused, as she was frightened. I later contacted RAF Valley. They told me no aircraft had been flying in the area at the time. Although over 20 years has passed since I saw the UFO, my memory of it is still clear."*

In January 2013 we spoke to Julie about her sighting, and of the fact that it was going to be in *Haunted Skies* Volume 8.

> *"All I know is what I saw. I thought it might have been a helicopter that made no noise whatsoever, maybe new technology. I contacted the police station and told them about it, they told me they had contacted the RAF and that there were no flights listed from RAF Valley and that nothing was going on – so it remains an unidentified flying object to this present day".*

Julie appreciates that unless you have seen something yourself it is all to easy to dismiss such sightings away, and that talking about the subject often attracts humour. Thank goodness there are people like Julie who have the courage to report what they have seen, now over 30 years ago but indelibly burnt into the memory of the person concerned.   **(Source: Police Constable Kevin Babb/Personal interview)**

GROUP	NUFON	BUFORA REF.	YEAR	NUMBER
/INV' EF	1/80/T1		1980	

SECTION B

1. Where were you when you saw the object(s)? Exact location....TABOR RD PENTREFELIN
Nearest town/village...PENTREFELIN Nr CRICCIETH...County/District:.....GWYNEDD

2. What was the date of your sighting?..............WEDNES day 22nd of OCTUBER 1980

3. At what time did you see the object(s)? Appx 7 *am/pm/midday/midnight. *Delete which ever does not apply. How did you know the time?....WRIST WATCH

4. For how long did you observe the object(s)?..............If not certain please state — for not less than 3 mins... and for not more than 5 mins

5. If each of the following objects were held at arm's length which one would just cover the object(s) you saw, i.e. have the same apparent size? (underline) Pinhead/pea/halfpenny/penny/ twopence/golf-ball/tennis-ball/other

6.

SMALL SIDE PLATE

Place an 'A' on the curved line in diagram (i) to show the altitude of the object(s) above the horizon when you first noticed it/them and a 'B' when you last noticed it/them. Also place an 'A' on the outside edge of the compass in diagram (ii) to indicate the direction in which you first observed the object(s) and a 'B' when you last saw it/them.

7. Did you see the object(s) at or near ground level? APPEARED 2000 TO GROUND

8. How did the object(s) disappear from view? TRAVELLED OUT OF VIEW DUE TO PASSENGER

9. If you took a photograph or made a measurements, give details — Nil

10. If you noticed any unusual effects on fire, animals, plants, objects or equipment nearby: Describe these Nil

11. What was the main feature of the sighting which made you feel that the object(s) was/were not natural or man-made? Not moving – unusually bright & no noise

12. How many other people at the same time saw the object(s)? one Give the names, addresses, age and relationship to you of other witnesses Aunty – Mrs Phylis Hughes 'BRISTOL HOUSE' LLANLLYN, CAERNARFON, GWYNEDD.

13. Give a brief description of the object(s) under the following headings:—
(a) Number of objects 1 or 7 (b) Colour 6 Fingernar green (c) Sound No noise
(d) Shape Not known was this sharply defined or hazy? no
(e) Brightness Very bright/B than Stars (compared to star, venus, moon, sun etc.)

14. What were the local conditions? Please tick in box where applicable.

Clouds		Temperature		Wind		Precipitation		Astronomical	
Clear Sky	☐	Cold	☒	None	☒	Dry	☒	Stars	☒
Scattered cloud	☒	Cool	☐	Breeze	☐	Fog or mist	☐	Moon	☐
Much cloud	☐	Warm	☐	Moderate	☐	Rain	☐	Planet	☐
Overcast	☐	Hot	☐	Strong	☐	Snow	☐	Sun	☐

Other conditions if any Just turned fully dark

R.E.P.O.R.T.

IR.1.
Ref   NE
CE1
1.80.T1.
22.10.80.
Pentrefelin.

General.

        See account.

6/3A/GR.0/SS/0/MNF

Witness.

The witnesses in this case are in fact close relatives, the number one witness
being my cousine (Mothers sisters daughter) and No 2 being my Aunty (Mothers
Uncles 2nd wife).
I can personally vouch for their integrity and truthfullness, neither are in
least ways interested in UFOs or anything Paranormal.
I have not obtained an account form from my aunty due to the fact that her
account is identical to my cousins.
Niether have any inclination to make up stories and in fact reported the
incident immediately to me, my cousin Julie Noutch was intreged and at the time
wanted to 'INVESTIGATE' further but my Aunty was afraid and talked her out of
investigating further.
I strongly believe they saw something unusuall and cannot see them making the story
up.
After the incident they both came to my parents house in Caernarfon, luckily they
chose the right time and I was home (unknown to them). Julie appeared very
excited and wanted to investigate further whilst my aunty was very wary and wasnt at
all keen, she kept trying to excuse the sighting as something normal such as a
helicopter or the such but she couldnt match the sighting up to any previous
experience.
I have examined what they have said not as a member of the family but as an
interested by stander and I personally believe them.

Both are healthy, bright and not inclined to lie or exagerate.

Area. - Local as to position of witnesses.

Lon Tabor (in English Tabor Road) is a very minor(more or less) single track road
which joins the A497 Criccieth to Porthmadog Rd with the A487 Caernarfon to
Porthmadog Road, the road is very bendy and bordered by high (Welsh type walls).
Whilst travelling up the road the hills and mountains of the Snowdonia Massive
are clearly visible as is the Aberglaslyn pass area.
there is only one village visible from Lon Tabor and this is Garn dolbenmaen which
is illuminated by orange phoresent lights, however this village was not in the
immediate line of sight of the witnesses.
I travelled about the area with Miss Noutch but could find nothing which
could account for what she saw.

Area. - General.

The area between the coast road is relativly sparsly populated between the coast
and the A487.
There are outlying farms and a couple of small villages but nothing to
cause the sighting.
The only unusuall object in the area is the Nebo TV mast but that was well away from
the area of the sighting and well known to the witnesses.
Nothing UFO wise is known of the area to me.

Background enquiries.

Aircraft.   NEGATIVE   R.A.F. Valley or Mona air field.

                 NEGATIVE   ████████████ No helicopters operational on the date by
                             the RAF or charter

```
                                            6.1.
                                            Ref      NE
                                            CE1
                                            1.80.T1.
                                            22.10.80.
                                            Pentrefelin.

           C O N C L U S I O N


    I have carefully  examined the area subject of this report and cannot find
    anything which could account for the sighting
    All enquiries locally and with the authorities have proved totally negative.
    I can only conclude knowing the integrity of  the witnesses that they
    saw somethingm unusuall which cannot be explained at present.

                                               Pc.1063.Babb
                                               Amlwch Police Station
                                               Anglesey,
                                               GWYNEDD.
```

UFO over London

At 4.40pm. 28th October 1980, Eric Rush, from London, was stood on the platform of Peckham Rye Station –

> *"I glanced up into a clear sky and noticed a 'bright light' almost directly above me, motionless in the sky. I knew it wasn't Venus, or Mercury. It was far too high to be a planet. I noticed there was a black smudge underneath it, which began to form a longer line as it corkscrewed downwards. I watched it for about five minutes, wondering what on earth it could have been – then I suddenly had this awful feeling . . . 'Was it an ICBM missile, with a nuclear warhead?' If it was, there wasn't much point in running anywhere. When the black line reached about 30,000 feet, it broke, or split, into three separate objects, that slowed in descent to about a 1,000 feet, before soaring like a Red Arrow bomb burst display, towards the East, South, and South-west – out of sight in seconds. I tried to telephone 'BUFORA' and Heathrow Airport but in the end, I gave up."*

(Source: Personal interview)

UFO over Anglesey

At 5am the 29th October, 1980, Police Constable David Philip Jones, from County Police Station, Llanerchymedd, Amlwch, was awoken by the sound of the family cat, crying to go out. While returning upstairs, his attention was attracted by a source of bright light filtering through the closed curtains. Curious as to the cause, he opened the curtains and recoiled from a glare so bright it pained his eyes to look at. Opening the window he looked out and, as his eyes adjusted slowly, he noticed:

> *"a large ball of silver light, with hazy rings around it, underneath which could be seen a smaller silver sphere."*

Excitedly, he called his wife – Helen Mary Jones. The couple then stood watching the dazzling object until the cold of the night proved too much, when they decided to go back to bed.

© Robin Drayton 2008

As a result of a visit made to the police station by local UFO researcher PC 1063 Kevin Babb, from Amlwch Police Station, (who had himself worked with the officer on various operational duties), it was established that immediately in front of the area where the sighting had taken place were several old buildings, including a large disused water tower, which was out of the line of Police Constable Jones' view but worthy of mention.

Enquiries made with RAF Valley and RAF Mona, (then leased to a Flying Club), revealed no aircraft were flying and that they had not received any other reports of UFO activity. However, Kevin did trace a woman, living a short distance away from the police station, who described having sighted *"two UFOs, floating downwards, before disappearing from view"*, during the same evening.

In 2012 we spoke again to Kevin Babb living in Mold Gwynedd. He confirmed the veracity of the people involved and was still interested in hearing about reported sightings of UFO activity.

We have nothing but praise for Kevin, who had the courage while a serving police officer, to investigate and document matters that most people would have regarded as being impossible to believe.

```
                                                          IR.1.
                                                          Ref      NE
                                                          CE1
                      R E P O R T                         2.80.T1.
                                                          29.10.80.
                                                          Llanerchymed
General.

            See acount.

                                         7/5A/w/B/o/N MNF

Witness.

    I have known the witness personally for approximately 1½ years, being
    a Police Officer in the same operational section as myself. I have worked
    closely with him during this time, we usually work together on criminal
    activities (detecting not perpetrating I hasten to add) and have found him
    to be a 'stickler' for the truth.
    He is not the sort to imagine things or to waste time contocting up a
    story, he has no strong interest in UFO or the Paranormal apart from the
    normal interest of any normal person.
    As far as I can see there is no reason to disbelieve what he has reported.
    His eyesight I believe is slightly defective but to no considerable extent.
    I would count Davy Jones as an A1 witness.
```

AREA. - Local as to position of witness.

```
    Looking from the window the witness viewed the objects from, you are faced
    by a row of old peoples bungalows, behind these houses are their gardens.
    Immediately behind these are fields which tend to be slightly elevated. these
    fields however cannot be see from the witnesses window.  there are several
    old buildings in the general area which include a large disused water tower
    but this tower was well away from the line of sight of the witness.
    there is nothing in the immediate area (line of sight) which could explain the
    objects seen.
```

AREA. - General.

```
    Llanerchymedd was the subject in the middle of 1978 of a bit of a UFO scare,
    this scare which was investigated by Mr Derek James took the form of sightings
    of UFOs in flight, a landing and a possible sighting of occupant(s). I believe
    physical eveidence was also found by Mr James.
    Llanerchymedd is also on what I believe to be a flight route which includes
    Parys Mountain approx 5 miles away. (Please see attached letter) - also a nearby
    village RHOSYBOL (Between Amlwch and Llanerchymedd) was the subject of a landing
    and occupant sighting scare in 77/78.
    Llanerchymedd is also nearly the centre of the Isle of Anglesey.
```

BACKGROUND ENQUIRIES

```
    Aircraft.     No planes flying from R.A.F Valley or R.A.F. Mona (Ex RAF Base now
                  leased to private flying club).
                  Likewise no Helicopters in use in area either by the RAF, Shell UK
                  or the electricity board.

                  Llanerchymedd is also well off the BLUE ONE Manchester/Dublin air
                  route.

    Weather.      Weather at the time very good, slightly cold, no clouds in sky

    RADAR.        NEGATIVE on RAF or TRINITY HOUSE RADAR.

    Stars etc.    No planets, stars or other heavenly bodies in area of sighting
                  moon not seen in area by witness.

    ( ALL OBSERVATIONS OBTAINED FROM RAF. TH. and LOCAL ENTHUSIASTS).
```

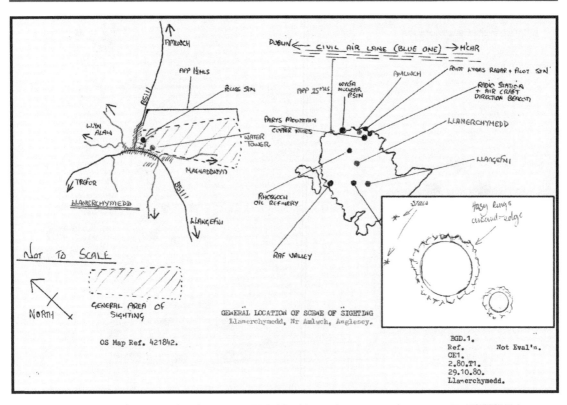

NOT TO SCALE

NORTH

GENERAL AREA OF SIGHTING

OS Map Ref. 421842.

GENERAL LOCATION OF SCENE OF SIGHTING
Llanerchymedd, Nr Amlwch, Anglesey.

BGD.1.
Ref.   Not Eval'n.
CE1.
2.80.T1.
29.10.80.
Llanerchymedd.

W H O   K N O W S

C.3.
Ref   NE
CE1
1.80.T1
22.10.80.
Pentrefelin

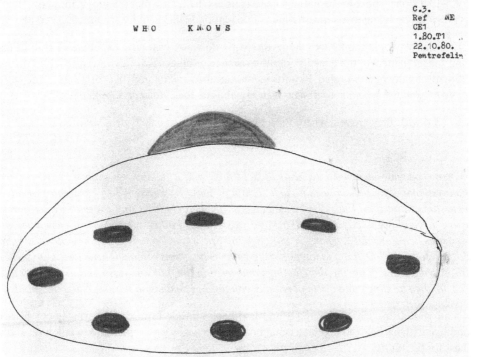

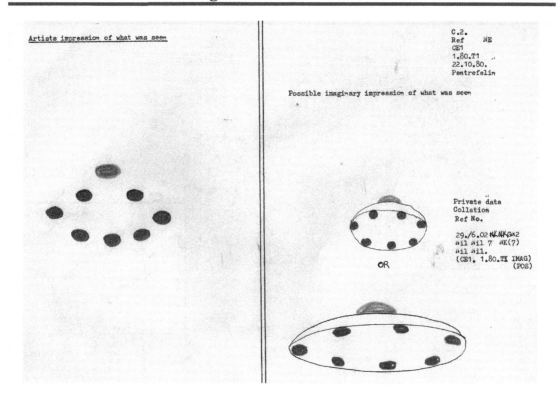

In January 2013, I (John) spoke to Kevin Babb once again about the case files (including the above illustrations) sent to us previously relating to his investigations into reported UFO activity around the 1980 period.

Despite what many people think, and claim, the MoD does not have any expertise or role in respect of UFO/flying saucer matters or the question of the existence or otherwise of extraterrestrial life forms, about which it remains totally open-minded. Reports were examined and logged (over 50 years) – they tell us they were *"solely to establish whether what was seen might have some defence significance"*.

Authors: . . . but what they are and where they come from – *the silence is deafening!*

Kevin:

> *"When I became involved I tried to look at this from a debunker's point of view, rather than automatically believing that such sightings could be attributed as examples of alien incursion. Naturally I was very sceptical and liked to rule out any rational explanations before accepting the possibility that there wasn't one. Rather humorously I remember an occasion being on duty driving a police Mini-Van when I received reports of what were claimed to be a UFO that had landed in the valley with aliens around it near Betws-y-Coed. I drove to the scene of the incident feeling some trepidation, but was surprised to find that this was no alien landing but a circle of people with torches flashing in the sky, collecting moths."*

Kevin, a man with a dry sense of humour and laid back attitude towards life, who hopes to realise his dreams and live with his beloved dog on a canal boat, was – as always – a pleasure to talk with and we wish him the best for the future.

CHAPTER 11
NOVEMBER 1980

UFO over Accrington

A T 5.45pm on 1ˢᵗ November 1980, Accrington resident – Mrs Maureen Turner – was stood outside her house, with her children, when she sighted:

". . . an object hovering in the sky. It looked like a Frisbee and then the shape of a lemon. It was orange to start with but then there was a blue flash which completely lit up the object, now metallic and blue-grey in colour. It made this loud humming noise and was in view for some time before moving slowly away."

(Source: Mr A Bramhill)

UFO over Oxford

We spoke to Wolvercote Oxford resident – Dave Packham, who had no problem recollecting what he and his mother saw, one evening in early November 1980, following the sound of an intense whining noise heard on their television set, which increased in pitch.

"I tried to turn the volume down on the set. It made no difference. I though it was going to explode. I went outside and looked around, wondering if there was something in the sky – like an airplane, or helicopter, and was staggered to see a round, bright green 'light', a few hundred yards away, about a thousand feet in height, hovering above power lines over *Port Meadow.

---

*Port Meadow is an ancient area of grazing land, still used for horses and cattle, and has never been ploughed. In return for helping to defend the kingdom against the marauding Danes, the Freemen of Oxford were given the 300 acres of pasture next to the River Thames by Alfred the Great, who founded the city in the 10th century. The Freemen's collective right to graze their animals free of charge is recorded in the *Domesday Book* of 1086 and has been exercised ever since. Because the meadow has never been ploughed, it contains well preserved archaeological remains, some of which survive as residual earthworks. Of particular note are several Bronze Age round barrows, an area of Iron Age settlement, and the foundations of 17th-century fortifications from the Parliamentary siege of Oxford during the English Civil War. It runs from Jericho to Wolvercote (where it becomes Wolvercote Common) along the east (left) bank of the *River Thames,* with the Cotswold Line railway, Oxford Canal and the suburb of North Oxford further to the east, and the village of Binsey to the west.

Port Meadow – © Wikpedia 2013

I watched it for ten minutes, as it silently stayed in the one position, until it moved to my right, hovered, and then returned to its original position. I went inside and alerted my mother. She and I watched it from the window, for a few minutes. Suddenly it moved away, at an incredible speed, and was gone – just a speck to be seen in the night sky. I checked the TV. The sound was still there but it gradually faded away – then gone. I did find out, a few days later, a crop circle had been found in the same field. Whether there was a connection I can't say."

(Source: *Oxford Mail*, 8.8.1996/Personal interview/Wikipedia)

On 11th November 1980, three people were driving along near Widecombe, Plymouth, when a large, purplish-red, sun-shaped object, with rays projecting from it, was seen in the sky. Within minutes, it had shrunk to the size of a star.

Close Encounter, Plymouth

At 12.20am on 12th November 1980, Plymouth resident – Mr Fredrick Collins, was walking to a taxi rank, when he happened to look up into the sky and see an object he described as:

". . . a 'spaceship', 2-300ft long, hovering about 200 ft above the ground; it was circular and showing four brilliant lights, which lit up the ground. Projecting from the central larger light was what looked like a central staircase of steps, as if pushed up some way from below. I looked around and was staggered to see a little green man, about 4ft high, stood in front of me, and heard a voice in my head inviting me to go on-board the ship. I tried to move but couldn't. When I replied in the negative, the next thing I knew was that I found myself walking towards the taxi rank."

The next morning, Mr Collins contacted the local radio station, *'Plymouth Sound'*, who suggested he speak to Plymouth UFO Investigator, Bob Boyd, who went to interview him, with Desmond Weeks – the secretary of the group. Mr Collins told them, agitatedly,

"I could accept the UFO . . . but little green men! It's just stupid. I just can't believe it. I'm asking you to believe it but I can't believe it myself. That's the trouble. I saw it with my own eyes and I don't believe it. It's driving me crazy. I mean, who would believe a little green man?"

UFO over Poole

At 4.30pm on 13th November 1980, six schoolboys – Richard Gilson, Lee Perkins, Anthony Rayment, Mathew Anderson, Vincent Jones and Abdul Shahid, were playing football on a stretch of land bordering Poole Harbour, known as Baiter Point, when they saw an object, resembling:

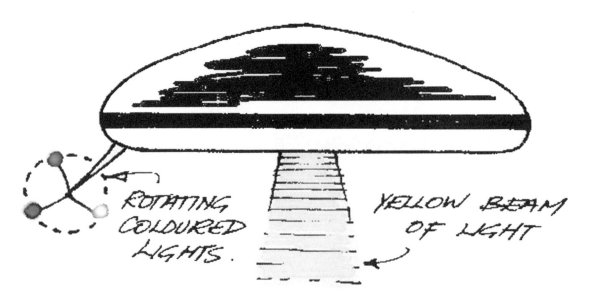

ROTATING COLOURED LIGHTS.

YELLOW BEAM OF LIGHT

"*. . . a hamburger, with 'bumps', bisected by a black line, showing red, yellow, and blue lights, apparently mounted on some sort of propeller projecting from the underneath, with a red poppy-shaped underside, out of which protruded a single central yellow light, twice the size of a helicopter, stationary in the sky, at a height of about 300ft.*"

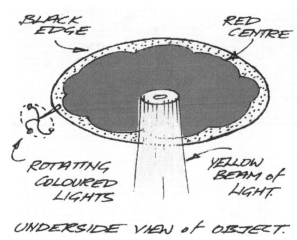

BLACK EDGE

RED CENTRE

ROTATING COLOURED LIGHTS

YELLOW BEAM of LIGHT.

UNDERSIDE VIEW of OBJECT.

After a few minutes, the object – making a low humming noise – rose upwards and flew away on a diagonal course. **(Source: Leslie Harris – Editor of *SCAN* Magazine, and Ron Lucas)**

Emphasizing the seriousness (on some occasions) in which the authorities viewed reports of UFOs, was brought home during a conversation with veteran UFO researcher and author – Nigel Mortimer. He has been involved in investigating reports of UFO phenomena for over 30 years and was the founder of the *Independent UFO Network* and regional director of investigations for BUFORA during the 1990s.

"I had my own encounter with a UFO, which started me off investigating this subject in November 1980, at Otley, and although it would be determined as just a light in the sky today, it merited a visit by a senior police officer to my home (in all his regalia!), with another bobby in hand, to interview me and my mother about what we had seen."

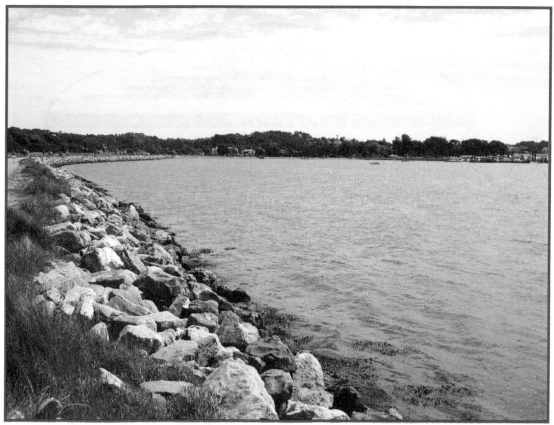

Baiter Recreation Ground / Parkstone Bay

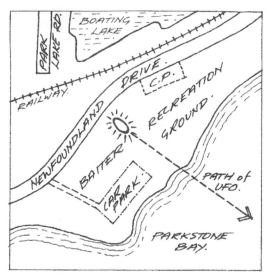

The location of the sighting near Poole Harbour.

*From left: Abdul Shahid, Richard Gillson and Lee Perkins –
three of the UFO spotters.*

UFO over Bodmin

Thanks to Jenny Randles, we were to come across an interesting account from Terry Cox and his wife, Pamela, who were then living in a remote location at Redmoor, near Bodmin.

Terry had spent considerable time experimenting with infra-red photography, trying to capture 'balls of light', after reading about the work of Trevor James Constable.

Jenny:

> *"I have seen many of his resultant images (always unseen by the naked eye) and have found them intriguing. He has photographed many things, not unlike my childhood – 'sky fish', in the air over the Cornish moors."*

On Sunday 15th November 1980, Terry was feeling ill to the point where the doctor was called to the house. He was given a strong sedative and sent to bed.

At 1am on 16th November, Terry was fast asleep but Pamela was unable to rest. She noticed a shaft of light stretching from her shoulder to her fingertips.

> *"It was clear white and made the veins in my arms stand out. I wondered if it came from the neighbour's farm lane, but it withdrew like a solid shaft or spear. It did not just go out. Ten minutes later it returned slowly, first lighting my shoulder arm and fingers. I looked through the window and saw an incandescent 'ball' of flaming coloured red light. It shimmered in a pattern resembling the crystal structure of a snowflake under the microscope. It filled half of the window frame in size. I raised Terry from his drug induced sleep, who sat up and saw it although it was receding; it pulled back across the fields, lighting up the hedges below it as it did so, shrinking to a tiny ball. The shaft of light followed it, also lighting up the ground. I guessed the sighting of whatever it was had lasted a minute or half. When I looked at my watch it was showing 1.20am."*

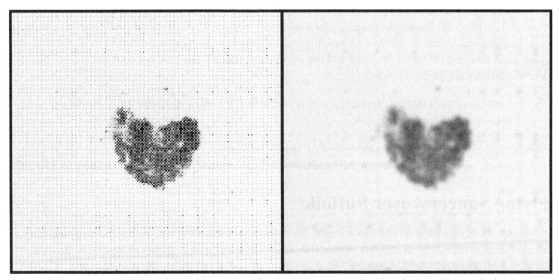

An object photographed using infra-red film. On the right, shown using a Gaussian blur, which reveals some further detail.

Close Encounter, Plymouth

On 16th November 1980, Plymouth resident – David Crouch (then aged 19) was walking the family dogs, with his mother, when they saw:

> *". . . a 'white thing' on the path – the height of a human, shaped like a pillar. The dogs cowered in fright."*

The couple summoned up their courage and followed the object, which was making a *'weird clonking noise'*, until they became too frightened to continue the pursuit and made their way home.

Was there a connection with a report from a lady motorist, who claimed to have seen a *'white thing'* in the road, *'like a man, with his head shrunk into his shoulder'*, a few days previously, approximately half-a-mile from where the couple had seen theirs? **(Source: Bob Boyd, Plymouth UFO Group)**

Explosions over London

At 6pm on 18th November 1980, residents living in Maroon Street, Limehouse, East London, heard what sounded like mass squadrons of aircraft passing overhead. Although they were familiar with the sound of aircraft moving over, this was completely different. Despite looking up into the sky, nothing could be seen. The noise continued unabated for the next two hours.

At 8pm a huge explosion was heard, causing many to wonder if a bomb had gone off, as walls shook and cups rattled. Then even louder explosions were heard, separated by the constant droning noise. One resident – Terry Mould – was convinced that they were witnessing the beginning of an IRA campaign. Some people thought that it might have been sonic booms, caused by RAF jets on exercise over the City – something the MOD strenuously denied.

Another witness to these phenomena was Jeannette Pretorious of Topmast Point, Millwall. She went to the window to have a look out, after hearing some loud bangs, but didn't see anything untoward.

At about 1.30am, after having watched a film which had started at midnight, she heard a loud droning noise. Frightened, she felt disinclined to look through the window, and got into bed. Without warning, the natural light entering the room dimmed and the room grew darker. She realised something very big and odd was hovering above the window.

> *"It was so close, I honestly thought it was going to hit the wall; it then created a spectacular light display inside the bedroom."*

The answer to the mystery remains unknown to this present day.

(Source: Mike Hallowell/*East London Advertiser*, 21.11.1980/28.11.1980)

'Flying Saucers' over Suffolk

At 8pm on 18th November 1980, Mike Boyle from Saxmundham, Suffolk, sighted a grey and orange coloured saucer-shaped object, heading across the sky over Butley, near to Rendlesham Forest. As it passed overhead, he heard a distinct *'whooshing noise'* before it passed out of sight, two minutes later.

(Source: Brenda Butler)

Did the object move behind something at any time particularly a cloud. ~~YES~~/NO.
If yes, then tell what it moved behind.

Did the object move in front of something at any time particularly a cloud YES/~~NO~~.
If yes then tell what it moved in front of.

.........Trees..

Did the object appear (a) (solid) (b) transparent..............

Did you observe the object through any of the following:-

    (a)   Eyeglasses
    (b)   Sunglasses   (e)   Binoculars
    (c)   Windshield   (f)   Telescope
    (d)   Window glass   (g)   Other _eyes_

What was the colour of the object... Greyas... Orange

Was there any sound coming from the object, if so give the description of sound.

...............Vhoosh...

Please draw sketch of object seen, giving as many details as possible:-   See R10 F.

The edges of the object were:-

    (a) Fuzzy or blurred   (c) Sharply outlined ✓
)b) Like a bright star   (d) Other....................

                     ....

Another witness to something strange in the Suffolk sky was now retired hotelier, Barry Rey, then manager of the Woodhall Country House Hotel, Shottisham, some six-and-a-half miles from Woodbridge, Suffolk – a popular venue for USAF servicemen from RAF Bentwaters and Woodbridge.

"It was in November, 1980 – definitely not connected with any UFO incidents that occurred at the end of December, 1980. I remember the sun was beginning to set, when I noticed a strange 'light' hovering over the village. I knew, from its shape and appearance, that it wasn't like any aircraft or helicopter I had seen before, so I jumped into my car and followed it, as it headed over fields towards the coast. It was disc-shaped, showing portholes of light projecting a powerful beam from its underneath. At one stage, it was only 50ft away from me

before it passed overhead, rose up slowly, and dropped down over some trees at the other side of the field, and landed. I drove along the road, for a short distance, and then saw it hovering over a house belonging to Robin Pendle, before it finally moved away for good."

Barry wonders, as a result of what he saw, whether the date given for the now world-famous incident, involving Colonel Halt, and others, is flawed – a supposition drawn rationally from his own experience. Unfortunately, Barry would not have realised, without the hindsight of many years research, that he was not the only one to sight UFOs over East Anglia – not forgetting other parts of the country, during this period.

(Source: Personal interview)

Bradford UFO

'Still fresh in the mind' was how Sheila Brooks remembered what she saw, at 10pm on 20th November 1980.

She was exercising the family dogs, at the bottom of her garden, in Bradford, West Yorkshire.

"All of sudden, I heard this voice – warm, melodious, and strangely beautiful – enter my head. Startled, I looked upwards to see a green disc-shaped 'craft', some 25ft above my head, with green pulsing lights around its perimeter. I was told telepathically to 'stay calm and not be afraid. You are not to be hurt in any way'."

Sheila slowly edged her way back towards the kitchen door, which was ajar, and called her husband – still keeping her eyes on the object, sensing that if she took her eyes off it, it would go away. When her husband failed to acknowledge her, she again called him, this time taking her eyes off the object, which raced off across the sky at an angle, before disappearing from view – the whole incident over in ten minutes.

(Source: Personal interview)

Close encounter, Cumbria

Mario Luisi in 2003 © J. Hanson

We were to come across a remarkable report, involving a 'close encounter' with an alleged alien 'craft', and its two occupants, during the late evening of the 21st November 1980, according to Mario Luisi – a resident of Burneside, Cumbria, whom we met up with in 2000, wishing to find out more about what lay behind his extraordinary claim.

Mario, an affable man, advised us, straightaway, that he didn't really care whether we believed him or not.

"I didn't have to answer your letter" he told us, and after some conversation, produced an elderly, poorly typewritten, but thorough, original, 5,000 word document, entitled, *'My Close Encounter'*, compiled a few weeks after the incident, showing the 'craft' and its 'occupants'.

Mario's close encounter

LANCS EVENING POST, Tuesday, November 25, 1980

Space invaders spoke to me — mill worker

PAPER mill worker Mario Luisi claims he's had a close encounter of the spine-chilling kind.

The 36-year-old father-of-three says he met and talked with two beings from another planet.

And he has given detailed descriptions of the aliens and their spacecraft to the "Post".

Mario has also showed us his melted torch — burned, he says, by some kind of ray gun they were carrying.

But he refused to reveal details of markings on their craft and emblems on their clothing, because he was warned against it.

Today, as he relived the amazing meeting that left him riveted to the spot with fear, Mario, at Hall Park, Burneside, Kendal, said: "I know I'll be the laughing stock of the village for this.

"But I'm not bothered because I know what I saw. I'm not looking for any

● Mr Luisi's sketch of the space man.

By David Jones

sympathy or anything — before, I might not have believed it myself."

He says he saw the human-like creatures one evening as he walked his dog on the banks of the river, near Croppers' papermill.

"I saw something that I thought must be a cow, at first. I swung round, and shone my torch and a light flashed back, melting it.

HOVERING

"Then I saw the craft, about 16ft long and 8ft deep and dark-coloured with a blunt nose and sort of glass windows, hovering just off the ground.

"A man and a woman stood next to it. They were the most beautiful people I have ever seen. Their hair was light-coloured, in a helmet style down past their shoulders.

"They wore skin-tight suits, a sort of back wet look, and she had a cloak over hers. They were about 5ft 6in tall.

"Their features were out of this world and they had very pale skins as though they were ill or something.

"I was with them about two or three minutes. The

would not harm me but that I must not tell certain things, like the letters on the craft.

"I wanted to run, but I couldn't. I didn't believe it was happening to me but it was. Then they got back into the ship up some folding-down stairs and it shot straight up into the sky in a red glow.

POLICE

Mario, who has been off work awaiting an operation since June, then ran as fast as he could until he reached home.

He reported the incident to the police and told his wife, Judith, and next door neighbour.

"I knew another woman in the village who says she saw something similar in the same field," he added. "But she doesn't want her name mentioned.

"I always believed in UFOs but never have any experience of them. I know its far-fetched, but how do you explain the torch?"

Judith added: "He never gets scared but he was that night."

A spokesman for Kendal police said: "Mr Luisi did report this to us and we sent a man out. He found nothing, so that's the end of the matter as far as we are concerned.

"We did have one or two reported sightings in the

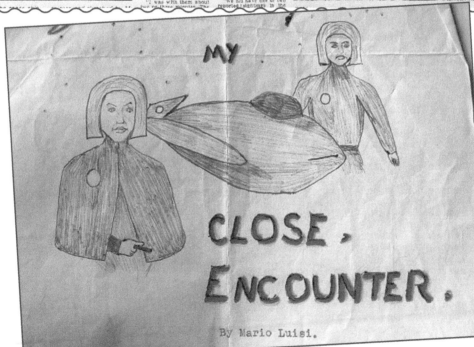

MY CLOSE. ENCOUNTER.

By Mario Luisi.

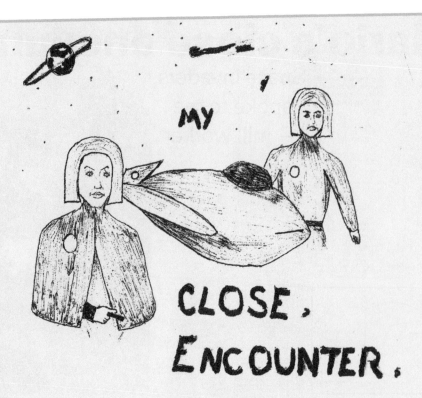

MY CLOSE, ENCOUNTER,

By Mario Luisi.

Did the Ancients know of worlds besides their own? And what are
the data of the Occultists in affirming that every globe is a
septenary chain of worlds, of which only one member is visible,
and that these are or where man bearing.

As we all know, life can be totally different in outer space,
but still there are few of us capable of even visualising what
it's realy like.
It is true that there has been millions of reports from around
the world on flying saucers, and it is also true that there have
been many of visits from space over the past millions of years,
But still we are know nearer as to why, or even know of their home
ground, for I beleave that U.F.Os. come from millions of miles
away, so far away that their distance is much more than we can
handle or even begin to think of reaching.

This I do beleave exaplanes the speed of their craft, which has
been on radar recorded speeds of 2,000 to 25,000 miles an hour,
and has been known to climb 12,000 feet in ten seconds, their
average speed is known to be a mile a second.
I dont beleave that there is anyone on our earth to day with that
sort of knowledge, for if there was then it would have been boested
about by now, and we must remember that this sort of thing has
been going on for thousands of years.

This is what he recorded:

"I stood next to a big tree on top of the slope, looking for a way to go, as I began to feel the rain coming down again and every second it seemed to be getting heavier. Out into the middle of the field I could see a large tree, which stood tall and dark in the distance, below a small ridge. To the right of it I could see something that looked like a cow, stood gaping into the night. I felt it was safe enough to head for that cow, as it would be on firm ground. Parts of the field were sluggish, as I walked – sometimes slipping and sliding on the mud with almost every step I took. I didn't want to use my torch as yet, in case someone saw me and that I didn't want to happen. In fact, the light from the Mill made it a little easier for me.

By now the rain had become very heavy, as the strong wind blew it hard against my face, making it harder for me to walk. As I came closer to the tree I could see what I thought had been a cow was not moving and wondered if it was a sheep pen, so I still headed for it. As every step I took came closer and closer to it, it wasn't long before I soon found myself standing about 6 feet away from what was neither any cow, nor sheep pen. For a second or two I stood looking at the object – a stoney grey in colour, cigar in shape, about 16 feet long and 8 feet deep which stood before me. I then decided to turn my torch on it, wondering what it could have been, noticing the rain didn't seem to be bothering it in any way. It all looked so real to me, rather than any dream. On one end of the object there was a large bulge – dark in colour – that looked like glass. It appeared to be a dome window, but it was too dark to see in. Every second I became more and more confused as to what it was that stood before me. I wanted to go closer to it, so I could observe it better, but something kept telling me not to.

On the other end there appeared to be some sort of very short wings, or flaps, which seemed to run almost straight back, and on top of that stood a short but sharp 'tail', which seemed to be pointing towards the dome of the glass. The more I looked at the object, the more I was amazed at its appearance. I couldn't see a farmer with an object like this one or, in fact, with anyone else's. Rain was still falling heavily, as I continued to observe. Below the dome of glass was some sort of markings, which were confusing – like I'd never seen before. I crept my torch along the object, towards the other end, and lit up the 'tail', which was short and pointed, and showing a sort of circular design on its surface.

At this point I sensed somebody else was present. I stood still, trying to listen above the noise of the weather – my eyes only moving from left to right, hoping to see who was there. I could only think of the police, or water bailiffs, and didn't want to be answering any of their questions. I grasped my torch tightly and, on the count of three, I swung round my light, which fell full onto two people stood before me. I was ready to run but somehow they caught my eye, which made me think again. I didn't know whether it was fear, or relief, that entered my mind. I sensed there was something wrong but what, I still didn't know. They were the most beautiful people I had ever seen in my life, standing about 5-6 feet away from me. I had no idea of who they were, or what they wanted.

Their hairstyles were identical – 'helmet style', unaffected by the strong wind as it blew around us. I could feel my body beginning to tremble beyond control, and my legs turning into jelly. I tried to run, noticing the reflection from the light made their eyes glitter, slightly, as they gazed upon me. Their clothing was dark – possibly black, worn tight – almost like our wet suits. The figure on the left of me, unlike the other, wore a short cape, which led me to think this was a woman, although their beauty was equal. I thought the other to be a man.

They were displaying a circular design on their clothing – the same as on the 'tail' of the object, but what it meant I had no idea. I heard a voice telling me never to disclose the nature of the design, as shown on their clothing – a promise I have never broken. I was puzzled to see the rain wasn't even affecting their clothing in any way. The cape the woman wore was still, despite the strong wind blowing. The couple were of average size, about five feet six. Their complexion was hard to make out, but I would have said they looked normal. When the light of my torch brightly dazzled their faces, I noticed the woman was holding something that looked like a pen, which she pointed at my torch; a flash of light, much stronger than my own, then hit the torch on the front. I felt no bang, or noise. A second or two later, my light went out. For a second or two, we gazed into each others eyes. In my case it was with fear.

As I gripped my torch so tight, I thought the blood had stopped circulating. I heard the tinkle of glass and something fell from my torch, landing into the muddy grass by my feet, but I dared not take my eyes off them to see what had happened. We stood facing each other, my torch still pointed at them. I waited, expecting a second 'shot', but it never came. I began to feel bothered and wanted to run, but somehow couldn't move, as I had seen enough by now. I began to sense there was something wrong but couldn't pinpoint what it was. I waved my torch over the object a dozen times, again and again, onto the puzzling markings – still unaware of its meaning. I realised, with amazement, the object, totally unsupported, was not actually on the ground but about 2-3 feet in the air.

I could feel the rain, which I had almost forgotten about, still falling, running down my neck. I began to let my mind get the better of me. I thought the last moments of my life were at hand. My heart was now beating as though I had just done a three mile sprint. Under the circumstances, I think I would have rather done that. I felt tightness in my throat, which made it hard for me to breathe – let alone swallow. First I would glance at one of them, and then the other, wondering what their next move was going to be.

The rain was still falling hard against my face and running down over my eyes, but I was too frightened to move my hand to wipe the water away, so I would have had clear vision, and I didn't think it was wise to make any sudden moves, in case the outcome became fatal. They kept their distance, which gave me the impression they were as frightened of me as I was of them. For a second or two they stood together, watching me for a moment. I thought they were going to ask me to enter their 'craft', but had the feeling they weren't going to let me see anymore than I had already seen.

Suddenly, the man turned and stepped into the 'craft' – out of sight. The woman waited a couple of seconds as she still observed me. I could see a faint but gentle smile on her face, as she turned and entered the 'craft' – and again out of sight.

I knew, then, this was the last time I'd see them as the door slowly closed to, and the step went in. For the first time (in which seemed hours) I could move my legs again, so I turned slowly, facing the 'craft', as it sat still in mid-air, but still had no movement, or noise, of any kind. My heart beat had slowed down but I could still feel myself trembling slightly, as I stood watching the 'craft' – waiting for something to happen.

A few seconds later it began to rise into the air, at a speed of fifteen to twenty miles an hour, but still there was no noise from it at all and no lights appeared on the 'craft'. There wasn't even any smoke, or flame, of any sort as it climbed into the rainy clouds above. My fear, now over, rapidly returned when, a few seconds later, a large glow of light appeared above the clouds, and I thought they were returning, but the light only lasted for about two or three seconds – then disappeared.

I took a deep breath and sighed; relieved it was all over, feeling the blood creeping back into my legs. I didn't know whether to laugh, or cry, at the thought of it all, but suddenly remembered my torch still held tightly in my hand, the front being destroyed, the glass smashed out, and the whole centre melted into a small ball of metal, in the muddy grass by my feet.

I wasn't sure in picking it up, or not, in case of radiation, or something to that effect was on it, but I knew at the same time I could not leave it there – a wave of emotion washing over me at the thought of what could have happened to me if I'd been hit by the 'beam'. I also wanted to get out of that field, fast, and away from the site altogether, and so reluctantly I bent down to pick up the middle part of the torch, being very careful not to touch it for too long, or too much.

I gently pushed it into my torch front, where it came from, sliding the whole thing into my jacket safely. The rain was still very heavy; the wind howled as strong. I grasped the torch under my coat and began to run. The field was like a skating rink. I slipped, a couple of times, as the grass was turning quickly into mud and slush with the rain. Panting heavily, I ran as fast as I could out of the field and through the village, towards home, soon finding myself at the back door of my house.

'I've seen something special & unreal'

UFO chases cop car and performs amazing stunts

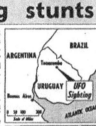

In one of the strangest UFO encounters ever, a huge, bright red disk followed a police chief's car for 90 minutes — and performed amazing aerial stunts whenever he flashed his headlights.

"I never believed in UFOs before, but I realize I've seen something special and unreal," says Miguel Costa, 30, police chief of Melo, Uruguay.

It was in the early morning hours that Costa, his wife, Carmen, and another couple, Armando and Maria Pena, saw the UFO as their car bumped along a gravel highway near the town of Tacuarembo. They were on their way home from a visit when the UFO, gleaming with bright yellow and orange lights, loomed up in front of them.

Costa stopped the car and, on an impulse, tried to communicate with it by flashing his headlights on and off.

"All of a sudden the UFO hesitated, then zigzagged up and back as if answering our code," he recalled.

"As soon as we started out again, it was there following us. I stopped the car again and flashed my lights — and again the UFO wavered in reply. We drove on once more on the twisting road and the UFO stayed with us, always about half a mile away. This went on for almost 30 miles.

"That's when the strangest thing of all occurred.

"We were all glued to the window watching as the red disk suddenly shot toward the earth as if it were going to crash. But it stopped 50 or 100 yards above the ground.

"We could all clearly see a

Miguel Costa, top and above, poses with passengers of car, left to right, Mr. and Mrs. Armando Pena and his wife Carmen.

type of ship now. It had a round, dome-like shape with a large flat plate underneath and there was a slight ring of cloud around the dome. The top was reddish but the bottom was a brilliant glowing white."

Overwhelmed by fear, they turned the car around, and headed back to Tacuarembo with the blazing light of the UFO hovering in their rear window. When they came to a truck parked in some trees along the road, Costa pulled over and they waited until the UFO seemed to be leaving. "We walked to a lit-

tle clearing and then looked up and saw a second disk, moving some distance behind the first one.

"They never touched but seemed to travel together. They moved up and down and clouds started to form. They passed over the top of the clouds and lit them up like a halo. Then they faded, getting smaller and smaller until they were finally gone.

"It was dawn. We looked at each other without speaking. We still couldn't believe what we had seen."

Gentle giant lives in misery

A sad but gentle 8-foot, 3-inch giant lives a virtual prisoner in a small religious shrine.

Mohammed Alam is 26 and weighs a healthy 400 pounds — but feels like a prisoner because his neighbors in Sehwun, Pakistan, consider him a freak.

The hundreds of people who mob him make his life so miserable that he prefers the peace and quiet of the shrine where he works as a maintenance man. He's made the shrine of Lal Shahbaz Qalander, a 13th century Islamic religious leader, his self-imposed prison.

When he ventures out he takes along two bodyguards to keep the crowds from pressing too closely.

Mohammed says even when

20 WEEKLY WORLD NEWS March 3, 1981

he is safe at home in the shrine, he still can't escape the cruel curiosity.

"Even at 2 a.m., strangers knock on my door and wake me up — just to see how tall I am," Mohammed says, sadly.

Mohammed says he was of normal height until he was about 10 years old. Then he suddenly began growing and he soon towered over everyone in the village.

"My mother, father, five brothers and three sisters are all of normal height. I don't know what happened to me," he says.

The gentle giant feels alone in the world, and doesn't believe stories told him of tall people — like basketball players — elsewhere in the world.

In his mind, doctors say, Mohammed feels everyone else in the world are midgets in

comparison to him. When Mohammed was made the subject of a Pakistani television documentary, he caught the attention of government officials. The bureaucrats decided the giant was somewhat of a national treasure — and, in appreciation, awarded him a $43-a-month allowance.

That's quite a bit of money in Mohammed's village — but the sad giant needs it.

Clothing, he says, is a major expense.

"It takes 15 yards of cloth just to make myself a shirt and trousers," he says.

But Mohammed's grocery bill isn't as high as you'd think.

"I'm perfectly happy and full if I just eat a small bowl of rice and meat," said Mohammed.

"It isn't food that makes me grow. It's something else — something strange."

Pauline Bendit's WORLD OF THE UNUSUAL

Researcher says magnetic changes make people burn

Mysterious changes in the Earth's magnetic field may cause people to burst into flames and die!

That may be the cause of some 290 known bizarre deaths, says researcher Larry Arnold of the ParaScience Research Institute in Harrisburg, Pa.

Arnold says the most bizarre such case was the death of Mary Reeser in St. Petersburg, Fla.

One day, he says, Mary was perfectly well and happy. The next day her landlady found a pile of ashes and her skull, charred and shrunken to the size of a tennis ball.

Arnold says it takes 24 hours of 3,900-degree heat to cremate a body and a house fire rarely gets hotter than 1,500 degrees.

Yet, Mary's body was almost completely cremated and — amazingly — her apartment showed no signs of such intense heat.

UFOs piloted by beautiful people

A paper mill worker said he had an amazing conversation with beautiful invaders from outer space as they stood beside their UFO.

Mario Luisi said he was walking his dog after dark when he heard a strange noise.

"Then I saw the craft, about 16 feet long and 8 feet high," said Mario, a resident of Preston, England. "A man and a woman were next to it. They were the most beautiful people I've ever seen."

He said both were blond and wore skin-tight suits.

Mario said the woman spoke to him in English and warned him not to reveal certain things he saw — particularly the markings on the UFO. Then he was released, unharmed.

Mario said he'll keep his promise to the space people and never disclose everything he saw or learned that night.

She keeps mom's corpse 10 months

A woman kept her mother's mummified body on a couch in her living room for 10 months and told stunned cops it was her voodoo doll.

Police Chief Addison Woods of Massillon, Ohio, says he went to Helen Merry's home after her uncle, Jim Harris, said she had been acting strangely. Jim said

the woman wouldn't let him in the house and he worried about her mother, his sister.

Cops said they entered the home and found Lena Merry, 88, dead on the couch. Her daughter, Helen, 60, told them the body was her voodoo doll and that she didn't know where her mother was.

Meteor or missile downed jet liner

Experts say a flashing meteor or a missile may have struck an airliner that crashed killing 81 persons.

That's the only possible explanation for the mysterious crash, said Judge Giorgio Santacroce in Rome.

The Italian airliner, a DC-9, disintegrated over the Mediterranean last year — and a lengthy investigation has yet to come up with a cause of the disaster.

Investigators say traces of strange chemicals have been found in the wreckage that indicated there was some kind of an explosion.

They added that immediately before the crash a radar operator picked up something flashing near the airplane in the sky.

Chinese Bigfoot fathers human baby

Chinese scientists investigating thousands of new monkey-man reports have found an astounding incident in which one of the creatures fathered a human child!

Professor Liu Minzhuang reported the poor creature was born in Sichuan Province in 1939 after its mother had been carried off by a monkey man — the Chinese name for Bigfoot.

The woman was never able to explain what happened, the professor says.

The child was kept alive for years, he says, but apparently died because of the mixture of ape and human genes.

He says monkey men reports go back 2,600 years in China's history — and recently there has been an upsurge in sightings.

Madame Bendit's prediction for this week

Famed Romanian psychic Pauline Bendit has shown amazing accuracy in her astounding predictions of the future. Madame Bendit makes this exclusive prediction for NEWS readers:

An incredible photograph of a UFO will be taken by Secret Service agents patroling President Reagan's California ranch.

My worry now was how I was going to explain it all to my wife and, even if I did, would she believe me? Was I going to tell anyone? I decided to phone the police, who told me that they were busy at the moment with the flooding, but would send someone out as soon as they could, but didn't sound too concerned about the matter. I wondered if I had done the right thing in reporting the incident to them. That night, and for the next few nights, I couldn't sleep too well, for every time I closed my eyes, I began to see and dream of the whole incident again, which I could do without. It was the Tuesday morning when the police finally arrived and took my torch away, but returned it later, the same afternoon, telling me they were satisfied with the situation – clearly not believing my version of the events that had taken place."

Mario told us, after the event, he was too frightened to go out and, whilst he had come to terms with what had happened, he hadn't visited the location for 20 years, but agreed to show us the scene of the encounter.

As we stood with him overlooking the River Kent, with the Paper Mill on the other side of the river, and the remains of the tree, where the incident had occurred, we wondered if there was any significance between the sighting and a curious cigar-shaped mound, jutting above the contours of the land, some 40ft in length. Was this an ancient burial mound, or long barrow? If so, was there a connection? Our hopes were dashed when we later discovered it was man-made, and constructed to protect adjoining fields from flooding.

Examination of the torch

The torch was submitted to a laboratory for examination by the North Lancashire UFO Group, when the following information was obtained.

Conclusions:

'It would seem likely the damage was created by some form of electrical discharge, or something of like nature. For simple physical heat, temperatures in excess of sixty-five degrees C would be necessary. This would also tend to blacken the plastic and leave sooty deposits, none of which is in evidence in this particular case. To achieve such an effect, by means of a blow torch, would require it to be set at a very high temperature, for a very short period of time, but this would also tend to distort the surrounding plastic of the casing, making it very difficult to achieve an effect similar to that of the 'Luisi' torch.

2171

THE NORTH LANCASHIRE UFO INVESTIGATION GROUP.

THE 'LUISI' CASE: Preliminary report on torch.

From the positions of the damaged areas of the torch, it could be assumed with reasonable certainty that the whole torch was intact when the damage occured, that is, the distortion on the surrounding area of the plastic component which held the glass is consistent with what would be expected were the central portion subjected to a certain degree of heat.

The main component of interest is the reflector, having sustained the most visible effects. This reflector would seem to be basically composed of a thermoplastic, electro-plated with chrome - or, more likely, sprayed with a thin coating of chrome to a density of not more than 7 microns (0,0015").

The reflector is most likely a polyacetal (formaldehyde polymer) plastic, which has a good heat resistance and excellent dimensional stability. Alternatively, a polypropylene plastic has an even better heat resistance - (service temperatures are in excess of 100 degrees C./Melting point - about 145 degrees C.). Temperatures above 65 dgs. C. after moulding distort most plastics.

In heavy plastic plating the object is immersed in a solution of copper in sulphuric acid for between 2 - 5 minutes at a current density around 5A/sq.ft. to cover contact areas with enough copper to withstand higher den - sities in the main plating solution.

It would seem most likely that the damage was effected by some form of electrical discharge, or something of like nature.

For simple physical heat, temperatures in excess of 65 dgs.C. would be necessary. This would also tend to blacken the plastic and leave sooty dep - osits - none of which is in evidence in this particular case.

To achieve such an effect by means of a blowtorch would require it to be set at a very high temperature for a very short period of time - but this would also tend to distort the surrounding plastic of the casing, making it very difficult to achieve an effect similar to that of the Luisi torch. However, a form of relatively 'cold' heat - such as with an Oxy -acetylene torch would produce more favourable results. This would, though, imply an in - genious and elaborate hoax, which, in the Luisi case, appears most unlikely.

However, a form of relatively 'cold heat' such as with an oxy-acetylene torch would produce more favourable results. This would imply an ingenious and elaborate hoax which, in the 'Luisi' case, appears most unlikely.

In conclusion it would appear that the source, 'electrical, or other', of the damage could be compared to a tube of heat, in which the highest temperature, or point of power, is concentrated in a localised area and the perimeter of that 'tube' would have a much lower temperature, or lesser charge, thus accounting for the minimal damage.'

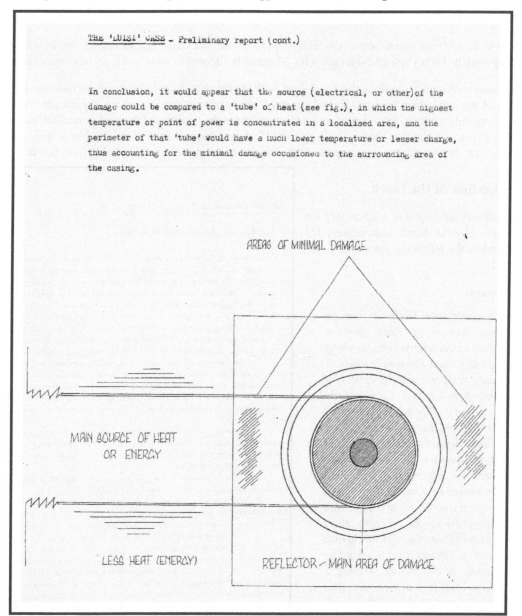

THE 'LUISI' CASE – Preliminary report (cont.)

In conclusion, it would appear that the source (electrical, or other) of the damage could be compared to a 'tube' of heat (see fig.), in which the highest temperature or point of power is concentrated in a localised area, and the perimeter of that 'tube' would have a much lower temperature or lesser charge, thus accounting for the minimal damage occasioned to the surrounding area of the casing.

AREAS OF MINIMAL DAMAGE

MAIN SOURCE OF HEAT OR ENERGY

LESS HEAT (ENERGY)

REFLECTOR – MAIN AREA OF DAMAGE

A second Close Encounter the following year

In Margaret Fry's excellent book *'Who Are They?'* published in 2004, she informs the reader that Mario and his wife together with another couple were returning from a rainy, misty evening out over Shap Fell, at about 10.40pm the 12th of August 1981when the car lights cut out and the vehicle came to halt. According to Mario:

> *"We noticed two men standing in the centre of the road coming towards us. They had light coloured zip suits and wore helmets with visors. The two women started to yell. I told them to keep the windows and doors shut as they wanted me, not them. I walked over to the two beings, and the next thing I remember was finding myself in a glass box in a room with roof and walls. The room had rounded corners."*

When further questioned about this incident he told of seeing another such 'box' containing someone whose leg was only visible.

> *"I could move my arms but my head was fixed. To the others side* (there was a gap of about 4ft either side of him) *I could see a shelf of glass above me, on this were boxes, part of which were black. I could see into the fronts, one contained a rabbit, the other a small mammal, the third contained, to may amazement, a single dandelion standing up".*

Mario described seeing a number of *'ordinary looking'* people moving in and out of the room via a sliding door. They wore helmets with holes in them and were wearing light coloured one-piece suits. He was then approached by an older man, about 50 years of age, who told him not to be afraid and that he had been chosen to be counsellor. He told Mario *"The planet we come from is Sorben, about the size of the earth".* Mario's next recollection was walking towards his car, when he arrived there, one of the women was hysterical and he had to calm her down. It was now 11.50pm.

Margaret says that when she interviewed Mario, his wife was moving in and out of the room but never chose to join the conversation, which we also noticed and thought odd during our visit. Further research into the matter failed to obtain any corroboration testimony from the other parties involved in the second encounter.

Following her return to Kent, Margaret was to receive further communication from Mario, who alleged that he was now receiving further visits from the 'beings' while in bed and that they had given him messages to give to the 'leaders'.

She then contacted the Earl of Clancarty, who initially agreed to meet Mario at his house with other members of the House of Lords UFO Study Group, but then changed his mind.

A hoaxed photo

Things went from bad to worse following the production, by Mario, of a photograph showing what was purported to be a silver suited alien. This was later discovered to be a hoax – it was, in fact, Mario wearing a silver foil suit. Tim Good himself, so we understand from Margaret, travelled to Kendal – where he spoke to Mario's sister – who told him the truth. Tim was understandably wary about any continuing association with Mario and returned to London.

Margaret believes, as we do, that aside from the crude hoaxing and attempts to make money after being ill-advised by a friend who suggested he make some money out of the experience by faking crude photographs, which were then offered for sale – a matter that Mario has always bitterly regretted having become involved in – but is adamant that the original event took place. We support Margaret's opinion that she believes the incident of the 21st of November 1980 was more than likely genuine, and that the rest was fabrication. Mario never told us about the second encounter during our visit to him, which seems odd. Unfortunately the only person who really knows the truth of what happened is Mario Luisi, who has found his place in history – but he is now unlikely to be believed.

UFO over Todmorden

While there may have been some doubt with the validity of what happened to Mario Luisi, the same cannot be said, for what happened to Police Constable 3961 Alan Godfrey, (33) who was on mobile patrol at Todmorden, Lancashire, during the early hours of Friday, 28th November 1980, in his Ford Escort patrol car, on what had been a cold, wet night, although rain had stopped falling earlier.

Alan Godfrey

Between 1am and 3am, Alan received a number of calls on his personal radio, reporting a herd of between 20-30 cattle roaming the streets on a local estate on the outskirts of Todmorden. After having made various searches of the area without finding any sign of the missing cattle, he continued on his patrol. Some reports suggest the cattle were disappearing and reappearing and that in some way they were transported to Centre Park, as if *"just plonked down"* according to Alan. It would be nice to know where the cattle actually came from, and whether there were any missing, not forgetting the witness testimony of some of the residents on the estate, who had occasion to telephone the police during the night.

At about 5.15am, Alan left Todmorden Police Station and drove a couple of hundred yards, west-north-west, along the A646 Burnley Road, towards the

Todmorden Police Station, Burnley Road, Todmorden. ©Humphrey Bolton 2013

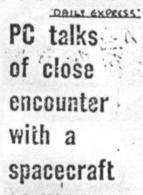

'DAILY EXPRESS'

PC talks of 'close encounter with a spacecraft

By ROGER TAVENER

A POLICEMAN told last night for the first time of his close encounter with a UFO.

And he claimed that up to 400 officers a year have similar sightings . . . but keep quiet.

Pc Alan Godfrey, 36, said he came face to face with an alien craft while on routine patrol. It was 5 a.m., November 28, 1980, when the officer was driving along a road near Todmorden, West Yorkshire.

Suddenly, in front of him he saw a diamond-shaped space-craft hovering five feet off the ground.

"I tried to send a message back to base," said Pc Godfrey. "But both my car and personal radios would not work.

"Suddenly I was on the other side of the craft, driving away from it."

Pc Godfrey is due to leave the force because of serious injuries sustained when he was assaulted on duty.

He said last night: "I feel now is the time to air the thing publicly and then get back to leading a quiet life."

A spokesman for West Yorkshire police said: "Pc Godfrey's claims were noted."

junction with Ferney Lee Road on his right, when he noticed a glow, low down, on the road in front of him, which he took to be an early morning bus, approximately 200 yards away.

> *"I quickly changed my mind when I saw this very strange object hovering about 5ft above the road, resembling a spinning top, with windows. It looked like a double-decker bus, side on. I estimated it had a width of 20ft, and was 14ft high. I drove up to 100ft away from it and stopped.*
>
> *It was dome-shaped, with the top more flatter than the base, and projected fluorescent light from the top. I saw it had a row of dark 'square' windows beneath it. The object was white in colour and rotating anticlockwise. The top of it came to within 2ft of the tops of nearby lamp-posts. The leaves on nearby trees were shaking, although there was no breeze. The headlights of the police car were reflected away from the object, showing me it was something physical. I tried to radio the Police Control – there was nothing, just static, although the area does have its 'black spots'."*

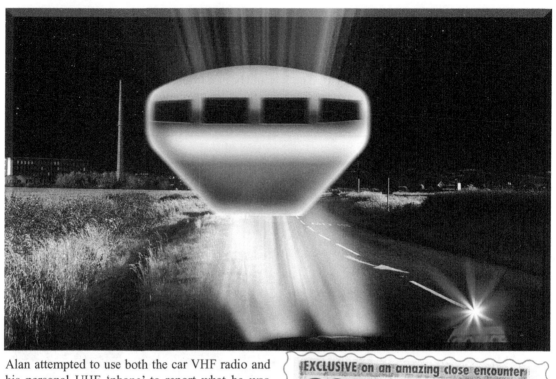

Alan attempted to use both the car VHF radio and his personal UHF 'phone' to report what he was seeing, but both failed to work.(Which may have been due to poor radio reception in the locality as opposed to interference from the UFO) Alan then took out a notepad, kept in the patrol car, and drew the object. The next thing that he remembers happening was a burst of light, and then driving his car further up Burnley Road, with no sign of the object seen earlier.

Alan drove back to the Police Station and picked up a colleague on duty (some accounts give two officers) and then returned to the scene of the incident.

When they arrived at the location Alan discovered a dried circular patch, on the roadway with a

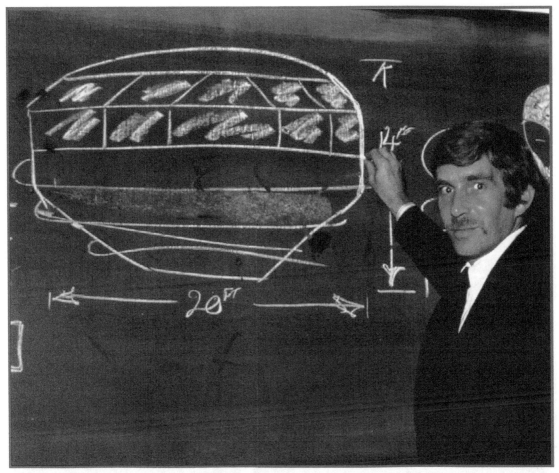

Picture of Alan Godfrey ©Janet & Colin Bord/Fortean Picture Library

swirled pattern. It is said his colleague later claimed he was unable to corroborate this. Alan then made his way back to the police station at about 5:30am and spoke to a colleague PC Malcolm Agley, who confirmed his agitated condition when he arrived, and that he said to him:

"You will never guess what I have just seen – a UFO, totally unbelievable".

Although Malcolm was unsure how to respond to what he had been told, he has publicly declared that he had no reason to disbelieve what Alan had told him, as he regarded him as reliable, and a trusted colleague whose integrity has never been in question as far as he is concerned.

A search along the stretch of road close to where the UFO had been seen revealed the presence of the missing bullocks in Centre Park.

Not wanting to be the subject of ridicule, Alan at first chose not to make an official report, but changed his mind when he discovered details of a UFO sighting, made by three other police officers, who were on duty at 4.53am, on what was *initially believed* to have been the same morning. It involved PC John Porter, PC Howard Turnpenny, and WPC Julie Baxter, who were out on a hill outside Halifax (8 miles to the east

Picture of Alan Godfrey ©Janet & Colin Bord/Fortean Picture Library

of Todmorden) looking for a stolen motorcycle, when they sighted a brilliant 'ball of light' approaching across the hills – low enough for them to instinctively duck as it passed overhead, heading off towards the direction of Todmorden in a series of angular turns, jerking from one side of the valley to the other. The matter was officially reported by telex to West Yorkshire Police HQ, Wakefield.

Another witness to sight something strange overlooking Todmorden, that morning, was a school caretaker. He was in the process of lighting the boilers, at 5.45am, when he saw:

> "*. . . a ball of white light, tinged with a blue streak, rise up into the sky, and move away fast*".

To Alan's surprise, the police released details of both sightings to the local weekly newspaper, the *Todmorden Times*, which ran a front page story under the headline: 'May The Force Be With You', and 'Amazing Encounter in Calder Valley'.

In an interview with one of the newspapers, he recalled that, as he sat watching the UFO, he heard a voice say:

"You should not be seeing this. This isn't for your eyes."

He told the reporter:

"Now whether someone was telling me this, or I was just thinking it, I don't know."

Sunday Express – November 1987

The *Sunday Express* newspaper, dated 22nd November 1987, published an article on the event and showed Alan at the scene of the incident. During conversation Alan said:

"It had chosen a spot where a drive into the car park of the *Old Mons Mill – a massive seven storey structure, standing back from the road – provided an extended hard standing."

If what he was looking at was some kind of hovercraft, it must have been manoeuvred over the mill and the engine room chimney that towered above it, avoiding the hills and trees with extraordinary skill. His incredibility turned to alarm when he realised that he was now a hundred yards down the road, way past where the object had hovered. He arrived at the Police Station, at 5.30am and wondered what had transpired during the missing minutes.

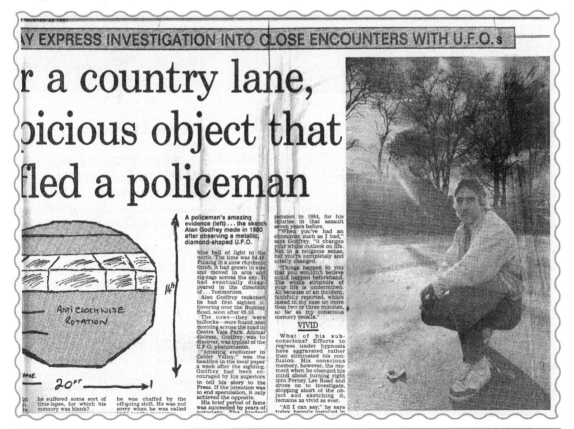

EXPRESS INVESTIGATION INTO CLOSE ENCOUNTERS WITH U.F.O.s

r a country lane,
ΰicious object that
fled a policeman

ANTI CLOCKWISE ROTATION

14″

20″

A policeman's amazing evidence (left) ... the sketch Alan Godfrey made in 1980 after observing a metallic, diamond-shaped U.F.O.

blue ball of light to the north. The time was 04.49. Pulsing in a slow rhythmic throb, it had grown in size and moved in arcs and zig-zags across the sky. It had eventually disappeared in the direction of ... Todmorden.

Alan Godfrey reckoned he had first sighted it hovering over the Burnley Road, soon after 05.10.

The cows—they were bullocks—were found next morning across the road in Centre Vale Park. Animal distress, Godfrey was to discover, was typical of the U.F.O. phenomenon.

"Amazing encounter in Calder Valley," was the headline in the local paper a week after the sighting. Godfrey had been encouraged by his superiors to tell his story to the Press. If the intention was to end speculation, it only achieved the opposite.

His brief period of fame was succeeded by years of notoriety. The kindest

pension in 1984, for his injuries in that assault seven years before.

"When you've had an encounter such as I had," says Godfrey, "it changes your whole outlook on life. Not in a religious sense, but you're completely and utterly changed.

"Things happen to you that you wouldn't believe could happen beforehand. The whole structure of your life is undermined. All because of an incident, faithfully reported, which lasted in my case no more than two or three minutes, so far as my conscious memory recalls.

VIVID

What of his subconscious? Efforts to regress under hypnosis have aggravated rather than eliminated his confusion. His conscious memory, however, the moment when he changed his mind about turning right into Ferney Lee Road and drove on to investigate, stopping short of the object and sketching it, remains as vivid as ever.

"All I can say," he says today happily installed in

he suffered some sort of time-lapse, for which his memory was blank?

he was chaffed by the off-going shift. He was not sorry when he was called

The Old Mons Mill

The article disclosed that Alan had taken two officers back to the scene and showed them how leaves and twigs under where the object had been were swirled into a circle. It appears the officers were sceptical and treated the incident with humour. Alan then went off duty without telling anybody else, such as his Sergeant or Inspector, about what had taken place. When he arrived home, he discovered his left boot was split open across the ball of the foot. On his left instep was a small burn, which the doctor later diagnosed as a skin infection – possibly brought on by shock; this was described as a small circle. (Similar marks are not uncommon to reports of this nature and have been seen on the bodies of witnesses to UFO sightings).

When Alan booked on duty, the next night, he was asked by the duty Inspector what he had seen. To Alan's surprise, the officer didn't laugh at him but ordered him to report the matter to Bradford, who would then telex it to the MOD. When Alan rang Bradford Police and told them he wanted to report having seen a UFO – the officer asked him if *"it was the one seen at Halifax, at 4.49am, by three other officers who had already reported it."*

According to a report sent to the Ministry of Defence by West Yorkshire Police (file released to the UK National Archives, in 2007) the date given by the officers was the 21st November 1980 – approximately one week earlier than Alan Godfrey's sighting. The sighting report was attached to a forwarding letter from West Yorkshire Police HQ, dated 24th November 1980 – four days before Alan Godfrey's report, which confirms the multi police sighting took place four days previously.

Hypnotic Regression

Following the matter being reported in the local newspapers, Alan was contacted by three members of the Manchester UFO Research Association – Harry Harris (39) a solicitor by occupation, Mike Sacks, tailor (well-known to the authors as a thoroughly nice man and most helpful) and Detective Chief Inspector Norman Collinson of the Manchester Fraud Squad. They asked Alan if he was willing to take part in a video-recorded hypnosis session. After agreeing to this course of action, which was under the supervision of psychiatrists, in August 1981, he underwent hypnotic regression by Dr. Jaffe, hoping to learn more of what had taken place.

The testimony that emerged may appear very odd, but it appears to have similarities with described events that we were to come across, over the years, involving witnesses who have been the subject of this method of memory recall.

Under regression, Alan told of the bright light stopping the car engine (an event he doesn't consciously recall) and engulfing him.

> *"I was then floated through an opening in the UFO, into something like a room in a house, oval yet with corners, and with a carpet on the floor; there was machinery, too, which pained me when I tried to look at it. In the corner of the room, I saw what looked like a bloody dog, the size of an Alsatian."*

Alan then tells of being persuaded onto a black leather bed, where he was studied by a frequently smiling, heavily bearded man, with a long thin nose, wearing a skullcap, and a robe – like a white sheet – who telepathically conveyed that his name was 'Yosef'. Something like 'bracelets' were then attached to Godfrey's right arm, left leg, and head.

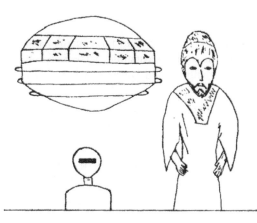

There was no intimate medical examination, as often reported by abductees, but assisting 'Yosef' was a group of about eight metallic, robot-like creatures, the height of *"a little five-year-old lad"*. Two of them *"plugged in"* to the bracelets. Godfrey described them as *"horrible"*, and as *"feeling my cloth"*. In one session he says they have heads *"like a lamp"*; in another he says he *"could not have seen their heads. They have a sort of lampshade on."* They made a noise similar to a robot.

Godfrey later told Jenny Randles:

> *"What I said under hypnosis is a mystery to me. I will accept the fact that it might be something I have read, dreamt, or seen. I just don't know."*

Police Constable Alan Godfrey's rough sketches show the "spaceship" (top left), "Yosef" (right) and one of the "lamp-headed robots" (bottom left).

Alan yearns for answers to the many questions that remain dominant to the background of his life, over 30yrs later, believing the intelligence, or influence, behind the orchestration of the UFO sighting was friendly, rather than hostile, and told us that he had not sustained any medical ailments of a physical nature, although he did discover the sole of his left boot was split, and of a small patch of inflammation on his foot, later diagnosed as Psoriasis.

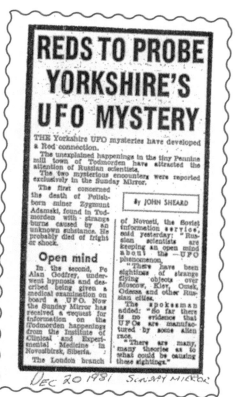

During our visit to see Alan in Todmorden, to discuss his involvement in the 'Adamski' case, of June 1980, we did not get the opportunity to have a look at the exact scene of the UFO incident. However, we can establish – looking at the newspaper cutting endorsed *'A Strange Encounter'* – that the building to the left, behind Alan, situated on the A646 Burnley Road, is next to the drive which leads to the Fielden Centre, opposite †Centre Vale Park. For those that may think there may be a connection with the saucer-shaped mobile home (parked there, for many years) this could not have been the case, as this was moved from the Fielden site, in 1971, to another part of Todmorden.

Many suggestions have been put forward to explain what Alan saw. They include imagination, altered state of consciousness, unidentified atmospheric phenomenon (UAP) which covers a range of light phenomena, such as earthlights, ball lightning, and atmospheric plasmas and vortices – similar to those proposed by Terence Meaden, as the source for some crop circles. There have been literally thousands of sightings of this type of UAP reported from the Pennine region, between Yorkshire and Lancashire, over the years. Sightings describe nocturnal lights that dance around, split apart, merge, and sometimes emerge from, or disappear, into the ground. (One wonders if the same phenomenon occurs in daylight).

Another suggestion on the physical plane, rather than the opposite, involves a prefabricated, plastic building, called the Futuro Home, which was the only one manufactured by *Waterside Plastics* (1971-1978) Waterside Mill, Rochdale Road, Todmorden. Prior to 1960 *Waterside Plastics* was a famous old textile spinning and weaving firm, called *Fielden Brothers,* whose business roots can be traced back to the sixteenth century.

©David Martin Photography   ©David Martin Photography

The house was exhibited outside the *Abraham Omerod Medical Centre* (now closed) in the town, near the railway viaduct (1971) for the town's centenary but previously functioned as an office for *Waterside Plastics,* for some years. Its present whereabouts are not known, although it was rumoured that it went to the Lake District.

The site of the mill is now a major supermarket. Laneside Cottages are still occupied as homes. The warehouse, offices and school, opposite the main site, are still standing, including the clock tower. There is apparently only one photograph of the Futuro Home of it being moved on a lorry – that was taken in 1971.

The 'saucer-shaped home' was parked at the side of Burnley Road, in a number of locations, between 1969 and the early 1980s. Initially, it was used as an information centre, when it was situated just a few hundred yards from Todmorden Police Station. Alan, of course, rejects this explanation as being *"bloody daft"*, which we concur with!

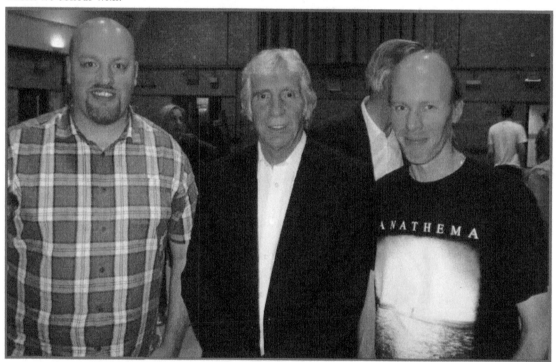

Alan Godfrey at Woodbridge Community Hall with Dave Hodrien (left) and Andrew Hodrien (right).

On the 17th June 2012, Alan gave what he declared as being his last public talk on the incident at the Rendlesham 2012 Conference, held at Woodbridge Community Hall, Suffolk.

The Alan Godfrey story, like the events of Rendlesham Forest, will continue to be the focus of attention, despite the years folding away. Each and every year brings new claims, as people strive to find what they believe to be the right explanation, feeling that logic and rationality dictates there has to be an answer. One thing is assured, if we find the explanation to what it was that Alan Godfrey saw then we will find the answer to what is, after all, still the most enduring question of the 20th/21st Centuries. As Gordon Creighton told us, *"it is still man's most enduring enigma of modern times and the greatest phenomena of all time."*

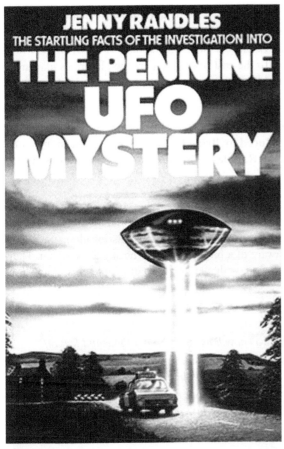

History of Mons Mills

*In June 1907, The *Hare Spinning Company* Ltd began construction of a cotton spinning mill in Todmorden, Calderdale, West Yorkshire, known as *Hare Mill,* Todmorden, this was completed in August 1912. Due to financial difficulties, it was sold to William Hopwood, in 1914, for half the original cost and renamed *Mons Mill* (1919) *Co. Ltd.,* which was then itself taken over by the *Lancashire Cotton Corporation* in the 1930s, and passed to *Courtaulds* in 1964, and production stopped in 1968. It was used into the 1990's by *Ward & Goldestone Ltd.* There was the logo of a white hare on the mill chimney – probably the reason for a number of roads known locally as Hare Court, Harehills Avenue, Harehill Street and Mons Road, which are found in the close proximity of where the Mill was part of which still survives to the present day. The site was cleared in 2000.

Centre Vale Park

†Centre Vale Park is located less than half a mile from Todmorden Town Centre and is used for public events since the first bowling greens were

The scene near to the Mons Mill building where Alan Godfrey's alleged UFO encounter took place

open in 1915, and continues today to be an area used for walking, sports and formal recreation, picnics, family outings and large scale events, including the Agricultural Show (one of the largest in the North of England) music events, the town's Carnival, Brass Band concerts, and the National Crown Green Bowling Club Championships, schools and educational events. To the east of the park are the children's play area, skate park and public toilets. The channelled River Calder runs along the north-eastern boundary of the park, adjacent to Burnley Road.

(Sources: Len Peltier, Todmorden. *Fieldens of Todmorden;* A Nineteenth Century Business Dynasty, Littleborough George Kelsall – Reproduced by Brian R. Law 1995/'A Policeman's lot', Jenny Randles, *FSR,* Volume 27, No. 2, August 1981)

UFO over Essex

In the same month, Mr & Mrs Jones were driving home, towards Southend-on-Sea, Essex, along the A127, close to the Brentwood junction, when they became aware of a bright 'light' in the sky above them. They then noticed a number of cars parked at the side of the road, with a large group of people gazing upwards into the sky.

Mr Jones:

> *"We decided to stop as well, because the 'light' was now hovering about a thousand feet off the ground, approximately a quarter of a mile away. After watching it for 30mins, or so, we decided to carry on our journey because the children were getting restless in the back. We drove towards the object and passed underneath it. I shouted at my wife to have a look, as I was concentrating on driving. She told me she could see lots of coloured lights inside a cigar-shaped centre. We later stopped and rang 999. By the time we got back to our location, there was nothing else to see."*

(Source: Personal interview/Brenda Butler)

We discovered another UFO report, which took place a few weeks later, at the same location, involving a motorist and his wife, who witnessed a gigantic glowing object, surrounded by an orange field, hovering in the sky. On this occasion, the object was seen to split into two – one part heading off towards the North, the other took up a position above the dual carriageway. According to one of the witnesses we spoke to:

> *"The calm of the night was then shattered by the arrival of two RAF Jet Fighters that shot across the sky, heading towards the UFOs, which moved away at tremendous speed, leaving the aircraft standing."*

(Source: Brenda Butler/Ron West)

CHAPTER 12
DECEMBER 1980

UFO over Poole, Dorset

A T 9am, 6th December 1980 – a cold, clear morning, with a blue sky and wintry sun – Jean Findlay, of Poole, Dorset, was walking along Turlin Road, a short distance from the house, when she had an urge to look upwards into the sky.

"Just ahead of me, over the A350 road, next to the railway track, was a saucer shaped object – oval, with a bulge on top – one end of the rim appearing to be more pointed than the other. It was about the size of a double-decker bus, in comparison, with a colour like that of the old dirigible balloon. I then saw it move slightly to the right – now hovering closer to the railway line – then it disappeared from sight."

(Source: Leslie Harris/John Ledner/Jenny Randles)

UFO over Basildon

At 6pm one Sunday evening in December 1980, a resident of Swallowdale, Basildon, Essex, was watching television, when two boys knocked on her front door and asked her to come outside to look at a strange object in the sky.

"On going outside with my husband and elderly mother, we saw this huge black object, showing a red glow in the centre, about 60 feet by 100 feet in size, and watched it until 7.00pm. – when it moved across the sky and disappeared from view."

UFO over Canvey Island

Anne Vanvlet, of Canvey Island, was watching a video film with her parents, at 11.30pm., in December 1980, when they saw a yellow *'glowing ball'*, motionless in the sky, through the French windows, overlooking the Thames Estuary.

"After fifteen minutes, it began to diminish to the size of a pinhead before disappearing. We contacted the police. They promised to send someone around to see the family, but they are still waiting, over 25 years later!"

(Source: Personal interview/Ron West, Brenda Butler–East Anglian UFO & Paranormal Research Association)

UFO over Parliament

On the 23rd December 1980 it was alleged by various newspaper reports that a spinning, shimmering, UFO was seen by Members of Parliament and police officers. Unfortunately, we were unable to obtain any further information on this alleged occurrence and wonder about the validity of an incident which, bearing in mind its position, should have attracted far more publicity – one would have thought?

Cosmos returns to Earth

At 9pm. on the 25th of December 1980, *'six or seven football sized objects, leaving a trail behind them'*, were seen heading across the UK skies, by people in Cricklade, Gloucestershire, and other parts of the Western Isles. It was later discovered to be the upper stage of a Russian Cosmos 749 rocket re-entering North West Europe airspace, at 9.07 pm. and breaking up, during re-entry – the last fragment believed to have burned out east of Clacton. (The satellite that it had launched came down three months earlier.)

One witness was Tony Pearce, from Millbrook, Southampton, who was walking his dog, at 9.07pm., 25th December 1980, and facing roughly south, when he saw: "lights in the sky, travelling towards the direction of Winchester. There were four or, maybe, five of them in line astern, glowing with a rocket trail behind each one. I watched them for about 20 seconds before they disappeared." **(Source: Personal interview)**

UFO over RAF Alconbury

As a result of an appeal made in the *'Cambridge News'*, seeking any information regarding unusual events having taken place at RAF Alconbury, we were contacted by Janet Lewis.

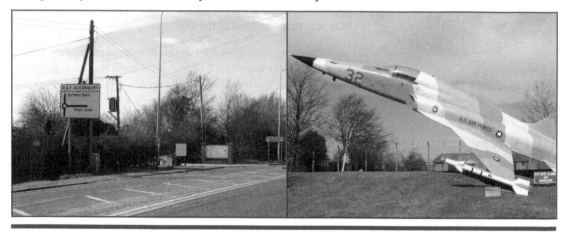

*"I can't be sure of the exact year, but it would have been approximately 25 years ago, (1980).
I was out walking the dogs near the airbase, on Christmas Day, when I noticed what looked
like a fireball circling around the sky. A few minutes later, it headed off towards the direction
of the airbase and was soon out of sight."*

The reader should be aware of some very mysterious incidents that took place at the airbase involving
a 'giant hairy figure in the early 1970's which was encountered by USAF servicemen. (See full story in

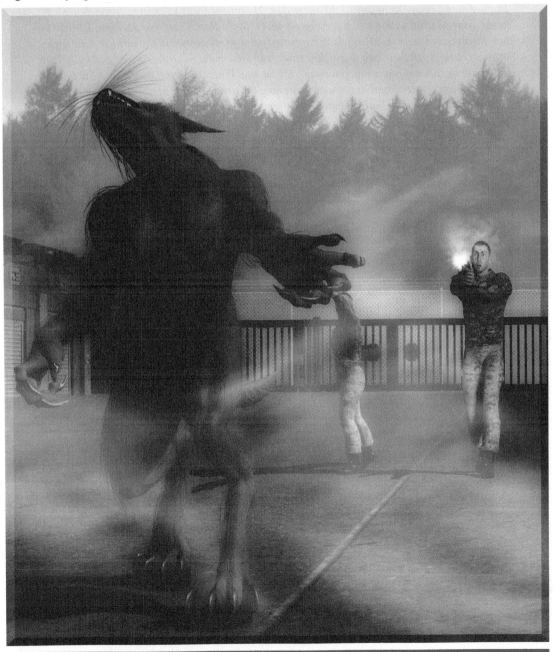

Volume 5 of *Haunted Skies* Page 143). An extract from that following personal interviews with retired officers tells us:

> *"I also heard about an incident involving two mechanics, who were working on an aircraft parked on the north side of the base – one of whom was so frightened by the appearance of a 'strange hairy creature' that he jumped into the cockpit of the aircraft and refused to get out for some time. I took such stories at face value, purely because I never encountered this 'leaping man', or spoke to any of the witnesses. My attitude was to change somewhat when, during conversation with my two regular partners, Sgt's. Randi Lee and Jackson, I learnt of their involvement in an incident which happened prior to my arrival at the airbase. One night, while on patrol with their two dogs, they saw some movement near the towers and called the main gate to check if any workmen were still on site. When told not, they asked for a truck response team to attend and assist with searching the area. As they approached a tower, they came face-to-face with a 'hairy figure'. The dogs stopped in their tracks, absolutely terrified, frantically trying to get away. One of the handlers urged the dog to go after the intruder, but was bitten by his own animal . . . that's how frightened the dogs were. The truck arrived just in time to see the 'creature' – whatever it was – climbing over the security fence, where it was last seen entering North Woods."*

RAF Alconbury

UFOs sighted over RAF Welford Airbase

In December 1967, we covered briefly a sighting that took place over RAF Welford Airbase, when USAF security officers had witnessed the over-flights of UFOs above the airbase. (See Volume 3, *Haunted Skies*)

In view of the fact that sketches and information pertaining to the Welford incident had been inadvertently omitted from Volume 3, of *Haunted Skies,* we felt it was of importance to bring this matter, once again, to the readers' attention, bearing in mind the events that were to take place 13 years later, in Suffolk – and of the fact that we were now in a position to show the images in colour.

USAF Sergeant John Roger Artie

Retired USAF Sergeant John Roger Artie, born 21st May 1935, now living in Reno, Nevada, USA – who was previously employed as a field investigator for the now defunct Aerial Phenomena Research Organisation (APRO) – told of a spate of UFO activity witnessed by him and other USAF security servicemen, while stationed at RAF Welford, Newbury, Berkshire, in 1967.

John Roger Artie's DD form

"I was on duty in the 'Z' area, looking out over the interior road and fields, when I noticed a security patrol vehicle, manned by Sergeants Nash and Brooks, slow down and stop. The two men then got out and looked up into the sky.

I was later approached by the two men, who reported having seen a strange reddish glow in the middle of low hanging clouds, although I did not witness it myself."

The main base at RAF Welford

Between 9pm and 10pm, the same date (11th November 1967) – a clear and bright night, with little or no cloud – USAF Security personnel Sergeants Coleman, Bean, Winston, Strickland, Knott, McDonald, and Lane – all from 'B' flight 7551st Support Police Squadron – were on duty at RAF Welford, when they sighted, *'a number of lights, moving erratically in the sky over the base'*. They reported what they had seen to Sergeant John Roger Artie, in charge of quarter duties that night.

John:

"I later learned that a report of the incident was written into the desk blotter – an official USAF document – and submitted, although I do not know the outcome of any investigations, but can tell you there was rumour going around that the night shift on the following night, the 12th November, also witnessed a similar phenomenon."

Further UFO sightings at the base

At approximately 8.30pm on 5th December 1967, USAF Security patrolmen, Sgt. Coleman and Sgt. John Roger Artie, were on duty at RAF Welford, when they sighted *'an orange circle of light, moving high up in the north-western sky – within two minutes it was gone from view'*. On this occasion, no report was submitted.

At 8.30pm, the following evening (6th December 1967) an orange circular 'disc', showing a light on top, blinking erratically, was seen hovering approximately 30ft above trees, in the vicinity of RAF Welford railhead gate, by security personnel – Sergeant's Coleman and Strickland. As the men made their way towards the UFO, it dropped downwards, behind trees, east of the railway embankment.

The men then drove towards a wooded area, close to building F-99, and alighted from the vehicle. By this time, the object was now out of sight. Sgt. Strickland flashed his lights several times, following which the UFO reappeared, rising straight up from a position estimated to be a couple of miles away, in the vicinity of Rowbury Farm. It then gained altitude, in an arc of movement across the sky, and flew over RAF Welford, passing along 'H' row, before turning up along an area known as 'Z', near the E3 complex.

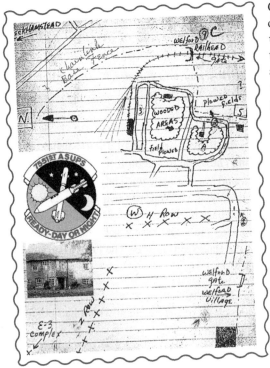

Coleman got out of the vehicle and saw the UFO, now displaying an erratic yellow light, heading southwards, towards the direction of Welford gate, once again. It then flew over the gate and vanished from view. After about 45 minutes had elapsed the two men made their way back to the wooded area by the railhead gate, and parked up by building F-99. At about 11.30pm, Sgt. Strickland looked through a pair of binoculars and saw:

> ". . . a glowing white mist in the sky over the Rowbury hill area, which I thought strange, as it was a clear, bright night, with no sign of any fog, or mist, elsewhere. The mist appeared to shroud an object shaped like an 'evergreen', or something like that. Coleman suggested we wait until day shift to check it out."

John:

> "Whatever it was I don't know, but it wasn't the same object we had seen earlier. Suddenly, I noticed the 'yellow light' (only visible through binoculars) was back in the sky over the direction of Rowbury Farm House – possibly much further away, perhaps the A34 Oxford-Newbury road, in the direction of Chieveley. It moved backwards and forwards in a north, then south, direction across the sky, for a few minutes, and then disappeared, leaving the other object still visible in the mist. At this point, we were called away. When we returned to the scene, just under an hour later, there was no sign of anything untoward in the sky."

The next night, 7th December 1967, John happened to be on duty and discussing the events with a RAF constable, known to him as 'Lofty', when he learnt that the officer had himself sighted a peculiar orange light in the sky over RAF Welford air base earlier in the week, while guarding the crash site of a RAF helicopter of the Queen's flight, which had crashed at Brightwalton. (The helicopter was on its way to RAF Yeovilton, at the time (approximately 3miles away from the Base).

Other UFO sightings for the 7th December 1967

Mrs Wilson of Woodland View, Sheffield, and her daughters, were stood on the drive of their house, at 5.10pm on 7th December 1967, when they noticed a red circular object, brighter than the moon, *"as big as a football in the air, with a dark patch on top,"* moving slowly through the sky, heading in a south-east to north-west direction.

At l0pm on 7th December 1967, Harrow Weald residents, Michael Redman and his wife, sighted three brilliant lights in the shape of a triangle, which were seen moving eastwards, towards Watford.

Mr Redman:

> *"Believe me! I hadn't been drinking that night! The lights were seen at tree level and maintained their triangular formation, the apex facing earth, as they moved across the sky."*

(Source: ***The Observer and Gazette**, 8th December 1967*)

History of Airbase

The history of RAF Welford began in October 1941, following the construction of a RAF airfield at the site being approved for use as an Operational Training Unit. The airfield was built in an 'A' shape, with three runways, a number of loops (which can still be seen), and two T2 hangars. The RAF took over the base on 10th June 1943, and passed it over to the USAAF in July. RAF Welford (also known as Welford Park) became USAAF Station 474 on 6th September 1943. The base itself was located on a hill just on the edge of the Berkshire Downs, 14 miles from RAF Greenham Common. The base was built around an 11th Century priory, which later became the official residence of the Base Commander. The Priory is rumoured to be haunted.

While not seeking to associate the helicopter crash to UFO activity, but in view of the UFO activity occurring a short distance away, we decided to check out the cause of the accident which had befell the Queen's flight.

The Pilot was Air Commodore Blount. He was one of four killed, when the QF Whirlwind they were travelling in, crashed in Berkshire, on 7th December 1967, while on their way to Westlands to discuss buying helicopters for the Queen's Flight, the official explanation being:

> *". . . it was caused by fatigue in the rotor shaft that allowed the head to separate. The fatigue was there from manufacture."*

(It was *alleged* the fatigue fault was caused by a short interruption of the cooling fluid when the shaft was being machined.)

From a contemporary newspaper account

Queen's Flight Accident "Baffling". The tragic accident to a Whirlwind HC.12 helicopter of the Queen's Flight which occurred last Thursday, December 7, is apparently unique and was described as "baffling" by an informed source. Crash site photographs show that an entire rotor blade was shed while the machine was airborne.

In the resulting crash the Captain of the Queen's Flight, *Air Cdre John Blount, was killed together with the other three occupants – the Flight Engineering Officer, Sqn Ldr. M. W. Hermon; the pilot, Sqn Ldr. J.

---

* On 9th April 1941, RAF Flying Officer John Hubert Lempriere Blount (DFC) (1919-67) son of Air Vice Marshal C.H.B. Blount, flew from RAF Oakington in Cambridgeshire in his Spitfire X4712. While engaged on photo reconnaissance over the port of Bremer, he was attacked by a Messerschmitt Bf 109 piloted by Rudolf Mickel. The Spitfire was seriously damaged and F/O Blount was forced into a 'belly landing' on the island of Texel. He was taken prisoner by the Germans and spent the remainder of the war in a prison camp.

H. Iiversidge; and the navigator, Flt Lt. R. Fisher. The Whirlwind HC.12, two of which were delivered to the Flight in 1965, is a specially-equipped version of the RAF's Gnome-powered standard Whirlwind10.

The Queen has never flown in them, since the policy is that she never flies in single-engine aircraft, but at the time the crash occurred the other HC.12 was with the Duke of Edinburgh in Germany. There have been suggestions from time-to-time that a twin-engine helicopter – the twin-Gnome Wessex – might be ordered for the Flight, for the Queen to enjoy point-to-point helicopter transport.

All RAF Whirlwinds were restricted to urgent operational flying immediately after the crash occurred, so SAR coverage, the Whirlwind's main service role, remains unaffected. There has apparently been no previous instance in British military use of a Whirlwind shedding a whole blade; in a previous instance where part of one rotor blade was lost, a safe landing was made. Asked whether, in this case, the "security" rules which normally inhibit public discussion of British military air-craft accidents would be waived,

an MOD spokesman said that he expected the findings to be published, though not the proceedings of the inquiry.

The Mk.12 was the first production example built in 1964 and one of only two VIP aircraft built for the Queen's Flight. The interior was fitted with special sound proofing, luxury fittings, chrome trim and a high gloss exterior finish. During its operational duty the museums example was piloted by HRH Prince Philip and The Prince of Wales. XR486 joined the Helicopter Museum at Weston Super Mare in June 2000.

In view of the fact that we had been unable to trace any of the other airmen involved, we discussed the matter at length with John Artie again in early February 2013. Although we were disappointed that neither of us has been able to trace his colleagues, we are satisfied there is no reason to disbelieve his version of events as being none other than genuine, and hope that in the fullness of time we will obtain additional corroboration of those events.

There were rumours that Prince Philip was intending to fly this helicopter himself but found something wrong with it, so he took the other helicopter. Following repairs being effected, Air Commodore John Blount took off on an air test on the 7th December 1967, and was killed with others when it crashed to earth at 9.10am on the 7th July, 1967.

John Roger Artie also sent us details of a UFO sighting which occurred on the 10th of October 1968, while he was guarding the remains of a downed SR-71 that had crashed on take off from Beale Air Force Base, California.

This aircraft ended its career in flames by skidding 1000 feet off the end of runway 14 at Beale AFB, California on 10th October 1968. The takeoff was aborted when a

On the 10th of October 1968 an SR-71 crashed on take-off at Beale A
AFB, Maryville, California. The aircraft (A/C) was about to take-off
on a mission when the engine began spewing parts out the tailpipe.
The A/C ran the length of the runway, crashed through the cable
barrier, cutting off it's gear. The plane slewed to a stop in the
Over-run area at the end of the runway where it burnt for a while.
The two crew ejected and only one fellow sustained a broken leg upon landing. The A/C was a write-off. Parts were salvaged and a very
large hole bull-dozed out of the red earth next to the hulk and the
wreckage pushed into it. The site was covered over. Much later a f
fellow told me the wreckage was unearthed and taken away. As I saw
the guy he was one of those guys who knows everything about anything.
I doubt he told the truth. Beale AFB is still an active Air Force B
Base, in paragraph two of Notes Two, I make reference to Beale in
it's present capacity.

As to my part in the above: Initially I was on Base Patrol and
saw the smoke. I drove immediately to the site. I was outside the u
runway fencing where (already) a crowd of "Looky-Lous" had gathered.
I parked with my "box" flashing and began sorting out the mess, (Come
On, Move It!...(I used my Sergeant Voice as my wife calls it) and began to get it moving away. The area had been a POW camp in WW II and
where barracks had been are open spaces. Through these I saw the
local Bread man's van bumping along to get a look! Got him turned
around and began directing traffic. I rather like that so stayed
there until it was over. The following nights our people were detailed
to provide guards on the wreck until it was disposed of and so on.

I was on the midnight shift and as my partner and I sat on the rim
of our Pick-up's bed we saw tiny yellow lights go by, back and forth.
They were over, so it seemed, the Sierra which is due east of Beale.
They were above the mountains as we saw them. They could have been
very tiny and relatively near-by, or quite large and very high up. It
was impossible to say. They were identical to the yellow lights I had
seen while at RAF Welford, flitting about the black sky. My partner and
I were very sure what we saw were not airplanes or high-flying bugs,
not any of the usual excuses the skeptics use to explain away that
which we clearly saw.

After my experience at Welford with the Air Force as to reporting
UFO's, naturally we did not report them.

Since I have lived in Florida and here in Nevada I've not seen
anything relating that might be of the UFO variety. Of course I was
not outside as much as when I was in Service. As a Security GUARD I
was concerned about my area of responsibility and had little time to
look up in the sky. To be sure I've seen the odd inexplicable vapor trail
and once saw a cloud formation that looked like the Star Trek's spaceship Enterprise. Nothing recently however.

wheel assembly failed. Capt. James A. Kogler was ordered to eject, but pilot Maj. Gabriel Kardong elected to stay with the aircraft. Both crew members survived.

9 Dec. '09, Sunday

P/S I write we are getting our first snowfall, about an inch on the ground. We are "promised" a "Bigger" storm Tuesday. Glad I'm retired & I don't have to go outside.

We are tending 2 feral cats & I feel bad for them. If I could get them to come inside I would. They refuse. They'll come outside our door but not inside. Of course we have five cats inside so that must put them off! Brendon & his sister Brenda are lovely "Moggies" as you call them, they're "Tabbies" here. I inherited them from a friend who had to leave Reno due to the economic situation.

Hope you have a very happy Holiday Season & milder weather than what I've seen on TV. All Best of the Season, Roger

John Roger sent us this Christmas card in 2009.
He is now 78 years old and still keenly interested
in UFO research – and loves his cats!

We are still attempting to ascertain if the original police blotters are in existence, and have written to RAF Welford Museum and left messages on various web sites, hoping to advance the investigation further forward. We will let the reader know if there are any further developments as time goes by.

Diamond UFO over RAF Coltishall

Recently retired Leicestershire Constabulary Police Constable 495 Brett Lynes (51) contacted us during the preparation of this Volume, in January 2013, to tell us about a very strange encounter which took place in 1980, whilst serving with the RAF Police at RAF Coltishall.

"In July 1979 (aged 18) I joined the
RAF Police and, after initial training,
was posted to "RAF Coltishall, in
Norfolk. This base is about 12 miles
north of Norwich and at that time had

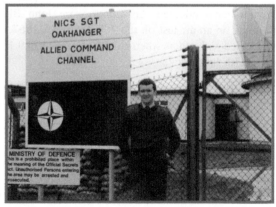

three squadrons of Jaguars and the 202 Search and Rescue helicopter squadron. The RAF Police Flight was quite small and my shift consisted of a substantive Corporal and two acting Corporals (one being me). Our office was situated on the side of one of the aircraft hangers – away from the runway and near to a fuel storage depot.

The incident occurred during a night shift in either late August or early September 1980. We started work at 10pm and took over from the afternoon shift. The evening was fairly mild, so we had the single door to the office open while we had the usual cups of tea before thinking about starting our security patrols."

Just before midnight there was a very loud boom from somewhere close outside. The men's initial thoughts were that the fuel depot had exploded, and the three of them ran outside and across the road to investigate further.

After ascertaining the fuel dump was obviously in order, they wondered if it could have been one of several others scattered around the base which had exploded.

They looked around the skyline to try and see if they could see any glow from a possible fire coming from those other sites, but saw nothing untoward, and wondered if it had been a loud thunderclap. Brett looked up at the sky and saw it was absent of clouds and the stars were visible. The weather was clear and mild and there had been no rainfall that day.

Brett:

"As we could not find any immediate cause for the sound of the explosion, we returned to the office and my shift commander – Corporal Dinning, rang the main guardroom, which was positioned at the entrance gate to the camp and staffed by a roster of airmen and one Sergeant taken from the other sections of the base. They would do one afternoon or night shift every couple of months, and their duty was to go out and check certain fire points once every hour or so. Cpl. Dinning asked if they had heard the 'explosion' and the duty Sergeant said no. Cpl. Dinning then asked that all fire patrols be sent out to check the base on foot, whilst we checked the airfield side in our police vehicles.

Cpl. Dinning and the other RAF police corporal went out together, and I went alone in my car to check various buildings and airfield installations. Nothing was found and, after about an hour, the fire pickets returned to the guardroom and we then settled back down to our normal routine of various security checks around the base."

Just before 5am in the morning, the shift was coming to an end and the men were winding down before being relieved. At 7am Brett volunteered to complete a task at the end of every night shift, involving the unlocking of the 'crash gates', situated on the far side of the runway used to allow emergency vehicles access, should they be required after an air crash on the base. (They are called crash gates, as the attending fire engines would drive through them to get into the base.)

"We had contractors working on the far side taxi way, repairing the concrete, and each morning they would come straight onto the airfield via one of those gates, which would be left unlocked for them. I said that I would drive over there and unlock the gate before they were due to arrive, around 6am. It was now light but a little overcast, with patchy clouds. This I did and I had just unlocked the padlock, when there was a terrifically loud 'boom'

directly over my head. I instinctively flinched down and then looked up at the sky, where the noise had come from. There were now intermittent clouds, but moving between two of them was a very large diamond-shaped craft. It's hard to say how big it was, but I would easily equate it to the size of a large naval vessel, destroyer or similar. It was certainly several times bigger than any aircraft I had ever seen and its shape was like nothing I'd seen before.

The whole underside of this craft was covered in equally spaced sets of diamond patterned lights. Several of the lights were of different colours, such as reds, oranges, purples, greens, yellows, but kept in groups of the same colour. There was no noise at all and the craft moved silently across the sky between two clouds.

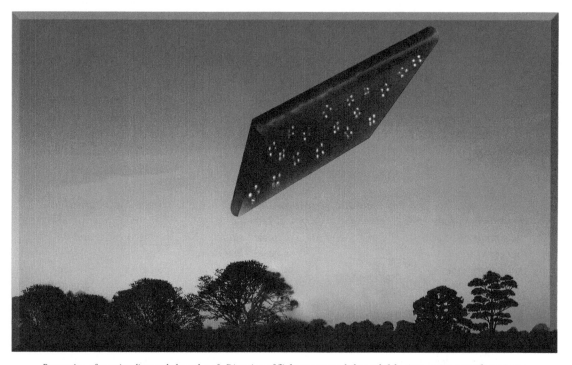

Recreation of massive diamond-shaped craft. Direction of flight was towards lower left horizon, going away from viewer.

Apart from being totally shocked, I managed to use my radio to call up the other two RAF policemen in our office.

I asked Cpl. Dinning to run across the road outside the office and look up at the sky directly above my position at the crash gate, and tell me if he could see anything. I think the tone of my voice prevented them from delaying, as he called back after just a couple of seconds, saying he couldn't see anything apart from clouds.

After about 20 seconds, or so, the craft disappeared fully into, or was hidden by, the clouds from my view and I didn't hear or see anything else of it, although I waited a few minutes just in case it should reappear. I drove back to the office and explained to the others what had happened and even drew a plan of the craft with the position of its lights and their various colours. Unfortunately I did not retain it, even though Cpl. Dinning suggested I submit an official UFO report. I had only been in service for 14 months and did not think it would do my career any good if people started to think I was a fantasist, or worse, so I declined.

I can say that the sound of the boom just before I looked up was pretty much the same sound we had all heard just before midnight, yet when I'd looked up at the sky then it seemed clear.

Many years later, sometime in 1997, or so, I recalled this sighting to another police officer friend and he told me about the Rendlesham incident, which I had never heard of. He lent me a book about that, but unfortunately I cannot remember the book's title, or author.

†In that book was a sighting prior to Rendlesham, by two men standing on the seafront at night, in Suffolk – about 20 miles or so from RAF Coltishall – when they sighted what appears to have been the same diamond shaped craft fly in over the coast from the sea and this, too, was silent. Their sighting was about 12 months after mine, in 1981.

I spent six years in the RAF, at various operational flying stations, and I've never seen anything similar to that craft before or since. Its size and the unusual lights set it apart from anything made public, such as Stealth bombers, etc."

RAF Coltishall Station and Squadron_showing crests on hangar.

*Royal Air Force Station Coltishall, more commonly known as RAF Coltishall is a former Royal Air Force station located 10 miles (16 km) North-North-East of Norwich, in the English county of Norfolk, East Anglia, from 1938 to 2006. It was a fighter base in the Second World War and afterwards a base for night fighters then ground attack aircraft until closure.

†Our records for 1981 contain this sighting. On the 23rd September 1981, Anna Sidali and her children were on holiday, at Lowestoft, in Suffolk, taking a breath of fresh air before night fell, when: *"I noticed a beautiful silver, diamond shaped object appear in the sky. I wondered if it had anything to do with the nearby USAF Airbase when, all of sudden, it was overhead. Frightened, I took the children and ran inside. The oddest thing is that I felt as if we were being watched. It's difficult to explain, but the sighting took place against a backcloth of oppressive atmosphere."* **(Source: Ivan W. Bunn)**

Previous sightings at the base:

Royal Air Force, Officer Gordon W. Cammell, now living in Canada, served at RAF Coltishall. He had this to say:

Gordon W. Cammell and wife.

> *"In 1953 I was based at RAF Coltishall, Norfolk, England, as a jet pilot flying Meteor night fighters. During a routine night flying exercise, Captain, F/O J. Allison and radar operator, F/OI Heavers reported sighting a cigar-shaped UFO, with internal green lights, visible through windows.*
>
> *When this crew entered our flight room, upon their return, they were both very excited and convinced that the object they had seen was extraterrestrial, because of its very high-speed and unusual configuration. The next day we learned that the crew of another night fighter jet of number 85 Squadron, flying near their base at RAF Maidstone, in Kent (over one hundred miles from Coltishall) had reported an identical sighting only three minutes after our crew's encounter. Three minutes to cover a distance of 100 miles meant that the UFO was travelling at about two thousand miles per hour, which was well in excess of the capability of any aircraft in the U.K. at that time in history."*

Illustration depicting a cigar-shaped object similar to that seen by Royal Air Force Officers in 1953.

The Rendlesham Forest Incident

DEPARTMENT OF THE AIR FORCE
HEADQUARTERS 81ST COMBAT SUPPORT GROUP (USAFE)
APO NEW YORK 09755

EPLY TO
TTN OF: CD   13 Jan 81

UBJECT: Unexplained Lights

TO: RAF/CC

1. Early in the morning of 27 Dec 80 (approximately 0300L), two USAF
security police patrolmen saw unusual lights outside the back gate at
RAF Woodbridge. Thinking an aircraft might have crashed or been forced
down, they called for permission to go outside the gate to investigate.
The on-duty flight chief responded and allowed three patrolmen to proceed on foot. The individuals reported seeing a strange glowing object
in the forest. The object was described as being metalic in appearance
and triangular in shape, approximately two to three meters across the
base and approximately two meters high. It illuminated the entire forest
with a white light. The object itself had a pulsing red light on top and
a bank(s) of blue lights underneath. The object was hovering or on legs.
As the patrolmen approached the object, it maneuvered through the trees
and disappeared. At this time the animals on a nearby farm went into a
frenzy. The object was briefly sighted approximately an hour later near
the back gate.

2. The next day, three depressions 1 1/2" deep and 7" in diameter were
found where the object had been sighted on the ground. The following
night (29 Dec 80) the area was checked for radiation. Beta/gamma readings
of 0.1 milliroentgens were recorded with peak readings in the three depressions and near the center of the triangle formed by the depressions.
A nearby tree had moderate (.05-.07) readings on the side of the tree
toward the depressions.

3. Later in the night a red sun-like light was seen through the trees.
It moved about and pulsed. At one point it appeared to throw off glowing
particles and then broke into five separate white objects and then disappeared. Immediately thereafter, three star-like objects were noticed
in the sky, two objects to the north and one to the south, all of which
were about 10° off the horizon. The objects moved rapidly in sharp angular
movements and displayed red, green and blue lights. The objects to the
north appeared to be elliptical through an 8-12 power lens. They then
turned to full circles. The objects to the north remained in the sky for
an hour or more. The object to the south was visible for two or three
hours and beamed down a stream of light from time to time. Numerous individuals, including the undersigned, witnessed the activities in paragraphs
2 and 3.

CHARLES I. HALT, Lt Col, USAF
Deputy Base Commander

The 'Halt Memo'.

Did a UFO land in Suffolk?

Despite the passing of over 30 years, the public still continue to be fascinated by the UFO events that reportedly took place in Rendlesham Forest, just outside RAF Woodbridge, near to the market town of Ipswich (often referred to by the media as *'Britain's equivalent to Roswell'*) as can be seen from the colossal number of web entries found on the Internet (2010) and numerous documentaries, books, and magazine articles, produced over the years.

'S OF THE WORLD PLUS **Sunday**

 STILL ONLY **25p** BEST VALUE FOR MONEY

BRITAIN'S BIGGEST SELLING SUNDAY NEWSPAPER   No. 7.291

- **Colonel's top secret report tells the facts**
- **Mystery craft in exploding wall of colour**
- **Animals flee from strange glowing object**

UFO LANDS IN SUFFOLK

A UFO has landed in Britain— and that staggering fact has been officially confirmed.

Despite a massive cover-up, News of the World investigators have proof that the mysterious craft came to earth in a red ball of light at 3 a.m. on December 27, 1980.

It happened in a pine forest called Tangham Wood just half a mile from the United States Air Force base at RAF Woodbridge, in Suffolk.

An American airman who was there told us there were three beings in silver space suits aboard the craft.

Farm cattle and forest animals ran berserk as the spacecraft, a sloping silver dish about 20ft across its base, silently glided to land in a blinding explosion of lights.

About 200 military and civilian personnel, British and American, witnessed

And that's OFFICIAL

NEWS OF THE WORLD INVESTIGATES

By KEITH BEABEY

over the base by a number of airmen.

It sounds like aliens coming to earth in the film Close Encounters, but the PROOF that an Unidentified Flying Object landed

two-metre high. It illuminated the entire area with a white light. The object itself had a pulsing red light on top and a bank of blue lights underneath. The object was

appeared elliptical through an 8-12 power lens.

They then turned to full circles. The objects in the north remained in the sky for an hour or more. The object to the south was visible for two or three hours and beamed down a stream of lights from time to time.

Numerous people, including myself, witnessed these events, Colonel Halt concluded.

Last week he declined to say anything further when we called on him at

[handwritten report section:]
toward the depression.

3.—Later in the night a red sun-like light was seen through the trees. It moved about and pulsed. At one point it appeared to throw off glowing particles and then broke into five separate white objects and then disappeared. Immediately thereafter, three star-like objects were noticed in the sky, two objects to the north and one to the south, all of which were about 10° off the horizon. The objects moved rapidly in sharp angular movements and displayed red, green and blue lights. The objects to the north appeared to be elliptical through an 8-12 power lens. They then turned to full circles. The objects to the north remained in the sky for an hour or more. The object to the south was visible for two or three hours and beamed down a stream of light from time to time. Numerous individuals, including the undersigned, witnessed the activities in paragraphs 2 and 3.

CHARLES I. HALT, Lt Col, USAF
Deputy Base Commander

EVIDENCE DETAIL from Lt. Col. Charles Halt's confidential report about the sighting of "unexplained lights" and a strange glowing object that lit up the forest

NO HOAX SAYS THE

It was never our intention to 'write-up' a comprehensive account of what had taken place, because the incident had been published in a number of books by popular authors, over the years. They included:

Sky Crash: A Cosmic Conspiracy. Brenda Butler, Dot Street and Jenny Randles – Neville Spearman (1984)

Above Top Secret. Timothy Good – Guild Publishing (1988)

Open Skies, Closed Minds. Nick Pope – Simon & Schuster (1996)

Left at East Gate. Larry Warren and Peter Robbins – Da Capo Press (1997)

You Can't Tell The People: The Definitive Account Of The Rendlesham Forest UFO Mystery. Georgina Bruni – Sidgwick and Jackson (2002)

The UFOs That Never Were. Jenny Randles, David Clarke & Andy Roberts – London House (2000)

In addition to these, we learnt of another two books being published this year (2013)

Rendezvous At Rendlesham. James Penniston, John Burroughs and Nick Pope.

Sky Crash Throughout Time. Brenda Butler and Philip Kinsella, Capall Bann Publishing.

However, we felt that the Haunted Skies series of books should contain some source material relating to our interest in the case following numerous visits to the Rendlesham Forest over the years talking to Brenda Butler, Chris Pennington, 'Dot' Street, and many of the USAF servicemen that had been involved including Colonel Halt.

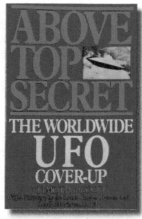

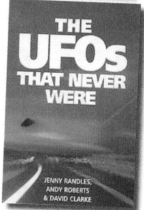

Gordon Creighton of *Flying Saucer Review*:

In 1984, Gordon Creighton of *Flying Saucer Review* (seen opposite with his wife, Joan) wrote to Bob Tibbitts of the *Coventry UFO Research Group*, wondering if the incident at Rendlesham would make an impact. Little did he realise just how big this case was going to be!

Bob Tibbitts:

"When reading news of the reported sightings and landing of a UFO in Rendlesham Forest near to RAF Bentwaters, I wanted to obtain a candid view from the then editor of 'Flying Saucer Review', *Gordon Creighton. His thoughts were important to me as I had been in contact with him on several occasions over the years, wanting his opinion regarding various incidents. The magazine was well regarded at the time and served as a vehicle for some splendid reports from all over the world.*

Although I had ceased publishing 'Syntonic', *I was still researching and gathering information about unidentified flying objects and similar phenomena. I was quite surprised by Gordon's response to my enquiry, as I felt that there was the potential that the incident could become as important as the often-cited Roswell, USA crashed flying disc case, of 1947. Surely, an intrusion into the airspace and countryside close to a military establishment of an 'unknown', with 'unknown' intent, apparently seen to aim beams of intense light downwards, near to a weapons storage area, must be of extreme significance. Gordon could not have guessed at the time what an impact the events around Bentwaters would have. The information contained in these pages of* 'Haunted Skies' *showing, that the debate continues – what happened to those involved and what are the real implications?"*

16 Cedars Avenue
Rickmansworth
Herts, WD3 2AN

16/10/84

Mr R.W.Tibbitts
50 Tudor Avenue
Radford, Coventry
COVENTRY, CV5 7BD

Dear Mr Tibbitts,

Thank you for your letter of September 24.

Publication date of the Rendlesham Forest book will be October 25. I don't think we can judge yet if the case will mark a watershed or make much impact.

As for the Institute- I think we made a great mistake in launching it, because nobody has shown any interest. Had I been the Editor then, I would not have launched it, as I had already perceived that the UFO problem is not a scientific problem and has nothing to do with human science. I think the Institute will have to be quietly phased out one of these days, but I don't think UFO research as a whole will last much longer, either.

Purely by "chance" - of course - both my typewriters packed up on the same day, and I am trying out a very cheap Japanese portable, which is not so hot and has in it a ribbon that seems dried out.

I say I think all UFO research will peter out because there is overwhelming evidence of MENTAL CONTROL of humans. Most folk already "don't want to know" about the subject, and this is evidently induced in them. The governments are naturally happy, because THEY don't want us to know either, and, as for the alien entities themselves, I don't see the slightest sign that any species among them is anxious to enlighten us about anything or to convince us of their existence. (The latter, I am sure, is the LAST thing that they would want!)

I visualize UFO research as continuing for a few years yet and then, I think, mankind will have such grave things to think about that he will forget all about it. They will like that!

All the best,
Yours sincerely,
Gordon Creighton

Lighthouse was the explanation

Despite the credibility of what took place outside RAF Woodbridge, there are still many that maintain the airmen confused the nearby lighthouse for a UFO. An example of this was an article published in the *East Anglian Daily Times,* on 30th April 1998, accompanied by a large photo of the lighthouse, and the text – *'Question: When is a UFO not a UFO? Answer: When it's the Orford Ness Lighthouse'.*

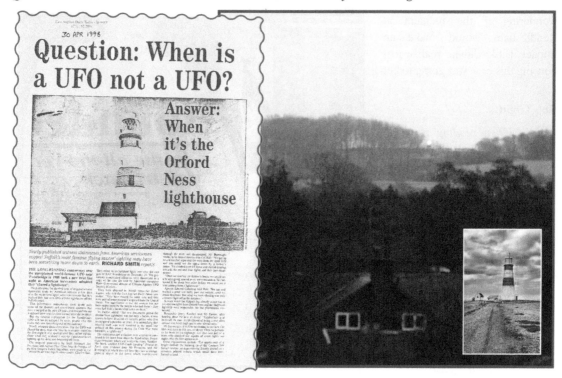

The newspaper article tells the reader:

> "The long running controversy over the unexplained world famous UFO seen near Woodbridge, in 1980, took a new twist last night as American servicemen admitted they chased a lighthouse. The publication for the first time of original witness statements made by American officers, a few days ago, after the mysterious lights were seen, reveals that they realised they had seen the Orford Ness Lighthouse off the Suffolk coast."

The foundation of this disclosure rests on the version of events given by airmen Edward N. Cabansag and John Burroughs, following documents obtained by British researcher James Easton, who disclosed to the newspaper:

> "The new documents prove the Orford Ness Lighthouse was not only a factor, it was known to have deceived security police who first investigated a possible air crash. It is astonishing that security staff who were involved in front line defence of this country during the cold war, were fooled by a lighthouse."

Those documents (according to the article) allege that John Burroughs, in his formal statement to Colonel Halt, says:

"We got up to a fence that separated the trees from the open field and you could see the lights down by a farmer's house. We climbed over the fence and started heading towards the red and blue lights and they just disappeared. Once we reached the farmers house {Authors: Mr Boast's house} we could see a beacon going around, so we went towards it. We followed it for about two miles before we could see it was coming from the lighthouse."

Edward Cabansag told Colonel Halt:

. . . and we walked a good two miles past our vehicle, until we could determine that what we were chasing was only a beacon light in the distance."

On 26 Dec 80, SSgt Penningston and I were on Security #6 at Woodbridge Base. I was the member. We were patroling Delta NAPA when we received a call over the radio. It stated that Police #4 had seen some strange lights out past the East Gate and we were to respond. SSgt Penningston and I left Delta NAPA, heading for the East Gate code two. When we got there SSgt Steffens and A]C Burroughs were on patrol. They told us they had seen some funny lights out in the woods. We notified CSC and we asked permission to investigate further. They gave us the go-ahead. We left our weapons with SSgt Steffens who remained at the gate,, Thus the three of us went out to investigate. We stopped the Security Police vehicle about]00 meters from the gate. Due to the terrain we had to on by foot. We kept in constant contact with CSC. While we walked, each one of us would see the lights. Blue, red, white, and yellow. The beckon light turned out to be the yellow light. We would see them periodically, but not in a specific pattern. As we approached, the lights would seem to be at the edge of the forrest. We were about]00 meters from the edge of the forrest when. I saw a quick movement, it look visible for a moment . It look like it spun XXXXX left a quarter of a turn, then it was gone. I'x advised SSgt Penningston and A1C Borroughs. We advised CSC and proceeded in extreme caution. When we got about 75-50 meters, MSgt Chandler/Flight Chief, was on the scene. CSC was not reading our transmissions very well,, so we used MSgt Chandler as a go-between. He remained back at our vehicle. As we entered the forrest, the blue and red lights were not visible anymore. Only the beacon light, was still blinking. We figured the lights were coming from past the forrest, since nothing was visible when we past through the woody forrest. We would see a glowing near the beacon light, but as we got closer we found it to be a lit up farm house. After we had passed throught the forrest, we thought it had to be an aircraft accident. So did CSC as well. But we ran and walked a good 2 miles past our vehicle, until we got to a vantage point where we could determine that what we were chasing was X only a beacon light off in the distance. Our route through the forrest and field was a direct one,x straight towards the light. We informed CSC that the light beacon was farther than we thought,, so CSC terminated our investigation. A1C Burroughs and I took a road, while SSgt Penningston walked straight back from where we came. A1C Borroughs saw the light again, this time it was coming from the left of us , as we were walking back to our patrol vehicle. We got in contact with SSgt Penningston and we took a walk threw where we saw the lights. Nothing. Finally, we made it back to our vehicle, after making contact with the #C's and informing them of what we saw. After that we met MSgt Chandler and we went in service again after termination of the sighting.

EDWARD N. CABANSAG, A1C, USAF
81st Security Police Sq.

Airman Edward N. Cabansag

How the Public learned about the Incident(s)

If it had not been for the early investigations carried out by Brenda Butler, Dot Street and then Jenny Randles, following information supplied by Brenda's 'informant' who was given the pseudonym 'Steve Roberts', the public's knowledge of this matter would have no doubt been severely depleted.

In March 1983 Larry Warren met with Larry Fawcett, a Police Lieutenant in the State of Connecticut. Following an interview, the famous *Halt Memorandum* was obtained after a FOI request by Larry Fawcett and Robert Todd of the *CAUS* (Citizens Against UFO Secrecy) on the 7th of May 1983.

A copy of this Memo was then sent to 'Dot' Street, who shared it with Manchester solicitor Harry Harris who had been involved in the Alan Godfrey case and other UFO incidents over the years. Harry then later sold it to the *News of the World*. According to Peter Robbins, *"A distorted version of the story was published on 2nd October 1983"*.

Larry Fawcett

Larry Warren at RAF Woodbridge, 1980

Larry Warren with Peter Robbins pictured on 28th October 2010 at RAF Bentwaters

One thing was assured, we felt we could rule out any likelihood of it being the Orford Lighthouse, taking into consideration that over the last thirty years, Brenda has been walking through the forest at least 3-4 times a week, for up to 8-10 hours a time, during the hours of darkness, and has never seen any examples of the lighthouse beam illuminating fields and moving about in the sky – and neither have we!

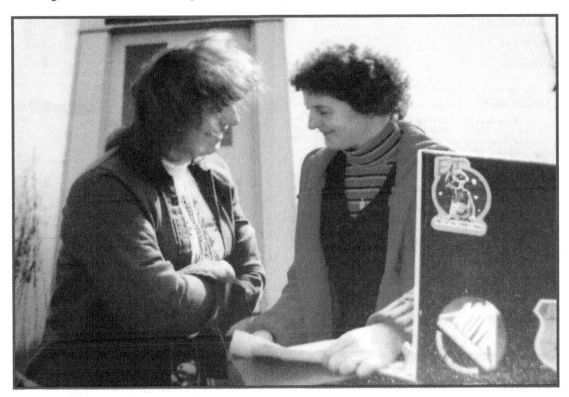

Brenda Butler and Dot Street. © Brenda Butler

Not forgetting that visibility would have been restricted ever further then, prior to many of the tall trees being blown down during the great storm of 1987. Over the years we have seen many instances of where, in the absence of any logical explanation, a ridiculous explanation has been offered by those in authority to explain what people have been seeing now for many years.

Letter to the MOD – It was the Lighthouse!

We decided to write to the MOD, enquiring about their knowledge of the matter, and subsequently received a reply on the 9th October 1993, from Mrs P.J Titchmarsh:

> *"There was no question of any 'alien beings', nor was there any confirmation that an object landed in the forest. You may be interested to know that the BBC recently carried out its own investigation into the incident and concluded that the UFO was nothing more sinister than the pulsating lights of the Orfordness Lighthouse, some 6-7 miles away, through the trees."*

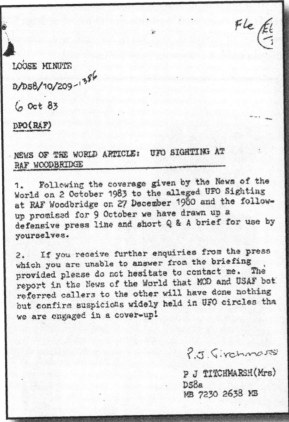

LOOSE MINUTE

D/DS8/10/209-1386

6 Oct 83

DPO(RAF)

NEWS OF THE WORLD ARTICLE: UFO SIGHTING AT
RAF WOODBRIDGE

1. Following the coverage given by the News of the
World on 2 October 1983 to the alleged UFO Sighting
at RAF Woodbridge on 27 December 1980 and the follow-
up promised for 9 October we have drawn up a
defensive press line and short Q & A brief for use by
yourselves.

2. If you receive further enquiries from the press
which you are unable to answer from the briefing
provided please do not hesitate to contact me. The
report in the News of the World that MOD and USAF both
referred callers to the other will have done nothing
but confirm suspicions widely held in UFO circles that
we are engaged in a cover-up!

P.J. Titchmarsh

P J TITCHMARSH(Mrs)
DS8a
MB 7230 2638 MB

UFO researcher Ron West who was a good friend of Brenda Butler and responsible for many investigations held around the Essex and Suffolk area, wrote to the MOD about this matter.

QUEST INTERNATIONAL
OFFICIAL INVESTIGATOR
Name   R WEST
Signature
Authorised by Tony Dodd
Director of Investigations
Date   1 / 8 / 91
WORLDWIDE UFO INVESTIGATION

Fn22/W-18/1   From: C R Neville   18/12/1980   30/12/80   2200

MINISTRY OF DEFENCE
Secretariat(Air Staff)2a   Room B245
Main Building Whitehall London SW1A 2HB
Telephone No: 01-218

R W West Esq   Your Reference
Chilburn Road
GREAT CLACTON ON SEA   Our Reference
Essex   D/Sec(AS)12/3
CO15   Date
                                      26 September 1988

Dear Mr West,

Thank you for your letter of 9 August 1988 which asked for details on the sighting
witnessed at Rendlesham Forest near Woodbridge, Suffolk on 27 December 1980.

The only information that we have on this incident is the report by the Deputy
Base Commander of RAF Woodbridge, Lieutenant Colonel Charles Halt, USAF. In
case you have not seen it before, I attach a copy of the report which may be
of interest to you. As you will see from Colonel Halt's narrative the witnesses
described the object as being approximately 3 metres long and 2 metres high.
In view of this small size it was and still is, considered highly unlikely to
have been a piloted vehicle. However, because we do not attempt to establish
the identity of unusual sightings, unless there are obvious implications on
the security and defence of the United Kingdom, I regret that I do not know
what was witnessed at Rendlesham Forest. Nevertheless, I can confirm that there
is absolutely no evidence to suggest that anything, including Stealth aircraft,
had landed or crashed there. I would also like to assure you that the MOD is
in no manner trying to cover up any UFO incident nor are we trying to in any
way, to obscure the truth about UFOs from the general public.

I hope that you will find this helpful.

Yours Sincerely,

Colonel Charles Halt

To those who maintain, in the face of adversity, that the lighthouse was responsible, we should take into consideration what Colonel Halt said:

"At this time we could see the lighthouse; it was off to the side of this object by about 30°. This object was no lighthouse; it was dancing about in the forest, woods and all."

Ridiculous explanations do not have to be believed, they just have to be offered. An example of this took place during the autumn of 1967, when hundreds of people saw what they described as an object resembling a *'Flying Cross'* moving through the sky over England, which was explained away as being Venus or Mars (See Volume 3, *Haunted Skies*, 1966-1967) But of course it doesn't matter how ridiculous the explanation will be, the majority of people will accept this rather than accept the unacceptable. This is why the lighthouse explanation abounds and will continue to do so.

Exact dates confirmed

For years arguments have ranged about the actual dates of when these incidents took place. According to Robert L. Hastings, in his book, *UFOs and Nukes: Extraordinary Encounters at Nuclear Weapons Site,* during 2009, Colonel Halt, told him:

> "We reconstructed the UFO incidents from memory, and inadvertently miss-stated the dates they had occurred.
> The first incident in the forest actually took place around 3am on December 26th; the second incident began late on the evening of December 27th and continued into the early morning hours of the 28th."

Brenda Butler – How it all began

Previous to the events that occurred in December 1980, were reports of an incident that took place in November 1979, near to Woodbridge airbase, involving Brenda Butler and Chris Pennington (an accomplished musician), who were socialising at the *Rod and Gun Club,* in November, talking to their friend – USAF security guard *Steve Roberts* – when the general alarm went off all over the base.

Brenda:

> "Suddenly there were blue lights flashing all over the place; outriders and security guards came to the Club. Steve had to go; he came back about half an hour later dressed in his security guard outfit, plus gun. He stood at the door and told everyone to sit down, as no one was allowed to leave for a while. I went over and asked him
>
> what was wrong. He said that he was not allowed to say, but it involved an aircraft and a lot of high ranking officers up on the flight line. We were kept there for about three hours, and then we were escorted off the base. There were still blue flashing lights all around and the alert conditions still held. Two days later, word had got around that a UFO had landed on the runway at Bentwaters, and high ranking officers had gone out to it. This was the night we were at the Rod and Gun Club."

Charles Halt was invited to comment on this in May 2013, he said:

> "This 'Alert' was a routine exercise held at regular intervals on the air base, not a UFO landing"

Author unknown: Similar to original illustration drawn by Steve Roberts

---

* Steve Roberts was the man who first told Chris Pennington about the UFO landing in 1980. We emailed 'Steve' in 2013, asking him if he would be willing to speak to us in confidence, but to the present date we have not received a reply – which isn't surprising. We have been aware of his identity for many years, and promised Brenda that we, like her, would never reveal publicly his true identity.

UFO and its occupants sighted

In November 1976, Brenda moved back to the family farm to look after her father, following the loss of her mother and husband, David – accompanied by her two children and partner Chris Pennington.

Brenda:

> *"In November 1979, my Dad and I saw a UFO and its occupants at the farm where we lived. It was 3.00 am when I was awoken by a bright light shining through my bedroom window. I got out of bed and looked out of the window; (first I looked at the clock on my wall) I saw a massive orb, hovering near some trees. The light was very bright and it hurt my eyes. I then looked to the left, as something caught my eye by the front gate. I saw a figure standing there. At the time I was not sure whether it was a man or a woman, as they had lovely long golden hair. They were dressed in a silver tunic, with writing across it. They had a gun, or a probe, hanging from a belt. They were beautiful. The figure knew I had seen him (later I knew it was a man); he told me not to be afraid. They were only here to collect some soil samples. This was given to me by thoughts into my head. I then returned to bed."*

The next morning Brenda thought it was all a dream, so did not say anything until her father surprised her at the breakfast table. He suddenly said:

> *"A funny thing happened at about three this morning. I saw a big white light shining in my bedroom window. I got out of bed and went over to the window. I saw a light by the trees on the front meadow. I then thought that somebody had told me to go back to bed. I think it might have been a dream."*

Brenda then told him what she had seen, but did not mention the figure, and asked him if he had seen anyone or anything by the gate. He said that he could not remember, but he was sure there was something else he had seen. However, he could not place it at that moment.

Brenda:

> *"He complained of a terrific headache, and his eyes were all red, so he said he was going to go for a walk to see if he could get rid of it. My father left, and came back about two hours later. He said that his headache was still there and that when he tried to remember the light, it turned into a pain. He felt his memory had, in some way, been erased of what happened the previous night."*

He told her he had discovered two large holes, about 12ft across and 10-12ft deep, in one of the top fields. All the soil had been scooped out – in steps – but no soil was found lying about on the ground. There were no footprints or tyre marks anywhere. Some of the trees had their tops burnt off and there were scorch marks on the trees themselves. He reported this to the police, who came and had a look, but would not comment.

Brenda contacted the local paper, asking if anyone else had seen anything that night, or if any other farmers had found holes appearing in their fields. A number of people came forward to say they had seen lights in the sky; some of these had been seen over Sizewell Power Station, near Leiston.

Several farmers contacted the paper to say they had found holes in their fields throughout Norfolk and Suffolk.

She suspects a connection between the light seen and the later discovery of holes found in the ground.

This was not the first time Brenda had been involved in a UFO sighting. In 1950, she saw an object moving across the sky, when aged 5, at Hall Farm, Martham, near Great Yarmouth. Her father came running out and speculated she might have seen a top secret experimental craft. (See page 62, Volume 1 *Haunted Skies*)

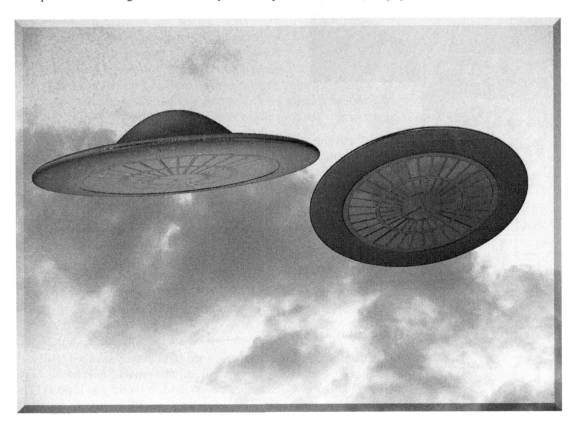

Triangular craft seen over Woodbridge Area – 1979

Brenda Butler:

> *"Several people had reported seeing lights and black shapes around that time. I went to interview several of them in Woodbridge and Hollesley, who had seen weird lights. One gentleman had seen a black triangular shape, with white lights underneath, going towards Woodbridge Base. Another witness told me that he had spoken to some Americans, who told him that a strange craft had landed on the base; followed by a strange unknown plane. (Could this be the same night that we were kept in at the Rod and Gun Club?)*
>
> *In November 1979, I was called out to many places of UFO sightings. One of these was*

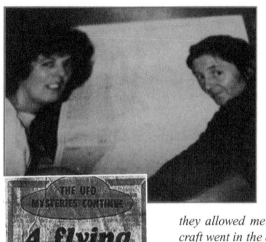

A flying triangle of fear

By KEITH BEABEY

TERRIFIED villagers near the scene of Britain's first "official" UFO landing have been buzzed by a new mystery craft.

The bizarre flying triangle hovered almost silently above the tiny hamlet of Hollesley in Suffolk for 20 minutes.

Frightened children fled indoors and stunned villagers watched open-mouthed as three bright white lights hung motionless in the night sky.

The UFO finally zoomed off making a high-pitched whining noise "nothing like an aeroplane or heli-copter," according to eye-witnesses.

Now villagers are demanding a meeting with American air force chiefs at nearby RAF Woodbridge to find out exactly what is going on.

One, John Button, said: "If they are experimenting, then we ought to be told."

Secret

"And if there's something flying around here which comes from outer space, we ought to be told about that, too."

The top-secret NATO airbase was the scene of the first ever UFO landing. But, as the News Of The World exclusively revealed, it was covered up by the authorities.

Many villagers are too frightened to talk about the latest incident, but baker Ron Macro was out on his rounds when the eerie lights came over the trees.

"We froze," said 41-year-old Ron, of St Austell Grove, Ketgrave, near Ipswich. "The talking suddenly stopped and all eyes looked skywards.

"The lights were in

RON MACRO: Froze

a triangle and re-mained perfectly still."

Several minutes passed. Then the lights moved.

"Whatever was in the sky flew over us. The lights beamed down and we heard a high-pitched whine," added Ron.

"It wasn't an air-craft. I've been delivering here for 20 years and I know the sound of jets and helicopters."

Mother-of-two Mary Potter was standing by Ron's van. She said: "I was really frightened."

Villagers bombarded the USAF with calls after the amazing sighting and were told the only aircraft in the area was a Her-cules transporter.

Captain Kathleen McCullom, at the air-base said: "Nothing was seen on radar. I cannot say more than that.

Car cut out

THE MOST frightening episode in the latest UFO incident was experienced by pretty Debbie Foreman and her pal Pauline Osborne. Strange things suddenly started happening to their car as they drove past Hollesley and saw the mysterious lights.

"The headlights on the car dimmed and the engine cut out," said Debbie, 21, of Heath View, Laiston, Suffolk. "Until then the car had behaved quite normally.

"It slowed down and almost stopped. Then, just as Pauline was going to start the engine again with the ignition key, the car started by itself. We drove home without saying a word."

---

over the base at Woodbridge; a craft was seen hovering over the runway. Another craft, or may be the same one, followed a young couple (Paul and Angela) along the Hollesley road. They described it as a huge triangular shape, with lights underneath. It gave off a weird atmosphere as it passed over them. They were on a motorbike at the time. They stopped and watched it before speeding off. When they arrived at Paul's home, they told his parents. His mother phoned me the next day. Although Paul and Angela were still in shock from this incident, they allowed me to interview them on tape. They said that the craft went in the direction of Woodbridge Air Base.

Another witness from the Hollesley area phoned to tell me that several residents had seen a craft flying towards the base, around the end of November. They had also seen the same thing a month earlier, in October – a large, triangular shaped craft, black in appearance, with lights underneath.

Nearly all the sightings throughout October, November and December 1979, were triangular crafts. Dot and I saw the exact same thing in 1983, while outside Col. Halt's house. It came over the top of us; it was silent. If they were test flying the stealth bomber around that time, I would say it was what we saw, as rumours were that it was being flown over Suffolk airbases."

Triangular UFOs

During many years' research into reported UFO activity between 1940 and the present, it is clear to say that in the mid 20th Century, while the majority of UFO sightings involved saucer-shaped objects, World War II pilots also described seeing craft resembling 'triangles' and 'flying Christmas trees' while on their bombing missions over Germany. On other occasions black triangular objects were seen in daylight.

People who have seen the underneath of these saucer-shaped objects sometimes observe three globes or balls, set at equilateral distance from each other, inset into the base. An excellent example of this occurred on the 17th of July, 1955 at Bexleyheath, Kent.

In the 1980's there were many reports of triangular objects seen all over Europe – some were chased by the Belgian Air force. In addition to this, many people (throughout the years) have sighted three lights (sometimes forming a triangle) moving across the night sky, these appear to dominate the background of UFO history. It is likely there is some connection between what we regard as different classifications of UFOs, and that at the end of the day they all stem from the same source.

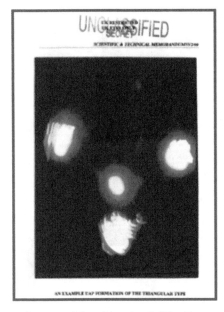

AN EXAMPLE UAP FORMATION OF THE TRIANGULAR TYPE

The Ministry of Defence enquiry into UFOs, code named *Project Condign* – released to the public in 2006, draws several conclusions as to the origin of *"black triangle"* UFO sightings. Their *unnamed* researchers conclude that most, if not all, *"black triangle"* UFOs are formations of electrical plasma – the interaction of which creates mysterious energy fields that both refract light and produce vivid hallucinations and psychological effects in witnesses that are in close proximity. We know where this line of thought would be going! If we presume this was the case surely it would not be too difficult to obtain scientific evidence in support of this hypothesis.

We do not believe this to be the answer, sightings of saucer shaped and triangular shaped UFOs were seen back in the 1950's.

It is highly possible there is probably no 'biological' difference between one type of UFO and the next, taking into consideration, while generally descriptions (and their later classification) depend on visual observations, one shouldn't forget that not only do people not see the same thing as their companions, but often only part of the object is visible. One presumes that this relies on certain criteria being met, involving not only the witness but geographical locations.

Triangular UFO over Staffordshire

One such sighting took place in 1964 over Staffordshire involving artist Mrs Mabel Till, who saw the following object flying over the garden of her house.

> *"It was dark metallic grey in colour and showed streaks as if paint had been applied too thickly. In the middle were a number of curious square panels illuminated by one panel in the middle, the colour of red hot metal but like Perspex in composition. A bar of brighter orange light moved along the panels 9 to 12 at half second intervals. I heard a gently singing noise which I identified as 'G' natural."*

(Full article and other information in *Haunted Skies* Volume 2)

Previous to the now-famous front page headline of the *News of the World* newspaper declaring: 'UFO Lands In Suffolk And That's Official', were found similar, stirring headlines in the *Daily Mirror,* in its edition of the 9.11.1967, during a heavy period of UFO activity. This time the banner-grabbing headline screamed out to the reader: 'It's Official!'

It's an amusing script of tongue-in-cheek references calculated to put the reader's mind at rest and show through the anecdotal exchange which took place between *House of Commons* Ministers – that there was nothing to worry about.

One might ask why it was that, while many local newspapers publicised those events, the nationals very rarely did – were they warned off by the Government? I think most of us who have carried out our own research into the UFO subject know the answer to that question!

EAST ANGLIAN U.F.O. & PARANORMAL RESEARCH ASSOCIATION

SECTION A — **SIGHTING ACCOUNT FORM**

Please write an account of your sighting, make a drawing of what you saw and then answer the questions in section B overleaf as fully as possible. Write in **BLOCK CAPITALS** using a ball point pen.

MY WIFE AND I SAW THIS BIG BLACK TRIANGULAR SHAPE CRAFT IN THE SKY. IT WAS LATE ONE EVENING. IT HAD THREE LIGHTS RED AND WHITE, IT MADE NO NOISE AS IT PASSED OVER OUR HOUSE — GOING TOWARDS THE BRENTWATERS AIR BASE. I THINK IT WAS AN USAF SPY PLANE GOING OVER. WE GET A FEW OF THEM HERE.

DRAWING*

Your full name (Mr/Mrs/Miss/Ms)
ERNIE GRANT ... Age 78
Address: 3 CORONATION AVE HOLLESLEY SUFFOLK
Telephone No. _____ (STD. ___)
Occupation during last two years. RETIRED

Any professional, technical or academic qualifications or special interests
_____

Do you object to the publication of your name?
*Yes/No. *Delete as applicable.
Today's Date: 8-9-88
Signature: E. Grant

* If preferred, use a separate sheet of paper.

Diary of Brenda Butler

Brenda was to keep a personal diary of the events that unfolded in 1981. Here are some of the extracts which allow us a unique opportunity to see for ourselves what happened during the early days of the investigation.

Witness — It came to my notice on Jan 6th 1981 that a craft had been sighted and had landed in Tangham woods Rendlesham nr Woodbridge base between xmas 1980 and the new year.

The informant a U.S.A.F. S.S. stated a local farmer had heard a noise over his farm + went out to have a look. His cattle were going crazy and one had got out + been hit by a taxi — he phoned another local farmer who came + helped him to calm his cattle.

Brenda Butler's Diary — He then phoned the base police as he thought it was a plane. He told them a plane had gone over his cattle + scared them — it had lots of lights on it — he told them it had gone over towards the Base — + the forest. The Base Police said they would go + check it out — they went out to the perimeter fence + reported seeing lights over the forest.

The Security Police, asked permission to go + check the lights out. They went out with the Base Commander, Chief of Security and some more High ranking officers. When they got to where the lights were they saw something, they stood watching it for awhile, it looked as though it was in trouble a craft of some sort. They saw 3 entities, who looked like they were suspended in shafts of light — trying to repair their thing — after awhile the craft took off. It hovered above the tree tops for a while then shot off at great speed.

A A10 was sent up to check for radiation

also to check for heat source. - as there was
supposed to be intense heat -
There was supposed to have been film taken
& photo's taken of the U.F.O & the scene. but these
have conveniently been misplaced.

Newspaper reporters were also supposedly been there
but warned not to print or say anything

Security guard also said there was communication
between commanding officer & the entities -

About a week later it came to my attention by a
Forestry worker that tops of trees were scorched and
burnt - and scorch marks had been found on the
ground, they had been told to keep quiet about
it.

I got in touch with my associate Dot Street &
told her what I had been told - we decided
to go down the base and check it all out -
I had been down before & met with S. Gaurd - he
had shown me roughly were it had happened - This
was on January 12th 1981. It was a vast
area & trees had been cleared - it was opposite about
to 2 little houses in the distance -

Dot & myself phoned up Base commander Moreland
to make appointment - on 18th Feb 1981. We thought
it was a long way ahead but agreed to that
we saw him at 6pm introduced ourselves & went
into his office - his Secretary & Moreland thought
we were M.O.D. his Secretary said " what the
incidents on 31st Dec 80'. I said 'No, on the 27th
of Dec' She said "the report was for the 31st"
we asked Moreland some questions - he asked us some -

& the car, whilst she went - but after awhile I
decided to drive down to the house - Dot was outside
talking to two old gentleman - I got into the car
& asked them some questions - They said there had
been a lot of activity in the woods between Dec 80
& Jan 81. with base alerts - they said about
30-40 Soldiers had been training in the woods -
also their T.V. had very poor reception over that
time. also their lights went on & off - a lot more
than usual - we talked for awhile then thanked them
they asked us to go again - they would ask around to
see what they could find out - we went back to
the car - Dot suggested we go back the same way as
we came - I wanted to learn as if the car broke down
we were miles from anywhere - we did go back the same
way. about a mile down the track we saw a empty
house - & stopped to investigate - the door was open- so
we went in dog & all. there was 3bags of white stuff
standing up the corner in one room some all over the floor-
I said it was probably lime or something to do with the
forest or a farmer.

Three weeks later we saw a piece in the local paper
where police had found some cocaine in that house - it had
been stored there from the coast - (we didn't know then at
the time though.)

we got back into the car & went another
300 yds or so we came to a clearing & stopped
as we saw a man walking to a white car
Dot wanted to ask him if he knew anything
but before dot could say anything he said - we're
we investigating the animals that had died in
the woods. he said there were deer, rabbits & squirrels
he thought we were from the environmental control
agency. Dot said "we were'

he told us "there were lights out there - just a few "
& some skins beings that looked just like Angels"
when he found out we were not from the M.O.D.
he stammered shut the U.F.O files which his Secretary
had brought in & told us to get in touch with the
M.O.D. in London as that is where all the U.F.O
reports go - he said 'he had said to much already!
But by him questioning us to what we knew, it
was obvious he knew something -

So far we had the S. Gaurds report & what
Moreland had told us.

When we left his office it was 9pm - we went up
to the forest to check out S. Gaurds directions - &
where I had been with him, it was snowing so
we didn't really go right to the place - we decided
to go to the other place - Friday Street where we had
been given directions to -

we entered a tunnel which lead through the woods
all went well until my car played up - as we went
further along my dog started jumping around in the back
the car was vibrating & going about 60 m.p.h.)
I thought it was going to shake to pieces - I was worried
about my dog & Dot was telling me to slow down - I told
her I couldn't do anything about it - as my foot was not
on the pedal - after about 5 mile the car stopped - I
was trembling & worried - Dot looked at me & said I
looked as though I had seen a ghost - The dog had
quietened down by this time but there was all
lumps of fur over the backing the car- I got out
& checked the engine nothing seemed to be wrong- I
had only had it serviced two days before -
we then spotted a house down in the forest- it
looked occupied - Dot suggested we go & ask some
questions there - I said I would stay with the dog

he said he came down to the woods every week - &
had seen lots of dead animals - we thanked him &
he left - we then got back into the car & started
off down the track - when my car started to play
up again stopping & starting lights flashing on & off
red ever- green ever- this was were it started to
play up going up the track - it also started to
vibrate again & came to a sudden halt as it
skidded - for no reason - we decided to go home as
it was beginning to snow again -

We phoned up the M.O.D in London when we
got home- they told us to write to them.

During the evening my dog started to growl &
show her teeth for no reason - I asked if she had
brought some more home with her. I had my car checked
by the garage next day. Nothing wrong with it !

great
Williams
Wed 18th
10.30pm Late wed night I received a phone call from
Lee who told me - The farmer phoned the police
police went out with Base commander - no C.T's
were seen - U.F.O. on 3 legs 30 ft apart -looked as
though it had some trouble - after awhile it took
off.
Next day A.10 went up to check for heat source
& radiation traces -
Security police & radiation teams checked woods
for radiation traces - opposite East gate found -
Radiation traces found also scorch marks on ground
where impressions were found
Lee told me the location in the woods where it
had landed. It was not far from where we had
been a few days before -

6

3rd witness:

Friday 20th 6pm

Had phone call from Shawn - didn't tell me anything new

Farmer phoned Bawe police. Saw craft reported it Bawe police. went out - Bawe Commander & Several other - 3 soldiers saw. repairing ship - after awhile it took off. A lot Sent up to check for radiation.

Next day woods searched for radiation traces some trees had tops scorched - branches knocked off & marks on trees where it had come down - the ground glowed when it took off with intense heat.

The area was cordoned off for several days & people told a sea aeroplane had crashed there.

＊ Funny thing was Friday Street was also cordoned off so people couldn't walk there for several days they were told bombs were found in the woods*

4th witness:
Tuesday 17th Feb

Travis phoned & told me something had landed in the forest by woodbridge base, he had been told one of their aircraft had gone down - which he didn't believe - there was a lot of activity in Rendlesham Forest - the people from Bentwaters were all in there doing something - he asked one of the soldiers what was going on - he told him Several unexploded bombs had been found - which they were blowing up just off Orford Island

＊ This coincided with about 20 mystery bangs which shook the area on 12th Feb. 20 minutes apart, the police received loads of phone calls but they didn't know what they were -

7

Tuesday 24th

Deb & myself decided to go down & have a good check this time of the landing site - First we went to the East gate it was up a road - there was a sign at the bottom reading For Authorized personal only - The Forestry Commission office was further on - we went up to the East gate & saw a barrier at the top - there was a guard house with a guard in it - when we reached the barrier he came out & asked what we wanted - had a long chat to him - he was quite nice - his name was Tom - he said an lot og the guys got bored & made the story up. so he heard -

we then left there & went up to the Forestry office - half way along the road there was a sign which said "No Entry Only by permission of the Bawe Commander" - we decided to keep going.

We got to the Forestry office & went in - there were two men inside - we asked them some questions - they said the farmer reported the U.F.O. to Bawe police because one of his cows got injured - he told them the craft made a loud humming noise & had lots of lights on it & it was supposed to have landed for 16hrs whilst being repaired. he said it was on Tuesday Dec 30th 1980 The forestry workers had searched the woods on the 28th & the 31st and found nothing as on the 28th through until 1st Jan forestry workers were cutting down trees & burning them.

They said we were not the first to go & see them - two men had been here asking questions two days after the incident supposedly happened The two forestry workers did not know who the men were only they looked official - they said

8

they didn't know who the farmer was - only that he had a smallholding in the area.

A third man then came in & said that he knew newspaper man had been at the scene. but had been told they must not report anything - all the trees around the site that had been damaged had been cut down & burnt.

They gave us permission to walk through the wood to where it landed, but said we wouldn't find anything as all traces had been removed. now -

we left there & went to several smallholdings in the area - the first one was down a road not far from the landing area.

We asked the farmer & his wife if they had seen or heard anything - he said they had it - only the English police who had been called. because - Several guys had set fire to some trees - as they were having a drag party & trying to cook a deer some one had shot - his wife said she had heard gorings in the village shop - about a craft landing by the bomb dump & lights being shown down the farmer then said - a man came by asking lots of questions - but his wife said "there was 2 men" he told us to go & see a farmer down the road on his own. same he was the farmer who reported it when we got there he was very uncooperative & looked very scared - he said he didn't know anything & didn't know what we were talking about - he told us to leave - as we left he watched us very closely.

Sat Feb 21st 81

Spoke to gentleman in pub Walford Bridge - said he travelled down to the Bawe regularly - & between 27th & 30th Dec - when coming back from the bawe one night

9

he saw a bright white light over R/F. area - he said he thought it was an aircraft, but got suspicion when it just hovered - he stopped & watched it for at least 20 mins - when he drove off the lights were still there He said it was on the 27th or 28th he couldn't remember which. but had seen no activity on other nights when driving past - no cars no trees no Soldiers nothing only the lights - this was between 11.30 pm - 1 am He said he had friends on base - & mentioned it to them. They said it was a secure alert out of that period of time -

Weds 19th Feb

Went to interview Brian from the base- worked. in the stores - he said some high ranking officer had come in & ordered parts for a car - which they did not keep on the base. So had to send to America for, Strange thing was he didn't know their High Ranking officer. & why did he come himself.

When Brian looked properly at the sheet of spares he wanted, they were aircraft components not for a car. Brian thought this very strange as he hadn't heard or seen some of the parts - but ordered them just the same - the telephone ho: he was given to ring was different from his usual no:

When he spoke to the man on the other end of the phone the men spoke in a broken American voice - like Russian or something Brian had a job to understand him.

Tom another person I met in the Walford Bridge was Brit manager on the base - he said it was a R.P.V. they were messing about with what it had electra sensitive equipment on it - that could watch Spies - & hear peoples conversation. it had a spy Camera

10

on it & could go in & out of the trees - they had been experimenting with this in the forest - it also had infra red cameras on it!

all our investigations led to the same place & the same story - at this time - Of course we heard rumours of plane crashing & satellite coming down or ...

The house owned by the Boast family. This is the closest habitation to the landing site, which is through the dense tree cover on the right hand side of the picture. Gamekeeper David Boast has proved an enigmatic witness during the investigation. A few days after the UFO landing he was visited by mysterious strangers. Despite its proximity to the house, the landing site is all but masked from view by trees

Brenda Butler (left) with Dot Street at the site, two years after the UFO event. The dog in the photograph is the one in the car when it underwent strange effects in the Friday Street/Fenn's Row area of the forest. The girls are in the area - then tree covered - when the security officers first encountered the UFO. From here it manoeuvred through the trees in the background to land on open ground beyond

Panoramic montage of the site in Rendlesham Forest. In the foreground is the area where trees were felled shortly after the events. The trace marks were somewhere in this vicinity. The boundary fence between the site and the field which hosted the landing is visible to the right of the picture. This is the one damaged by the security officers during the close encounter

Dead trees on the boundary between the forest and the field where the landing occurred. Speculation abounds that the radiation left by the UFO was involved in their death. Vic's house is visible centre right of the picture on the far edge of the field. The cattle were in front of here. The Boast home is at the extreme left of picture, also on the far edge of the field. One of these two houses was said to have 'glowed' during the encounter

Close Encounter in the forest:

In November, a Mr Jolly – then employed as a rabbit catcher on base – telephoned Brenda to say he had seen some *'little brown monk figures'* around the bomb dump on Woodbridge Base, whilst out shooting rabbits. This is what he told her:

> *"I was driving along to the bomb dump, one night at 11.30pm, when I thought I saw movement in the forest, stopped my jeep, got out, and hid behind a tree and looked through my gun-sight. I saw what I first took to be four children, dressed in monk habits, but thought it strange as I could not see any feet, or faces, and wondered why four children should be playing around at that time of the night. I telephoned the security guards on base and told them what I had seen. They told me to stay where I was and they would send two security policemen out to meet me. They arrived within 10-15mins, and got out of their car with their guns, making a lot of noise. They looked through their sights and started to walk towards the four 'children', who immediately disappeared somewhere behind the bomb dump. When we arrived at the spot, all what was left was a green, sticky, gooey mess. They picked some up and it dematerialised in their hands."*

Mr Jolly was then taken to the base security hut and asked to make a statement, which he did. He was then advised not to talk about this to anyone. He didn't, until another man, working on base, saw the same thing in a copse of trees – four little *'monk'* figures, watching him. He first thought they were children, dressed-up. He told the other workmen, but they did not report it to the authorities. After the sighting of the little *'monks'*, Mr Jolly was not allowed to go to the bomb dump area without guards being present.

Brenda:

> *"One night, after the guards had left, he was driving down the road to a different area; he saw an orange orb-light following behind him. He could see this in his wing-mirror. He stopped his jeep and got out. As he did so, the 'orange light' came up to him over his head and then whizzed off at a great speed. He did not report this.*
>
> *Another man walking his dog around the area also saw orange 'balls of light' on a regular basis coming from the Woodbridge base area, so much so that he was disappointed if one day he did not see one."*

Authors: We have ourselves spent many hours walking through the forest in recent years and have seen some odd things in the forest and captured them on camera. We cannot say there is any connection with these 'anomalies' and what Mr Jolly and the other men encountered, but found them intriguing.

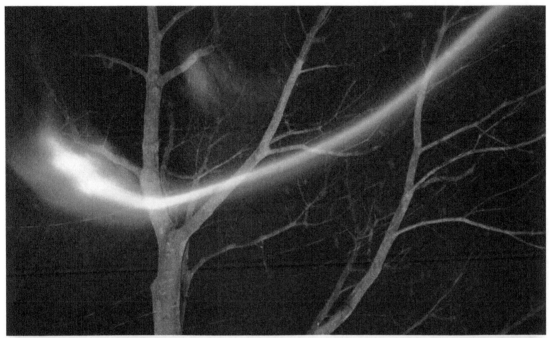

Apparent 'little man' photographed in the forest area by David Bryant

Brenda:

"So . . . there was quite a lot happening in November 1979, right through to November 1980, where once again, crafts were seen hovering over the base and bomb dump. One allegedly landed on the runway, in November 1980. Several witnesses saw crafts flying over Melton and Woodbridge, also in November 1980. Maybe they had come to pick up the little 'monk' figures, after dropping them off a year earlier.

I am still being contacted by witnesses, who wish to tell me about what he or she saw, during December 1980, forming an even bigger picture of something which will not go away, despite declassification of MOD documents pertaining to the case.

Actually, the first person who was told about a UFO having landed in the Forest, at Tangham Woods, Rendlesham, near Woodbridge Airbase, between Christmas 1980 and the New Year, was not me but my partner at the time – Chris Pennington – during a party held at the family farmhouse, at Aldringham, on New Year's Eve 1980."

Airman Steve Roberts

"Chris was approached by an airman, who asked his identity be kept secret (referred to as Steve Roberts). 'Steve' asked Chris whether he should tell me. Chris told him to go ahead.

On 2nd January 1981, 'Steve' came to my house and told me about something having come down in Tangham Woods, involving a UFO, which crash-landed just outside the perimeter of Woodbridge. They had to send to Germany for spares; two days later it was repaired and then took-off. According to 'Steve', I learnt that a local farmer – Mr Higgins – heard a noise over his farm and went out to have a look at the cattle, who were going crazy, one of whom had escaped and been hit by a taxi.

Another farmer – Mr Flemming – was summoned. He came and rendered assistance. Mr Higgins telephoned the police and told them a plane, showing lots of lights, had gone over the cattle, frightening them, before heading off in the direction of the airbase and forest. The base police sent some service personnel out to the perimeter fence, who reported seeing lights over the forest, as a result of which security officers from the airbase went out into the forest, accompanied by the base commander and some high ranking officers.

When they approached closer to the lights, they saw what looked like a 'craft' of some sort, in trouble, accompanied by three 'entities', suspended in shafts of light. Shortly afterwards the 'craft' took off and hovered over the treetops for a while, before heading at great speed across the sky. An A10 was sent up to check for radiation and heat source. There were supposed to have been films and cine film taken, but these have been currently misplaced. Newspaper reporters were also supposedly to have been there, but were warned not to publish anything. The security guard said there was communication between the commanding officer and the 'entities'."

Landing area pointed out:

Following a visit into the forest with 'Steve', on the 12th January 1981, where the 'landing area was pointed out', Brenda was approached by a forestry worker, who told her he had found some of the branches and trees in the forest burnt and scorched, and that he had been warned to keep quiet.

Brenda:

> *"Next time we saw 'Steve Roberts' he tried to deny it all but, by that time, the housing officer on base had been telling people about the UFO in the bar on base. He even came to us and told us the same story. The story was getting bigger – then, all of a sudden, he was sent back to the States. Nobody knew why, or how – he just went.*
>
> *Was it because he was talking out of term? It seems strange he was sent back so quickly."*

Our enquires revealed his return back to the States was due to personal commitments rather than through any association with the UFO incident.

During the week of the 10th February 1981, Brenda went to the base and interviewed Brian, who worked in the stores. He told of being approached by a high ranking USAF officer, who came in and ordered parts for a car, which they didn't keep on the base.

Oddly, Brian had never heard of the officer and, when he examined the order, discovered it was for *aircraft components*, which he had no knowledge of, but carried out the instructions and ordered the parts, using the telephone number given (which was not the regular number used) from a man who spoke in broken American, believed to have been possibly Russian.

Another version of events was give to Brenda by Tom – a bank manager on the airbase. He heard that it was *"a remote propelled vehicle, carrying sensitive equipment that had gone astray".*

RAF LIAISON OFFICE
Royal Air Force Bentwaters Woodbridge Suffolk IP12 2RQ

Telephone Woodbridge 3737 ext 2257

MOD (DS8a)

Your reference

Our reference BENT/019/7
AI
Date *15 January 1981*

UNIDENTIFIED FLYING OBJECTS (UFO's)

I attach a copy of a report I have received from the Deputy Base Commander at RAF Bentwaters concerning some mysterious sightings in the Rendlesham forest near RAF Woodbridge. The report is forwarded for your information and action as considered necessary.

D H MORELAND
Squadron Leader
RAF Commander

Copy to:

SRAFLO, RAF Mildenhall

February 1981 – a visit to see Squadron Leader Donald Moreland

Brenda revisited the base with Dot Street, after having telephoned Squadron Leader Donald Moreland, who agreed to see them on the 18th February 1981. When they arrived at the base they were shown into the office – after introductions, Squadron Leader Moreland and his secretary erroneously presumed the two women were from the MOD and that their visit was with regard *to an incident on the 31st December 1980.* Brenda said, *"No . . . the 27th December".*

The secretary replied: *"The report was for the 31st".* Brenda and Dot asked Squadron Leader Moreland some questions. He replied: *"There were some lights out there – just a few, and some shiny 'beings' that looked just like angels".* When he discovered they were not from the MOD, he slammed shut the UFO file, which his secretary had bought in, and told them to get in touch with the MOD in London.

After leaving the office at 5pm, the two women intended to return to the scene of the incident, previously shown by 'Steve Roberts' but, as it was snowing, set out along Friday Street, when they encountered a problem with the car being driven by Brenda.

> *"While driving along a track through the woods, the car began to vibrate – as if it was going to shake itself to pieces. The dog in the back started jumping up and down. Dot told me to slow down, as the car was moving at 60mph. I told her I couldn't do anything about it, as my foot wasn't even on the pedal. After about half a mile, the car came to a stop. I was trembling with fear. There were lumps of fur in the back of the car from the dog. I got out and checked the car. Dot suggested we go to a nearby house and continue our investigations. I declined, saying I should stop there, but after a short period started the car and drove down to where she was stood outside, talking to two elderly gentlemen. They told us there had been an increase in activity in the forest between December 1980, and January 1981, involving the appearance of 30-40 soldiers seen on a training exercise, and that they had experienced poor reception on the TV and power cuts."*

Television and electrical interference

Two old brothers who lived in the heart of Rendlesham Forest and very near to the airbase of RAF Woodbridge were visited by DS and BB as part of their investigations in the immediate area. The two men did not actually see anything, but said that their television and lights kept flickering during the month of January 1981. Inaddition to this they had noticed an increase in the military activity during this time.

SCUFORI investigator Martin Shipp, with Dot Street talk to one of the brothers outside the house where they had been troubled by television and electrical disturbances.

Brenda and Dot thanked the two men and made their way back along the same route, when they came across an empty house with the front door open. Curious, they went inside and noticed three bags of white powder in the corner of the room, which they presumed was lime or some other chemical used by forestry commission workers.

While on the way back along the track, the car began to stop and start. Fortunately, Brenda was able to coax it home. An examination by the local garage revealed no problems with it.

They were shocked to discover, a few weeks later, while reading the local newspaper that the police had seized a quantity of cocaine, stored at the same house they had gone into. Over the next few days, Brenda was to receive a number of telephone calls from other witnesses, who told of rumours about something having landed in the forest near the airbase, believed by some to be an aircraft which had crash-landed, and that a number of soldiers had been seen in the forest.

One man asked the soldiers what they were doing in the forest and was told they were blowing up *'several unexploded bombs'* found in the forest at the nearby Orford Island – no doubt the explanation for a number of calls made to the police on the 12th February 1981.

Brenda Butler:

> *"Dot and I decided to go down into the forest and re-examine the landing site. First, we went to the East Gate barrier and chatted to 'Tom' – the armed guard on the gate, who thought the incident was just a story, fabricated by bored personnel. We then set off into the forest, ignoring a sign that read 'No Entry – Only By Permission Of Base Commander', and made our way to the Forestry Office, where, during a conversation with them, they divulged that the farmer had reported the UFO to the base police because one of his cows had been injured, and that the 'craft' had made a loud humming noise, had lots of lights on it, and was supposed to have landed for four hours, whist being repaired, on Tuesday 30th December, 1980."*

The East Gate barrier at the airbase.

Brenda and Dot continued their enquiries at various smallholdings in the forest. On one occasion, a farmer and his wife spoke about having been contacted by the police, who said they were investigating a drugs party held in the forest, when trees had been set on fire and someone had tried to cook a deer which had been shot.

His wife told the two women it was common gossip in the village that a 'craft' had landed by the bomb dump and lights had been shone down.

Centenary House, Leeds – Lecture by Charles Halt

Colonel Halt served several combat tours in South East Asia. He was a USAF F-16 Base Commander in both Korea and Belgium, and served 28 years in military commission service. He holds BSc's in Economics, Chemistry and a Master Degree in Business Administration. His final assignment was Director of the Inspection Directorate for the US Department of Defense with overall responsibly of the entire military establishment. He retired in June 1992.

A CLOSE ENCOUNTER OF THE THIRD KIND NEAR WOODBRIDGE, SUFFOLK? by Dot Street

(An account of this case initially appeared in "Lantern", Summer 1981, pp.17-18).

Early in February this year (1981) I heard from my friend and associate, Brenda Butler, about an alleged UFO landing near Woodbridge in Suffolk. We arranged to meet and visit the area, and our initial visit took place on Wednesday, February 18, 1981.

Brenda told me of what she knew at that time, namely that she had heard from several people who claimed to have witnessed a UFO landing in Rendlesham Forest some- time around the beginning of January this year. She had very little information regarding the sighting at this time, save that an object with three legs together with 'entities' who appeared to be doing something to the craft had been seen and that she had also heard that communication had been made between these 'entities' and personnel from the nearby USAF base at RAF Bentwaters.

On February 18th, Brenda and I went to the air-base and made an appointment to see the Base Commander. Whilst we were talking to his secretary and arranging to see the Commander, we mentioned that the sighting took place in January, to which his secretary replied (without prompting), "The beginning of January?" When we confirmed that this was so, she seemed more determined for us to see the Commander whom later that day we did see.

The Commander asked us for some form of identification. I showed him my BUFORA membership card, but he obviously did not accept it and said that without proper identification he could not say anything. As we told him what we knew of the sighting he told us, smiling all the time, that he didn't know anything about it. He then asked us if we were going to continue our investigation. I replied, "Yes." What would we do with our information, he asked. I said we would do the same as them - file it!

Although the Base Commander would not say anything concerning the report, we left his office with the distinct impression he knew far more than he had been saying.

We then went to the part of the forest where the landing had allegedly taken place, but we saw nothing out of the ordinary.

Several days later, Brenda heard from a man. He refused to give her his name, but said that the report was true and gave her directions as to how to get to the site where the object had landed. At a later date, this witness said that he had been told to speak to no-one about the sighting, and later still he denied all knowledge of it!

On February 24th, Brenda and I decided to pay another visit to Rendlesham Forest in an attempt to locate the landing site using the directions given to us by the anonymous caller. Unfortunately, owing to the fact that the directions were somewhat vague, we could not locate the place. Finally we went to the Forestry Commission's office where we had an interesting conversation with the man on duty. He told us that he had been working in the office on January 1st, when a man walked in and said that he had just been talking to a farmer who, on December 29th, 1980, had heard a very loud noise which had frightened his animals. The farmer also said that at the same time the area around his farm had been illuminated by a very bright, white light. He (the farmer) then telephoned RAF Woodbridge who sent men out to investigate. The whole episode, he said, lasted about four hours.

Unfortunately, no one seems to know who this farmer is, and we have heard that he has been told (presumably by the security people at the air-base) not to say anything about what happened. We have also been unable to trace the man who told this story to the Forestry Commission employee.

While we were in the office, another forestry worker came in and told us that his wife's friend's husband had also seen a UFO that same night, and that his account tied in with that of the other witnesses. He then showed us on a map exactly where the whole incident was supposed to have happened; he also said that his men had been right through that part of the forest but had not seen anything untoward, although it is worth noting that since the incident tree-felling has taken place in that part of the forest.

After leaving the Forestry Commission's office, we went to talk to people living in the immediate area. At one farm-house we were told that the residents had been visited by two men on January 1st, who had asked the same questions as us. One of these two unidentified visitors also mentioned that they had interviewed Forestry Commission workers. The people at this farm also told us that they had heard that something had happened that night, on the air-base bomb disposal site which is nowhere near the site pointed out to us by the Forestry Commission man. At all the other houses we visited everyone else said that they knew nothing of the report.

Although I am still investigating this report, with all the pieces of information gleaned so far the account of the sighting seems to be as follows:

On the evening of December 28th, 1980, a farmer living near Rendlesham Forest was woken up by his restless cattle. He went outside to see what was wrong with them and noticed that the sky was lit up as bright as the day. At the same time he heard a loud and unusual noise unlike that of any aircraft (living next to an operational air-base he is very familiar with the sounds of aircraft). He contacted RAF Woodbridge/ Bentwaters who sent out security men to investigate. The farmer then became aware of an object, seemingly in some sort of trouble, hovering over the forest. When the security men arrived, they too saw the object and contacted the base who acknowledged by sending more personnel. By this time the object had landed and three 'entities', surrounded by a white glow, were seen floating around the 'craft', which stood on three legs some 30 feet apart. These 'entities' appeared to be doing something to their craft. It is said that some sort of communication took place between the base personnel and the 'entities' and that the former were instructed to leave their weapons behind and to assist with the damaged craft. One report suggests that the craft was, in fact, removed to the air-base. While this was happening a member of the public witnessed it all and what he says ties in with reports from other witnesses. The incident lasted about four hours and we have also been told that during this period there were power failures in the area. Because of the involvement of the British Government, all of the witnesses who initially contacted us (some of them were air-base personnel) now refuse to talk further - and one witness has actually denied any knowledge of the incident! They say that they have been told to keep quiet and fear for their jobs if they do not. I myself know one of the witnesses personally and can vouch for his honesty, but even he now refuses to discuss the incident. For obvious reasons I have not revealed the names of the witnesses.

On February 18th Brenda Butler 'phoned the Ministry of Defence about this incident and was told to write. She later received a reply to her letter in which the MOD denied any knowledge of the incident and said they were unable to give any further information.

N.B. Contrary to any rumour or reference to the above case that may be found printed elsewhere, "Earthlink" possesses no more information about it than has already been made freely available in widely circulated publications. (Ed.)

In 1988, Colonel Halt travelled to England to attend a number of media engagements, which had been arranged by Manchester based Solicitor – Harry Harris. Colonel Halt addressed a small gathering at Todmorden, Lancashire, before travelling to Centenary House, Leeds, where he spoke to 150 people about his role in the incident. (Tickets at £4.50pence)

Colonel Charles Halt also gave a further illuminating personal account during a lecture held at St. George Community College, England, in August 1997, following a visit to London, made on the 27th June 1997, when he took part in a 'Strange But True' live TV debate.

> *"In the spring of 1980, I was finishing my tour and had been hand-picked to go to Oslo, in Norway, to be Commander of US Forces there. However, it seemed the CINC in Europe, the Commander-in-Chief's Executive, wanted the job and had a little more pull than I did, so I was given the option to go to Italy, Bentwaters, England, or two or three other places. Fortunately, or unfortunately, I picked Bentwaters, England, arriving in the summer of 1980. At that time, it was the peak of the Cold War. There was an awful lot of activity. Bentwaters-Woodbridge twin base complex was home of the 81st Tactical Fighter Wing, which possessed six squadrons of fighters – being the largest fighter wing in the free world, charged primarily with stopping the enemy armour as they came across Germany, should that ever happen.*
>
> *Just before Christmas, in 1980, I was in the habit of going out and spending evenings riding around with the police, visiting the fire department, going to the dining hall, into the medics,*

the clinic, just trying to be the eyes and ears of base, finding out what was going on, when a *strange incident was brought to my attention."

John Burroughs:

"We saw some weird red and blue flashing lights in the trees, east of the gate, and decided to go and have a look. We went down the East Gate road, turned right at the stop sign, and walked along the tarmac road, ten or twenty yards, before turning left along the forest road. At this point I saw a white light shining down onto the trees, accompanied by the red and blue flashing ones. At this point, we decided to return to East Gate and report the incident to the base."

John Burroughs

The cleared area of Rendlesham Forest

Lt. Fred Buran was on duty at Building 679 Central Security Control, when he received a call at 3am from AIC John Burroughs who told him he had sighted some strange lights in the wooded area east of the runway, at Woodbridge, and that following the arrival of Sgt. Penniston and his rider Airman Cabansag, Lt. Buran directed Staff Sgt. Coffey – the Duty Security Controller, to ask Jim Penniston whether they could have been marker lights.

Jim Penniston:

"I have never seen lights like this before. They were red, blue, white, and orange lights, no further than 100yds from the road east of the runway."

Jim Penniston

---

*This strange incident involved Airman John Burroughs who was on guard duty at the East Gate entrance when Sgt 'Budd' Steffens pulled up in his truck and invited him to join him on security patrol. The two men then entered the Forest.

Fred Buran:

> *"Jim Penniston then asked permission to investigate and was joined by Security Flight Chief MSgt. Chandler. I monitored the progress of Penniston, Burroughs and Cabansag, as they entered the wooded area, and appeared to get very close to the lights."*

John Burroughs:

> *"By the time we arrived, the lights were still in the sky above the woods. A security patrol turned up and we asked to go with them. After parking the truck, we went on foot across an open field, when we heard what sounded like a woman screaming and many animal noises. The area was lit up with light. All three of us hit the ground, when whatever it was started moving back towards the open fields. After a minute or two, we got up and moved into the trees and the lights moved out into the open field."*

In an interview held in 1990, John described the object as:

> *". . . a bank of lights; differently coloured lights, that threw off an image of, 'like a craft'. (Other reports refer to an object showing a bank of blue lights on it). I never saw anything metallic, or anything hard. Everything seemed like it was different when we were in that clearing. The sky didn't seem the same . . . it was like a weird feeling, like everything seemed slower than you were actually doing, and all of a sudden, when the object was gone, everything was like normal again. To be honest, I was hoping that when I got out there, after reporting it, that basically I would see nothing – there would be no tell-tale evidence of anything which would make it easier for me to accept, but when you get out there and you find damage to the trees, and depressions in the ground, that makes it even more unexplainable."*

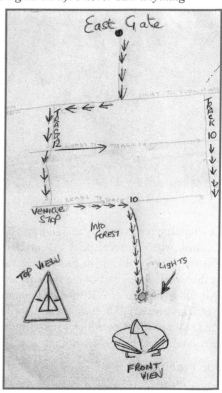

Philip Mantle Interview:

Speaking to Philip Mantle a few years ago for an article (later published) in *Matrix Magazine* Volume 1 Issue 3, John was asked a number of questions about his recollection of the incident, now 30 years previous.

During the interview John says the incident lasted between 3am and was finished by 5 and 6am and that he only went into the forest twice.

Illustration: Author unknown

> *"I did not hear any rumours or conversations the next day about the incident as I lived off base. I was not officially told to keep quiet, threatened, interrogated or that I could not talk about what had transpired. People have accused us of telling lies and then they tell us that it was this or that. We were hung out to dry"*

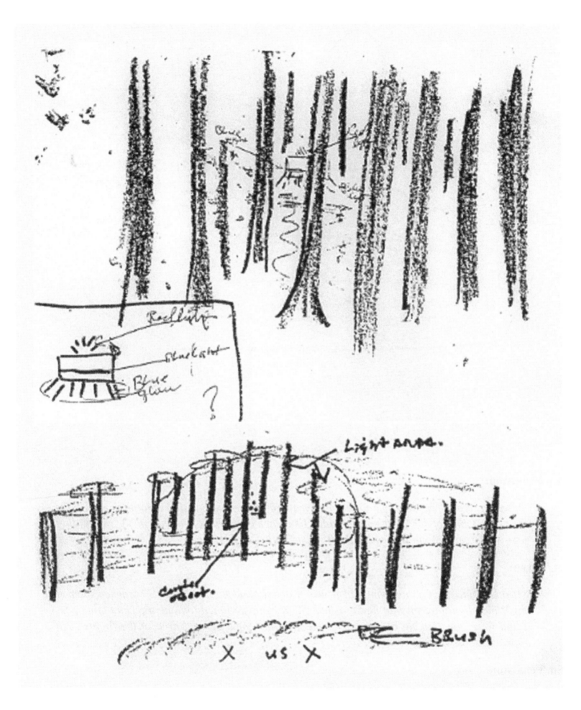

Jim Penniston made sketches of the incident.

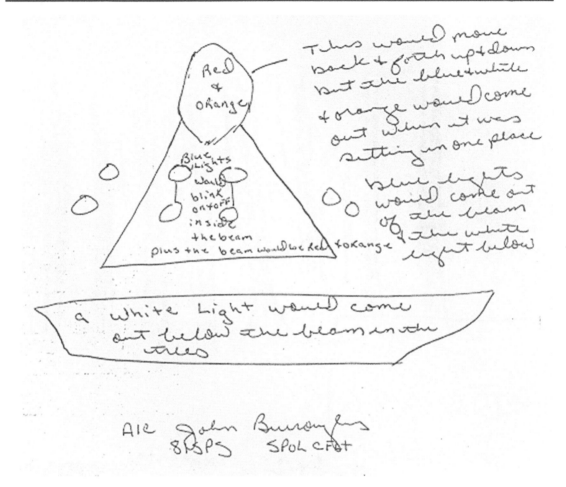

Jim Penniston:

> *"It was a 'craft'- the size of a tank – and triangular in shape, with a smooth surface, like glass. The fabric of the 'craft' was moulded like black glass, but opaque or misty. No landing gear was apparent, but it seemed like it was standing on fixed legs."*

Lt. Buran:

> *"At one point, SSgt. Penniston said it was a definite mechanical object. I warned them it might be a light aircraft that had crashed. SSgt. Penniston then told me they had gone past it and were now looking at a marker beacon in the same general area of the 'lights'. He appeared somewhat agitated."*

Jim Penniston:

> *"I walked around the 'craft' and finally walked right up to it and noticed it had an outer surface, consisting of what appeared to be smooth, opaque, black glass, with bluish lights fluctuating from black to grey, to blue.*

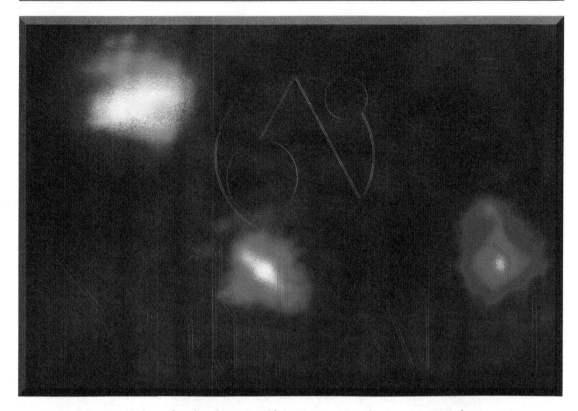

I was pretty much confused at this point. I kept trying to put this in some sort of perspective, hoping to find some logical explanation as to what it was and what was going on, against a background of silence – not even the noises of animals anymore. I felt like as if I was moving in slow motion. I had my notebook and camera with me, so began to make written notes of the object now in front of me, which was triangular in shape, with a top portion producing mainly white light, encompassing most of the upper section of the 'craft', with a small amount of white light spilling out of the bottom.

On its left side centre was a bluish light; the other side was red. The lights seem to be moulded into the exterior of the object, rather than any additional attachment, and were smooth, slowly fading into the rest of the outside of the structure of the 'craft'. I also made a point of memorizing as much detail as I could of the object in front of me, for what seemed like hours, but in fact, was only minutes. Finally, I unleashed my camera case cover and brought the camera up to focus. I began snapping photo after photo, and took the full roll of 36 pictures.

On the 'craft's' smooth exterior shell there was writing of some kind, but I couldn't quite distinguish it, so I moved closer, seeing three-inch lettering, rather symbols, that stretched for the length of two feet – maybe a little more. I then proceeded to touch the object, but was only able to for a short time. I touched the symbols and I could feel the shapes, as if they were inscribed, or etched, or engraved, like a diamond cut on glass. Suddenly, the white light on the object instantly grew brighter. John Burroughs and I jumped backwards in defence, and threw ourselves onto the floor for cover."

Now almost blinding the men with white light flooding out from the top, the object moved upwards off the ground, about 3ft, and then silently started to move slowly, weaving back through the trees – maybe half a foot per second. Within a couple of minutes, it rose to a distance of about 200ft off the ground and, following a momentary pause *'in the blink of an eye'*, was gone.

After the object had gone Burroughs and Penniston, dazed and confused from their encounter, became aware of everything returning to normal, seeing the lighthouse in the distance, and stars – almost as if time had slowed down while the experience had taken place.

As they walked back to the logging road, Burroughs noticed *'three triangular indentations in the forest floor, each about three metres apart, in the same place as the object was first sighted'*, and assumed *'it had been caused by the object sitting on the ground'*. After making a note of the three indentations, the two men continued on their way back to the base, where they met Cabansag, and went back to the base.

Lt. Buran:

> *"At 0345hrs, I terminated the search and ordered them back to the base. After talking with SSgt. Penniston, face-to-face, I was convinced he saw something out of the realm of explanation. I found him to be a totally reliable and mature individual. Later that morning, I discovered there had been several others sightings."*

After returning to the base, they were instructed to report to the shift Commander's office, and were told, according to John Burroughs:

> *"It is best you keep quiet about what you have just seen. You saw something. Heathrow tower confirms you saw something. You should go out and look for some physical proof of what happened."*

Penniston and Burroughs went back into the forest, to check for any evidence to support their story. Burroughs was hoping there would be nothing out there, but discovered what appeared to be scorch marks on the trees, along with branch damage and the three indentations, which they had found earlier, so they decided to leave the area.

Jim Penniston made his way to a friend's house, near Ipswich, and collected the necessary ingredients to make plaster casts, and made his way back to the forest, where he took plaster casts of the three indentations.

Colonel Charles Halt brandishing a plaster cast of one of the impressions left in the soil following the incident in the forest

Brenda Butler:

> *"When I lectured with Colonel Halt, in 1996, he produced a plaster cast – the size of a football, made of the marks/impressions found on the forest floor. It looked like concrete to me, with small 'fish tank stones' sticking out of it – the sort of thing you would have found on*

a gravel path, rather than a forest, with pine needles sticking out of the top. This 'evidence' was carried in a shopping bag, as shown on a photo sent to you, which I thought was rather unprofessional. Colonel Halt wouldn't let anyone handle the cast, as he thought it might be damaged, although he allowed me to handle it. My impression was it appeared to be a lump of small, shapeless, concrete and heavy. I have to be honest I don't think people were impressed with the showing of this item at all, although I mean no criticism of the Colonel, whom I have every respect for."

Colonel Halt 2013: *"Jim Penniston gave one to me; they were not the size of a dinner plate."*

Mark Birdsall, of the Yorkshire based UFO Society, was also very interested in the events that had taken place outside the airbase and wrote to the RAF Bentwaters during the early 1980s, asking them if they had any information regarding the matter.

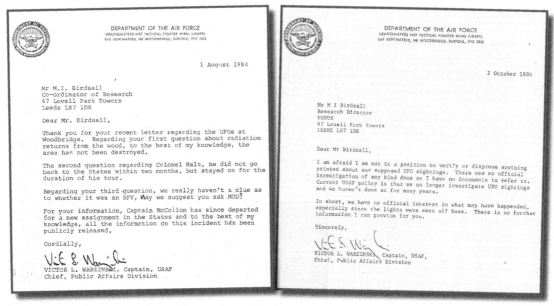

Colonel Halt: (In an interview with Jonathon Dillon)

> *"I decided to take two plaster casts of these cavities and naturally, I still have one left today. Jim Penniston also made three others without telling anyone he had them, until someone stole them from his luggage while going through customs. I gave him another one, which he buried at the bottom of his garden in the States. They didn't get mine though, so I'm currently having some tests done on that, plus other soil samples I kept from the forest."*

Dennis Porley

At 2.30am on 26th December 1980, Dennis Porley from Harwich, Essex (a mate on a tug boat) was driving along the A137, and had just passed the turn-off for Alton Water, on his left –

> *". . . when I saw what I took to be a marine distress flare, or rocket, going up over Mistley Quay, but then realised this could not be the case, as it did not explode in flight.*

I continued on my journey – now descending a steep hill, at which point I lost sight of whatever it was. As I ascended the hill on the other side, close to a nearby railway line, I saw the object again in the sky. It looked like a rocket, or plane on fire, about the size of a full moon, but more red in colour. I lost sight of it, once again, due to the contours of the countryside, but then saw it again – this time behind me. I decided to pull-up halfway between Brantham and Stutton, to obtain a closer look, as it slowly moved over Stutton Point, before descending over Hollesley Bay, where I lost sight of it.

When I returned to work after the Christmas period, I happened to mention what I had seen to a colleague. He suggested it might have been a large meteorite, which I don't believe was the case. Neither could it have been the *Cosmos 749 Russian Satellite, as this had splashed down one day previously."

Dennis Porley,
————— Lane,
Gt. Oakley,
Harwich,
Essex.

1068

Tel. 01255 ———

18/06/02

Dear Sir,

I am writing in reply to your letter in the Evening Gazette about your interest in UFO sightings, I don't know if what I have to say is of any use to you but it concerns the Rendlesham Forest sighting in Dec. 1980. I did write a letter about this to the News of the World after their article a few years after the sighting but got no reply, apart from this I have only talked about what I saw with a few colleagues at work and friends and family who have shown some interest in the subject.

Early on the morning of Boxing Day 26th Dec. (it was definitely the 26th) I was returning home to Great Oakley from Ipswich after taking my parents home, they having just spent Christmas Day with us, I cant remember what the time was, although I would have thought it was between 2 & 3 O'clock give or take 30mins or so. I was at the time driving an old FX4D London Taxi so its speed was not great, about 40 to 45mph much slower up hill. As I reached approx. point "A" on the map I saw what at the time I thought was a marine distress rocket over Mistley Quay, I soon realised it wasn't because it didn't explode it just seemed to hang there although it was probably moving, its difficult to say because I was driving at the time. Shortly after point "A" on map "1" the road goes down quite a large hill to the stream on the map then up a steep hill to the R/H bend before the rail line. I lost sight of the object going down the hill and didn't think very much of it at this time but as I was getting near the top of the hill on the way up I saw it again, it seemed a bit more to the East than when I first saw it, over the river, so I slowed down and drove slowly watching it. It looked a bit like a rocket but not quite, perhaps like an aeroplane on fire although I've never seen one, just a ragged edged glow about the size and brightness of the full moon, a bit more red, no structure. By this time I was thinking "That's strange, what the devil is it". I then lost sight of it again behind The Bull pub and having turned the corner it was now about 45 degrees behind me on my left, I drove on to point "B" on the map and pulled up across the entrance to a farm driveway. From here I could see it through my rear window travelling quite slowly over Stutton Point, it then disappeared behind trees between the Point and Stutton village. It must have been at least 4 mins between first seeing it and losing it behind the trees, I then drove quite quickly to the bridge over the river at Cattawade and stopped for a few seconds to look down the river; Nothing. I was interested enough to drive home along the South of the river, not my usual way home but a good view across the river from higher ground; Still nothing. I went home wondering what I had seen, it wasn't like anything I had seen before or since.

I was at this time working for ARC Marine who were running a ballast dredging operation in the river, I was Mate on the Tug "Pen Deben" I later went on to become Engineer then Master of their Dredger "Arco Stour". When I returned to work after the Christmas holiday I was talking about what I had seen when someone said there had been reports of a large meteorite seen over the South Coast, I then got the charts out and said something to the effect that I was sure it wasn't a meteorite and that whatever it was came down in the Hollesley Bay area, I was then told by someone that this was strange because a ship in that area had reported over the radio during the holiday that they could see a strange light. They were told either by The Coast Guard or Harwich Harbour that it was probably a fishing boat. Ships in this area see fishing boats all the time, they know what they look like. No one would report something so common and I think the authorities would also know this. I have traced the approximate trajectory of what I saw onto the maps in red from the point where it appeared to be when I first saw it, to where I lost sight of it and then on to where from the charts I thought it would have come down. I had also several years previous to this when working at sea seen a large meteorite which travelled over about a 90 degree arc of sky, it was nothing like what I saw that night, the meteorite looked like a meteorite, it was also much faster. I have also seen reports that what was seen during this incident was the Orford Light House. We see this reflected off the clouds over the area on occasions and know exactly what it is. I really can't remember if there was cloud that night or not, so couldn't say at what height the object was but it appeared to be low in the atmosphere and getting lower all the time.

Dennis Porley

It was discovered that a brilliant fireball (meteor) was seen over much of southern England at 2.50am on that day (as recorded in the BAA (Meteor Section, Newsletter No. 4, Feb 1981).

(Source: Personal interview)

---

*Actually we learnt that it was the upper stage of a launch rocket, not a true satellite, and would not have had a nuclear plant on board – unlike the nuclear powered Cosmos 954, which crashed over Canada, in 1978.

Chris Arnold:

> *"My flight chief, at Bentwaters, asked me if I wanted to head out to Woodbridge to meet up with Burroughs and see what was up. I grabbed the back gate keys and took the back way to RAF Woodbridge. I met Burroughs at the East Gate of Woodbridge. We left our guns with the guy riding with Burroughs and drove to the end of the long access road. We left our vehicle and walked out there. There was absolutely nothing in the woods. We could see lights in the distance and it appeared unusual, as it was a sweeping light (we did not know about the lighthouse on the coast at the time). We also saw some strange coloured lights in the distance, but were unable to determine what they were. Contrary to what some people assert, at the time almost none of us knew there was a lighthouse at Orford Ness. Remember, the vast majority of folks involved were young people, 19, 20, 25 years old. Consequently it wasn't something most of the troops were cognizant of. That's one reason the lights appeared interesting, or out of the ordinary, to some people."*

(Source: James Easton)

Involvement of the Suffolk Police

On the 25th December 1980, Police Constable David King and PC Martyn Brophy were posted to night duty.

During that shift, if it was quiet, they would call in at RAF Bentwaters Law Enforcement Office Desk. They normally did this between 2am and 5am.

David King:

> *"While we were there the Security Police telephoned through, reporting strange lights in the forest at East Gate, RAF Woodbridge."*

(The 999 call was made at 4.11am on the 26th December, by Chris Arnold – the USAF Law Enforcement Officer, at RAF Bentwaters – reporting:

> " . . . *some unusual lights in the sky. We have sent some unarmed troops to investigate. We are terming it as a UFO at present."*

David King:

"We were on the way there when we were redirected to Otley Post Office, after a report of a burglary in process. After arriving, we followed the security airmen in our police car into the forest, in an easterly direction, until the track stopped. We were then shown the direction in which other security personnel had gone on ahead of us, in search of the 'lights'.

We decided to make our way into the forest on foot, leaving the escorting airmen to return to base. We had no problems navigating our way through the forest, due to the lack of lower growth on the pine trees, which were close together. All we saw was a white flashing light in the distance, which I worked out was the Orford Lighthouse, and made our way back, where I noticed the airmen had all gone. I forgot about the incident until the next night, when I came on duty, at 10pm, and read through the logs for the day, when I came across a message, timed at 10am, 26th December 1980 (6 hours after our attendance) to the effect that the Security Police had returned to the forest and found marks in the ground, which could have been made by a UFO. The 'message' indicated an officer, from Woodbridge Police Station (PC Creswell) had attended and written-up the log as, 'the indentations' (marks) appeared to have been made by animals."

DAVID KING

TRIMLEY St MARY
FELIXSTOWE
SUFFOLK
IP11

TEL. 01394

Dear JOHN.

A Reply to your letter to me about the UFO. sighting or sighting's at Rendlesham Forest Near Woodbridge on 26ᵀᴴ December 1980. and days to follow. I, like yourself Retired 3½ year's ago at 55 having served 26 year's in the Suffolk Force. Most of the time in the Woodbridge area.

2

I will answer your question's first

'Yes' I did attend, with a young officer Martyn BROPHY He left the force a few year's after the incident. (Nothing to do with the incident) Martyn lived at Newmarket. I don't know what he is doing now or where he is. I did not sense any mood of the USAF airmen, and we both felt we were on a 'wide Goose chase'. (I will explain later.) We never took any photographs because we never saw anything. and Never carried a camera anyway in those days. We were the only two officers on duty in the area at the time and "no one" else would have attended being Bank Holiday and as you know we were short of staff for 2 days.

THE INCIDENT.

(as far as I was concerned.)
Martyn and I were teamed up to cover the whole area of Woodbridge all very quiet, a clear and dry night. No wind.
Around 4am we were contacted by Headquarters to attend the "east Gate" entrance of RAF Woodbridge as strange lights were seen in the forest by security airmen.
We arrived and were escorted into the forest in a easterly

4

direction. We followed the security airmen in our vehicle until the track stopped.
We were then shown the direction in which other security airmen had gone off ahead of us in search of the strange lights.
We went on foot into the forest. The airmen who had taken us, must have gone back to base.
We walked for 15 - 20 minutes we could see quite clearly through the trees because fir trees close together do not have lower branches.
"All we saw was a white flashing light in the distance, which I worked out was "Orford Light House"

5-

on the coast.
Being a Beach sea fisherman I have often seen and fished close to the Light House.
WE NEVER HEARD OR SAW ANYTHING ELSE. IT WAS QUIET AND CLEAR NIGHT. A STILL NIGHT
We made our way back to our vehicle. all other airmen had gone, there were no other vehicles to be seen. We went back to Woodbridge Police station. giving FHQ an update, who had in turn contacted Various airways and all said. no aircraft was or had been flying in the area.
I forgot about the incident.
Reporting back on duty at 10pm

---

that following evening. I checked through the logs for the day and found a Message / log. timed at about 10am 26/12/80 (6 hours after I attended) that the security Police on RAF Woodbridge had Returned to the forest and found Marks on the ground which could have been made by a U.F.O. [maybe smaller?]
an officer from the Woodbridge Police station attend and Resulted the log. as, indentation's appeared to have been made by animals.
In the early hours of 27th December 1980. 2-3 am. Martyn and Myself called at RAF Bentwaters Law enforcement Desk

as we normally did. (on nights)
While there the security Police
of RAF Woodbridge contacted the
Law enforcement Desk stating
Strange Lights again in the Forest.
at East Gate RAF Woodbridge.
As we had Nothing better to
do we decided to attend.
Because Nothing was seen or
heard 24 Hours Previous I did not
inform F.H.Q. that we were going.
Before we arrived at RAF
Woodbridge we received a call
from our F.H.Q. of a Post office
being broken into (a Burglary) at
Otley which was in the opposite
direction to RAF Woodbridge
so we attended the Burglary and

8.
Finished our shift there. (6.am)
The Next thing I Knew about
the incident was 4 or 5 years later
when I was told about the book
"SKY CRASH" with contents about
the UFO sighting in Rendlesham Forest.
In the Book no one can make up
their minds what Night it happened
on. Some say it happened on 2 or 3
Nights.
I was interviewed by a Journalist
"HANK" (Can not Remember his surname)
from America about a year later
and in 1997 1995 I was interviewed
by LWT (London Weekend T.V.) for
their "Strange But True" Programme
I did not hear from either of them
again. (I didn't say what they

(wanted to hear I suppose.)

My comments about the incident.
I found it Strange that the
Base Commander was on duty at
the time and that security Police
from Base went beyond their
Perimeter fence to find out what
it was BEFORE we arrived. They
never did before, they would always
tell us and wait for us to arrive.
Even Col Halt's Report states
3 am on 27 December 1980. which
it could have been because we were
called on the second night at that
time but were diverted as explained
earlier.
I always found the americans

10
quite a friendly lot but also
found them stranger than the
UFO sightings. They even set up
flood Lights in the forest on the
second Night in case the UFO.
came back so they could get a
Better Look!! or so the book
State's. Perhaps I am strange

I have enclosed a Paper cutting
about the "Strange But True?" programme
on T.V. 2 weeks ago. Did you see it?

Sorry I have gone on and on and
my english is Not perfect. or spelling.
But I just write what I want to
Say.
                    David King
anything else you want to Known Ringme

David King:

"I never gave the matter any further thought, until some years ago, when I learnt about the book 'Sky Crash', and can only comment that I found it personally strange that the Deputy Commander was on base duty at the time, and that the security police went beyond their perimeter fence to investigate the matter before we arrived, taking into consideration the policy then in existence, being that they would always wait for us before venturing out into the forest, as this area was outside their jurisdiction. It was quite common for the English police officers to spend a lot of time on base. In fact, there was an office designated for their use on Bentwaters, specifically, as it was 'quite common' to call into the airbase at least once a night, to check if there were any matters that should be brought to their attention. I don't know what to make of the now well publicised incident. I never saw anything myself, although I did see some strange red lights, low on the horizon, near the village of Burstall. What it meant I don't know, but it was strange."

We wrote to Dave, asking him some further questions, and he wrote back with the following answers – which are self-explanatory.

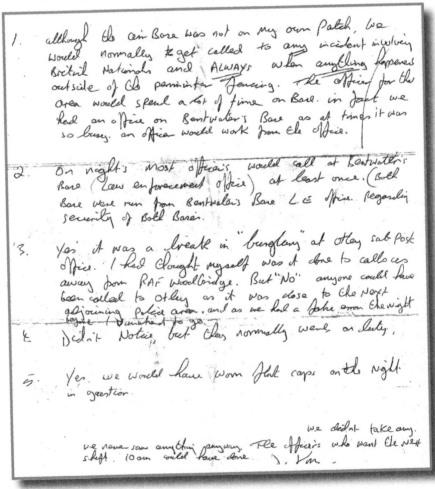

Suffolk Constabulary

In November 1983, a letter sent to the Suffolk Constabulary, enquiring about their knowledge of the incident(s) was answered by the Chief Constable.

> *"Police knowledge of this matter is limited to a telephone call of the alleged incident, timed at 4.11am, 26th December, and received from a person at RAF Bentwaters, together with the two subsequent visits to the location by police officers. The first visit followed immediately the reported incident and the two officers who attended made a search of the area with a negative result. A note on the log indicates that Air Traffic Control, at West Drayton, was contacted and that there was no known knowledge of aircraft in that area to coincide with the time of the sighting. Mention is also made on the log of reports received of aerial phenomena over Southern England, during that night. The only lights visible to the officers visiting the incident were those from Orford Lighthouse. A further report was received at 10.13am, 26th December 1980, from a staff member at RAF Bentwaters, indicating that a place had been found where a 'craft' of some sort could have landed, two miles east of East Gate, at Bentwaters."*

Letter to Georgina Bruni

In a letter, dated the 28th July 1999 sent to Georgina Bruni, Mike Topliss an Inspector from Suffolk Constabulary Planning and Operations Department confirmed:

> *"There is no documentary evidence that police officers were involved in similar incidents on 27th to 31st December that year.* (1980) *I have tried to be as objective as possible with the answers provided, like yourself, would undoubtedly be pleased to see a local incident like this substantiated as an authentic UFO experience. PC (name blocked out S40) holds similar views to myself and returned to the forest site in daylight, in case he had missed some evidence in the darkness. There was nothing to be seen and he remains unconvinced that the occurrence was genuine. The immediate area was swept by powerful light beams from*

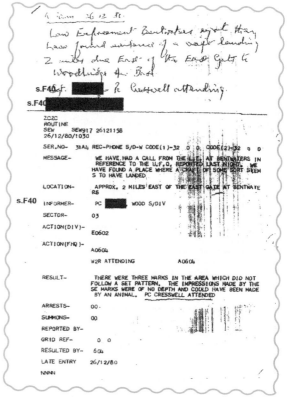

a landing beacon at RAF Bentwaters and the Orford Lighthouse. I
know from personal experiences that at night, in certain weather and cloud conditions, these
beams were very pronounced and certainly caused strange visual effects."*

(Source: Declassified MOD Documents)

SUFFOLK CONSTABULARY

**FORCE HEADQUARTERS, MARTLESHAM HEATH,
IPSWICH IP5 7QS Tel. Ipswich (0473) 624848 Telex: 98120**

All official correspondence should be addressed to the Chief Constable

Your Ref.

Our Ref.   25(3)3/83 DJ/SRP   23 November 1983

Dear Sir

SIGHTING OF UNUSUAL LIGHTS IN THE SKY AT WOODBRIDGE ON 26 DECEMBER 80

With reference to your letter dated 3 November 83 which related to the above mentioned incident.

Police knowledge of this matter is limited to a telephone report of the alleged incident timed at 4.11 am on 26 December and received from a person at RAF Bentwaters together with the two subsequent visits to the location by police officers.

The first visit followed immediately the reported incident and the two officers who attended made a search of the area with a negative result. A note on the log indicates that Air Traffic Control at West Drayton were contacted and that there was no known knowledge of aircraft in that area to coincide with the time of the sighting. Mention is also made on the log of reports received of aerial phenomena over Southern England during that night. The only lights visible to the officers visiting the incident were those from Orford Light House.

A further report was received at 10.30 am on 26 December 80 from a staff member at RAF Bentwaters indicating that a place had been found where a craft of some sort could have landed. An officer attended and the area involved did bear three marks of an indeterminate pattern. The marks were apparently of no depth and the officer attending thought they could have been made by an animal.

It is considered little more would be gained by you making direct contact with the officers involved as the above information constitutes the sum of their knowledge in relation to this matter. It is hoped the information supplied will be of assistance to you in formulating your intended account of the circumstances.

Yours faithfully

R. Kitson

Chief Constable

Police visit the Forest again:

Later that morning (26th December 1980) PC Brian Cresswell made his way to the forest, following a telephone call made at 10.13am from the base, reporting three unusual marks in the forest floor. The marks were apparently of no depth and the officer attending thought they could have been made by an animal.

Thanks to some good investigative work by Georgina Bruni, whom we had the pleasure of talking to, during walks through the forest, she discovered a photograph taken by Master Sergeant Ray Gulyas, which shows PC Brian Cresswell examining a triangle of marks on the ground with Capt. Mike Verrano on the morning of 26th December, 1980.

It appears that this was the officer Jim Penniston spoke to, while walking back to his vehicle, after making the plaster casts, accompanied by John Burroughs. The two men explained to the officer what had taken place and, according to Penniston, the police officer refused to write any information relating to a UFO incident in his notebook – only recording a sighting of *'strange lights'*, which could have been from the nearby lighthouse, along with an entry explaining away the landing marks as looking like *'rabbit scratchings'*.

Letter to Georgina Bruni

Inspector Mike Topliss also disclosed, in his letters of communication with Georgina Bruni, that two local police officers (King and Brophy) were in the Law Enforcement Agency Office, at RAF Bentwaters, when they were told of 'lights' being seen in the forest. (This was on their second night's shift, during the early hours of the 27th December). They were intending to check this out, when they were directed to a burglary at Otley Post Office. (This is where we believe a man was apprehended).

Georgina Bruni

Curiously, Mike Topliss was to experience his own sighting of a UFO, some years later – not that this may necessarily be associated with the events which had occurred in December 1980. However, it is well worth bringing to the attention of the reader; firstly, because this UFO sighting took place in Suffolk, and secondly, we were impressed, during our conversations with him, about the way in which he had recorded an incident that may well have attracted ridicule, irrespective of his rank.

Followed by strange lights

Inspector Mike Topliss, of the Suffolk Constabulary – then in charge of Leiston, Saxmundham, and Aldeburgh communities – was driving home from Leiston, at 10.45pm on 18th November 1993, along the B119 road, towards Saxmundham, in a gold coloured Rover Montego saloon. The night was clear, with a bright moon that illuminated the countryside – bright enough to have driven without headlights.

> *"I was driving at approximately 45-50mph and slowed down to negotiate two 'S' bends between Leiston and Saxmundham, when, about a kilometre from the outskirts of Saxmundham, I came up behind a slower moving vehicle – a Morris Marina saloon, containing four occupants, travelling at about 40mph.*

Knowing the road well, I checked my rear view mirror, intending to overtake, when I noticed what I presumed to be a set of headlights in the distance behind me, apparently gaining on me very quickly. I had hardly rounded a left-hand curve when the 'headlights' rushed aggressively up behind me, slowing suddenly to match my speed, about a car length away. The two 'lights' were consistent with the height, spacing, colour and brightness, of normal headlights on dipped beam. They were circular in shape, with no sign of any vehicle to which they were presumably attached to. There was a noise consistent with the hiss of tyres on the road surface, but nothing unusual. My impression was of an impatient driver, waiting for the first opportunity to overtake me.

About a hundred metres after the left-hand curve, the 'lights' suddenly moved out to my offside, disappearing from the rear view mirror and appearing in my offside wing mirror. I glanced over my right shoulder and briefly caught a glimpse of them, about a metre away, as if the actions of an overtaking vehicle, but I heard no engine noise or saw any actual vehicle.

Suddenly both the 'lights' and road noise disappeared, as if someone had flicked a switch off. I instinctively performed an emergency stop, thinking that the 'overtaking vehicle' had lost control and crashed.

The Marina driver in front of me also stopped. I got out and looked around; there was no sign of the mysterious 'lights' – just the skid marks made on the road (clearly visible in the moonlight). I looked at my watch. It was 10.25pm. I immediately got out of the car and looked all around me. There were no hedges. The fields were flat and bare. I could see for several hundreds of metres in all directions. There was no sign of any tyre tracks, or marks, which would have been left from a vehicle leaving the road.

The middle-aged Marina driver came over to me and asked me what happened to that car. I asked him, 'what exactly did you see?' He replied, 'there was a car overtaking you. It suddenly disappeared. I thought it had gone into a ditch'. After he had left the scene, I felt there was something about this whole incident which I found strangely embarrassing and this appeared to compromise my judgement.

In retrospect, I believe this was caused by the frustration of not being able to understand what had occurred and, at the same time, not wishing to be seen as some sort of weirdo. I wondered if perhaps the incident could have been the result of a ghostly manifestation of a previous serious accident, although my enquiries, made later, revealed that no serious accidents had occurred at that location (Map Reference: TM394632, Landranger Series Sheet 156) – precisely where the 30 metre contour line crosses the B119 Road on the attached map. The offside verge is marked by a leaning concrete post. The following day, in daylight, I returned to the scene. There was nothing further to be seen, other than the skid marks."

(Source: Personal interview)

He was not the only police officer who was to sight something strange in the Suffolk area.

UFO over Woodbridge, Suffolk

We contacted retired Police Constable Martyn Brophy, who was the partner of PC David King. He remembered the incident clearly and expressed surprise that a Colonel should have been on duty over the

Christmas period. Unfortunately, he had nothing else to add with regard to what Dave King had told us. However he was to describe something highly unusual that took place a few months later.

> *"I was driving a police car through Woodbridge, accompanied by another officer, during March/April 1981. I happened to look upwards and see the amazing sight of a massive bank of lights, forming a rectangular shape, moving slowly across the sky. I felt the hairs on the back of my neck rising. I knew this was no aircraft and watched, in silence, unable to comprehend the sheer size of the 'craft'. From the look on my colleague's face, I knew he had also seen it."*

The officers made their way back to the police station and sat down, trying to retain their composure. All of a sudden there was a frenzied knock at the front door, followed by the entrance of a man, wearing a crash helmet, who was shaking with fright. He told the officers:

> *"You'll never believe what I've just seen. I was riding towards Woodbridge, when this huge UFO swooped down over the top of me. I thought it was going to strike me – then it disappeared."*

(Source: Personal interview)

Sgt. James Penniston's narrative continues . . .

> *"I told the officer (PC Cresswell) about having seen an actual 'craft' and of discovering three identical indentations in the ground, all the same distance apart. The PC would not listen. I asked him why and he said, 'because I'm not going to put anything other than that in my report'. We found that just totally absurd. The ground was frozen and it was just impossible for that to happen."*

Sgt. James Penniston

Colonel Halt's narrative continues . . .

On one occasion Colonel Halt happened to be visiting the Security Police Operations Centre, known as 'the Desk', between 5.30am and 5.45am, to pick up the 'blotters' for the previous 24 hour period – something he did if he happened to be out early and near the Police Station.

"The desk sergeant on that morning was Staff Sergeant 'Crash' McCabe. We called him 'Crash' for a very good reason – that's why he was on the 'Desk', instead of a patrol car. He said, 'Colonel, you're not going to believe this. Burroughs, Penniston, and Bustinza, were out in the woods last night, chasing a UFO'. I said, 'What?' We both had a chuckle. I said, 'Now, be more specific'. He replied, 'Well, the Lieutenant said (the Lieutenant being the Flight Commander for the evening, or that early morning shift) he didn't put it in the blotter'. I said, 'What happened? You got to put something in the blotter'. He said, 'I know they saw some lights, and something happened out there, and they think they saw something'.

I knew Penniston was very credible . . . Burroughs probably so. I didn't know Bustinza, so I said, 'Well, why don't you just put in the blotter that they saw some lights in the forest', and, uh, I got a chuckle out of it and didn't think too much about it. I picked up the blotters and went up to the office and read through them. Didn't see anything else too exciting in there, shared them with my boss, and we kind of had a chuckle – UFOs in the woods, oh great – and didn't think too much more about it. I interviewed the three young airmen individually, who were involved in the incident, at the Base Commander's office, and obtained statements from them. Basically, what they said was that Airman John Burroughs was patrolling Woodbridge Base, as was one other patrol.

We normally kept two patrols, Police 4 and Police 5, Law Enforcement type, on Woodbridge Base, and three on Bentwaters Base, due to it being a little larger base – more aircraft – and he had to do hourly, or semi-hourly, whatever it was, checks at the back gate and was going out to the East Gate, to check it for security, bearing in mind it was a combination lock, but sometimes the combination would be 'leaked', and people would take a short cut. He went out and rattled the gate; it was locked, when he noticed something out in the woods.

John Burroughs reported having seen 'some red, green, blue and white, lights in the woods, about 300 yards out, so I called back to Law Enforcement and said 'It looks like there's been a crash – looks like an airplane, probably a helicopter's gone down'.

The Law Enforcement Desk Sergeant, Sergeant McCabe, immediately responded. He called our Woodbridge and Bentwaters Control Tower, but they were both down. Although there was manning there, they just weren't up and operational. They both said the same thing, 'There's nothing flying in the vicinity'.

They contacted Wattisham Air Defence sector, and asked them if they had any knowledge of anything happening in the Bentwaters area, but were told nothing. Similarly, the same response was obtained from ATC London Heathrow. In the meantime, Police 4 comes up and joins John Burroughs, and he sees it, so he calls back.

About this time, the Security Patrol – the people that guard the airplanes – Jim Penniston, comes up. He and several other Law Enforcement people, including the Flight Chief Master

Sergeant, confirm they can see it as well. The Master Sergeant is pretty smart. He says, 'Well, I'm not going out there. How about three, or four, of you guys go out there and see what happened? Check your weapons with me', so J.D. Chandler takes the weapons, bearing in mind you don't carry a gun in England.

Penniston and Burroughs, and Bustinza, troop out into the woods. They go down the forest service road, turn on a kind of a trail, and go up in the pines and actually approach something, describing it as 'approximately nine feet in length on the side, triangular in appearance, with a tripod-like set of legs, showing various coloured lights.

James W. Penniston

12

April 10, 2000

Mr. John Hanson
P.O. Box 6371
Birmingham, UK
B48 7RW

Dear Mr. Hanson;

I received your letter and the photographs of your model, thanks for an interesting view on your interpretation of what the craft might look like. I understand there has been a lot of misinformation published in book form over the years. There is also a flurry of media articles and in the form of television shows, which are extremely misleading.

Even despite the mass of misinformation released about RAF Bentwaters/Woodbridge incident, I never tire of listening or pursuing bonified explanations about the event. Truly, a sensational and well-documented case, with far reaching consequences, yet to be publicly realized.

The United States Air Force, completing an official investigation on a craft-of-unknown-origin. Is quite remarkable by it self. I find the aftermath of the incident, a stand-alone event by its self. Mainly, on how governments and people in "official" positions do business, and react to the "unknown".

I am currently under contract with other primary witnesses and an established writer, so any discussion about the event is highly curtailed and in some incidences, prohibited. However, I will be glad to comment on your model.

I find your depiction, in the model, is not physically close to the craft-of-unknown-origin, my team, investigated that night in December 1980. I am not sure what your information source(s) were, but I strongly recommend that you treat all information *out there* at this time as, dubious. The exception to the information *out there* is the Microsoft project done a few years back on the incident, which I do wholeheartedly endorse.

I hope this helps answer some of your questions on this subject, and may your research continue, unabated.

Best regards,

James W. Penniston, USAF/Ret.

They came very close to it. At this point, their stories become somewhat muddled. They are not really sure whether they were onboard, whether they touched it, or exactly what happened. We do know they were out there for probably three to four hours – in fact, to the point where people were very, very, concerned on the base as to what happened to them. Penniston can describe to this day the hieroglyphic-like symbols he saw on the side of the object that appeared to be raised – sort of like they were burned on, with a welding rod or something."

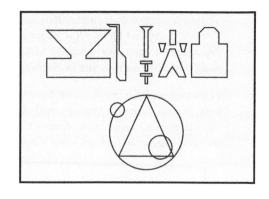

Although Jim had rejected any similarities with the craft seen by Colin Saunders nearly 20 years later we thought this was an exceptional sighting and should be contrasted against what the airmen saw, understanding the curious marks seen by the witness on the outer surface, that have been the foundation of many other reports brought to our attention over the years.

Triangular UFO over Leicestershire:

On the 31st March, 1999, Colin Saunders – a design draughtsman, having worked on aircraft design for Airbus Industries in Germany, Saab in Sweden, Chevron Petroleum in the North Sea and flown on many helicopters was travelling home in the family car after having visited the *White Lion* in Pailton for a drink celebrating Madge's birthday, heading towards the Fosse Way, Leicestershire.

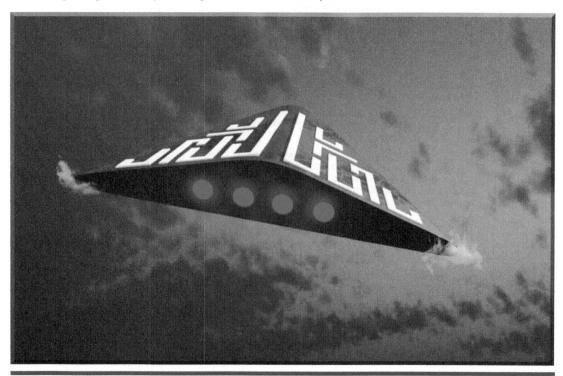

As they turned onto the Fosse Way, (half a mile away exactly from the village of Monks Kirby) they noticed a cluster of deep 'rose' red lights, with a hint of white, hovering in the sky about half-a-mile away.

Colin (who was sat next to his wife in the front passenger seat):

> *"My daughter Victoria (12), who was sat behind my wife Karen (44) driving, said: 'There's been talk of a headless horseman down here,' my mother, Madge (62), behind me in the back jokingly replied we should look out for him.*
>
> *We all commented on the lights. My wife said it was too low for a plane and too many lights for a helicopter. We drove down the road parallel to the lights that I estimated to be only eighty feet away.*

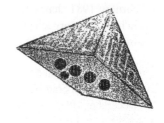

> *I noticed the lights were in a row but not level with the ground, tilted at approximately twenty-five degrees to the horizon. I stared into the light on the far left. This light was the highest side of the tilt, with the far right light being the anchor point for the twenty-five degrees angle. I then noticed a fifth, smaller, spurious light off to the left-hand side. (This turned out to be the one underneath the front of the 'triangle'.)*
>
> *In the middle of the end light I could see a criss-cross of lines – a bit like a traffic light lens. Somehow hypnotic, it seemed to pulse very rapidly in a digital fashion. I began to see a shape start to appear around these lights. The edges looked like the sky was rippling, due to what I believed was their transparency at the time. I could see the shape of a diamond around the lights.*
>
> *You needed a sharp eye to make out the shape. At some point, I thought I saw a mist – like cotton wool, around the wing tips. The whole thing then tilted upwards in a most peculiar fashion to reveal a large 'triangle'. The tilting action was not from the centre of the 'craft' but from the rear, i.e. the rear end stayed where it was and the 'nose' rose in the air.*

> *The surface of the 'triangle' looked to be alive. It was like a lake of dark grey liquid, similar to Mercury, with waves running up and down the surface – like ripples on a lake in a breeze. On top of this 'lake' were silver lines that looked like box sections raised off the surface, interlocking like an old-fashioned maze.*

> *I thought to myself, 'My God, aliens do exist and abductions must be true. This explains why we have ancient mysteries'. The next thing I recall is shouting to my wife, who was driving, to stop the car, as my view of the object was being restricted by a large hedge. When we got out of the car, it was gone.*

> *We could see a large 'craft' in the distance, with strange red lights at the rear. It seemed enormous to me, with a huge wingspan. At the end of each wing was a white light shining up along the top surface. We couldn't decide if it was conventional, or not. There were no smells of any burnt fuel in the air at all."*

Colin telephoned Coventry Airport, the following morning, but was told there had been no other UFO sightings reported to them. He told us his daughter Vickie had felt a sensation like sunburn to both of her ears, noticeable as dark and light patches, after the event, which was attributed by her doctor as an allergy, caused by something like hairspray, and wondered if this was connected with the appearance of the UFO.

(Source: Omar Fowler/PRA/Personal interview)

The Object was tracked on Radar

In February 1981, Jenny Randles received information from Paul Begg, the author of *Into Thin Air,* who was in his local Norwich public house, one evening, when he entered into a conversation with a man known to him – then employed as a radar operator at RAF Watton, in Norfolk.

This man had not been on duty himself, but told Paul about a conversation which was told to him by one of the other radar operators. This man claimed having tracked an unusual object on the radar screen, during 27th December 1980. Watton lost the target about 50 miles south, to the east of Ipswich and in the vicinity of Rendlesham Forest.

On the 29th December 1980, the same operator received a visit from USAF Intelligence Officers (which one may think odd, as this was a British tracking station) and asked for the log books and film of the radar recording, covering a period of several days. The men told him that a UFO had crashed in woodland near RAF Bentwaters and that Watton may have tracked it on radar. (*UFO Crash Landing? Friend or Foe?,* Jenny Randles)

Another account from *Sky Crash* describes a more in-depth conversation made . . . (page 35)

> *"The radar men were told that it was possible that what they had tracked was an object that had crash landed into a forest near Ipswich. This had been a metallic UFO, a structured device of unknown origin. Men who had gone out to confront it from a nearby base had found the engine and lights of their jeep failing. They then had to continue on foot. The object was on the ground for several hours before repairs could be undertaken by the aliens who had crewed it; during this period, high ranking officers from the base went into the forest and the base commander himself had conversed alone with the occupants."*

According to the authors of *Sky Crash,* the informant alleged that RAF Bentwaters had contacted Watton during the time the visual sighting was taking place.

Jenny Randles, in original notes made, following a conversation with the radar operator, reported that the man told her:

> *"The Intelligence Officers had informed the Base Commander, and several officers had been called out into the forest from a party on base, which they were attending. This was in response to the original discovery of a landed UFO. They took with them a battery operated portable tape recorder and made a transcript."*

Irrespective of the version of events supplied by Steve Roberts, Larry Warren and Adrian Bustinza, one would naturally be suspicious of conversation made by unidentified USAF Intelligence Officers, during a visit to Eastern Radar on 29th December 1980, involving extraordinary admissions of a crash-landed UFO, and that it was on the ground for several hours while repairs were effected under the supervision of the Base Commander. We do not believe this took place – others may believe it did.

Jenny describes having found the previously mislaid original notes she made from her conversation with 'David Potts' (Malcolm Scurrah) in 1984, and identifies the date as 27th December 1980. Brenda Butler confirms this was a mistake and that it actually took place in November 1980 (corroborated by Malcolm Scurrah).

Although we have no doubts about accepting the validity of Jenny's investigation, a professional lady of immense knowledge and well-respected throughout the UFO community, we felt wary of accepting this alleged statement of UFO crash-landing events, as corroboration of anything. Others may think differently.

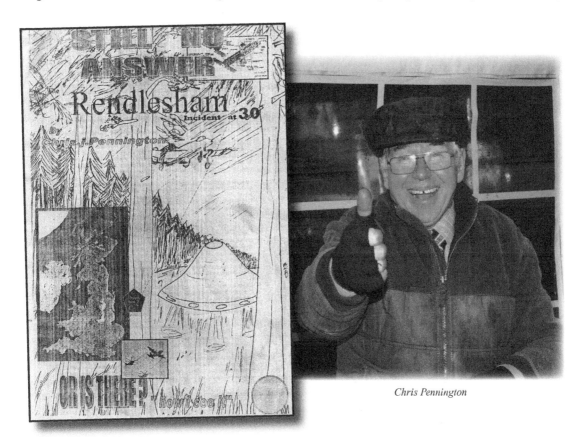

Chris Pennington

Air Traffic Controllers tracked down and interviewed

We spoke to Robert Hastings, considered a leading researcher on nuclear weapons-related UFO activity. Robert has interviewed over 120 witnesses to date, including former and retired US military personnel, and has lectured on the UFO-Nuclear connection at over 500 colleges and universities in the United States.

His authoritative book, ***UFOs and Nukes***: ***Extraordinary Encounters at Nuclear Weapons Sites,*** was published in July 2008. He has appeared on CNN's *Larry King Live* on 18th July 2008, together with three former US Air Force officers, who spoke about their involvement in classified UFO-related incidents.

In 2007, Robert Hastings interviewed the two now-retired USAF air traffic controllers, who had been on duty in the week of the UFO events at Bentwaters – James H. Carey and Ivan 'Ike' R. Barker. During a taped telephone call, Carey told him:

"At the time, I was a tech sergeant, an air traffic controller with the 2164th Communications Squadron. The other controller was named Ike Barker. A major named -------- was also there. What I remember seeing was a very fast object on the radar we had in the tower. The scope was variable – it had a zoom as far as its [displayed] range, between 5 and 60-miles radius, but I think it was set at 60-miles when the object appeared. It came in from the east, went straight west across the scope and disappeared off the left side. It took maybe four sweeps – each sweep was two or three seconds – to cross it entirely. So it covered 120 miles in [approximately eight to twelve] seconds. In the 15 years I was an air traffic controller, I'd never seen anything travel across the scope that fast. A few seconds later, it came back on the scope, retracing its course, west to east, at the same speed. Then – I think it was maybe half or three-quarters of the way across – it did an immediate right-angle turn and headed south, off the bottom of the screen. I mean, it turned just like that, instantly. We couldn't believe it! I told Ike, 'Okay, that was not one of ours!'

So, that's all I remember, except for the chatter on the radio. I think it was on the Major's hand-held radio, which was tuned to the Command Post Net. That's who he always talked to [on other occasions]. I wasn't really listening to it, so I don't remember any of the details, but I do know that [the radio] was pretty quiet all night – then, all of a sudden, they're just yakking back and forth. They were kind of excited but that's all I recall. Besides, if they were going to discuss UFOs or security problems, or that kind of stuff, they would have gone to a restricted channel, which they scrambled. But the chatter did start up a little while after we tracked the object. Anyway, I only saw the unidentified object on radar, but Ike told us that he saw something out the window."

Robert interviewed Barker on audio tape. This is what he had to say:

"There was a visual on [the UFO we were tracking]. When it hovered, I saw it out of the window. It was basketball-shaped, and had a sort of an orange glow – not bright orange, uh, sort of dim, maybe like the full moon would look behind a thin layer of clouds. There seemed to be something across the center of it, lighter-colored shapes, like – don't laugh – portholes or windows, or even lights, in a row left to right, across its center – maybe six or eight of them. They were stationary, not moving across the object, but it seemed spherical, not flat like a 'flying saucer'. I couldn't hear any noise. It wasn't huge, but I think it was bigger than an airplane. I would say it was maybe twice the size of an F-111.

Now, there's a water tower at Bentwaters. If you were in the air traffic tower, facing the runway, the tower is almost behind you. [From my vantage point] the object was directly over the top of the water tower, or just past it. The object [appeared] larger, maybe twice as large, as the tank on the water tower. It stopped in mid-air for a few seconds, probably 500ft, uh, maybe a 1,000ft above the tower, and then it left. I didn't see it turn, uh, rotate or anything like that before leaving, but what impressed me most was the speed this thing had. I have never seen anything so fast in my life! It was zoom . . . gone!"

When Robert Hastings told Barker that Carey had said he did not remember seeing the UFO out of the window, Barker replied emphatically,

"Oh, he saw it! They both saw it! But we weren't going to admit that. Just after I saw the object out the window, I turned to Jim and --- and said, 'I didn't see that, did you?' One of them responded, 'No, I didn't see it either.' I don't remember who answered me, but they both saw it. But we made no log entries on anything, including the fast-moving target. We didn't really have a discussion about not telling anyone, because that was already understood."

Barker then mentioned an earlier UFO incident, at a USAF base in Japan, during which he had been grilled by Air Force investigators.

"The controllers were harassed to the point that they said the object they saw was only aircraft lights. That taught me a lesson: Never go on the record. Never open your mouth. So, at Bentwaters, I think we were all scared to discuss it. I know I was. As I said before, we didn't even record it in the log."

Barker added:

"After the object left, uh, maybe an hour later, we could see lights, actually a glow, in the direction of Woodbridge, but the trees blocked our view so we couldn't see what was causing it. Now that I think about it, I'm not sure if --- was still up [in the tower] at that time, but I know Jim was. The glow seemed like it was coming out of the forest; it wasn't like lights in the air. It could have even been vehicles on the ground, but I know one damn thing – it wasn't a lighthouse!"

Robert Hastings:

"Importantly, a British radar unit apparently tracked the same object. Barker told me that he or Carey had called a British radar unit, known as Eastern Radar, to ask whether they were tracking anything anomalous.

The importance of the radar tracking revelations can not be overstated. Two independent military units tracked an anomalous aerial object during the peak week of UFO reports at the twin bases. Moreover, one of those units – the USAF controllers at RAF Bentwaters – had a visual on a hovering, spherical object, which correlated with that tracking. I finally asked Ike Barker for his opinion about the object he tracked. He replied: 'I can tell you that this was no manmade technology. I was very familiar with all types of aircraft, obviously, and I can tell you that what I saw was not from any country on Earth. I will never forget it!'"

(Source: Robert Hastings)

Colonel Halt:

> *"Another interesting thing is that the Command Post, the Senior Command Post not the Police Command Post, the one that my radio tied into (which only talked to the Commanders and the other agencies outside of the base) had a 12 hour 12 inch commercial tape recorder. This recorded everything said last night and everything said in the Command Post. Every shift that came on duty looked at that tape and turned it over if there was nothing of any great significance.*
>
> *I know for a fact that somebody kept that tape. They copied that transmission or wiped that portion of the tape because a friend of mine heard it from somebody else in intelligence, so I'm aware that someone took that off and picked it out of the tape for some reason. Somebody told me that one of our agencies had it!"*

In an interview conducted with Jonathon Dillon, following the publication of *Left at East Gate*, Colonel Halt says:

> *"Sgt. Coffey, from Bentwaters Air Traffic Control, contacted Heathrow Airport, in London, and Eastern Radar, who'd both seemingly tracked the manifestation on radar, first picking it up roughly 15 miles out over the east coast, but as it dropped beneath radar contact they couldn't identify it. In addition, RAF Watton reported a strange object on their scope as well."*

In a letter sent to the authors, in 2012, Colonel Halt disclosed:

> *"The two air traffic controllers on duty that night I was out, actually saw the glowing object, tracked it on their radar, and saw it descend into the forest where we were. They didn't tell anyone until they both retired, for fear of being decertified."*

Larry Warren

At 11.45pm (approximately), 28th December 1980, USAF Security Officer Airmen Lawrence 'Larry' Warren – then 19 years of age – was standing guard at Bentwaters perimeter post 18, when he overheard some radio transmissions being broadcast between the Bentwaters weapons storage area and Woodbridge control tower.

A young Larry Warren

> *". . . something about some funny lights having been seen, bobbing up and down over the forest, near Woodbridge Airbase, some five miles away. (I had no knowledge of the previous incidents that had occurred over the previous nights). Suddenly, out of the darkness came five deer, clearly panicked by something. Two of them actually jumped the fence and were out of sight in seconds."*

A few minutes later a Security Police truck arrived, driven by Sergeant Adrian Bustinza, accompanied by Second Lieutenant Bruce Englund, and two other Security Police Officers. Larry was then told to radio in. He was being relieved from his post, which he did so. Bustinza told him they were going to collect light-alls (generator mounted spotlights) from the motor pool. After collecting these, they arrived at the main gate at Bentwaters, which was attended by at least five or six other vehicles containing other security police personnel.

Larry asked where they were all going and was told Woodbridge Airbase. Was it an Exercise, he wondered?

The 'convoy' sped on through the Suffolk countryside, past Eyke, and then onto a sharp curve on the East Gate road, where they were forced to slow down, due to a law enforcement car blocking half the road.

"As our vehicle was waved forward, past the makeshift road block, with emergency red flares being placed onto the ground, I noticed a white Ford Cortina car, containing a woman, sat in the driver's seat, with a child asleep on the front passenger side. As we drove past, I heard the Law Enforcement Officer advising the woman that there might be some unexploded ordnance in the area and that she shouldn't be delayed too long.

The vehicles moved along a road with a pine forest on the left (Rendlesham). Somebody in the vehicle ahead shouted out, *"Where are we supposed to go?"* The reply was, *"turn left at East Gate."*

Following a drive of approximately half a mile, the trucks entered a large clearing and Larry got off, where he stood awaiting orders. After handing over their weapons, which were collected by a truck from the armoury, Larry checked his watch. It read 12.30am (29th December 1980).

A Flight Commander with the rank of Captain approached and joined the group, now consisting of Warren, Bustinza, and two other airmen, and instructed them that radio silence was to be maintained. They were then ordered to follow the Captain down the footpath and into the woods. Approximately a few hundred yards along the path, the group turned right and deeper into the forest.

Larry Warren:

"I heard a radio transmission, 'You people have to avoid those hot spots. Remember they're marked October Number One, over'. I knew the code they were referring to – the First Officer at the scene. I thought, perhaps, we were going to be fighting a forest fire, but why is it not fire personnel? I started to feel uneasy. Things seemed almost surreal. The forest was, by now, deathly calm, although radio traffic was increasing. We continued on our journey into the forest, until we came up to field separated from the forest by a broken wire fence, about a hundred feet in front of us."

Beyond that could be seen military personnel apparently walking around something on the ground, which grew bright and then dimmed. As they approached the location, Bustinza whispered to Larry, *"That's what happened to me in Alaska"*. Larry wondered what on earth was happening, after noticing an airmen clearly distressed, with his head in his hands, crying, being comforted by a Master Sergeant.

"We moved even closer, enabling me to see what looked like a localised yellow/green, almost transparent coloured ground fog, about a foot in height, with something glowing very brightly inside. Close by were two disaster awareness officers, carrying yellow Geiger

counters. Another man was taking photographs of the object, while others were filming; this was the sight that greeted me and about forty other service personnel. I heard what sounded like a pilot's communication, followed by, 'here it comes, here it comes'. Over the far end of the field, towards the direction of the North Sea, a red light appeared in the sky at this time. I felt as if my physical movements had, in some way, slowed down. The light cleared the pine trees bordering the field and descended in an arc, until approximately twenty feet above the object, when it exploded in a blinding flash, shards and particles of light raining down onto the object on the ground.

In its place, occupying where the fog had been, appeared what looked like a machine – almost the shape of a pyramid – showing an off-red glow on the top, with a pearl white body, creating a rainbow effect, and a base of bright blue cobalt lights, and what looked like boxes, pipes, and strange extensions, covering its surface – its image constantly distorting, best seen on the edge of peripheral vision. My impression was it looked old, but advanced. I never saw any insignia, flags, windows, or identifying marks on it. From the main body of the object were three delta-like appendages protruding, giving it an almost threatening appearance."

An officer approached Bustinza and Warren, ordering them to walk with him close to the object, which they did until about ten to fifteen feet away, by which time Larry's eyes were watering. At this point he and the others were ordered back to their original positions.

Larry says he saw two English policemen from Woodbridge, one of whom was taking photographs, but that security personnel had seized the camera after much argument. Even in the middle of what may well have looked like chaos, Larry felt the situation was being organised along lines of previously laid down procedure.

According to Larry, a staff car arrived, containing Colonel Gordon Williams and other officers, some dressed in civvies, who liaised with other officers already there.

Georgina Bruni pictured here with Colonel Gordon Williams

"A glowing ball of bluish gold light moved slowly, with apparent purpose, from behind the right 'delta' of the object and came to a halt about ten feet away from the 'machine', enabling me to see, in the glow, what looked like kids. It then split into three separate glowing cylinders, each containing what appeared to be a living creature I would described as 'small, 3-4 feet high, ghostlike in appearance, showing large heads, with black eyes, wearing bright silvery clothing'. Oddly, I never felt frightened while watching the drama unfurl in front of me. Colonel Williams approached them slowly and stood looking down at them. They cocked their heads at him and I felt the impression they were communicating with him in some way.

Suddenly, behind us, a loud noise was heard – as if something heavy, like a tree, had fallen. Immediately, the 'Entities' moved their arms up to the front of their chests and floated backwards to almost under the craft, before slowly returning back towards Williams, who turned towards another officer, who handed him something I was unable to make out."

At this point, Larry and his comrades were instructed to return to the trucks and wait. As he did so he looked back, seeing the object and entities were still there, with Colonel Williams still in conversation with other officers.

Somebody else who claimed that Colonel Williams was present was Steve Roberts, the confidential informant of Brenda, Jenny, and Dot. He told Brenda about:

"... three small identical figures, just over 3ft tall, wearing all-in-one silver suits, hovering close to the ground, suspended in the shaft of light which emerged from the underside of the craft.

Wing Commander Williams went forward, close up to the entities, while others were ordered back. He seemed to communicate with the aliens, although no words were heard. After the craft had been repaired (it had been there for several hours) it took-off, unsteady to begin with, but then picked-up speed and shot off at an angle, towards the sea, and vanished from sight. After it had gone, all cameras used were seized by the senior officers."

Many years ago we wrote to Mr David Boast, whose farm is situated a short distance from where the incident took place, hoping that he may be inclined to assist further, and received this reply . . .

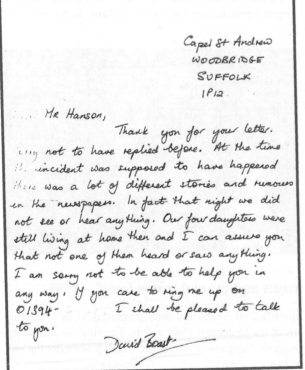

Capel St Andrew
WOODBRIDGE
SUFFOLK
IP12.

... Mr Hanson,

Thank you for your letter. ... not to have replied before. At the time ... incident was supposed to have happened there was a lot of different stories and rumours in the newspapers. In fact that night we did not see or hear anything. Our four daughters were still living at home then and I can assure you that not one of them heard or saw anything. I am sorry not to be able to help you in any way. If you care to ring me up on 01394- I shall be pleased to talk to you.

David Boast

Larry Warren

We first met Larry at Cheltenham, many years ago, when he and Pete Robbins launched their book, *Left at East Gate*, and, on another occasion, in Rendlesham Forest, Suffolk, on 27th December 2000, when we captured a UFO on film in the sky (over the same general direction nominated by Larry) in a temperature of 10° below zero, which we believe was off the coast.

We met up with Larry Warren again (now living in Liverpool) at the Midland Red Social Club, in Birmingham, during April 2010, when he had been hired to speak by the Birmingham Group, about an event which he obviously still feels very passionate about, despite it having happened nearly 30 years ago. Although primarily Larry spoke about his general background and his service in the Air Force, showing various documents and

personal letters, accompanied by the occasional quip of humour directed at the audience, he did not discuss the incident itself – no doubt presuming that most people, by now, would have learnt of his account, which was published initially in *Sky Crash,* referred to by the name of *Art Wallace,* and then, in more depth, in his and Peter Robbins' book, *Left At East Gate* – not forgetting the uncounted number of times he has appeared in television documentaries, over the years.

UFO landing at Bridgnorth with occupants and ground traces found – 1969

We felt it was important to include reports of other landed 'craft' and their perceived Alien occupants, whatever the year, bearing in mind the implications of the December 1980 events. The purpose behind this is not necessarily to add weight to what the USAF serviceman saw, but to show that they were not the only ones to report incidents like these, over the years.

The witness – a schoolteacher from Bridgnorth, Shropshire – was interviewed by West Midlands UFO researcher Derek Samson, with regard to what she saw on 12th April 1969:

> *". . . the amazing sight of an object, resembling a spinning top in appearance, on three legs, around which stood three figures, moving about in front of the 'top', bending down, picking something up from the ground, and placing whatever it was into an object that looked like a large mirror, situated beneath or close to the front of the craft, that I estimated to be approximately the length of two cars."*

(Source: *Haunted Skies*, Volume 4)

Could there have been a connection with what the USAF Officers saw, over 10yrs later?

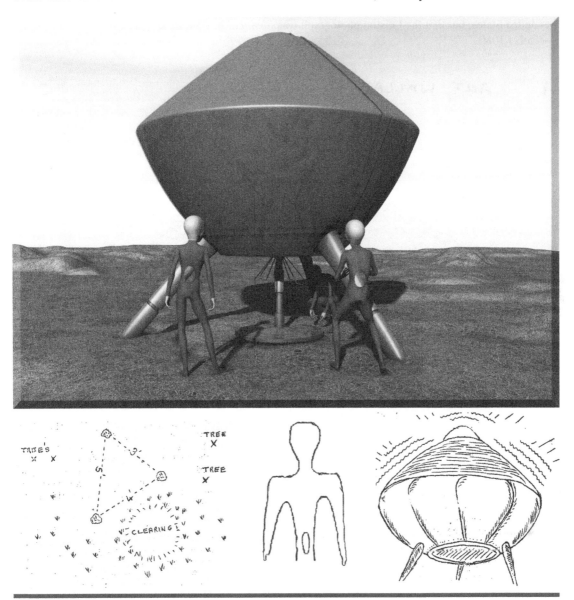

Larry, feels he had been the target of some unwarranted criticism directed at him, over the years, by those who had claimed he was never there, at the scene, which included Colonel Halt, who maintained, in an edition of *UFO Magazine* (January 1995) that: *'Larry was not there'*, but in June 1997, told Jenny Randles: *"I thought he was out there on a third night, when I was not present, because I certainly knew he was not with my group. All I will say is that he was not there officially."*

(Source: Page 104, *UFO Crash Landing, Friend or Foe?* Jenny Randles, 1998, Blandford Publishers)

During a visit to Rendlesham Forest on 27th December 2000, we took the opportunity to speak to Larry Warren about his drawing of the distinctive 'turtle back' UFO image *(1)* as shown on the front page of the *News of the World,* released in 1983. He was then shown the UFO photograph *(2)* captured over Leiston, in November 1979. Larry disclosed that the image was prepared by *Betty Luca, under his guidance, in the United States, but that the Leiston photograph was *identical to what he had seen in the forest,* during December 1980.

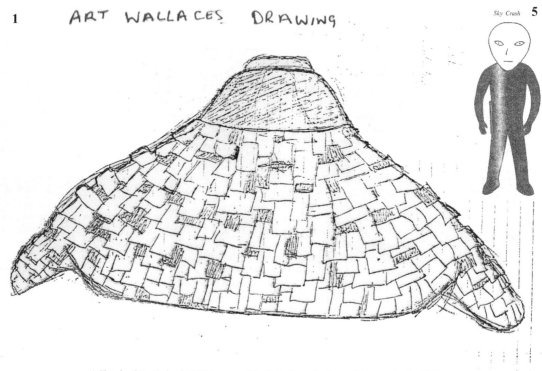

1 ART WALLACES DRAWING

Sky Crash **5**

1 *Sketch of 'turtle back' UFO prepared by Betty Luca for Larry Warren, aka Art Wallace*
5 *Inset: Sketch made by Art Wallace for 'Sky Crash'*

Does this add any weight to the version of events given by Steve Roberts, who handed over a sketch *(3)* of what he saw in the forest to Brenda and Dot, dated March 1981? This image was not used in the original *Sky Crash* (Neville Spearman Books. 1984) but instead (on page 73) a very professional image, endorsed *'based on a sketch by Steve Roberts',* was used. *(4)*

---

*Betty Andreasson nee Betty Luca alleged an incident of alien abduction at her home in South Ashburnham, Massachusetts, on 25th January 1967.

- Colonel's top secret report tells the facts
- Mystery craft in exploding wall of colour
- Animals flee from strange glowing object

UFO LANDS IN SUFFOLK

And that's OFFICIAL

A UFO has landed in Britain—and that staggering fact has been officially confirmed.

Despite a massive cover-up, News of the World investigators have proof that the mysterious craft came to earth in a red ball of light at 3 a.m. on December 17, 1980.

It happened in a pine forest called Tangham Wood just half a mile from the United States Air Force base at RAF Woodbridge, in Suffolk.

...board the craft.

From inside the forest climax rushed-back as the watercraft, a dazzling silver ball about 200 yards away, silently glided to and in a blinding explosion of lights.

About 200 military and civilian personnel, British and American, witnessed the astonishing event. The craft said the stalkers appeared to be expected.

Two nights later a series of fast-moving objects emitting powerful lights northward were spotted

NEWS WORLD INVESTIGATES

By KEITH BEABEY

over the base by a number of airmen.

It sounds like aliens coming to earth in the film Close Encounters, but the PROOF that an Unidentified Flying Object landed in Britain is irrefutable.

The key witness is Lt. Colonel Charles I. Halt, deputy commander of the USAF 81st Tactical Fighter Wing stationed alongside the RAF at Woodbridge.

With the help of UFO experts in Britain and the US we have obtained a copy of his official report on the incident, part of which is reproduced on the right.

On official USAF notepaper and headed "Unexplained Lights," Colonel Halt wrote:

Early in the morning two USAF security police patrolmen saw unusual lights outside the back gate at RAF Woodbridge.

PULSING

Thinking an aircraft might have crashed or been forced down they called for permission to go outside the gate to investigate.

The on-duty flight chief allowed three patrolmen to proceed on foot.

The individuals reported seeing a strange glowing object in the forest.

The object was described as being metallic in appearance and triangular in shape, approximately two to three metres across the base and approximately

two metres high. It illuminated the entire forest with a white light.

The object, as it moved, cast no light on top and a bank of blue lights underneath. The object was hovering or on legs. As the patrolmen approached the object it manoeuvred through the trees and disappeared.

At this time the animals on a nearby farm went into a frenzy.

The object was sighted approximately an hour later near the back gate.

The next day three depressions one and a half inches deep and seven inches in diameter were found where the object had been sighted on the ground.

The following night, the colonel reported, the area was checked for radiation and readings were found in the depressions and near a tree.

His report goes on:

Later in the night a red sun-like light was seen through the trees. It moved about and appeared to throw off glowing particles and then broke into five separate white objects and disappeared.

Immediately thereafter three star-like objects were noted in the sky, two objects to the north and one to the south, all of which were about 10 degrees off the horizon. The objects moved rapidly in sharp angular movements and displaying red, green and blue lights. The objects to the north

appeared elliptical through an 8-12 power lens.

They then turned to full sparkles. The objects to the north remained in the sky for an hour or more. The object to the south was visible for two or three hours and beamed down a stream of lights from time to time.

Numerous people, including himself, witnessed these events, Colonel Halt concluded.

Last week he declined to say anything further when we called on him at the base.

"This is a very delicate situation," he said.

"I have been told very clearly that I could jeopardise my career if I talk to you about it."

But before filing his report Colonel Halt sought advice from the RAF base commander, Squadron Leader, Donald Moreland, who told me:

"The Colonel sat in my office and was a very worried man.

TRUTH

"The first I knew of these events was when he came to me and related what he had seen. I know Col. Halt well and respect him and I fully believe he was telling me the truth.

"Whatever it was, it was able to perform feats in the air which no known aircraft is capable of doing.

"I put the events the Colonel related to the down as inexplicable phenomena."

He was sent to the site in a convoy of military vehicles from member

EVIDENCE
DETAIL from Lt. Col. Charles Halt's confidential report about the sighting of "unexplained lights" and a strange glowing object that lit up the forest

NO HOAX: Brig. Gen. Williams

NO HOAX SAYS THE AIR CHIEF

THERE has been no hoax, says the man who was in charge of the USAF base at Woodbridge when the UFO came down.

The Wing Commander, now Brigadier-General Gordon Williams, said back home in America: "I recall Lt. Colonel Halt's report.

"I don't know exactly what happened. It is all there. He is not a man who would make the British Ministry of Defence — the American Air Force Department."

Despite official silence, News of a World reporters discovered that the UFO was tracked on radar by RAF Watton, 50 miles from where it landed.

Radar technicians reported "Tracing unidentified object."

They followed its progress across the east coast until it disappeared off the screen.

USAF intelligence officers later checked the tapes of all radar installations in the area.

Bentwaters that night and describes what he saw:—

"We looked up in the sky and saw a red ball of light coming towards us from over the forest.

"There was no noise, no sound at all. We were all mesmerised. All of a sudden, the red light exploded.

"The place was filled with explosions of colours, all kinds of colours.

"We were momentarily blinded and when the colours died down there was a machine."

Art said there were beings in the craft, but he could not see them as he was on the wrong side.

SILVER

"But colours did. They said there were three, wearing silver suits.

Art Wallace we have chatted his name (for security reasons—tells his story on Page 1 told—

One theory is that the craft was a visitors space vehicle returning to earth from a top secret mission but that would hardly explain why Colonel Halt knew nothing of it.

Last week one of our gamekeeper Hector Gouse, who lives in his cottage near the airbase:

"Something happened in the wood. The earth is churned up and there are roots from trees the woods.

"It is all very strange."

VEHICLE LOOKING like a giant tortoise, this is airman Art Wallace's drawing of what he saw when the pulsating craft came to earth in the Suffolk countryside

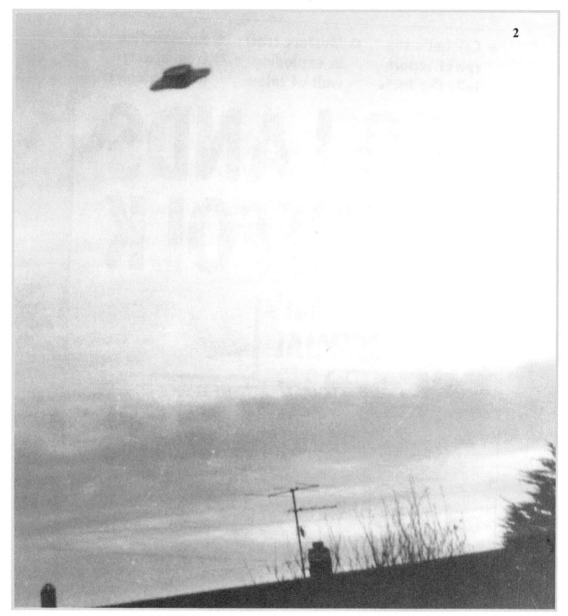

2 *UFO photograph captured over Leiston, in November 1979*

However, in the next issue of *Sky Crash* (Grafton Books, 1986) while the same image is shown endorsed *'based on a sketch by Steve Roberts'*, there is an additional image attributed to Steve Roberts, showing the same saucer-shaped sketch but now replete with aliens, on page 115 titled, *Steve Robert's view of the alien contact with the base commander'*

In her book – *UFO Crash Landing? Friend or Foe?*, Jenny Randles (Blandford Press, 1998) – Jenny uses the same image *(4)* but now endorsed *'sketch of the UFO seen in the forest by original witness Steve Roberts'*

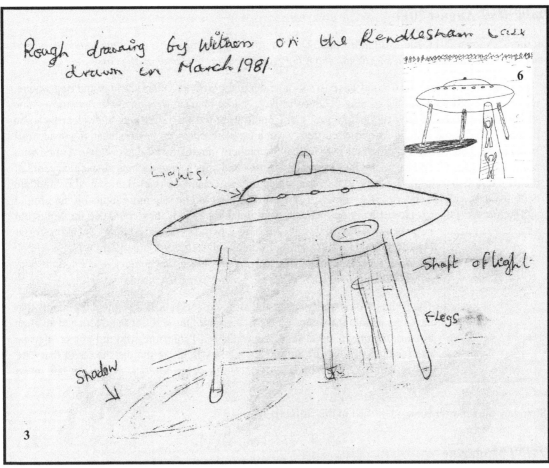

Rough drawing by Witham on the Rendlesham bash drawn in March 1981.

Lights

Shaft of light

Flegs

Shadow

3

3 *Steve Roberts handed over this sketch to Brenda and Dot, of what he saw in the forest – dated March 1981.*
Inset: **6** *is a drawing based on the original by Steve Roberts, origins unknown.*

4

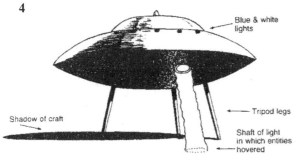

Blue & white lights

Tripod legs

Shaft of light in which entities hovered

Shadow of craft

The 27 December 1980 UFO on the ground. Based on a sketch by Steve Roberts

4 *Professional sketches that appeared in 'Sky Crash'.*

Daily Mail, August 2011

On the 8th August 2011, the *Daily Mail* published an article – *'Suffolk UFO sighting could have been a hoax: U.S. commander talks about Rendlesham Forest incident for first time in 30 years'*. –

'U.S. Air Force Colonel Ted Conrad was base commander of the airfields at Woodbridge and Bentwaters, near Ipswich. At the time the base is believed to have stored nuclear weapons. After spotting some strange lights in the sky two nights in a row, Col Conrad went to investigate and, after clearing some bushes, found some strange markings on trees, which he believed could have indicated a spacecraft landing. He then picked a group of his own men and sent them into the forest that evening. Armed with night vision goggles and a camera, they searched the area and after seeing nothing suspicious some of the men returned to base. However, Col Conrad's deputy, Lieutenant Colonel Halt, stayed behind and kept in touch with his superior via radio. Lt Col Halt then reported he saw more lights on the ground and in the sky. Other senior officers on the base went outside to see if they could see the lights but nobody was able to, despite it being a perfectly clear evening. Speaking to Dr David Clarke, UFO adviser to the National Archives, Conrad said: *"He should be ashamed and embarrassed by his allegation that his country and England both conspired to deceive their citizens over this issue. He knows better."*

The former Commander has also dismissed Sergeant Jim Penniston's claims that he had gone into the woods on the first night of the sightings and touched an alien aircraft. Colonel Conrad said he interviewed Penniston, who did not say that he had touched the aircraft but did say he saw lights in the distance, and that *"we saw nothing that resembled Lt. Col. Halt's descriptions either in the sky, or on the ground."'*

Col. Theodore J. Conrad

(Strangely the reporter is not identified in this article).

OMNI Magazine

˙In an interview conducted with journalist Eric Mishara, published by *Omni* magazine (Volume 5/6) in March 1983, Ted Conrad , (who was alleged to have spoken with the aliens) recalled:

> *"At 10.30pm on that fateful night four air policemen spotted lights from what they thought was a small plane descending into the forest. Two of the men tracked the object on foot and came upon a large tripod mounted craft. It had no windows but was studded with brilliant red and blue lights. Each time the men came within 50yds of the ship, it levitated six feet in the air and backed away. They followed it for almost an hour through the woods and across a field until it took off at phenomenal speed."*

Acting on the reports made by his men Colonel Conrad began a brief investigation on the incident in the morning. He went into the forest and located a triangular pattern obviously made by the tripod legs. He claimed he had never observed any aliens but did interview two of the eyewitnesses and concluded:

> *"Those lads saw something but I don't know what it was."*

How strange that this same newspaper had apparently used the illustration from *Sky Crash* and labelled underneath it: *'Sighting: 'Lieutenant Colonel Halt's sketch of the alien spacecraft he claims to have seen in Rendlesham Forest'* – which is completely false and misleading. The illustration is endorsed with the copyright © *Corbis*. The article also includes a photograph of Lt. Col. Halt, on the left, and Kevin Conde.

Under the photograph of Charles Halt is the banner: *'Lt. Colonel Halt, on the left, filed a report to the MOD and said he believed the lights were extraterrestrial, while Kevin Conde, right, admitted to the BBC that he had played a prank on a colleague while he was working at the base'*. Once again, further inaccuracies! We were intrigued about the copyright and searched the *Corbis* website for this image, but found no trace of it – so we emailed *Corbis Images* at 111, Salisbury Road, London NW6 6RG, United Kingdom, asking them if they had any images pertaining to the Rendlesham Forest UFO incident of 1980.

On the 14th February 2013, Yuliya Stuart from *Orbis* replied:

> *"Unfortunately we do not have any images matching that description."*

In another email, she responded:

> *"I tried to find an image of a UFO in Rendlesham Forest, but there wasn't any on our website."*

We then sent her the original image and asked if they could explain why their corporate copyright was affixed to the image. Yuliya Stuart stated:

> *"Not sure about the image, as I couldn't find it. Perhaps it is on our site but has a different keyword."*

One might think that they would know where this image was on their website, understanding its importance. The firm quoted us approximately £70 for copyright fee to use any of their UFO images. Had they purchased the image; if so, from whom? If so, why weren't they more forthcoming with the details of the person acknowledged as original copyright? One presumes that they charged the *Daily Mail* a fee? Will they charge us a fee? Time will tell.

We brought this to the attention of Colonel Halt who had this to say:

Colonel Halt:

> *"Another good reason to take anything you read in the media with a grain of salt. Remember their goal is to sell their publication the truth be dammed. The only investigating Conrad did was to listen to the participants when I took them to him after interviewing them and taking statements. His only trip to the site was when I took him and his family out to look. Apparently he's not aware, or ignoring, all the witnesses such as the Air Traffic Controllers, cops and civilians. You might want to talk to Tony Cossa, the then Communications Group Commander, who ordered his two repairmen that also witnessed the event to keep quiet. Apparently the spooks took it seriously when they used hypnosis and drugs on the airmen to get the whole story and apparently 'plant' false memories. Conrad's such a coward – he didn't want his name involved; hence I was told to do the memo, which he read and approved. I was then hung out to dry when it hit the Press. Everybody above me hid when it hit the Press. Disappointing! What you're seeing is some very skilful disinformation. You have no idea the ends some agencies will go to discredit this."*

Authors comment: It is clear that evidence gathered from various people indicates that Ted Conrad knew far more than he was letting on to the *Daily Telegraph,* as the reader will see for themselves as they read further on into the book.

On August 6th 2011 *The Daily Telegraph* published Jasper Copping's article "Rendlesham Incident: US Commander Speaks For The First Time About The Suffolk UFO". The article is centred on Colonel Ted Conrad, ex-base Commander of the twin airfields of Woodbridge and Bentwaters, and his views on the Rendlesham Incident.

Copping writes in his article that:

> *"Just after Christmas (1980) mysterious lights were seen in the sky above nearby Rendlesham Forest, and after a second night of reports from his men, Col Conrad investigated himself."*

> *Col Conrad said: 'The search for an explanation could go many places including the perpetration of a clever hoax. Natural phenomenon such as the very clear cold air having a theoretical ability to guide and reflect light across great distances or even the presence of an alien spacecraft. If someone had the time, money and technical resources to determine the exact cause of the reported Rendlesham Forest lights, I think it could be done. I also think the odds are way high against there being an ET spacecraft involved and almost equally high against it being an intrusion of hostile earthly craft', Conrad added."*

In an email sent to Jasper Copping of *The Telegraph*, in August 2011, Colonel Halt had this to say:

From: Halt@xxx.com
To: jasper.copping@telegraph.co.uk
Subject: Re: Press query, Sunday telegraph, London.
Date: Tue, 9 Aug 2011 09:40:52 -0400 (EDT)

Jasper:

I will have to assume you're looking to print the truth, not 'sell' a sensational story. Ted Conrad is having memory problems, has his head in the sand or continuing the cover up. Even his son has admitted to family talk substantiating the incident. Let's start with his investigation. I interviewed the witnesses, collected their statements (I still have them) and then took the witnesses to Conrad to tell their account. I took Conrad and his family to the site in the forest and showed him the depressions.

When I talked with Gordon Williams, neither he nor Conrad wanted their name mentioned with the incident. Thus, I was directed to get with Don Moreland (RAF) and see what he wanted as it was to become a British affair. I did so and he asked for a memo. I wrote it and it was typed by Conrad's secretary. Conrad read it, showed it to Williams and both approved. It was never meant for public dissemination.

Conrad has his chronology mixed up but that's understandable. Through the years Conrad has made conflicting statements about the events. First he stated he never went out to look in the sky. Then stated he never saw anything. Apparently he doesn't remember talking to me on his radio [about seeing a UFO sending down beams of light onto the base].

He and you need to read Robert Hastings book UFOs and Nukes. Hastings has gotten confirmation from the Air Traffic Controllers on duty that saw the object flash by and go into the forest and even observed it on their scope; He's gotten statements from SP's as well as a Communications man working in the WSA stating their sightings. He's even dug up the RAF Controller that picked up something on his scope.

Remind Conrad of his article in the OMNI Magazine dated March 1983. It's on page 115 and titled UFO Update. In the article he describes the first incident in detail and concludes, 'those lads saw something, but I don't know what it was'. Now he's smearing those involved. It's pretty clear there was a very intense confrontation with something in the forest. Does Conrad want to talk about how the airmen were then subjected to mind control efforts using drugs and hypnosis by British and American authorities?

Yes, Burroughs and Penniston have issues that relate to the events. There are a lot more details substantiating the event but I'm not going to bore you. I suppose having to look for details or the truth is less important than the 'story'. It's sad but I've come to understand how the main stream press works.

'UFO Enthusiasts Admit The Truth May Not Be Out There After All – Declining numbers of "flying saucer" sightings and failure to establish proof of alien existence has led UFO enthusiasts to admit they might not exist after all'. Jasper Copping of the *Daily Telegraph* Newspaper 4.11.2012, published another story on the UFO subject:

'But having failed to establish any evidence for the existence of extraterrestrial life, Britain's UFO watchers are reaching the conclusion that the truth might not be out there after all. Enthusiasts admit that a continued failure to provide proof and a decline in the number of "flying saucer" sightings suggests that aliens do not exist after all and could mean the end of "Ufology" – the study of UFOs – within the next decade. Dozens of groups interested in the flying saucers and other unidentified craft have already closed because of lack of interest and next week one of the country's foremost organisations involved in UFO research is holding a conference to discuss whether the subject has any future.

Dave Wood, chairman of the Association for the Scientific Study of Anomalous Phenomena (ASSAP), said the meeting had been called to address the crisis in the subject and see if UFOs were a thing of the past. *"It is certainly a possibility that in ten years time, it will be a dead subject,"* he added. *"We look at these things on the balance of probabilities and this area of study has been ongoing for many decades. The lack of compelling evidence beyond the pure anecdotal suggests that on the balance of probabilities that nothing is out there."*

"I think that any UFO researcher would tell you that 98 per cent of sightings that happen are very easily explainable. One of the conclusions to draw from that is that perhaps there isn't anything there. The days of compelling eyewitness sightings seem to be over." He said that far from leading to an increase in UFO sightings and research, the advent of the internet had coincided with a decline.

ASSAP's UFO cases have dropped by 96 per cent since 1988, while the number of other groups involved in UFO research has fallen from well over 100 in the 1990s to around 30 now. Among those to have closed are the British Flying Saucer Bureau, the Northern UFO Network, and the Northern Anomalies Research Organisation.

As well as a fall in sightings and lack of proof, Mr Wood said the lack of new developments meant that the main focus for the dwindling numbers of enthusiasts was supposed UFO encounters that took place several decades ago and conspiracy theories that surround them. In particular, he cited the Roswell incident, in 1947 when an alien spaceship is said to have crashed in New Mexico, and the Rendlesham incident in 1980, often described as the British equivalent, when airmen from a US airbase in Suffolk reported a spaceship landing.

Mr Wood added: *"When you go to UFO conferences it is mainly people going over these old cases, rather than bringing new ones to the fore. There is a trend where a large proportion of UFO studies are tending towards conspiracy theories, which I don't think is particularly helpful. The issue is to be debated at a summit at the University of Worcester on November 17 and the conclusions reported in the next edition of the association's journal, Anomaly."*

The organisation, which describes itself as an education and research charity, was established in 1981.

Its first president was Michael Bentine, the comedian and member of the Goons. It contains both skeptics and believers in UFOs and has been involved in several notable sightings and theories over the years.

Lionel Fanthorpe with Dot Street at the BUFORA Conference in 2012

Its current president Lionel Fanthorpe has claimed in its journal that King Arthur was an alien who came to Earth to save humans from invading extraterrestrials. The summit follows the emergence earlier this year of the news that the Ministry of Defence was no longer investigating UFO sightings after ruling there is "no evidence" they pose a threat to the UK.

David Clark, a Sheffield Hallam University academic and the UFO adviser to the National Archives, said:

"The subject is dead in that no one is seeing anything evidential. Look at all the people who now have personal cameras. If there was something flying around that was a structured object from somewhere else, you would have thought that someone would have come up with some convincing footage by now – but they haven't. The reason why nothing is going on is because of the internet. If something happens now, the internet is there to help people get to the bottom of it and find an explanation. Before then, you had to send letters to people, who wouldn't respond and you got this element of mystery and secrecy that means things were not explained. The classic cases like Roswell and Rendlesham are only classic cases because they were not investigated properly at the time."

But Nick Pope, who ran the MOD's UFO desk from 1991 to 1994 and now researches UFO sightings privately, said there was a future for the subject: *"There's a quantity versus quality issue here. So many UFO sightings these days are attributable to Chinese lanterns that more interesting sightings are sometimes overlooked. The same is true with photos and videos. There are so many fakes on YouTube and elsewhere, it would be easy to dismiss the whole subject out of hand. The danger is that we throw out the baby with the bathwater. And as I used to say at the MOD, believers only have to be right once." '*

> **John Hanson:** *"We would like point out that we have been researching the UFO subject for almost 20 years. During that time we have spoken to many UFO researchers, who have spent a considerabe part of their life researching something that we are told doesn't exist! It is obvious, despite the clamour from those sceptics to the contrary, that we are looking at the presence of a phenomena whose actions have clearly influenced the affairs of mankind. We cannot identify the source of the manifestation, due to our inability to prove its origin but it continues to make its presence known to us. Despite extensive research into the recorded activity, the only thing we have learnt is that it is more or less predictable in its actions. Whether it is from another plane of existence, as some believe, or incursions by aliens from outside the planet, is not worth arguing about. It is here and will continue to show itself, irrespective of the affairs of man."*

Simon Sharman, a professional, with background media experience, and member of the on-line Manchester UFO Truth Group – A Political Campaign – is currently helping to organise an official petition in the UK against the UFO cover-up. In November 2012, Simon wrote the following email to Mr Tony Gallagher, Editor of the *Daily Telegraph:*

Mr Gallagher (Editor of *The Daily Telegraph*),
I want to bring to your attention Jasper Copping's piece on the end of ufology dated 4.11.12. Having covered my main issues with his shoddy journalism in my online response found here, I must inform you of my concerns. It would appear that his entire article was based upon a statement made by Dave Wood, Chairman of something called the Association for the Scientific Study of Anomalous Phenomena (ASSAP). Considering this organisation, if it can even be called that, was the centre of Copping's argument one

would assume that we were hearing from 'experts' in the field. Unfortunately for your night editor this couldn't be further from the truth. Here's why:

1) the group hold their meetings in pubs
2) they publish reports on anything from vampires to fairies
3) they have NO coverage of ufo's to be found in their online literature barring the most mundane of generic pieces, the most recent dated 2010

To publish statements on matters of the state of UFOlogy from a group such as this is can only be described as 'Page 1 Google Journalism'. It simply isn't good enough for someone who's job description is night news editor, as I see no editorial skill on display. On top of that, Copping also wrongly cites a previous incorrect Telegraph 'report' concerning the date that the government UFO hotline was shut down (and clearly more page 1 Google investigation). A two minute effort would have ascertained that this occurred in 2009.

The reality is that ufology is far from dead and there needed to be more balanced input from active and more qualified experts in the field. Dr David Clarke does not come under this category as, although he may be qualified, he is well known for his sceptical and debunking views.

All in all to put out such badly researched and incorrect content, to a global audience, is no where near the mark. Having been a broadcaster myself for many years I would never get away with such lacklustre efforts in my films or programs, and the printed word is often much more powerful (and therefore damaging) being far less transient.

I hope you take this criticism in the tone that it is intended which is that I would like to believe some form of internal follow action will be taken. I look forward to your reply.

Sincerely, Simon Sharman (*Truspiracy* blog 2012), a member of the *Manchester UFO Truth Group*

Simon Sharman also felt it was necessary to write to Tony Gallagher, editor of the *Daily Telegraph* on the 15th of November 2012. A reply came from Assistant Editor Hugh Dougherty, a few hours later, in which he thanked him for the email but defended what Jasper had written as a fair and balanced piece of journalism.

Fair and balanced it may be, but the evidence of what *Haunted Skies* has published so far – between 1940 and 1980 – shows a completely different aspect to that presented by the National Newspapers, and occasional TV documentaries, with regard to their presentation of matters pertaining to the UFO subject.

They seek to continually denigrate reports of UFO activity with 'tongue in cheek' comments, drawn from ill-conceived conceptions about a subject which, sadly, they know little about.

Despite having published literally thousands of sightings of inexplicable objects that continually appear in our skies, which involve pilots, police officers, and people from all walks of life, we have been, and are, completely ignored by the media. This was the same media that asked us for free books to review when we published Volume 1 (1940-1959) but this never took place and is unlikely to do so, irrespective of how many volumes we publish.

Perhaps it is because we have, against impossible odds, collected, catalogued, and assimilated, all this immense amount of material and have published it, because we believe it forms part of our important social history and should be preserved accordingly.

> *"I (John) was invited to talk at the ASSAP 'summit' held at the University of Worcester, on the 17th of November 2013, for 60 minutes.*
>
> *When asked what I would be talking about I was then directed to include a paranormal aspect to the talk, rather than discussing reports of UFO activity, as they didn't want to hear*

the same old cases! When speakers' details were uploaded onto the internet, advertising the forthcoming venue, mine were not there. When I brought this omission to the attention of the organizer I was told not to worry but would be squeezed in for a 30 minutes talk on the day. I felt embarrassed to be treated this way, especially after having cancelled a talk at another lecture earlier in the year when I was ordered at my own expense to go to London to take part in a podcast and then told I wouldn't even be paid travelling expenses! Suffice to say, I did not attend. As for the statistics that 98% of UFO reports are explainable, I regard this as the biggest load of rubbish I have ever come across!"

Email from Simon to Hugh Dougherty, 15/11/12:

Simon Sharman

Dear Hugh,

Firstly I would like to thank you for taking the time to respond to my concerns so promptly, and for considering my issues with what appears to be some degree of thought.

Unfortunately I believe that when one considers the title of the article was "UFO enthusiasts admit the truth may not be out there after all" and the sub heading being, "Declining numbers of 'flying saucer' sightings and failure to establish proof of alien existence has led UFO enthusiasts to admit they might not exist after all" I think it's safe to assume that the general premise of Copping's piece is quite clear. The story is quite literally based upon the words of Mr Wood as I have previously said. If there was another basis for the piece which I somehow missed I would very much like to know what it was.

Although I thank you for pointing out the full name of attributed to the ASSAP, I am completely aware of what it stands for and in fact it is their wide area of interest that concerns me the most. To suggest the state of ufology is dead based on comments made by an organisation that discusses the nature of fantasy figures such as vampires and fairies is utterly incongruous if one knows anything about the nature of *some* UFO incidents, which are not mere 'fairy tales'. I'm not talking about the 90% of explainable cases that are misidentifications, natural phenomena or hoaxes. I'm referring to very serious incidents such as the RAF Woodbridge case of 1980, which was definitively a real event that even the late Hill Norton, Admiral of the Fleet, became involved with. So concerned was he about the reality of the incident and its significance to our national security that he repeatedly made a fuss in parliament in search of answers. Of course there are many more real incidents I could make reference to, where corroborative evidence exists such as radar confirmation etc, which definitely takes the subject well out of the 'ghosts and paranormal' arena.

With reference to your question of relevance regarding their meeting spot being a public house, and your comparison to literary greats such as Tolkien and CS Lewis, I feel it necessary to point out just one thing. Those creative geniuses were famous for precisely that – creating incredible works of fiction and fantasy, a process which is undoubtedly assisted by varying degrees of intoxication of some sorts or another. I for one am very grateful for their time spent in the pub if it helped them write those amazing books. On the contrary, any organisation which makes use of the words 'Scientific Study' in its very title cannot be expected to be taken seriously or 'scientifically' by conducting meetings in houses of intoxication. Also, as I pointed out previously there appears to be no evidence of any scientific thought, work or papers on UFOs published anywhere on their website that I could find (there are a total of 3 very old pages on UFOs on their entire website, none of which have any real substance). This does not constitute a body that can legitimately call itself a scientific UFO body, and therefore could never be cited as a credible voice for ufologists across the UK.

Sincerely, Simon Sharman

Brenda Butler

Somebody who offers us a different perspective is Brenda Butler. In her personal diaries we learn that at 3pm on Tuesday, 16th August 1983, she and Dot called to see John Warburton – the curator of the Anglo Saxon burial site and museum at Sutton Hoo, and a personal friend of the Base Commander, Ted Conrad.

Brenda:

> *"He told us he was a friend of *Ted Conrad's and that Ted had told him we are not allowed to say anything about what happened, as it would cause embarrassment to world Governments; everyone was sworn to secrecy and the UFO story was put out as a cover-up. After a while, John told us 'something had fallen off an aircraft, which was very sensitive and that the aircraft shouldn't have been in our airspace'. John said he was having dinner with Conrad soon and would try to find out more, but he said it definitely was not a UFO as we know them."*

Brenda later spoke to John again, when he told her during a conversation with Conrad, at a dinner party he attended, the officer mentioned about being a machine – *a silver, long shape*. John did not know what it was, but guessed that someone did. He thought it was part of an aircraft but was not sure what.

Colonel Halt's narrative continues . . .

> *"Burroughs thinks he may have been onboard, or so he has told me. They didn't tell me this initially, by the way, they were very secretive. They were concerned it was going to affect their military career, as we all were.*

*Colonel Theodore J. Conrad (Ted) was the Base Commander at RAF Bentwaters/Woodbridge. He was in charge of the overall running of the Airbases.

They managed to find their way back onto the base, after claiming the 'craft' levitated and went off at a high speed. They managed to find their way back onto the base, just prior to shift change, which would have been around four or five o'clock in the morning. Nobody knew quite what to do, so the Lieutenant, the Flight Lieutenant, decided nothing would happen – there would be no entries, although there was an entry made in the Law Enforcement Blotter at my insistence.

Charles Halt with Jim Penniston

I don't know what was entered in the Security Blotter because when I went back a year and a half, or two years, later, to try and recover from the archives, both the Security Blotter, the record of what happened that night, and the Law Enforcement Blotter, were gone. Somebody had picked them up. I suspect one of the individuals involved in the incident, probably, or a curiosity seeker, or somebody I don't know. I don't think it was an act on the part of any agency, or anything of that nature, because at that time, it was pretty secretive. It didn't really get too far out, other than the base. Later that day, I started getting all sorts of reverberations from the Police Squadron or various agencies on the base about this UFO, and wondered if there was something to this. I still didn't think too much about it. It was just before Christmas and there was a lot of activity. Quite a few people were on vacation back to the States and off on the Continent."

John Burroughs

Soon after the incident, Jim Penniston asked Lt. Col. Halt if he could be transferred to another base, as he was shaken after the event. John Burroughs, who had been far more affected by the earlier UFO sighting, stayed out in the forest for days, waiting for the UFO to return. Charles Halt recalls sending out blankets and food to Burroughs, but he didn't accept them.

> *"Some five hours after the sighting, I informed my Commanding Officer about having seen 'red and white lights flying up into the trees, over the forest'. He then said, 'Let's go and see if we can find any physical proof of what is happening', and, following a visit into the forest, we found damage to the trees and three depressions in the ground, forming a triangle, measuring 3.4 metres between each depression."*

In 2010, John Burroughs contacted us and said:

> *"Now that I have had a chance to look at things, I have a funny feeling that what went on was to do with some sort of military testing."*

Film taken of the UFO encounter

A roll of 35mm film was taken on the same night by Sgt. James Penniston. When developed, it was found to be fogged. Ray Boeche, an investigator, alleged that he had heard from a highly placed USAF official, at the Pentagon, that photos were indeed taken, *but not all of them* came out fogged.

From the left: John Burroughs, Jim Penniston, David Bryant and Nick Pope at Rendlesham. © David Bryant 2010

In an interview, conducted with James Archer (a pseudonym used by Jim Penniston, published in an edition of *UFO Magazine,* in 2001) he described the object as being,

> *"triangular and supported on three legs. I wasn't sure whether I actually saw alien beings, but was convinced the 'robot' shapes seen were non-human and inside the craft."*

(Source: *UFO Magazine,* January/February 2001)

The landing sites

Maps drawn by various airmen, identifies the route taken by vehicle from the security hut at East Gate, and then cutting across the Forestry Commission road, down track 12, before stopping at the junction with track 10. The occupants of those vehicles then made their way on foot along track 10 and headed away into the forest at an oblique angle, for 150yds, before coming across the UFO – a route confirmed by Colonel Halt, who wrote the following letter to Brenda Butler, in 2002:

> *"When I went out with the police, we went from Bentwaters to Woodbridge (as I remember) by way of the public road (through Eyke) onto Woodbridge, and then out the East Gate, down the road. We turned right onto the forest service road for a hundred or more feet – then left on the dirt road towards the sea. After several hundred yards, we turned left on a trail and continued for several hundred feet. From there we went right into the trees, towards the fence line. The 'landing site' was about 200-300ft from the fence, ahead, and to the left was the 'Boast' home."*

The route

The photo, showing PC Brian Cresswell, taken at the 'landing site' on the morning of the 26th December 1980 (referred to in the Suffolk Police Log as *'two miles east of the East Gate to Woodbridge Airbase'*) is generally accepted as the location identified by Colonel Halt, in the forest adjacent to Mr Boast's house.

An original sketch not used in *Sky Crash* (believed drawn by James Easton) endorsed, *'path taken from RAF Woodbridge to the site of the encounter',* appears as a 'cleaned up' illustration used in *Sky Crash.* On the left-hand side of this map, someone has drawn a small 'flying saucer' showing its flight over the forest, before passing over the landing lights next to Folly House, then heading out towards the coast.

The reader can see that the original 'plot' of the UFO (as shown in these maps/illustrations) falls into the same general area of forest referred to by Brenda and Peter Parish as *Area 1,* where they believe the UFO came down, causing damage to the canopy and burn marks to the trees.

We have to say that this location appears very similar to the location shown on the 'Brian Cresswell' photograph. However, during our walks through the forest, another similar site was pointed out as to where this photo was taken, located between track 10 and 12 – not too far away from the stretch of forest where Colonel Charles Halt and his colleagues followed the UFO. While we see no reason to dispute what Brenda and Peter claim, there is an inherent problem in trying to identify stretches of forest and pinpoint locations which may have looked completely different over 30 years ago.

Another map taken from a visit to the location by Martin Shipp and Charles Affleck shows a location close to that nominated by Colonel Halt.

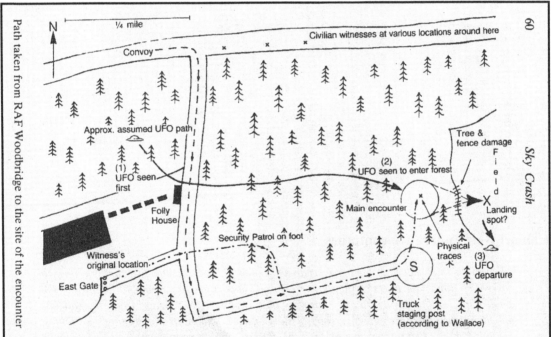

The fact that, periodically, the Forestry Commission have cut down large swathes of trees (as they have done in Area 1, and other parts of the forest) never mind changing the track numbers themselves, can obviously lead to confusion. These points should be borne in mind, particularly as these sightings took place in the darkness.

Brenda:

> *"I have read all manner of different directions taken to the so-called UFO landing site over the years, including a mention of an open field on the right-hand side of East Gate. There is*

no open field. I agree that, generally speaking, the locations nominated by the airmen are in the same general area, but there doesn't appear to be one place universally nominated by everyone as being where the 'craft' landed, which just adds to the confusion – especially when you bear in mind that they were all supposed to be together on the nights when this happened."

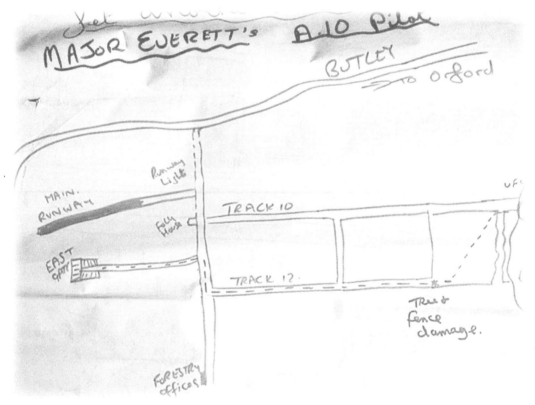

Colonel Halt's narrative continues . . .

"Two night later we were having Christmas dinner [27th December], a family dinner, a cover dish dinner for all the Officers and combat support group – about 40 families at the small Club, at Woodbridge Base, known as the 'Twelve O'clock High' Club. We had just finished dinner and were getting ready to start dessert, and enjoy the evening's festivities, involving things like annual awards and the recognition for people who had done special things, when Bruce Englund the on-duty Flight Lieutenant for the Security Police Squadron came bursting in, with his Ml6, and all red-faced and upset, and said to me, 'I've got to talk to you privately, right now'. So I got hold of Ted Conrad, who was my boss – the Base Commander – and we went into the cloakroom. It was the only private place to talk in the Club, at that time. He said, 'It's back'. 'What's back, Bruce?' He said, 'The UFO's back'. I said, 'How do you know that?' He said, 'I've seen something'. I said, 'Where?' He said, 'Outside the East Gate, in the woods'. 'So what are you doing out in the woods in the East Gate?' . . . bearing in mind England was a foreign country, as far as we're concerned.

We were guests there, and our mission was not to patrol the woods but to maintain the perimeter of the base. He said, 'Some of the guys saw something, so we sent a patrol out there. We took some light-alls with us. (The NF2 light-alls were motor generators. They were nothing but a small, I think, a five horsepower 'Briggs & Stratton' engine with a couple of big mercury vapour lights on top, and a gas tank, and a lot of sheet metal.) The lights wouldn't work. The radios were acting up. When we looked in the woods with a starlight scope, we saw some strange things'. 'What did you see?' 'We saw a glow and some red lights.

Ted Conrad and I looked at each other, as he had to make all the presentations, or maybe that was his excuse. He said, 'Why don't you go out and see what this is all about. Ok, I wasn't too excited, but I realised the cops had become preoccupied with this – both the Security Forces and the Law Enforcement – and they were more attuned to what was going on in the woods probably than what they should be doing; in other words, guarding the perimeter of the base and providing law enforcement. So I went to the Disaster Preparedness Officer and said, 'Would

Staff Sergeant Nevels

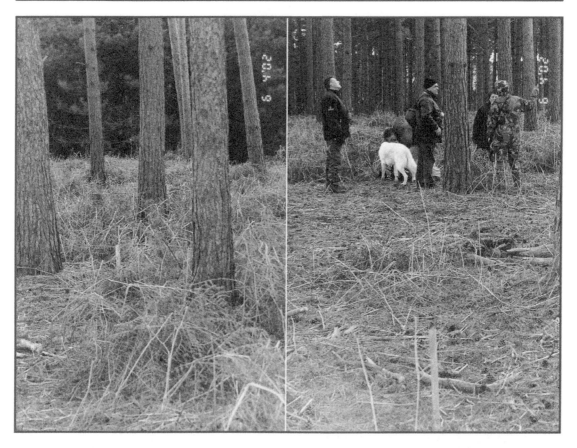

you have one of your key NCOs – whoever is on standby – go over to your office, pick up an ANP-27 Geiger counter and calibrate it', and I knew who. She told me who was on duty. It was Sergeant Nevels. I knew he was a professional photographer, and had a degree in photography, so I said, 'Have him bring his camera along too', so she got on the phone and called him. I drove home.

The police came by in a jeep and picked me up (Master Sergeant Bobby Ball) and I don't remember who else. We then went over and picked up Sergeant Nevels. I watched him calibrate two ANP, ANP-27's, and we picked what I thought was the better. Actually, they were both probably very good . . . then we bundled into the jeep, and drove across the flight line. The two Bases are about a mile and a half apart – a little closer if you drive right across the flight line and in the back gate. We unlocked the back gate and drove across, and to what, what's known as East Gate, at Woodbridge. Lo and behold, there's a crowd out there. Well, I was quite concerned, so I said to them, 'Let's keep all these people back. We don't need the publicity.

We are kind of trespassing. This was the Queen's forest – sort of like a National Forest. There's a lot of private property around here. We don't want to cause a lot of concern, or get people upset. They're going to wonder what we're doing stomping around out here in the woods', so he said, 'Ok'. At this time there were probably 30 or 40 people in total, with three or four light-alls which were acting up. They wouldn't run right, kept flickering off and on. I could hear comments: 'He didn't refuel them' and somebody else said, 'Yes, I did refuel them; I took them down to the motor pool before we brought them out'.

Bruce says, 'Let's look into the woods there', and he had a first generation starlight scope. We looked into the woods and, sure enough, in one area there was a dull glow. When you look through a starlight scope you don't see things as you normally would. It's a greenish-yellow tinge to them. It's a different spectrum, or different, uh, frequency and there was something I could see in there, but I wasn't really sure what it was. It didn't make a lot of sense to me . . . and I'm not sure it's of great significance, but there was something.

I had taken my small cassette recorder along with me, not specifically for this instance. It's just that any time I went around the base, I would take this little recorder along, record things that need to be done, a fence that needed to be mended, or a road needing to be paved, or whatever I noticed, or something out of the ordinary . . . and I'd bring it back and flip it to the secretary, and she'd type it up, then, at the next staff meeting, would mark who had the action on the items, and pass it them out for tasking . . . so I'd taken it along that night, just because I thought I might need to take some notes and it was probably 35, 40 degrees, with a stiff wind blowing off the coast, and quite cold . . . and I made a tape, which was later inadvertently released by a co-worker. I can't exactly repeat what's on there.

It's 1980, but I'll just go through what happened. I was afraid that wouldn't be too good, but the little pocket recorder I had has long since worn out. It gave up the ghost, and they've changed the format on tapes now so I put it on big tapes, while I could. Basically what happened, I took the pocket recorder along and just dropped it in my pocket, and I'd pick it up, and every few minutes I would say what was going on.

When we approached the site, we found the three indentations. We measured them, and you can hear the distance on there. I think there were eight or nine, seven feet apart, very triangular, and the dosimeter was picking up definite readings which were above background radiation, seven to twenty times, dependant upon whom you talk to, and it was, the site was hottest, so to speak, in the centre formed by the triangle. Also the trees, the pine trees that were there, were approximately, I would say, anywhere from 8 to 15 inches diameter.

There were some marks on them. There were two, two sets of marks, or types of marks. There were blade marks that were done with an axe, that were very clear. Someone had come through the forest not too long before, and marked trees – probably for cutting, but there were some big rub marks and, if you looked overhead, branches were broken as though something could have come up or come down, although I can't say that for a fact. It appeared that way. You could see the sky there and you couldn't see it anywhere else. We were walking around.

We identified one of the indentations as point one and I'm measuring them and taking readings, so we have a record of all this, when suddenly, Bruce Englund, the Lieutenant who was with me, looks out and says a few words I won't repeat, and says, 'There's something out there – look at that', and it was a red thing. It's the only way I can describe it. It looked like an eye. It was oval and had a black centre, and it was winking. It just looked like an eye is what it looked like. And it moved back and forth through the trees, horizontally, and not necessarily in a level plane. It was moving through the trees. It was in the forest at that time. We watched it blink. Now some people have equated this to the Orford Ness lighthouse, which we were all very familiar with.

The lighthouse has three different beams. It has a white rotating beam that does go around about every five seconds; it has a red light, and a green light. The white light revolves. The red light and green light are fixed at sea. They cannot be turned, even manually, toward the land . . . and I've gone back and talked to the lighthouse keeper personally to verify this, thinking, you know, there's got to be an explanation of the red light. The lighthouse could not have been what we saw.

It moved through the forest, moved through the trees. We stood there in awe for quite a while, watching this thing . . . and, finally, I said 'Let's try and get closer', so we worked our way through the forest and, as we did, it receded. It moved out into the field. There was a large field on the other side of the forest. We came up to a barbed, an old barbed wire fence, and watched there for a few minutes. And it seemed to be centred almost in front of a farmer's house, and the farmer's house had a glow in all the windows, as though it were on fire inside. It's the only way I can describe it. It may have been a reflection off the glass in the windows. It probably was, but I didn't know for sure.

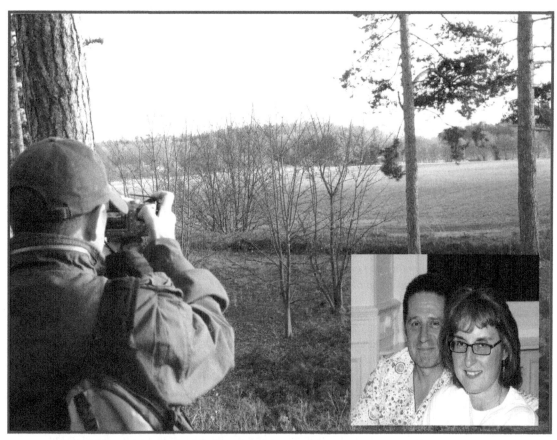

David Sankey and Erica Williams looking over on the field adjacent to the farm owned by Peter Greenwell.

I was quite concerned for whoever was in the farmhouse, if anybody was there, and it was an active farm. The animals were just going crazy on the farm. The horses, the cows, the pigs – everything was just making all kinds of noise. There was no activity that we could discern in the farmhouse at all. It was quiet. The object was there, probably for, I'm guessing, 30, 40 seconds – maybe a minute, and all of a sudden, it just silently exploded into five white objects and they disappeared – just gone like that! While we were watching it, it appeared to be dripping the equivalent of a molten metal. Something was, like, dripping off it, so when the object disappeared, I said, 'Let's go out in the field and see if we can find some burned evidence, or some spots on the ground where something has fallen – there has to be something'. . . and we went out, of course. It was in the dark, and about all we did was step in cow pies, but we didn't find any evidence at all. We went around the farmer's house, went on out into a ploughed field, to get a better view, and all this time we could see the lighthouse. In fact, there was another lighthouse further down the coast we could see at that time, too. We're standing out in the ploughed field. We crossed it, and we all fell into a stream we didn't see and got good and wet.

We came out of that, into another ploughed field, and, I don't remember who, but somebody said, 'Look!', and we looked up to the North, and there were objects in the sky, to the North. In the meantime, we're having great problems with the radios. Uh, there were five of us there. We all had radios, and each (three of us) were on different nets.

I was on the net with the command post. There was a cop on the security net with the Security Police, and one of the cops was on the Law Enforcement net, so we were talking to three different control centres, so to speak, all the time. Generally, we would have to relay, through one of the people that were back by the light-alls, because the radios would not carry that far and they were in the line of sight, yes, pretty much, but we were out in the open, in the clear, which was kind of puzzling because normally we should have gotten a good transmission right through.

It was a clear night, standing in the field, and somebody said, 'Look up there!', and here are these objects in the sky. The best way I can describe them – they look like a half, or a 'Cherokee' moon, and they were well-illuminated, with multiple coloured lights, and they were moving about in sharp, angular, patterns – very fast, and as we watched them, they turned, from the equivalent of a 'Cherokee' moon into a full circle. It was very amazing . . . and the way they were going, it appeared that they were doing some type of grid search, or doing some type of a pattern, or seemed to be some type of logic to their movement – really wasn't sure.

We probably watched them for twenty, thirty minutes, and suddenly, we noticed an object to the South. This was a round object and it was approaching us at very high speed. It came in – and it's real clear on the tape. That's an interesting part of the tape, if you could hear it – it came in very, very close, I'm guessing within a quarter to a half mile, and stopped two, three, four thousand feet up, and sent down a beam. The best way I can describe the beam is a laser beam, because a light beam normally radiates out. This came down instead and it was six to eight, or maybe nine, inches in diameter and fell right at our feet. Well, that really had us upset because we weren't sure whether it was a warning, whether it was, you know, a shot at us, whether it was somebody trying to communicate, or what it was. We had no idea, and we just stood there and looked and nobody said anything and, all of a sudden, as fast as it came on, it was gone. The object receded. Now the object, when it receded, was back over Bentwaters Base and we could see beams of light coming down there, near the weapons storage area, and we could hear the chatter on the radio.

The people over there could actually see the beams of light, too, so we stayed out there in the forest – I'm guessing, a total of about three and a half, maybe four hours. Now I can account for all our time, and you know, I, I've had every possible explanation, from an air inversion to ball lightning, to a meteor shower, to just about the lighthouse.

Everything you can think of. And really, my original intent when I went out, was to put the whole thing to rest, so the 'cops' could get on with business, and here I was, kind of in a dilemma, and wishing 'Gee', I wish I hadn't got involved in this – this is the end of my military career', so I came back to the base and briefed my boss on it. I played the tape for Wing Commander Gordon Williams – he was then a Colonel, now he's a retired three star General – and he just raised his eyebrows. He said, 'Gosh, Can I borrow the tape?' Of course you can borrow the tape, boss'. I gave him the tape. He took it out and played it for the Third Air Force Commander, who was the Commander for US Forces, in England – General Bazley, he listened to it at a staff meeting and turned to his staff and said, 'Well, what do we do now?' There was silence.

Third Air Force Commander, Major General Robert Bazley (left) with Welford Commander Lt. Col. Jim Wadell

He said, 'I guess this is a British affair. It happened on their turf. Give it back to them', so he brought the tape back and handed it to me, and says, 'Tell the 'Brits' about it'. It's exactly what he told me. Gosh. So I went over and the Liaison Officer – Don Moreland, who we called the British Base Commander (we had two British Officers stationed with us) – uh, was on vacation, so I told his assistant and he didn't want to touch it with a pole, so Don came back, a few days later, and I went over and said, 'Don, uh, why don't you make some calls and see what your Government want. I'm sure they'd want to investigate this'. So I waited, and waited, and waited, and a week or so went by . . . and I kept asking. He said, 'I haven't heard, I haven't heard'. Finally, he and I agreed I'd write a brief memo, so I wrote a brief, one-page, cleaned up, so to speak, version of what happened, to see how much interest there were, or was, and, uh, what would happen. I gave it to him.

He sent it off the Ministry of Defence, in London, and it was never heard or seen again. A copy found its way to his boss, at Mildenhall, Third Air Force Headquarters. Somehow or other, that copy survived for several years and, two or three years later, a gentleman by the name of, uh, Larry Fawcett heard about it from a friend, and a friend, et cetera, and he came in under the Freedom of Information Act for release of that document. At that time, a friend of mine was Third Air Force Commander, Pete Bent. He called me up and said, 'I'm going to have to release this document'. I said, number one, 'How did you get it?' He said, 'Boy! It beats me, but it's in the file here'. I said, 'Well, it wasn't addressed to you. It was addressed to the Ministry of Defence'. He said, 'Well, we have it, and we're going to have to release it', and I said, 'Please, don't. Your life, and mine, will never be the same'. He said, 'I'm sorry, we're going to have to'. Well, I was right on. I can tell you that because, the day after it was released, I met BBC1, BBC2, ITV, Japanese TV, German TV, every local radio station, every reporter worth his salt. It was unbelievable what happened the next day. I had to go into hiding, almost, and I almost became a recluse after that, so that's how the story came out, and that's in essence what happened.

Now there's a lot more to it. I've told people through the years, probably the biggest story is what happened afterwards. There's been an awful lot of interesting things happen, and I don't want to go into too many details here, but I am firmly convinced that there're an awful, there's an awful lot of interest, at an awful lot of agencies in the Government, that compete for, how shall I say, information and access to certain data. And, uh, there's all, there's been an awful lot of intrigue. I do know one or, if not, two of the original participants were given injections and some, how shall I say, hypnosis, uh, right after the incident occurred. There was a lot of clandestine, uh, sleuthing around, by various agencies, both from this side of the pond and the other side of the pond.

I have never been officially approached, although people from Kirtland and various sundry agencies have invited me to lunch that had an interest in this subject and things, and I played games with them, like they did with me. I think the only thing that has kept me out of, out of the middle of it, so to speak, is that I have some very, very high contacts, including probably the most senior Senator in Washington, and, uh, my last position as the Director of Inspections, Director for the DOD IG, where I had total inspection oversight for the whole Department of Defence, and had some very good contacts there. It's probably protected me, but some of the other people have been bothered and meddled with and, unfortunately, it's caused a lot of personal problems for them.

What really happened at Bentwaters? I honestly don't know. Something very strange happened. I've been back several times. I've gone back to the site. I've sat down with any and everybody I can think that, you know, could shed some light on it. I've batted this around with Jacques Vallee. I've met the foremost Astrophysicist, from Great Britain, and gone through things with him, and I have a lot of unanswered questions, and probably we'll never have them answered. I'd like to have them answered. But, it was a very interesting experience. I'm not sure, if I had the opportunity to go out again, whether I'd do it again or not. I haven't looked for publicity. I haven't written any books. I haven't gone on talk shows. I have done a couple of TV documentaries, but the agreement is in writing has been beforehand that it would be honest, factual, above-board, and that I'd get to review it before they publish because there's some real interesting people out there, including one who, as far as I'm concerned, wasn't there and has been telling a distorted tale.

So that, in essence, is what I know of what happened at Bentwaters. Now, I say, there's a lot of other intrigue and so forth that happened after the fact. I was telling somebody at lunch that I've been accused of everything, from cohorting with the devil to having participated in the second coming of Christ, so you meet some very strange people sometimes! Awful lot of credible people, an awful lot of very interested people that have some of the same questions I have, so, where do we go from here? I really don't know. I was hoping, maybe, to learn a little more today. I have, through the years, prised some more information out of some of the other participants, because they, for very personal reasons, didn't come completely forward on everything; in other words, they were concerned for their career, for their health, for their family, et cetera, so its unfortunate things have to be that way, but I think most of you probably understand that."

In an email sent to us in 2000, Colonel Halt had this to say, after we asked him whether he had suffered any ill effects following the incident:

Colonel Halt, 2012

"Further, I did not experience any sustained ill effects. I cannot speak for the other individuals involved, as I'm told that several feel they have sustained lasting health problems.

I talked with John Burroughs and Jim Penniston; they are now convinced that military experiments caused us to experience what we did, but I'm not convinced. The guys that hypnotized and drugged them are probably gloating over their success with all this disinformation. I did meet with Mike and Harry about 1982 and we all agreed not to reveal the meeting. General Williams was never involved. There were certain government agencies playing games with us. I'm firmly convinced of that, but I can't prove it – they're very discreet. Over the years I've also been approached by certain intelligence people, one from a certain installation in New Mexico. We had lunch. He asked me questions about what I had witnessed. I asked him what he wanted to do with it. He said 'it's classified'."

In an email sent to Brenda Butler, the Colonel said:

"It was too horrendous beyond belief to ever let people know what I saw. It happened at East Gate, right from day one."

September 25, 2000

Brenda Butler

Leiston, Suffolk

England

Dear Brenda:

Your wild experiences really sound like something is really heating up at "the East Gate". It's hard enough to believe what happened to us back in 1980 let along what's going on now. I would suggest you try hard to establish a dialog with what ever you've come in contact with. I would be most interested in hearing the results. If you do establish a dialog and I can help, I'm willing.

When I warned you to be careful I was not talking about something beyond us. My concern was that an agency with secretive powers might do something. You be the judge of that. I do know several of the airmen were hypnotized, drugged and threatened.

I have to assume that now you realize that other than when I gave up on your original Sky Crash trio, I have been telling the truth.

Keep in touch and be careful.

Chuck Halt.

Colonel Halt, during interview with Robert Hastings

In another interview conducted with Colonel Halt, Robert Hastings (Author of *Nukes and UFOs*) asked him to briefly summarise his experience. He replied:

> *"We saw objects that were under intelligent control."*

Robert asked:

> *"What was the source of the intelligence?"*

He replied:

> *"I don't know. It had to be something beyond [human technology] because of the way the objects moved — the speeds, the angles they turned, and the things they did."*

Could the objects have been remotely controlled?

> *"Certainly."*

He asked Colonel Halt:

> *"So you're saying that it was a technology beyond anything any country on Earth would have?"*

Colonel Halt replied:

> *"I never saw any little green men, but it's possible it was alien technology. I sure would like to have the answers, but don't think I'll ever get them.*
>
> *We could very clearly see the UFO. It sort of danced about in the sky and it sent down beams of light. I noticed other beams of light coming down from the same object, falling different places on the base. My boss, Col. Ted Conrad, was standing in his front yard in Woodbridge and he could see the beams of light falling down, and the people in the [Bentwaters] Weapons Storage Area and several other places on the base also reported the lights.*
>
> *The objects appeared elliptical and then they turned full round, which I thought was quite interesting all three doing that. They were stationary for a while and then they started to move at high speed in sharp angular patterns as though they were doing a grid search. About that same time, somebody noticed a similar object [in the southern sky]. It was round – did not change shape – and at one point it appeared to come toward us at a very high speed. It stopped overhead and sent down a small pencil-like beam, sort of like a laser beam. It was an interesting beam in that it stayed – it was the same size all the way down the beam. It illuminated the ground about ten feet from us and we just stood there in awe wondering whether it was a signal, a warning, or what it was. We really didn't know. It clicked-off as though someone threw a switch, and the object receded, back up into the sky. Then it moved back toward Bentwaters, and continued to send down beams of light, at one point near the weapons storage facility. I wondered if it was searching for something."*

Visit to see Colonel Halt

Brenda Butler and Dot Street went to see Colonel Halt, at 2pm, on the 12th August.1983. They were welcomed into his office and then asked if they had a tape recorder on them, to which they replied in the negative.

Brenda:

> *"Colonel Halt told us he was annoyed about his 'memo' ever having been released and that he had been promised by 'they'(whoever they are) that it would never be released. He remarked, 'The craft was triangular in shape, under some sort of control. There were no entities; I only know what the men have told me'."*

When Dot showed him Larry Warren's statement, he said that *"it was rubbish; only bits and pieces made sense."* When we showed him Steve Roberts' statement he said *"That's more like it, but no entities were seen".*

When the two women asked which bits were right, he replied *"That's for you two to figure out".* Laughing he said *"The truth is there somewhere!"* He took out a map and showed them where the landing site was, which was the same location as shown by Steve Roberts.

Colonel Halt, in 2009 said:

> *"I wish to make it perfectly clear that the UFOs I saw were structured machines, moving under intelligent control and operating beyond the realm of anything I have ever seen before or since. I believe the objects that I saw at close quarter were extraterrestrial in origin and that the Security Services of both the United States and England were, and have been, complicit in trying to subvert the significance of what occurred at Rendlesham by use of well practiced methods of disinformation."*

Bob Tibbitts, former head of Coventry UFO Research Group

> *"If there was no 'real' UFO incident at Bentwaters, and that it was all disinformation put about on the urging of a clandestine body, is it likely that the long silver object mentioned by Colonel Conrad was the 'M' word missing at the end of Charles Halt's tape recording?*
>
> *As this was a period when certain 'ordnance' was stored on British soil (with good reason at that time) it seems a logical assertion that the source for all the activity was caused by an experimental aircraft that needed repairs and the 'M' would have been a 'missile' of some description, that had become detached from the aircraft as a result of some malfunction.*
>
> *I wonder if there exists some type of co-operation between the major powers of our planet and a 'human' counterpart that has access to technologies that span 'time', 'space', and other 'dimensions of being'.*
>
> *Such an alliance would have profound implications for all people on Earth, especially if there is some form of skullduggery going on, impacting our own evolution. I can understand just why there would be such a tight lid placed around this incident and I wouldn't want to go on the record as being critical – but at the same time ask: Should we be left in the dark?*
>
> *Would most people be able to handle the 'extraterrestrial' explanation more readily (considering the onslaught of popular media and 'Hollywood' influencing our judgement) – as opposed to the 'real truth' (if that is what it is), of humankind from a distant place and distant time, involving themselves with the affairs of their ancestors ('us' at this moment) with an inevitable, but possibly, unsavoury outcome? This, constituting a part of the whole 'tapestry' that is being embroidered by the 'visitors' and parties from who-knows-where – who also have an ongoing interest in human affairs going back in history. Set against this scenario, even though our questions about 'The Rendlesham Forest Incident' are valid and should be asked – I cannot see that we will be furnished with an honest answer from those who do know the truth – any time soon."*

Nick Pope's comments on Georgina Bruni

"One cannot overstate the contribution made by Georgina, who ran a number of businesses in areas such as fashion, PR, and events organising. She was a former Director of the Yacht Club, where she was involved in hosting social events for MPs, Diplomats and MOD officials. She was also involved in various charities, mainly relating to injured Service personnel.

It was through some of her political and military contacts that she first heard about the Rendlesham Forest incident. It intrigued her and she spent several years researching it, using her contacts to track down and interview many of the military personnel who had been involved – who had never previously spoken about what had occurred.

Georgina Bruni obtained the MOD file on the incident, using the Code of Practice on Access to Government Information – a forerunner of the Freedom of Information Act. She then wrote the definitive book on the case – 'You Can't Tell the People'. The title was taken from a conversation about UFOs that Georgina had with former Prime Minister Margaret Thatcher, in 1997, when they met at a charity fundraising event. The book won praise not just from the UFO community but from Gordon Williams, who had been Commanding Officer of the twin bases of Bentwaters and Woodbridge when the incident occurred, and from former Chief of the Defence Staff, The Lord Hill-Norton, who asked Georgina to brief him on her research and draft a number of questions, which he subsequently raised in Parliament.

There was controversy too. Some UFO researchers were suspicious of Georgina's establishment contacts and her friendship with me. They wondered why the launch party for her book was held in the King Henry VIII Wine Cellar in Ministry of Defence Main Building, Whitehall. And she attracted more than a little jealousy when she managed to find witnesses and acquire documents that ufologists had been trying in vain to locate for years. Georgina acted as consultant and contributor to numerous TV documentaries on the case. Indeed, much of what we know about – arguably the most significant UFO case aside from Roswell – we know through the efforts of Georgina."

Courtesy of the Disclosure Project

The Lord Hill-Norton, former Chief of the British Defence Staff, wrote in a letter to us:

"I have no doubt that something landed at this US Air Force Base and I have no doubt that it has got the people concerned into a considerable state. The Ministry of Defence has doggedly stuck to its normal line, that nothing of defence interest took place. Either large numbers of people, including the Commanding General, at Bentwaters, were hallucinating – and for an American Air Force Nuclear Base, this is extremely dangerous – or what they say did happen."

WITNESS TIMELINE

Meteor display over Europe 25th December 1980

At 9.07pm on the 25th of December 1980, a number of people living in the Kent and Thames estuary contacted the authorities after sighting a formation of six objects emerging from a larger one moving across the sky eastwards towards the North Sea. Other reports described blazing debris as if a plane on fire. The phenomenon which was in view for over 5 minutes was later explained away as a brilliant meteor.

UFO sighted over Airbase – 25th December 1980

Carl Thompson Jr. – former radio communications specialist at Bentwaters – was interviewed by Robert Hastings. This is what he had to say:

> *"At the time, I was a Senior Airman with the 2164 Communications Squadron. I was a radio relay repairman. On the first night – Christmas night, if I'm not mistaken – I was at the Weapons Storage Area working on a piece of equipment in the security tower, trouble-shooting it. I think it was a motion-detection component, used for the security of the weapons. At midnight, the guy who was going to relieve me called and said that he would come out to the area.*
>
> *So, I went back to the wide-band radio shop and finished up some paperwork. Now, I don't remember how much later it was, but he called me at the shop and said, 'We just saw a UFO!' He meant himself and the security guards. He was in the security tower cab at the time he called. You could plainly tell he was excited and maybe kind of anxious. He sounded matter-of-fact but also kind of half-scared. I asked, 'What did it look like?' He said, 'It was so bright that you couldn't look directly at it.' So I didn't get any details about its shape, how large it was any of that. It was just a really bright light. He said it was hovering there for just a few seconds, then it went toward Woodbridge so, maybe, that would be in a south-westerly direction. 'Did everybody see it?' He said that everyone had. Then he asked me, 'How am I going to report this?' I said, 'Is anyone else going to report it?' He said, 'No, they're not going to report it.' So, I said, 'How are you going to look, if the others who were right there in the area aren't going to report it? You're going to be on your own. If it were me, I would let it go.' I was the ranking person on that night, so I told him, 'I would advise against it, but it's up to you.' When I saw him later that night he had to order a part for the tower, so we crossed paths – he told me that he'd decided not to report the incident. At the time, we didn't know that the other base was involved. We had no idea that there had been some security police hunting it down, or whatever, in the woods.*

Authors: (John Burroughs sights strange lights over the forest at 2 am 26th December 1980 while with his watch-supervisor Budd Parker – he then meets up with Jim Penniston and the two men experience a close encounter a short time later). Carl Thompson continues:

> *I guess it was two nights later, the part for the equipment in the tower came in. We got notified*

about that just as my colleague was coming on shift, at midnight, so he said he would go out and install it. I stayed at the radio shop. A little while later (it had to be past 12:30, since he had to pick up the part first), he called, really excited, and told me that he had just seen another UFO. It had followed the runway, which runs more or less east and west, then it turned, uh, then it turned again and flew directly over the Weapons Storage Area.

He said it came right at the tower and was so low that he and the guard hit the deck! He said it had hovered [nearby] for a few seconds. He couldn't say how long, and then it slowly moved off, over the trees. He said it was just above them, but then it dropped down into the trees. He didn't see it come back up, so that's when he called me on the landline. He said he heard a bunch of chatter on the radio in the tower – the guard there was talking to someone – and said [the Security Police] were going to have to report it this time, because it went down into the woods."

Official response following debriefing

The next time Carl saw his colleague, he told him he had to file a report with the Security Police at their headquarters, approximately 30yds away from the Weapons Storage Area.

About a week or so later, the man was called by his Squadron Commander – Major Cossa – and told to report for a briefing. He was gone most of an afternoon but when he came back he was really agitated.

Carl asked him: *"What's up?"* He replied, *"We are not to speak about the UFO."* Angrily he declared, *"I know what I saw!"*

He told Carl that during the briefing, someone – he assumed it was OSI (Office of Special Investigations) told everyone there that night they hadn't seen anything.

Carl:

> *"I think that upset my colleague more than anything. According to him, they called all the police liars. My colleague said, 'They told us that we did not see it, and were never to speak of it. He was really upset. He said (the OSI agents) had talked to them as a group and then talked to them individually. You know, went over their statements with them. He said they told him he was a liar, that he would never have a career, and all that. You know, threatening him. But he told me that he couldn't go into the details. We never talked about it again."*

A while later Carl tried to ask some of the Security Police about the incident, when he saw them at the Weapons Storage Area, but they were fairly tight-lipped about it.

> *"They told me that they went into the forest on the night of December 27th/28th; they took light-alls with them, all of sudden the lights and vehicle engines quit. The radios picked up a lot of static on them; after a few minutes everything just started working again. I don't know much more than that, until I saw all of the reports from Colonel Halt and the others on TV, that's about all I can tell you"*

Robert Hastings asked Thompson:

>*"How do you know the first incident happened on Christmas night?"*

Answer:

>*"Well, I'm not positive it did, but it was definitely during the holidays, the 25th, the 26th, because '.....', and I, were working a longer shift on both of those nights. We were single and our sergeant asked us to volunteer for that, so the married guys could be with their families during Christmas. In return, we got some days off in January."*

Robert then asked Thompson if '............' had described seeing one or more beams of light coming from the UFO, down into the Weapons Storage Area, on either night.

Answer: *"No, he didn't say anything about that."*

 ## Anne Hopton-Scott

Other witnesses to something strange seen happening during the 1980 Christmas period included Anne Hopton-Scott, who was driving back from Woodbridge, one evening, when she saw a bright object moving through the sky, which appeared to follow the curve of the road.

>*"Suddenly, it came up and went straight over my car, making a terrific whooshing noise."*

 Gary Collins was heading home, at 11.30pm, when he saw 'lights' moving across the sky. He stopped and parked up.

>*"When my eyes became adjusted to the light, I was able to see the front was triangular in shape, with portholes underneath, and then it shot away from zero to a terrific speed over me and into the forest."*

(Source: Georgina Bruni)

 ## UFOs sighted over Ipswich between 9-11pm, 26th December 1980

Wayne Burgess (12) and his family were in Bennett Road, near Ipswich, when they spotted half-a-dozen mysterious lights in the sky over Ipswich.

Wayne:

>*"I have never heard of another account from anyone else that resembles mine; however this is 100% accurate, as I was quite excited about it at the time. The one thing I am not certain about is the number of lights that were there (5, 6 or 7) but I can say that they were individually moving, just slightly enough to know that they weren't part of the same object."*

The family watched the lights which showed an aura around them for about 5-10 minutes and appeared to be individually moving across the sky, at a very slow speed. After a while, the family decided to move on, and left – the lights still slowly moving across the sky.

It was later suggested that Wayne and his family could have seen meteors, or a satellite, re-entering the atmosphere. Wayne rejects this as an explanation and said:

>*"I remember that following the sighting, when the newspapers were released after Xmas, my*

father saying that he had read a report of a meteor shower in the Press. However, the lights in the sky that I saw, although slightly moving, stayed in the same position in the sky, whilst we stood and watched it. Although I understand it is always a temptation to connect it with something mysterious, I do not believe, in my humble opinion, that this is what I saw.

These lights/objects did not have fiery tails, as a meteor or a burning-up satellite would do, only a slight haze around each 'globe of light'. Additionally, the meteors were only reported to have been visible on the 25th December, not the 26th in this case.

I did not realize until several years later, whilst reading an account of famous UFO sightings in the Sunday Times Magazine *in the UK (during the high profile Roswell case) that this was connected to the famous Rendlesham Forest sighting. I had, on several occasions, recounted my story to friends, and was quite excited that, at last, my sighting coincided with an official UK mystery in print".*

Strange Lights seen over the Airbase – 11pm on 26ᵗʰ December 1980

Gerry Harris was then living in a house situated in the centre of Rendlesham Forest, overlooking the twin bases of RAF Bentwaters and RAF Woodbridge. At 11.00pm on 26th December, he happened to look out of the window and notice some unusual lights in the sky.

"The lights were going at a nice steady speed and were moving about in the sky. I walked out into the front yard and stood watching them. I couldn't hear any sounds at all. They were bobbing up and down, and moving from side to side; they continued to move about in this manner for three-quarters of an hour when, all of a sudden, they disappeared. However, just before they disappeared, there was a lot of activity on the base. I could hear vehicles driving about, and see flashing lights of vehicles moving about and people shouting. I could hear their voices calling to each other, which at that time of night was unusual."

A few days later, he visited Rendlesham Forest and spoke to some of the Forestry Commission workers. They told him an area of trees had been felled and that there was an area contaminated with radiation, which he must stay away from.

Gerry Harris and his wife in 1983

In February 2013, we had the opportunity to speak to retired mechanic Gerry Harris (79) whose friendship with Brenda and her first husband goes back many years. We discussed his sighting. He reiterated what was written above and then said:

> *"What I can't understand is that there were three objects in the sky, I must have looked away because then there was only one, whether they combined I can't say, I got a bit fed up watching them. The bigger one in the middle descended down behind the trees. I thought to myself it's crashed. All of a sudden it came back up and rose up into the sky until I lost sight of it. After haring all the noise from the base I went down to have a look and found a military policeman there standing next to a uniform civilian police constable. They wouldn't let me on to base. I had customers come to my garage afterwards to pick up their cars; some of them were base personnel. I asked them what the hell had gone on at the base that night. One of them told me "It's more than my life to talk about it."*

A few days afterwards Gerry noticed that large area of trees in the nearby woods had disappeared almost overnight. When he asked a forester who called into the garage what had happened, he was shocked by the answer – *"The trees were radioactive. They had to go."*

Strange Lights seen and security alert – 11pm 26th December 1980

 The Landlord of the *Ramshott Arms* Public House, Ramshott, near Woodbridge, was driving on the outskirts of Woodbridge, at 11.00pm on 26th December 1980, on his way home, after collecting his wife and children from Butley.

> *"As I came up the road, past the* Butley Oyster *Public House, I could see lights across the trees, over Rendlesham. Curious as to the cause, I turned up the forestry road and saw trucks and jeeps, with men getting out of them. I thought it was an exercise and carried on up the road. A security guard then stopped me and ordered me to turn around and leave. I asked him what was going on. He refused to answer, and again ordered me to leave. I noticed more jeeps and lorries arriving up the road, and drove away, but decided to park up at the side of the road, when I heard lots of shouting and saw bright lights over the forest. After about ten minutes, I decided to go home."*

(Source: Brenda Butler)

Strange lights over the Forest – 11pm 26th December 1980

Travelling salesman Arthur Smekle from Essex was driving past Woodbridge air base when he noticed an object in the sky heading low down towards the direction of Rendlesham forest –

> *"I first thought it was an aircraft but the lights were unlike anything I had ever seen before; they were both extensive and brilliant. I stopped my van to get a closer look but it went out of view behind trees."*

(Source: Sky Crash page 87)

UFO seen and security alert – 26th December 1980

On Boxing Day 1980 evening, local resident Graham Tilt was having a drink at *Woodhall* – formerly an Elizabethan priory, (now Hintlesham Hall Hotel) –

"I was in the bar with Barry, who owned the place. He went over to open the window, as it was getting hot, to let some air into the room, when we both saw a strange bright white 'light' fly silently across the sky. Barry said to me, 'How strange, there is no noise. I'm going to go and have a look'. He then drank up and went one way, while I went the other.

I made my way toward the direction of Felixstowe, and diverted off towards the Woodbridge Airbase. When about two miles along the Bawdsey road, near to the communications centre, I was stopped from driving further by armed members of the USA Police, who told me, 'There has been an incident'. I then turned around and drove away. What amazed me was what on earth they could be doing outside the Airbase. After all, they had no jurisdiction on English soil, and surely would not have been allowed off base."

(Source: Personal interview)

UFO seen over the Forest – exact date not ascertained

Former security patrolman officer on D Flight, Robert 'Charlie' Waters, who had been on duty at the Weapons Storage Area during the week of the UFO activity, was interviewed by Robert Hastings.

"There was some commotion in the Weapons Storage Area that night. Someone saw this object. I don't remember who, and called out to us. I think my ART partner was Rob Isbell, but I'm not certain, but we looked and saw this spinning light – multicoloured light. I can't really remember the colours – anyway, this craft was hovering and then slowly descended toward the forest.

We ran up on one of the beams to get a better view of it. We then reported it to Central Security Control. I remember I used a couple of expletives and was warned not to use profanity on the radio. I think I was talking to a guy named Alfred Coakley. Anyway, he's the one I remember talking to most of the time that night. The next morning, I talked to one of the operations officers, who told me that a small group of security police had gone out to the woods and had seen some burn marks on trees, about three feet off the ground. He said it looked like, whatever it was, had bounced from tree to tree coming down. The person who told me that wasn't our flight's shift commander. He was another officer, but I don't remember his name. I also think I saw something sticking out on the bottom, uh, like a rod, or something like that."

Marks alleged found in Rendlesham Forest – 26th/27th December 1980

An unsigned letter from a woman staying with friends on an unidentified USA Airbase describes an incident brought to her attention by a friend. She telephoned her, reporting that her husband had been on patrol when he heard, over his portable radio, of a UFO which had landed inside the Airbase on the late night of 26th December/early hours of 27th December 1980.

The man concerned told her the other men had been frightened and moved away from the object. The woman, her curiosity aroused made her way to the designated location but it had been cordoned off. However, a short time later, she went back for another look and discovered three large marks, in a triangular position, where the alleged object had been seen. Unfortunately, as we do not know any further details, or the identity of the people concerned, we can only take this information on its face value.

(Source: Brenda Butler)

Was the woman mistaken? Could these have been the events described as happening on the evening of the 25th of December 1980, followed by the visit to the forest by PC Creswell at 10.13am on the 26th?

Alert at the airbase 27th December 1980

Airman Steve Wilkins phoned Brenda Butler on Thursday 6th October 1983 and told her he was working on the flight line on the 27th December 1980 when he noticed lots of lights and increased activity occurring in the forest involving many lorries and jeeps heading up the flight path. He asked what was going on and was told it concerned *"Aliens but not like 'Aliens'"*.

Brenda:

> *"Steve Wilkins phoned again on Saturday 8th October and told me the men who went to the area were briefed on what to say and it definitely was not a UFO. He said the men were told to say it was a UFO and to let people think it was something from outer space. To the men it was a UFO because they didn't know what it was. He wouldn't say anymore. He was worried the phone was being monitored."*

According to *Sky Crash*, Steve also mentioned that during the next afternoon while talking to a colleague about the incident:

> *"I was told by one man that a small craft had come down in the forest, it had stood on legs, four robot creatures were in control of it, and that twenty four men including senior officers had been allowed to go near it".*

UFO seen over Woodbridge – 2.30am on 27th December 1980

Woodbridge resident Mrs Webb was driving her car, at about 2.30am on 27th December 1980, on the outskirts of Rendlesham Forest, accompanied by her husband, Roy, who had their daughter, Hayley, on his knee. Hayley brought her parents attention to a 'star' that was following them.

Mrs Webb:

> *"I saw what looked like a bright 'star' following our car. All the time it stayed level with us. When we stopped in a lay-by, it remained with us. We sat there for a minute in the lay-by – then the light went up and vanished."*

(Source: Brenda Butler)

Highpoint Prison placed on alert – evening of 27th December 1980

George Wild – a resident of Ossett, in West Yorkshire, who had been employed as a senior prison officer at Armley Prison, Leeds – spoke to Graham Birdsall of *UFO Magazine*, in 1995, with regard to a conversation held with a fellow prison officer, then based at *Highpoint Prison, Suffolk*.

The man told George that during the early evening of 27th December 1980, he and his fellow members of staff, received instructions warning them they might have to evacuate the prison, due to an incident late that night. When staff questioned this, they were told it was a matter of National Security.

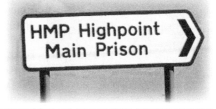

Questions raised in the House, by The Lord Hill-Norton – 26ᵗʰ April 2001

The Lord Hill-Norton later asked questions in the House:

> *"Further to the written answer, by Lord Bassam of Brighton, on the 23ʳᵈ January, Whether their search for evidence of any instructions concerning the possible evacuation of Blundeston Prison and Hollesley Bay Young Offenders Institution included an examination of the Governors journals for these two establishments and whether these journals have been retained."*

Lord Bassam

Lord Bassam, Parliamentary Under-Secretary of State, Home Office:

> *"Governors Journals are the most likely source of this information so long after the event. The Governors Journal at Blundeston remains in existence and was examined. The relevant Governors Journal for Hollesley Bay could not now be found, and in the absence of any written record, long serving staff, including the Governor's Secretary, were consulted. They did not recall any instruction to prepare for an evacuation, although they well remembered the local events at the time, which prompted speculation about such an instruction."*

(Sources: *BUFORA Bulletin*, No. 004, Dot Street, Page 20-21, *Northern UFO Network -Case Histories*, Jenny Randles, *Flying Saucer Review*, Volume No. 27, Jenny Randles, *The Unexplained*, Volume 9, Jenny Randles)

This was not the last time we were to hear of Lord Steven Bassam.

In June 1998, Elaine Waite (now a personal friend of the authors) was head of Southall-based UFO group UPN, and had occasion to complain to the Post Office about personal mail having gone missing and mail being damaged in transit. Feeling that nothing was being addressed, she reported the ongoing postal interference to the police in 1999. In 2001 she brought her grievances to Baroness Trixie Gardner, knowing that she had asked a question in the House of Lords recently on this matter.

Lord Steven Bassam

Elaine Waite

Baroness Gardner (Rachel Trixie Anne Gardner) wrote to Lord Steve Bassam of Brighton, at the Home Office, about the situation. Lord Bassam in turn wrote back to Elaine, enclosing a covering letter:

'*Dear Trixie,*

Thank you for your letter of 12th February, following up your question of 1st February, and enclosing correspondence from Elaine Waite, Manaton Crescent, Southall, Middlesex, about whether anyone is entitled to know that an interception warrant has been issued.'

[He then outlined the provisions of the Regulation of Investigatory Powers (RIPA) quoting Part 1 of the Act, relating to it being a criminal offence to intercept a person's telephone calls, or mail, without his/her consent]

'*Of course it is possible to intercept a telephone without the authority of a warrant. This will be generally unlawful and anyone who suspects that his or her telephone calls are being unlawfully intercepted should report the matter to the police. Much as I would like to be able to reassure UPN Investigations about whether or not the intelligence law enforcement or security agencies may have an interest in them and whether their telephones or post is being intercepted under warrant, I am sure that you will understand that I cannot do so. It has been the policy of successive Governments not to comment on such matters. This is not because the Government has anything to hide but because if for the sake of argument we were to reassure you that UPN Investigations was not under investigation, then we should have to be similarly open with everyone who has made such enquiries. As I am sure you will appreciate, word would soon get around and before long I would be receiving letters from the few people, who because they present a threat to national security or because they were suspected of involvement in a very serious crime are subject to these measures. That would clearly defeat the purpose of covert investigations.*

Yours, Steve Brighton'
Lord Bassam of Brighton

We accept, unequivocally, what Lord Bassam of Brighton has said here in his letter to the Baroness Gardner. Clearly there cannot be one law for one and another law for another, but we know from communication with Elaine and her family, at the time, that a number of strange vehicles, with occupants, were often seen outside her home, and that she was followed to Wiltshire, Woodbridge, and even Yorkshire.

> "*Even strange vehicles were parked outside my place of work, at the school; I cannot give you an exact figure, it was happening so often*".

Knowing 'Elly', we remain puzzled why she should attract this level of surveillance interest from the intelligences services, conducted crudely rather than covertly. Presumably 'they' wanted her to know that she was being watched.

Silver 'Missile' seen in Rendlesham Forest – evening of 27th December 1980

Ron Gladstone – a resident of Woodbridge – was walking his dog in Rendlesham Forest on the evening of the 27th of December, 1980 when he came across a crater in the ground, with what looked like a silver missile sticking out of it. Next to it were three men wearing silver suits (believed firemen). Ron decided to leave and went home.

Brenda Butler:

> "*The* News of the World *heard about his sighting and tried to interview him. Sadly Ron's wife died in mysterious circumstances aged 26. The location where Ron saw the missile was identical to the location nominated by Colonel Halt.*"

(Source: Recorded interview)

Later the same evening (27th December 1980) Mr Tony Sorrell, employed as food production manager at Thetford, was on his way home after locking up the business premises when he saw:

> "... a sharply defined triangular-shaped object, like frosted glass, moving through the clear night sky as it moved the stars above dimmed, it was not moving very fast, and was gone from view twenty seconds later".

Bright 'light' seen over Rendlesham Forest –11pm on 27th December 1980

 Michael Simms – the son of an American serviceman, then living in Marlsford, Woodbridge – contacted Brenda and told her that he and his two friends saw a big bright 'light' over the forest, then coming towards Parnham at about 11.00pm on the 27th December 1980. They watched it for 45mins. He said:

> "We tried following it on foot. After a while, it split up into 3 lights and sped off."

At 11pm on the 27th of December 1980 Mrs Sadler from Leiston was driving along the road, when she sighted a red ball of fire over Tangham Forest, Rendlesham. **(Source: Brenda Butler)**

Bright 'light' over Rendlesham Forest – 11.30pm-1.00am on 27th December 1980

Brenda:

> "We spoke to one witness in a pub, at Wilford Bridge, who said he was travelling down to the Airbase, between 11.30pm and 1.00am on 27th or 28th December, when he saw a bright 'light' over the Rendlesham Forest area. He thought it was an aircraft, but couldn't understand why it remained motionless in the sky for twenty minutes. When he asked some of his friends on the base, they told him it was an exercise alert. Importantly, he added that he had seen no sign of any activity, such as vehicles or soldiers."

(Source: Brenda Butler)

Georgina Bruni:

> "Colonel Halt refers to two nights of events, the first of which took place at 3.00am on the 27th December, and the second on the 29th. In my book, You Can't Tell The People, the first event actually took place much earlier, on the 25th December, and there is also evidence that at least two other events occurred during that week. It is clear that Charles Halt gave the wrong date for the initial encounter and has since confirmed that this was the case."

Does this confuse or clarify the dates, bearing in mind that Robert Hastings was told by Colonel Halt previously that the first incident occurred around 3am on 26th December, and the second on the evening of the 27th which continued into the early hours of the 28th?

Chuck Daldorf – 27th-28th December 1980

Between December 1977 and 1981, Chuck was employed as an airman/aircraft field systems technician, at RAF Woodbridge, an E-5 Staff Sergeant, assigned to the 81st Tactical Fighter Wing. His duties included the repair of fuel tanks, in-flight fuelling and drop tanks from A10s, at Bentwaters and Woodbridge. He shared a very small despatch/tool shop building 307, with the 67th Aerospace Rescue and Recovery Squadron fuel repair crew. The 67th ARRS operated HC-130N/P fixed wing aircraft and heavy duty HH-53 Helicopters, used for combat search and rescue.

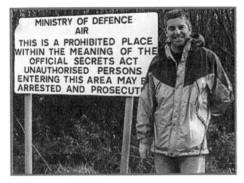

"Our building was located between the 67th ARRS helicopter hanger and the 81st EMS Hanger 202. During the time of the purported incident, both the 81st TFW and 67th ARRS were operating on a very limited duty due to the holiday. Both operations generally had used their allocated flying hours, but kept a very small amount in case of an emergency. I was on duty on the 27th December, during the swing shift 4pm-1am, but on my own time, helping to organise and lead a hired coach through Big Ben Travel up to Scotland for the hogmanay celebrations. This trip would have been cancelled if there had been a military operation taking place as I was part of the 67th personnel group, which included 28 people consisting of security police, mechanics, para-rescue staff and admin clerks, supporting the 81st TFW Commanders.

The trip went off well, with no problems or delays, two days after the alleged incident. No one discussed the incident, or rumours of an incident, which occurred at the base. I never heard of the UFO story until almost May 1981. This happened when an enlisted woman, who shared my rented cottage at Tunstall, employed on the 31st Weather Squadron team, which worked 24 hours a day, seven days a week, with an unblocked 360° view of the airfield and surrounding area told me what had taken place. I would swear, under oath, that no aircraft took off that evening. During that year, the HH-53s did engage in special ops and rescue simulations in the forest and on the coast. They carried out many low level hovers and dropped men into the forest and extracted them. British Special Forces also conducted operations in and around the area (they still do, despite the twin bases having been closed for some years).

The lighthouse at Orford is certainly one possibility of creating weird light effects, caused by drifting coastal fog and rain. The British Department of Defence also ran a secret compound at Orford Ness. God knows what they did there.

I believe it would have been impossible to have kept the UFO story quiet – there would have been rumours flying. I never heard anything until May, and it was said 'tongue in cheek'. It wasn't till the middle 1980s that I began to hear of the stories surrounding what was said to have happened."

(Source: Richard Conway)

 Security Patrolman Rick Bobo, interviewed by ©Georgina Bruni

"I think I was the first to report the sighting that night. I was on the tower at Bentwaters; you get a good view from up there. There were several lights and there was this huge ship over the forest."

G. Bruni:

"Can you describe the object?"

R. Bobo:

"I'd say it looked circular but, remember, I was over at Bentwaters and this was happening over at Woodbridge. I was instructed to watch it and can tell you that it was up there for about five hours, just hovering.

I would say it was quite low in the sky."

G. Bruni:

"Were you alone in the tower?"

R. Bobo:

"Someone came to the tower and watched it through a scope. I don't know who he was; he was from a different department. I wasn't told anything and I didn't get to look through the scope."

G. Bruni:

"Could you hear the radio transmissions from your location in the Bentwaters tower?"

R. Bobo:

"I heard some of the radio transmissions, not all of them, you understand, because there were different frequencies. I heard over the radio that London had spotted something on their radar. I heard some of the radio transmissions from some of the men who were out there. They were reporting a 'light' going through the woods, it had bumped into a tree and they were getting radioactive readings from the area. They were discussing three impressions and stuff moving through the woods, toward Woodbridge. They kept switching to different frequencies, so I couldn't hear everything. I know there was a Colonel with them."

Robert Hastings contacted Rick Bobo and interviewed him, some years later; this is what he had to say:

"As you probably know, the night I saw [the UFOs] I was in the tower at the Bentwaters Weapons Storage Area. The main object hovered out there for a long, long time. It never really moved anywhere else. It was kind of hard to see, but it was slightly oblong, I guess, and I seem to recall it had bluish and reddish lights on it. Not really lights, like aircraft lights, just a tint. It wasn't a star or planet, and it wasn't a lighthouse, as some people claim."

He then asked Bobo:

"If you held a dime at arm's length, was it larger than that?"

He quickly said:

"Oh yeah, it was larger than that! I would say it was, maybe, as large as a half-dollar coin, held out at arm's length, but I don't know how far away it was; it was so dark that night, I could just make out the forest. Anyway, at the same time, I was listening to all of the radio communications coming from our sister Base, Woodbridge.

There was lots of chatter on the radio. I think I heard that Heathrow [Airport] had it on radar. I'm surprised no-one scrambled a fighter. And, of course, I talked to people too, at our CSC. It was my job to keep an eye on the UFO and to report it if anything happened. Tim [Egercic] had taken [CSC] over before all this started happening, so I was talking to him. And he let me hear some of the chatter from Halt's team in the woods. I couldn't switch my radio frequency over to that, but when I called Tim, I could hear some of that on the phone. And I think I talked to Charlie Waters, but I'm not sure about that, but I did talk to our area supervisor. That was either Sgt. 'Willie' Williams or Sgt. 'Clarence' George that night. He told me to keep a close watch on the object. When the object first caught my eye, it was already stationary. I didn't see it move to where it was and I didn't see it leave. I never left the tower and I kept a close eye on the object most of the time, you know, trying to figure out what it was and what it might do next."

Robert asked Bobo if he had observed anything resembling beams of light coming down from the object at any time. He paused a moment, then said:

"No, not beams of light, but after it was hanging there a long while, I saw things shooting off it, really, really fast, like little sparks or something, maybe four or five of them – little pieces of light, all leaving within a minute [of one another] like they were getting out of there. I hate to say it, but they looked like little ships, like drones maybe, but I don't know. They were shooting off in all directions, but up into the sky, not down to the ground. Right after that, the big object just disappeared. I was watching it, at least I thought I was, but it was just gone. I don't know what happened to it."

USAF Security Patrolman Officer Bill Ferris

He was living off-base at the time, and carrying out a patrol with another serviceman, when he learnt, from a colleague, of an incident, involving strange 'lights' seen by other Security Police in Rendlesham Forest, and that they had gone out to investigate.

"When they got there, they radioed the Base Commander to tell him that a craft had landed, as a result of which the Officer had met up with the beings from the craft. The next night there was another UFO incident. When the man first told me I thought it was incredible, but nobody else said anything to me, so I blew it off. I figured if it was that amazing, the base would be buzzing and it wasn't."

Richard Kirk – 28th December (approx)

Richard Kirk was an NCO on loan from Martlesham Heath, and in charge of the Bentwaters Telephone Communication Facility, located next to the Base Commander's hut, a few days after Christmas 1980.

"All I can say is that radio traffic became really heavy. I had problems finding a spare channel to carry out daily testing of the appliances. There was also an increased volume of personal traffic between the Telecommunications Facility and the Base Commander's hut, suggesting that an 'Alert' was in progress, although I am unable to say what the cause of the build-up was."

(Source: Richard Conway)

UFO sighting on the 28th or 29th of December, 1980

STATUATORY DECLARATION

I, GORDON LEVETT, of Munday Lane, Orford, in the county of Suffolk, Department Manager, DO SOLEMNLY AND SINCERELY DECLARE as follows:-

1. I make this declaration realising that it is a document on oath and in the knowledge that it may be shown to the general public.

2. On or about the night of 28 or 29 December 1980 at approximately 7 pm to 8pm, whilst residing at White Lodge, Sudbourne, in the county of Suffolk, I was in the garden putting my dog into its ~~shed~~ kennel. When my attention was aroused by some unknown means I looked towards the coast and observed a light which moved on a steady path towards me. My dog also reacted and its attention became focused on the object. The phenomenon glowed with a phosphorescence and was unlike any conventional object with which I am familiar. It descended and hovered for a few seconds immediately above us at a height of no more than twice the rooftop of the house and its size, were the object to be placed on the ground, would be similar in size to the rooftop. The object then moved away and disappeared over the woods in the direction of Butley, Rendlesham Forest and RAF Woodbridge. ~~My dog was terrified by the presence.~~

3. The following day there were still evident signs of distress in my dog. It cowered within its kennel and was not keen to come out. Having told my wife, June, immediately following the experience I subsequently discussed it with several friends, including Ron Macro, a baker from Kesgrave in the county of Suffolk.

4. I exhibit here, marked "A", a drawing of the object which I saw.

AND I MAKE this solemn declaration conscientiously believing the same to be true and by virtue of the provisions of the STATUTORY DECLARATIONS ACT, 1835.

DECLARED at Orford, in the county of Suffolk this 17th day of July 1984.

Before me,

A solicitor.

This is the exhibit "A" referred to in the attested Declaration of Gordon Levett Harry Harris

Brenda Butler:

"I received a telephone call from June Levett and Gordon, who I knew about this sighting. After speaking to them I contacted Jenny Randles. Jenny then told Harry and Jenny, Harry, Dot and I were present when that interview took place"

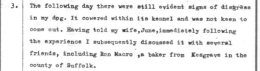

Harry Harris (left) interviews Gordon Levett (right).

'Lights' seen over the Airbase – 1-3am on 28th December 1980

Between 1am and 3am on 28th December 1980, twelve-year-old Sarah Richardson, from Woodbridge, was up late and happened to look out of the window, when she saw:

> ". . . *three bands of red, blue and yellow, 'lights' appear over the woods at the side of the runway. They were star-like; one in the north direction, the other two in the south. I thought someone was having a party and they were fireworks. It was a cold and clear night; the lights were low in the sky.*
>
> *I opened the window and leaned out. The lights appeared solid and looked metallic. No moon was shining. The light kept changing colour. They were there till well after 3am or 4am, when they suddenly shot straight away and disappeared from sight."*

(Source: Brenda Butler)

 Gordon Levett from Sudborne was another witness to UFO activity in December 1980. He was later interviewed by Harry Harris and signed a statement to that effect. (See previous page for statement).

First World War UFO sighting, Suffolk

A few miles away from where Gordon Levett had his sighting is the coastal town of Aldeburgh – the scene of a most unusual occurrence that took place during the First World War. We felt it was right to include

Agatha Maitland and her husband Roy

this incident, especially bearing in mind what was to happen in Rendlesham Forest, over 60 years later. Was there a connection? We shall probably never know!

In 2008 we met up with Aldeburgh woman Mrs Agatha Maitland (88) and her husband Roy. Her mother was Mrs Agnes Whiteland. She was to often tell of what she saw, one morning, during the middle of the First World War, while looking out of the bedroom window, at 10 Leiston Road (where she lived for 59 years)

Her brother Alfred E. Whiteland, (died 1989) of Saxmundham, Suffolk felt convinced his mother had seen something extraordinary, and wrote a letter to the *Daily Mirror,* which was published on 8th August 1968.

This was seen by Charles Bowen – Editor of *Flying Saucer Review.* Accordingly, details covering the sighting were later published in the magazine.

(Source: Gordon Creighton, The Aldeburgh Platform, *Flying Saucer Review*, Vol. 15, No. 1, Jan/February, 1969)

> *"My mother has often told the following story over the years and, as she is eighty-four, I would like to find out for her who these mystery men were and what they were doing. This is her story....*

It was about the middle of World War I and on a weekday she had gone upstairs just before dinner, opened the casement window, and looked out to see who might be on the road. Having looked up and down and noticed there was no one in sight, she was about to step back when something urged her to look again. A little above the level of the house, eight to twelve men appeared on what seemed to be a round platform, with a handrail around it. This they were gripping tightly. She could see them so clearly. They were wearing blue uniforms and little round hats, not unlike sailors. She heard no sound from the machine as it came off the marshes. It turned a bit and went over the railway yard to disappear behind some houses. Have you any explanation for this?"

The letter was to attract the attention of two readers, who wrote back to the newspaper suggesting that a possible explanation could have been an observation car, lowered from an airship. Another man – Mr Carl Grove – then wrote a comprehensive letter to Mr Whiteland, asking a number of pertinent questions, which were answered in the following letter by Mr Whiteland: (We have had to reduce some of the text bearing in mind the constraints of space, but have included what we feel is of importance)

"Dear Sir,

Thank you for your letter via 'Daily Mirror'. I will give you as much of the details as I can.

My mother has answered your questions as I put them to her.

Question: "Had they beards or moustaches?" I asked her.

Answer: "I was looking at them and not thinking about their faces so much."

Question: "What about the uniform? Was it like a tunic, tight up to the neck, or not?"

Answer: "I'm not sure. There they were, but somehow it might not have been a dark blue uniform, a little bit lighter ('grey', I said) yes, maybe a bit of grey in it. The hats were pulled on like sailors, with no rim – just a band and soft top."

Question: "How quickly did it move?"

Answer: "It might have been going as fast as a man can run after about three or four minutes, maybe longer. It seemed a good while but it went straight away from me into the distance, until the trees or houses hid it. This was about 12 miday on a bright day."

Question: "What time of the year?"

Answer: "I don't know – must have been around summer time. I know it was a nice day and bright. I can see them now... how they came along and turned straight for here."

Question: "How fast was the object moving, as compared with a car or a man?"

Answer: "It seems to be just higher than the telegraph wires and when it turned and went towards the station yard, I did think it would hit the shed roof or side." (This was the cart shed ground floor and first floor with the top of ridge, 25ft or so, above road level)

Question: "How high was the object above the ground?"

Answer: "30ft, not much more."

Question: "Were the men doing anything? What were they looking at?"

Answer: "The men were looking straight out, as all were clustered around the platform and could well have been looking for anything.

At that time, as she said, I went off to school at 3½ years (I was born 1910). She doesn't quite know what made her take another look, but there it was coming along from the marshes on her right, straight along the road, "not wobbling", and then right in front of her it turned sharp right and went between the back of the Railway Hotel, and the cart shed, with a room above it (about 20ft-25ft between) over the top of the other cart shed mentioned, over the railway, which had on the railings of the station platform a large printed sign, about 8ft long, blue background, with white letters ALDEBURGH. This may have been spotted by them and that is why they turned off so sharp, instead of going along the road. There was a camp for soldiers, about 300yds further along, with trees around it; this might also have been the reason."

Question: "What were your mother's feelings, as she watched the object?"

Answer: "Had no real feelings – was thinking more about how it could move without an engine, as no sound was heard. I looked up in the sky to see if anything was holding it up. Couldn't see anyone kneeling between the men to work it, and watched it go for a long while."

Question: "About how long was it visible? At what time was it first seen? What did your mother think it might be? What was it made of?"

Answer: "Thought it was something to do with Zeppelins, but as no rope or anything was to be seen or heard, was quite puzzled. Did mention it to my father when he came home that night, and next day to a neighbour; both said that the Germans were supposed to have people looking round from Zeppelins, and as no-one else ever spoke or mentioned anything, it was only talked of when different happenings were read over the times that mother would tell of what she did see."

Question: "Did anyone else in the area see anything unusual during World War I (or in that general period)?"

Answer: "Never did hear of anything like it, or know of other people seeing it, or anything else around here. There were plenty of soldiers about. Why didn't one of them see it? I don't know why. Perhaps they didn't believe them."

Not unnaturally the article caught the attention of others who wrote to Mr Whiteland, eager to provide an explanation for what his mother has seen. They included Mr Graham, who wrote telling him what his own mother – then living at Aldringham fen, about one-and-a-half miles from Aldeburgh – had seen.

"During the First World War – an airship lowering an observation device, suspended hundreds of feet below it."

Mr Winslow of South Lambeth, London, also spoke of the platforms suspended beneath the baskets carried by airships, carrying several men, for accurate placing of the small bombs in use at that time, and that he and others had buried the crew of a Zeppelin, which crashed at Harrow.

Charles H. Gibbs-Smith – the Aviation Historian at the Victoria & Albert Museum, during 1968 – then regarded as the leading authority on aeronautical history in the UK, said:

"There is not the remotest possibility that what Mrs Whiteland saw was anything to do with Zeppelins!"

and enclosed a copy of an observation device, as used by the airships, which according to him,

". . . was used when the airship was flying above cloud cover, never suspended near the ground, since they could be easily attacked by gunfire. There are many other reasons why

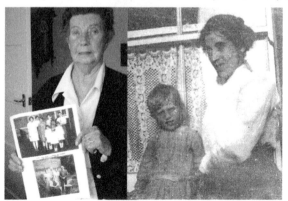

Agatha 2008 showing family photos of Mum at bottom (seated) Agness taken in the 1914 with son Alfred

the platform could not have been hanging from the Zeppelin. As you point out, a turn of 90 degrees would have been impossible. I find your remarks about the thickness of the rope required to support such a platform of great interest."

We obtained a copy of a booklet showing the Zeppelin crash at Theberton, and visited the local church, which still displayed pieces of the airship inside the church porch.

We were to discover the cloud car or sub-cloud car was essentially a small cigar-shaped, one-man observation platform, (resembling a 'flying bomb' or rocket) mainly used by the German Army Schutte-Lanz airships, constructed of wood as opposed to the Naval Zeppelin model, which were made of aluminum. Their use by the German Army airships were generally discontinued by 1916, which tells us that whatever Agness saw is certainly not likely to have been any airship, or sub-cloud car, in our opinion, bearing in mind that there appears to have been only one raid over England involving the lowering of a cloud car (as alleged above.)

In March 2013, we again spoke to Agatha (now aged 94) about the incident witnessed by her mother. Agatha remains puzzled by the event – now nearly a hundred years ago!

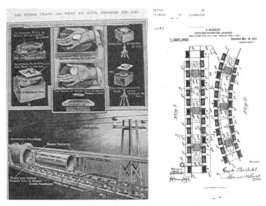

Bechelet Levitating Transmitting Apparatus

We naturally rejected any suggestion this object could have been the result of human construction, but were surprised to discover that an early example of a Maglev vehicle took place during 1914, in London, by French-born inventor Emile Bachelet.

Winston Churchill in London at Bechelet Lab

He later moved to the United States, in the 1880s, where he worked as an electrician.

After discovering the therapeutic qualities of magnetic fields, especially with arthritic patients, he began to commercialise this practice. While doing so, Bachelet began to experiment with magnetic fields. He was awarded a patent for his 'Levitating Transmitting Apparatus', which was meant to transfer mail and small packages on a cart levitated above a track of magnets. Interestingly, we found out that he had opened an exhibition at 151,152, Great Saffron Hill, Holborn Circus, London, in the same year, and had invited members of the British Admiralty to the exhibition, which involved the levitation of Keith Alderton in a wicker chair.

One of the guests on the 11th May 1914 was Winston Churchill, shown here on some photographs kindly sent to us by Christine Windheuser, National Museum of American History Suitland, Maryland. We know this could not have been the explanation for what Agnes saw, but it is intriguing to discover that human technology, even in 1914, was capable of levitating the weight of a small boy and wicker chair, a few feet up in the air. What did the Admiralty make of it?

Nearly 40yrs later, on the afternoon of 18th October 1955, The Reverend Pitt-Kethly was travelling on the Uxbridge train line to East Harrow, London. When the train had stopped at the West Hampstead viaduct, he noticed:

> *". . . a reddish-brown and grey platform, the size of a small bus. It was silent and travelled at a height of about 120ft. There were approximately 20 helmeted men, dressed in khaki uniforms, standing on the platform – like a German troop carrier – which moved at about 20mph and was in sight for three or four minutes."*

The Halt tape-recording

There seems little point in reproducing verbatim textually the whole of the tape recording, but to hi-light paragraphs of interest with regard to the actual sighting itself. The described characteristics of UFO behaviour, in this case, have formed the background of many other UFO sightings brought to our attention over the years. We do not believe this was a one-off case, despite the pronounced scepticism of some people who refuse to accept the evidence of thousands of other sightings that surely must corroborate, to some degree, what was observed by the witnesses.

Colonel Halt: *"We've just bumped into the first night bird we've seen. We're about 150 or 200 yards from the site. Everything else is just deathly calm. There is no doubt about it – there's some type of strange flashing red light ahead."*

Bruce Englund: *"Sir, it's yellow."*

C.H: *"I saw a yellow tinge in it, too. Weird! It appears to be maybe moving a little bit this way? It's brighter than it has been. It's coming this way. It is definitely coming this way."*

Voice: *"Pieces of it shooting off . . ."*

C.H: *"Pieces of it are shooting off."*

Voice: *"At eleven o'clock."*

C.H: *"There is no doubt about it. This is weird!"*

Voice (Nevels?): *"To the left."*

C.H: *"Definitely moving."*

Voice (Nevels?): *"Two lights – one light just behind [?] and one light to the left."*

C.H: *"Keep your flashlights off. There's something very, very strange. Get the headset on; see if it gets any stronger."*

Nevels: *"I have."*

C.H: *"OK. Give us your . . ."*

Nevels: *"Make a notation that this is on a beta reading, too."*

C.H: *"It's on a beta reading?"*

Nevels: *"The beta shield has been removed."*

C.H: *"OK. Pieces are falling off it again."*

Englund: *"Sir, it just moved to the right."*

C.H: *"Yeah!"*

Englund: *"Off to the right."*

C.H: *"Strange! One again left. Let's approach to the edge of the woods up there. Do you wanna do it without lights? Let's do it carefully. Come on."*

C.H: *"OK, we're looking at the thing. We're probably about two to three hundred yards away. It looks like an eye winking at you, still moving from side to side. And when you put the Starscope on it, it sort of has a hollow centre, a dark centre, it's . . ."*

Englund (?): *"Like a pupil"*

C.H: *"Yeah, like a pupil of an eye looking at you, winking. And the flash is so bright to the Starscope that it almost burns your eye."* (Garbled security communication) *"we've passed the farmer's house and are crossing the next field and now we have multiple sightings of up to five lights with a similar shape and all but they seem to be steady now, rather than a pulsating or glow with a red flash."*

C.H: *"We've just crossed a creek."*

Voice: *"Here we go."*

C.H: *"And we're getting what kind of readings now?"*

C.H: *"We're getting three good clicks on the meter and we're seeing strange lights in the sky. We're at the far side of the farmer's . . . the second farmer's field, and made sighting again about 110 degrees. This looks like it's clear off to the coast. It's right on the horizon, moves about a bit, and flashes from time to time . . . still steady, or red in colour."*

Where is the rest of the alleged two hour tape made by him, the contents of which – according to Brenda Butler, following a conversation with Colonel Halt – will never be disseminated (it is alleged) due to its frightening content?

Georgina Bruni, in *UFO Magazine*, dated September 2001, said:

> *"Much controversy has surrounded the tape, with researchers offering various opinions, but it now seems certain that the *18 minute recording is an edited version of an event that lasted approximately 4 hours. In 1999, Retired Colonel Sam Morgan – then the Commander of the Airbase – sent me a cassette, which he said had been copied from Colonel Halt's original tape. This is a much clearer copy than the one that had been in the public domain since 1984, and reveals background voices which offer new vital evidence."*

***Authors:** A typed copy of the statement made by Colonel Halt gives duration of 17 minutes, 50 seconds recording.

Brenda:

> *"Even the tape that Colonel Halt made out in the forest is suspect. We have had it analysed twice. On both occasions, we were told that it was done inside a building. Sam Morgan found the tape in Colonel Halt's desk and could not make head or tail of it. When he asked Halt what it was, Halt said 'I don't want to talk about it', so Morgan listened to the tape again and questioned some of the men. After this he decided that there was nothing to it, only a bunch*

of guys messing around in the woods. He (Morgan) said, 'They should not have left the base and Halt had no right to have been out there'."

Colonel Halt, 2011

> *"There is no missing or withheld section of tape; I wish Brenda would get over this. I wasn't sure how good the batteries were or how much tape I'd use, so I only turned the tape on when I wanted to record something. As far as the horrendous belief to ever let people know what I saw is a bit of an excess. At the time Brenda and her gang were pestering me no end. They even literally kidnapped my teenage son and plied him with drink to learn details. On one occasion, I had to have them forcibly removed from my home by the police. I may have misled them out of frustration. Brenda should remember how they hounded me."*

Brenda:

> *"When he was absent from the base, we were contacted by his son and Ted Conrad's son, who came around to see us and spent some time in the forest assisting us; this was of their own free will. The fact that we allegedly kidnapped his son has been a standing joke between the two of us right to the present day."*

In February 2013, Brenda released a number of her personal diaries pertaining to *conversations held with Colonel Halt and investigations carried out by her and Dot onto the *Lone Ranger* website. (Some of

---

*Colonel Halt commented on her material, saying that: *"50% of it was accurate, I was disappointed this had been placed on the internet."*

this information had been previously published in *Sky Crash*.) Brenda also referred to the incident at the airbase, involving the police who were called out by Colonel Halt; she also included sheets of binary code, received telepathically, following visits to the forest over the years.

Copies of Halt's tape recording were first released to UFO researchers in 1984 by Colonel Sam Morgan, who was successor to Colonel Ted Conrad as Base Commander and Halt's superior. However, the tape did not enter general circulation until 1985. Colonel Morgan had found the tape in a desk when he took over as Base Commander in mid-1981. Although he had been on the base at the time of the incident as Assistant Chief of Maintenance for the A-10 aircraft, Morgan had not heard of the events before. He spoke to Halt and the UK Base Commander, Don Moreland, and decided, as he told American researcher Philip Klass, in 1984, that it was *"just a bunch of guys screwing around in the woods"*.

Colonel Halt (2013): *"Sam Morgan found the tape and gave a copy to Harry Harris and suddenly it was public. I never gave the tape to the MOD if General Charles Gabriel was given a copy, I was not aware of it"*

Mike Sacks

Jenny Randles

Harry Harris

Brenda Butler

In *Sky Crash* (page 186) we were intrigued to hear of a secret meeting held between Colonel Halt, Mike Sacks and Harry Harris, at the airbase, sometime in August 1983. Although that meeting was kept secret from Jenny, Dot and Brenda, they learnt of it from another source. When tackled, the two men explained that they had been sworn to secrecy by Colonel Halt and were not willing to discuss the matter further. For many years we remained curious as to the exact nature of what was discussed with Charles Halt.

According to Mike Sacks, in an interview conducted in February 2013, he told us that:

> *"Harry had telephoned General Gordon Williams, in the States, seeking permission to listen to a copy of that tape. Subsequently this was arranged and we were then allowed onto base, where we met up with Colonel Halt. After discussing UFOs generally, we sat around the table and he played the tape. We then signed a contract forbidding us from talking about what had been discussed that day, but chose to ignore the agreement made."*

Colonel Halt confirmed to us, in February 2013:

> *"I did meet with Mike and Harry, it was about 1982 and we all agreed not to reveal the meeting, although I would refute any arrangement was made with General Gordon Williams. I was very disappointed when the gang – Brenda, Dot, Jenny, Harry and Mike – sold the story to the *News of the World. That wasn't supposed to happen and it took years before I trusted Harry and Mike again. If you're talking with them, say hello. I did forgive them, but it took a lot of time. Chuck."*

(*The story was sold to the *News of the World*, and a contract provided to Mike, Harry, and Jenny.)

Colonel Halt, during a lecture at Scaitcliffe Hall Country Hotel, Todmorden, West Yorkshire, in the 1990s, had this to say:

US Air Force colonel tells of UFO chase

ROSSENDALE ufologists are to get the chance to quiz witnesses to two of the country's foremost flying saucer mysteries.

In one incident PC Alan Godfrey reported being apparently abducted onto a spaceship in a Todmorden suburb in the early morning hours.

Later the same year — 1980 — American Air Force colonel Charles Halt and three of his men claimed to have chased a UFO through a forest near the RAF Woodbridge base in Suffolk.

The second incident was reported to the Ministry of Defence which allegedly refused to pursue the incident further.

Both PC Godfrey and Colonel Halt are to address a four-hour meeting next Friday (29 July) at Scaitcliffe Hall, Todmorden, which has been organised by solicitor and prominent ufologist Harry Harris.

Mr Harris, who has spent many hours observing the unexplained in

By NEIL GRAHAM

Rossendale's skies, said: "Both the sightings were bizarre to say the least.

"PC Godfrey was driving through Todmorden at 5am when he saw lights illuminating the road. He thought it was a works bus but it turned out that he was within 30 yards of a flying saucer.

"It was the size of a double decker bus and the bottom was rotating. His radio wouldn't work. Then he found himself on the other side of the UFO with 20 minutes of his life gone."

Experiments

Under hypnosis later, PC Godfrey recounted an apparent experience on board the spacecraft where aliens conducted medical experiments.

His feet — being a policeman, perhaps appeared to be of particular interest to them.

The meeting starts at 7.30pm. Mr Harris has paid for Colonel Halt to fly over from America for the meeting and is charging a £4.50 entry fee.

● *ARTISTS impression of a UFO seen over the Waterfoot area in 1980*

"I used a small tape recorder to log the night's events, mainly because it was a lot more practical than using a small note pad and pen, but I never intended for it to be made public and become second generation, like it has done now. The pocket recorder only holds about twenty minutes or so, so how did I manage to tape record over 4 hours commentary? Sure the tape recorder shows over two hours has elapsed, but that's because I had to be as brief as possible because I didn't have more tapes with me. I assure you that the tape is genuine and I would be willing to undergo a polygraph test to prove it hasn't been tampered with. When the CNN Network in the States did their own analysis, a couple of years ago, they came away firmly convinced that the voice stresses of the people on it couldn't have been fabricated."

Colonel Halt was asked about the odd interruptions that appeared in the first few minutes of the tape. He replied:

"Well I must admit that one of those is just a bar of music I managed to record accidently pressing the play and record button together, whilst my daughter was playing the piano one day. The other voice I've no idea – perhaps it's been added by an investigator or somebody along the way."

Following his arrival at the airbase, Colonel Halt was asked about the audio recording made. He then handed it over to General Bazley of the 'Third Air Force', Commander of US Air Force activities in England at that time. Later, in another discussion about what to do with the tape, Colonel Halt was instructed to hand the tape over to the MOD. When he asked if they wanted a complete report of the events, personnel and measures taken, he was surprised to learn that this was not necessary.

The summary was taken by Squadron leader Donald Moreland and then sent to the MOD. The tape was circulated around the States and later released to Robert Todd of the Citizens Against UFO Secrecy (CAUS). It then fell into the hands of Sam Morgan, Ted Cochran, and Harry Harris. Ironically, the tape was played at some cocktail parties and treated with merriment before being returned to Colonel Halt, copies having been made – presumably without the knowledge of Colonel Halt.

According to Donald Moreland, the tape recording made by Colonel Halt was handed over to General Gabriel, during a visit to the airbase. This would tie in with what Georgina Bruni suggested in her book – *You Can't Tell The People* – that this evidence was *"most likely to have been dispatched to Ramstein Airbase"*. We believe, from other sources of available information, that she was right.

We sent Colonel Halt a newspaper cutting relating to reports of ghosts being seen on base, in one of the buildings which was previously used some years ago as a morgue.

April 18, 2000

Mr. John Hanson
P.O. Box 6371
Brimingham, B48 7RW
England

Dear John:

Thank you for the newspaper article. I found it most interesting. I have had numerous people state they had similar experiences to that which we were exposed to during the events in East Suffolk.

I would like to comment further but am working on a book and have agreed to withhold comment until its in print.

Perhaps we can discuss the issue at some future date.

Say hello to Brenda.

Sincerely,

Charles I. Halt

RAF Neatishead – The faulty Radar tape

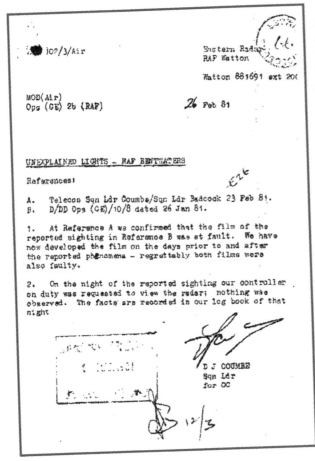

Squadron Leader Derek Coumbe was on duty as RAF Commander of Eastern Radar on the same night when Colonel Charles Halt telephoned, requesting confirmation of his sightings.

> *"They were very jumpy and panicky on the phone, but I personally checked the radar picture and there was absolutely nothing to be seen. They kept coming back and implying there should be something, but we kept a watch on it through the whole period and nothing was seen."*

Coumbe impounded the radar tapes. In January 1981 they were removed by a joint RAF/USAF team from the Military Air Traffic Operations centre (MATO) at Uxbridge. This was not unusual but quite a common procedure that followed incidents such as a near-miss involving aircraft.

In an interview with Dr. David Clarke, in 2001 and 2003, he confirmed being on duty when the UFO report was received in the early hours of 28th December, following a direct call transferred through from Bentwaters tower, reporting a *"flashing light"* over Rendlesham Forest. The MOD file contains a note from Coumbe, which confirms a check was made by the duty controller, but nothing was observed. The facts were then recorded in the log book of that night.

In 2003, Derek was interviewed by *BBC Radio 4*. He confirmed that several calls had come through from Bentwaters, asking them if they were seeing anything unusual in the Bentwaters and Woodbridge area.

> *"We scrutinized the radar time and time again completely, and kept a watch on it through the whole period when these phone calls were going on, and nothing was seen – Nothing at all."*

UFO Display over RAF Neatishead

This was not the only time when unidentified objects were brought to the attention of RAF Neatishead. Ex-RAF senior Air Craftsman Malcolm Scurrah, who had previously served at RAF Coltishall as a RAF Radar Operator, in the 1980s, described what took place while on duty at nearby RAF Neatishead, located five miles away from the village of Neatishead, during November 1980.

⊙ **ROYAL**
AIR FORCE

Mr Ceri Baker
HEADQUARTERS AIR COMMAND
Spitfire Block
Royal Air Force
High Wycombe
Buckinghamshire
HP14 4UE

Mr A Russell
xxxxxxxxxxxxxxxxxxxx@xxxxxxxxxxxxxxx.xxx

Our Ref:
AirCmdSec/11-11-2010-144649-001

25 November 2010

Dear Mr Russell,

Thank you for your e-mail of 15 November clarifying your Freedom of Information request of 11 November 2010. You state that you wish to know which radar was operating at RAF Neatishead in December 1980 and how radar returns were recorded. Your e-mail was treated as a request for information under the Freedom of Information Act 2000.

I have been unable to identify records that deal with this matter. However, one of my colleagues recalls that RAF Neatishead operated T84 and/or T85 area search radar and HF 200 height finders around the time in question. They also believe that the search radar would have been recorded onto film by radar recorder camera. These films would have been routinely destroyed after one month. Therefore, it appears highly unlikely that any radar tapes from December 1980 would still remain, particularly since there would be little practical requirement for the MOD to retain them. However, I have not been able to locate any records confirming this.

It is possible that information concerning RAF Neatishead has been passed to The National Archives who can be contacted on their website www.thenationalarchives.co.uk. You may also consider contacting the RAF Radar Museum. This is a non MOD museum adjoining RAF Neatishead. Although it is currently closed, you can e-mail them at xxxxxxx@xxxxxxxxx.xx.xx as they may be able to confirm the type of radar in operation in December 1980.

I am sorry I could not be more helpful.

...ied with this response or you wish to complain about any aspect of
...r request, then you should contact me in the first instance. If informal
...ssible and you are still dissatisfied then you may apply for an independent
...ontacting the Head of Corporate Information, 2nd Floor, MOD Main

INVESTORS IN PEOPLE

LOOSE MINUTE

D/DD Ops(GE)/10/8

DS8

UFO SIGHTING - RAF WOODBRIDGE DECEMBER 1980

1. At Reference you ask if the suggestion that the USAF be asked for the tape recordings was followed up by this Deputy Directorate. It was considered that the tapes would reveal no better report than that already received, and no further request was made. However, it is considered that your approach to the RAF Liaison officer, will produce any considered views on the event.

2. I believe your outlined response is the right one; Neatishead, which is the Sector Ops Centre responsible for that area had nothing unusual to report, and nothing more substantive has come to light. I have received no evidence that any radar reported unusual tracks. MISS Randles appears to have "evidence of radar tracking", and provided that it can be managed without undermining our position, I would like to have a look at this radar evidence.

(Mar 83

D BADCOCK
Sqn Ldr
Ops(GE)2b(RAF)
MB 4258 7754 MB

LOOSE MINUTE

D/DD Ops(GE)/10/8

DS8

UNEXPLAINED LIGHTS

Reference: A. D/DS8/72/1/2 dated 20 Jan 81.

1. At Reference you forwarded a report from RAF Bentwaters for information and asked if anyone else might have an interest in the content. You will see from the attached LM, I forwarded a copy to D155 and PS/ACS(G)(RAF). I have had no response.

2. SOC/CRC Neatishead regret that the radar camera recorder was switched off at 1527Z on 29 Dec 80 and an examination of the executive logs revealed no entry in respect of unusual radar returns or other unusual occurrences.

3. I have spoken with Sqn Ldr Moreland at Bentwaters and he considers the Deputy Base Commander a sound source. I asked if the incident had been reported on the USAF net and I was advised that tape recorders of the evidence had been handed to Gen Gabriel who happened to be visiting the station. Perhaps it would be reasonable to ask if we could have tape recordings as well.

16 Feb 81

D BADCOCK
Sqn Ldr
Ops(GE)2b(RAF)
MB 4258 7274 MB

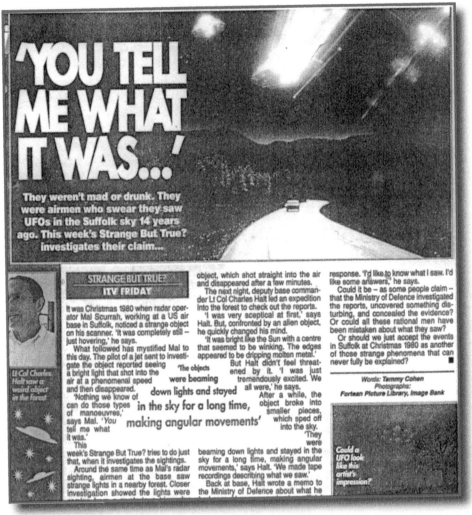

'YOU TELL ME WHAT IT WAS...'

They weren't mad or drunk. They were airmen who swear they saw UFOs in the Suffolk sky 14 years ago. This week's Strange But True? investigates their claim...

Lt Col Charles Halt saw a weird object in the forest

STRANGE BUT TRUE?
ITV FRIDAY

It was Christmas 1980 when radar operator Mal Scurrah, working at a US air base in Suffolk, noticed a strange object on his scanner. 'it was completely still – just hovering,' he says.

What followed has mystified Mal to this day. The pilot of a jet sent to investigate the object reported seeing a bright light that shot into the air at a phenomenal speed and then disappeared.

'Nothing we know of can do those types of manoeuvres,' says Mal. 'You tell me what it was.'

This week's Strange But True? tries to do just that, when it investigates the sightings.

Around the same time as Mal's radar sighting, airmen at the base saw strange lights in a nearby forest. Closer investigation showed the lights were object, which shot straight into the air and disappeared after a few minutes.

The next night, deputy base commander Lt Col Charles Halt led an expedition into the forest to check out the reports.

'I was very sceptical at first,' says Halt. But, confronted by an alien object, he quickly changed his mind.

'It was bright like the Sun with a centre that seemed to be winking. The edges appeared to be dripping molten metal.' But Halt didn't feel threatened by it. 'I was just tremendously excited. We all were,' he says.

After a while, the object broke into smaller pieces, which sped off into the sky.

The objects were beaming down lights and stayed in the sky for a long time, making angular movements

'They were beaming down lights and stayed in the sky for a long time, making angular movements,' says Halt. 'We made tape recordings describing what we saw.'

Back at base, Halt wrote a memo to the Ministry of Defence about what he response. 'I'd like to know what I saw. I'd like some answers,' he says.

Could it be – as some people claim – that the Ministry of Defence investigated the reports, uncovered something disturbing, and concealed the evidence? Or could all these rational men have been mistaken about what they saw?

Or should we just accept the events in Suffolk at Christmas 1980 as another of those strange phenomena that can never fully be explained? ■

Words: Tammy Cohen
Photographs:
Fortean Picture Library, Image Bank

Could a UFO look like this artist's impression?

Malcolm (on duty from 5pm to midnight shift) was monitoring night flying exercises being conducted 50 miles out to sea, over The Wash, involving two RAF Phantom fighter aircraft, using height finding radar apparatus.

Just after 8pm a single 'target' appeared on the radar screen, at a height of 5,000ft, and stationary. Checks were made with Eastern Radar Air Traffic Control to ascertain if this could have been a civil aircraft helicopter from one of the oil rigs. However, nothing had been brought to their attention.

Suddenly the target accelerated upwards, from several thousand feet over the next 15 minutes, and was then plotted in a series of 'jumps' to an altitude of 100,000ft, which Malcolm and his colleague found amazing and unheard of in their experience, before being lost from the screen (presumably off the height indicator band). The only aircraft capable of reaching such high altitudes was the Lockheed SR71Blackbird, but this was no steady climb – just a series of jumps, with nothing between them.

Air Craftsman Malcolm Scurrah

During his break, the incident was the subject of much discussion with his colleagues.

> *"I learnt that the unknown target had been tracked on the main radar screen, and seen to perform manoeuvres that defied all convention. If this had been an aircraft, the G forces involved would have rendered them unconscious or killed them. Following the appearance of the unidentified target, the night exercise was temporarily postponed.*
>
> *One of the RAF jets was then ordered to investigate. The fisher controller, his assistant and supervising officers, were listening in on the radio frequency of the aircraft and guiding the pilot towards the unidentified target. They asked me for the height of the object, but at the time I thought I was giving height on the other jet because I thought they were into the night flying exercise. I didn't know it was hovering because on the height finding radar you can't see movement – all you can see is height. The pilot had described seeing a very bright light in front of him on his voice intercom, from a distance of some half a mile away from the object; suddenly it just flew off very fast."*

The day after, it became common knowledge that two senior RAF Controllers, at the main Section Operations Centre had been interviewed by high ranking RAF Officers from London. From then onwards, they did not talk about it. They took the radar tapes with them.

Malcolm:

> *"This was an unfamiliar occurrence. Tapes were normally removed in either a near miss or an accident. I do know that video images had been transmitted in 'real time' to the command centre at West Drayton."*

Malcolm was a frequent guest at UFO meetings, held by Graham and Mark Birdsall, during the 1990s. Philip Mantle (2013), who met Malcolm several times, spoke very highly of him and described him as a friendly, down-to-earth man, who was completely genuine.

(Source: Graham Birdsall, *UFO Magazine,* May/June 1995)

Ex-RAF serviceman Nigel Kerr

Nigel Kerr was stationed at RAF Watton, during 1980. Sometime near Christmas 1980, he received a phone call from RAF Bentwaters, enquiring if anything unusual had been plotted on the radar screen, as strange 'lights' had been seen falling from the sky.

Nigel checked his radar screen and noticed a strange blip in the sky over the Woodbridge area which was visible for three or four sweeps on the screen, before disappearing. No report was logged of this matter.

We know that Jim Penniston spoke to John Coffey, who then contacted RAF Watton (he may have spoken to Nigel Kerr). Coffey confirmed that RAF Watton had tracked an object, which had disappeared into the forest area. Minutes after hearing this, Jim and John were out in the forest looking for the source of the strange lights they had seen earlier.

Ex-RAF serviceman Gary Baker

Another man who had the courage to come forward in the blanket of officialdom that seeks to deny the existence of UFOs and their continual visual sightings, and being tracked on radar, was ex-RAF Senior aircraftsman – Gary Baker, who was stationed at RAF Neatishead from 1979-1981. He contacted Russell Callaghan after reading an article by Georgina Bruni, in which she examined claims made that RAF Neatishead's radar camera was switched off around the Christmas period of 1980. In an interview, later published in *UFO Magazine* (November/ December 2001 & February 2002) Gary said:

Gary Baker

". . . RAF Neatishead had not one primary Air Defence Radar in 1980, but two! This means that if the primary radar camera was down for maintenance, then the second one would have been in operation as back-up.

These radar cameras would always work together, apart from routine planned maintenance, but you don't have both going wrong at the same time. Maintenance is planned well in advance, so that one is always operational. Radar 'air pictures' are recorded on film to provide evidence of any incursion of UK airspace by unknown aircraft. It is used as evidence in the event of air accidents or near misses.

You cannot have equipment that goes wrong simultaneously and at separate installations. That's why we used two radars, and even then, other overlapping stations would take over if RAF Neatishead were ever taken out. I find it absolutely inconceivable that both radar cameras could go wrong, but the files don't mention two cameras or two radars, just a camera. At no time in my service at the base do I ever recall both radars being unserviceable at the same time. In the unlikely event that this occurred, other Air Defence assets would provide cover. Be under no illusions, a radar record of what transpired in and around Rendlesham Forest, in December 1980, must exist at best or did exist at worst.

That smells of a 'cover-up' and from my own point of view, I distinctly remember rumours flying around at the time, within the operations room, of a UFO incident and a UFO flap. It was common knowledge amongst personnel that the MOD had come down to remove the tapes. I should add that I was personally not a witness to the Rendlesham Forest incident, but I never heard any other rumours about a UFO flap during my time at RAF Neatishead; there would definitely be film of radar of the incident at the time.

I've been aware of the Rendlesham incident for some time, but always felt that I didn't have anything to add to what was known, but when I read 'UFO Magazine' and saw what Georgina Bruni had to say about the newly released documents, I felt I had to comment. With regard to the explanation made that the Radar was switched off at RAF Neatishead, and poor and unusable radar film at RAF Watton? I find this totally unacceptable. Remember this was the time of the 'Cold War' and the importance of RAF Neatishead and RAF Watton to NATO. On the international stage the political situation was extremely grave; Warsaw Pact forces were aggressively poised, the Soviet Union had just invaded Afghanistan, and tensions were running high over Poland. So potent was this threat that Britain, together with its allies, was secretly preparing for war."

Authors: It is obvious that despite an attempt by the MOD/RAF to convince us that the radar tapes were faulty, this was clearly not the case according to the evidence obtained from both USAF & RAF radar operatives which shows the official stance was seriously flawed, although the public would not have known about it at the time.

Visit to the MOD, 1983

On Thursday, 18th August 1983, Dot Street, Brenda Butler and Jenny Randles met up with DS8 representative, Pam Titchmarsh, at the MOD, Whitehall, in London.

Brenda:

"Following an appointment with the publisher at 2pm. We left there at 3.30pm and went to Whitehall, MOD. We spoke to Pam Titchmarsh. Jenny did most of the talking, asking Pam questions about Radar and UFOs. Dot showed Pam some of the documents we had in our possession from The Deputy Base Commander, Charles Halt, to the MOD, which had been passed on to the USA Government. Pam said she didn't know how the USA Government had received these documents, as the MOD had not sent them.

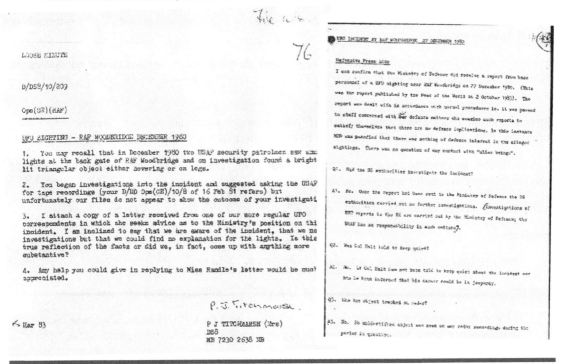

The meeting went on for two hours. We were all talking about the Rendlesham Forest case. Pam said the MOD had checked it out, as far as they could, and found no case to proceed any further with their investigations, as they found that whatever it was, was no threat to our security. She said she didn't know much about the case, as she had only been there (at the MOD) for six months, so she probably only knew what she had been told. When Jenny cross-examined her, she kept repeating the same thing. She said basically, the MOD hadn't really investigated it, as they had been satisfied there was no reason to suspect that whatever happened was of no threat to any of our bases. She told us she had no knowledge of any radar tapes or radar traces. We were asked to sign a document . . . Dot said, 'No'. Jenny and I said we would, if they could prove that what happened would harm our defence system. They couldn't, so we wouldn't sign anything."

Ralph Noyes

Ralph Noyes was brought up in the West Indies. He served in the RAF from 1940 to 1946 and was commissioned as aircrew, engaging in active service in North Africa and the Far East. He entered the civil service in 1949 and served in the Air Ministry and subsequently the unified Ministry of Defence. He was head of Defence Secretariat 8 (DS8) at the MOD, for four years, which handled reports of UFO sightings from the public. He was very much a 'believer' rather than sceptic, presumably dictated by his own sighting of *"three yellowish-white balls of light moving across the sky one evening, in a triangular formation"*, near Elstree Studios, London, in May 1985.

In 1977, he retired early from the civil service to take up a writing career, leaving in the grade of Under-Secretary of State. He has since published several pieces of shorter fiction, most of them on speculative themes.

Like The Lord Hill Peter Norton, Noyes was convinced that the MOD was hiding something, but discovered nothing further than the standard line given out that Halt's report had been examined and dismissed as 'of no Defence interest'.

Noyes also asked his successor about the fate of 'some interesting gun camera clips' taken by RAF pilots, during the 1950s, shown to him at Whitehall, in 1970, but was told that no trace of the films could be found!

In 1985, *Ralph Noyes wrote a novel based on the Rendlesham Forest incident, and used the publication of *A Secret Property* to quiz his successor as head of DS8, Brian Webster.

In an interview conducted by David Clarke and Andy Roberts, Ralph Noyes was asked:

Question:

"What's your standpoint on the Rendlesham Forest incident?"

Answer:

"There is no doubt at all that the MOD played a thoroughly dishonest game over the Rendlesham affair. I have already put some of my reasons on record in the afterword to my

science fiction novel, 'A Secret Property', and in a paper, 'UFO Lands In Suffolk', printed in Timothy Good's 'UFO Annual', 1990 (Sidgwick & Jackson, 1989).

We know – the responsible Minister even admitted as much in the British House of Commons after more than two years prevarication – that the MOD received an astonishing report in 1981 from a responsible USAF officer (Lt. Colonel, now Brigadier General, Charles I. Halt) of very weird phenomena which (as he believed, and seemed in part to have witnessed) had taken place in the vicinity of a major military establishment in the UK, in December 1980.

The MOD had flatly denied the existence of this report in response to enquiries put to them in 1981 and 1982. We would probably still be faced with this bland denial but for the action taken by American citizens under the US Freedom of Information Act, in 1983. In response to enquiries made to the USAF by CAUS (Citizens Against UFO Secrecy) the USAF obtained a copy of Halt's report from the MOD and released it into the public domain, in mid-1983.

The case itself is complex. I have given my own views about it in the papers mentioned above – essentially that Halt and several others came face-to-face with a striking manifestation of the 'UFO phenomenon' (whatever that may be) in the December of 1980. Other commentators may disagree; alternative theories abound. My only immediate point is that the MOD have resisted all attempts to obtain a sensible statement, even under sustained pressure to the Defence Secretary from The Lord Hill-Norton. Why? Simply, I think, because it embarrasses them. Either they must admit that a senior USAF officer at a highly sensitive base in the UK went out of his mind in December 1980 (with unthinkable potential consequences in Defence terms) or they must acknowledge publicly that weird things occur for which no explanation is at present possible. Can we be surprised that they stalled and cheated? I would have done the same had I had the ill luck to be in post at the relevant time! (Let others among you who are without sin cast the first stone).

The Rendlesham incidents remain open to debate. I will merely add that they could not possibly have been a mere military misfortune – e.g. the loss or crash in Rendlesham Forest of a bit of troublesome hardware. I have given my reasons more fully in the papers mentioned above. Perhaps I may be forgiven if, in this paper, I merely summarise my conclusion by the assertion (based on hard MOD experience) that major military mishaps can't be concealed, anyway in this country, and that not even the stupidest of officials would attempt concealment by seeking to over-excite local UFOlogists.

There was never, in my day, a deliberate policy of concealment or a deliberate plan of obfuscation. We received hundreds of reports from the public of unidentified sightings – just as I receive, today, from a cuttings service to which I subscribe, hundreds of similarly vague reports of things seen in the sky (if I may parody) worthy citizens who have seen something on the outskirts of Wigan, while walking the dog. I and my staff dealt as courteously as we could with these well-intentioned communications, and we invariably considered (often with a sigh) whether they just possibly reflected some Russian breach of the 'rules of the game'. They never did . . . Only very occasionally (and usually from Defence establishments) did we receive anything definite, for example from Bentwaters/Lakenheath, in 1956, and from RAF West Freugh, in 1957. And they also, alas, never provided solid evidence which Defence scientists could get to grips with. They never happened twice in the same place; they never did us perceptible damage; we never had the faintest idea of what had occurred; we were very glad that the public never got to hear of them; we would have stone-walled like crazy if Parliamentary Questions had ever been asked."

Question:

"What is your viewpoint on the nature of the UFO phenomenon, and how best should it be studied or investigated in the future?"

Answer:

"It is only since I left the MOD (in 1977) that I have seriously tried to consider what may possibly lie behind the 'UFO phenomenon'. It was impossible to discuss it seriously within the Department: I would merely have 'rubbished' my working relationship with the RAF and scientific colleagues if I had disclosed the interest I felt in the better reports which reached us. What I retained from my MOD experience – greatly reinforced by much that I have since read – is that the 'phenomenon' is veridical and important, and that the expert methodology developed over the past century by scholarly people in the field of the so-called 'paranormal' may possibly be relevant. I wouldn't put it higher than that at present. I can't even define 'paranormal' to my own satisfaction! All I can be quite sure of is that we, in UFOlogy, are dealing with transient and somewhat insubstantial events of a bizarre character, and that we are not alone in doing so. I think they matter. I also think that we and the 'parapsychologists' might have some useful exchanges."

(Source: © David Clarke and Andy Roberts, WWW. 2003)

It was the Lighthouse!

Authors: Common sense dictates that the lighthouse was not responsible for what Colonel Halt and the airmen saw, although Jim Penniston and John Burroughs appear to have later confused the beam of the Orford Ness lighthouse following their encounter in the forest, which they do not deny. It therefore seems pointless to waste any further time on this explanation.

Chris Pennington – A Russian aircraft landed!

Somebody else who showed an interest in the events that took place at Rendlesham Forest, right from the beginning, was Brenda's partner, at the time, Chris Pennington – an accomplished musician – whom we first met while he was still living with Brenda. Unfortunately, the couple have now gone their separate ways but still remain the best of friends.

Chris, a well-spoken, intelligent, friendly man – with no particular interest

Chris Pennington

in the UFO subject, but naturally curious about the incident which was to occupy so much of his partner's time – has his own particular theories as to what lay behind what is now indisputably the UK's top UFO mystery, attracting TV crews from all over the world, intent on interviewing Brenda right up to the present date.

For those of you that may feel some understandable suspicion regarding the testimony given by Texas-born Airman Steve Roberts, who brought the 'UFO landing' to the attention of Chris, it is only right to outline that this was not the actions of a man hitherto unknown to Chris and Brenda.

Brenda Butler

Chris tells of meeting a 'giant of a man' way back in 1976, at the *Weybread Crown,* where he was performing as a four man band. According to Chris, a 'party trick' of Max the piano player was to play something appropriate when someone walked through the door. For example if Max suspected he was Dutch, he would play *Tulips From Amsterdam,* if he was American it would be *Yankee Doodle Dandy,* and so on. Following the entrance of Steve into the pub, and the appropriate music, the 'new arrival' Steve strolled over and struck up a conversation. He was to become a personal friend of Chris and Brenda's from that time on, and has remained so despite having left the UK some years ago.

From conversations held with Chris and access to a personal five page document, entitled, *What Happened In Tangham Woods?*, produced in 1993, he outlined a number of possible explanations. They included: *Was it a 'craft' from another planet? a crashed aircraft? defecting Russian Tupolev TU 142 'Bear'? or the re-entry of a Russian satellite, or even a drugs party?*

Chris:

> "The 67th came to Woodbridge Airbase in about December 1969, with a complement of 250 personnel and their equipment, HC 130 Hercules and HH53 Jolly Green Giants (helicopters) with in-flight refuelling capabilities, and were responsible for aerospace rescue operations over almost a million square miles. It was the biggest Search & Rescue Squadron in the World. These units were set up primarily to pick up astronauts, wherever they may come down around the world, as back-up to US Space Operations, NASA.

Maybe it was just an excuse for the 67th to practise their arts. They never seemed to advertise their connection with the Space Race. They must have had equipment to practice with – if not the real thing, simulated models – which brings me to a conclusion that a Re-entry Module looks remarkably like some of the UFOs that were reported. If it were only a practice, why did John Warbiton tell us that Colonel Halt's boss, Colonel Ted Conrad, said, 'not allowed to say what happened, as it would embarrass Governments'.

As one may or may not know, for some reason or another, many things that Brenda Butler and Dot Street wrote in the original 'Sky Crash' were not included – just to mention two examples. (1) It was reported an aircraft was sent to Germany, in order to pick up spare parts for the craft.(2) Should the truth ever be revealed, then Governments would topple. I believe that we secretly let a Russian Aircraft land in the UK. There were reports on the National News a Russian aircraft carrier had passed through the English Channel and that Russian spy planes were seen flying deep into the funnel of the North Sea. (Were they looking for a lost satellite, maybe?) One must remember that courtesy exchanges between Russian and French Air Forces were being made at around that time, and one possible route was North Sea, English Channel. So long as they remained in International Airspace, one could do nothing.

How can you ignore the evidence of Ron, who visited the Rendlesham area at about midnight on the 27th December 1980, after being told by a mate, who lived near Woodbridge, of unidentified lights sighted over the area? Ron told Brenda he was walking along the forestry trail, somewhere near the eastern perimeter of RAF Woodbridge, when he saw a lighted area in the woods. The next thing that happened was he was escorted away from the area by two armed security guards and the film from his camera confiscated. He was then taken to Woodbridge Police Station, but later released without charge. They (SCUFORI) sent people down to the forest, who met up with Brenda and Dot, but following their investigation into the alleged incident, they concluded there was nothing to it and dismissed it as being of no importance, which I felt was a personal slight on Brenda and Dot, who might have been only 'a couple of housewives' but knew something of importance had occurred.

What you have to realise is that I was involved in all of this. Dot, by this time, was in touch with an American Group. They wrote to her and said, 'Hey, some of your stuff has been released under the USA FOI Act'. They sent Dot a copy of the information, which included Colonel Halt's letter. We then went to High Wycombe, when the UFO Congress was on. It was obvious they were going to make fools of us, bearing in mind the visit by SCUFORI. In fact, I believe that's why they were invited. Harry Harris saw the document and came over to us and offered to be spokesman, on our behalf, at the meeting, as he was a member of BUFORA, which we weren't. They started 'booing' Brenda and Dot, and saying they didn't know what they were talking about – things like they didn't have the experience etc. – but when the document was brought to the attention of the audience by Harry, they changed their tune".

Brenda Butler:

"I heard of a Russian Tupolev military aircraft seen off our coast, and also on the TV News broadcast (in December 1980). When we contacted the TV Station, they said it was a mistake and it should not have been broadcast. In 2010, during the preparation of a documentary on the incident, Colonel Halt came to see us. In conversation with Chris Pennington, who showed him his research work relating to his theory that it was a satellite, Charles said to him, 'You are on the right track. I told Brenda to be more scientific, in 1983'. He then took the pamphlet and later left."

It was a Russian Satellite!

In 1986, Brenda was contacted by a woman identified as Karin. She said she was employed at RAF Woodbridge as a secretary, and knew Colonel Halt, and wanted to tell the real truth of what had taken place at the base (over 6yrs previously).

Brenda and her colleague – Derek Newman – picked up Karin and interviewed her on tape, which we have listened to and also obtained a script.

'Karin' alleged that the UFO story was engineered to camouflage the recovery of a Russian satellite or aircraft. Why she left it so long before bringing this to the attention of Brenda and her companion, Derek Newman, is anybody's guess.

We understood that Brenda made a note of her real name, but promised her that a pseudonym would be used.

We discussed the contents of the tape-recorded interview with Brenda many times over the years – and also forwarded a copy to Colonel Halt for his comments, in 2013.

While we remain intrigued by what 'Karin' alleged, we decided that it would be inappropriate to outline the whole of that lengthy interview in this book, as it falls outside the boundaries of what our research is about.

As the reader will see from the reply given by Charles Halt, some of those allegations made by 'Karin' relate to issues of a domestic nature, involving personal grievances with other employees on the airbase. She also claimed that Colonel Halt was an OSI agent.

Colonel Halt:

> *"John, there are bits of truth in some things she says. We did, from time to time, have classified planes land but almost always at Bentwaters, not Woodbridge. We did have classified convoys but not UFOs, or Russian planes/satellites – just routine weapons movements. This was common and they were treated with great care. Photography was not allowed and large areas secured. I liked the part of my replacement firing his secretary because she was too tall. My replacement was quite tall so I can just imagine how tall she must have been . . . Me, an OSI Agent? Her story isn't worth much comment."*

Apollo Command Module

Some people – including researcher Jan Roth – believe it was the botched recovery of an Apollo Command Module, housed covertly at RAF Woodbridge, for training exercises (fitted with lights for recovery purposes that could be either programmed or remotely switched on, and equipped with a distress flare system to assist recovery from the sea).

Jan:

> *"It weighed about the size of a small family car, and was the same size and pyramidal shape that Jim Penniston and others had described. The Module was smooth to the touch and had a ceramic type surface designed to withstand re-entry heating. The navigation lights were under the surface skin of the object, and shone through Pyrex type glass panels. It stood on three short legs, with concave disc-shaped feet. Some of the pilots took off in a HII53 (Jolly Green Giant Helicopter) after hooking the capsule on underneath, intending to place it on one of the Airfields as a practical joke, but while flying low over Rendlesham Forest, the Module collided with one of the approach landing lights, causing it to start swinging, which made the helicopter unstable, so they dropped the capsule into the forest.*
>
> *A search was made of the forest with spotlights, by the helicopter, which hovered over the forest for some time – an action seen by people in the Bentwaters control tower. As there was no sign of it, a search was carried out on foot, when it was located and covered over.*

The following evening, the lights on the Module were switched on to aid those on foot. Would this explain the large presence of servicemen who had gathered to witness the spectacle, after somebody suggested it resembled an alien spaceship and the cover-up started? Orders were given for the Module to be taken back to the Airbase, so as not to attract attention from the locals; accordingly, it was lifted up and flown back to the base on the second night.

Apollo Module on Airbase © David Bryant

They then decided to fabricate a story about a UFO having been seen, knowing that if the matter was brought to the attention of the High Command and the British Authorities, some of them would have been court-martialled – not forgetting the fall out of any political aftermath, which could have comprised the further use of the airbase and have endangered the good relations with the British. I believe Lt. Colonel Halt and a few others were initially ignorant of what had taken place, but later became part of the cover-up. Shortly afterwards, the Apollo Command Module was shipped out to an undisclosed destination."

Was it a UFO that crash landed and needed repairs?

In 2009, USA UFO researcher, Mary Margaret Zimmerman, contacted Philip Mantle, following a telephone call made to her from a John Traylor – formerly a resident of Greyfriers Road, Woodridge, in Suffolk now living in the States. He claimed that the object seen by the airmen in Rendlesham Forest was an alien craft, and that repairs were made. Philip then asked us to look into the allegations made by John Traylor. We spoke to John, and this is what he had to say:

> *"Following the sighting of a triangular UFO over the nearby Porter's Wood, towards the end of December 1980, my brother-in-law's father, Ken Pratt, who had connections with the Ipswich-based Company – Ransome & Rapier – owned a factory in Ipswich, which made the skeletons for Tesco Stores and supplied the steel for the bridge over the River Orwell. He was approached by someone who asked him to manufacture a piece of machinery for a 'spaceship, stored at RAF Woodbridge, in December 1980, and was shown a piece of metal he had never seen before. Unfortunately, Ken later committed suicide."*

We spoke to John's mother, Yvonne, now living in the Berkshire area (who asked us not to reveal her full name) on a number of occasions about this matter, over the telephone.

> *"They closed the airbase down at the back of Rendlesham Forest. Reports had it that the 'spaceship' was actually in one of the hangers. All of the airmen who saw it were shipped off back to the States. My husband was sworn to secrecy. Everybody was talking about it. I made the kids come indoors. It was real strange."*

The sighting of the UFO, as seen by her son and friends, was something Yvonne found easy to talk about. However, there appeared to be some, perhaps, understandable reluctance to discuss, in any depth, the extraordinary claims made by her son, regarding Ken's role in repairing a landed 'craft' at the airbase. Yvonne could only tell us that *'the spacemen wanted a piece made of strange metal'* and seemed unwilling to discuss his involvement further.

Whether her attitude was due to a subsequent break-up in the marriage and, later, divorce of her (unnamed) daughter to Ken's son, some years ago, or her husband's current employment with the US Government is anybody's guess. Perhaps they feared attracting the attention of the media once this story was published.

Yvonne:

> *"It was in wintertime. The nights were drawing in. About 4pm, my youngest son at the time – John (now over 40) arrived home. I asked him where he had been. He told me he had been out playing with some other boys in Porter's Wood, one of whom was Johnny Cracknell (who died*

some years later, aged 20). Johnny told him about a 'spaceship' in Porter's Wood. As dusk fell my children came in and asked whether they could go to Porter's Wood and have a look, because some other friends of theirs had told them the Dr. Who series was being filmed about a 'spaceship' in a clearing and two people 'like us' got out."

I told my son it was getting dark and I wasn't going to let him go and have a look in the woods but said he could play outside in the street, where I could keep my eye on him, and that when the tea was ready they would have to come in. They were playing 'spotlight', or something (shining torches at cars). When I went outside to get them in, they came running up the street and told me about a spaceship hovering overhead. It didn't make a sound. The kids kept shouting, 'Mum what is it?', so I fetched John out, my husband, and he picked up a camera – then this 'thing' just shot up in the sky, towards Rendlesham Forest.

It was about four stories high above the houses in height, covered in bright lights, triangular in shape, and lit up the road as it hovered overhead. The 'craft' went toward the direction of Rendlesham Forest. By the time my husband clicked the shutter, it had gone. When we developed the picture, all it showed was a bright star in the sky. The problem is that if you told people it was a spaceship they wouldn't believe you, as it looked like a star in the sky – it went so fast.

The next day, John went into work. When he came home, the news of the spaceship landing in the forest was all in the news. All the trees were down where it had landed. The animals had left the forest. There were lots of things going on at that base. The airmen that were there (one of my friend's husband's) got sent back to the States. They weren't allowed to speak to anybody and tell them why they were going home.

Lots of civilian people saw that spaceship, as well as my kids. (Do you remember Johnny Kemp? He was a children's presenter. He used to make films for children's television – some of them at Woodbridge. One of the presenters from Blue Peter *used to live there. I thought they must be making a film."*

Yvonne believes the 'spaceship' and 'men' were real and that the children thought it was a movie set, although they didn't see any equipment lowering the spaceship.

She told us trees were broken in the forest, but was unable to remember who the other children were, but that *"many people who lived in Woodbridge, at the time, saw the craft"*. She recommended the local newspaper archives and suggested we speak to David Jenkins, one of the 'boy' witnesses, who still lives in Woodbridge.

We then telephoned John Traylor, in the States, and spoke to him about the allegations during mid-2009. He corroborated the sighting of the triangular UFO over Porter's Wood, and confirmed the information given regarding Ken Pratt.

"He had connections with the Company, in Ipswich, Suffolk, named Ransome & Rapier. *This was the Company that made the part for the UFO, held at RAF Woodbridge. Although I think the son would rather not be contacted regarding why his father died, perhaps he would*

respond to a query regarding any knowledge he may have as to the part made for a UFO by Ransome & Rapier.

As for Kingston Middle School (where the UFO landed and then took-off again) if you have the opportunity to visit the location of the School for yourself, you may want to take a Geiger counter with you. I believe Mr Spicer was the Headmaster of the School. He may now be residing in Kesgrave. Finally, as for Ransome & Rapier, *I was under the impression that the Company was shut down after the part was made (though some accounts state the Company simply changed its name) yet all senior bosses left very quickly."*

Authors:

Whilst we believed, from conversations held with Yvonne and her son, John, that we were dealing with genuine people, as opposed to any orchestrated deception, we felt some concern of not having been allowed the opportunity to interview them personally at their home address, despite offering to visit them on a number of occasions. We asked her if we could examine the photographic slide of the UFO and were told that she did not know where it was. She asked us not to reveal her name because of possible repercussions to her husband, (who still works for the American Government) although he confirmed the UFO sighting had taken place He declined to comment on the information regarding *Ransome & Rapier*, but confirmed he had photographed the triangular UFO, and said he had served under Colonel Halt at the Airbase, in 1980.

John Traylor also suggested we contact David Jenkins – a lifelong friend of his, living in Woodbridge – who was a witness to the sighting of the UFO. Unfortunately, we discovered that Mr Jenkins had passed away, a few years ago, although he was well-known in the locality and a regular at the local Public House – *The Red Lion* – and left a daughter, as far as we know.

Despite appeals made in the local Newspaper, the *Evening Star,* asking for any information on the whereabouts of Ken and his son – apparently still employed as a metal fabricator in the Ipswich area, who was believed to be connected with *Ransome & Rapier* (without any mention of the UFO connection) – we never received any reply. A letter, sent by recorded delivery to a business address in Ipswich, asking Ken to contact us with regard to this matter, was also not answered.

Was his refusal to enter into correspondence with us due to the acrimonious domestic situation that had existed between him and Yvonne's daughter, following a divorce, or was there another reason? Could we even be sure this was the same man we wanted to interview? His evidence and knowledge is vital to this enquiry. The last thing we wanted was to cause any embarrassment to somebody who had the misfortune to have the same name as the person we sought to interview.

Without some corroboration, we effectively had nothing to support the claims made regarding Ken and John's part in this incident, given by John Traylor and his mother, but felt we had done as much as we possibly could under the circumstances.

However, we did receive a large number of letters and telephone calls from former employees of *Ransome & Rapier*, all of whom denied any knowledge of Ken Pratt and his son – which may not come of any surprise, understanding that it was never suggested they were employed directly by *Ransome and Rapier* but were connected through another company, which may well have independently supplied material to that firm.

We discovered that Orwell Bridge – which carries the A14 road (then A45) over the River Orwell, south of Ipswich, Suffolk – was constructed under contract to *Stevin Construction B.V.*, a Dutch company, in October 1979, and was opened to road traffic in 1982.

Enquiries made with them, to establish if they had subcontracted to any Ipswich-based manufacturers (including Mr Ken Pratt and his son, David) to supply any steel, or work on the bridge, proved unsuccessful. Yvonne told us she had no knowledge of the 'spaceship' having landed at the nearby *Kingston Primary School*, (as alleged by her son), but claimed the school, which was of recent construction, had to be demolished afterwards, following conversation with her son, John, who told her this course of action was orchestrated following the landing of the UFO, in the school grounds. This was the same UFO which then took off and later crash-landed in the forest.

We asked her if we could examine the photographic slide of the UFO and were told she didn't know where it was. Yvonne asked us not to reveal her surname because of possible repercussions to her husband, John, (an ex-USAF serviceman of undetermined rank and position within the USAF) who, in a separate conversation to us, albeit brief, said he knew Colonel Halt and had served under him at the airbase in 1980. John declined to discuss any information regarding *Ransome & Rapier*, but confirmed having sighted and photographed the triangular UFO.

We visited Porter's Wood and the site where *Kingston Middle School* had stood, off Cherry Tree Lane, Woodbridge, in 2009, in company with Brenda Butler and Peter Parish. We took some photos of the 'school playing field' – now a grassed area of land belonging to the nearby Care Home for the elderly which lies adjacent to the nearby railway line, but saw nothing of any note, either on the grass or in the surrounding locality.

While it would be easy to believe the information corroborated what Brenda had been told initially by her contact 'Steve Roberts' about parts being manufactured to repair a 'craft' which had landed in the forest and of other sources which may or may not back up this version of events, we should be careful about jumping to the wrong conclusions. It is not that we necessarily disbelieve what Yvonne had told us – far from it, but we weren't prepared to accept such a sensational claim without being able to interview them personally, especially bearing in mind their general reticence to allow this course of action to take place.

The media interest has also sparked off various claims made by those who wish to perpetuate the myths by admitting they were responsible, and become the focus of media attention. Such claims have included hoaxing, by driving a police car around the base, and more recently, a lorry load of fertilizer which was set alight by an Ipswich man! These admissions were to attract considerable worldwide media attention, but should not be treated seriously.

Another explanation involved an allegation that the UFO story was concocted to cover-up a crash of an aircraft carrying a nuclear device, or the testing of military hardware – extremely sensitive issues during a period of great public concern over the threat of nuclear deterrent, with crowds of protestors camped outside the USAF Airbase, at Greenham Common.

Could this suggestion have been given some credibility, following information received by Brenda Butler and Del Newman, in November 1987, from 'Karin' – the wife of an airman, based at RAF Woodbridge (formerly Sutton Heath), who alleged *"An aircraft was sent to Germany, to bring back some spare parts for a Russian aircraft that had landed!?"*

While Brenda and Derek Newman believe the woman was sincere, are we really expected to believe the military authorities had intercepted a Russian aircraft with a satellite on board – then constructed an elaborate version of events, involving airmen on the Base, to release a story about a UFO to cover-up an action, which if discovered, would have precipitated some hostile action by a foreign power?

None of 'Karin's' claims have ever been corroborated by any other USA service personnel stationed at RAF Woodbridge or Bentwaters – this seems odd, understanding the nature of an alleged incident, the magnitude of which would have surely, in time, instigated other people to come forward wishing to reveal what they knew behind what is still regarded by many, as the most important UFO mystery of the 20th Century.

If the Russians had lost an aircraft off the Suffolk coast towards the end of December 1980, through ditching, having sustained engine/mechanical failure, or even landing at the Base following defection, what a fantastic coup that would have made for the British/American authorities.

Others claim it was a satellite film return capsule ejected from a KH-9B Hexagon 'Big Bird' satellite which was picked up off the coast.

'Karin' maintains there was a deliberate cover up and deception, orchestrated by someone to camouflage the 'real truth' behind the leaked UFO story, which was given credibility following the release of the Halt memorandum. But what if 'Karin' was deliberately or unknowingly manipulated by someone to disseminate information, knowing that this 'evidence' could have caused some embarrassment, never mind the serious implications of such an allegation, unfounded or not, against the USA Government.

If we accept that what 'Karin' alleges is true, why should an American citizen want to betray her Country?

She mentioned she had been suspected of an arson allegation on the base involving damage to the ladies toilets, so presumably her name and criminal actions were known to security police on the Base. Was this the reason why she didn't 'leak the information' until some years later. Knowing that disclosure would have 'blown her cover' following the December events being public knowledge within the air base – never mind the embarrassment caused to her, her husband who she claimed was a pilot on the Base, or was this a case of 'sour grapes'? We shall never know! If the UFO story was a ploy to cover up some covert activity, what does this mean for the integrity of the airmen concerned, who still maintain to this present date that UFO activity was sighted over separate nights in December 1980?

Probe Group and their investigation, 1982

The Swindon based UFO Group, 'Probe' – run by Ian Mrzyglod – asked Martin Shipp and Charles Affleck, of SCUFORI, to visit the locality in late September 1982. The two men spoke personally to Dot Street and Brenda Butler, in order to find out what lay behind various stories circulating in the media, *alleging that a UFO had landed in the forest*, wondering whether this was a story fabricated to conceal something else, such as a 'live' nuclear bomb having fallen from one of the aircraft en route to the airbase, or was it a hoax?

They also felt there was a need to determine exactly 'where the landing site was', although their objectives were not to investigate the story but to determine the sequence of events alleged to have taken place, during December 1980.

Charles Affleck:

> *"Prior to my visit to the forest, I had spoken to Dot, who told me, following a recent visit to the landing site it was still devoid of any plant growth, over two years later."*

After parking the car, they accompanied Dot to the 'landing site', as shown on the OS Map Reference Sheet 169, 362 488, where they were amazed to see a huge area devoid of any plant growth.

> *"The ground was very dry and covered in pieces of branch and leaves. The location was directly in line with the end of the runway, at RAF Woodbridge."*

Using a Geiger counter, the ground was tested for radiation but did not detect anything untoward. The ground was closely examined and there was found to be several examples of plant life sprouting through the dead leaves. The question that stunned the researchers was *what could have caused such a huge area to be devoid of life?*

A further examination of the locality revealed similar cleared areas of trees, from which it was surmised, from the stacked up piles of timber nearby, that they had been felled by the Forestry Commission, as opposed to damage caused by an object crash landing. The investigators then examined other matters pertaining to the case. They included a complaint made by Brenda of an out-of-character vibration to her Ford Cortina estate vehicle, while driving along the forest track to visit witnesses, with Dot, which was suggested to be attributed to the proximity of overhead power cables, or water running down the track. A drive along the same track by Martin and Charles failed to recreate the same conditions, but it was of significance to see the height of the forest wall then (before the great storm of 1987).

(How on earth would one have been able to see the beam of the lighthouse through this dense foliage?) Ironically, no-one could have guessed, in their wildest dreams, of the huge 'wave' of media interest which was to swamp the Suffolk area, following the disclosures later made by Colonel Halt, Larry Warren and others, although, of course, none of this was known at the time by 'Probe', who concluded, from their investigation into the matter, quote:

> *'As previously stated, it was not 'SCUFORI's' intention to investigate the sighting, only to attempt to determine if the case was worthy of a detailed follow-up.'*

Timothy Good with Dot Street

Brenda Butler:

Brenda Butler later wrote to 'Probe', after reading their 'write-up' of their visit.

> *"Dear Sir,*
>
> *I am one of the Investigators on the Rendlesham case and half of what you have printed is untrue, and I would like to put it right. The landing site – the UFO did not land where these four Investigators went. I cannot understand why Dot Street took them there, as Dot knows where it landed (supposedly). The*

witness showed us where the landing site was and it was certainly not at the place in the photographs. Dot says the Forestry men told her where the site was on the map – the map I saw was covered in little green trees and you could not tell one place from another."

The Group also brought to Brenda Butler's attention their misgivings that she was the only person told of the events by a person whose identity had been concealed.

"My witness asked me to keep quiet about the UFO, on behalf of him. This I did for five weeks, but I had permission to use this information if I also got it from someone else. After I was told the same story by a forestry worker, whom I knew, I released the story, so I did not betray my confidence to the witness."

As it was questionable, in the Group's opinion, whether something unusual had occurred at RAF Woodbridge, in late December 1980, owing to what they saw as discrepancies raised (which cast doubts on the entire case) they decided the matter did not warrant further investigation. In hindsight it is all too easy to criticize SCUFORI – an organisation which was run very professionally under the guidance of Ian Mrzyglod – for failing to accept something extraordinary had *apparently* taken place in this remote part of the forest, but how could they have possibly known the extent of information still hidden from British view, including the report submitted by Colonel Halt, in January 1981?

Acceptably, mistakes and discrepancies occurred, but none of this should detract from the professionalism of all of the parties concerned.

(Source: Martin Shipp, Charles Affleck/Ian Mrzyglod, Jenny Randles (Northern UFO Network)/
***BUFORA Bulletin* 004, Page 20-21, Dot Street, *Flying Saucer Review*, Volume 27, No. 6,**
by Jenny Randles, p.4-48 & *The Unexplained*, Volume 9, Jenny Randles, p.2101-2105A)

Robert Hastings and interference with Nuclear Missiles on Base

"I am not condemning any government agency for its policy of secrecy regarding UFOs, but I believe that the public should be given the facts. I believe that UFOs are piloted by visitors from elsewhere in the universe who, for whatever reason, have taken an interest in our long-term survival. These beings are occasionally disrupting our nukes to send a message to the American and Soviet/Russian governments that their possession and potential large-scale use of nuclear weapons threatens the future of humanity and the environmental integrity of the planet.

In 1994, 12 years before my interview with Halt, another retired US Air Force officer told me that following the UFO incident at the Bentwaters WSA, two of the weapons had been removed from one of the bunkers for inspection.

That individual once held a high-level position with NATO's nuclear weapons security program. I had been introduced to him by a mutual friend who knew of my longstanding interest in nukes-related UFO incidents. I was aware of the retired officer's background, so I hesitantly asked him if he had ever heard about the Bentwaters/Woodbridge UFO incidents.

After warily staring at me for a few seconds, he acknowledged that he was familiar with them. Figuring that I had nothing to lose, I plunged ahead and asked him if he had heard the rumours about the UFO sighting at the Bentwaters Weapons Storage Area. Much to my surprise, he confirmed the presence of a UFO near the WSA, confirmed that it had directed a beam or beams of light downward into the bunker complex, and – without any prompting from me – said that he had once read a report stating that two tactical nuclear bombs had been removed from one of the bunkers shortly after the incident and shipped by the Air Force to the U.S. for inspection. I must admit that I was somewhat taken aback by this individual's candor.

He concluded his remarks by saying that he was unaware of the findings of this inspection because it had taken place several years before his tenure with NATO. Regardless, in light of these comments, it appears that the US Air Force was sufficiently concerned about the condition of the two bombs after the UFO incident to remove them from their bunker for inspection.

Unfortunately, I am not at liberty to reveal the retired officer's identity. However, his credentials relating to his previous involvement with the US military's nuclear weapons security program, are a matter of record and I consider his statements to be highly credible."

Colonel Halt, interviewed by Brenda Butler – 1996

In August 1996, Colonel Halt and Brenda had lunch together in Manchester, during which time she asked him a number of prepared questions.

Q "Why was only one sighting picked up on radar when, according to the witnesses, there were three sightings?"

A "The radar had closed down as it was over the Christmas holidays."

Q "Why, when we phoned up Watton Radar Station, did they tell us that they had not picked up anything on radar over those days in December 1980?"

A "They were told to say that."

Q "What fell off an aircraft that was so sensitive that it had to be covered up?"

A "No comment."

Q "Why, on your first tape, are there no forest noises, birds, or the sound of men walking? We have gone through the forest at night with a Walkman, and we got noises on our tape. We could hear rabbits and deer running about, birds flying out of the trees, and our own footsteps quite clearly."

A "I had them cut out of the tape."

Q "I think that the tape was made in a building, as there is an echo-like sound rebounding off a wall."

A "Maybe. I don't know."

Q "Why is the Department of the Air Force withholding seven documents, which consists

  of inter-agency memoranda?"

A *"I don't know anything about these documents."*

Q *"Why did you tell your son, Chuck, to say it was a UFO?"*

A *"Is that what he told you? Wait till I see him!"*

Q *"By it being referred to as a UFO, does that mean that it was of unknown origin to you, but not a space vehicle?"*

A. *"I do not know what it was."*

Q *"Was it a cosmic incident, or were they practising with a lunar command module or landing probe?"*

A *"They do have a module they keep in practice with, the Aerospace Rescue and Recovery Squadron."*

Q *"Were the Aerospace Rescue and Recovery Squadron involved in any activities on the 26th and 27th December?"*

A. *"They were all off base, as it was a holiday."*

Q *"Is it true that you and Conrad shifted the dates for a cover-up to misdirect people?"*

A *"No!"*

Q *"A witness said that it was a silver object in a crater in the ground, with five men covering it up with a tarpaulin. The object looked like a missile."*

A *"That's not what I saw."*

Q *"The MOD said that it was of no threat to our security."*

A *"It wasn't."*

Q *"How do you know it wasn't a threat to our National Security if you didn't know what it was?"*

A *"No comment."*

Q *"Why were the Army, Navy and Air Force, all involved and why was HMS Norfolk off the coast?"*

A *"I don't know. It's news to me."*

Q *"Why were the men allowed to touch the craft when they didn't know what it was, with the added danger of radiation?"*

A *"It was up to them; no senior officer was present to stop them."*

Q *"Why was the Russian Tupolev TUZU 'Bear' aircraft off the coast over international waters?"*

A *"The 'Bear' is always going up and down the coast."*

Authors: Regarding this question, Jonathon Dillon in his interview with Colonel Halt suggested to him that a Tupolev TU14 Russian 'Bear' Aircraft suffered a gearbox failure on one of its four sets of rotating props and its vibration caused a fire and fuel leak, following which a decision was made for it to carry out an emergency landing at the airbase.

Colonel Halt:

"I think there's more to be heard. Something very strange happened that night that I think a lot of people don't want out. An awful lot of people tend to overlook our testimony, but others want to know what's going on, not only with this but with other occurrences."

Q "Is it true that American and Russian scientists are working together in diverse fields of biology, medicines and space biology?"

A "We do work alongside them, yes."

Q "Why were the British MOD not involved in the incident; yet it took place on British soil?"

A "We phoned the MOD; they were not interested and told us to handle it. We did call the British Police and they attended."

Q "Why was there a Russian submarine off the coast over Christmas?"

A "I don't know!"

Q "I phoned Mildenhall and spoke to their PR officer. He told me that you would not be allowed to talk about an incident; if you did it would mean a heavy fine, imprisonment, loss of pension, or a discharge from the service. This applies to all servicemen."

A "You certainly have done your homework, haven't you?"

Q "Was it a nuclear powered UFO, American, or Russian?"

A "No!"

Q "Do you know what 'Project Moondust is?"

A "No!"

Q "Do you know what Remote Viewing is, as I know someone who has this ability?"

(At that point he got quite concerned and said that they were still experimenting in the USA and Russia with it)

Q "I was told that the 141 Starlifter Transporter Aircraft had secret intelligence men on board. What did they want?"

A "I didn't know about this until a later date."

*Project Moondust

First initiated by the US Air Force, in 1957, as a secret-level program for the recovery and analysis of foreign (particularly German) aircraft and anomalous objects, MOONDUST is still in operation today and is managed by the USAF Foreign Technology Division. While most of its duties still pertain to the study of weapons and air/space platforms of terrestrial powers, the project's mystique stems from the far rarer, investigation of suspected extraterrestrial objects. To the disbelief of many on the outside, both missions are handled by the same personnel; there is no 'above secret' detachment within MOONDUST to handle objects of unknown origin, nor is there much distinction made between the investigation of the two. Most analysis is done through the collection of disparate intelligence and reports (including sometimes videos and radar tracking) received from the field. Actual recoveries, whether from crashes, shoot-downs, or (even more rarely) capture raids, are infrequent. **(Source: Wikpedia, 2013)**

Material recovered from the landing site

Many years ago we were allowed to take a sample of what looked like blue foam, from Brenda's possession, after we learnt that some larger items of material were recovered from the 'landing site' shortly after the event being brought to their notice. In addition to this, she handed over a photograph showing the larger pieces. We had a tiny piece examined and understood it was likely to be a foam based chemical in origin. We have no idea what its purpose or use was – presumably it was connected with something on the Base but we really don't know, unless it was dumped there.

UFO Conference in the Nebraska USA 1983

Jenny Randles described a journey undertaken by her and Dot Street, to the United States, on a four day UFO conference, held at the University at Lincoln, Nebraska.

On the 6th November 1983, Jenny and Dot met at a London hotel. They spent the evening discussing various UFO related matters with a number of other investigators. The next morning, they caught a flight to Chicago. Rather charmingly, bearing in mind the way in which air flights have changed, Jenny, in her own meticulous manner, 'paints a picture' of Dot exercising her interview techniques on board with the other passengers.

Dot even brought the pilot back (we presumed she meant the co-pilot) and introduced him to Jenny, followed by a conversation about UFOs. One cannot even visualise such a thing happening now. Jenny confessed she felt some trepidation,

> *"after realising that at 35,000ft, if something went wrong, how he would get back to the cockpit! I was not reassured to learn that a computer was flying the 747, especially after finding out that the in-flight movie was War Games, which was about how a nuclear holocaust was nearly caused by a computer."*

After a safe landing, the couple made their way to the home of Allen and Mimi Hynek at Evanston (headquarters for the Center for UFO Studies) – what a privilege that must have been.

Jenny:

> *"I felt pleased to have discovered that even the vastly efficient Dr. Hynek and CUFOS have data retrieval problems; their case reports and materials tend to form lots of little piles on stairs, in boxes, and in any little nook and cranny they can find."*

At the conference, they met up with Larry Fawcett (he had obtained the Colonel Halt memo from the MOD, under the Freedom of Information Act) and Linda Moulton Howe. Lectures were given by Allen Hynek, Budd Hopkins and John Scheusler (Cash/Landrum case, from Texas) who showed photographs of the gruesome effects of radiation sickness, caused by a UFO.

After the conference, Dot flew on to Connecticut with Larry Fawcett and Jenny headed for the University of Boulder – home of the Condon Report, where she spoke to some of the scientists involved – then back to Chicago, where she spent time with Jerome Clark, at the Office of *FATE* magazine.

Jenny:

> *"I had travelled over 13,000 miles and over 4,000 by road and rail, but it was well worth it and I would do it again like a shot!"*

(Source: *BUFORA Bulletin* of February 1984, The Freeway to American UFOLOGY)

UFOs over Suffolk, 2000

The East coast has laid claim to many sightings of UFOs, over the years. In addition to this, there have been a number of occasions when UFOs have been plotted on radar, moving eastwards, over East Anglia.

On the 30th January 2000, London-based UFO researcher – Tony Spurrier – travelled to Sizewell Power Station, in Suffolk, accompanied by Susan Addison, and colleagues, to conduct a 'sky watch'. Tony and four colleagues set up an observation point behind the main bank of the power station, while Sue and a colleague made their way to the main

site. At 12.50am, Tony received a message from Sue that a 'flying triangle' was approaching from the North, but was unable to see what Sue was watching because of their restricted view. The situation was made worse by the arrival of the police, who stopped Sue and her colleague, and after asking them what they were doing, instructed them to leave the area. At this point a huge formation of lights forming a 'V' in the sky, were seen moving overhead – large enough to block out the Ursa Major constellation of stars.

The group decided to continue their observation from a southern position, away from the power station (which was now no longer visible) and were lucky enough, during the early hours, to see 'flying triangles' and other shaped craft, moving above an approach road, towards the power station. Tony told us that the footage we took was identical to what he filmed.

At 8.29pm on 27th December 2000, a group of us – including Brenda Butler, Jack Solomon (Head of the Norwich UFO Group) and members of the Essex UFO Branch – were stood talking on an

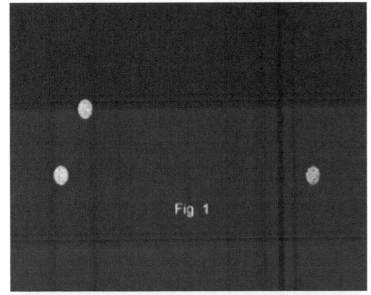

Fig 1

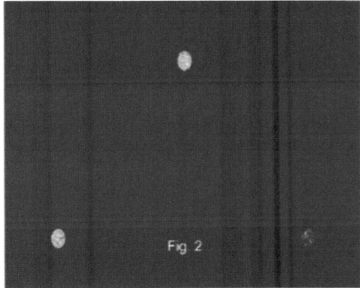

Fig 2

elevated section of the forest, near to the end of track 10, opposite to the field nominated by Larry Warren (who was himself in the forest that night) as being the one where he saw the UFO land, 20 years ago.

A yellow 'light' was seen just above the horizon, towards the direction of Orford Ness Lighthouse, followed by a number of others which appeared in the sky, forming a horizontal line, approximately four to five miles away, apparently over the coast, or out at sea. We do not maintain this was any 'alien craft' – all we can say is that we have never seen any strange 'light' like this over the forest before, at this particular location.

Fortunately we managed to video the effect (by using a Sony Handycam Video Camera, with night light 72Xdigital zoom). See opposite page, showing stills from the footage.

Photo of the area from where the author's video was taken. The cross marks the approximate spot where the object was seen.

The following day we were interviewed by the local TV Station, *Look East,* and *Suffolk Advertiser,* but it was not until many months later, that we discovered we were not the only ones to have witnessed something unusual occurring at that time in the forest, during that evening, one of whom was Mark Doulton and members of the Southend UFO Group.

> *"We arrived in the forest at about 8pm, and were immediately struck by the intense cold (some 15° below freezing). We walked down track 12 but, finding nobody about, decided to look down track 10. Following consultation with Chris Martin, who was in our group and had been successful in capturing UFOs previously on film, we decided to meditate as part of an experiment. Much to our surprise, some 20 minutes later, we were rewarded by the sight of a strange flashing in the sky above our heads. This 'flashing', whatever it was, had certainly not been visible before – apart from this, the sky was relatively clear. We watched this strange 'flashing' for some minutes, before deciding to move to track 12, in order to meet up with other groups. We noticed the 'flashing' seemed to be concentrated in one area of the sky only. Not being experts on weather phenomena, we cannot say what this was, but having been to many countries and experienced severe storms I have to say this was nothing like what we saw that night."*

Following publicity, Mrs Butler was contacted by people who reported having seen strange lights over Woo Way, Orford, at about 8pm, along with a report of an orange 'ball of light' seen hovering over the sea, at 10.45pm, accompanied by the arrival of a helicopter, which appeared to be looking for something. Whether it was the UFO could only be speculation. However, one should bear in mind that strange 'lights' seen over the coast would attract the attention of the Coastguard.

The waters around Orford Ness have several strange stories attributed to them. In 1749, *The Gentleman's Magazine* claimed several fishermen were attacked by a winged crocodile-like creature, which snagged in their nets, while off the coast. It is alleged that the beast killed one man and disabled another, before being slain. The 'sea-dragon', as it came to be known, measured just over a metre in length; it had two legs, with cloven feet. A fisherman travelled the county of Suffolk displaying the creature, though what became of the oddity is unknown.

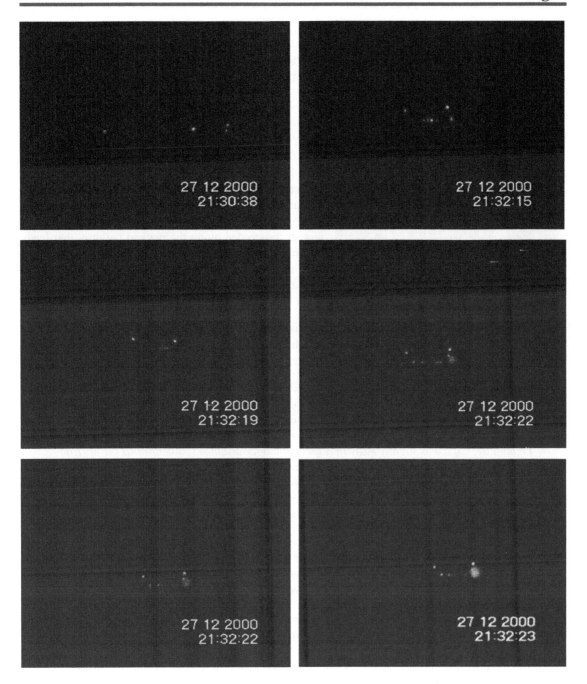

The 1197 case of the Orford Merman is well documented (albeit a short while after the event, by Ralph of Coggeshall) and still talked about locally. There is even a local pub named after him. The story is that the 'man' was caught in the sea and then held in the castle for a period of six months, before finally escaping back into the ocean. The 'merman' never talked during his captivity, and appeared to have a preference for fish over other types of food.

Most tales of this nature can be explained away as cases of mistaken identity, but what identified sea creature resembles a winged crocodile? What 'man' spends six months in a castle before escaping back into the wild? Britain's first atomic weapon, *Blue Danube*, was developed and tested in large pagodas, which dominate the coast. The skeletal remains of other buildings, used during the two World Wars and Cold War, are scattered across the shingle.

UFO over Suffolk, 2011

Matt Lyons – head of BUFORA, was invited to speak at the recent UFO conference, at Woodbridge Hall, Suffolk, England, in September 2011 and took time out to visit the area, during daylight. Matt, who was accompanied by his mother, proceeded along the marked pathway that leads towards East Gate, on what was an overcast day but with good illumination from a slowly clearing sky to the south, with a slight occasional drizzle of rain.

After some camera shots were taken of East Gate and the landing site, they made their way to the small clearing, which opened out into the large field, identified by Larry Warren as where his UFO sighting took place.

"On looking directly towards the lone farmhouse, central as a marking in the field in the mid-distance, we noted no birds or typically identifiable flying craft of any description. My mother noted the quiet stillness, with no whirr of microlights, helicopter, or any type of aircraft noise. We were interested to observe the soon to be decommissioned Orford Ness Lighthouse, but it was slightly misty in respect of longer distance vision towards the horizon line. After two minutes of observance and looking across the opening, we noticed a small blip in the distance to the airfield direction of the field, at a left bearing. By pure good fortune, it happened to be just when my mother was taking some pictures with camera already poised across the wide rural field panorama. I recommended her to focus on this area and she took one photograph.

We had to wait until the following day to get a closer look at the object captured on this afternoon's encounter, as my mother's camera did not have a substantial LED review window pane on this particular camera design she owned.

On attendance and speaking at the conference at Woodbridge, I decided to refrain from mentioning this at the time, as I was certain we had both seen something which would later be explained as a typical object. The following day, the camera card was downloaded and we were both surprised to see that the object retained a high degree of strangeness. The object can be seen to be of a rounded disc shape, with some light distortions on the outer edges. This can be seen clearly before the pixels go to the extreme. There are hints of faint lines on the upper top centre of this daylight disc but they are so slight as to not give any further clues. With the scope for all sorts of new drone technology and perhaps even advanced light reactive fuselages, this could offer a possible explanation for the object."

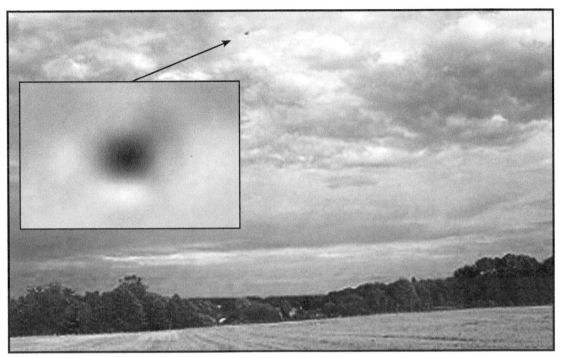

The picture that Matt Lyons' mother took in September, 2011 in the field nominated by Larry Warren as to where his encounter took place. Inset: Enlargement of 'small blip' seen by Matt and his mother.

Silvery 'balls' – June 5th, 2012

David Bryant:

> *"The 'balls' were on a photo I took on June 5th, 2012 to the south of RAF Woodbridge; we'd parked along Heath Road and walked north along a wide forestry track towards the perimeter fence. As I always do, I took lots of random photos, including an AWACS aircraft and escort, which flew over the base shortly afterwards! The balls were on a panorama of the track."*

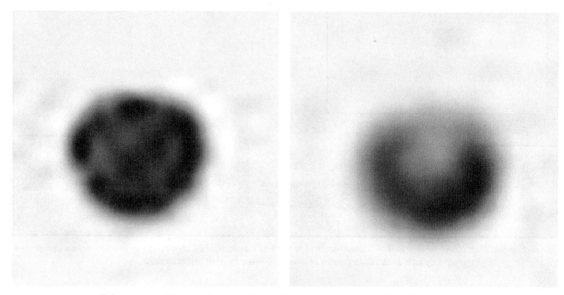

Enlargements of the two silvery 'balls' that where photographed by David Bryant in 2012

UFO Display over Suffolk 2004

We learnt of a UFO, captured on film at 2.00am on 26th October 2004, by Mr Peter Saxon – the Licensee of The Swan Inn, at Alderton, near Woodbridge – and decided to visit him in 2006, when he told us what happened.

Peter:

> *"I was awoken by shouting, coming from outside, and after getting dressed, went into the back car park, where I saw what I initially thought was a helicopter, hovering in the sky over the houses opposite to* The Swan. *I soon realised that this could not be the case, as the 'light' began to move erratically in the sky, at which point I could see it had a jet black dome, with a long rectangular bar underneath,*

and a group of lights at each end. I could see it 'shaking', from side to side, and moving up and down.

I rushed into the pub and picked up my Sony camcorder hi 8 video camera and rushed out, expecting to see it; there was nothing there, but looking upwards into the sky, I spotted it once again – now much higher, surrounded by a luminous blue field. I then took a short clip of film, lasting a few minutes, before loosing sight of it."

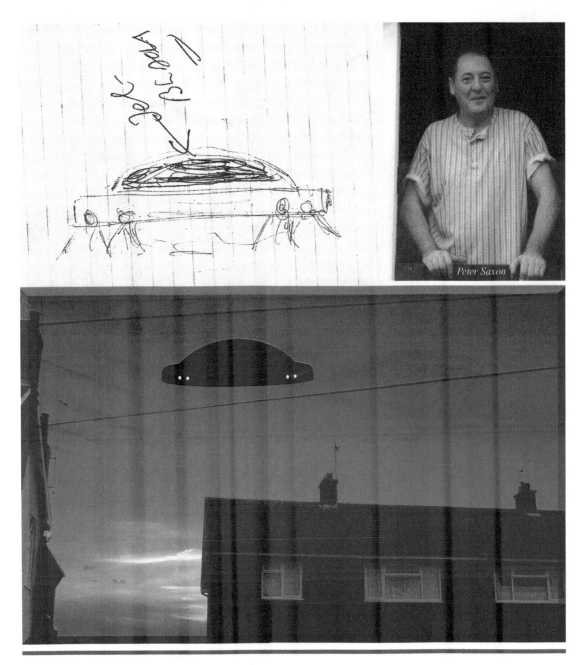

Peter Saxon

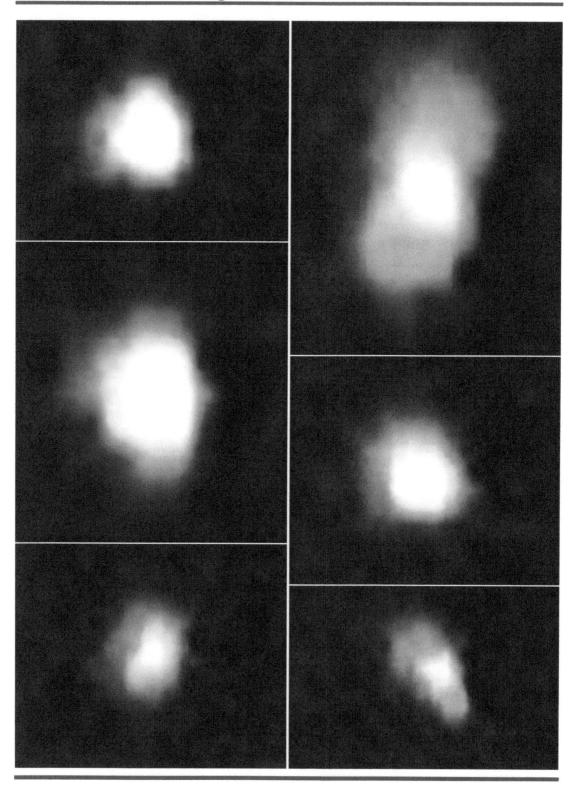

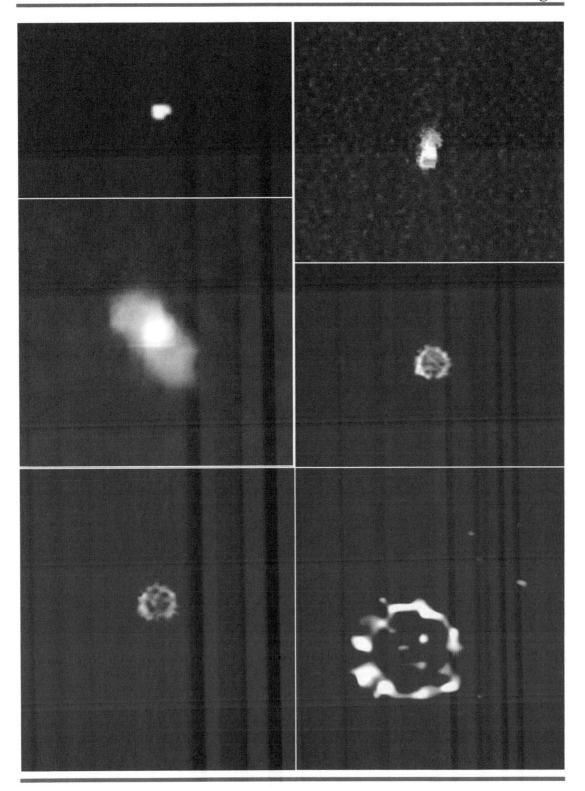

Peter contacted the *Evening Star*, who published an article on 26th November 2004 – *'Were Bright Lights Over Village A UFO? X File Is Opened By Residents'*. We spoke to another witness – Rick Thompson. This is what he had to say:

> *"I was awoken by my six month old baby; I looked out of the window and saw a bright light, stationary in the sky. It was too bright to be a helicopter, and too big, and was completely silent – then it began to move erratically in the sky, making these peculiar up and down, backwards and forwards, motions. I found it quite frightening."*

By the time we were in a position to examine the film taken by Peter, two years later, time had taken its toll. A good portion of the film (some 9 minutes, towards the end of the clip) had been inadvertently erased, leaving us with a total footage of approximately 65 seconds. Prior to us obtaining a copy of this now degraded piece of film, Peter told us that he had allowed a UFO researcher to take away the film and conduct an initial examination as to whether there was anything of value on the footage. He was disappointed to receive the item back through the post with a brief note advising him to the contrary, which was rather unprofessional in our opinion.

Of that 65 seconds, the first five seconds showed a brightly-lit object darting about in the sky. This was large enough, without the application of a zoom lens, to show something fairly substantial, viewed at an angle of approximately 90° off the horizon – possibly 5-10 miles away, and likely to have been over the sea – conceding the difficulties faced with trying to establish distances and sizes without any other frames of references, bearing in mind that this clip of film was taken after the object rose upwards in the sky.

Our examination of the film showed us an object that had the propensity to extinguish its outer illumination but was still visible (under extreme scrutiny) in the sky. One again, we are left with the feeling that while we may not be dealing with any alien spaceships, we are dealing with an unidentified phenomenon. What it is and where 'it' or 'they' come from, we just don't know. However, what we do know is that they continue to behave in the same manner, irrespective of how much time passes us. Generations may flourish and die, but UFOs appear timeless.

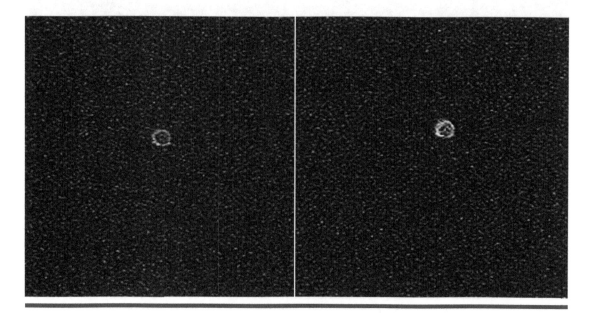

Falls of stones and even an elephant!

Incidents relating to complaints of spontaneous materialisation of objects, however bizarre and unlikely they first appear, are impossible to believe unless you, yourself, have experienced the disquieting thud, as a warm stone falls inexplicably onto the ground in front of you, wielded by an invisible person, or agency.

In Sir Arthur Clarke's book, entitled: *World of Strange Powers*, by John Fairley & Simon Welfare (published in 1984, by Book Club Associates) they outlined an investigation into incidents involving falls of stones, reported to the West Midlands Police, during early 1981, and included interviews with some of the officers, including Detective Sergeant Brian Laurie (known to the author) and Chief Inspector Leonard Turley, who are shown holding some of the stones.

Chief Inspector Turley:

> *"My team had spent more than 3,500 hours in a fruitless investigation. In that time the police have solved five murders, but the file on Thornton Road was still frustratingly open."*

This matter will be covered extensively in the next Volume of *Haunted Skies* (Volume 9). Whether those falls of stones, that caused extensive damage to the houses concerned, are anything to do with what we experienced in Rendlesham Forest is anybody's guess, but unlikely in our view.

During our visits to Rendlesham Forest, Suffolk, where all manner of strange anomalies have been captured on film, we saw for ourselves, on at least two occasions, milky-white 'orbs' floating above the forest tracks, close to the East Gate entrance, which we captured on photograph. This confirmed to us that our eyes were not playing tricks. On another occasion we photographed the reflection of one of the 'orbs' in a puddle, close to the same location.

Space prevents us from writing about the many occasions when people, who treated such claims with scepticism, were staggered to see, and photograph, such anomalies during their own visits to the forest. Even stranger was what befell professional photographer/golfer Paul France, and his wife Denette Valerie France (sadly no longer with us) from the Redditch area.

Paul France, and wife Denette

After photographing objects which were not dust, lens faults, or the other myriad of scientific explanations put forward to rationalise the capture of these strange 'lights', some of which were seen with the naked eye, Paul's attitude towards his previous scepticism was changed forever. On their return to Redditch, the following evening, they discovered the house was covered in 'orbs'. Within a few days, the 'orbs' had gone. Had they brought 'them' back from the forest to the house, or was there another explanation?

From our own visits to the area, we always found it to be a pleasant, warm, place by day but very eerie at night, when thick mists swirl around the forest tracks, blotting out sound and vision.

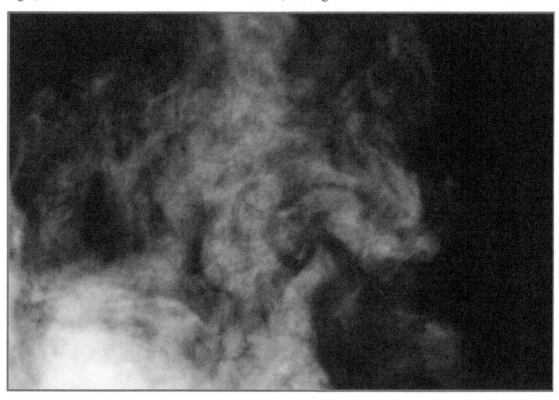

John Hanson and Dawn Holloway

Even stranger were the falls of stones, which we witnessed personally, on a number of occasions. To those who have not experienced these phenomena, they invariably always suggest that there must be a natural explanation, such as a meteorite or the work of hooligans, which we reject out of hand.

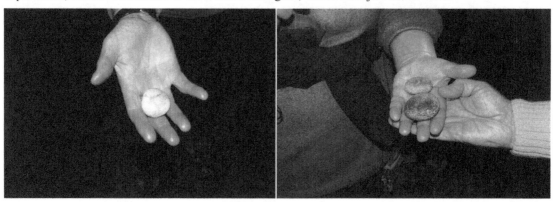

Apports is the name given to various objects, such as flowers, jewellery, and even live animals, which have allegedly materialised in the presence of a medium. During the first hundred years of Spiritualism, the appearance of foreign objects literally from nowhere, referred to as apports, was one of the most prominent and effective features of Spiritualistic séances. Sometimes these apports flew through the air and struck the faces of sitters; other times they appeared on the table or in the laps of those present. Occasionally, their arrival was endorsed by heady perfume, branches of trees, armfuls of fruit and flowers, money, jewels, and live lobsters are among the more extraordinary apports.

There appears to be two theories which attempt to explain the phenomena of apports. One is the fourth dimension; the other, favored by Spiritualists, is the disintegration and reintegration of the apported objects. The former was first advocated by German psychical researcher Johann Zöllner to explain the phenomenon of interpenetration of matter, which he claimed to observe with Henry Slade. It was accepted by Cesare Lombroso and Camille Flammarion and later endorsed by W. Whately Carington, in Britain, and Malcolm Bird, in the United States.

Johann Zöllner

Zöllner's theory implies that there is a higher form of space, of which we are totally unaware. Apported objects are lifted into this dimension, before being launched into our three-dimensional space.

Martin Beech in *The Physics of Invisibility: A Story of Light and Deception* wrote: 'Zöllner presented his book as a physical investigation into the paranormal, including clairvoyance, matter transfer, ghosts and natural spirits. The main thrust of Zöllner's argument was that all these kinds of mystic phenomena could be explained if ghosts (spirits of the dead) inhabited a "real external world" composed of four spatial dimensions. On this basis, he argued that what we see as ghosts are really just shadows projected into our three dimensional spatial realm'.

John:

"Each and every time we have experienced this phenomena the stone was found to be very warm, in complete contrast to 'control stones' lying on the ground in the surrounding locality, which were cold. We believe the energy required in moving the stone through the air creates heat to the object itself. On another occasion during April 2004 while in the forest close to the location of the 1980 UFO landings, we were sat in a densely packed part of the forest. As I stood

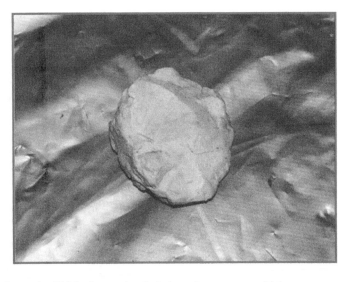

up I felt something strike my back gently. If I had remained sitting, the stone would have dropped behind me onto the ground. This stone was not a round polished pebble like the others but a piece resembling the chalky flint found in Wiltshire."

Gordon Goodger

"Brenda, myself, Ronnie Dugdale and Beverley Plumridge, were returning from a walk in the forest, during late September 2012. We reached the road from track 12. Ronnie and Beverley were approximately 8ft away from us. At about 12.20am, we heard a noise; it sounded like a stone, hitting the tarmac, about 6-8ft behind where Brenda and I were standing. I turned around and went looking for whatever had landed. I found a large stone and picked it up. It was the only stone of its size in the immediate vicinity. It was warm to the touch, slightly warmer than body temperature.

A short time later, we saw a white light on the track that leads down to East Gate; one moment dim, the next bright. This moved towards us, then away. We stood watching it for several minutes, when it suddenly divided into two intensely bright lights – one red, the other green/blue – before shooting up into the sky."

Don Ramkin

One late Saturday evening, in 2008, Don Ramkin from Bexley Heath, Kent – a UFO/paranormal investigator – and his companion, Terry, made their way to Suffolk to meet up with Brenda Butler and walk around Rendlesham Forest hoping to obtain further examples of photographic anomalies.

"The sky was a combination of clear patches with cloud, which was slowly moving away. Earlier that evening rain had fallen, so the forest was damp. After walking along some of the tracks, we ended up at the spot named locally as the 'alien tree' (on which an ET looking face naturally formed on the bark).

We stood next to the base of the 'alien tree' and carried out some meditation (quiet contemplation) listening for sounds, waiting to see if anything was heard out of the ordinary. As a paranormal investigator, I have no qualms in saying that often it would be one of the strange shadows, which resemble figures – a phenomenon that has been witnessed by us, many times previously, around the forest on our weekend visits. It may sound incredible, but we weren't the only ones to have sighted what became known locally as the 'shadow people'. What they are and where they come from I can't say, but they have been seen many times, over the years.

We started to take a few random photographs, hoping to capture some anomalies, but only picked up moisture droplets in the air. We then heard a crackle through the branches of the surrounding trees, followed by a thud on the ground – quite close to where we were stood. We knew from our past visits to the forest, over many years, that this probably meant that an apport had just occurred. We searched the surrounding area with torchlight and discovered, lying on top of the wet leaves, a fairly large white 'cheese cutter type stone', very warm to the touch – as if it had been near heat.

Over the space of maybe 20 minutes, a further two stones come down in our vicinity. I can clearly recall saying out loud, perhaps a bit sarcastically, 'Ok, we know you can throw stones but is that all you can do?' Within the space of maybe three minutes of my asking, behind us but to the right of the tree, we heard something that sounded like an object had dropped onto the forest floor, although not as loud or pronounced as a stone would have made.

We began scouring the ground with our torches in the area we thought it came from. Just in front of me, I saw a small grey object. I walked forward. Bending down, I picked it up and was amazed to see a plastic toy elephant – not only that, but it was very warm to touch. You can imagine my excitement when I showed it to Brenda and Terry. I guess the spirits (if, indeed, it was a spirit) had answered my question."

Authors:

We asked a friend of ours – a scientist – to examine the apport and a control stone (found in the same location) under the electron microscope. We were surprised to see that the 'control stone' showed a rough surface with cracks and fissures commensurate with its age while the 'apport stone' was clean and smooth. But to the eye they looked more or less the same in composition. We shouldn't draw any conclusions from this but felt it was important to introduce this as a point of some discussion. Is this phenomenon indigenous to Rendlesham Forest? Or would one find similar 'manifestations' at other wooded locations. Do the stones fall when nobody is in the forest? Are human beings in some way orchestrating their levitation off the ground? Whatever the answer – one thing is assured – the stones will continue to fall!

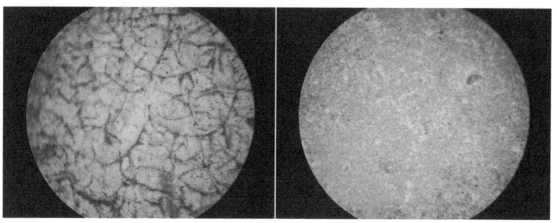

Control stone   Apported stone

Orbs, Mists and Lights Phenomena

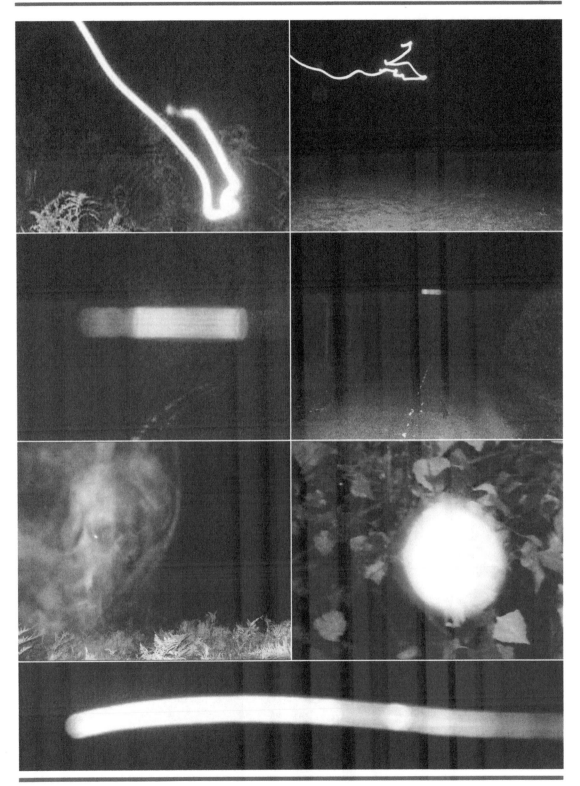

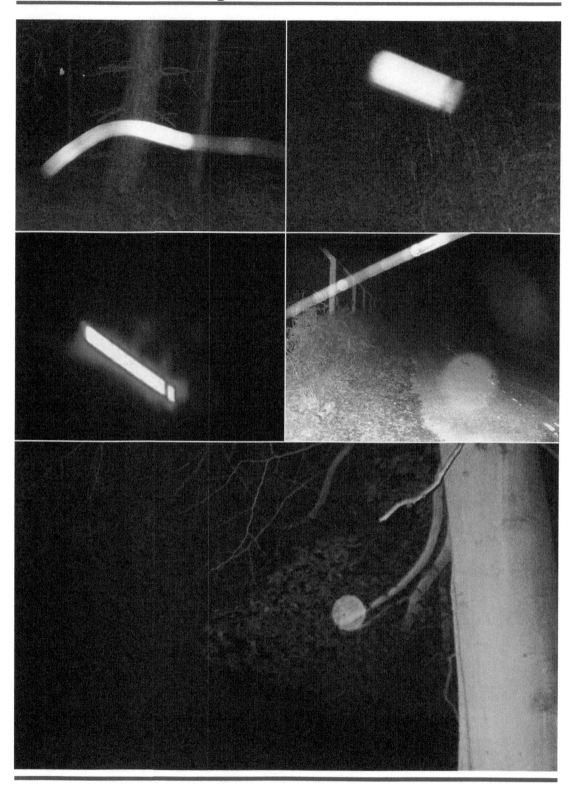

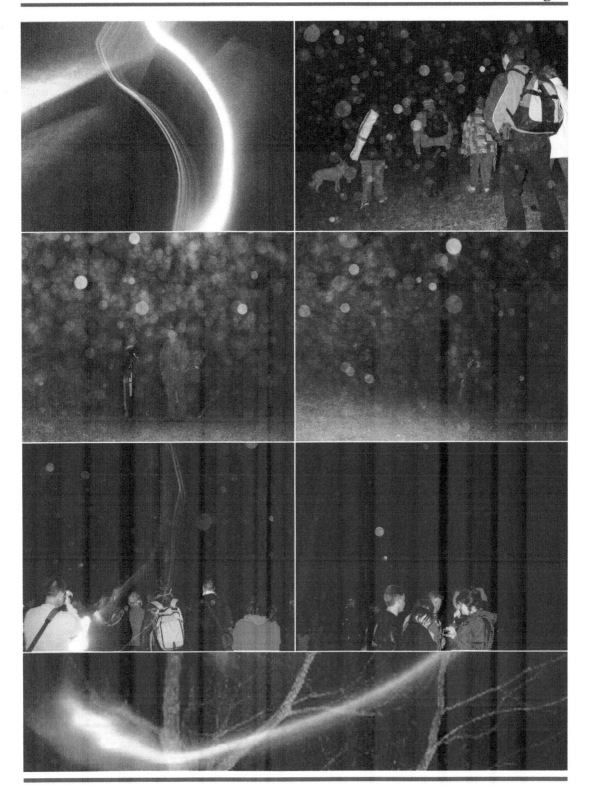

Glowing object over Bentwaters – 1995

Paul Pittock was driving from Woodbridge to Melton, Suffolk, one evening in January 1995, when he saw a bright 'light' hovering in the sky above the now closed RAF Woodbridge/Bentwaters Airbase. Curious, he stopped the car and was surprised to see that the 'light' had now began to move from side to side in the sky. Rushing home he picked up his telescopic sight and, accompanied by neighbour Richard Warnock, drove back to the airbase just in time to see whatever it was drop down towards the flight line and disappear.

> *"As we stood by the entrance gate to the base, wondering what was going on, over thirty military vehicles drove up; they included a military ambulance and a larger white vehicle, covered in aerials. After unlocking the gate, the convoy drove onto the Bentwaters Airbase (closed some 16 months ago). With tyres screaming and lights flashing, the vehicles drove around the airbase pointing searchlights into the sky, as if looking for something; there were even helicopters hovering overhead.*
>
> *We saw an orange-red glow emanating from the flight line – then a glowing triangular shape appeared. It had a distinct outline and could be seen clearing the slope. It stayed for a while and then left."*

(Source: Personal interview)

Reports of UFO activity continue to be brought to our notice. At 7am in February 2013, a bright light was seen in the sky over Hintlesham near the fish market by Vicky, partner of Peter Parish, while on her way to work. She tells of seeing two smaller 'globes' next to the larger object – one of which was then seen to separate and roll downwards.

Even at this late stage we were still obtaining additional evidence, for inclusion in the book. Here is another UFO newspaper cutting of interest with regard to what Mr Peter Saxon from *The Swan* Inn saw in 2004.

Were bright lights over village a UFO?

X-file is opened by residents

By GRANT SHERLOCK
grant.sherlock@eveningstar.co.uk

SIGHTINGS of unexplained lights in the night sky above Alderton have got the village buzzing with talk of strange crafts and UFOs.

Residents have been left puzzled by stories of brightly lit flying objects illuminating the sky.

At least two residents say they spotted what they have described as an object capable of travelling at speeds faster than any craft they have ever seen.

Landlord Pete Saxon was so amazed at what he saw after being woken by shouting outside his pub, the Swan Inn in The Street, at 2am, that he ran to get his video camera and caught the object on tape.

"I walked out the back and came up at the back end of the car park. There was what I

WONDERING: Landlord Pete Saxon outside the Swan Inn in Alderton.

out as it was quite bright. What happened next is unbelievable. It shot to the left at an alarming rate.

"It was really erratic movement. I couldn't understand anybody actually being inside it. It was some sort of structure but the movement wasn't what a helicopter would do."

The incident will evoke memories of an alleged sighting of a UFO in nearby Rendlesham forest in 1980.

On that occasion, an American airman spotted bright lights at 4am on December 26, sparking a heated debate which still carries on today between the cynics and those who believe alien spacecraft could exist.

In the latest incident at Alderton, Rick Thompson, 27, had been woken by his six-month-old baby when he looked out of a window in his Mill Hoo

thought was a helicopter," Mr Saxon said.

"I watched it because it stood

home and saw a bright light. Mr Thompson said: "It was too bright to be a helicopter and too big a light and it was quiet.

"I didn't hear any noise. I suppose it was stationary for a couple of minutes, then it started doing things it shouldn't do.

"It was up then down, forward then back, left then right. It was frightening really."

Mr Saxon, 52, said the video images he captured have become the most talked-about subject in his pub.

"It was really, really unusual," he said.

"Along the bottom of it was a long strip with a bright light on the end.

"It was as big as a low jumbo. What made it a bit weird was that there was no noise. You could see the dome top and you could see the bottom was flat. It was luminous blue around the outside."

Swan Inn regular Brian Foster, a former coastguard from Bawdsey with experience of spotting lights at night, has seen the video and said: "The speed is so extraordinary that it's got to be something. We haven't got the technology to move at that pace.

"The movement was totally erratic, so it couldn't be one of the sea marks."

THE INVESTIGATION CONTINUES

WE know that two Suffolk Constabulary Police Officers – PC David King and PC Martyn Brophy – attended the forest, during the early morning of 26th December 1980, and that a follow-up visit was made to the forest at 10.30am, by PC Creswell.

In the first paragraph of his memorandum (see page 222) Colonel Charles Halt refers to the incident which took place during the early morning of 27th December 1980 (involving Jim, John, and others, who were not named at the time) when this should have been during the early morning of 26th December 1980.

The incident, involving Charles Halt and other servicemen, took place on the late night of the 27th, going into the early morning of 28th December 1980. This was down to a simple error and should not be construed as anything else.

This means that the second paragraph of the memo, which relates to a depression being found, the next day (inferring the 28th, following on from the alleged 27th) actually refers to 29th December 1980.

In 2009, Charles Halt was asked about the date of the first UFO incident (involving Penniston and Burroughs) by Robert Hastings, and confirmed the 26th as now being correct. He also amended the date of the second incident (involving him) as being the night of the 27th into the early morning of the 28th December. On page 413, Colonel Halt now considers that Larry Warren and Bustinza were out in the forest before he arrived. The problem is that Larry refers to 11.45pm on 28th December 1980.

Additional information

In March 2013, Matt Lyons – Head of BUFORA – contacted us about some additional information received from East Anglia resident David Morgan, following conversations held with David's father, who served in the USAF armed forces in the area of Shingle Street, during the Second World War.

The information (which was obtained by the son, during a recent visit to California, in the United States, after having tracked down his father) is split into two separate parts; the first relates to an abandoned village, situated close to Orford Ness:

> *"If the public knew what lay beneath Shingle Street to this day, all hell would break loose because it's nothing like that's been said and unlike anything anyone could imagine."*

The second then alleges a connection between this and the event that took place on Woodbridge runway, on the 28th December 1980.

This was obtained from a conversation with a friend – a retired USAF Sergeant – during a social drink, who was employed on the A10 aircraft at RAF Bentwaters. Following transfer to RAF Mildenhall, this man disclosed that he was a member of a team, stationed at RAF Mildenhall, whose job was to retrieve aircraft from crash sites.

In response to questions put to him by Matt Lyons, David Morgan outlined that on the night of the 28th December 1980, he and a team of men (seven) which included three low ranking officers, flew from RAF Midlenhall to RAF Woodbridge, in response to what they believed was a downed aircraft.

They were confined to the aircraft and not allowed off. A friend (unidentified) who was a member of the recovery crew, states that it was 10.00pm when they landed at RAF Woodbridge, and that upon their arrival, two jeeps and four to five personnel approached them. Three or four hours later the men flew back to RAF Mildenhall. During a debriefing, they were informed that the base was on 'red alert' and that standard rules of no discussions applied. It appears they were also warned not to say anything about what had happened that night. It was then alleged the airbases of Mildenhall, Bentwaters and Woodbridge were placed on 'high alert'.

Authors: We contacted Colonel Halt and asked him if he could remember any specific occasions of unscheduled aircraft having landed on the base, which took place while he was in command.

He told us that he had no knowledge of any special aircraft movements, but that . . .

> *"I do know I was told by one of the security officers (I believe it was Burroughs or Penniston) years later, that they were aware of a 'special' mission. Highly classified missions were fairly common due to weapons movements, the 67ARRS activities and Aerial Recon activity. The only time in the entire time I was at the base that I was in a jeep was the night I went out into the forest. I stand by my statement that I had no personal knowledge of any special aircraft movement related to the incident. It might have happened but I have no first-hand knowledge of such. The use of 'red alert' was not a used in the Air Force"*

The version of events given by Matt Lyons is an interesting one but what exactly is the nature of the speculative claims made? Are we expected to really believe that a clandestine operation was mounted by another USAF air base to recover – what?

At the end of the day we should rely on the evidence given by Charles Halt and his colleagues – theirs is the real evidence which won't go away.

UFOs sighted over Rendlesham Forest 2013

David Bryant sent us these photographs (presented on the page opposite) of an object he saw during a night spent with friends in Rendlesham Forest. He reported the area

> *'. . . exhibiting lots of amazing orbs and mists'.*

The photos were captured at 10pm on Sunday, March 31st 2013 and reveal what David describes as

> *". . . an authentic UFO: A bright, circular object that moved from the North to the zenith, where it paused – dancing about and pulsing, before disappearing to the East".*

The light display was also seen by Jason & Jane Hughes, and David's wife Linda.

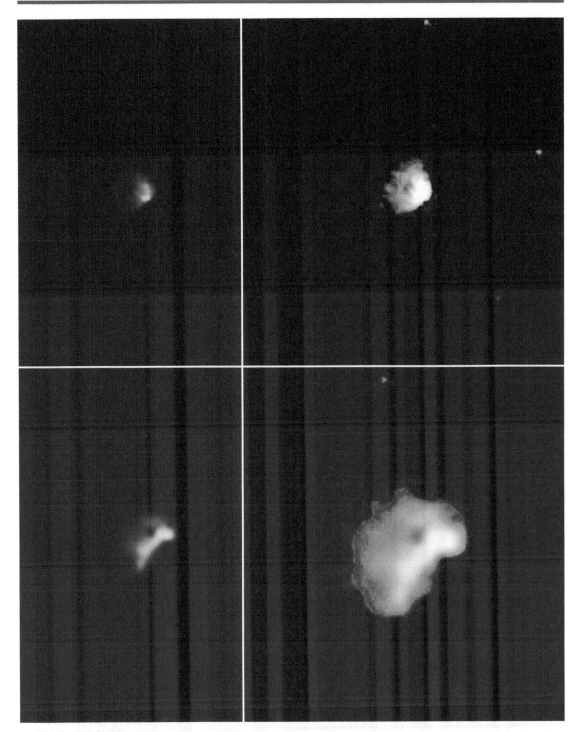

The object sighted by David Bryant on 31-03-2013 over Rendlesham Forest. Images on the right are adjusted for levels and brightness with a view to reveal further detail.

Squadron Leader Donald Moreland

Even at this late period of the book we are pleased to present a unique photograph, showing Squadron Leader Donald Moreland and Lt. Colonel Halt, at RAF Woodbridge, during a ceremony marking the retirement of the Squadron Leader.

Thanks to the assistance of Colonel Charles Halt, we had the opportunity of speaking personally to Donald Moreland, in June 2013.

When we told Donald about the subject matter of the book we were writing he became sceptical, which wasn't surprising given the way in which the media sensationalise such accounts.

We sent him Volume 1 of *Haunted Skies*, and hope that he enjoys it.

Brenda Butler, 2013

Brenda continues to keep the focus of public attention on the UFO subject through countless television interviews and documentaries. She has now written an E Book, *Out of this World* – published by Monique Elton – and also, co-written with Philip Kinsella, *Sky Crash Throughout Time* – which has now been published by Capall Bann Publishers, Somerset, UK.

During a period of now over 30 years, Brenda (and Dot) has accumulated a massive amount of personal correspondence, tape-recorded interviews, letters, photographs and documents, from members of the public and servicemen. For someone who believed initially that this was a UFO incident, she now wonders, after many years of research, why it is that so many did not hear or see anything of significance during that Christmas weekend.

"In 1987, during ongoing investigations into the matter, following visits to the breakfast bar, supermarket, and the 'Stars and Stripes' on base, with Dot, many of the men said they had no knowledge of anything untoward having happened and pointed out if that was the case, then why wasn't the base closed down or put on alert? We talked to people who walked around the forest with their dogs; none of them had heard or seen anything strange in the woods, or been denied access. I heard from one source of a 'drugs' party in the woods and that it was all hushed up. We spoke to local farmers, and learned about a crash with trees being brought down, and men seen wearing special suits to take the trees away, but I thought this happened in New Year 1981.

In June 1987, I met a man in his early 60s, from Bawdsey, who was exercising his dog in the forest. Following discussion of my interest in the matters that had taken place in 1980, I learned that he had previously been employed on the MoD Secretarial Staff in London. This man confirmed his knowledge about a lot of activity which had occurred out at sea, involving a helicopter seen searching the sea, close to a ship moored off Orford Island. We spoke about a Russian Sub and a Tupolov (Russian aircraft) being seen on the same weekend."

Taken 1st May 2004 by Brenda Butler looking over Folly House towards runway at RAF Woodbridge.

Brenda Butler 1 Mafking Place
Leiston, Suffolk IP164EN
England

Dear Brenda:

Thank you for updating me on happenings in Rendlesham Forest. I was sorry to hear you received what sounds like radiation burns. I hope you are ok. In several similar cases in the States the victims suffered badly. I suspect you now believe me and the fact that I was not trying to hide anything or part of a cover up. I'm convinced now that certain agencies left me out there to take the heat and look foolish.

I am also convinced that whatever is going on is much more than mind control although that appears to factor for some of the participants. Be careful, as there could be some real danger in what you are doing.

Keep me posted, as your experience sounds so familiar.

Chuck

Previously unpublished information now shown

Brenda has now decided to include a previously unpublished document, and two photographs in *Haunted Skies*, from a person who, in 1987, claimed the UFO story was engineered to cover up something else which had happened in December 1980 – and that the photographs offered proof of something recovered off the coast and winched into a helicopter.

[THIS FORM IS SUBJECT TO THE PRIVACY ACT OF 1974 — SEE REVERSE]

TRAVEL VOUCHER OR SUBVOUCHER
[Complete by typewriter, ink, or ball point pen (PRESS HARD) do not use pencil]
READ PRIVACY ACT STATEMENT ON REVERSE PRIOR TO COMPLETING THIS FORM
LAST NAME, FIRST NAME, MIDDLE INITIAL — GRADE/RANK — SSN

10. FOR DO USE ONLY
DO VOUCHER NO.
SUBVOUCHER NO.

CHECK MAILING ADDRESS (Include ZIP Code) — DUTY PHONE NO.

PAID BY

ORGANIZATION AND STATION
Classified

TRAVEL ORDERS (Paragraph, S.O. No., Issuing Hq., Date) (Include amending orders)
Top Secret

PRIOR TRAVEL PAYMENTS OR ADVANCES UNDER THESE ORDERS (Amount, DO Voucher No., Date received, Place paid, or DO Station No. If none, so state)

1. ITINERARY (See Item 25 for Symbols)			2. MODE OF TRAVEL	3. REASON FOR STOP	NUMBER OF MEALS		4.
DATE	LOCAL TIME (24 Hour Clock)	PLACE		COST OF LODGING	GOVT	OPEN MESS	POC MILES
22	DEP 0200	Sembach AB GE					
	ARR 0600	RAF Woodbridge UK					
28	DEP 0500	RAF Woodbridge UK					
29	ARR 1200	Sembach AB GE					
03-28	DEP 200	Sembach AB GE					
	ARR	Kirtland AFB USA					
03-29	DEP						
03-29	ARR 1200	Sembach AB GE					
	DEP						
	ARR						

COMPUTATIONS

5. REIMBURSABLE EXPENSES/CHARGE FOR DEDUCTIBLE MEALS* (See Item 24)

DATE	NATURE AND EXPLANATION	AMT CLAIMED	ALLOWED

6. Long distance telephone calls are certified as necessary in the interest of the Government.

APPROVING OFFICER (31 USC 680a)

7. TR'S/MTA'S/MT'S (If none, so state)

NUMBER	FROM	TO
24H-0011	Sembach AB GE	Kirtland
496-1110	Woodbridge	Sembach

8. LEAVE STATEMENT: _____ days _____ hours taken between _____ and _____
9. POC TRAVEL ☐ OWNER/OPERATOR (See Item 22a) ☐ PASSENGER

SUMMARY OF PAYMENT

Per Diem
Actual Expense
Mileage or Transp Allowances
Reimbursable Expenses
Total Entitlement
Less Previous Payments
Less Voucher Deductions
Amt Charged to Acctg Class

11. PAYMENT DESIRED ☐ CHECK ☐ CASH
12. ☐ PER DIEM REQUESTED
13. BAS RATE

PENALTY: The penalty for willfully making a false claim is: A MAXIMUM FINE OF $10,000 OR MAXIMUM IMPRISONMENT OF 5 YEARS, OR BOTH (U.S. Code, Title 18, Section 287.)

I hereby claim any amount due me. The statements on face, reverse, and attached are true and complete. Payment or credit has not been received.

14. CLAIMANT — DATE 03-29

15. ACCOUNTING CLASSIFICATION
67 ARRS   TOP SECRET $1335

16. COLLECTION DATA

17. COMPUTED BY — 18. AUDITED BY — 19. TVL RCRD POSTED BY — 20. RECEIVED — 21. AMOUNT PAID $335

DD FORM 1351-2 (1 JUN 78)   PREVIOUS EDITION IS OBSOLETE.
Exception to SF 1012 and 1012a approved by NARS, GSA April 1978.

Even if we could prove the document (dated 27th December, 19??) is an authentic record of flight movement between airbases, it only confirms that flights took place; it does not identify if any cargo was carried, and it certainly does not prove the USAF carried out a recovery of a terrestrial object offshore or on land.

Curiously, the year and the name of the claimant on this travel document have been blotted out, which seems unusual rather than suspicious. One can imagine that the absence of this information would have caused problems with their finance department in approving the necessary payment of expenses, to the officer named, unless this was either a simple mistake or deliberately inked over to hide something.

This document is endorsed 3677.SN. *67th ARRS Top Secret – summary of payment, see file. Was this the serial number of the officer, or social security number? Who was the officer? Was this 1980 or not?

We speculated whether it was possible if it was December 1980 that it could have related to the visit made by General Gabriel CINCUSAFE to RAF Woodbridge from Sembach Airbase, Germany, arriving there at 0210hrs, 27th December, following the report of the UFO landing. On the 28th, a return flight was then made from RAF Woodbridge to Sembach. This was followed by a flight from Sembach to Kirtland Air Force Base, or was this just supposition or conjecture?

General Charles A. Gabriel

According to Wikipedia 2013, Charles Gabriel travelled to RAF Bentwaters, after having been told about the UFO sighting. Gabriel was promoted to full General on August 1, 1980, and retired on July 1, 1986.

We sent a copy of the document to Charles Halt, who had this to say on the 10th June 2013:

> *"John: I am suspect of the travel voucher. Gabriel didn't come to B/W on Dec 27th – It was much later. Besides, he would have come from, and gone to, Ramstein AB. I don't have issue with your using my correspondence with Brenda. Chuck."*

We sent a copy of the document to the Director of MUFON, in order that it could be examined by one of their specialists, in early June 2013. Once again, we reiterate that even if this was December 1980, it only confirms that flights took place.

As for the photos, these could be from any date and, once again, offer no new evidence, unless one believes that the drum-shaped object aboard the helicopter (which Jim Penniston thought might have been an aero engine) was either a satellite or some alien craft – it is highly probable they are neither.

---

*On 15 January 1970, the 67th ARRS transferred to RAF Woodbridge, UK. The unit operated the Lockheed HC-130 fixed wing (also used as rotational support for their Detachment of H-3 helicopters stationed at Keflavik, Iceland) and Sikorsky MH-53 rotary wing aircraft. On 1 June 1988 the unit was split into two units re-designated the 67th Special Operations Squadron for the HC-130 aircraft and the 21st Special Operations Squadron for the HH-53 rotary wing. **(Source: Wikipedia)**

Above and opposite page: The two photographs provided to Brenda Butler in 1987.

Colonel Halt addresses audience in 2012

In September 2012, at the Smithsonian-affiliated National Atomic Testing Museum, Las Vegas, Charles Halt accused the government of a UFO cover-up that involves a secret agency to deal with what might be extraterrestrial visitations.

"Folks, there is an agency, a very close-held, compartmentalized agency that's been investigating this for years, and there's a very active role played by many of our intelligence agencies that probably don't even know the details of what happens once they collect the data and forward it. It's kind of scary, isn't it? In the last couple of years, the British have released a ton of information, but has anybody ever seen what their conclusions were, or heard anything about Bentwaters officially?

When the documents were released, the time frame when I was involved in the incident is missing – it's gone missing. Nothing else is missing, I have never been harassed over the reports I made about the Bentwaters UFO incidents, probably for a couple of good reasons – number one, my rank and some of the jobs I've held, but also very early on, I sat down and made a very detailed tape and made several copies of everything I know about it and they're secluded away. Maybe I'm paranoid. I don't know, but I think it was time well spent when I made the tapes."

Project Blue Book

Another speaker making a rare public appearance was retired Air Force Colonel Bill Coleman – the former chief spokesman for *Project Blue Book*, between 1961 and 1963. (The controversial study ended in 1969, concluding that there was nothing about UFOs which represented technological developments or principles beyond the range of present-day scientific knowledge.)

Colonel Bill Coleman

Bill described his encounter with a UFO, while the pilot of a B-25 bomber, in 1955, when he saw an unknown circular object, descending from an estimated height of 20,000ft, and attempted to pursue it.

> "We were moving at maximum continuous power for the B-25, about 300 miles an hour; we got right down to the treetops and I closed in on it very rapidly. I said I was going to overtake it – 'hang on and put your seat belts on'. I made a hard 90° bank to try and pull up alongside of the UF0 and it wasn't there. I zoomed up to about 1,500ft, and could see the object right on the deck, over a freshly plowed field, moving at a pretty good speed, and trailing two vortexes."

When Coleman dropped down and flew behind the trees to try and head the object off, it was gone *"It was"*, he said, *"a typical 'flying saucer'."*

Colonel Bob Friend

During the time that Coleman was the *Project Blue Book* spokesman, the director of the Air Force study was Col. Bob Friend. He disagreed with the Air Force's negative conclusions about UFOs, in 1969.

> "My primary explanation for these things is that, yes, they're real, and I think it would be much better if the government, or some other agency, was to take on these things and to pursue the scientific aspects of it. UFO sightings are real and you will not be ridiculed by any honest organization that investigates it. Just come forward, quote your case, and allow people to investigate what they can to make some determination about what it is that you've seen. In the future, just remember that we're on your side."

Another UFO speaker was retired Army Col. John Alexander – a former military insider – who convened a special group in the 1980s, called the *Advanced Theoretical Physics Group*, whose members were recruited from the military services and the aerospace and intelligence communities. They concluded that while there had been numerous cases of credible UFO encounters, the group could not find any evidence of any actual government cover-up.

Alexander cited a variety of intriguing UFO cases, involving pilots, and told the audience that UFOs are:

> "real and is a global phenomenon -- not something that just happens in the U.S. We need to make it permissible for scientists to discuss and research these topics. ... There are no simple answers, and not only do we not have the answers, we're not at the point of asking the right questions yet, and that's what we need to do."

Colonel John Alexander

DEPARTMENT OF THE AIR FORCE
WASHINGTON D.C. 20330

OFFICE OF THE SECRETARY

1 SEP 1977

Lieutenant General Duward L. Crow, USAF (Ret)
National Aeronautics and Space Administration
400 Maryland Avenue
Washington, D. C. 20546

Dear General Crow:

    Inclosed are the UFO Fact Sheet and standard response
to UFO public inquiries you requested.

    I sincerely hope you are successful in preventing a
reopening of UFO investigations.

                      Sincerely,

                      CHARLES H. SENN, Colonel, USAF
                      Chief, Community Relations Division
                      Office of Information

Attachments

Action Copy to AOA
File Copy to

A35481 AB.AC.
S.FL, W.C
AE

Rec'd in NASA 9-2-77

Suspense Date NONE

MUFON Report on Travel Voucher –

Received from David MacDonald, Executive Director, following examination by Bob Wood (see page 388).

> *"Dear Dave, whereas having the original would give me a warmer feeling, my guess is that it will appear to be "old" paper, and that a comparison with watermarks of similar forms would show consistency. The thing about TOP SECRET missions is the money has to come from somewhere, so it is reasonable that such docs exist so the traveller can be compensated.*
>
> *In this case there is a TO (Travel Order, probably) number of 668412. Also, I suspect that there IS an accounting classification 67ARRS.*
>
> *There seem to be two different forms, the 1351-2 and the 1351-2C, probably used by different locations in the military establishment, probably Air Force, since Kirtland is an AF base. The dates of 1981 seem clear on the -2C order and I think I see a "03-24-81" on the -2 voucher as well as 03-29 meaning March 29. The -2C seems to date around September 21, 1981.*
>
> *There are inconsistent spellings of Kirtland and Sembach in different places. In this case, I would say they favor authenticity. Also, the fact that a Lt. Col was involved in the "computed by" calculation would lend a bit of authenticity, too. Interesting, the SSN is 36976xxxx, or 369-76-xxxx. This number was probably issued by Michigan. (See Social Security Numbers Issued by State on the Internet) I see no reason to assume that either of these documents is a forgery."*

Bob Wood, 12 June 2013

'Spinning top' UFO over the Forest, 27th December 1980

Brenda suggested we contact Neville Caley, who runs a farm in the Butley area of Suffolk with his father, about what he sighted while on the way back home, at 2am on 27th December 1980.

We spoke to Neville, who had this to say…

> *"I was on my way home in a local taxi, after a night out, when we saw this 'thing' coming in fast over the brow of a hill. It looked like a spinning top and was glowing red in colour. As it came over, a part of it fell off and landed in the nearby forest, close to Barrow Mound. Our curiosity aroused, we drove over to the location but were stopped by a Yankee copper, who was stood there. There were other guys about, some of them on the radios. I formed the impression they were waiting for something, but had to leave."*

Mystery men now identified – 30 years later!

Bristol-based veteran UFO investigator Terry Hooper of *The Anomalous Observational Phenomena Bureau* was able to finally supply the answers to another piece of the 'jigsaw' with regard to the mysterious visit made by two men, who called in at the Forestry Commission office and spoke to Mr. James enquiring about the whereabouts of a local farmer (Mr. Boast).

Over the years, rumours have abounded that these two men were representative of the infamous 'Men in Black' whose reputation for threatening and intimidating UFO witnesses is well documented. It appears Terry and his colleague, spoke to farmer David Boast, who later admitted to Brenda and Dot that he had received a visit by two men, although he then denied this visit had taken place.

Terry Hooper:

"I received a telephone call from two UFO International investigators – Dot Street and Brenda Butler (I think it was Brenda) about some USAF men, who reported seeing a UFO near Rendlesham Forest. I asked them to look into it further, which they did, but I remained puzzled why they involved Jenny Randles.

As I was going to RAF Honington, I asked my driver if he could divert and have a look at the locality around the Orford Lighthouse and the Forest, where it was alleged that some form of UFO activity had occurred. We checked out the lighthouse and ascertained that it did not cast light overland. (I had lived a while on the Kent coast and know the trouble caused by lighthouses casting beams of light into people's homes!) We checked the rough location of the 'landing' and the Geiger counter showed nothing above normal background radiation; a magnetometer did give a slightly high reading. No ground traces were found – or none were very obvious – although we discovered plenty of rabbit's traces and marks.

We then talked to various people and said we were looking into a possible 'low level flight' incident (if you started saying 'we're looking at a UFO report', people either walked away, or you got every loony who had seen a satellite inundating you) as this was all part of being 'discreet'. We said that people might have seen a red or a blue or white light in the area - nothing. There was a farm, with some cattle in a field, but no-one there reported seeing anything (though they would have been in direct sight of the forest).

We spoke to some USAF personnel who, on seeing our AOPB IDs (Anomalous Observational Phenomena Bureau) saluted us. We quickly pointed out that was not necessary! It seems that two black suited men with ID cards turning up and asking questions made it seem we were very official. I don't think any official report had been made at that time (even more 'suspicious'!). No mention of aliens, or even a constructed craft with lettering on, at that time. We were pretty much convinced a natural phenomenon had been seen – even if impressive. We wrote a report and a copy went to the MOD.

I am quite shocked at all the stuff added to the event since that time – including the fact that the two of us have now been called MIB and the things we were supposed to have done.

Unofficially, the MOD let it be known the conclusion we reached was 'accepted' – we heard via Sir Victor Goddard, who had talked to 'one of the chaps'. I think natural phenomena were involved – I've seen these things myself – and a heck of a lot got made up since that time. But, yes, I and the driver (I've heard that he passed away recently) were the first real investigators there and neither of us believed an alien craft was involved!"

Between 1974 to the present date, Terry has acted as a wildlife consultant to UK Police Forces on exotic animals living in the UK, and is a noted naturalist. In the same year (1974) Terry set up the Bristol UFO

Investigation Team (BUFOIT) and joined the British UFO Research Association (BUFORA), covering the West of England as an investigator and Regional Investigations Coordinator

In 1976, Terry joined the oldest UK UFO group, the British Flying Saucer Bureau (formed 1952) and later became Head of Research & Investigation and also editor of the *UFO News Bulletin*

In 1977, as an attempt to promote more scientific approach to UFO investigation, Terry set up *UFO International,* having established contact with Lord Clancarty and Air vice Marshal Sir Victor Goddard (a former head of RAF Intelligence and outspoken UFO believer).

In the same year Terry, along with late colleague Franklyn A. Davin-Wilson, visited London for a meeting with Lord Clancarty, Goddard and others, having submitted a document calling for a National Aerospace Commission [NaComm]. Hooper was asked to mount an unofficial investigation into all aspects of the UFO phenomenon – a limited fund for travelling and living expenses was agreed upon.

In January 1978, the Anomalous Observational Phenomena Bureau [AOPB] began its work building up a database on every aspect of UFOs – historical cases, trace, physiological and psychological, animal disturbance, EM cases and much more. Original members of the AOPB were Graham F.N. Knewstub [deceased], Dave Cowdy [deceased], Franklyn A. Davin-Wilson [deceased], and Terry Hooper.

Between 1978-1984 there was much unofficial assistance given to the Bureau by professional astronomers [some publicly sceptical] and former members of the Armed Forces, Air Ministry, Ministry of Defence, as well as serving members of the Armed Forces and Police Forces.

Franklyn A. Davin-Wilson

A network of UFO investigation and research groups was set-up, including GUFOI&RG [Gloucestershire], Wessex UFO I&R Group [Somerset], Wiltshire UFO I&R Team, and so on. Much of this cooperation continued well past the closing of the Bureau in 1995, though Governmental changes in policy since then have restricted any cooperation. In 1984 a 2,000 pages *British Report on Unidentified Flying Objects* [UFOs] was completed. This was later reduced to 1,500pp on editing.

Britain's Project Blue Book

Lord Clancarty, Sir Victor Goddard, and others, including members of the House of Lords UFO Study Group, stated the report was *". . . the closest thing the UK will ever have to a Project Blue Book".* Although copies went to the Ministry of Defence and Sir Victor passed copies on to former subordinates and ex-heads of RAF Intelligence, private UFO groups condemned the Report without even having seen the summary offered. The report is currently being updated with more contemporary evidence being added.

Alien seen on the Airbase

At 6.15pm on 20th November 2000, Brenda received a telephone call from Bury St. Edmunds resident – retired USAF serviceman Mr. Masters – who told her that he had read Georgina Bruni's book and was shocked that she had been allowed to enter certain buildings on the airbase. He said he had decided to tell

Brenda what he had witnessed because of his age and debilitating illness.

> *"When I was working on the base there were a lot of things that I heard and saw, which I wasn't allowed to talk about, especially after the Second World War. One place we weren't allowed was a closed off section, which housed decontamination rooms for soldiers who had come into contamination – some of whom died; others were sent home – but the strangest thing was the building that housed the tall spindly-type people, who used certain doorways to go to part of an underground building. They never spoke and had their faces covered with breathing apparatus. When I saw them I felt they were in control, without them even speaking. These people were still on base for years after the war."*

Brenda asked him if he thought these 'people' were aliens. He replied:

> *"They certainly were not human; they were dressed in white and had gloves on and long arms, and wore helmets over their heads."*

We traced a number of men, called 'Masters', from the Bury St. Edmunds area, but were unable to identify the man that had telephoned Brenda (presuming this was his real name) and interview him for ourselves. Was his story just a figment of imagination, disinformation, or is there a glimmer of truth? Ironically, Mr Masters (if that was his real name) was not the only person to report sightings of aliens at the base!

(Source: Brenda Butler)

Lieutenant Alan Brown

According to Georgina Bruni in her book *'You Can't Tell The People'* – on Sunday 28th December 1980, Gordon Williams was playing golf with, then Lieutenant, Al Brown. The two men were good friends and often played golf at the local club. Alan Brown told Georgina:

> *"I only heard rumours on the base and at the golf club, but I can tell you that there was definitely not any alert at the time. I know that's been mentioned. The week it happened (I think it was a Friday) I played golf with Gordy Williams on the Sunday. He was a good golfer. I asked him outright. I said, 'Come on, Gordy, tell me what happened'. He said, 'You got to be kidding me. I know nothing. No-one told me anything. Some guys, a bunch of young people, got a bit scared in the woods. Something scared the hell out of them, that's all I know, but I can tell you that something happened, but what it was, I honestly don't know. So something happened and those that were higher rank than me asked and they didn't know. I had heard that an air traffic controller saw weird lights and things and one of the officers was out there around the Woodbridge base; it wasn't near Bentwaters. I asked Donald Moreland about it, but he really didn't know much. By the way, Orford Ness lighthouse theory was bullshit."*

We decided to contact retired USAF Major Alan Brown, now living in the Suffolk area but found he was away until July 2013. Alan Brown's wife, Sally – a pleasant, well-spoken woman, who seemed very interested in the UFO incident – confirmed she and her husband had first heard about the December incident during a radio broadcast, rather than information obtained by her husband, from personnel at the airbase. [Authors: We believe this to be 1983]. Sally:

> *"My husband and I were good friends of 'Gordy' General Gordon Williams. We were saddened to learn that Georgina Bruni had passed away. I can remember taking Georgina and her bodyguard, Jacqueline, to the forest to show them the alleged landing site."*

She pointed out she had read Larry's book, and remarked humorously it should have been right at East Gate, not left! She was asked about whether her husband was in the Control Tower the night of the UFO incident; and said he was off duty.

[Friday would have been the 26th December, which would have been the morning Colonel Halt was out in the forest.]

Colonel Halt believes that General Gordon Williams was listening to the radio transmissions while the event was occurring. Georgina Bruni questioned Gordon Williams about this but felt he was evasive with answers. Was this due to accountability issues? After all, he was the man in charge of the joint bases and should, one would have thought, known exactly what was going on all of the time.

Georgina Bruni also spoke to Sgt. Rick Bobo, as he was mentioned in Sgt. Randy Smith's account as being stood next to each other in the security tower, watching '*UFOs*' that night.

> "*He (Bobo) positively insisted that nobody was with him in the tower. Only later did somebody (not Smith) visit to check out the situation. I do not wish to discredit Smith's testimony. All I can say is that Bobo, in my opinion, is a good, stable witness – no frills, straight to the point – wouldn't say anything that he wasn't sure of and never changed his story. Nobody I talked to, including those in the WSA, saw the beams and Tim Egercic was on duty there for three nights – 26/27, 27/28, 28/29 Dec. Rick Bobo was actually in the tower and Egercic confirmed this. I think Halt was not sure what was going on. Don't forget he was out near Woodbridge and only heard the chatter. According to the witnesses the UFOs were not visible from the WSA, except the tower of course.*"

Transcript of interview with Sgt. Randy Smith

Randy D. Smith is an Honor Graduate from Air Training Command. A Security Specialist, Randy's Certificate of Appointment confirms he was assigned to RAF Bentwaters with the non-commissioned rank of Sergeant, on 1st September 1980.

> "*I was either a [Senior Airman] or Sgt. at the time. It was Christmas time, 1980. 'D' flight had been working the 3-11pm shift, while 'C' flight had been working the 11pm-7am shift. It was a quiet, clear night. I believe I was working 'Whiskey 5', which was the alarm response team in the weapons storage area on Bentwaters. I am unsure of my partner that night. I had free range of one half of the WSA and I was driving a pick-up truck. Clarence George was my area supervisor. Rick Bobo was the SPCDS [Small Permanent Communications Display Segment [a 'computerized alarm system'] tower operator in the WSA. The next thing I recall, not long after the shift began, perhaps midnight or so, I heard Bob Ball come over the radio and request that the aircraft control tower give him permission to cross the active runway; it saves 15 minutes driving time, as opposed to driving the perimeter road. At that point I knew SOMETHING was happening because no-one ever crossed the active runway unless there was an extreme emergency.*
>
> *Bob, perhaps logically, accompanied by Lt. Bruce Englund, crossed the runway on Bentwaters. They picked up Lt. Col. Halt, and some equipment, and returned by the same route. I would say that between 30 minutes to an hour had passed since Bob made his first request to cross. They then proceeded to re-cross the runway and went out the back gate, headed toward RAF Woodbridge. After that, the radio was quiet for a long time.*

It was a very quiet night – no planes, no helicopters flying. Clarence George came by to talk to me and he said that everyone in the WSA was in the SPCDS tower watching 'lights' and did I want to come check it out? So I did. Clarence thought they were all crazy. It's a small tower and people were jammed in there, body to body, overloading the tower I'm sure. More people than I've ever seen in the tower at one time.

I asked what everyone was looking at, and they pointed out three objects that appeared like stars to the naked eye. Binoculars were being passed around and when I had my turn I saw VERY CLEAR images of three triangular-shaped craft that were hovering a few miles away, and above treetop level. They were triangular in shape, larger than a fighter jet, but smaller than a C5 – Definitely triangular, with lights that were arranged around the bottom that were perhaps different colors, but unable to distinguish at that distance. I only stayed in the tower for an hour or so, and heard one of the guys with a turn on the binoculars, say: 'Wow, it just took off'. Two of the craft left at a high rate of speed. The one remaining craft was still in position when I left the tower. Regarding sound – very quiet, no motor sounds whatsoever.

I also remember hearing the radio traffic regarding the light-alls [these were petrol powered, portable lights, which it's known were being used that night and proved problematic] and not working – replacing them didn't work, and then much later they all worked fine.

The following night, I went on duty. At Guard Mount, Bob Ball was very serious; he's almost never serious, a very jovial person. He said, 'I saw something last night, but I'm not at liberty to discuss it', and that was the 'end'. I later heard that the morning we got off our first midnight shift, an A-10 was scrambled and sent to Ramstein, Germany, by Lt. Col. Halt.

Randy described the object as effectively an upright pyramid, but was uncertain whether it may have been flat-surfaced or conical. However, he believed the objects were cone-shaped, as they "didn't look to be as flat as an actual pyramid. The lights underneath, which created somewhat of a backlit effect, enabling the shape of the crafts to be seen clearly were observed as 8-10 rectangular blocks, arranged in a circle".

(Source: James Easton, *Pulsar Newsletter*, No. 4, 6/4/1999)

The description of the UFO is actually quite common to many other sightings we were to come across during the intervening years, especially the reference to the rectangular blocks, as described by the witnesses, as seen forming the exterior structure. As we have said before, many UFO reports contain references to three objects seen and which on occasion have demonstrated the capability to split into separate sections before reforming together. Whether these sighting are connected with what Randy saw, we cannot say.

Colonel Halt:

"Randy Smith was there and reliable. I'm not convinced he and a crowd were allowed in the WSA tower. He was part of the Immediate Response Team and should have remained on post. However, he could have gone up into the tower. I don't know of anyone else claiming to have gotten in the tower with Bobo. The remainder of his account sounds reasonably correct. The only film from either night was Penniston's and Nevels" and you know about them. I never handled any film. A plane did go Germany soon after the event but it was supposedly to take some late promotion papers to a board. Last week I heard from a former Security Cop that was on 'D' Flight. He was off the night of the event but told me Bobby Ball was so

shaken by the event that the next day he went to the hospital for medication to calm down. This is the first I heard this.

Carl Thompson was not an Air Traffic Controller – he was a Communications Specialist that told of he and a co-worker working on the tower sensors in the WSA the nights of both incidents. His co-worker told of seeing the UFO both nights and was frightened into silence. I have his name but not with me."

Control Tower, Bentwaters – 1983

We spoke to Lee Southgate, who was employed as a civilian under the Official Secrets Act, at Bentwaters, with top secret clearance about what he remembered from his time there. Lee explained he was not there in 1980, but recommenced employment in 1983.

"The event that happened in 1980 was still occasionally talked about in the Bentwaters Control Tower. People suggested all manner of explanations. I remember that on the shelf, in the middle of all the flight manuals and other technical books, was a copy of Sky Crash that stuck in my memory.

Security was good at Bentwaters, but not quite the same at Woodbridge. I remember forgetting my pass, so I stuck an old farm pork sticker, green in colour, on the windscreen. The guy on the gate just waved me in."

Invariably, there was also tragedy. Lee told of Sergeant Carr – an ex-Vietnam Vet – who drove home one evening, in his Ford Cortina, the worse for wear.

"He hit a fence and was impaled on the railing, and died later.

The next day I went to look at the car, which was hardly damaged. The railing had come through the front of the car, under the windscreen, and struck him – a chance in a million. Sorry to see him go; he was a really nice man and had plenty of tales to tell while serving in Vietnam."

Declassified Documents of interest

Nick Pope

In June 2013 we contacted Nick Pope, regarding the question of what date General Charles Gabriel visited the airbase.

He said:

"I don't know the exact date of General Gabriel's visit. All I can tell you is that the relevant MOD document is dated 16th February, so we know the visit was sometime between the incident and that date."

Nick Pope is currently working with Jim and John on a new book, entitled: *Encounter in Rendlesham Forest,* which is due to be published in March 2014. Nick himself questioned the authenticity of the report

```
.OOSE MINUTE

D/DD Ops(GE)/10/8

DS8

UNEXPLAINED LIGHTS

Reference:   A.  D/DS8/72/1/2 dated 20 Jan 81.

1.    At Reference you forwarded a report from RAF Bentwaters for
information and asked if anyone else might have an interest in the
content.  You will see from the attached LM, I forwarded a copy
to DI55 and PS/ACS(G)(RAF).  I have had no response.

2.    SOC/CRC Neatishead regret that the radar camera recorder was
switched off at 1527Z on 29 Dec 80 and an examination of the executive
logs revealed no entry in respect of unusual radar returns or other
unusual occurrences.

3.    I have spoken with Sqn Ldr Moreland at Bentwaters and he considers
the Deputy Base Commander a sound source.  I asked if the incident
had been reported on the USAF net and I was advised that tape
recorders of the evidence had been handed to Gen Gabriel who happened
to be visiting the station.  Perhaps it would be reasonable to ask
if we could have tape recordings as well.
```

Feb 81

D BADCOCK
Sqn Ldr
Ops(GE)2b(RAF)
MB 4258 7274 MB

submitted by Colonel Halt, during July 1992, and the tape-recording, in May 1983, as can be seen from now declassified documents.

Even the date was in question, as we can see from a document referring to the 29th December 1980, which gives the 29th December 1980 as the one involving Colonel Halt.

On the 17th November 1983, Pam Titchmarsh wrote to Squadron Leader Moreland, bringing his attention to information received following the *News of the World* article, stating the date given by Colonel Halt was wrong.

Squadron Leader Donald Moreland wrote back to Pam Titchmarsh on 25th November 1985, making reference to unexplained lights seen at Woodbridge.

A declassified MOD document, dated 7th December 1983, from Pam Titchmarsh, gives the dates of the sightings. She confirms no radar tapes were confiscated and that they had no knowledge of any Constabulary

From:  Secretariat(Air Staff)2a, Room 40

MINISTRY OF DEFENCE
Main Building Whitehall London SW1A 2HB

Telephone   (Direct Dialling)
             (Switchboard)   Section 40
             (Fax)

Your reference

Our reference
D/Sec(AS)12/3

Date
14 May 1993

Dear  ,

Thank you for your letter dated 28 April, and for sending me a copy of the tape recording allegedly made by Lt Col Halt.

I listened to the tape with interest, but can offer no definitive view. Personally, I suspect that the tape is a hoax, albeit an extremely well constructed one. My main reason for saying this is that I find the whole scenario extremely unlikely; I have never heard of any instances of military personnel investigating an incident, whilst simultaneously making an audio recording. The fact that the tape has been edited down and re-recorded (complete with two very non-military interruptions) also suggests that the recording was made by enterprising members of the public. Furthermore, if the recording was genuine, I would expect that the ufologist to whom the tape was supposedly first made available would be able to produce an official covering letter; I have never heard of such a letter. Finally, it is perhaps significant that there is no reference to the tape recording in Lt Col Halt's memo.

I have never heard any official mention of the tape, so I do not believe that any official UK or US department would be able to obtain a full length copy of the recording.

I hope this is helpful, and I wish you luck with your research.

Yours sincerely,

E2

From: N G Pope, Secretariat(Air Staff)2a, Room 8245

MINISTRY OF DEFENCE
Main Building Whitehall London SW1A 2HB

Telephone (Direct Dialling) 071-21-8 2140
(Switchboard) 071-21-89000
(Fax) 071-21-8

Sqn Ldr P Rooney
RAF Commander
RAF Bentwaters
Woodbridge
Suffolk
IP12 2RQ

Your reference

Our reference
D/Sec(AS)12/2/1

Date
2 July 1992

Dear Sqn Ldr Rooney,

1.   I am writing concerning the background to the UFO sighting near RAF
Woodbridge on 27 December 1980, and the report that was subsequently made by the
USAF Deputy Base Commander, Lt Col Halt.

2.   I have attached a copy of a letter from one of your predecessors,
together with a copy of Lt Col Halt's report, and I have two requests:

a.   If you have files going back this far, could I have a copy of the
original covering letter, BENT/19/76/Air dated 15 January 1981. I believe our
copy was archived some time ago.

b.   I would be grateful if you would confirm that Lt Col Halt's report is a
genuine USAF report; this may sound a strange request, but over the years there
have been a very clever series of hoax documents produced on the subject of
UFOs. These often relate to official government/military knowledge of UFOs, and
often appear to be on official notepaper – presumably using genuine official
letters sent to members of the public, with the hoax text placed over the
genuine text, and then photocopied again. In the absence of all the background
papers, I am unsure as to the exact circumstances under which this report first
surfaced. I do not know what standard practice would be, but would such a
report not have been submitted on paper with a Bentwaters/Woodbridge address?

3.   This may all seem like ancient history, but this alleged incident has
become the best known UFO story in the UK, being mentioned in dozens of books on
the subject (including one entire book relating the story of how USAF personnel
repaired a crashed flying saucer and communicated with its alien occupants!).
We still receive a steady stream of telephone enquiries and letters on the
subject even to this day.

Yours sincerely,

17

N. Pope

RESTRICTED

7274

RAF Neatishead
Eastern Radar
RAF Watton

D/DD Ops(GE)/10/8

26 January 1981

UNEXPLAINED LIGHTS

1.   The Deputy Base Commander of RAF Bentwaters
has reported sightings of airborne phenomena on the
evening of 29 Dec 80 in the Rendlesham forest area
near Woodbridge. We would appreciate a statement
of radar observations, or lack of them, in the area
and at the time concerned.

J D BARCOCK
Squadron Leader
Ops(GE)2b(RAF)

RESTRICTED

MINISTRY OF DEFENCE
Main Building Whitehall London SW1A 2HB

Telephone 01-218 2638 (Direct Dialling)
01-218 9000 (Switchboard)

Sqn Ldr D H Moreland RAF
RAF Liaison Office
RAF Bentwaters
Woodbridge
Suffolk IP12 2RQ

Your reference

Our reference

D/DS8/10/209-1873
Date

17 November 1983

Dear Squadron Leader

I attach a copy of a letter received from
a member of the public following publication of
the News of the World reports on the Woodbridge
"UFO" sightings.

████████ has written twice before on this
subject and now alleges that the date given in
Lt. Col. Halt's report of the initial sighting as
being on 27 December 1980 is inaccurate. I would be
grateful for your comments on this.

I would also be grateful if you could discover
whether the second sighting mentioned in the report
took place on the same night or a subsequent night,
and if so, the date of the second sighting.

Yours sincerely

Pam Titchmarsh.

P J TITCHMARSH(Mrs)

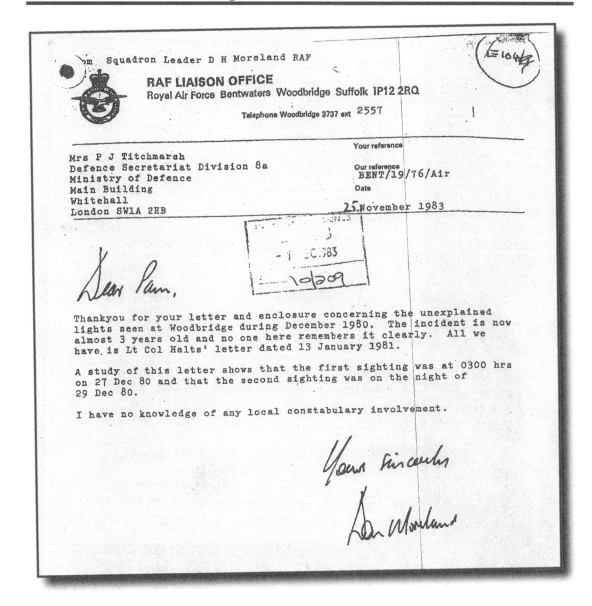

From Squadron Leader D H Moreland RAF

RAF LIAISON OFFICE
Royal Air Force Bentwaters Woodbridge Suffolk IP12 2RQ

Telephone Woodbridge 3737 ext 2557

Mrs P J Titchmarsh
Defence Secretariat Division 8a
Ministry of Defence
Main Building
Whitehall
London SW1A 2HB

Your reference

Our reference
BENT/19/76/Air

Date
25 November 1983

Dear Pam,

Thankyou for your letter and enclosure concerning the unexplained
lights seen at Woodbridge during December 1980. The incident is now
almost 3 years old and no one here remembers it clearly. All we
have is Lt Col Halts' letter dated 13 January 1981.

A study of this letter shows that the first sighting was at 0300 hrs
on 27 Dec 80 and that the second sighting was on the night of
29 Dec 80.

I have no knowledge of any local constabulary involvement.

Yours sincerely

Don Moreland

involvement, which is strange. (It is more likely nobody bothered to check, knowing that if they had, they would have learned more about the involvement of the police.)

Ralph Noyes wrote to MP David Alton on the 31st March 1985, asking why the only document then available from the MOD in respect of the incident that had taken place in Suffolk, during December 1980, was the Halt memo? Also why was it that the MOD did not have a copy of the tape-recording, which was made only available several months later?

Ralph Noyes wrote to MP David Alton on the 14th May 1985, explaining about his previous role within the MOD department and bringing their attention to what he referred to as a *"puzzling and disquieting case"*.

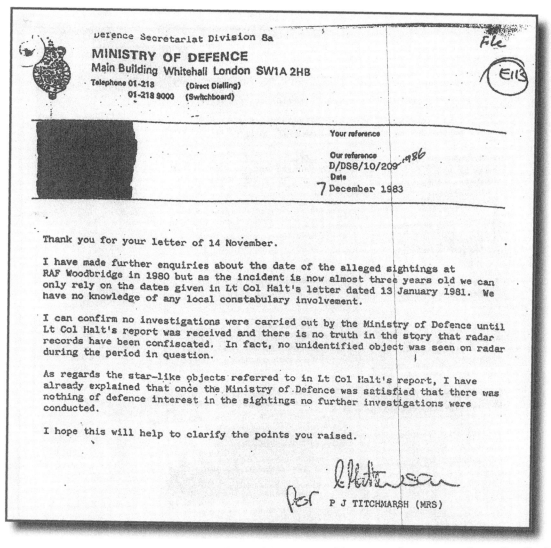

Defence Secretariat Division 8a

MINISTRY OF DEFENCE
Main Building Whitehall London SW1A 2HB
Telephone 01-218   (Direct Dialling)
    01-218 9000   (Switchboard)

Your reference

Our reference
D/DS8/10/209 1986
Date
7 December 1983

Thank you for your letter of 14 November.

I have made further enquiries about the date of the alleged sightings at RAF Woodbridge in 1980 but as the incident is now almost three years old we can only rely on the dates given in Lt Col Halt's letter dated 13 January 1981. We have no knowledge of any local constabulary involvement.

I can confirm no investigations were carried out by the Ministry of Defence until Lt Col Halt's report was received and there is no truth in the story that radar records have been confiscated. In fact, no unidentified object was seen on radar during the period in question.

As regards the star-like objects referred to in Lt Col Halt's report, I have already explained that once the Ministry of Defence was satisfied that there was nothing of defence interest in the sightings no further investigations were conducted.

I hope this will help to clarify the points you raised.

P J TITCHMARSH (MRS)

A copy of that now declassified letter is shown. (We presume his unnamed source was Jenny Randles.) Ralph points out that he disagrees with the opinions expressed by Lord Trefgarne to David Alton of there being no defence interest in this case.

The Lighthouse was not the answer!

This is an interesting document, as it refers to the following points of interest: Soil, tree samples, infra-red readings and photographs were taken.

Quote:

> *"Neither the MOD or the USAF will accept the lighthouse theory officially because they are as well aware as I am that it is easily refutable by the facts. Ian Ridpath actually stated on television (in a debate with me) 5th March 1985, that he regarded his investigation as*

31 March 1985

Dear Mr Alton,

Thank you for your enclosures (undated) which reached me on 30th inst.

May I comment on the reply of Lord Trefgarne to yourself.

His letter is virtually a word-for-word repeat of the standard MoD line (it must save money to keep churning them out of the word processor!) However, he does add a couple of points not previously noted. These are the specific references to not covering up "any incident or mishap" and not "in any way to obscure the truth". That said, and it presumably being true, I would have thought that it was of interest to know from the MoD why they only have the memo from Col Halt (and note he is refered to in Trefgarne letter _as_ Colonel Halt, his rank now, although on the memo he is Lt.Col.).

Bear in mind that this incident (whatever it was) occurred on BRITISH soil (_not_ base land) and just outside the perimeter fence of an RAF owned base. Consequently British citizens have a right to expect to have been kept informed of matters, especially as then British commander (Squadron Leader Donald Moreland) was specifically on base for that purpose.

YET - according to the MoD stance - we are lead to believe the following data was at no time made available...VIZ

i) The tape recording made by Halt, the base security chief and several other senior officers, which describes in detail the taking of soil samples, tree samples, photographs radiation readings, infra-red readings etc AT THE SITE ON BRITISH SOIL. Subsequently (as the tape records) a "UFO" reappeared. This tape _is_ in our hands and Moreland personally told me in January 1984 (several months before we got it from the US commander in America) that he was aware of its existence.

How come the MoD have no copy? How come the activities recorded on it took place on British soil without MoD knowledge? How come Moreland never advised the MoD of this _vital_ evidence?

ii) The photographs and samples recorded on the tape (which is officially accepted as genuine by the US) are, again, crucial evidence. Under a recent Freedom of Information US) request they _have_ been admitted and are likely to be made available in the USA very shortly. Again, I think we are entitled to ask why the MoD appear not only to be unaware of these but have no copies or copies of the analysis results which must accompany them. Again Moreland was aware that these samples and photographs were taken

IF, as the MoD contend, the events do not bear any relationship to a secret test or experiment (and if they _do_ they have lied both to you, as an MP, and to me) then that is an admission that they involve an Unidentified Object (which is all I contend the UFO to be). Indeed in the letter to me of 13 April 1983 DS 8 _do_ say that the lights are unidentified and have "no explanation".

It seems to me that there are questions here concerning the inter-relation between the US Air Force on British soil and our country IF, as contended, several senior officers from a USAF base can be involved in protracted work outside the base and on British land without such facts being known by the MoD or the results of their work being made available.

It is an interesting question as to who legally owns the samples of allegedly

irradiated soil and tree bark taken from BRITISH land (owned by the Forestry Commissi‹
in fact)! I doubt very much that the USAF have carte blanche approval to do what the‹
like on our shores. And if they do I for one am very concerned about it!

Finally, you will note that the official response makes no reference to the lighthouse,
normal background radiation theories propounded by Ian Ridpath in the Guardian (on th‹
strength of almost no evidence). Yet the Trefgarne letter to you does try to convince
you this is the answer,

Neither the MoD nor the USAF will accept the lighthouse theory officially because the‹
are as well aware as I am that it is easily refutable by the facts. Ian Ridpath
actually stated on television (in a debate with myself)(5 March 1985) that he
regarded his investigation as more objective. His investigation, as he admitted, has
consisted of interviewing not a single one of the 17 eye-witnesses from the USAF now
traced as being present during the events. Instead it consisted of speaking to one
forestry worker who found some holes in the ground one month after the sightings and
has presumed they might have been connected! I have spoken to that worker also, on
the site itself, and he is less than convinced of his theory himself.

None of this takes into account the various BRITISH CIVILIAN eye-witnesses who saw
the events, some in positions where it is literally impossible to see the lighthouse,
others looking in the opposite direction from it, and one who had the decidely
curious experience of the "lighthouse" flying right over the top of his house!

I am trying to force no explanation onto anybody. But frankly the lighthouse idea
is utterly ridiculous and the MoD must know that.

Besides which — what does it do to the USAF/RAF/MoD inter-relationship if all these
senior officers (base commander, deputy commander, chief security officer, on-duty
night command officer and control tower chief amongst them!) do not know what a
lighthouse looks like, which has stood five miles from one of our bases for decades
and still stands today?

It seems to me this proffers defence implications should these men (or men like them)
ever be put into a situation where they have to defend this land!

In connection with which comes the question of the radiation. Ridpath insists this
was ordinary background stuff. The forest was not irradiated, The "peak" readings in
the alleged ground traces (samples taken) are quoted as seven-tenths on the point
five scale. And I am reliably informed these are significant.

But again — assuming they are not — are we to take it that none of these senior
USAF officers have received any training on radiation monitoring? If so — are YOU
satisfied to leave them in charge of cruise missiles and nuclear weapons on our
shores?

I know that I am not happy, and I am convinced that such factors pose even more
serious defence implications than if a genuine bona-fide UFO was involved. The MoD
have steadfastly refused to make any comment on these matters. Perhaps you, Er Alton,
can get them to do so?

I pass this letter to Ralph Noyes for forwarding to you, with a letter I trust he will
write you. Ralph, as former head of the DS 8 section handling UFO enquiries, knows the
situation better than I ., supports our call for more information on this affair,
and will I hope open your eyes to the truth about what is being obscured here.

Please do not be put off. There are important civil liberties issues at stake.

14th May, 1985

David Alton, Esq., MP,
House of Commons,
Westminster,
London SW1

Dear Mr. Alton,

▮▮▮▮▮▮▮▮ has kept me informed about her corres-
pondence with you on the unusual incidents which were reported to the Ministry
of Defence by USAF authorities at RAF Woodbridge in January 1981. I have also
seen Lord Trefgarne's letters to you of 19th March.

▮▮▮▮▮▮ decided to write further to you about this puzzling
and disquieting case, and she referred to me her enclosed letter of 31st March,
which is addressed to you, in the hope that I might be able to add useful comments. Much to my regret I have had to spend much time out of London on other
business in recent weeks and it is only now that I am able, very belatedly, to
send on ▮▮▮▮▮▮▮▮▮ letter to you.

My own background, in brief, is that I served in the Ministry of
Defence from 1949 to 1977, leaving in the grade of Under Secretary of State.
From 1969 to late in 1972 I headed a Division in the central staffs of the MOD
which had responsibilities for supporting RAF operations. This brought me into
touch with a proportion of the many reports which the Department receives about
unidentified traces in British airspace.

I believe that ▮▮▮▮▮▮▮▮▮ is right to remain very dissatisfied
with the official line which the MOD has adopted on the Rendlesham Forest incidents of December, 1980. I have myself said so on a number of public occasions,
and I have pursued the matter in correspondence with the MOD — wholly without
success.

At the risk of burdening you with an excessive amount of paper, I
attach the most recent of my letters to the Ministry of Defence. You will see
that this is dated 25th February 1985. I have so far received no answer, despite
reminders. On a previous occasion it took the Department three and a half months
to send me a wholly perfunctory reply.

▮▮▮▮▮▮▮▮ claims much collateral evidence for her own views; on
this I am not competent to comment. My own position is, quite simply, that an
extraordinary report was made to the Ministry of Defence by the Deputy Base
Commander at RAF Woodbridge early in 1981; that the very existence of this report
was denied by the MOD until persistent researchers in the US secured its release
under the American Freedom of Information Act in 1983; and that the MOD's responses to questions since that time have been thoroughly unsatisfactory.

I cannot accept Lord Trefgarne's view that there is no Defence
interest in this case. Unless Lt.Col. Halt was out of his mind, there is clear
evidence in his report that British airspace and territory were intruded upon
by an unidentified vehicle on two occasions in late December 1980 and that no
authority was able to prevent this. If, on the other hand, Halt's report cannot
be believed, there is equally clear evidence of a serious misjudgement of events
by USAF personnel at an important base in British territory. Either way, the

case can hardly be without Defence significance.

The dates in question are now rather remote, but I doubt that this should be taken to excuse the very perfunctory manner in which Lord Trefgarne has dealt with your letter. I hope that you may feel able to pursue the matter further, either in correspondence or in a PQ. The essence of the questions to be pressed seems to me to lie in my preceding paragraph. Seen in these terms, ▓▓▓▓▓▓▓▓ article in the GUARDIAN (which Lord Trefgarne rather surprisingly falls back upon) is wholly irrelevant. If the USAF really are capable of hallucinations induced by a lighthouse which must surely be very familiar to them, then I shudder for that powerful finger which lies upon so many triggers...

My own letter to the MOD (enclosed) raises other more detailed questions. But I do not suggest that you should necessarily concern yourself with them, anyway at this stage. It would be nice if the MOD would answer letters, of course ! But the essence of the Defence interest which I suggest a responsible Member of Parliament might reasonably raise lies in the argument I have tried to present above.

If I can be of any assistance in discussion with you, I am at your disposal.

Yours sincerely,

more objective. His investigation, as he admitted, has consisted of interviewing not a single one of the 17 eye-witness accounts from the USAF now traced as being present during the events. Instead it consisted of speaking to one forestry worker, who found some holes in the ground one month after the sightings, and has presumed they might have been connected. I have spoken to that worker also on the site itself, and he is less than concerned of his theory himself. None of this takes into account the various BRITISH CIVILIAN eye-witnesses who saw the events, some in positions where it is literally impossible to see the lighthouse; others looking in the opposite direction from it, and one who had the decidedly curious experience of the 'lighthouse' flying right over the top of his house."

On the 11th June 1985, Lord Trefgarne wrote to Merlyn Rees MP, in which he pointed out that the events reported by Colonel Halt on 13th January 1981, were not of any defence significance.

Colonel Halt comments on the taped interview with Adrian Bustinza and Larry Warren – 1984

In June 2013, as this book was finally coming to a close, Charles Halt told us about a tape he had come across, relating to interviews held with Adrian Bustinza and Larry Warren, in 1984. This tape was dated 18th April, 1984.

Telephone 01-218 ~~2397~~ (Direct Dialling)

01-218 9000 (Switchboard)

file 12/4
copy to

ARLIAMENTARY UNDER-SECRETARY OF STATE
FOR THE ARMED FORCES

D/US of S(AF)DGT 4884

11 June 1985

Dear ~~Mr~~ Rees,

Thank you for your letter of 14 May which enclosed a further letter from ▓▓▓▓▓▓▓▓

I am afraid I have little to add to what I said in my letter of 20 February 1985 in reply to your original enquiry on this matter. We remain satisfied that the events reported by Colonel Halt on 13 January 1981 are of no defence significance. The report was, like all other UFO reports, examined at the time by those in the Department responsible for the air defence of the UK and we have since seen nothing to alter our views.

Turning to ▓▓▓▓▓▓▓▓ request for copies of all UFO reports we have received since 1980, I am afraid that the Department could not justify the effort involved in acceding to this request. However, ▓▓▓▓▓▓ will already know that we are prepared to release reports of specific incidents to interested parties and, if he has any particular reports in mind, ▓▓▓▓▓▓▓ can obtain copies of these from Sec(AS)2 in my Department, whose address is room 8249 Ministry of Defence, Main Building, Whitehall SW1A 2HB.

Yours sincerely,

Trefg ─

Lord Trefgarne

Rt Hon Merlyn Rees MP

Colonel Halt:

> *"According to Bustinza, he and Larry were out in the forest before I arrived, and then came back and went out with me; he never told me what he saw. He claims they saw a craft. Obviously, if this is true, it is of some importance with regard to the chronology of what happened down there. This may well have been the reason why Bruce Englund came out to get me on the evening. I must reiterate that apart from the report of yellow fog being seen by Larry Warren, there is no evidence to support the claims made that an alien craft landed and that Gordon Williams entered into some sort of a dialogue with the entities. This is completely untrue."*

The tape referred to by Colonel Halt relates to an interview conducted with Adrian Bustinza, by Ray Boeche and Scott Holburn, on 15th April 1984. This was three years before the interview with Larry Fawcett and only four years after the event.

Adrian tells of responding to a report of a fire seen in the forest area with Lt. Englund, who then called Colonel Halt, and after telling him about it was given permission to investigate further. Adrian identifies Colonel Halt as being there.

> *"He pointed to the individuals he wanted to go with him, so we went back to Bentwaters, grabbed two lights-alls and had a patrol refuel them."*

(He then says that when they go to point 'A' – the sighting of the UFO – the light-alls and the truck wouldn't run.)

> *"We started to search. One individual said he had spotted the object like sitting on the ground. We proceeded to look and found triangular tripods burn into the ground at three different standpoints. They took radiation readings of the holes and they got a radiation reading, as I recall.*
>
> *Then I recall we were walking through the woods and we came upon the lights again, and that's when I first saw the object. We got, I think it was flight Chief Sergeant Ball and another individual officer. We kept searching the area, trying to follow the object moving through the trees. In the process we came across a yellow mist, about two or three feet off the ground; it was like dew, but nothing I've seen before. We ignored it . . . we were worried about the [other] object to see if we could locate it again, or catch up to it again.*
>
> *We did see the object again. It was hovering low, like moving up and down anywhere from 10-20ft, back up, back down. There was a red light on top and several blue lights on the bottom. There was also like a prism [rainbow lights] on top and several other colours. It was a tremendous size. It even surprised me that it was able to fit into the clearing – a tremendous size, and I use the word carefully. It was round, circular shape. I hate to say like a plate, but it was thicker at the centre that at the edge."*

Bustinza:

> *"We were ordered to form a perimeter around the object at 15ft intervals. After about 30 minutes of observation, it suddenly took off, and was gone in a flash. When it left we were hit by a blast of cold wind, which blew towards us for 5-10 seconds. It was a really scary feeling. I was just frozen in place, at first. My life actually passed in front of my eyes."*

According to this interview, Bustinza neither denied nor confirmed the presence of alien beings. But he did confirm that the Base Commander – Gordon Williams – arrived at the site. He also claimed that photographs and films were taken by both British and American personnel.

> *"There was two 'Bobbies' there. Colonel Halt approached myself and Larry Warren (was it Larry? I'm trying to remember) I'm not too sure of the other guy's name. Halt told us to approach the individuals who were standing in the grass area; they had some sophisticated camera equipment, which wasn't unusual for the British. Halt told us to confiscate the material from them, which we did, and he (Colonel Halt) put it into a plastic bag, telling us it would be dealt with at the highest level of command. He didn't say exactly at what level or anything. I assume it went to the photography department on base; it could easily have been the intelligence department as well."*

Ray Bouche

According to Ray Boeche, Colonel Halt told him personally that a *Captain drove General Gordon Williams from the landing site to a Jet Fighter at Bentwaters He was in possession of cine film of the UFO, contained in a canister. This was flown to Ramstein AFB, West Germany.

Ray Boeche said he was told by a highly placed USAF records management official at the Pentagon that photos were taken and some of them – but not all – were fogged, but that officially their records would not show the existence of any photographs taken at all.

Colonel Halt has denied he said this to Ray Boeche and claims there was a misunderstanding.

Peter Robbins:

> *"Georgina told me, in person, that when she asked Williams, face to face, whether he had been involved, he told her he would 'neither confirm nor deny' his involvement in the events of 12-80. I think the best source as to the film canister being uncovered was by CNN's Military Correspondent, Chuck DeCaro, and put on the record in the then-fledgling news network's 3-part 'Special Report' on the Rendlesham incident. We refer to it on page 178 of 'Left at East Gate'. It was *Capt. Mike Verrano who verified for CNN that 'motion-picture film' of the UFO had been taken to a waiting aircraft by Gordon Williams – then flown on to Germany."*

Ray Boeche, June 2013:

> *"I was pleased to have found and spoken with Adrian Bustinza on, I believe — without digging out my files — two or possibly three occasions. One very brief conversation was taped by my colleague, Scott Colborn. The other conversation(s) were not taped, as those calls were made from my office at work, in an attempt to reach Adrian at a time convenient for him. I was also quite frustrated that Adrian would not share much, and even 30 years ago, stated exactly what he has told you; that this event traumatised him so badly that he just wanted to forget about it.*
>
> *Adrian's mother really gave me a piece of her mind when I called once for Adrian and he wasn't home."*

Ray Boeche

She was quite upset that I was trying to convince Adrian to dredge up memories which he found quite unsettling, and had impacted his life in an extraordinarily negative fashion. My single conversation with Col. Halt (which was not recorded, regardless of Harry Harris' insistence that I was keeping the tape a secret from him) certainly did include his assertion that 'film' (I don't recall whether he indicated if it was movie or still film) was taken and was flown directly to Ramstein Air Force Base, in Germany.

I'm unsure what tape Col. Halt may have. I was attempting to interest the late U.S. Senator for Nebraska, James J. Exon in this case, as he sat on the Senate Armed Services Committee at the time. At one point, while I was attempting to clear-up some rather odd things that seemed to indicate some sort of surveillance of my personal communications, one of his aides in Washington stated 'We have a file on you here that's just huge!"

Chuck De Caro

Following various conversations between Larry Warren and Chuck De Caro of CNN, in 1984 (approx), Larry says in the book *Left at East Gate* that he received a telephone call from Lee Spiegel – a producer with WNBC radio, in New York. He told Larry that he had interviewed Colonel Halt at Tinker Air Force Base, in Oklahoma, and *"that Halt had been very candid about the events of December 1980"*.

It is alleged by Lee Spiegel that when he asked Colonel Halt about the role of Colonel Gordon Williams and the '*beings*', Colonel Halt became defensive and asked the crew to go outside. According to Spiegel, in 'off the record' comments:

> *"Halt told me that beings were seen on the third night of activity and that Gordon Williams had been involved. Colonel Halt said he would only tell what he knew of the whole story if Congress subpoenaed him to testify."*

(Colonel Halt denies saying this).

On 25th February 1985, *Cable News Network* televised the first of three '*Special assignments'*.

The first one included the evidence of Jerry Harris and Gordon Levitt, followed by an interview with Master Sergeant Gulias who described the three depressions in the ground, making a perfect 12ft triangle. Halt's document (memo) was then read; the first part was then concluded with an interview with Airman Greg Bartram. The second part featured interviews with Greg and other witnesses. Although faces were obscured, Larry confirms that they were Master Sergeant Ball, Sergeant Gulias, and Captain Verrano, who confirmed that a motion picture film of the UFO was taken to a waiting aircraft by Gordon Williams and flown to Germany. The third part included interviews with Larry Warren, who spoke about the life forms he had seen.

Previous to this, Chuck De Caro had written to the Department of the Air Force on 8th October 1984, asking a number of pertinent questions about the incident, and received an answer dated 23rd November 1984. There seems little point, as space is in short supply, of including the questions and answers made, other than to say most of the answers were negatives, and offer nothing further of interest.

The Office of Special Investigations

A copy of this document, obtained from the USA Government by Larry Fawcett (CAUS) was sent to Dot Street. It contains a list of servicemen named as being involved in the incident. We were curious about two

CAUS

CITIZENS AGAINST UFO SECRECY INC.

10T Street   June 23, 1983
1; Black Berry way
Oulton Broad
Lowestost Sussolk England

Dear Dot,
          Enclosed you will find the documents that I promised
to send you.
Document #1- Letter From Colonel Henry J Coohran Base Commander to me dated April 28, 1983. Note admission " There was
allegedly some strange activity Near RAF Bentwaters at the
approximate time in question"
Document #2 Drawing made by AIC Larry Warren of object that
landed in the Rendlesham Forest. Larry Warren was a member
of the 81ST Security Police Squadron at RAF Bentwaters.
Document# 3 Letter to me from Robert Todd CAUS Research
Director Dated June 20, 1983.
Document #4 Letter to CAUS Research Director Robert Todd
From Colonel Peter W. Bent Commander 513 Combat Support
Group USAFE. NOTE Document #5 was obtained from your Gover-
nment by OUR AIR Force.
Document 5 Letter to your government RAF/CC by CHARLES
I. Halt LT COL USAF Dated 13 Jan 81 Paragraph 1 talks about
the landing in the Rendlesham Forest on Dec 27, 1980.
Paragraph 2 talks about depressions made in the ground by
object in Paragraph 1. Paragraph 3 talks about objects seen
on Dec 29, 1980 and was witnessed by LT COL CHARLES I HALT.
I now have a witness to the event in Paragraph #3 his name
is Steven LA PLUME former Member 81ST Security Police Sq
USAF RAF Bentwaters.
Also enclosed are 6 photos numbered on the back 1-6
PHOTO #1 SIGN at RAF Bentwaters
PHOTO #2 Sign erected after landing Rendlesham Forest
PHOTO #3 Landing Sight Rendlesham Forest AIC Larry Warren
pictured showing were object sitting on ground
PHOTO #4 Showing area around landing site Note road to right
of picture.
PHOTO #5 Close up photo of that road.
Photo # 6 AIC Larry Warren our witness to the Rendlesham
landing.
Dot please return all the pictures to me for they are my
only copys. You can keep the Documents for your file.
Listed below are all the names that we have uncovered
who were present from the USAF on the night of the landing
in the Rendlesham Forest.
AIC Lawrence Warren *81st Security Police.
Capt Michal Verona 81ST Security Police
Major Malcolm S Zickler Commander *81ST Security Police
SGT Adrien Bustinza 81ST Security Police
Staff SGT Maida 81 ST Security Police
Capt Graham 81st Security Police

CAUS
CITIZENS AGAINST UFO SECRECY INC.

SRA Malenga 81ST Security Police
AIC Marzy Steffenhagen 81ST Security Police
LT. Robert England 81st Security Police Not sure of first
name is right.
AIC John F Burrough 81ST Security Police this man took
pictures of the object when it landed but had his film an
camera taken away by USOSI.
AIC Mark Thompson 81ST Security Police
SGT COMBS USOSI and T SGT INGRAHAMS USOSI.
Also present during the landing were members of the RAF
we have no names or what units they belong to.
Dot please hold all names supplyed to you in strick confi
dence. If these names should leak out my government will
keep these men from talking about the incident.
well I hope the information I supplyed in this letter wil
help you in some way in our search for the truth.For our tw
governments to continue to maintain that UFOs are NON-
existent in the face of the documents already released,
and of other cogent evidence as the Rendlesham Incident,
is purile and in a sense an insult to the American and Br
itish people. For, as one national newspaper in AMerica
proclaimed in front page headline, " IF there are no UFOs
why all the secrecy?"

Your Friend in search of the truth
Lawrence Fawcett
Lawrence Fawcett
ASS't Director (CAUS)
CITIZENS Against UFO Secrecy
471 Goose Lane
Coventry, Conn 06238 USA

of these, as they were identified as being OSI (members of AFOSI) who are claimed to have conducted their interviews vigorously and administered sodium pentothal during interviews with the airmen, following their encounter with the UFO.

Colonel Halt:

> *"These operatives harshly interrogated five young airmen, some of them in shock at the time, who were key witnesses. Drugs, such as Sodium Pentothal – often referred to as a truth drug, used with some form of brainwashing or hypnosis – were administered in those interrogations, and the whole thing had damaging and lasting effects on those men."*

AFOSI investigates a wide variety of serious offenses – espionage, terrorism, crimes against property, violence against people, larceny, computer hacking, acquisition fraud, drug use and distribution, financial misdeeds, military desertion, corruption of the contracting process, and any other illegal activity that undermines the mission of the US Air Force, or the Department of Defense. AFOSI units are located at most Air Force bases worldwide. They are a Federal law enforcement and investigative agency operating throughout the full spectrum of conflict, seamlessly within any domain; conducting criminal investigations and providing counter-intelligence services.

AFOSI was founded August 1, 1948, at the suggestion of Congress, to consolidate investigative activities in the Air Force. Secretary of the Air Force, W. Stuart Symington, created AFOSI and patterned it after the Federal Bureau of Investigation (FBI). He appointed Special Agent Joseph Carroll, an assistant to FBI Director J. Edgar Hoover, as the first AFOSI commander and charged him with providing independent, unbiased and centrally directed investigations of criminal activity in the Air Force. As of 2007, the AFOSI has 2,900 employees. AFOSI focuses on five priorities: Develop and retain a force capable of meeting Air Force needs. Detect and provide early warning of worldwide threats to the Air Force. Identify and resolve crime impacting Air Force readiness or good order and discipline. Combat threats to Air Force information systems and technologies. Defeat and deter fraud in the acquisition of Air Force prioritized weapons systems.

In 1984, Major Kathleen O'Day – director of public affairs – refers to an enquiry made by a reporter about OSI involvement, after having obtained sight of a leaked document, published by the MOD, which outlines the result of OSI investigation into the incident.

Major O'Day denies any involvement by OSI and concludes it to be a hoax

Interestingly, the alleged forgery refers to the landing of an alien craft. The appearance of entities and repair work being carried out to the craft.

This apparent 'leaked' document was sent to Brenda, Dot and Jenny, in early 1984. However, enquiries made revealed it to be a deliberate fake, manufactured by certain parties, after it was ascertained that the MOD letterhead was of a style not used on public letters until late 1983. On 19th June 1984, Andrew Mathewson – head of DS8 at MOD – contacted Harry Harris and told him that he found the memo interesting, but concluded it was a forgery and probably intended as a joke (unlikely, we would have thought). The three women felt this had been an attempt to sow disinformation, with a view to impugning their credibility.

MINISTRY OF DEFENCE

Main Building, Whitehall, London SW1A 2HB

Telephone (Direct Dialling) 01-218 ▓▓▓

(Switchboard) 01-218 9000

Dear ▓▓▓▓ ,

As you know, OSI has completed a report on the landing of a craft of unknown origin crewed by several entities near RAF Bentwaters on the night of December 29/30 1980.

Interestingly, OSI reports that the entities were approximately 1½ metres tall, wore what appeared to be nylon-coated pressure suits, <u>but no helmets</u>. Conditions on the night were misty, giving the appearance that the entities were hovering above ground level.

Tape recordings were made on which the entities are heard to speak in an electronically synthesized version of English, with a strong American accent. Similar transmissions intercepted irregularly by NSA since 1975.(See attached - Flag A)

According to OSI, entities had claw-like hands with three digits and an opposable thumb.

Despite original reports (Flags B - G), OSI said the craft was not damaged but landed deliberately as part of a series of visits to SAC bases in USA and Europe. Reports that craft was repaired by US servicemen or was taken on to the base are not confirmed by OSI.

Landing is not considered a defence issue in view of the overt peaceful nature of the contact, but investigations by DS8 are to be continued on ▓▓▓▓▓▓ authority. Precautionary plan for counter-information at a local level involving ▓▓▓▓ and a ▓▓▓▓▓ ▓▓▓, is strongly recommended.

Sincerely

E

JOINT MESSAGEFORM					SECURITY CLASSIFICATION UNCLAS E F T O						
PAGE	ETC RELEASER TIME			PRECEDENCE		CLASS	SPECAT	LMF	CH		ORIG MSG IDEN
	DATE TIME	MONTH	YR	ACT	INFO	EEEE					
01- 02	041837Z	DEC	84	RR	RR						

MESSAGE HANDLING INSTRUCTIONS "U"

FROM: HQ AFOSI BOLLING AFB DC//PA//

TO: AFOSI DISTRICT 62 UXBRIDGE UK//CC//

INFO: AFOSI DETACHMENT 6205 RAF BENTWATERS UK//CC//

UNCLAS E F T O

SUBJ: NEWS MEDIA QUERY

1. FYI, MR. AL TERZI, WTNH-TV, CONN., (ABC AFFILIATE) IS RESEARCH
STORY REGARDING AN ALLEGED UFO LANDING, DEC 29-30, 1980 WHICH MAY
HAVE HAPPENED NEAR RAF BENTWATERS. THEY HAVE A DOCUMENT ALLEGEDLY
FROM THE UK MINISTRY OF DEFENSE WHICH MENTIONS "OSI" MAKING A REPOR
ABOUT THE INCIDENT.

2. REPORTER ASK THAT AFOSI VERIFY OSI INVOLVEMENT OR VERIFY IF IT
IS A FALSE DOCUMENT.

3. AFOSI/PA RESPONSE (WHICH WAS COORDINATED WITH DISTRICT 62/CC WA
RELAYED TO TERZI 1100 HRS, 4 DEC 84. "THE RESPONSE TO QUERY WAS AS
FOLLOWS: "HQ AFOSI AND ITS FIELD UNITS IN THE UNITED KINGDOM HAVE N
RECORD OF THE DOCUMENT YOU DESCRIBE AND DID NOT PARTICIPATE IN THE
ALLEGED INCIDENT. BECAUSE WE ARE NOT FAMILIAR WITH DETAILS OF THE
ALLEGED INCIDENT, AFOSI CANNOT VERIFY THE DOCUMENTS' AUTHENTICITY.

"POSSIBLE FOLLOW-ON QUESTION: BECAUSE OF PREVIOUS FOIA

DISTR:

DRAFTER TYPED NAME TITLE OFFICE SYMBOL PHONE
KATHLEEN M. O'DAY, MAJOR, USAF
DIRECTOR OF PUBLIC AFFAIRS PA/74728

SPECIAL INSTRUCTIONS

TYPED NAME TITLE OFFICE SYMBOL AND PHONE
MAJ KATHY O'DAY PA/74728

SIGNATURE
Kathleen M. O'Day

SECURITY CLASSIFICATION
UNCLAS E F T O

DATE TIME GROUP

DD FORM 173/2 (OCR) PREVIOUS EDITION IS OBSOLETE

© U.S. G.P.O. 1992-383-

JOINT MESSAGEFORM

SECURITY CLASSIFICATION: UNCLAS E F T O

PAGE	DATE-TIME	MONTH	YR	PRECEDENCE ACT	PRECEDENCE INFO	CLASS	SPECAT	LMF	CIC	ORIG. MSG. IDENT
02- 02	041837Z	DEC	84	RR	RR	EEEE				

MESSAGE HANDLING INSTRUCTIONS

REQUESTS FROM THE CITIZENS AGAINST UFO SECRECY, CAUS, AFOSI HAS MADE A THOROUGH SEARCH OF THE HQ AFOSI INVESTIGATIVE FILES, FINDING NO RECORD OF THE INCIDENT OR AFOSI INVOLVEMENT BY ITS FIELD UNITS ASSIGNED IN THE UK."

FYI: AS YOU MAY KNOW, THE AIR FORCE ENDED ITS UFO EXAMINATIONS IN DECEMBER 1969 (PROJECT BLUE BOOK) BECAUSE NO EVIDENCE COULD BE FOUND THAT THE SIGHTINGS WERE A THREAT TO NATIONAL SECURITY OR REPRESENTED VISITS FROM OUTER SPACE.

4. ALTHOUGH TERZI TOOK OUR STATEMENT, BE ADVISED THAT WTNH-TV FILM CREW MAY TRAVEL TO UK THIS WEEKEND TO FURTHER RESEARCH STORY. THEY HAVE BEEN IN CONTACT WITH A UK MINISTRY OF DEFENSE OFFICE WHICH STATED THE DOCUMENT WAS A HOAX.

5. PLEASE SHARE THIS INFORMATION WITH YOUR 81 TFW PUBLIC AFFAIRS OFFICER AND FOLLOW HIS GUIDANCE.

6. IF YOU HAVE ANY FURTHER QUESTIONS PLEASE PHONE MAJOR O'DAY, AV 297-4728.

6
5
4
3
2
1
0

DISTR.

DRAFTER TYPED NAME TITLE OFFICE SYMBOL PHONE

SPECIAL INSTRUCTIONS

RELEASER TYPED NAME TITLE OFFICE SYMBOL AND PHONE

SIGNATURE K.M. O'Day

SECURITY CLASSIFICATION

DATE TIME GROUP

DD FORM 173/2 (OCR) PREVIOUS EDITION IS OBSOLETE

*U.S. G.P.O. 1981-323-77

Larry Warren tells of being told by Zickler of a debrief, the morning following the UFO incident, and that he and a dozen other men were instructed by OSI Staff Sergeant Jackson to sign a document, explaining that they had only seen a few lights in the trees.

Larry:

> "We were instructed to sign the documents again. I did so reluctantly. They moved us to another room, in which three official-looking men were standing; one in a naval officer's uniform. We were told to sit on the folding metal chairs and co-operate fully with the debrief. Malcolm Zickler then left the room.

> The Navy officer introduced himself as Commander Richardson of the Office of Naval Intelligence. He also introduced the other two men as members of the Armed Forces Security Service. He began explaining how what the men had seen in the forest 'represented technology far advanced to our own'. Richardson carried on adding that 'numerous civilizations visit this planet from time to time'. He continued saying that none of them could discuss the incident with anyone at the bases and added that they were not to discuss the matter over the phone or in letters."

We emailed Nick Pope, in June 2013, wondering if he had any knowledge of the identity of OSI personnel, based at Bentwaters/Woodbridge, at the time of the incident, and received this reply:

> "I am not able to make any further comment on this matter, in view of the sensitivities involved."

One should bear in mind that Nick has himself been carrying out his own investigation into the events of Rendlesham Forest, for some years now, and we wish him and the other two co-authors the best with the book.

Interview with Adrian Bustinza – 1987

In this interview (of which relevant extracts involving reference to Colonel Halt are included, rather than the whole) Larry Fawcett outlines the version of events given to him by Larry in his previous interview and asks (Bustinza) to corroborate those events, which he does.

Rather than asking Adrian to describe in his own words his own memory of what happened, Larry outlined segments of the story previously given to him by Larry Warren, and then invited comment.

Larry Fawcett interview

Adrian agreed that Major Zickler, the Squadron Commander, was there and that they split up four men teams; they included John Burroughs, Sergeant Medina, Captain Verrano, Sergeant Ball, Mark Thompson, Airman Palmer, and Sergeant Combs.

LARRY FAWCETT – OK. Now, let me get back to the field part, OK? We put Larry under regressive hypnosis. Now, what came out under hypnosis was, while he was in the field and he was standing next to that machine, he was like petrified – frozen – that he couldn't move, you know? And he could see beings, small type of creatures. And they were talking to an officer there. He gave me the officer's name – Williams; I can't remember who the hell it was now. It was a big guy, whoever it was.

ADRIAN BUSTINZA – Lieutenant Colonel Halt.

LARRY FAWCETT – Halt. OK. And he said the beings were conversing with Halt. And at this point, something happened on the other side of the craft because all the beings like got defensive. They all lined up. Larry said he could hear a commotion on the other side of this machine, and all the beings' eyes got real big, and they all lined up in a straight line, real quick, like a defensive move. And then they dissipated a little bit, you know. It seemed to calm down whatever was going on the other side of the ship. At this point, one of the beings floated over the top and came over by him, and that's the last thing he remembers. Does it sound anything like you remember?

ADRIAN BUSTINZA – OK. Oh, boy, let me see. I remember the conversation. I don't remember word-for-word conversation, OK?

LARRY FAWCETT -Yeah

ADRIAN BUSTINZA – What was going on? I was shocked.

LARRY FAWCETT – You saw the beings?

ADRIAN BUSTINZA – Hold on, let me see. Colonel Halt, when we approached the machine, I remember Colonel Halt said – I remember Larry. I don't know why they picked Larry, but I remember Larry was going up there, and I was so scared I don't know what to think. I was in a foreign country, you know.

LARRY FAWCETT – Yeah Larry said you made a comment, and you said something like, *"Oh, no, not again!"* Yes . . . and Larry said, *"What do you mean?"* And you said, *"I went through this"*. See Larry had it mixed up though. He said, *"I went through this in Alaska once before."*

ADRIAN BUSTINZA – Yeah, OK. It wasn't Alaska. When I was talking to them and I was telling them about it, I had just come from Alaska TDY.

LARRY FAWCETT – Yeah.

ADRIAN BUSTINZA – It was in California where it actually happened.

LARRY FAWCETT – This was at Davis?

ADRIAN BUSTINZA – Mather Air Force Base. Yeah.

LARRY FAWCETT – OK. So go ahead, you started to say something.

ADRIAN BUSTINZA – I said *"Oh, no, not again."* Colonel Halt said – he mentioned a couple of names to me. We walked up toward the craft.

LARRY FAWCETT Yeah.

ADRIAN BUSTINZA – When we walked up there, Colonel Halt started talking, and it was like, it was instant communication between personnel.

LARRY FAWCETT – Between the men

ADRIAN BUSTINZA – The men.

LARRY FAWCETT – How about the beings?

ADRIAN BUSTINZA – To tell the truth, I remember seeing the craft. I remember Colonel Halt talking, and I remember looking to who he was talking to and I couldn't see nobody, I couldn't see what, I mean, who he was talking to, and for a minute there I thought everybody there was going crazy here or something, you know… and I do remember him saying he would contact the electronics division, which would be CRF, I think it was, the call letters for the group… and they would possibly have to get the part from another world. And I just looked at, I couldn't hold my, you know. Who are you talking to, what are you talking about, you know?

LARRY FAWCETT – Right.

ADRIAN BUSTINZA – It was like, when something like that's happening right before your eyes, you want to try to keep track of everything, but it's hard because everything is happening so fast.

LARRY FAWCETT – Yeah.

ADRIAN BUSTINZA – More or less, it was like Larry says. I remember that, and then after that, you know, I woke up in the morning.

LARRY FAWCETT – You don't know how you got out of the field?

ADRIAN BUSTINZA – I don't know, well, yes, I remember. I got back in the jeep and lieutenant who was in the jeep; they kept telling us that we were better off not talking to anybody about this at all.

[Authors: Was this Bruce Englund?]

ADRIAN BUSTINZA – Not even among ourselves. He said people would think different about us and everybody. Lieutenant looked at me. He said, *"You're a supervisor, you ought to know better"*, and he said, *"You keep an eye on these guys. If anybody says anything, you report to Colonel Halt"*.

LARRY FAWCETT – OK.

ADRIAN BUSTINZA – And then personnel affairs would handle the whole situation.

LARRY FAWCETT – OK. Now, you did see Halt talking to somebody though, but you could not see who he was talking to.

ADRIAN BUSTINZA – Right.

LARRY FAWCETT – What, do you remember, basically, what was he saying? Just that we can get parts from the electronics division, or we'd try to get parts?

ADRIAN BUSTINZA – The electronics division, that's all. I'm sure, I remember. Because I looked at him real funny, I remember, I said, *"Electronics division? Who is he talking to? What is he talking to?"* I asked myself those questions.

Colonel Williams denies knowledge

ADRIAN BUSTINZA:

> *"No, they didn't." Colonel Williams' words were, quote unquote: "Whatever you saw out there, I don't want to personally know anything about it. That's between you and whoever's handling the case. Well, no-one ever told me what that machine was. I just took it for granted. Since it was nothing I had ever seen, I took it for granted – I labelled it a UFO. What I thought afterward was that these supposedly UFOs, with beings and stuff, they're far more intelligent supposedly than we are. How is the Air Force going to help them fix the machine? How are they going to help? I remember the words Colonel Halt said, 'We'll get you the parts from our electronics division', and that kept ringing a bell and ringing a bell, like how can we help them? You know?"*

Sgt. Adrian Bustinza describes the alien machine

> *"It was the first time I've seen one like it. It was circular-shaped; it looked like a pancake. It was thick in the middle, and it would narrow out toward the edges – a blackish-gray colour. I saw lights, all kind of lights. It would have been a beautiful sight, you know. The lights were so bright that I could only see certain parts of the craft, and there were a bunch of little gadgets on it, too, like some planes got, and other little gadgets that I never even seen on aircraft before."*

Further questions elicits the following information:

> *"Assumed to be made of metal, got within 6-10ft; it wasn't a humongous thing, but it was of a very good size – about as wide as an A-10. From what I could see in the beginning, it was very big, but I couldn't really tell exactly how big – as big as a medium-sized house – I would say 12ft x 40ft? When it took off, it was, like, hovering. It went up and, like, took off at about a forty-five° angle, and if you would have blinked, you would have missed it. And we got a cold draft of air that lasted about a good ten seconds. You know, like when you get a good blow of dust or wind. No noise though; I do remember that. The colours were constantly changing while I was there. I remember, it was different colours, and they just, like, go on and off or go to a lower shade."*

According to Georgina Bruni, in her book she claims that snatches of conversation on the tape-recording made by Colonel Halt, confirms the presence of three other airmen – Lieutenant Bruce Englund, Sergeant Munroe Nevels and Master Sergeant Robert Ball. She says that while Colonel Halt admitted having seen strange lights, he denied any landing.

Georgina:

> *"I spoke to former Sergeant Adrian Bustinza, who was in his patrol and swears on his life there was a landed UFO. Halt at first said Bustinza wasn't with him, but I later came across a tape with Bustinza's voice on it."*

Georgina says that during interviews with Bustinza, he claimed that Colonel Halt was already there by the time the UFO landed.

We contacted Adrian Bustinza, in June 2013, after learning he was going to come over to the UK last year and speak about his involvement in the matters, and were surprised to hear him tell us:

> *"John, I have blocked everything I could possibly block from my memory bank on this subject. I have no desire to talk and/or remember anything more of this. It has been 33 years come this December, and I would love none other than to remember everything that happened on those nights to us. However, our wonderful Government has managed to somehow make us forget some of the details and I will not guess at this and only want to be left alone on this subject."*

Steve Roberts

During early investigations held into this matter, one may have presumed that the version of events given by 'Steve Roberts' to Brenda Butler, alleged from him to have happened during the early morning of 27th December 1980, would have been the same morning when Charles Halt and his men witnessed the strange lights.

'Steve Roberts'

In view of the fact that *Lt. Colonel Halt now confirms the date as the early morning of 28th December, it is pointless to pursue such an association but one is bound to wonder why Colonel Halt, or any of the other airmen, involved over the various nights running have never identified 'Steve Roberts' as being present?

Especially following Steve Roberts claim of having witnessed a landed craft with its alien occupants, and their meeting with Colonel Gordon Williams and other USAF service personnel, during the early morning of 27th December 1980.

Surely they cannot all have been sworn to secrecy not to reveal his part in the matter. We found this suspicious and speculated whether he had been there at all.

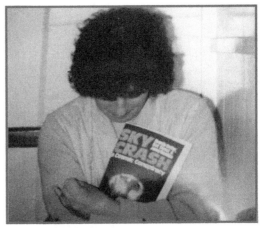

Brenda Butler clutching a copy of her book 'Sky Crash'

Colonel Halt:

> *"Steve Roberts had worked in the same office as Jim Penniston. He was not there and picked up the story from Jim. Even Jim will tell you that."*

Further 'unidentified illustrations' are now shown; the first bears a strong resemblance to the original 'Steve Roberts' illustration (on this one the aliens are even more pronounced.) The second one shows a similar object to that described by Jim Penniston – although Jim denies any association with these sketches.

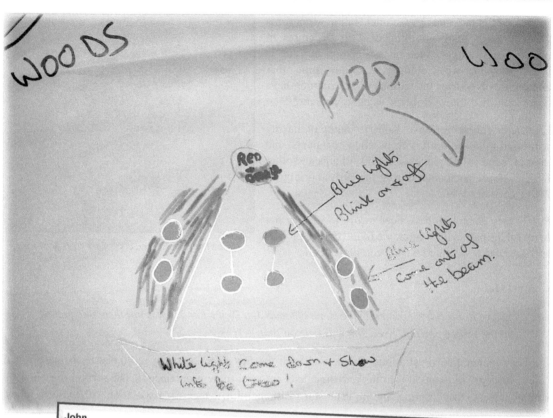

John

From:
To: <johndawn1@sky.com>
Sent: 20 May 2013 14:09
Subject: Re: Emailing:

John:

I have enough information to back up my thoughts that Jim and John were messed with either in the forest or in the "debriefing" afterward or some combination there of and that they have reality and fantasy confused. It's too bad as all they are doing is spreading disinformation. For example the cop that sat next to Jim on the crew bus the morning of their encounter while riding back from Guard Mount at CSC has been found. He talked with Jim and Jim took out the "notebook" and drew what he saw. He didn't see other drawings or any code or inscriptions in the book. In fact, we did numerous programs together and the notebook never was mentioned until at the National Press Club 3 years ago. Several years ago when Jim and I were doing a program on site he took us to the wrong site and insisted it was correct. We know that to be wrong as he and John had taken me to the original site. Plus, we know where the plaster casts were made. There are other inconsistencies. **Steve Roberts** was not there but worked in the office with Penniston and picked up the story from him and others. Even Jim will tell you that. That we agree on.

An interesting book that has some parallel things similar to what we experienced is Hunt for the Skinwalker by Keller and Knapp. I personally know several of the NIDS (National Institute for Discovery Science) researchers. They are very talented and professional. You'd be impressed. Another book well worth reading is by my good friend John Alexandra- UFO's myths, conspiracies and realities.

In 2009, Charles Halt was asked about the date of the first UFO incident (involving Penniston and Burroughs) by Robert Hastings, and confirmed the *morning of 26th December as now being correct. Larry Warren refers to 11.45pm on the 28th December 1980, and of meeting up with Adrian Bustinza and Lt. Bruce Englund. Just after 12.30am on 29th December, Larry and his colleagues sighted a yellow-green fog, with something glowing inside it. This was followed by a red light, and the arrival of a pyramidal *'alien craft'*. Larry maintains Colonel Williams was there, along with other officers [unnamed] and that aliens were seen floating down from the *'ship'* over Colonel Williams. The *'ship'*, which had been there for some hours, then took off after repair work had been carried out.

In *Above Top Secret,* published in 1988 by Tim Good, he gives the date of the incident involving Larry Warren as having taken place on the 30th December 1980. In *Left at East Gate,* Larry claims it was the 28th December, going over into the early morning of the 29th December 1980.

We discussed these issues with Colonel Halt in mid-June 2013, and were not surprised by his answer.

> *"As I said to you before, there is no evidence to support the claims made that an alien craft landed and that Gordon Williams entered into some sort of a dialogue with the entities. This is completely untrue. Major Zickler was not present as he stayed at the party with Conrad, as he didn't want his name in it. Verano, Palmer, Combs and Thompson were not there and John Burroughs was held back and ordered to stay back on the service road. Now he talks about all kinds of things that I know didn't happen. The account from Bustinza is one of fabrication. I never ordered anyone to surround an object! There were no 'Bobbies' there. No-one, to my knowledge, was taking pictures (other than Nevels) and no film was confiscated. It appears from this version of events that Larry may not have been present.*

> *John, you have no idea how skilled these people are in fabricating disinformation. My advice is to be very cautious with regard to claims of this nature made, as they are untruthful.*

> *Carl Thompson was one of the Air Traffic Controllers on duty that night (he and his partner saw the object both on the screen and visually). There's no way Bustinza could have known his name, as he didn't come forward until recently and their duty roster is not known but to a few. Just further evidence that someone messed with Adrian. The plot thickens! I can only recommend that you proceed with caution. Warren, Penniston, Burroughs, have been given confusing and distracting memories. Even Larry has admitted this possibility to me. Perhaps you have read the recent news about NSA. What the paper has, only scratches the surface. I did an orginational inspection of them 22 years ago and I was shocked with the little bit I found.*

> *It is clear, from the information I have gathered, that Jim and John were messed with either in the Forest, or in a debriefing which took place afterwards, or some such combination, and that as a result of this they have reality and fantasy confused. It's too bad, as they are unintentionally spreading disinformation. For example, the 'cop' that sat next to Jim on the crew bus the morning of their encounter, while riding back from Guard Mount, at CSC, has been found. He talked with Jim, and John took out a notebook and drew what he saw. He didn't see any other drawings or any code or inscriptions in the book. Jim and I, did numerous programs together and the notebook was never mentioned until at the National Press Club, three years ago.*

> *Several years ago, when Jim and I were doing a program on site, he took us to the wrong*

AFFIDAVIT OF CHARLES I. HALT

(1) My name is Charles I. Halt

(2) I was born on ▓▓▓▓▓▓▓▓▓▓▓

(3) My address is ▓▓▓▓▓▓▓▓▓▓▓▓▓▓

(4) I served in the U.S. Air Force for 28 years, retiring in 1991 with the rank of Colonel. In December 1980, I was the Deputy Base Commander at the Anglo-American base, RAF Bentwaters, in Suffolk, England.

(5) Late in the evening on December 27th, and continuing into the pre-dawn hours of December 28th, in response to reports of unusual lights in nearby Rendlesham Forest, I led a team of USAF Security Policemen into the woods to investigate. This was the second such incident in as many days and rumors of UFO activity were rife on base. By going into the forest, my intention was find a logical explanation for the mysterious lights.

(6) While in Rendlesham Forest, our security team observed a light that looked like a large eye, red in color, moving through the trees. After a few minutes this object began dripping something that looked like molten metal. A short while later it broke into several smaller, white-colored objects which flew away in all directions. Claims by skeptics that this was merely a sweeping beam from a distant lighthouse are unfounded; we could see the unknown light and the lighthouse simultaneously. The latter was 35 to 40-degrees off where all of this was happening.

(7) Upon leaving the forest, our team crossed a farmer's field. As we did so, someone pointed out three objects in the northern sky. They were white and had multiple-colored lights on them. At first, the objects appeared elliptical but, as they maneuvered, turned full round. They were stationary for awhile and then they started to move at high speed in sharp angular patterns as though they were doing a grid search.

(8) About that same time, someone noticed a similar object in the southern sky. It was round and, at one point, it came toward us at a very high speed. It stopped overhead and sent down a small pencil-like beam, sort of like a laser beam. That illuminated the ground about ten feet from us and we just stood there in awe, wondering whether it was a signal, a warning, or what it was. It clicked-off as though someone threw a switch, and then the object receded back up into the sky.

(9) This object then moved back toward Bentwaters, and continued to send down beams of light, at one point near the Weapons Storage Area. We knew that because we could hear the chatter on the two-way radio. Several airmen present later told me that they saw the beams. I don't remember any names at this point. From my position in the forest, it appeared that one or more beams came down near the WSA. At the time, the object was just to the north of the facility. I had great concern about the purpose of the beams.

(10) In keeping with official U.S. Air Force policy, I can neither confirm nor deny that the Weapons Storage Area held nuclear weapons. However, I am aware that other former or retired USAF Security Police who worked there at the time of the incident are now on-the-record confirming the presence of tactical nuclear bombs at the WSA.

(11) I believe the objects that I saw at close quarter were extraterrestrial in origin and that the security services of both the United States and the United Kingdom have attempted—both then and now—to subvert the significance of what occurred at Rendlesham Forest and RAF Bentwaters by the use of well-practiced methods of disinformation.

(12) I have not been paid nor given anything of value to make this statement and it is the truth to the best of my recollection.

Signed: _____

Date: 6/17/10

Signature witnessed by: Katherine C. Shaw

Notary: K.C. _____ My commission expires April 30, 2011

site and insisted it was correct. We know that to be wrong, as he and John had taken me to the original site. Plus we know where the plaster casts were made. There are other inconsistencies."

The News of the World article, released in 1983, also contained some glaring errors. These included reports of Colonel Halt having spoken directly to that newspaper. He did no such thing. The report was not classified Top Secret, as was suggested. They also quoted Donald Moreland and Colonel Halt, which was incorrect, and also stated that there were 200 personnel in the forest that night; the list goes on......

On the 17th June 2010 Colonel Halt made an affidavit relating to the incident, which was countersigned by Katherine Shaw of the Commonwealth of Virginia, which we enclose for the information of the reader.

Bob Tibbitts:

"Will there ever be a definitive statement claimed as the real 'truth' of what went on at Rendlesham? Maybe not. However, what 'Haunted Skies', Volume 8, has strived to accomplish, is to lay before the reader as much evidence as can be found at this present time from which to arrive at the shores of at least some of this 'truth'. Navigating the waters can prove difficult. No doubt, subsequent to this volume being published, there will be misinformation and 'guided' proclamations to further fog the issue. My personal insight is that Colonel Halt may know more than he remembers, or than he is allowed to admit, and that certain 'agencies' prefer to keep it that way. Perhaps they won't succeed.

I haven't met any of the witnesses myself or been to the site of the events in question but raise my views based on the information I have been privy to over the years. Having said that, many others have posed their theories about what may or may not have occurred there and have felt that their views are worthy. We should listen carefully to what has been said by the witnesses themselves and take on board the new information coming to light from them, especially from Colonel Halt. Any closeness to the 'truth' will lie with them. New revelations from Jim Penniston and John Burroughs will also need to be absorbed by the reader while trying to gain clarity of the events in 1980 at Woodbridge/Bentwaters.

Somewhere amongst the tangled web of dates, times and differing recall of the witnesses, lies the reality of what happened. Was it a craft in difficulties that needed some assistance, which the men at Bentwaters were able to give, and, if so, was that craft manufactured on our planet or elsewhere? If, as some have speculated, it represented our own technologies from way, way into the future (or the past) . . . would it have been possible to recognise it as such and would the men at the airbase have been able to communicate with the intelligence controlling it? We shall probably never know whether the incursion was deliberate, or a forced landing with little choice, caused by failure of the operating system onboard, bringing the device down into the forest on that fateful evening and into the lives of so many people."

Authors:

It has taken us an enormous amount of time to sift through documents, and spend endless hours talking to Brenda, over many years, and visiting the forest on numerous occasions. Thanks to Brenda we were able to build up a rapport with Charles Halt, who has entrusted us with his opinions and personal memories of those events – now over 33 years ago – not forgetting the assistance of Jim Penniston, John Burroughs and Larry Warren, whom we have met personally . . . and so many others.

Colonel Halt's description of what he saw has many similarities with other sightings we were to come across, during our research. Charles Halt continues to try and clear his name, with regard to what he sees as a slur on his character and his integrity. He maintains vigorously to this present day, of having no knowledge of involvement with any alien species following a UFO landing or knowledge of other senior officers being involved in any communication with any alien species.

He continues to raise public awareness about what he and his men witnessed, through public speaking, despite continuing disinformation orchestrated by certain agencies to discredit the UFO subject – examples of which can be seen on most days, by the media, who still, in the main, continue to treat UFO reports as being the butt of humour, and more in keeping with the annals of science fiction than the stark reality of what is continuing to happen on an everyday basis.

As far as the events that took place in the forest are concerned, it is clear – apart from the inconsistencies between the given dates, some of which have been clarified – there is a vast difference between what Colonel Halt and his colleagues witnessed – and one, if not two, close encounter claims made by the other servicemen.

During many years research, we have interviewed people from all walks of life (including police officers and pilots) with regard to sightings of all manner of strange flying objects.

In addition to this, we have spoken to a number of other people who report incomprehensibly of having sighted, on occasion, '*small figures*' stood around or inside a landed object. These people do not claim this is substantive proof of extraterrestrial presence – just that '*this is what we saw – make of it what you will*'.

However, we have never come across one other example involving direct communication with human beings, asking for assistance with their broken-down craft – but this doesn't mean to say that this did not happen. Don't forget there was a time when we were sceptical that UFOs existed. There was also a time when we believed UFOs existed but were sceptical about them having any occupants. Not any more!

In June 2013 MOD declassified its UFO files

Declassified files, released by the National Archives in late June 2013, reveal that the MOD closed its UFO desk in 2009, claiming that any investigation into sightings *"would be an inappropriate use of defence resources"*. The 25 files included 4,400 pages and cover the work carried out in the final two years of the MOD UFO desk – from late 2007 until November 2009.

Officials decided to close the 'UFO hotline', as it was deemed to have no '*defence benefit*' and resources devoted to it were taking staff away from '*more valuable defence-related activities*'. They include accounts of alleged abductions and contact with aliens, as well as UFO sightings near UK landmarks, including the Houses of Parliament. In a briefing to then Defence Secretary – Bob Ainsworth – in November 2009, Carl Mantell, of the RAF Air Command, suggested the MOD

> *"should reduce the UFO desk, which is consuming increasing resource, but produces no valuable defence output".*

He said that, in more than 50 years,

> *"No UFO sighting reported to (MOD) has ever revealed anything to suggest an extraterrestrial presence or military threat to the UK".*

An official MOD statement declared,

> *"The Ministry of Defence has no opinion on the existence, or otherwise, of extraterrestrial life. However, in over 50 years, no UFO report has revealed any evidence of a potential threat to the United Kingdom."*

Commenting on the release of the files, Dr. David Clarke, author of the book *The UFO Files*, said:

> *"The last files from the UFO desk are now all in the public domain. People at home can read them and draw their own conclusions about whether 'the truth' is in these files or still out there."*

Typically sightings recorded in the newly-released files include a letter from a schoolchild, asking for the truth about UFOs, after she had seen some strange lights; a report, via the UFO hotline, by someone who had been '*living with an alien*', in Carlisle, and a man from Cardiff, who alleged a UFO had abducted his dog, car and tent. In addition to this, there were reports of UFOs seen over the Houses of Parliament, Stonehenge and Blackpool Pier.

We ask the reader to form their own conclusions on the many thousands contained within the pages of the *Haunted Skies* books, sometimes involving the sighting of what appears to be an alien craft and their occasional perceived non-human (in the main humanoid) occupants, rather than misleading information, which tries to convince us that such things do not exist. If they did not, the books would never have been written!

SKY CRASH THROUGHOUT TIME

A Continued Investigation into the Rendlesham UFO Mystery

by Philip Kinsella and Brenda Butler

Very few of these reports ever appear in any downloaded Public Records Office files. Why is that we wonder? We feel this is an inaccurate representation of what has taken place over the years. However, having said that, one should take into consideration many people did not report their sightings to the MOD but to other UFO organisations. It is apparent certain 'low grade sightings' have been carefully selected and presented to the media – mostly in a humorous vein, which can only denigrate the real truth of what lies behind it all.

We cannot prove the existence of any alien incursion onto our planet; all we can say is that this is what people have been seeing and will continue to see, irrespective of the everyday affairs of mankind.

Whatever '*they*' are, '*they*' appear to have time on their side and, in all probability, have been here on this planet alongside us as an invisible indigenous species, for eons.

We are not sure what the necessary criteria are for the UFO sightings to occur and, occasionally, interact with human beings. However one thing is assured, whatever your beliefs, sightings of strange objects have been recorded in history since man first looked at the night sky and will continue to happen.

David and Linda Bryant of *Spacerocks* website

We are now nearing the end of what has turned out to be a momentous volume, but felt we wanted to pay our respects to a couple who have given us so much encouragement and support all the way through the volumes of *Haunted Skies*.

Former helicopter pilot, David Bryant and his wife, Linda, are the UK's only full-time professional dealers of meteorites, and have been involved in their sale for now over 15 years. http://www.spacerocksuk.com

The couple hold Degrees in Astronomy and Biology and are more than capable of being able to discuss their inventory with experience, enthusiasm, and knowledge; they supply most of the UK's wholesalers, museums and educational institutions, and are members of the IMCA, and offer a lifetime guarantee of the authenticity of purchases to their clients.

David and Linda were also instrumental in introducing John personally to many Astronauts, during their visits to the UK. John feels privileged in being able to talk to people, like Dr. Edgar Mitchell, Buzz Aldrin and retired General Charles Duke.

David is an accomplished lecturer and musician. He is frequently invited to talk by the media and professional institutions about his knowledge of meteorites and astronautics.

During those talks he often recommends purchasing *Haunted Skies,* because he passionately believes, as we do, that reported UFO activity forms part of British social history and should be preserved.

His expressed opinions about the existence of UFOs invariably will, and does, attract ridicule by those from academic and scientific institutions, who strongly feel there is no evidence to support such views.

We know personally, from conversations with David, that his UFO beliefs have occasionally influenced decisions by certain sections within the media, who have chosen not to engage his services fearing possible embarrassment should he inadvertently make references to the UFO subject.

David does not claim that aliens or 'flying saucers' exist; all he has ever claimed is that there is ample evidence from many responsible people (including astronauts) – some from senior ranks within the RAF and Government – of the existence of a mysterious phenomena that continues to attract the attention of the media.

History will record men of courage like David Bryant for his efforts to raise some public awareness of the existence of UFOS (whatever they are and wherever they come from) in the face of adversity, rather than those who thought the opposite! All he seeks are the answers to what is, after all, the most enduring enigma of modern day times.

David and Linda Bryant are regular visitors to Rendlesham Forest, Suffolk, and have been fortunate enough to capture some strange anomalies on photograph – as can be seen on pages 242 and 385.

In July 2010, the couple also captured something strange.

"Myself, my wife – Linda, and three friends, spent much of the day, until shortly before midnight, walking the paths at the northern end of the wood, from East Gate car park and Folly Cottage to the various landing sites. We made three anomalous observations, photographing two of them.

The first was a bright triangular object that appeared in a photograph, taken along Track 10, looking west, towards East Gate, from the main path. Nothing was noticed at

the time the picture was taken (the woods were much darker than the camera suggests!) but on magnifying and brightening the central section, a curious object, flanked by apparently humanoid figures, was apparent. I should add that the photo was taken looking back from where we had just walked, and that all five of us experienced a powerful sensation of being watched at the time. The other object we photographed was a bright oval light, moving silently above the field to the east of the picnic table, at Capel Green.

This object is one of several strange images that have appeared on photographs we have taken at the forest, over the years; I make no claims as to its identity, or origin. For all I know, there may be a natural explanation. As a keen amateur astronomer and lecturer on Astronautics and Meteoritic, I am completely familiar with the more normal things one would expect to see in the sky and remain intrigued as to the cause."

DISCLAIMER

In respect of the images in this volume, which include sketches, photographs and personal memorabilia, obtained over many years' research, we have tried our utmost to identify exactly who individual copyright lies with. Should we have got it wrong, we unreservedly apologise and will credit the copyright in *Haunted Skies* Volume 9. Last, but not least, our thanks go to Robert Townshend for his hand painted images which he has submitted for use in this volume.

INDEX

(Also includes source references)

C

COPYRIGHT/PERMISSIONS

Page 231 – © (photo) author unknown

Page 231 – © (drawing of craft) author unidentified

Page 233 – © (image) David Sankey, 2006

Page 234 – © (photo) Brenda Butler

Page 235 – © (image) David Sankey, 2006

Page 235 – © (photo of UFO) www, 2013

Page 239 – © (photos) *Sky Crash* (1983) Randles/Butler/Street

Page 240-241 – © (photos) Brenda Butler/John Hanson

Page 242 – © (photo) David Bryant, 2012

Page 244-246 – © (photo) Charles Affleck, SCUFORI, 1980

Page 247, 248 – © (photos) Brenda Butler, 2013

Page 251 – © (photos) Jim Penniston/John Burroughs, www, 2013

Page 252 – © (photo) Philip Mantle, 2013

Page 252 – © (sketch) author unknown

Page 253 – © (sketch) Jim Penniston

Page 254 – © (sketch) John Burroughs

Page 255, 256 – © (images) Wayne Mason, 2012

Page 257 – © (photo) Colonel Charles Halt

Page 259 – © (photo) Dennis Porley, 2012

Page 260 – © (photo) Jason Chapman, 2012

Page 261-264 – © (letters) David King, 2006

Page 267 – © (photo) Nick Pope, 2012

Page 269 – © (photo of scene) www.internet, 2013

Page 269 – © (photo) James Penniston, 2012

Page 271 – © (image) Colin Saunders, 2012

Page 272 – © (symbols) David Sankey

Page 272 – © (image) David Sankey, 2006

Page 273 – © (sketch) Colin Saunders, 2012

Page 275 – © (booklet) Chris Pennington, 2010

Page 275 – © (photo) John Hanson, 2008

Page 276 – © (photo) Robert Hastings, 2012

Page 278, 279 – © (photos) Larry Warren

Page 280 – © (photo) Nick Pope, 2012

Page 282 – © (letter) John Hanson, 2010

Page 282 – © (photos) John Hanson, 2010

Page 283 – © (image) David Sankey, 2006

Page 283 – © (sketches) Derek Samson, 1969

Page 284 – © (sketches) Larry Warren, 1980

Page 286 – © (photo) Chris Whitewick, 1979

Page 287 – © (sketch) Steve Roberts, March 1981

Page 287 – © (sketches) *Sky Crash*

Page 292 – © (photo) John Hanson, 2012

Page 294 – © (photo) Simon Sharman, 2012

Page 295 – © (image) David Sankey, 2006

Page 296 – © (photo) www.internet, 2013

Page 297 – © (photo) David Bryant, 2010

Page 299-302 – © (maps) Brenda Butler, 1980

Page 299 – © (photo) www.internet, 2013

Page 302 – © (photo) Dawn Holloway, 2002

Page 304 – © (photo inset) Erica Williams

Page 304 – © (photo) John Hanson, 2005

Page 306 – © (photo) www.internet, 2013

Page 310 – © (photo) Brenda Butler

Page 312 – © (photo) John Hanson, 2006

Page 312 – © (photo) Disclosure Project, 2012

Page 316 – © (photo) Gerry Harris, 1983

Page 320 – © (photo) Elaine Waite, 1997

Page 320 – © (photo) www.internet, 2013

Page 323 – © (photo) Chuck Daldorf, www.internet, 2013

Page 326 – © (photo) Harry Harris, 1980

Page 327 – © (photo) John Hanson, 2006

Page 328 – © (image) David Sankey, 2006

Page 329 – © (photo) John Hanson

Page 330 – © (photo) Agatha Maitland, 2006

Page 331 – © (photos) *National Museum of American History*, 2013

Page 334 – © (photo) Brenda Butler, 2010

Page 340 – © (photo) Graham Birdsall, 1995

Page 342 – © (photo) Gary Baker, www.internet, 2013

Page 344 – © Ralph Noyes interview, Dr. David Clarke, 2013

Page 344 – © (photo) Brenda Butler, 1980s

Page 346 – © (photo) John Hanson

Page 347 – © (photo) John Hanson, 2007

Page 347 – © (booklet) Chris Pennington

Page 350 – © (photos) David Bryant, 2013

Page 351 – © (photo) John Traylor, 2012

Page 351 – © (photo) John Hanson

EXAMINING THE EVIDENCE

AS we entered the final pages of this book, sightings of strange objects reported over RAF Woodbridge still continued to be the focus of our attention. Some of them seemed apparently inconsequential – worthy perhaps of further investigation at a later date; others demanded immediate further scrutiny, in order that at least we could try and separate the myths, disinformation, and occasional fabrication, which have wrapped itself around this story – now 33 years old.

Strange light seen, December 26th 1980

Strange lights and mysterious mists have been captured on camera in the sky over Rendlesham Forest, during recent years, many of which have been brought to the attention of the public (including mysterious falls of stones) in the forest. Another witness to strange luminous phenomena seen during December 1980, over the airbase, was security patrol officer Lori Buoen from Fridley, Minnesota. She was posted to RAF Woodbridge, following basic training at Lackland AFB, after leaving high school.

On December 26th 1980, Lori was on 'D' flight guard duty at the Woodbridge East Gate, and remembers Base Commander Ted Conrad bringing Christmas dinner to her and other members of the night shift.

Lori:

> *"While looking north over the Rendlesham Forest, from the small wooden East Gate guard shack in which I was standing, just after midnight on the 27th December 1980, I noticed a large, orange-red 'ball' of fiery light; it resembled three handfuls of coloured fire put together, as they flew through the sky – not blinking, but rotating – over towards RAF Woodbridge Control Tower, on my left, about a mile from the East Gate guard shack. It was heading in a straight north direction across the dark flight line above Rendlesham Forest, before descending slowly into the forest. At the east end of the runway was a UK residence, called the Folly House. About six miles straight east was the Orford Ness Lighthouse. This fiery sphere was in front of me on the north side of the runway, above the woods, where there is nothing but darkness from the trees, and, as I said before, the light just slowly disappeared (into the trees)."*

In addition to this, Lori remembers a radio conversation held between security Police Lt. Bonnie Tamplin, Master Sergeant Ball, and others, talking on air, during the same shift.

Lori Buoen with colleague c1980

"From the way in which radio protocol was broken they were frightened and calling each other by first names, such as 'Bob Bob', where are you? I remember wishing I had brought a cassette tape, so I could have recorded it. I found out that Bonnie had gone out into the woods to see what the lights were and her vehicle quit running. Some kind of blue light flew through her vehicle. She totally lost her composure and was so upset they sent her home for the evening."

She was not the only one; apparently Bob Ball was also to suffer some stress as a result of his experience – bad enough to seek medical assistance from a local hospital. (See page 399)

"All I know about Bonnie Tamplin is that she lives in Italy. If only I could find Joy Harper. She was my supervisor. I did contact Adrian Bustinza, two years ago; he didn't want to talk about it. He said he would share pictures with me, but we haven't talked much since."

Other accounts suggest Bonnie may have lost a loaded handgun, whilst out in the forest. Some people have speculated that the UFO story from the first night was used as a cover-up to give the USAF time to find a weapon. We discovered, from a reliable source, that she had lost an M-16 rifle presumably the weapon was recovered. The problem is that we haven't spoken to her personally, but we are hoping to do so and will update the reader in due course.

Bonnie Tamplin

According to the website (www.UFO Mystery.co.uk) John Burroughs, during an interview conducted in 2009, told of hitching a lift back to the airbase, while off duty, at 6am (27th December 1980?). He spoke to the desk sergeant, who told him:

"Whatever you saw was back tonight! He then spoke about how again they'd seen lights out in the forest. They had sent the shift commander out. She went out into the woods to see what the lights were again and her vehicle stopped running – some kind of blue light flew through her vehicle. She totally lost her composure, as it had upset her a lot, and they sent her home for the evening. At that point I decided I was going to go back out that night and see what went on. I hung out with some guys at the dorm. At that time we had no idea there was going to be another incident."

Statements taken: John Burroughs

Obviously, it was of importance to examine some of the original documents, submitted by the servicemen, following the reported UFO events, rather than statements obtained many months or years later, when on the night of 25-26 Dec at around 0300 while on patrol down at east gate myself & my partner saw lights comming from the woods due east of the gate. The lights were red & blue the red one above the blue one & they were flashing on & off. Because we never saw anything like that comming from the woods before we decided to drive down & see what it was. We went down east gate Road & took a right at the stop sign & drove down about 10 to 20 yards to where there is a road that goes into the forest. at the road I could see a white light shining onto the trees & I could still see the red & blue lights. we decided we better go call it in so we went back up towards east gate. I was watching the lights & the white light started comming down the road that lead into the forest. We got to the gate & called it in. The whole time I could see the lights & the white light was almost at the edge of the road & the blue & red lights were still out in the woods. a security unit was sent down to the gate & when they got there they could see it to. We asked permission to go & see what it was & they told us we could. We took the truck down the road that lead into the forest. as we went down the east gate Road & the road that lead into the forest the lights were moving back & they appeared to stop in _____ bunch of trees. We stopped our truck where the road stopped & went on foot. We crossed a small open field that lead into the trees where the lights were comming from & as we were comming into the trees there were strange noises, like a woman was screamin also the woods lit up & you could hear the farm animals making alot of noise & there was alot of movement in the woods. All three of us hit the ground & whatever it was started moving back towards the open field & after a min or 2 we got up & moved into the trees & the lights moved out into the open field. We got up to a fense that seperated the trees from the open field & you could see the lights down by a farmers house. We climbed over the fense & started walking towards the red & blue lights & they just disappeared. Once we reached the farmers house we could see a beacon going around so we went towards it. We followed it for about 2 miles before we could. It was comming from a lite house. We had just crossed a creek & were told to come back when we saw a blue light to our left in the trees. It was only there for a min & it just streaked away. After that we didn't see anything so we returned to the truck.

memories can fade or even play tricks. What shocked us as we slowly came to the end of this volume, was realising just how many people had been involved in this matter whose accounts we hadn't covered. This was sobering, and left us feeling slightly dispirited perhaps we should have made more space available, but where does it all end – if, in fact, there is an end to it all?

It is not our intention to take anyone to task because, at the end of the day, we were not there and to do so would imply criticism. Neither are we questioning anyone's account of what they witnessed, but we felt some comments should be made of the statements taken that are available so far.

First of all, we are curious as to why John Burroughs' statement was not countersigned by a supervising officer, and why it is not dated and signed. The sketch (see page 254) that accompanies his statement may give an impression that we are looking at a triangular object, sat on a base, from fairly close by, when, in fact, our interpretation is of a triangular swathe of light, seen from some distance away. In his sketch of the UFO, John describes the object as seen to move back and forth and up and down – a pattern of behaviour reported countless times throughout the years, but normally reported at some height rather than low down in the sky.

John has always denied seeing any 'craft' but says he saw a bank of lights that threw off an image like a craft (see page 252) not forgetting his interview with Phillip Mantle, a few years ago, when he told Phillip he had *"never been told to keep quiet, threatened or interrogated"* – only that he had been *"left out to dry"*, which presumably means he failed to receive the appropriate support from his senior officers. However, on page 257, John says that he was advised to keep quiet about what he had seen, after having reported to the Shift Commander's office. Burroughs was to later allege he was taken aboard, or been aboard the craft, according to Colonel Halt (see page 295) although this was not known about initially.

We emailed John Burroughs in July 2013 and asked him whether he was prepared to confirm the originality of his written statement. He told us, *"Nice try John, and you will have to wait for the book to come out just like everybody else. Oh and then you can add what we have to say to your book your working on. The problem is you will have to start from scratch after we release everything we know!"*

Following this exchange of information in late July 2013 our email account was blitzed by emails from John saying *'Goodbye tin soldier'* which we interpreted as rather childish.

John Burroughs

Jim Penniston

In Jim's short typewritten, undated and unsigned statement, he doesn't mention the *lighthouse at all. He confirms his closest approach to the object was 50 metres and that he and John were 15-20 metres apart,

---

*Georgina Bruni says, on pages 272 to 273 of her book, *"I would hope there is now enough of a reason to dispel the theory that the lighthouse was the culprit. Having been presented with more facts, both Vince Thurkettle and former policeman †Dave King have reconsidered their original theory and have now admitted they are no longer certain that it was the lighthouse the witnesses saw. Let us also consider the testimonies of the witnesses themselves. Adrian Bustinza was forced into agreeing it was the lighthouse when interrogated by special agents. Edward Cabansag denies he typed the witness statement, which claims they were chasing a lighthouse beacon. Charles Halt, Jim Penniston, John Burroughs and others are in no doubt that the lighthouse was not what they saw. Therefore, it looks as if the sceptics will have to turn to the AFOSI for support on this matter."*

†(See 1998 newspaper article about Dave King on page 526 Scrapbook)

STATEMENT

Received dispatch from CSC to rendzvous with Police 4 AIC Burroughs, and Police 5 SSgt Seffens at east gate Woodbridge. Upon arriving at east gate directly to the east about 1 ¼ miles in a large wooded area. A large yellow glowing light was emitting above the trees.(refer diagram) In the center of the lighted area directly in the center ground level, there was a red light blinking on and off 5 to 10 sec intervals. And a blue light that was being for the most part steady. After receiving permission from CSC, we proceeded off base pass east gate, down an old logging road. Left vehicle proceeded on foot . Bonroughs and I were approx. 15-20 meters apart and proceeding on a true east direction. from the logging road. The area in front of us was lighting up a 30 meter area. When we got with in a 50 meter distance. The object was producing red and bl ue light. The blue light was steady and projecting under the object. It was lighting up the area directly under IMexstending a meter or two out. At this point of positive identi- fication I relayed to CSC, SSgt Coffey. Postitive siting of object...1..color of lights and that it was defidently mechaniclal in nature. This is the closes point that I was near the objet at any point. We then proceeded after it. It moved in a zig-zagging manner back through the wood then lost site of it. On the way back we encounterd a blue streaking light to left lasting only a few seconds. After a 45 min wal k arrived at our vehicle.

while walking through the forest. The sketches drawn by Jim show a box-shaped object, on what appear to be legs or stilts, and was described as being a mechanical object. There is also another sketch, endorsed with the words *'glowing, yellow object'* that appears to accompany the unsigned statement.

Georgina Bruni had actually already asked Jim Penniston about this in her book – *You Can't Tell The People,* on page 183. She says: *"The following typed statement is part of the file of alleged witness statements that were officially made for Lieutenant Colonel Charles I. Halt, in January 1981. When I told Jim Penniston of its existence, he told me, 'My statement was handwritten; if the one you have is typed, then it was not done by me'. After sending him a copy of the typed statement, he responded: 'Statement seems original in content; however, the original was not typed. I think Halt summarized statement'."*

Some people have remarked on the difference between this apparent original version of events and the more up-to-date statement reproduced by him; an example being one which was submitted for the *National Press Club*, Washington D.C., in November 2007, as used in the documentary *'I Know What I Saw'*, produced and directed by James Fox. Participants involved included Jim, Charles Halt, and over a dozen others.

JAMES PENNISTON

My name is James Penniston, United States Air Force Retired.

In 1980, I was assigned to the largest Tactical Fighter Wing in the Air Force, RAF Woodbridge in England. I was the senior security officer in charge of base security.

At that time I held a top-secret US and NATO security clearance and was responsible for the protection of war-making resources for that base.

Shortly after midnight on the 26th of December, 1980, Staff Sergeant Steffens briefed me that some lights were seen in Rendlesham Forest, just outside the base. He informed me that what ever it was didn't crash…it landed. I discounted what he said and reported to the control center back at the base that we had a possible downed aircraft. I then ordered Amn. Cabanzak, AIC Burroughs to respond with me.

When we arrived near the suspected crash site it quickly became apparent that we were not dealing with a plane crash or anything else we'd ever responded to. There was a bright light emanating from an object on the forest floor. As we approached it on foot, a silhouetted triangular craft about 9 feet long by 6.5 feet high, came into view. The craft was fully intact sitting in a small clearing inside the woods.

As the three of us got closer to the craft we started experiencing problems with our radios. I then asked Cabansag to relay radio transmissions back to the control center. Burroughs and I proceeded towards the craft.

When we came up on the triangular shaped craft there were blue and yellow lights swirling around the exterior as though part of the surface and the air around us was electrically charged. We could feel it on our cloths, skin and hair. Nothing in my training prepared me for what we were witnessing.

After ten minutes without any apparent aggression, I determined the craft was non hostile to my team or to the base. Following security protocol, we completed a thorough on-site investigation, including a full physical examination of the craft. This included photographs, notebook entries, and radio relays through airman Cabansag to the control center as required. On one side of the craft were symbols that measured about 3 inches high and two and a half feet across.

These symbols were pictorial in design; the largest symbol was a triangle, which was centered in the middle of the others. These symbols were etched into the surface of the craft, which was warm to the touch and felt like metal.

The feeling I had during this encounter was no type of aircraft that I've eve seen before.

After roughly 45 minutes the light from the craft began to intensify. Burroughs and I then took a defensive position away from the craft as it lifted off the ground without any noise or air disturbance. It maneuvered through the trees and shot off at an unbelievable rate of speed. It was gone in the blink of an eye.

In my logbook, (that I have right here) I wrote, Speed: IMPOSSIBLE. Over 80 Air Force Personnel, all trained observers assigned to the 81st Security Police Squadron, witnessed the takeoff.

The information acquired during the investigation was reported through military channels. The team and witnesses were told to treat the investigation as "top secret" and no further discussion was allowed.

The photos we retrieved from the base lab (two rolls of 35 mm) were apparently over exposed.

© James Fox

Jim said this at the National Press Club

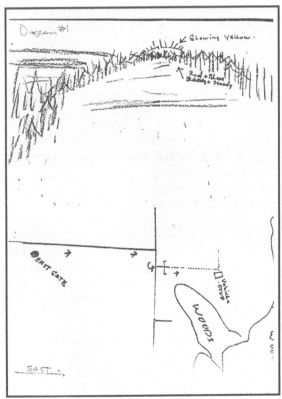

"We completed a thorough on-site investigation, including a full physical examination of the craft. This included photographs, notebook entries, and radio relays through airman Cabansag to the control center, as required. On one side of the craft were symbols that measured about three inches high and two and a half feet across. These symbols were pictorial in design; the largest symbol was a triangle, which was centered in the middle of the others. These symbols were etched into the surface of the craft, which was warm to the touch and felt like metal."

Likewise, the object originally drawn by Jim, in his sketch (see page 253) appears different from the sketch endorsed 27th December 1980, with Jim's home address, showing top front and side view of the object, which he advised us was not in the public domain.

In late July 2013, we e-mailed Jim and asked him if he was willing to clarify this situation. Jim confirmed the typewritten document was not his original statement. He did, however, promise information would be made available in the book *Encounter At Rendlesham Forest* being prepared by himself, Nick Pope and John Burroughs, which would include previously unpublished, official statements, taken by the investigating officers, following the event having taken place.

Charles Halt, 2013:

> *"None of the original statements given to me were classified. In fact, nothing I know of was classified. I do more than suspect there was a lot of behind the scenes investigation that was classified but I was never privy to that."*

While admittedly having no access to any original signed statements, we should bear in mind the content of the first paragraph, outlined in Colonel Halt's memo, following interviews with James Penniston and John Burroughs, shortly after the event (although not named at the time). This, to some degree, corroborates Jim Penniston's account of his encounter with a metallic, triangular-shaped object in the forest. However, there is no information identifying the distance involved, during the pursuit of the UFO, and whether physical contact was made.

Ted Conrad remarks on Penniston and Burroughs

Previously in this book (see page 288) we reported that the *Daily Mail* (8.8.2011) published details of an interview, held between researcher Dr. Dave Clarke and Colonel Ted Conrad, with regard to Penniston and Burroughs' account, when they followed an unidentified light through the trees, which disappeared behind a low rise in the direction of a farmhouse.

Ted Conrad:

> *"There was no mention of an encounter, or a notebook. Penniston said he didn't get close enough for a detailed look."*

Jim's facebook entry response to Conrad

Jim Penniston of the 'Justice For The Bentwaters 81st Security Police' facebook.com – 11th August 2011 – 1.13am made this response:

> *"Thank you for indirectly posting something on this page. Good Grief, I see that you have bitten off too much with this one . . . David some advice. Remember David, short dogs don't run through tall weeds. An old saying I have, and I think that it applies with you . . . The other piece of advice is: 'If you tell the truth, you don't have to remember anything.' You must have forgotten about your emails where you said you did not have permission to publish Colonel Conrad's private letter.*
>
> *We are not upset with anyone. We are pretty used to the B.S. and s.o.s. from the skeptics and naysayers . . . Let me remind you why we are a little disappointed about your lack of integrity. I guess you have to stick with your story since you got caught telling something that was not true.*
>
> *As for the Conrad letter that was written to you (original, unaltered) we are fine with it. We always have been . . . ever since its unauthorized publishing back in the fall of 2010. Colonel*

Conrad was very supportive of us in the letter. He told as much as he could. I think everyone forgets the details of this incident are still classified and remain classified. So it restricts how much these officers can actually tell . . . He was somewhat hard with Halt though. David we have many emails from you and others . . . I think the public would be shocked with the way you and others do business. We must think about making these public. That will be an eye opener for your paying public, I am sure.

As far as the extraordinary things, which have happened with us and Rendlesham, you will have to wait until we figure out a format for that release. Your first and biggest mistake is, Rendlesham is not about UFOs (ET/Alien) and never was.

David, let's bring these issues you claim on our page public . . . for everyone to hear and evaluate. How about an international radio or a national TV show. We will consist of John and I . . . and you can bring Colonel Conrad with you since you think you have some kind of relationship that transcends our military relationship with him, and what he has told us. I think you would be very surprised what he would say if he actually went on the record. I personally would like Rob Simcox radio program to do it . . . Or we can go face-to-face in a television studio. The choice is yours.

So let's arrange something, David. And as far as your childish comments of mob action and such, I think what you really mean is, I like to throw stones from the keyboard, but, I can then retreat behind the keyboard at any time and hide, without being responsible for what I say . . . Keep in mind, we are only responding to disinformation which has been placed in British papers and the internet. You don't have to remind us that this is the way you make your living . . . But, what we are saying, you're not going to publish rubbish and make money out of our situation by making things up and doctoring documents to meet your marketing needs . . . We will not allow it any more . . ." Jim.

With regard to Jim's comments, as above, we believe that he is not referring to any military covert aircraft, satellite re-entries, or downed Russian aircraft, but to visits from human beings from the future. Georgina made a reference to this matter on page 181, from her book – *You Can't Tell The People.*

"The most amazing part of the regression deals with an alien encounter at the scene of the incident. When asked about the possibility of being present, Penniston begins to talk about 'the visitors'. He describes them as being from our future, a dark and polluted world with many difficulties. He explains that they are visiting in teams and each team is assigned a different task. Apparently, the teams know exactly which people they are to target when they arrive in our time. Penniston reveals that some of them are coming here to take sperm and eggs, which are necessary in order to help their species survive. It seems they have a serious problem with reproduction . . ."

During the December 2010 event held at Woodbridge Hall, Suffolk, we were surprised when Jim claimed that, following his close encounter with the landed craft, he had written down in his notebook many pages of binary digits, received telepathically.

We asked him whether he had any opinions on where the *'craft'* had come from, bearing in mind his close proximity to the object and that he had undergone regression, in 1994. He told us he believes the *'craft'* is from the far off future and that it contained our distant descendants, returning as time travellers, to obtain genetic material to keep their ailing species alive.

We can neither disprove nor prove this hypothesis but whatever you believe, something extraordinary happened in the forest over the Christmas weekend, involving an object(s) that has made its appearance in our sky and on the ground, many times previously, worldwide. While some people feel they have the answers, the truth would probably defy our most vivid of imaginations. One thing is assured UFOs will continue to be reported, despite the MOD closing its desk.

Major Drury, who was interviewed some years previously by Georgina Bruni, as outlined in her book, *You Can't Tell The People*, had this to say:

Jim Penniston

"I was in the shift commander's office, but not technically on duty at the time, when some of them were making statements; there was a pile of them, because I recall going through some of them. On reading the statements, I understood that it was a very big object – bigger than a mini. There were marks in the trees quite high up, and someone said they had walked up to the object and it had left depressions. I went out the next day and saw the marks on the trees and the ground depressions, which weren't that deep, and I suggested we send someone to do some Geiger counter readings."

Georgina Bruni talking with the late Prime Minister, Margaret Thatcher, at a charity dinner party in spring 1997

Deep Throat

We asked Brenda about page 183 of *Sky Crash*, which showed an intriguing sketch endorsed *'based on the contents of the files of Colonel Halt'* from a *'deep throat source'* (deep throat is the pseudonym given to secret informants), wondering where this had come from, as it referred to the 29th/30th December 1980. Brenda thought it may have been John Burroughs' sketch.

We contacted Colonel Halt, who denied ever having seen it. The only sketch he associated with John Burroughs was the one submitted by him, which has been previously shown in this book.

We emailed Jenny Randles about the identity of the sketch in late July 2013.

"Something at the back of my mind suggests it came from one of the face-to-face meetings that Halt had, in June 1983, with the small group of people who met him then. I was not one of them and did not know these meetings had occurred until Dot told me, a few weeks later. Allegedly, the Halt tape was played there also – a year before it was ever released to anyone – though the description of what was supposedly on it seems wrong. If I recall this was a sketch one of those attendees did, based upon the testimony they were shown during a visit to Halt from then unreleased evidence like the tape held on base. So not actually (a fake) a sketch directly by a witness but based on the account of a witness then not in the public

domain (which in June 1983 was still pretty well everything). I think it is meant to portray the part on the tape where the lights 'explode' from the winking eye. It is certainly from the Saturday night – Halt reconnaissance site encounter – not the Burroughs/Penninston episode."

Mike Sacks

Knowing about the 'hush hush' meeting with Colonel Halt, by Harry Harris and Mike Sacks (page 335), we asked Mike if he had any knowledge of this, in July 2013, feeling that it was important to clarify the author of the sketch – for all we knew, it might have been one of the servicemen involved, if so it would have been a vital piece of evidence. We were delighted to hear that it was, indeed, Mike's . . .

> *"Well I appreciate that time has passed; it's now over 30 years ago, but I feel that inexplicably, for whatever reason, we were totally written out of the loop. Harry and I went down there, after the initial enquiries made by Brenda and Dot (who were banned from the base, at one point).*
>
> *When Charles Halt played the audio tape to us, I remember another Commander was there; I think his name was *Jack. The tape was played and we had a chat in Colonel Halt's office afterwards. When I arrived home I drew the sketch from the description given on the tape. Tim Good also used the sketch in his book, 'Need To Know' (page 331)."*

(*Jack being Colonel Jack Cochran). (The date is not included in this version).

Mark Birdsall, Harry Harris and Jenny Randles at a YUFOS Conference

Brenda also sent us a document which we believe to contain alleged details of a telephone conversation made with Colonel Sam Morgan on the 30th of December 1984 by Philip J Klass (November 8, 1919 – August 9, 2005) who was an American engineer, journalist and UFO researcher, known for his scepticism regarding UFOs. Klass, declared that "roughly 98 percent of people who report seeing UFOs are fundamentally intelligent, honest people who have seen something – usually at night, in darkness – that is unfamiliar, that they cannot explain." The rest, he said, were frauds.

HIGHLIGHTS OF TELCON with Col. Sam Morgan   12/30/84 :

1. Incident happened before Morgan got there, as Base Commander. At time of incident,
    Col. Conrad was base commander and Lt. Col. Halt was deputy.

2. Going thru desk, found dictaphone tape recording, decided to listen before erasing.
    "I called Halt in and said what the hell is that about, and he said well he really
    didn't want to talk about it. I said well that's really not one of the choices.
    So he told me about it, I listened to the tape (again), talked to a number of guys
    and decided there wasn't anything to it.

3. When I left England, I dumped all the stuff in a box. ...guy named Harry Harris called
    me 8 months ago...so I sent him copy of the tape...he sold to Japanese, they tell me,
    for 20 grand.

4. Thing supposedly landed outside the base. Bentwaters and Woodbridge are about 7 miles
    apart, and Rentlewood Forest is in-between. The guy on the gate at Woodbridge said he
    saw something going on in the forest, but he didn't have any authority to go out and do
    anything about it. Well, Halt rounded up a few guys, the next night or so they're out
    there messing around in the forest. And they took a guy named Nettles, who was a
    disaster preparedness NCO and he takes along a geiger counter, and they take along a
    couple of cops and they take along one of these starlight scopes.

    And Halt has this tape recorder in his pocket and he has this thing running. So
    you can hear them, Neveills says he's reading .05 roentgens, well, shoot, that's
    background radiation. Then you've got the guys looking through the starlight scope
    and they're ohing and ah-ing about this and that, and while they're doing that they
    see a light and they suspect whatever it was it is now coming back. Well they take a
    look at it thru the starlight scope--and any kind of light at all will overwhelm
    a starlight scope, so they get this blacked out circle in the middle of the image
    and you hear them talking about it looks like a giant winking eye--just exactly what
    you get....

5. Subsequently three of the enlisted troops, who just casually knew about it, left the
    service. And these guys got with the British people...(PJK recounts Warren's story)
    Those guys, they're just making that up. They're now telling people about a triangular,
    shaped, metallic spaceship . Fact of the matter is that Halt wrote it down in a 2 or
    3 piece of paper, he gave it to squadron leader Don Moreland, who was the RAF base
    commander.

    As far as U.S. was concerned, that was the end of it. Halt really had no authority
    out there in that forest that night anyhow. So he was a kind of hobby-est on his own
    our lurking around. When I first became aware of it and looked into it I concluded
    that it was just a bunch of guys screwing around in the woods. Fact that Don Moreland
    knew about it so the proper channels had been informed. So that's the last I heard of
    it until I started getting all these calls from England and this guy Harris took the
    (tape) and sold it to the Japanese

    (discuss his skepticism and mine, he was former fighter pilot

Bob Tibbitts – Consultant for *Haunted Skies*, comments

*"It is said that Conrad has claimed the whole 'UFO incident' was a 'hoax' but, at the same
time, we are being advised that matters pertaining to these events are 'classified' and cannot
be commented on further.*

*So, if it was a hoax, as some people allege, why is it still classified and not included in
the recent MOD release of files? This indicates that it is, indeed, classified and as such,
something that cannot be released to the public.*

Could the 'hoax' refer to stories about UFOs being propagated to camouflage an incident that was deemed very sensitive then, and still is? Why would the MOD classify a hoax? Why would radar tapes 'go missing'? Would cine film have been taken by a base photographer within the woodland area without the aid of lightalls (which were said to be malfunctioning)?

Was the helicopter activity, during this Christmas period, routine? What of the photograph of a 'part' inside a helicopter and claims of an object suspended beneath a helicopter that collided with runway lights? What of the claims of parts being sent to and received from Sembach, Germany?

Was the visit by General Gabriel a scheduled event, or merely a Christmas time social call? If not, what was his visit all about? Why did Charles Halt supply 'sandwiches' to Burroughs at a time when he was said to have been absent and 'living' in the woods? Was Burroughs legitimately on leave, or was he asked to stay in the woods by Charles Halt for some unspecified purpose.

Why would Sgt. Penniston state that it was never about UFOs ('Rendlesham is not about UFOs and never was') but then state that he saw symbols on the side of a 'craft' and that he received certain binary codes directly into his mind and made drawings in his notepad of a craft? If he claims it isn't about UFOs, one can only assume that the 'craft' was identified. Bearing in mind comments made by Ted Conrad: 'Penniston said he didn't get close enough for a detailed look'.

If it was recognised as a craft of earthly origin (or from the future, as Jim believes) then perhaps there had been some reason for it to be in the airbase vicinity and so stories of UFOs were encouraged by certain agencies to cover that fact. Who was it that reported seeing 'aliens' in the vicinity of the craft? Were these 'aliens' actually 'known' to the authorities and so, therefore, posed no security threat?

Was the Russian presence in the air an indication that they were very interested in the 'craft' and its origin and purpose near to a nuclear-weapons equipped airbase at a time of heightened cold war sensitivities? Or was this merely a routine, regular patrol near to our airspace, and merely a coincidence? If the incident is still classified, then there must be a good reason for it to be so . . . and not necessarily because there may or may not have been UFO activity. Of course, it is quite possible that 'both' could have been the cause of all the activity, a prototype aircraft and a craft from 'elsewhere'!

As in other cases where nuclear missiles were said to have been affected by the presence of 'unknown lights', are there any known documents that have been released, showing that the weapons stored at Woodbridge/Bentwaters were compromised in any way? If they had been, then that is a 'good reason' for the incident to remain classified.

There seems to be an ever-increasing deluge of questions about all of this. There is no definitive, clearly-stated, 'cause' that can be identified as the reason for the events at Rendlesham . . . if there is one, then I guess that this remains 'classified' and probably with valid reasoning. Of course, if it is 'classified', then Nick Pope, James Penniston, and John Burroughs, can only really fuel further speculation . . . because they cannot break their security oaths – or can they?"

David Bryant

Another piece of vital evidence, which was re-examined and appears to support the events involving Jim and John, came from Mr Porley (see page 259). We asked David Bryant what he believed Dennis had seen.

"Assuming that Mr Porley's account is accurate (and that his recollection of dates and times are correct) it doesn't sound like any meteor or fireball I've ever seen or heard of! Some points:

1 – The object he witnessed seems to have followed a similar W-E path to the one reported 24 hours earlier, which was apparently observed for five minutes or so.

2 – From when he first saw the object, Porley travelled around 3km before stopping: he then watched it descending in the east, over Hollesley. Assuming a speed of around 60kph, this sighting would also have lasted around five minutes. Bit of a coincidence, isn't it? – TWO fireballs on the same trajectory, a day apart?

3 – Porley's object seems to have moved quite slowly: I would have thought a meteor (which would typically travel between 10 and 70km per SECOND!) would have taken no more than 10 or 15 seconds to have travelled from the southern horizon (at Mistley) to the eastern, at Hollesley Bay.

Some years ago, I witnessed a brilliant green fireball descending from S-N over the North Sea, before exploding: it took no more than five seconds to travel 2/3 of the way across the sky. The same is true of a re-entering satellite, which might travel at 30,000kph (around eight km per second).

The British Astronomical Association Meteor Section Newsletter No. 4, dated February 1981, contains a brief report on the fireball that apparently sparked the Rendlesham Forest UFO incident. The BAA report notes that this fireball was seen at 02.50 UT (five minutes) on Boxing Day 1980, by four witnesses, locations not given but seemingly in southern England, all of whom estimated its brightness as comparable to the gibbous (i.e. three-quarter) moon and of three to four seconds duration.

In that bare information lays the genesis of one of the most celebrated UFO cases of all time. The identification of the object seen falling over Essex, on the 25th December, as the top stage of the Cosmos 749 launch rocket, has always struck me as a bit dubious; scientists love being able to put names to things!"

Master Sergeant J.D. Chandler

In his statement, dated 2nd January 1981, there is a reference to a conversation held with Jim Penniston, involving misidentification later made with the beam of the lighthouse, following the initial sighting of the mysterious lights. He confirms Jim told him it was a mechanical object, and gives a distance away from the object as being 50 metres.

STATEMENT OF WITNESS

_____ (Place)

2 ꞁꞔꞗꞇ 1981
_____ (Date)

I, ___J.D. CHANDLER, mSgt. USAF___, hereby state that

~~has identified himself to me~~

as _____ USAF.

(Special Agent AFOSI, Security Police, Other--Specify)

I do hereby voluntarily and of my own free will make the following statement without having been subjected to any coercion, unlawful influence or unlawful inducement.

At approximately 0300 hrs, 26 December 1980 while conducting security checks on RAF Bentwaters, I monitored a radio transmission from AIC Burroughs, Law Enforcement patrol on RAF Woodbridge, stating that he was observing strange lights in the wooded area just beyond the access road, leading from the east gate at RAF Woodbridge. SSgt Penniston, Security Supervisor, was contacted and directed to contact Burroughs at the east gate. Upon arrival, Sgt Penniston immediately notified CSC that he too was observing these lights and requested to make a closer observation. After several minutes, Penniston requested my presence. I departed RAF Bentwaters through Butley gate for RAF Woodbridge. When I arrived, SSgt Penniston, AIC Burroughs, and Amn Cabansag had entered the wooded area just beyond the clearing at the access road. We set up a radio relay between SSgt Penniston, myself, and CSC. On one occasion Penniston relayed that he was close enough to the object to determine that it was definitely a mechanical object. He stated that he was within approximately 50 meters. He also stated that their was lots of noises in the area which seemed to be animals running around. Each time Penniston gave me the indication that he was about to reach the area where the lights were, he would give an extended estimated location. He eventually arrived at a "beacon light", however, he stated that this was not the light or lights he had originally observed. He was instructed to return. While enroute out of the area, he reported seeing lights again almost in direct pass where they had passed earlier. Shortly after this, they reported that the lights were no longer visable. SSgt Penniston returned to RAF Woodbridge. After talking to the three of them, I was sure that they had observed something unusual. At no time did I observe anything from the time I arrived at RAF Woodbridge.

AF FORM 1169 PREVIOUS EDITION WILL BE USED   Page 1 of _____ Pages

CONTINUATION SHEET FOR AF FORM 1168 and 1169.

I further state that I have read this entire statement, initialed all pages and corrections, and signed this statement, and that it is correct and true as written.

WITNESSES:

F.D. Chandley
(Signature)

81 Security Police Sq
(Address)

Subscribed and sworn to before me, a person authorized by law to administer oaths, this

_____
(Signature)

_____
(Address)

_____ day of _____ 19 ___

at _____

_____
(Signature)

(Signature of Person Administering Oath.)

_____
(Address)

(Type Name, Grade & Title of Person Administering Oath.)

U.S. GOVERNMENT PRINTING OFFICE: 1977-241-130/1322

STATEMENT OF WITNESS

Bldg 679, RAF Bentwaters

2 Jan 1981 *(Place)*

(Date)

I, _____ Fred A. Buran _____, hereby state that ~~has identified himself to me~~

as _____ USAF.

(Special Agent AFOSI, Security Police, Other-Specify)

I do hereby voluntarily and of my own free will make the following statement without having been subjected to any coercion, unlawful influence or unlawful inducement. The following statement is general in nature and may be inaccurate in some instances due to the time lapse involved and the fact that I was not taking notes at the time of the occurrence. At approximately 0300 hrs, 26 December 1980, I was on duty at bldg 679, Central Security Control, when I was notified that A1C Burroughs had sighted some strange lights in the wooded area east of the runway at RAF Woodbridge.

Shortly after this initial report A1C Burroughs was joined by SSgt Penniston and his rider, AMN Cabansag. SSgt Penniston also reported the strange lights. I directed SSgt Coffey, the on duty Security Controller, to attempt to ascertain from SSgt Penniston whether or not the lights could be marker lights of some kind, to which SSgt Penniston said that he had never seen lights of this color or nature in the area before. He described them as red, blue, white, and orange.

SSgt Penniston requested permission to investigate. After he had been joined by the Security Flight Chief, MSgt Chandler, and turned his weapon over to him, I directed them to go ahead. SSgt Penniston had previously informed me that the lights appeared to be no further than 100 yds from the road east of the runway.

I monitored their progress (Penniston, Burroughs, and Cabansag) as they entered the wooded area. They appeared to get very close to the lights, and at one point SSgt Penniston stated that it was a definite mechanical object. Due to the colors they had reported I alerted them to the fact that they may have been approaching a light aircraft crash scene. I directed SSgt Coffey to check with the tower to see if they could throw some light on the subject. They could not help.

SSgt Penniston reported getting near the "object" and then all of a sudden said they had gone past it and were looking at a marker beacon that was in the same general direction as the other lights. I asked him, through SSgt Coffey, if he could have been mistaken, to which Penniston replied that had I seen the other lights I would know the difference. SSgt Penniston seemed somewhat agitated at this point.

They continued to look further, to no avail. At approximately 0354 hrs, I terminated the investigation and ordered all units back to their normal duties.

I directed SSgt Penniston to take notes of the incident when he came in that morning. After talking with him face to face concerning the incident, I am convinced that he saw something out of the realm of explanation for him at that time. I would like to state at this time that SSgt Penniston is a totally reliable and mature individual. He was not overly excited, nor do I think he is subject to overreaction or misinterpretation of circumstances. Later that morning, after conversing with CPT Mike Verano, the day shift commander, I discovered that there had been several other sightings. Any further developments I have no direct knowledge of.

AF FORM 1169 PREVIOUS EDITION WILL BE USED

Page 1 of 2 Pages

CONTINUATION SHEET FOR AF FORM 1168 and 1169.

NOT USED

I further state that I have read this entire statement, initialed all pages and corrections, and signed this statement, and that it is correct and true as written.

WITNESSES:

Fred A Bryant
(Signature)

81 SECURITY POLICE SQUADRON
(Address)

_____
(Signature)

Subscribed and sworn to before me, a person authorized by law to administer oaths, this

_____
(Address)

_____ day of _____ 19 ___

_____
(Signature)

at _____

_____
(Address)

_____
(Signature of Person Administering Oath.)

_____
(Type Name, Grade & Title of Person Administering Oath.)

AF form 1170   ☆ U.S. GOVERNMENT PRINTING OFFICE: 1977-241-130/1323

Fred Buran

His statement, contained on Form AF 1168/1169 (witness suspect) is also dated 2nd January 1981. He confirms that Jim Penniston also described the object as mechanical and that they (Jim and John) went past the lights and later found they were looking at a marker beacon in the same general direction of the lights. When the men arrived back at the Base, Fred directed Jim Penniston to make notes of what had happened, and says he was convinced Jim had seen something out of the realm of explanation for him at that time. It seems strange that while this form appears to be specifically issued for recording witness/suspect incidents, it was not countersigned by a senior officer. One is also bound to wonder why there is no uniformity between this form and other documents used to record the incident.

Monroe Ruby Nevels

Sgt. Monroe Ruby Nevels, of the RAF Bentwaters Disaster Preparedness Office, was with Colonel Halt, in Rendlesham Forest, during the early morning of 28th December 1980 UFO incident, and can be heard on the tape made by Charles Halt. Monroe corroborated the events that unfolded in the forest and was responsible for operating the Geiger counter. Monroe also took numerous photographs of the lights and object; unfortunately these photographs, when developed by Monroe himself, were found to be fogged.

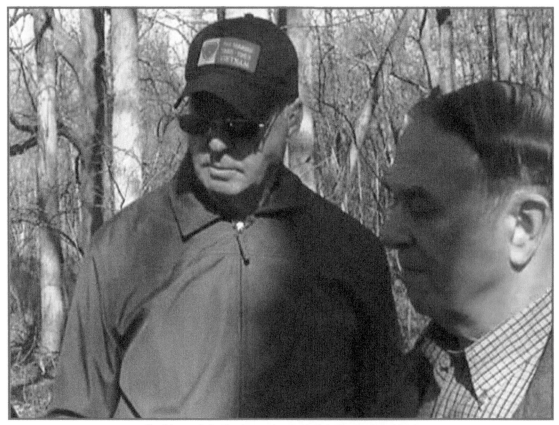

Sgt. Monroe Ruby Nevels seen here with Col. Charles Halt (right)

> *"There were three objects or lights. The largest light was the leading or command vessel. The lights were three vessels that moved independently of each other. They were moving and were able to jump from Woodbridge and show up over Bentwaters in less than a second. While the craft was on the ground, pieces of flying debris were being shed, which appeared to be like molten steel in a boiler pot. It seemed to get hotter as the object was approached."*

As the men crossed a farmer's field, the object seemed to head straight for them – then disappeared. This was followed by the sighting of three *'craft'*, visible in a grey-white sky. Colonel Conrad directed Monroe to scan the skies for several days after the incident.

Two days later, around 1300-1400hrs., Monroe spotted a series of bright lights approaching at a very high speed. These lights were moving so fast that it was difficult for him to obtain enough time to observe them. These lights were unlike the ones observed by Monroe on 28th December 1980. He never witnessed the lights again.

> *"I took photos with a Nikon F3 and a 105mm f/2.8 lens, with TriX @ ASA 400. I processed them myself in my home photo lab. They were fogged, and after a few years I realized the reason: Radiation detected around the sight and on the trees. This is why none of the photographs could be viewed. By the way, I was and am a Professional Photographer. I was methodical with my work, and as a Disaster Preparedness Tech., I knew and did my job professionally. I KNOW WHAT I SAW!"*

He reiterated, in a following email:

> *"Col. Halt and myself, along with the others on that night, saw, over to the left of the farmer's field, a yellowish object from a distance that looked as though it might be a very hot metal, or steel, burning at very high temperatures. It seemed to get brighter as we went over the fence, but suddenly was gone. As I looked up, I pointed out to Col. Halt they were in the sky. As I know how brightness can make the eye/brain think all sorts of things, I saw them moving, so to make sure my statement was accurate I lay down on my back, closed my eyes and opened them again, several times. They were indeed moving. There were three of them. And, as sure as they were there, they were gone; they were also seen overhead by an excited group at RAF Bentwaters"*

Major Malcolm Zickler

We emailed Colonel Halt, in August 2013, to tell him we had not been able to trace Bonnie Tamplin yet.

Charles Halt:

> *"Something happened to Bonnie, and that gave them an excuse to get rid of her. The real answer would be to find Edward Drury. He knows a lot and will probably talk. Major Mal Zickler screwed him, as he was a bright academy graduate and Zickler couldn't stand that."*

Lori Rehfeldt:

> *"Major Zickler was all about intimidation . . . you did not talk to him casually. He was not friendly. It is a shame that he railroaded so many airmen's careers. He was the cause of much bad feeling."*

According to Brenda Butler, she was told by Steve Roberts that Zickler – then Head of the Police – was sent back to the United States, after he failed to complete a clear-up operation of the landing site.

Georgina Bruni:

> *"Lt. Colonel Zickler retired from the USAF in 1989, and lives with his wife in Florida. He runs a business called 'Woodbridge Engineering'. The fear imposed upon those individuals connected with the incident is still embedded deep in their minds. Major Edward Drury remembers exactly how he was silenced."*

In April 1990, a copy of the police log was retrieved from the files of the *History of the 81st Tactical Fighter Wing, Maxwell AFB, Alabama*. Several incidents were recorded but no mention of any UFO or aircraft accident. We will attempt to obtain an interview with Bonnie, in due course. If we are successful, it will be published as an update in *Haunted Skies* Volume 9.

It was also suggested that Major Malcolm Zickler ordered Sgt. James Penniston to report to the Air Force Office of Special Investigations (AFOSI) for a meeting, to tell his story to an AFOSI Special Agent and a US Air Force Major. Although officially AFOSI were not involved, others claim that he led the investigation into The Rendlesham Forest Incident – which one imagines would have been correct, if Head of Police Security at the time.

Major Malcolm Zickler

Georgina Bruni herself describes the AFOSI agents as having a lot of power, with the ability to detain virtually anyone in the force, including very senior officers. No wonder many of the young airmen were reluctant to tell their stories afterwards. It seems, from the accounts given by some of the airmen involved, that those alleged interviews were conducted vigorously and included being given injections of *Sodium Pentothal (after permission had been sought) – the trauma of which is still being experienced to this present day.

On page 301 of *Sky Crash*, we learn that Larry Fawcett, and Dot Street (during her visit to the United States with Jenny Randles) telephoned Malcolm Zickler (now a retired Lt. Colonel) while in Florida, to interview him regarding the allegation made that he had cleared the landing site by removing all traces. He was not in, but his wife Linda was. When they told her of the nature of their enquiry, she replied, *"Oh, you mean the UFO landing?!"* During a discussion that lasted about 90 minutes, Mrs Zickler confirmed she and some of the officers' wives had seen the damage to the tree, although according to her, the big event was on the first night and some photos had been taken.

---

*Sodium thiopental, also known as Sodium Pentothal (a trademark of Abbott Laboratories), thiopental, thiopentone, or Trapanal (also a trademark), is a rapid-onset short-acting barbiturate general anesthetic. Sodium thiopental is a core medicine in the World Health Organization's essential drugs List, which is a list of minimum medical needs for a basic healthcare system. It is also usually the first of three drugs administered during most lethal injections in the United States. Thiopental (Pentothal) is still used in some places as a truth serum to weaken the resolve of the subject and make them more compliant to pressure. The barbiturates as a class decrease higher cortical brain functioning. Some psychiatrists hypothesize that because lying is more complex than telling the truth, suppression of the higher cortical functions may lead to the uncovering of the truth. The drug tends to make subjects loquacious and cooperative with interrogators; however, the reliability of confessions made under thiopental is questionable. Sodium thiopental features as a truth serum in several Hollywood films, in comics and other literature, and even in popular music. Psychiatrists have used thiopental to desensitize patients with phobias, and to facilitate the recall of painful repressed memories. In 1963 the USA Supreme Court ruled that a confession produced under the influence of truth serum was unconstitutionally coerced, and therefore inadmissible. We presume this would also cover witness testimonial evidence obtained by these means as well. **(Source: Wikipedia 2013)**

The couple then telephoned Colonel Sawyer, who also was not available, but his wife spoke to them and confirmed having seen the damaged tree and that she, herself, had taken children into the forest to look for UFOs and that in early January 1981, had taken some cine film of a light in the forest. When they asked her to send the film to them, Mrs Sawyer appeared to change her mind and suggested it might have been the Moon! She promised to send the film to Larry Fawcett but this never happened.

On New Year's Eve, there was a party in the forest. Around 15 people were looking for UFOs. According to Mrs Sawyer an airman was arrested for taking drugs and sent home. (Not forgetting that Brenda and Dot were told by local farmer – Mr Boast, and his wife – that the police told the 'Boasts' they had been investigating a drugs party in the forest, when a deer had been shot.)

Colonel Halt:

> *"I am aware of this information. Mrs Sawyer came on to the scene a few days later. In my judgement the claims made by her that she had taken photos and seen things was unsubstantiated; you should take anything she says with some suspicion, unless proved otherwise. Zickler knew a lot more than he was ever willing to say. He was very much a guy that worked in the background at the base and I believed he would have liaised with the AFOSI and other British and American agents to provide a cover story to explain what had taken place. He had to know that John, Larry, Jim and Adrian, were messed with during the investigation held after the events."*

Malcolm Zickler was interviewed by Georgina Bruni, on 11th June 1998, and asked about his involvement.

> *"No I wasn't there on any night. I was advised on what they saw – an object. I went to the woods during the day and saw none of these things. When I knew Halt was out there I chose not to go, as I didn't see eye to eye with him. I was subordinate to him in rank, but I didn't work directly for him but for the base commander."*

He was asked what he thought happened in the forest, and replied:

> *"I don't know. Halt seemed to think this was a major problem. I knew he did a report, but I was not privy to that and I've no idea of the response to that."*

On another occasion he told Georgina:

> *"The consensus of those that investigated it – the AFOSI – came to the conclusion that 'something happened', but there was insufficient evidence."*

A different version of events was given by Adrian Bustinza in the book *Left At East Gate*.

Adrian who was interviewed by Larry Fawcett recalls an amusing incident involving Major Zickler, his squadron Commander, who stepped out of the jeep while alighting and fell into mud, much the amusement of the other servicemen. Adrian also recalls hearing Major Zickler saying *'scramble two'* a short time later. Adrian also says that he was later interviewed by Major Zickler and Lt Colonel Halt, and that he had three meetings with the base Commander.

Malcolm Zickler was in charge of the police and security at both airbases. It seems highly improbable in our opinion, bearing in mind his role, that he was unaware of the events which had taken place. One thing is assured – his wife seems to know far more of what went on than him!

Bob Tibbitts:

"Senior Master Sergeant Ray Gulyas and Captain Mike Verrano are said to have taken photographs, on December 26th, of the UFO landing site. Ray Gulyas shot a whole roll of film and handed it to Verrano, who sent it higher up the command structure. Ray was later then told the film was completely fogged. Two days later he returned and took further photographs as well as plaster casts for his own curiosity. He handed the film over to Richard Nunn. This film turned out fine.

In the spring of 1981, when returning to the US, the film, negatives and plaster casts, disappeared from his personal possessions. Bruni managed to get a contact strip of these shots. In one shot was a tall policeman. Ray's film also contained Mike Veranno. That was December 26!"

Claim of piece of metal found at Rendlesham landing site

In late July 2013, we entered into e-mail communication with Ronnie Dugdale – a laboratory technician and nurseryman, from Great Yarmouth. Ronnie has a long-standing personal interest in the UFO events reported to have taken place, in 1980, at Rendlesham Forest, and has more recently witnessed his friend – Brenda Butler – receiving and writing a binary download, during one of their night-time visits to the forest.

Brenda Butler has entrusted him to post many stories, entries and interviews, from her diaries and journals, on the *'Lone Ranger'* Facebook page. He is also the UK representative for Paul and Ben Eno's *'Behind The Paranormal'* radio show, and has been instrumental in introducing onto those shows many witnesses and investigators, including Brenda Butler.

In June 2013, while serving on his plant stall at Campsey Ashe market, in Suffolk, he struck up a conversation with a customer, when he noticed her American accent.

"I asked her if she was from one of the airbases and she told me she was once married to an American airman and now living at Wickham Market, but she had previously lived, for many years, near Rendlesham Forest. I asked her if she had seen any UFOs, to which she smiled and told me she hadn't but knew that others had. I then told her of my interest in the event that had taken place in the forest at the end of December 1980, and after exchanging pleasantries she left. On the same morning she returned and handed over to me a bright metal object, which looked aluminum in composition and appeared extremely light for its size. I asked her what it was, to which she replied 'It's from your UFO; it came from the field'."

Ronnie handed it back, but she told him to keep it. She said she had some '81st' ephemera that Ronnie might find interesting and then left. Ronnie cannot say whether she is a regular to the market or not, as he has only been trading at that market for a few weeks. He describes her as:

". . . smartly dressed, blond hair, well-spoken, and in her early sixties. She was wearing a distinctive red white and blue neckerchief, similar to what an air hostess would wear, so it may well have been a uniform. She paid for her plant and then left."

We discussed the matter with Brenda Butler, who agrees with us that there is no evidence at the present time to prove that this metallic object was recovered from Rendlesham Forest, 33 years ago, to which she agreed.

Even if we could prove the piece of metal was recovered on that date, and in that manner, it does not provide proof of anything, as the areas around RAF Woodbridge and Bentwaters must still be littered with parts of aircraft debris, understanding the role in which the runways played during the Second World War.

What is of interest is why this woman should wait 33 years before picking up the object from her house, and then handing it over. If the sample had been a lump of insignificant, irregular-shaped steel or iron, which could have come from anywhere, we would not have shown as much interest. However, the photographs of the piece of metal, sent to us by Ronnie, appear to have superficial similarities with other incidents involving alleged pieces of metal recovered after UFO sightings.

Ronnie is open-minded about the artefact and makes no claims as to its authenticity, but he believes that the charming and friendly woman was genuine and disagrees with our suggestion that her actions were deliberately orchestrated to disseminate false disinformation about the incident, and points out that it was he who entered her into conversation regarding Rendlesham, rather than the other way around.

He is convinced that had he not brought up in their conversation about the subject of Rendlesham Forest, she would have simply paid for her plant and left. Ronnie has kindly agreed to allow us to have the artefact tested. The result will, hopefully, be published in an update in a future Volume of *Haunted Skies*.

In *Haunted Skies* Volume 5, we reported about the recovery of a piece of metal from Wentworth Drive, Harborne, Birmingham, by police officers Margaret and Geoffrey Westwood – then head of the Birmingham UFO Group, UFOSIS, in 1974. This took place after a number of UFO *'displays'* had taken place over the suburb, which were brought to the attention of the MOD.

Margaret:

"I was told by the babysitter that she had seen a vivid lime green coloured light shoot over the house. The following morning, I discovered the top of a young eucalyptus (transplanted 12 months previously) was blackened, as if burnt. At the base of the tree, I found a fragment

of material, about two inches in size, that I hadn't seen there before. When later analysed, it was found to be rich in aluminum, with large traces of silicon and smaller amounts of iron. I don't know whether it was connected, but the leaves on the tree grew very elongated. The tree itself grew to a height of 16ft over 12 months – an abnormal growth rate."

Unfortunately, Margaret had mislaid the sample, and its present whereabouts are not known.

Dawn Holloway with Margaret Westwood

We discovered MOD officials had written to several people, living in the Harborne area, confirming that their reports were *". . . being examined, to see if there are any Defence implications"*. Needless to say we have never seen any of these declassified documents, despite this having happened now 39 years ago!

We were intrigued with the composition of the metals found at the scene, and contacted Nick Reiter – a scientist at a solar research facility in Toledo, Ohio – who has also spent over 20yrs researching UFOs and anti-gravity concepts. A copy of the incomplete graph, supplied by Margaret, was sent to Nick, who has worked on numerous cases involving the alleged recovery of UFO debris, in 2012.

He told us:

> *"I did some comparative study of the old Harborne plot versus known sample plots of my own. Attached is the annotated version. It looks like that metal was magnesium primarily, with aluminum and sodium being the other two main missing peaks. I would call it a magnesium alloy, with Al, Fe, Cu, and Ge added. It makes for a strange blend, I'll give you."*

Nick has had the opportunity to work with many well-known investigators and authors, including Bud Hopkins, David M. Jacobs, PhD, and Linda Moulton Howe, and was one of the 'behind-the-scenes', formerly anonymous analyzers, asked by Linda Moulton Howe, to examine the alleged Roswell UFO metal fragment that appeared on the *Coast to Coast* radio show, in the mid-1990s.

Nick's many original technical developments, and instruments, are currently being tested in the field for their effectiveness in providing solid, quantum physics-based solutions to anomalous experiences. You will find Nick's innovative techniques mentioned in the *Fortean Times*, *New Energy News*, *Journal of Borderland Research*, *UFO Forum*, *The Bulletin of Anomalous Experiences*, and *Nexus* magazines. He has also been featured in *Glimpses of Other Realties* (Volume II) by Linda Moulton Howe, and *Electric UFOs: Fireballs, Electromagnetics and Abnormal States*, by Albert Budden.

Examination of metallic debris found in Ohio, USA

In March 2003, Nick Reiter received a phone call from his father, Bruce Reiter, concerning an interesting piece of news from his old rural neighborhood, north of Tiffin, Ohio.

His father related to Nick that his nearest neighbour – 'Ed' – had found a mysterious piece of metal in his side yard, while raking up the last fall's leaves and twigs. The object had been obscured over the winter by two heavy snowfalls and numerous lesser ones. 'Ed' had no explanation for the irregular metal blob, which was roughly six inches by two and a half inches, with a maximum thickness of one half inch, or so.

The blob had very apparently been molten at some point, and had solidified against a fairly flat or solid surface. While the piece had been found in the yard on the earth, the bottom side of the blob when found was generally smooth, with some white oxides present. By reviewing the weather, over the course of the winter that year, he concluded that the 'blob' of metal – if it had not been placed by artifice at a later post-snow date – had apparently fallen onto a hard packed ice crusted snow drift that had remained there since January of the year, up until the thaw in March. The blob may have then melted into the snow and ice a ways, but then apparent, that same month. Nick interviewed 'Ed' carefully, and borrowed his blob of mystery metal after being granted permission to cut it open as desired.

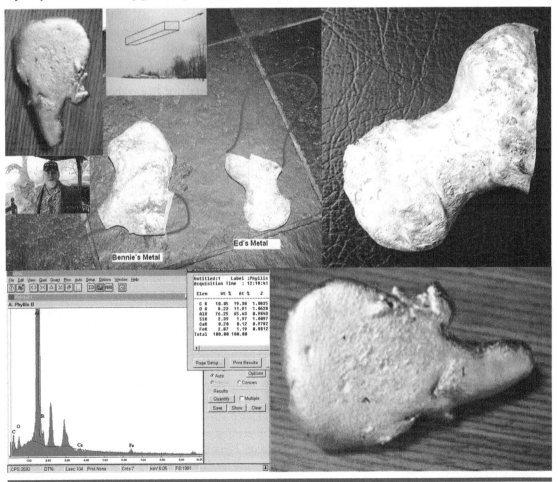

Bennie's Metal

Ed's Metal

Nick ended up sawing a roughly 2ins. portion from the main blob. The interior of the metal appeared homogeneous. A small shaving was taken from both the interior and the surface and analysed by Nick with a Jeol 840 scanning electron microscope, fitted with EDS.

The sample was originally analysed using EDS (Energy Dispersive Spectroscopy) by Nick, which determined the metal was primarily aluminum, with traces of carbon and silicon. A crude Archimedean test of density indicated that the aluminum was within a couple percent of appropriate mass weight, thus meaning it was likely not an unusual isotope. It was not noticeably radioactive when surveyed with our Baird Atomic rate meter (Geiger counter).

Metallic debris falls from UFO Ohio

In late 2006, an uncannily similar account came to Nick's attention, by way of the Ohio UFO investigative community. The witness to this event was a Vietnam veteran, named Benny Foggin, living in rural central Ohio, southeast of Newark. He told of sighting:

> *". . . a large, dark, box-like UFO – the length of a commercial airliner – glided silently over my home, at an estimated altitude of 100 to 200ft. I say silent, but I did hear a rhythmic sound near one end that reminded me of the drum of a washing machine, scraping on bad bushings. As this noisy end of the craft passed over, I heard a dull 'thud' from somewhere nearby, but was transfixed by the dramatic object above."*

It was only after the *'craft'* had vanished to the west, over the tree-line, that Benny thought to look for the source of the thud sound he had heard, a few minutes before, and discovered what appeared to be a blob of solidified and still hot aluminum lying in his gravel and dirt driveway. The material was recovered and placed into in a box, intending to show it to some of the Ohio UFO research community.

However, domestic and personal issues at the time prompted him to delay, and within a few months, the box had been misplaced and Benny and his wife had, by that time, moved to a new home in the area.

In 2006, the piece was re-discovered by the owner, and was analysed by EDS and IR spectroscopy. In early 2006, Benny found the box containing the mysterious metal and took it to Ohio researcher, Joe Stets, in Columbus. Joe apparently had an unnamed party at his own work establishment to take an informal analytical look at the material. However, another piece of the aluminum blob was also sawed off and sent to Phyllis Budinger, of Frontier Analytical Services, Cleveland, who has done high quality analysis on 'unusual event' residues and artifacts, for some years. Phyllis used Infrared Spectroscopy on the sample then performed, in turn, by a colleague of Phyllis' – Dr. Sampath Ayengar. Dr. Ayengar is also well-known as analytical expert on matters of unusual or anomalous artifacts and materials.

Nick, 2013:

> *"As you mentioned before, that certainly is similar in form to not just Benny Foggin's metal, but the 'Ed' metal, as well as two others I have now seen photos of. If ever there is a chance to get a small sample of Brenda's substance sent to me I will cover the cost to get it analyzed or re-analyzed as the case may be. You might be interested to know that a couple of months ago, I had some isotopic ratio analysis performed on Ben's sample. Two values – Nickel 62 and Strontium 84 were interestingly out of bounds from textbook numbers. Odd that."*

Nathan's Metal

"Nathan contacted me in early 2011. He and his young son found this cooled 'blob' in a meadow, close to a park, near the city of Youngstown, Ohio. There was no UFO story associated with it. Unfortunately, before I could get a sample for comparative testing, Nathan fell out of touch, due to divorce and childcare issues in his life. He never replied back to later e-mails sent to him from me.

Belmont County Metal, found by Nick in 2008   *Nathan's metal*

Oddly, here is the other Ohio artifact (discounting Bennie's metal, or Ed's metal) which I found in 2008, when out walking through a field in extreme south-eastern Ohio, with some friends, exploring old house ruins in a region torn up for coal mining in the 1920s. It was simply lying on the grassy, weedy ground, away from anything else. I thought it looked like Ben's metal in form (although smaller) and picked it up. I have done no testing on it yet, other than some simple chemical tests to say it is mostly aluminum (like all the others)."

In addition to these developments was an article published by the *Sun*, on 13th May 2011, showing UFO researcher Russ Kellett, holding a piece of metal that he claimed was recovered from the Berwyn Mountains, in January 1974. We covered this incident in *Haunted Skies* Volume 5 and are satisfied, from having conducted our own research, that the events described are fictitious, although Russ clearly believes the opposite, which of course, is his prerogative.

We also wanted to remind the reader about some pieces of metal (now shown in colour) that were sent to

Bristol researcher, Terry Hooper, by an unidentified RAF serviceman, which he alleged came from the Berwyn Mountains in the same month. Terry a regards as we do that this was a hoax and represents further evidence of disinformation.

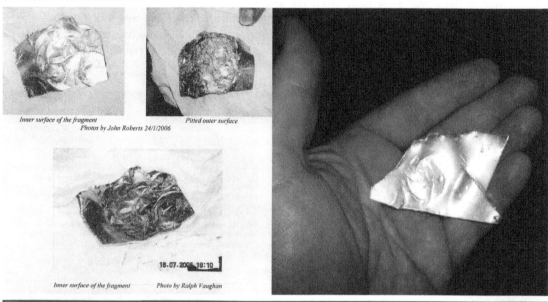

Inner surface of the fragment

Pitted outer surface

Photos by John Roberts 24/1/2006

Inner surface of the fragment

Photo by Ralph Vaughan

UFO researcher Russ Kellett holding a piece of metal he claims was recovered from the Berwyn Mountains, in January 1974

Saturday, June 28, 2008 **Sun** 23

SPACE ODDITY

Riddle of molten lump off 'crashed spaceship'

Heavy metal . . . Russ with the UFO debris

Out of this world . . . melted blob found in Wales

By ALASTAIR TAYLOR

ALIEN hunter Russ Kellett yesterday revealed a lump of mystery metal which he says was recovered from a crashed UFO 34 years ago.

The shiny one-and-a-half inch melted blob was found near Llandrillo in Berwyn Mountains, Wales, after reports of a spaceship plunging to earth.

Russ says it is similar to melted aluminium, yet heavier.

Police logs described a "terrific explosion" shaking houses on January 23, 1974, and locals said hundreds of cops and military personnel ordered everyone off the mountain.

It has been claimed that alien spacemen were whisked off to a secret military installation — all hushed up by the Government.

Former building worker Russ said: "That and this piece of metal from the spaceship proves in my mind the existence of aliens.

"The metal was picked up by someone who was on the mountain at the time. They have since died and it was passed to me about a year ago.

"I passed it to a jeweller who showed it to an expert but they have no idea what it is."

Russ 45, of Filey, North Yorks, has amassed more than 30 years of data about flying saucers — but only unveiled the shiny metal after reading recent UFO reports in The Sun.

We told of three sightings in five days earlier this month — in Shropshire, near Cardiff and over the Brecon Beacons.

Russ, who started studying UFOs after being surrounded by inexplicable lights while on a motorbike in 1988, said: "None of these incidents surprise me.

"It is only a matter of time before we get conclusive proof."

a.taylor@the-sun.co.uk

Sunspot . . . page 1 story   LLand of Llegend — P34&35

The piece of black matter in my hand felt curiously light and alien. UFO researcher Peter Guy told me it was found on the lawn of a house in Birmingham, shortly after a mysterious, pulsating light had been seen hovering above trees at the bottom of the garden.

"There were several pieces scattered over the lawn. We had the material analysed at a university and it was found to have a rather peculiar make-up," said Peter.

"There was nothing in it that couldn't be explained by normal chemistry. It was just peculiar. It was extremely rich in aluminium with a large amount of silicone and smaller amounts of iron. I can see no earthly reason for that."

I looked at the black lump with a genuine sense of awe. Could it really be connected with the strange, pulsating light which amazed several witnesses in Birmingham — and was that light a UFO? If so, where did it come from? Who controlled it?

Peter Guy would also like to know the answers to these and many other questions that arise from the unexplained sightings of lights and objects in the sky.

He is a member of the British Unidentified Flying Object Research Association and a dedicated investigator for the Birmingham - based UFO Studies Information Service.

DIRTY

Mention flying saucers to Peter and he frowns. "That's a dirty word to us." Even the object seen over Olton about two years ago and drawn by Peter from the evidence of eye - witnesses, is described unemotionally as an alleged unidentified flying object, although it has all the characteristics of the traditional "saucer" — high dome, with small round windows and a base like an up - turned saucer.

Talk of invaders from other planets will provoke a similar reaction. "We are extremely wary if anyone reports a contact. The last thing we want to hear of is little green men.

"We have got contact cases, of course. One is under serious investigation at the moment. A professional psychiatrist has offered to interview the witness under hypnosis."

Peter, who lives in Chelmscote Road, Olton, has never seen a UFO. At least, his unbiased and scientific mind will not allow him to accept his own sightings as positive evidence.

Most sightings, he will tell you, can be put down as natural phenomena —

aircraft and other lights in the sky, meteorites and metal from man - made satellites re - entering the earth's atmosphere.

But his studies and investigations — "I once traced a UFO from North Yorkshire to the Thames estuary" — have brought him to the conclusion that some UFO's could be manufactured craft, possibly the product of extra - terrestial intelligence.

Peter has scientific and technical know - how which helps him in his research into UFO's. He works for a major oil company and is reading for Open University degrees in mathematics and geology.

He has designed a spectroscope to be fitted to the cameras of UFO spotters and is optimistic that some day the researchers will receive official recognition for their work.

FUTURE

"We hope it will produce at some time in the future, once and for all, a solution to the problem. I want to know what these craft are, and how they are powered. And I want to know something about the technology that produces them."

So far, official recognition has not been forthcoming. "We write to the Ministry of Defence and get absolutely no reaction. All we get is a stereotyped letter, 'Dear Sirs, this matter is being attended to ...' and that's the last you hear. If you write again, you're sent exactly the same letter. We find it very frustrating."

Peter Guy with his spectroscope designed for UFO spotters, and his drawing of the Olton UFO. "Flying saucer's a dirty word to us."

A visit to the Forest in August 2013

In late August 2013, we travelled down from the West Midlands to meet up with Brenda Butler, who handed over to us the piece of metal given to her by Ronnie Dugdale We photographed this and the lightweight material handed over to her 30 years ago, by 'Steve Roberts', which were claimed, by him, to have been recovered from the UFO landing site.

Later that evening, we met up with Brenda's friend Jean, Derek Savory and Bernie, before setting out on a walk through the forest. Since our last visit, made a few years ago, already changes had occurred. Alongside what was track 10, opposite Folly House, was no longer a wooded area but a great swathe of cut down trees. Sadly, we discovered that the

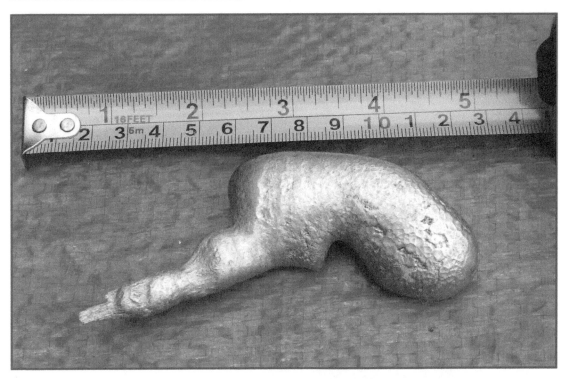

The piece of 'metal' given to Brenda Butler by Ronnie Dugdale who acquired it from an American lady at his market stall.

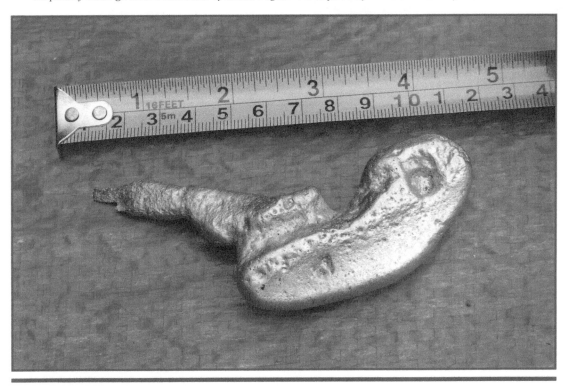

The lightweight items allegedly found at the UFO landing site, given to Brenda Butler by 'Steve Roberts' over 30 years ago

lady who lived at Folly House – then a regular visitor with her dogs in the forest – had passed away . . . the area now eerily quiet.

We noticed the field belonging to Mr Boast had been fenced off all the way around and that the location identified by Colonel Halt (a short distance away from the previous site) bore no resemblance to the original site, as shown to us by Brenda, many years ago, as the reader will see for themselves by the photographs taken. In years to come, this will no doubt be identified as where Jim Penniston had his sighting! Bizarrely, the Forestry Commission has announced plans to build a half scale model of the UFO that Jim saw and site it at this location.

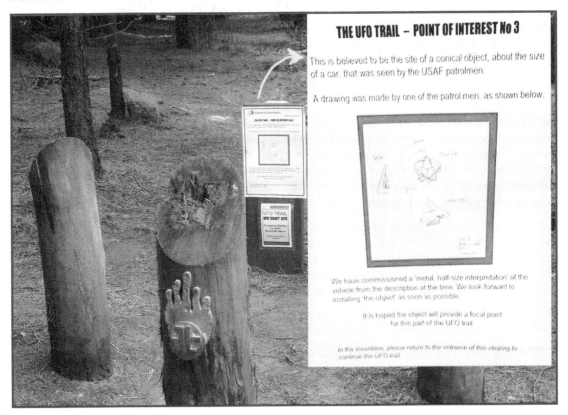

Landing at Midnight

After a few hours sleep, we returned to the forest with Brenda in the afternoon and made our way once again (this time in the daylight) to what is generally referred to as Colonel Halt's site. During conversation with Brenda, we were astonished to discover from documents on our filing system that she and Peter Parish had experienced falls of stones, in 2002. We thought this had started in 2006! We also learnt from Brenda that Neville Spearman wanted to title the book (*Sky Crash*) as *Landing at Midnight* with subtitle!

Ipswich Fire Service

We asked Brenda about the role of the civilian Fire Service, as we understood they had attended at the base, following an incident reported to them during the end of December 1980, but were refused entry.

> *"I interviewed a retired fireman, some years ago, who told me that fire tenders were sent to RAF Woodbridge and RAF Bentwaters, following the UFO incidents reported in December 1980. Both appliances from Ipswich were refused entry and the firemen were warned that if they talked about their involvement, they would lose their pensions. Another thing that has crossed my mind, so many times, is to wonder why (if those marks found on the forest floor were rabbit marks) did they seal off the area and place posts in the ground, in the presence of a local police officer and USAF official?"*

Georgina Bruni speaks at UFO Conference – 2002

With regard to the authenticity of the original statements tended by the airmen involved, it was of interest to discover the following comments made by Georgina Bruni, at a UFO Conference held in 2002. The first was:

> *"According to the Deputy Base Commander of OSI for Bentwaters, such typewritten statements would not be regarded as official; only handwritten statements were deemed acceptable in order to avoid potential fraud."*

She cites Lieutenant Fred Buran's *'fact and fiction'* statement and points out that, although his signature appears real, he never read it but just signed it – which seems a strange thing to do, unless you are being coerced or threatened, and can only be speculation at this stage. Georgina also revealed to the audience (and to us in conversation during her visits to the Forest with Brenda) that Jim Penniston told her that he had seen *"alien life forms, transparent and human looking"* and he was positive Lt. Colonel Halt had communicated with the aliens by using telepathy – which, Colonel Halt has categorically denied.

In *New Alien Mysteries*, as shown on *Sky* in 2013, Jim Penniston tells of receiving a telephone call, after his UFO sighting, to report to OSI. During a subsequent interview he was then directed by them to write down a full account, leaving nothing out. After this was done Jim handed over his statement, which was then taken away. They returned some ten minutes later, and handed Jim a typed copy, prepared from his written statement, which only contained about a quarter of the account put down on paper.

He asked them for the rest of it and, although he says he did not like the situation, signed it after stating that *"OSI operate outside the chain of normal command. Orders are orders – that's how it worked"*.

In 1994, Jim underwent hypnosis. From those sessions he learnt there was more to the UFO encounter than first thought, and that he was given sodium pentothal by the OSI officers during the interrogation. We are not saying that Jim or John is guilty of any fabrication; far from it, we have the greatest respect for them. However, we have some misgivings about the reliability of this evidence gained through regression techniques, rather than direct memory after the event.

There is no denying something highly unusual took place, involving what appears to be close encounters with unidentified flying objects, over some nights running, this isn't in issue. However, accounts of binary code, along with stories of lost cities and visitors from the future, seem to have more in common with a Hollywood science fiction film.

While it would be easy to dismiss Jim's claims as *confabulation, we should not do so until we can prove otherwise, especially bearing in mind that Brenda Butler has also claimed of having received messages and binary code, telepathically, during her visits to the forest since the early 1980s.

---

*Confabulation is a memory disturbance, defined as the production of fabricated, distorted or misinterpreted memories about oneself, or the world, without the conscious intention to deceive. Confabulation is distinguished from lying as there is no intent to deceive and the person is unaware the information is false. Although individuals can present blatantly false information, confabulation can also seem to be coherent, internally consistent, and relatively normal. Individuals who confabulate present incorrect memories, ranging from subtle alternations to bizarre fabrications, and are generally very confident about their recollections, despite contradictory evidence.

Tim Egercic of the 81st Police Squadron

Colonel Halt recommended that we contact Tim Egercic, of the 81st Police Squadron, who was posted to 'D' Flight at RAF Bentwaters, in December 1980, working under the supervision of Ray Gulyas, Robert F. Ball and Edwin Kearney. We emailed Tim in mid-August 2013, seeking permission to use some photographs of the Base, taken while on a visit over here, some years ago, with other colleagues.

"On December 25th, I was finishing up a Swing Shift (3pm-11pm). After midnight, in the early mornings of 27th, 28th, and 29th December, members of 'D' Flight radioed in about strange lights seen in Rendlesham Forest. M.Sgt. Bob Ball was the only one I knew who went over to investigate all three of those nights. Within the past few years I learned the first night/early morning (27th December) involved Bonnie Tamplin and the final night/early morning (29th December) involved Ball, Halt, Bustinza and a lot more people. I would change 3rd night running to 4th night running, since members of 'C' Flight had their encounter on 26th December and 'D' Flight witnessed the lights on 27th, 28th and 29th December."

On the early morning of 29th December 1980, someone from the Weapons Storage Area was asked to go to the tower and see if they could see the *'lights'*, now reported for the third night running. Training Sgt. Clarence George asked Tim if he wanted to go over and have a look – but he declined, not wanting to miss out on radio transmissions.

Tim:

"I was posted all night in the alarm monitor building, so Sgt. Bob Sliwowski made his way over to the Alarm Monitor building. After returning from three days off, on 1st January 1981, someone (not me) on 'D' Flight asked M.Sgt. Ball during guard mount what happened, at which point he said he wasn't allowed to say what he saw. Charlie Waters, who was posted in the Weapons Storage Area, only stated he saw the object hovering before he saw it descend into the forest. At no point since the December 1980 UFO sightings have I come across anyone who claims a *UFO hovered

---

*Colonel Charles Halt, 2013: *"I never told anybody any structure was penetrated by beams. I was several miles away. From my view, a beam or more came down near the Weapons Storage Area. I don't know for a fact that the beams landed there. I know they were in the area. I was too far away but relied on the radio chatter, which indicated the beams landed there."*

over the Weapons Storage Area, including the tower operator – Rick Bobo.

Several UFO accounts relating to Rendlesham state this happened. I can't say for certain that it didn't occur, because no one in the Weapons Storage Area was looking up in the sky at every given moment, but who was the first person to state this and who was working in the Weapons Storage Area that will back up that claim now?"

Gary Tomoyasu, Base Photographer

"I worked at the photo laboratory during the UFO incident. We did process film that was brought in by someone from SF or OSI – can't remember exactly. I do remember that an alert photographer was called out, but don't remember which day and if it was at night during the sojourn through the woods. I do remember someone from the shop went out during the day with SF, or one of the investigators, and I remember seeing photos of round indentions that were in a roughly triangular pattern. We gave the negatives and the proof sheets to the requestor, as was standard operating procedure. We kept some negatives from the Information Office (now Public Affairs) and some other types of jobs. I've always wondered about the UFO sightings, though we did kind of make light of the incident.

I do remember a CNN three-part report the year after I got back to the States – 1983 – each part was only about three to five minutes long. We never really thought about printing copies for ourselves; after all, it was just pictures in the forest and dimples in the ground. Sorry this isn't much help. I do remember staying at Woodhall, in 1984, when on Temporary Duty Assignment from the States. The barman told us that Lt. Colonel Halt was back in England because of the UFO incident."

The Hull connection, December 1980

During an interview with the secretary of Colonel Richard Spring – Chief of Base Operations and Training, at Woodbridge/Bentwaters – Georgina Bruini was told of a visit made by Hull police officers, with regard to a UFO incident under investigation by them, and that Colonel Spring had himself gone to the railway station to pick up the officers. According to Colonel Halt, 2013:

"The last I knew of Dick Spring, he was back to flying as a Navigator with AWACS at Tinker AFB, in Oklahoma City. I think he retired there. I'll try and find out more."

Initially, when we read about this, we were puzzled as to why the Hull police should have contacted Colonel Richard Spring about any UFO incident which had taken place hundreds of miles away from them. The problem was that we did not know in which year the *'Hull incident'* had taken place. If it had been the end of December 1980 or early January 1981, one would be bound to query how the Hull police could have known what happened outside the airbase, as this was not readily known to the public until publication of the *News of the World* article in 1983.

We now have every reason to believe the visit by the Hull officers was as a result of a UFO incident which took place at Ganstead, near Hull, during early January 1981. This involved members of the local CB Radio – the 'Hull Citizens Band' – who, after hearing of the incident (no doubt through picking up the police transmissions) made their way to the location concerned.

Details of this incident were covered in an article published in the *Hull Star*, on 16th January 1981. The very nature of its presentation was hardly likely to be taken seriously. Enquiries into this matter revealed that there may well be far more to this than meets the eye. In 2001, Humberside Police Officer P.C. Darren Parr, and Andy McCartney – members of the *Hull UFO Society* – decided to conduct their own investigations into the matter, following information received from local boxing coach, Michael Bromby.

We retraced their journey in 2013, and spoke to Mike Bromby Snr., who told us of a conversation held with Peter – then a serving police officer – about two police officers known to him that had been directed to the UFO incident. As a result of what they had witnessed, it was alleged that the woman officer suffered some trauma. Both of them were warned not to ever discuss the matter again.

14 HULL STAR, JANUARY 16, 1981

Strange tale of Tin Man's UFO

TIN MAN caused quite a stir when he had a close encounter in the East Hull area with an extra-terrestrial craft from another galaxy.

Tin Man, codename for a member of Bridgetown Breakers' Club, the Hull area's Citizens' Band radio users, claimed to have sighted a stationary UFO in a field near Ganstead.

Even though it was late at night, he alerted his CB radio colleagues, who still operate illegally, and soon Sandpiper, Red Knight and Mustang joined an expedition to Tin Man's glowing orange dome.

A Bridgetown Breakers spokesman explained: "Tin Man said the thing was larger than a house with antennae on top and a ring of orange lights circulating around it. Smaller 'craft' seemed to be buzzing round with white lights to the front.

"It was decided that extra equipment would be needed, so the expedition returned to base to pick up binoculars, torches and a floodlight."

Metro and Butterfly had joined the expedition by now and Magic Mushroom was planning to charter a helicopter from South Humberside.

The spokesman added: "When the party finally made it back to the UFO, it was gone. A search was carried out on foot.

"Butterfly, Mustang and Sandpiper ended up in about 2ft. of water, but they could not see anything suspicious—no tell-tale scorch marks, no burnt vegetation."

After four hours, the frustrated Breakers headed home, but they decided to return the next morning. And the daylight revealed that the fearsome UFO was ... a giant heap of sand with workmen climbing about all over it!

Mike Bromby:

> *"Peter told me of a cover-up involving the army, who had driven onto the Ganstead site and cleared the whole area. Two officers that were in attendance were warned to keep silent."*

Andy told us that, following his original enquiries, he was able to determine that one of the CB enthusiasts was a Shaun Moxon. Obviously his information, like that of the two police officers, was vital. We knew that other accounts identified the location as being off the A165 at Skirlaugh, Hull. Unfortunately, we were unable to trace Shaun initally, but hoped, as time went on, that he would contact us. As we suspected, this

Darren M Parr

Harvey Street
Lincoln
LN

10th December 2001

Mr Peter

Analaby
Kingston-upon-Hull

Dear Mr

I am writing to you in the hope that you may be able to offer your kind assistance to my colleague, Andrew McCartney and I in our research concerning two incidents back in 1980/8. Both incidents concern unusual aerial phenomenon observed in the Hull/Holderness areas of the former North Humberside region.

We have been informed by a long-time colleague and friend of yours, Mike Bromby, that you may have some knowledge of the first incident. This concerns an unusual aerial object sighted in or around the Skirlaugh area of the A165 by members of a radio club, and also by at least one Police Officer. Mike also tells us that, quite possibly, you may be party to knowledge of a visit made by Police Officers from Hull to a Suffolk-based United States Air Force base in January 1981, again concerning a similar sighting made in or near to Hull and also in Suffolk.

Mike tells us that you share our deep interest in unusual and unexplained activity, including that of the UFO phenomenon, hence our anticipation that you might be able to contribute to our research. It is our intention to eventually release the findings of our research into the public domain, however, as with all our cases anything relating to your personal identity will treated with the utmost of confidentiality.

We can be contacted through the Hull UFO Society (HUFOS) on 01482 219887 or by email at *hullufosociety@yahoo.co.uk*. Thanking you for your help and assistance.

Yours sincerely

Darren Parr

was the reason for the Hull police officers' visit to Bentwaters Airbase, sometime during the early 1980s. Ironically, this was not the only report made of UFO activity for the end of December 1980. On 26th December 1980, Andrew McCartney aka then as Andy Barb (19) from Hull, East Yorkshire, was on his way home at about 11.30pm, after having visited the Wellington Club, which was a popular nightclub, catering for people with an interest in punk rock music.

Andy:

"I'm the lad with the short black hair, dark black and blue stripy pants, shouting. Think I have a red and white scarf on, on the left front.

I had drunk a couple of bottles of beer and decided to take a short cut home. Approximately 15 minutes later, I saw what I thought initially, was a large, bright white marquee, or dome tent, with what looked like a dry ice machine at its base, on the ground in Waterloo Street Park next to a children's play area, close to a concrete tube. It was about 20ft across. I lit a cigarette near the tube, which was a drainage tube – probably put there for the kids to play in. My first impression was that someone had put it up for a party.

It was very icy on the ground. I slipped over and fell on my back. I then realised that this was no tent or marquee; there was a strange eerie silence about. It was very white and bright inside – too bright to see anything, other than what I thought was a long table type thing – that's all I remembered, until the next morning, when I woke up on the settee and hearing my mum shout my name 'Andrew'!

My mum was standing in front of me. I was laid on her living room sofa, and she was pointing at my lack of attire! I still had my leather jacket on, though my T-shirt was back to front. My brand new black, canvass, Levi's were gone, as were my undergarments. How the hell had this happened? My calf length Para boots were still on, and laced right up. It would have been impossible to remove the skintight jeans without removing the boots first.

All I was concerned about was my missing Levi's; they had cost me a tenner! Also embarrassed at being found that way, I told my mum I had walked home like that for a bet (The alternatives were not an option for me). For years after that, at family gatherings, now and then, someone would utter 'Remember when you walked home naked for a bet?' (ad nauseam) I eventually forgot about that strange Christmas night, until a friend mentioned an event at an Airbase, in Suffolk.

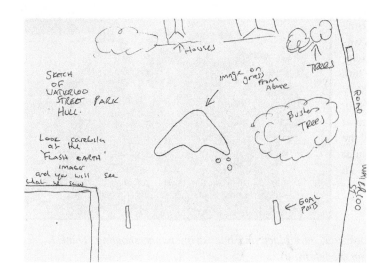

I met up with Sean Tierney – now a good friend of mine, who runs HUFOS (Hull UFO Society) – who is neither a doubter nor a believer, but a very well respected nice man. I read a lot about the incident at Rendlesham Forest and the more I read about it, I began to wonder why it seemed familiar. My dear mum said, quite matter of fact to me, 'Didn't you have something strange happen to you that Christmas week?'

The walking home naked bit surfaced again, and I said 'Mum, I didn't walk home like that' . . . and it all came back to me in a flash – the tent, my hair standing on end, the fierce nosebleeds in 1981, the unexplained mark on my thigh that has never faded! Part of me thought there must be a rational answer to what I had experienced. Surely incidents like this only happened in science fiction comic books, not real life. Perplexed and unsure of how to deal with this and progress forward, I spoke to Larry Warren and felt that some of what he experienced felt very similar."

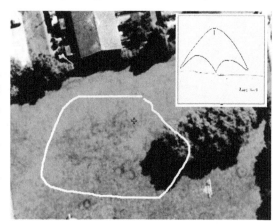

In early August 2013, we spoke to Sean Tierney – a highly respected UFO/paranormal researcher – about the incident, bearing in mind his experience within the field of UFO research and personal knowledge of Andrew (who was an old school friend). Sean agreed with us that there was no reason to dispute the authenticity of Andrew's encounter and that he had been a regular at their meetings.

Andy:

"After listening to my account, Sean introduced me to my good friend – Darren Parr – then a police constable, who agreed to assist me in conducting further research. We ascertained the archives containing Humberside police records for the year 1980 were stored at the 'Beverley' archive. We visited them and Darren produced his warrant card and requested the 'general notes files' for December 1980. The usher politely agreed and produced a dusty folder, adorned with a ribbon. He then asked, 'Are you wanting to look at these in a professional or private capacity?' Darren answered, 'Private'. The file was immediately withdrawn. He was told that if he wanted the file, he would need permission from above.

(We emailed the Beverley Archive, in 2013, asking if they could confirm they were in possession of such a document, they told us no such file existed.)

HUMBERSIDE POLICE
'D' Division
Police Headquarters
Queens Gardens
Hull HU1 3DJ

Tel No: (01482) 220177
Facsimile: (01482) 220459
DX No: 708882, Hull 10

Your Ref:

Our Ref: D/T/SUPT/PG/JVDE

Mr Sean Tierney
Hull UFO Society
62 Egton Street
New Cleaveland Street
Hull
HU8 7HU

25 January 2001

Dear Mr Tierney

I am replying in relation to your letter requesting information about the visit of police officers to Suffolk in 1980.

I am afraid that the records you refer to have been destroyed. Our policy is only to keep such administrative records for a maximum period of 7 years. The only way to find the information you want would be to try and contact the police officers themselves who have now retired and moved to various addresses around the country.

I am sorry we are unable to provide information you require at this time.

Yours sincerely

P GEENTY
Superintendent
Operations
D Division

Web Site: www.humberside.police.uk

A friend also put me in touch with a retired policeman who, unfortunately, sounded terrified and politely declined to speak about it, although he knew what I was talking about. A letter sent to the Humberside police produced a reply, which did not deny the event but told me the police involved were retired and moved to other areas! Darren also placed an advert in the Lincolnshire Echo, *in October 2001, asking for any information on the UFO sightings.*

The technique of regression is something I have never really considered but I decided to try it, wondering if any additional information might be recovered from my subconscious memory. In 2002, I contacted hypnotherapist *Steve Burgess, C.M.H C. H<small>YP</small> C .CPNLP MNCH (A<small>CC</small>) of The Natural Therapy Centre practice, Beverley, East Yorkshire, and explained to Steve about what had happened; he was intrigued enough not to charge me for the first session. In conversation with him, I discovered a friend of his had also seen a UFO (a policewoman). I believe she was one of the officers who saw it approach Hull from the Wetherby area.

I found the hypnosis session unlike that portrayed on the stage; it was very relaxing, although I tried to fight it. As far as answers were obtained there were no little 'green men', but it did clear up a few things and now I knew I was not going mad, or had imagined the whole thing. I saw the 'tent thing' very bright, and then I remembered the word 'stepping stone' clearly said to me as I approached the 'thing'.

Help us solve UFO mystery in the skies

MYSTERIOUS happenings took place in the skies above twin USA airbases in Suffolk sometime between Boxing Day and New Yea Eve, 1980.

A number of US airmen alleged have seen something unusual, bot in the sky and on the ground in a clearing, in a nearby forest.

These events gave rise to the Rendlesham Forest UFO mystery.

Now, almost 21 years after these strange events took place, people coming forward to say that they t saw unusual objects flying above east and eastern coastal regions o England at the end of the year in 1980.

Two researchers are investigati potential connections between th Rendlesham incident and these n claims and are seeking others in Lincolnshire area who might hav observed the unusual aerial even Christmas 1980.

If you know somebody who saw something, or you are one of thos who witnessed the events, we wor like to talk to you about them. We can be contacted through Hull UFO Society, by post to 62 E Street, Hull, East Yorkshire. Or telephone (01482) 219887. Alternatively email on hullufosociety@yahoo.co.uk.

DARREN PARR, Harvey Street, Lincoln.

When peering in, it was so bright. All I saw was an empty long white table. Feeling hands on me, and being a petulant young lad, I remember lashing out and jumping down off something – a platform, or other. When exiting, I ran for some yards, looking back; the 'thing' was not where it originally was. It was now at the bottom of Chapman Street Bridge – that's when I realised certain items of clothing were gone. Compromised and cold, I ran to a railway embankment close by (Dansom Lane). This way I knew I would not be seen.

This railway is elevated and my mother's house faces it at the rear, a safe passage so to speak. Nearing my Mum's and over the tracks, in the air, there seemed to be an angry red cloud. As I climbed over the fence into my Mum's garden, the privet hedge, which was six feet high, was shaking violently.

The red cloud was now a lot of bright light above the house. I realised that I could not get in – no pants, no keys.

I can't explain this next bit, so be patient with me. I was lifted by the elbows, like a child. The locked door opened, like a movie. I could see the living room getting nearer, and I was gently laid on the sofa. I did ask, whoever they were, a question. 'What's going on?' The reply was short and matter of fact – 'You are just a boy. You would not understand'.

Also during the regression, when exiting the 'tent' and running down Chapman Street, I looked back, and †Services – either firemen, police, or perhaps army, were surrounding whatever was now at the foot of Chapman Street Bridge, with lots of lights flashing and what looked like a cordon.

This filled the gaps in for me, but not who or what was responsible. It did not feel alien, or anything like that, but yes – very strange. Steve said he was impressed and said it would be natural to question the validity of the outcome. He saved me asking 'Where did all that come from?' I even remember calling him, a few days later, saying something like 'was that all bullshit?' Steve has had experience enough to know the real from the false. He said it was a real event and my subconscious had either put it away to protect me, or something else had!

Billy Rhodes (Wedgner) also saw, over Newbridge Road Park, a triangular-shaped craft hovering over the park near the railway line (same one I ran along!) His mum initially thought a helicopter was on fire over the park and woke Billy to show him. He said it slowly turned at an angle, with red lights rising and falling on its rear, and headed off towards the 'Chimney', which is the direction of my mum's house and the railway line."

(We learned that at about 10pm on Boxing night 1980, following a fault in an underground 11,000 volt cable, parts of Bridlington sustained a power cut and a number of premises were plunged into darkness. The next morning there was a report of flooding, following the collapse of a 21ins water pipe in Hull Street, Hull, which necessitated the area being cordoned off to the public while repairs could be carried out).

2013 – *Steve Burgess

We contacted Steve Burgess – a very pleasant and helpful man.

> "Andy typifies other ET abductees, who have desperateness about them to try and understand what's happened to them, or to share their experiences in order to make sense out of things, that they often come across as slightly intense. Although I can't find my notes on Andy's session and therefore the details of it are hidden behind a veil of time, I remember thinking that the memories he expanded in the regression session were real and not imagined.
>
> This is because of the way he was when in hypnosis, which

Boxing Night blackout

A FAULT in an 11,000 volt underground cable plunged a large area of Bridlington into darkness at about 10 o'clock last night — putting a damper on Boxing Night celebrations.

A YEB official said the fault shut down a feeder from the

PHONE NEWS TO HULL 27111

Brett Street sub station, cutting off the supply to about 1,200 homes in the Trinity Road, Tennyson Avenue, Victoria Road, part of Promenade and part of Quay Road, Flamborough Road and the Sands Lane area. Houses in the Queensgate area were also affected. The supply was not restored until midnight.

Mr Roy Whiting, landlord at the Half Moon, who is also president of Bridlington and District Licensed Victuallers' Association, said seven public houses were affected.

CANDLES LIT

He said there was a rush to get candles lit before customers decided to leave. The blackout had a disastrous effect on the night's takings, he said.

More than 500 youngsters attending a disco at the Three B's Theatre Bar were sent home when the lights failed. Younger children attending the function were allowed to remain until their parents called for them.

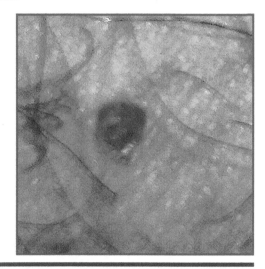

Drawing by Sean Moxon.
3rd October 2001

was a typical regression session for me. Having completed many thousands of regression sessions (not, obviously just connected to possible ET experiences) I can usually tell very quickly whether the person is simply fantasising and making memories up, as these fantasy experiences have a different quality to real memories. I do not believe this to be the case with Andy. As for the policewoman, I'm sorry to say I have no memories of this person at all. It may have been someone who I'd heard about at the time, but now I honestly can't remember who that was."

Andy:

"Later we spoke to CB enthusiasts, who were pursued by the same thing, and postmen, on a Christmas night out, who saw something hovering over the college, emitting sparks of light or metal. I spoke to neighbours who had seen this over another park in Hull, on the same night. The local paper put an article in about cordoning off a one mile area, because of a burst water pipe, on December 26th/27th. I checked this – no such occurrence. Also I spent the whole morning of the 27th searching for my Levi's! The area was not cordoned off, at least not in the daytime!

There were other strange things that happened. While researching this, my phone acted up. Even moving address three times, this still happened. Mail tampered with. Was I being paranoid? Perhaps I was not the only one to have their phones/mail intercepted. And my good friend, Darren Parr, had been followed all the way to Stoke. A policeman knows when he is being followed. There are, I am sure, other witnesses in Hull who witnessed this event. I remember hearing a rumour in the 80s – 'Remember the UFO that landed in James Reckitt Avenue?' – not realising, at the time, his was the one!

I still have the blood red mark on my thigh from that night, which has never faded; it is a perfect rounded off triangle. I was only 19, at the time, and never appreciated just what happened, and I still have strange nightmares from time to time. I just hope, one day, someone who knows will tell us all what went on and why. Perhaps Colonel Richard Spring may. This man was mentioned in Georgina Bruni's book 'You Can't Tell The People', *in which the Hull police are mentioned, more than once, visiting Bentwaters to compare notes on 'a similar incident there' and at the same time. Someone, I am sure, knows who they were and what they wanted."*

UFO sighted – Interference with Motor Vehicle

We eventually managed to speak to Shaun Moxon, now the owner of a successful cleaning company in Hull, during September 2013.

"I was out with a friend and two girls that night, when we saw this domed shape with orange lights, in the distance – then it lifted up and moved along. It stopped again and came down and had bright lights coming out from it. We saw these things coming towards us, heading across the field.

We left and I told my dad about it, and he went to the upstairs bedroom window to see if he could see it. He said it was there but not moving. I got into my car – a 1960 Volkswagen Beetle – and drove around the area, looking for this 'thing'. I had a 12 volt battery in my car, connected to a Citizens Broadband radio, which was illegal and hidden under the seat. I didn't want the police to see it, if stopped by them on a routine check. As soon as I saw it again I lost power. The lights went out on the car and the CB radio (on a separate feed) also stopped working. I checked the wiring and found it to be ok, but still no power – the battery was dead. The UFO then moved upwards into the sky and vanished from sight. As it did so, my car lights and the CB radio came back on again. This really 'freaked me out'. I then started the engine of the car and drove away. I contacted my fellow CB enthusiasts, using my code name 'Tin Man', and explained what had happened. The next night they were all out looking for the UFO, using high powered torches. The Press found out and inferred, in the newspaper article published about the incident, that they had mistaken the huge heap of sand at Ganstead, lit up at night in the winter, for a UFO. I didn't report the UFO incident to the police because I was frightened, at the time, that I would be prosecuted for using the CB radio illegally."

Billy Rhodes (Wedgner)

Andy told us another witness to a UFO sighted around that period of time was Billy Rhodes (Wedgner) from Newbridge Road, who mentions having seen a triangular-shaped *'craft'*, hovering over the park near the railway line. His mother had initially thought it was a helicopter, on fire over the park, and woke Billy to show him.

He said, *"It slowly turned at an angle, with red lights rising and falling on its rear, and headed off towards the 'Chimney', which is the direction of my mum's house and the railway line."*

We discussed this matter with Brenda Butler, who had, coincidently, in her possession, a written letter from Billy, sent to her in 1994, outlining what he had seen.

Following an appeal in the *Hull Daily Mail*, in August 2013, regarding any witnesses to UFO events that took place in Hull in 1980, we received a telephone call from Billy Rhodes, who had this to say:

"I was aged 15 and it happened sometime towards the end of December 1980, or early January 1981. I lived in Newbridge Road, Hull, with my mother. She slept in the rear bedroom overlooking a small park, which now has a school built on it. One morning, about 3am or 4am, I was awoken by my mother, who seemed very agitated. She told me to come and have a

MR W.R. [SIGNER]
NEWTOWN COURT
SOUTHCOATES LANE
HEDON ROAD
HULL
NORTH HUMBERSIDE
HU9

TELEPHONE CONTACT NO.
HULL (0482)
ext...

MISS L...

8.11.94

Dear Ms. Butler,

I am writing to you in connection with a UFO I saw in 1980/81. At the time I was 15 years of age and living at number 27 Newbridge Road, Hull.

I was asleep in the upstairs front bedroom of the house when I was woken up by my mother who had seen the object. At first she thought it was a helicopter on fire.

When I looked out of the window at the back of the house I saw a triangular shaped object which was red/orange and seemed to be throbbing in and out. The object was approximately 100-150 FT away and 70-80 FT off the ground. The object made no sound at all. It was approximately 30-40 FT long, 15-20 FT wide and 10 FT high. I estimated the travelling speed at 25/30 MPH.

It was between 3am and 4am and it was very clear. I could see two or three port-hole shaped windows at the front of the object.

The object was in sight for approximately 10 minutes, and travelling in the direction shown on the enclosed map.

We did not know what the object was but we were certain that it was not an aeroplane or helicopter.

One or two weeks later a headline was printed in the Hull Daily Mail paper which read, "Government cover up?" "UFO lands at Army Barracks".

I think that the paper read that the UFO was surrounded by Army Patrol men. It also stated that it was tracked on radar travelling over the east coast of Britain.

I kept the article from the Hull Daily Mail for quite some time but never thought of contacting anybody about it until just recently when I saw an episode on 'Sightings' on SKY T.V. They did a piece on the UFO which landed at the Army Barracks in Brentwater. I have this episode of 'Sightings' on tape.

I knew that this was the same UFO I saw when they said they tracked it over the east coast of Britain at approximately 3.30 AM. It was not mentioned that the UFO was seen travelling over Hull or any other area.

Myself and my mother, Mrs. J. Fallon, has since moved from 27 Newbridge Road, Hull.

I understand that you are investigating this case and I hope you find this information useful.

I would appreciate it if you could let me know if the information I have given you has been of any use to your investigation.

Please do not hesitate to contact myself at the address given, or my girlfriend on the contact number given between 9AM - 4pm.

Thank you,

Yours sincerely,

W. R. [Signature]

look out of her bedroom window. I went into the bedroom and looked out. I was astonished to see an object, which I estimated to be 150ft long, hovering over Victor Street park, about 60ft off the ground. It was completely still. The 'body' of this diamond-shaped object was glowing red hot and reminded me of metal that has been pulled out of a fire. The light coming off the object illuminated the park and surrounding houses. I opened the window and looked out into the cold, early morning sky, onto the side of the object, and thought what the bloody hell is it?!

I could see what looked like 4-5 portholes along its side, with bright yellow light spilling out. After 30-40 seconds, it began to move slowly left from right, and turned, moving towards a block of flats at the top of the road, enabling me to see it from the back. The end of the object was shaped like a pyramid. In this 'pyramid' were two panels. In each panel there was a light moving from top to bottom inside it, going from large to small in size. I believe this formed part of the propulsion system of whatever it was. We watched it continue on its way, until it was a small dot in the sky."

UFO sighted over Hull

Derek Lewis was 15 years of age at the time, and living in Kingston-upon-Hull.

Sometime in 1981 he was with a group of other boys, playing football in the street. All of a sudden, they heard a sound – like a helicopter, flying at very low altitude. The boys looked up and saw nothing. By this time the noise had stopped just as suddenly as it had started. Then it started again, but sounding much lower, before stopping abruptly again after a few seconds. The boys carried on playing football – all thinking it was a helicopter, now out of sight, and thought nothing of it.

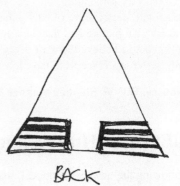

Derek:

"As I went to retrieve the football from the other end of the road, a very bright star like point of light caught my eye. I remember thinking to myself, I'll get my telescope on that later, when it rises, thinking it was the planet Jupiter, but after a few seconds, I realised it wasn't Jupiter, as it was in the wrong place and swaying to and fro. I looked at it, thinking it was some kind of airplane, and continued the game. As soon as I took my eyes off the distant object, it caught my eye again as it was swaying to and fro – faster than anything I had ever seen. I called out to my friends in the street to come and take a look at it. They all said it was a helicopter, with an extremely bright light on it and ignored it.

A few minutes later, the object came hurtling silently across the sky towards us. As it approached closer, I was startled to see a classic saucer-shaped craft, something we had never seen before, but the weirdest thing about it was that at that precise moment EVERY boy on the street turned around and looked at it at precisely the same time, as though this object wanted us all to look at it.

It was grayish-silver in colour, with yellow windows all around the dome. We all looked at it dumbstruck! None of us could move. (Whether it was through fear I do not know) After about

10 seconds, it shone the brightest light I had ever seen resembling a constant discharge from xenon light. It was so bright that it cast shadows of the parked cars in the street! At that point we all took to our heels and ran into our own houses, petrified."

Derek rushed into the house and alerted his parents, telling them about the huge UFO hovering in the sky outside. Within a short space of time his younger brother came rushing into the house, saying exactly the same thing. His father fetched a camera to take a photo of it. Whilst he was busy looking at the UFO, and taking off the lens cap, the UFO slowly and silently drifted off towards the other end of the housing estate and was lost from sight.

The next day Derek was at school, thinking *'Who do I tell about this?'* and *'Will they ever believe me?'*– *'I know what I saw!'* He overheard a conversation about the same thing in his physics classroom, amongst some other boys whom he did not know.

Apparently the UFO had drifted off towards a field in which they were playing and, according to one of them, they all just turned around at the same time and saw what the other boys had seen earlier. One boy, who was clearly a staunch disbeliever, was busy goading the other boys – until Derek told them he had seen the very same thing. This boy informed him, and all the kids that saw it, to go to opposite ends of the classroom, out of sight of each other, and draw what they supposedly saw. They all drew what they saw and EVERY picture had matched up in great detail. One boy went a bit pale and said that he had no other option but to believe them all. Derek is now 43 years of age and he still remembers that day as if it were only yesterday. It seems to have left an indelible memory on his mind and all those who saw it.

(Source: WWW. Stephen Wagner Paranormal Phenomena. About.com 'UFO over Hull' 2013)

UFO over Hull – January 1987

Following the newspaper appeal, made in 2013, we received an email from Hull residents – Phil and Jan Readymartcher – who were with two others when they sighted something very unusual, one evening in early 1987.

The couple described what they had seen.

"Two of us saw it first. It came from our right, moving quite slowly. My mate said, 'What's that?' I said, 'I don't know, but there is another'. He then said, 'There's another'. This one was much further away."

The three of them were heading in the same direction. There was one white light at the back and seemingly two at the front. One of them seemed to be moving like a lighthouse beam, in a circular motion, sweeping the ground and sky.

Phil:

"This was also reported to the Hull Daily Mail *by a woman from Newbridge Road, Hull, who said she saw it over her house. We rang her to confirm what she had seen. As for size, the only way I could describe it would be as a BIG airship. With it being a dark sky, no shape was visible – only the lights. Another time I would try to look through the object to try and see if it blotted out any stars.*

The Hull Daily Mail *published two articles. As usual, they got things wrong. There were four of us at High Farm who saw the flying objects. The second article, 'Aircraft theory in Hull link big bang Mystery' was misleading, as there were no bangs and it says TWO tanker aircraft. We saw THREE large objects and no smaller objects, and certainly no flashing aircraft navigation lights."*

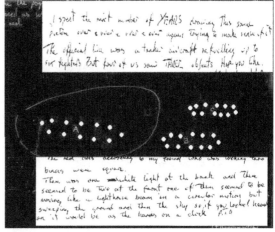

A farmer from Fitling, Hull, North Humberside, also said he had seen over 50 lights, moving through the sky.

John, "these are the fields to the left of the house. It is over these fields that I watched the objects (now three) disappear into the distance towards Coniston and Skirlaugh to be seen over Fitling."

Phil, "I am stood in the doorway looking to my right, you can see the roof of the houses of Bilton estate this is where the first object appeared from. The trees and bushes have grown a lot since then"

Further Documents

Even as this book was in its final completion, we acquired further documents of interest from Brenda Butler.

The first, from her friend – Peter Parish, shows another map of the Rendlesham Forest area and is endorsed with several key locations that the reader may find useful.

The second document is another (previously unpublished) travel

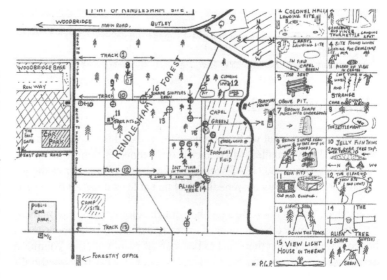

voucher, handed to Brenda by the 'whistleblower', 'Karin'. Whether there is any significance, we cannot say.

Final, few words

Reluctantly, we feel that we have come to the end of this book and want to thank Charles Halt, Brenda Butler, Dot Street, Jenny Randles, Mike Sacks, Jim Penniston, John Burroughs, Larry Warren, Peter Robbins, and many other civilian and USAF witnesses, for their assistance over the years. We are not naïve enough to feel we have determined any answers, but feel that at least it has all been recorded.

In hindsight, we did not realise just how much colossal information there was relating to these events, which still attracts an incredible amount of interest, and how much time we would spend on it. The more we delved the more we found, but there had to be a cut-off point with this Volume. Until all of the classified documents are released in this matter, the 'real truths' behind what happened will never be known. If the documents pertaining to the events that took place there suffer the same fate as the majority of other UFO documents which have never been declassified, or made available to the public, then the situation will remain unchanged.

Obviously, we would be delighted to hear from anyone who has additional information regarding any of the matters discussed in this Volume. The authors can be contacted by email: **Johndawn1@sky.com** or by writing to: **31, Red Lion Street, Alvechurch, Worcestershire B48 7LG**.

Update on samples

In October 2013, we were contacted by Nick Reite. He told us his colleague – Phyllis Budinger – had contacted him, following her examination of the 'blue foam like material' (see page 361 and 488), and has concluded, from her analysis so far, that *"The Rendlesham sample is polystyrene. Not surprised, especially when you said it was soluble in MEK. I don't detect any other components."*

With regard to the sample of metal sent to him from the possession of Ronnie Dugdale, Nick had this to say in an email sent to us:

> *"Potentially important – I was able to do some crude chemical and flame analysis on the metal bit. It is NOT a magnesium alloy; it indeed appears to be aluminum of some alloy or blend – so therefore, it does not match that old plot you had shared last year, from back in the 1980s (the one that showed magnesium). Maybe it will match Ben's alloy. The material here, in this picture, looks like a granular sintered metal, or glassy substance – is this the same material seen in the earlier pictures from a couple of weeks ago (that looked like a melted and solidified metal blob)? Well, we have an interesting match it seems."*

In an update, a few days later, Nick had this to say:

> *"The 'rough' analysis by my colleague's SEM and EDS came back in. I've attached his report. You may use this – it looks like he 'sanitized' it by removing the company name, as is best. The upshot – the metal appears to indeed be similar (in rough terms) to Ben Foggin's metal alloy – aluminum, with the main minor component being silicon. Also seen was some magnesium, in about the same ratio as Ben's. The next step will be to do ICPMS on this, which would be the fine analysis. Ben Foggin and I both agreed that if this sample came back resembling his, we would pay for the ICP. Interesting finding!"*

VOLUME 9 1981-1986 – Peek into the future . . .

Haunted Skies Volume 9 (1981-1986) was, bizarrely, completed before Volume 8, due to the ongoing investigations centred around the incidents which took place at Rendlesham Forest. This Volume contains many reports of 'Close Encounter' cases, and has much fresh information. Anticipated release date: late November 2013. Volume 10 (1987-1988). Anticipated release date: January 2014.

Ron West and Brenda Butler

We would also like to bring the readers attention to the research work carried out by Essex-based Ron West, of the East Anglian UFO and Paranormal Research Association, who was also Head of the Essex UFO Research Group and his colleague, Brenda Butler.

Thanks to their commitment in preserving the history of the UFO phenomena, during the late 1980s onwards, we are now able to document the result of that evidence, collected and painstakingly catalogued by Ron, fully in Volume 10 of *Haunted Skies* – which will be on sale in January 2014. In this book, which is currently under construction, the reader will learn of a colossal number of sightings, of what is now referred to as the *Triangular UFO,* which was first brought to the attention of the public during the early 1980's. This could so easily have been lost from history.

Brenda Butler and Ron West at Leiston

Thanks should also go to Miss 'G' from Essex, who has looked after the files following the death of Ron and now his wife Dorothy. Miss 'G' does not wish to be identified, but has asked that her beloved pet be shown in Volume 10, which will be done, it is the least we can do!

Ron wrote to Prime Minister Tony Blair, in 1997, reminding him of his promise to make available information pertaining to the incident which took place at Rendlesham Forest, in 1980. He also wrote to the Rt. Hon Paddy Ashdown MP, asking for information about the same matter, and received the following replies:

The Rt Hon Paddy Ashdown MP

HOUSE OF COMMONS

LONDON SW1A 0AA

Mr Ron West
95 Chilburn Road
Gt. Clacton
Essex
CO15 4PE

4th August 1997

Our Ref.: JR/Views

Dear Mr West

Thank you for your recent letter addressed to Mr. Ashdown who has asked me to reply on his behalf.

Mr. Ashdown is grateful to you for taking the time to write to him, and for giving him your views.

Thank you once again for writing.

Yours sincerely

David W.R. Lees
Senior Correspondence Officer

1O DOWNING STREET
LONDON SW1A 2AA

From the Correspondence Secretary   30 September 1997

Mr R W West
Essex UFO Research Group
95 Chilburn Road
GT CLACTON
CO15 4PE

Dear Mr West

I am writing to thank you for your recent letter and I am very sorry that your original correspondence addressed to the Prime Minister has not been acknowledged. He has received an enormous amount of correspondence since the Election and it has been found necessary to delegate the responsibility of answering the great majority of them to the Departments of State.

As your letter was referred to the Ministry of Defence I have passed this further letter to them and asked them to ensure a reply is sent to you as soon as possible. Meanwhile, please accept my sincere apologies for the unfortunate delay.

Yours sincerely

MISS J GORMAN

HAUNTED SKIES

SCRAPBOOK

A document released by the U.S. Air Force under The Freedom of Information Act confirms that a landed and entities were seen near Rendlesham Forest in Suffolk on December 30, 1980. However, the case has been safely explained away as caused by a distant lighthouse.

Southern Evening Echo, Southampton
26 APR 1988

UFO sleuth aims to uncover top level conspiracy

FLYING SAUCER REVIEW

Vol 29 No 3 1984 March

Annual subscriptions (six issues): UK and Overseas: £7.50 USA $15.00 (bank exchange commission in US dollars or personal cheques in US dollars drawn on banks in the USA is covered by this amount). **Single copies:** £1.50 (US$3.00).

OVERSEAS SUBSCRIBERS ARE RECOMMENDED TO REMIT IN £ STERLING BY INTERNATIONAL (OR BANKERS') MONEY ORDER.

IMPORTANT NOTICE: Subscribers in the Republic of Ireland and in Canada are requested to remit the sterling amount by International Money Order, or by Giro (FSR) Publications Ltd., Giro No. 356 3261) and **NOT** by personal cheques drawn in sterling (unless these are drawn on a bank in the United Kingdom), or drawn in US dollars (unless these are drawn on a bank in the United States of America).

Airmail extra: for USA South Africa, Argentina, Brazil £4.74 (US$9.50) Australia, New Zealand etc., £5.34. Middle East £3.90, all annually.

Overseas subscribers should remit by bank draft or personal cheque drawn on a bank in the United Kingdom, by personal cheque in US dollars drawn on banks in the USA only, or by International Money Order in Sterling (our preference). If remitting by Giro then FSR's account number is 356 3261.

All mail, editorial matter and subscriptions should be addressed to:

The Editor, FSR Publications Ltd., West Malling, Maidstone, Kent ME19 6JZ. England.

Remittances should be made payable to 'FSR Publications Ltd.'

Gordon was not to guess *then*, just how much media interest would be generated over the years.

He would have been amazed by Colonel Halt 's admission of having seen an Alien and reports of binary code by Jim Penniston. Will the real truth ever come out?

Artwork: Eve and Contributors

UFO INVESTIGATOR: Dot Street is determined to find out more about close encounters with alien life.

Close Encounters of a UFO writer

SCHOOLTEACHER turned author, Jenny Randles, makes no secret of her intention in researching into and writing about Unidentified Flying Objects. It is not just to sell books, reports CHRIS CHILD.

JENNY RANDLES'S fourth book, The Pennine UFO Mystery, just published, investigates the many sightings and reports of unexplained objects and incidents in the Pennines area of Yorkshire.

But Mrs. Randles said she had never gone out with the intention of writing a book that was going to sell. "I don't say the things that people often want to hear about UFOs," she admitted. "People who are interested in the subject like to believe there really are aliens at the heart of this, and it is not very nice for them to have to face up to the realities, and I tell the realities."

27th July 1983

The day the aliens landed... in Suffolk

Jenny Randles ... I have no doubt at all that there are several unexplained phenomena at the heart of reports.

The Weekly News, April 6, 1996. 13

EX-COP CLAIMED HE WAS KIDNAPPED BY ALIENS

A new six-part BBC series alleges secret government departments are treating these 'X-File' cases seriously

BY TOP PARANORMAL EXPERT PETER HOUGH

UFO LANDS IN SUFFOLK
And that's OFFICIAL

EAST ANGLIAN DAILY TIMES
UFOs can lead you up the forest path...

IS THERE ANYONE OUT THERE?

'Spectacular' UFO sightings recalled

SIGHTINGS of a UFO near two Suffolk air bases are being billed as "probably the most spectacular and convincing UFO story ever".

A 30-minute programme featuring the dramatic events in 1980 at Rendlesham Forest, near Woodbridge, will be shown on television this week.

The final programme in the *Strange But True?* series will be introduced by Michael Aspel and features the 14-year-old mystery that still attracts worldwide interest.

People fascinated by the claims that a spaceship landed close to RAF Woodbridge are still anxious to uncover the truth. Americans still ring up investigators with information, and visits are occasion-

ally made to the remote site.

The Japanese printed 35,000 copies of a book by Brenda Butler, of Leiston, and co-author Dot Street, which quickly sold out and a second run of 39,000 copies was also snapped up.

Just after Christmas in 1980 a security patrol reported bizarre lights and Suffolk Police, called to investigate, confirmed indentations in the ground. Americans found they formed a perfect triangle.

More lights were reported in the forest a few nights later. Woodbridge base deputy commander Lt Col Charles Halt set out with a team of men equipped with a Geiger counter, night vision scope

and tape recorder, to investigate.

They claim they also saw a UFO. The Geiger counter recorded 25 times the normal background radiation, the night vision scope picked up heat readings from the trees.

The Ministry of Defence investigated the incidents. It found there was no military or defence significance.

But Lord Hill-Norton, a former Chief of Staff with the MoD, believes there was a cover-up, and a former American military intelligence officer claims a top secret investigation did take place.

The London Weekend Television programme is on Friday at 8.30pm on ITV.

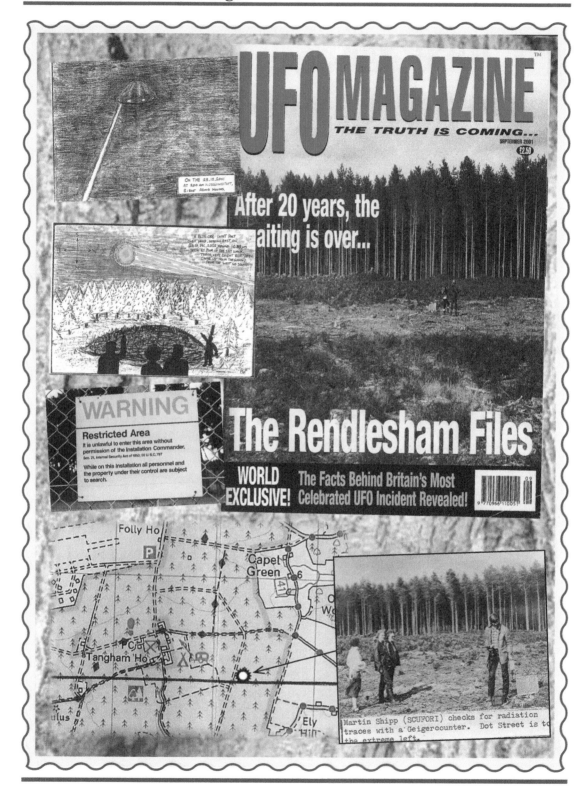

Alien craft theory is dismissed officially

By RICHARD SMITH

THE Ministry of Defence has ruled out holding an investigation into the world-famous Rendlesham UFO which has hit the headlines for the past 20 years.

The House of Lords was told no new information has come forward and, therefore, there was no reason why the MoD should conduct an inquiry.

The announcement was made after Admiral of the Fleet, Lord Hill-Norton, former Chief of Defence staff, asked a series of questions concerning the UFO which Americans claimed to have seen close to RAF Woodbridge after Christmas in 1980.

Lord Hill-Norton asked the questions following the publication of new information contained in Georgina Bruni's book *You Can't Tell The People*.

Ms Bruni has claimed her 400-plus page book is the most definitive account of the UFO mystery.

Lord Hill-Norton has taken an interest in the subject for many years, but his question and answer session in the House of Lords did not produce anything new to stimulate the thousands of ufologists.

Replying to his questions, Baroness Symons of Vernham Dean, minister of state for the Ministry of Defence, denied there were any underground facilities at the nearby former RAF Bentwaters base.

It has been claimed by Larry Warren, a former member of the American security forces, that after seeing the UFO, he was drugged and taken to an underground installation where he saw the same object.

Ms Bruni, who has visited Bentwaters, disputed last night the statement made in the House of Lords and claimed there were underground facilities at the base that were sealed.

"The security chief at the installation, who gave me a guard and permission to investigate the buildings, told me the underground facilities were sealed when the MoD put the base up for sale," she alleged.

"He had written several times to the MoD requesting details of these, but although they promised to look into the matter, he received nothing.

"I also discovered a door in the main command post

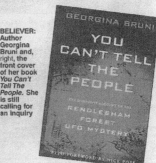

BELIEVER: Author Georgina Bruni and, right, the front cover of her book *You Can't Tell The People*. She is still calling for an inquiry

that was clearly an entrance to an underground facility because it could not lead to anywhere above ground."

Baroness Symons said the MoD was not aware of any involvement by the MoD police in the alleged UFO sighting.

The MoD's knowledge of involvement by Suffolk police was limited to one letter dated July 28, 1999, and contained in Ms Bruni's book.

She added: "No additional information has come to light over the last 20 years to call into question the original judgement by the Ministry of Defence that nothing of defence significance occurred in the location of Rendlesham Forest in 1980. Accordingly, there is no reason to hold an investigation now.

"As a matter of courtesy, the Ministry of Defence informed Headquarters 3rd Air Force at RAF Mildenhall about the (Georgina Bruni) book. The US authorities have not subsequently approached the Ministry of Defence on the issue."

Lord Hill-Norton raised the issue almost four years

ago with the then minister of state Lord Gilbert.

At the time he wrote to Lord Gilbert, saying: "My position, both privately and publicly expressed over the last dozen years or more, is that there are only two possibilities.

"Either an intrusion into our air space and a landing by unidentified craft took place at Rendlesham, as described.

"Or the deputy commander of an operational, nuclear-armed, US Air Force base in England and a large number of his enlisted men were either hallucinating or lying.

"Either of these simply must be 'of interest to the Ministry of Defence', which has been repeatedly denied."

Ms Bruni argues if the MoD had read her book and it was concerned enough to alert the Americans, then the incident must have had extreme defence significance.

INTERNET LINK
www.parliament.the-stationery-office.co.uk

be caused by exceptionally strong magnetic fields.

Whatever the cause, we can be sure that reports of abduction by aliens will continue and these will undoubtedly be the subject of further detailed studies.

Rendlesham Forest

Britain's most highly publicised UFO incident occurred at Rendlesham Forest, Suffolk, between the adjoining Woodbridge and Bentwater air bases.

At 3.00 am on a December morning in 1980, the members of a security patrol guarding the perimeter of the Woodbridge base noticed strange lights in the forest, which were bright enough to convince them that an aircraft had crashed. A three man patrol was sent into the forest and they claim to have discovered a triangular shaped object hovering above the ground in a clearing, which bathed the entire area in a brilliant white light. [As they] approached the object, it moved off and was lost from sight.

A further brilliant object was observed [above the] trees, which [moved a]bout [...]

[Various theories have been put forward to] explain the strange lights. Even in the forest and many investigators believe the guards were fooled by the beam from the Orford Ness lighthouse on the coast and possibly the lights from a passing police patrol car. However, Colonel Halt strongly disputes the fact that anyone would be misled by the lighthouse and says that base personnel were fully aware of it. It has also been suggested that a very bright meteor and the re-entry of Cosmos 749 above England may have contributed to events.

Mysterious lights beyond the trees. Photo by [...]

[R]eal flying saucer? No, just a foil dish tossed in the air. Photo by Bill [...]

While there definitely was unusual activity taking place in this area during December 1980, many of the reports which took [...]

The last UFO of the '70s?

THE peace of New Year's Eve at Ilkeston was disturbed by a UFO — sighted by two police officers.

A policeman and a policewoman reported sighting an unidentified flying object at about 1.20am on Monday morning.

For five seconds they saw a bright oval green object with a white tailback above Boyah Farm, Dale Abbey.

It travelled in a straight line, east to west, at a low altitude above tree height in the clear sky.

Details of the sighting were passed from Ilkeston police station to county headquarters at Ripley.

It is understood they will be sent to Manchester Airport where information on such sightings is collated.

fic fills our skies. [...] low level air activity is military in nature [...] occasionally this will include secret [...] aircraft which are mistaken for [...]

Trevor Parker who found the mystery body

From Page One

they interviewed the policeman who spoke of the sighting.

They say he agreed to undergo hypnosis and while in a trance he recalled seeing a flying saucer earlier on the day that Mr Adamski was found.

West Yorkshire police would not allow us to interview the officer.

This is the unbelievable story uncovered by Sunday Mirror investigators.

Mr Adamski vanished on June 11 last year after setting off on foot from his home to buy potatoes at a corner shop.

Pile of coal

Coal merchant's son Mr Trevor Parker found his body in a hollow on top of the pile of coal in Todmorden, where Mr Adamski had no known connections.

There was no indication as to how he got there.

His face, cheeks, forehead

Coroner James Turnbull

and clothes were NOT marked by the corrosive substance, suggesting that when the burns were inflicted the top half of his body was naked.

Mr Adamski, who became a soldier and later a miner after fleeing Poland in the war, was found wearing a jacket but without a shirt.

His watch and wallet were missing but he had £5 in his pocket.

Consultant pathologist Dr Alan Edwards said death was caused by heart failure, possibly due to "a severe shock or fright".

Police probed Mr Adamski's background in an attempt to find clues to his death.

But they found that he drank little, did not gamble, and was unlikely to have enemies.

Coroner Mr Turnbull adjourned the inquest three times and appealed for anyone who could solve the riddle to come forward.

Then he recorded an open verdict.

Worldwide

Mr Turnbull told us: "An open verdict means that this case is still technically under investigation."

"It is an intractable mystery. The police, too, have not closed their file."

Mr Graham Birdsall, area co-ordinator for Contact International UK, the largest UFO study movement, said: "There is worldwide interest in this case. It is the biggest UFO story for many years.

"The fact that the police

have even considered the possibility of UFO involvement is unique."

Mr Birdsall and Mr Walter Reid, of the British UFO Research Association, confirmed that the PC involved underwent hypnosis.

"There is no obvious explanation why the body was there" said Mr Reid. "It would seem he was literally dropped there".

Mr Adamski's widow, who is confined to a wheelchair, said: "He was a good man with no enemies.

"He must have been kidnapped, by who or what and for what reason, I don't think I will ever know."

UFO enthusiasts class list him as a CE-3—Close Encounter of the Third Kind.

New threat to Times

SUNDAY TIMES journal[...]

Interest in UFO book is growing

INTEREST in the world famous UFO sighting at Rendlesham Forest, near Woodbridge, has been rekindled by a new book by one of the eyewitnesses. Woodbridge Books has sold nearly 200 copies of Larry Warren's first-hand account entitled Left At East Gate since it went on sale during the summer.

The shop in the Thoroughfare sold 100 copies in 90 minutes when Mr Warren and his co-author Peter Robbins attended a book-signing session.

Now the shop has organised a second signing session on August 23 from 11am until 12.30pm to satisfy demand from the public to meet the authors and discuss the dramatic events in 1980 close to RAF Woodbridge.

In June up to 100,000 national television viewers said they believed aliens had visited Earth after watching evidence on the UFO. Eyewitnesses claim they saw a space ship on three legs and small beings alight in the forest near the east gate of the air base.

Speculation is expected to mount further in January when UFO investigator Jenny Randles publishes new evidence in a book about the sightings.

21 AUG 1997

ANGLIAN

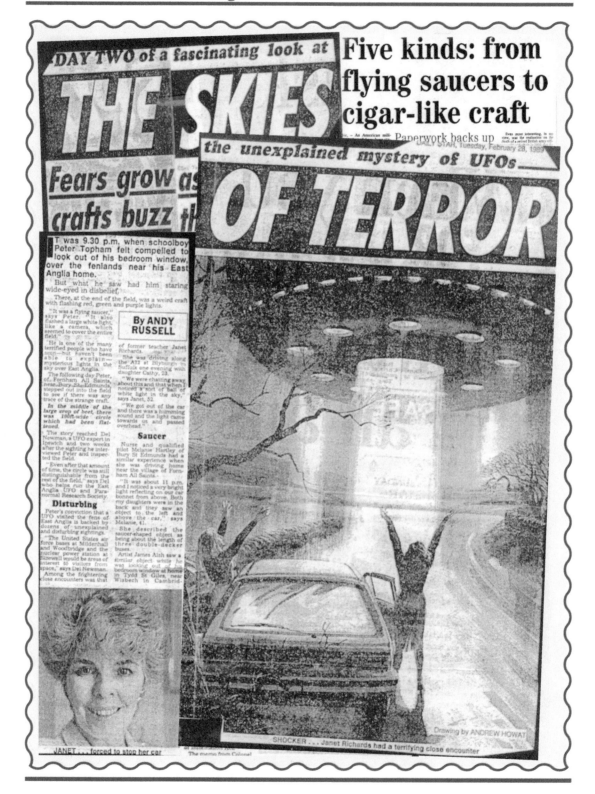

DAY TWO of a fascinating look at

THE SKIES

Five kinds: from flying saucers to cigar-like craft

the unexplained mystery of UFOs

OF TERROR

Fears grow as crafts buzz t...

...r, – As American mili- Paperwork backs up

DAILY STAR, Tuesday, February 28, 1989

I T was 9.30 p.m. when schoolboy Peter Topham felt compelled to look out of his bedroom window, over the fenlands near his East Anglia home.

But what he saw had him staring wide-eyed in disbelief.

There, at the end of the field, was a weird craft with flashing red, green and purple lights.

"It was a flying saucer," says Peter. "It also flashed a large white light, like a camera, which seemed to cover the entire field."

He is one of the many terrified people who have seen—but haven't been able to explain—mysterious lights in the sky over East Anglia.

The following day Peter, of Fornham All Saints, near Bury St Edmunds, stepped out into the field to see if there was any trace of the strange craft.

In the middle of the large crop of beet, there was 100ft-wide circle which had been flattened.

The story reached Del Newman, a UFO expert in Ipswich and two weeks after the sighting he interviewed Peter and inspected the field.

"Even after that amount of time, the circle was still distinguishable from the rest of the field," says Del who helps run the East Anglia UFO and Paranormal Research Society.

Disturbing

Peter's conviction that a UFO visited the fens of East Anglia is backed by dozens of unexplained and disturbing sightings.

"The United States air force bases at Mildenhall and Woodbridge and the nuclear power station at Sizewell would be areas of interest to visitors from space," says Del Newman.

Among the frightening close encounters was that

By ANDY RUSSELL

of former teacher Janet Richards.

She was driving along the A12 at Blythburgh in Suffolk one evening with daughter Cathy, 23.

"We were chatting away about this and that when I noticed a sort of ball of white light in the sky," says Janet, 51.

"We got out of the car and there was a humming sound and the light came towards us and passed overhead."

Saucer

Nurse and qualified pilot Melanie Hartley of Bury St Edmunds had a similar experience when she was driving home near the village of Fornham All Saints.

"It was about 11 p.m. and I noticed a very bright light reflecting on our car bonnet from above. Both my daughters were in the back and they saw an object to the left and above the car," says Melanie, 41.

She described the saucer-shaped object as being about the length of three double-decker buses.

Artist James Aish saw a similar object while he was looking out of his bedroom window at home in Tydd St Giles, near Wisbech in Cambrid...

Drawing by ANDREW HOWAT

SHOCKER ... Janet Richards had a terrifying close encounter

JANET ... forced to stop her car

The memo from Colonel

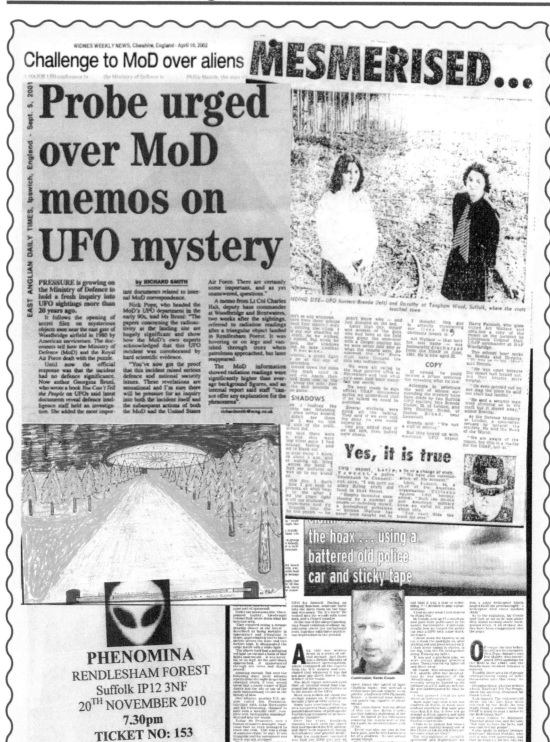

WIDNES WEEKLY NEWS, Cheshire, England - April 18, 2002

Challenge to MoD over aliens

MESMERISED...

EAST ANGLIAN DAILY TIMES, Ipswich, England – Sept. 5, 2001

Probe urged over MoD memos on UFO mystery

by RICHARD SMITH

PRESSURE is growing on the Ministry of Defence to hold a fresh inquiry into UFO sightings more than 20 years ago.

It follows the opening of secret files on mysterious objects seen near the east gate of Woodbridge airfield in 1980 by American servicemen. The documents tell how the Ministry of Defence (MoD) and the Royal Air Force dealt with the puzzle.

Until now the official response was that the incident had no defence significance. Now author Georgina Bruni, who wrote a book *You Can't Tell the People* on UFOs and latest documents reveal defence intelligence staff held an investigation. She added the most important documents related to internal MoD correspondence.

Nick Pope, who headed the MoD's UFO department in the early 90s, said Ms Bruni: "The papers concerning the radioactivity at the landing site are hugely significant and show how the MoD's own experts acknowledged that this UFO incident was corroborated by hard scientific evidence.

"You've now got the proof that this incident raised serious defence and national security issues. These revelations are sensational and I'm sure there will be pressure for an inquiry into both the incident itself and the subsequent actions of both the MoD and the United States Air Force. There are certainly some important, and as yet unanswered, questions."

A memo from Lt Col Charles Halt, deputy base commander at Woodbridge and Bentwaters, two weeks after the sightings, referred to radiation readings after a triangular object landed in Rendlesham Forest. It was hovering or on legs and vanished through trees when patrolmen approached, but later reappeared.

The MoD information showed radiation readings were significantly higher than average background figures, and an internal report said staff "cannot offer any explanation for the phenomena".

richardsmith@ncng.co.uk

LANDING SITE— UFO hunters Brenda (left) and Dorothy at Tangham Wood, Suffolk, where the craft touched town

PHENOMINA
RENDLESHAM FOREST
Suffolk IP12 3NF
20ᵀᴴ NOVEMBER 2010
7.30pm
TICKET NO: 153

SHADOWS

Yes, it is true

the hoax ... using a battered old police car and sticky tape

Confession: Kevin Conde

520

BERWICK ADVERTISER
14 FEB 80

Berwick textile worker saw a U.F.O.

Textile worker, Yeoman Redfearn, is not just spinning a yarn when he says he saw a U.F.O. in the early morning sky on Monday.

Yeoman, who works at Pringles of Scotland Ltd., on the Tweedside Trading Estate, spotted the object on his way to work.

At 6.45 a.m. he saw a flashing light in the sky.

It was following the rail-

above the One Tunnel'
ng to the Trading Estate.

Yeoman said it wasn't

the U.F.O. for about
10 minutes.

SPACESHIP RIDDLE DEEPENS

MINISTRY of Defence officials confirmed last night they had received an amazing report that a UFO landed near an air base.

The sighting claim was filed by American air force colonel Charles Halt, who said he saw bright lights and a space machine at Woodbridge, Suffolk, in December 1980.

A Ministry spokesman said no record of the colonel's report had been kept.

But he added: "All

UFO sightings are passed on to the RAF staff for further investigation."

In the private report, Colonel Halt said he and others saw a red ball of light in the sky.

He went on: "All of a sudden it exploded. The place was filled with an explosion of colours.

"When they died down, there was a machine, hovering on legs."

Daily Star - Sept 83

Flying saucer or secret experiment?

This is the second sighting...

latest research on Rendlesham Forest's UFO mystery suggests the encounters reported by many witnesses on two successive nights were caused not by aliens from outer space but by a more sinister, earth-bound force. **DAVID BARRETT** spoke to the author who has been investigating the case for 18 years.

WHAT HAPPENED?

DEC 1980 near RoF–USAF
BENTWATERS & Woodbridge
Air Base.

An open air event
Saturday 20th November 2010

7.30pm - 8.00pm: Mediumship with Philip Kinsella
8.00pm - 9.00pm: Talk on UFO's - Interactive discussion with Brenda Butler
9.00pm til late: Sky watch walk

Tickets: £10.00 - Tel: 01728 830757
email: nigel.turner@forestry.gsi.gov.uk
web: www.philipkinsella.com

Something so strange that the world Media took an interest in investigation into the mysterious PHENOMENON that occurred at RENDELSHAM FOREST

"A triangular craft landed in Suffolk"

"I had contact with an ET and then there was the Yeti"

Ex-policeman relives UFO close encounter
By Kelly Thornham

RETIRED policeman Alan Godfrey, who had a close encounter with a UFO, relived the experience before an audience of more than 100 people.

Mr Godfrey took some of time filming a programme for the BBC to talk at a charity event when the day in 1980 when he spotted the UFO while on patrol in Todmorden.

THE UFO MYSTERIES

THE Sunday Mirror last week revealed astonishing evidence that Whitehall has been keeping UFO sightings secret from the British public.

Today we look at how this cover-up extended to investigations into a remarkable incident at a Suffolk airbase. An incident witnessed by senior military men. We examine this mystery, and below give case histories of other "close encounters" reported in Jenny Randles' book The UFO Conspiracy.

Jenny—"The truth is being hidden."

By CHRIS MOORE

A WEIRD, unearthly light in the forest puzzled the security patrol at a Suffolk air base.

Three men went to investigate — and came face to face with what they are convinced was a UFO.

There, in a clearing, they found a brightly-lit object the size of a small car, apparently hovering just above the ground.

Baffled, the three patrolmen approached the strange craft and one, John Burroughs, tried to touch it.

Later, he was dragged from the forest in a state of shock.

Just what happened

Strange UFO attracts experts

SITINGS of a strange object seen hovering in the sky near Charterhouse School has sparked off an investigation by a Surrey UFO group.

The Surrey Investigation Group on Aerial Phenomena is hoping to obtain a full and detailed description of what happened on the night of February 15 in Godalming.

And what was seen in the sky the following night by a motorist driving along the Shere Bypass.

Group investigation co-ordinator Mr. Omar Fowler said it was too early to have a theory on the cigar-shaped objects spotted in the sky.

But he said the sitings two weeks ago were "very similar" to the sitings of UFOs in Ash two years ago, which attracted wide publicity both locally and nationally.

A group of schoolboys from Charterhouse were the first to see the latest object in the sky. They described it as "cigar-shaped" which hovered silently.

The next night Mr. David McCarthy and three friends were driving along the Shere Bypass towards Albury when they spotted something similar.

"We want more identity details from the witnesses," said Mr. Fowler. "Whether the object had multi-coloured lights, whether it accelerated rapidly, etc."

Forms have been sent to the witnesses by the Surrey investigation group for full details. "We will then classify and file the forms or personally visit the witnesses," said Mr. Fowler.

SURREY DAILY ADVERTISER
5 MARCH 80

'Aliens' in silver suits

When the flying saucer took off

Guest on a space ship

Encounter with real-life terror

MILLIONS of movie-goers thrilled to an alien landing in Steven Spielberg's Close Encounters of the Third Kind. They thought it was great science fiction. It was really very close to being science fact.

Nothing was closer to the truth than the sequence where car engines cut out in the path of a UFO.

Jenny Randles claims there have been 1,000 UFO-related car break-downs around the world during the past 14 years, including us in Britain.

One night, in Levelland, Texas, in 1957

The Rendlesham

By Don Ramkin

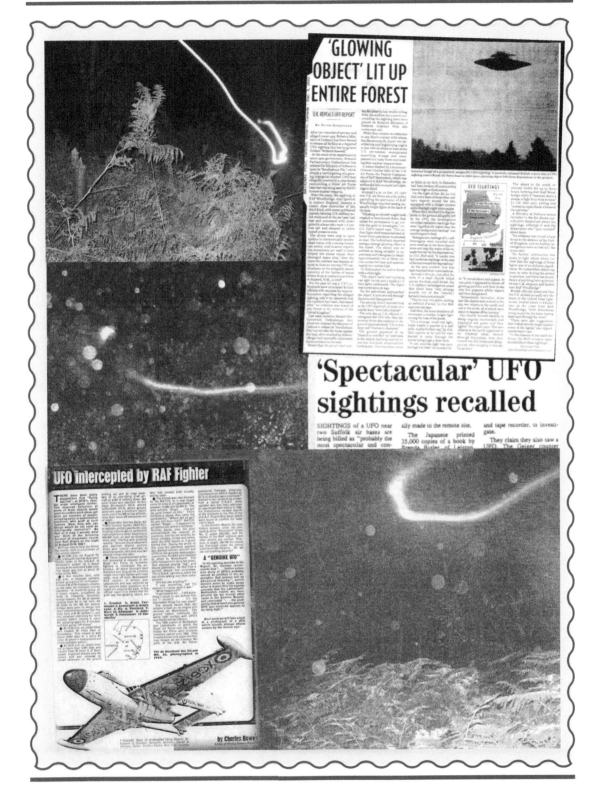

'GLOWING OBJECT' LIT UP ENTIRE FOREST

U.K. REVEALS UFO REPORT

By Peter Goodspeed

'Spectacular' UFO sightings recalled

SIGHTINGS of a UFO near two Suffolk air bases are being billed as "probably the most spectacular and con-s?ually made to the remote site.

The Japanese printed 35,000 copies of a book by Brenda Butler, of Leiston, and tape recorder, to investigate.

They claim they also saw a UFO. The Geiger counter

UFO intercepted by RAF Fighter

A "GENUINE UFO"

by Charles Bowen

Forest UFO 'was just lighthouse'

2 APRIL 80

...e may have picture of U.F.O. A523.

Ex-Pc rails against far-fetched stories

By RICHARD SMITH

A FORMER policeman who investigated the world famous Rendlesham Forest UFO in 1980 has claimed that the incident was nothing more sinister than the light from Orford Ness lighthouse.

He has spoken publicly about the 18-year-old mystery for the first time and says he decided to break his silence after becoming annoyed that people worldwide were making money from elaborate and far-fetched stories.

David King, 59, says they have been trying to come up with a mysterious explanation to cover their tracks after they were fooled by the lighthouse.

Mr. King, of Stennett's Close, Grimley St Mary, says the only other explanation for the lights in the forest near RAF Woodbridge was the breaking up in space of the Cosmos 749 Soviet satellite.

Alerted

Mr King spent 26 years with Suffolk Police, with most of his time stationed at Woodbridge where he was on night duty over the Christmas period in 1980.

He was alerted to investigate lights seen in the forest, near the east gate of RAF Woodbridge, and set off in pursuit with another constable, Martin Brophy.

The call to their police car was made at 4.11am on December 26 and they followed an American vehicle into the forest to try to trace the lights.

"It was a quiet, mild night, with not a soul around. It seemed dead in there. As we

see a light flash and I knew that was the Orford Ness lighthouse flash. I said to Martin, there is nothing here. We only saw the lighthouse."

He came on duty again in the evening of December 26 and looked through the police messages at Woodbridge. Mr King says that there was a message from RAF Bentwaters saying that they thought they had found the place where the UFO landed.

"Another policeman went out to the site and confirmed at 10am on December 26 that there was nothing there," said Mr King.

Mr King was making a routine check with the law enforcement desk at RAF Bentwaters late on December 26 when a call came through from RAF Woodbridge to say that strange lights had been seen for the second consecutive night in the forest.

Mr King wanted to have a look – but he was diverted to an emergency at Otley Post Office and did not investigate the second sightings.

"I have said all along that it was the lights from Orford Ness, but no one wants to take notice of that as it doesn't fit in with what they want to believe," he added.

His crucial evidence comes a few weeks after the publication for the first time of original witness statements made by American officers a few days after the 1980 sightings.

The statements made by Staff Sergeant Jim Penniston and Airman First Class John Burroughs, of the 81st Security Police Squadron, were made to the Bentwaters air base deputy commander, Charles Halt. They admit that they 'chased a lighthouse.'

BROKEN SILENCE: Former policeman David King speaks out. Picture: JOHN KERR

Mr Bert Perrie, Jubilee Cottage, Baldovie, thinks he may have a photograph of the U.F.O. sighted in the area recently.

Last Wednesday evening, about six o'clock, he caught sight of a shining object fairly high in the sky.

"At first glance, I thought it was an aeroplane, but I nipped out to the garden for a closer look," he said yesterday.

"Then I noticed something hanging from the object in the air and thought it must be a parachute or weather balloon as it was travelling north with the clouds.

"It stopped slightly north of Baldovie for about twenty minutes before moving off in an easterly direction and eventually rising out of sight."

Mr Perrie and his wife, Isobel, both tried to film the object with their cine camera. It was difficult to focus on it with the camera lens although they could see it with the naked eye.

Mr Perrie next day told his colleagues at work and the local policeman about the incident. They were sceptical, as no other sightings had been reported at that early date.

BEST MYSTERY PROGRAMME

● **Strange But True?** ITV, 8.30pm.

The series ends with the best story by far — a UFO sighting at a U.S. Air Force base in East Anglia which is very well corroborated, very hard to explain and seems to have been the subject of a deliberate cover-up. A genuine mystery, properly expounded — if only the rest of the series had come up to this standard.

Lori Buoen

BARNSLEY CHRONICLE
BARNSLEY, YORKSHIRE
ISSUE DATED 31 OCT 1980

Space invaders over Barnsley
Martin Oxley checks up

Good Lords! – it's a UFO

BOOKS: In 1979, the Earl of Clancarty addressed the Upper House on the subject of flying saucers – while Britain was on the verge of collapse. By **Jay Iliff**

Authors invited to UFO summit

Did this man see a UFO in Suffolk 20 years ago?

COVER UP: Larry Warren was warned not to talk about his experiences. 'Bullets are cheap,' he was told. Inset: Larry in 1980

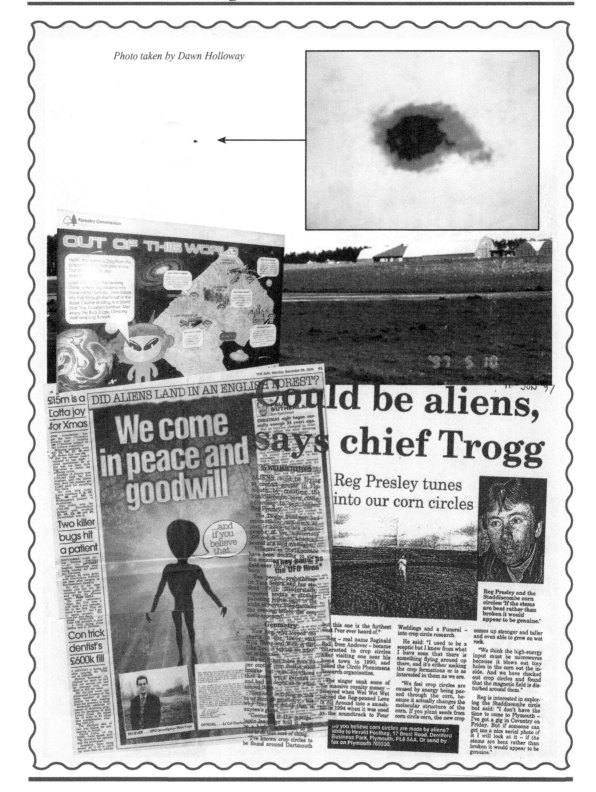

Photo taken by Dawn Holloway

Flying saucer or secret experiment

Latest research on Rendlesham Forest's UFO mystery suggests the encounters reported by many witnesses on two successive nights were caused not by aliens from outer space but by a more sinister, earth-bound force. **DAVID BARRETT** spoke to the author who has been investigating the case for 18 years.

Eastern Daily Press - Norwich
(Circ: 80,968)
5 FEB 1998

There is one thing that Jenny Randles wants to get straight from the very beginning. The phrase "Unidentified Flying Object" does not have to refer to little green men. In fact, 95 per cent of UFO sightings have a rational, natural explanation which has nothing in common with Mulder, Scully, Close Encounters or Steven Spielberg's little brown men who was good with plants.

"A lot of researchers believe in UFOs but not in alien spaceships," said Randles.

"A UFO does not have to be extra-terrestrial, it merely has to be unexplained."

In her new book – UFO Crash Landing? Friend or Foe? – Randles sets out a number of earth-bound theories to explain the series of encounters by military and civilian witnesses across East Anglia at Christmas 1980.

It is Randles' second book on the subject, and her latest research throws out a lot of the information contained in the first book she co-wrote in 1984.

"It's a case that has almost obsessed me as I try to get at the truth," said Randles.

"We were unable to get any official verification at the time of the first book and I'm afraid we probably brought a lot of rumour and tall tales to the public, which I now believe was misleading, perhaps deliberately so."

On Christmas night, 1980, the civil aviation radar base at Watton tracked an object heading from the Wash to Rendlesham. It was also tracked by military radar teams at Neatishead and both bases independently reported their sightings to the London Air Traffic Control Centre.

"A routine patrol from RAF Woodbridge was led by the 26-year-old USAF airman John Burroughs, who observed this object coming down from the sky and landing in the forest," said Randles.

Believing what they had seen to be an aircraft coming down, the patrol was joined by air accident specialist Jim Penniston, and from the edge of the forest they could see strange lights.

Penniston described them as "chemical fires" and "multi-coloured" while Burroughs thought they looked like Christmas tree lights.

to find this machine in Jane's Book of Aircraft.

The two men's descriptions vary. Penniston said it was a craft with a physical structure with a surface like smoked-glass, and that it had some black markings on it, while Burroughs said it was more like a glowing mass of lights.

"Both men say when they got within 10 feet, it was surrounded by an aura, like a huge electro-magnetic field. Their hair began to stand on end, their skin was tingling and their eyes were watering. Every step seemed to defy the laws of time and space, like trying to walk through treacle it was more and more difficult to get closer to the craft.

"Then it shot vertically upwards, hovered over the trees and darted off at an acute angle, at great speed."

The team, gripped by what they had seen, returned the following day and found three marks in the ground and a huge hole in the tree canopy, which Randles

Deputy base commander Charles Halt (who later went on to hold a top job at the Pentagon) first heard about the night's excitement at breakfast on Boxing Day, said Randles, and later had a chance to experience the things at first hand.

The lights were seen again on December 27, and Halt led an investigation team armed with Geiger counters, arc lights and cameras. They investigated the first site, with Halt dictating notes into a tape recorder, then at 1.38am they saw lights in the sky.

"Halt described a huge object like an eye, winking at them and projecting a beam of light towards the ground. They literally chased it through the trees, following some star-like lights for two hours before fatigue made them give up and turn back to base.

The Monday after the sightings, United States Air Force intelligence officers flew away from the Watton and Neatishead bases, explaining they were required for analysis.

At Watton, the intelligence spooks also said something very strange and out of character, according to a witness interviewed by Randles.

New twist in UFO mystery

CONSPIRACY: Did top-level military officials use the UFO sightings near local air bases to hide the extent of their work at Orford Ness? Pictures: LIBRARY

Face to face with black-eyed aliens

"AS MY mind tried to register what I was looking at, the ball of light exploded in a blinding flash. I couldn't move; I tried to cover my eyes, but was too late. Now, right in front of me was a machine occupying the spot where the fog had been."

No, this isn't an excerpt from some science-fiction novel. They're the words of Larry Warren, former United States Air Force security guard and self-proclaimed UFO eyewitness, in his new book Left at East Gate.

At a West Midland theatre tonight,

By SALLY-ANNE SWIFT

he will be describing his experiences.

Warren claims to have seen first-hand the arrival of a UFO in a field, not in some obscure New Mexico town, but in the heart of rural Suffolk.

He also claims to have seen its alien occupants: "They were small, about three to four feet tall, and somewhat ghostlike in appearance. They had large heads with cat-like black eyes."

Warren, together with ufologist Peter Robbins, has spent the past ten years documenting his experiences and the result is the hefty 490-page

volume. In it they claim to have more evidence to support their story than was ever found at Roswell, New Mexico, where the remains of a crashed UFO were said to have been found exactly 50 years ago.

And they claim the whole thing was the subject of a massive cover-up operation on behalf of the British and American governments. Warren was stationed at RAF Bentwaters, one of Suffolk's largest Nato bases, in December 1980. One night he says he was ordered to drive to the east gate and turn left (hence the title of the book) to join other security personnel.

His story, in brief, is that he saw an alien craft land and strange beings emerge from it. Afterwards, he says,

he and his colleagues were debriefed and told to forget everything they saw.

Warren went public about his experience after he received an honourable discharge from the Air Force. Seventeen years later it has been set down in black and white for all to see.

ROBBINS says: "We have not written this book for UFO buffs. We have written it for everyone. It's a very human story."

Sceptics have put the alleged sighting down to a distant lighthouse, the planets Jupiter and Saturn, stars, a fireball or satellite re-entry. But Warren says he is unperturbed by the fact that some people will dismiss his book as nonsense.

"When they get a sense of the amount of evidence we have got they should know that this one can't be challenged," he says.

And he denies he is after a place on the best-sellers list.

"We do not care about best-sellers, that's not the issue. We have spent most of the money we had on this and I have experienced repercussions because of my public position. There has been a price to pay but it's worth it to change people's attitudes."

• Left At East Gate is published by Michael O'Mara Books (£15.99). Larry Warren and Peter Robbins are touring the UK talking about the book and will be at the Red Rose Theatre in Taylors Lane, Rugeley, at 7.30pm tonight.

MoD accused of 'UFO cover-up'

DEFENCE chiefs will today be accused of a cover-up over reported sightings of a UFO near a Suffolk airbase.

A former top civil servant at the Ministry of Defence claims officials have concealed information about a spacecraft landing at RAF Bentwaters near Woodbridge.

About 200 people reported seeing some kind of craft landing near the base in 1980. A confidential report on the landing was made by Lieutenant Colonel Charles Halt, then deputy commander of the base, according to a national newspaper.

Lt Col Halt's report referred to "unexplained lights" and a strange glowing object that lit up the forest that surrounded the base, the paper said. The landing is supposed to have happened on December 27, 1980.

Ralph Noyes, a former top civil servant said to have responsibility for UFO sightings, is to tell a TV station that the MoD imposed a news black-out about the landing. Mr Noyes will claim the MoD said nothing about the alleged landing because it wanted to save any embarrassment.

But a spokesman for the MoD reacted coolly to the suggestions. "I would treat all this with some caution," he said. "As far as I am aware we don't have people who are responsible for UFO sightings. We do take an interest in what might be a threat to national security."

Night I saw a UFO land at my airbase

Ex-US military chief tells all on British Roswell

From **David Gardner**
IN LOS ANGELES

A VETERAN air force chief has spoken out for the first time about what he saw in the only British UFO sighting to be documented by the Ministry of Defence.

Dubbed Britain's Roswell, the 28-year-old mystery sighting over East Anglia's Rendlesham Forest has been at the centre of X-Files-style claims of a cover-up by the Government.

Charles Halt, now retired, was the lieutenant colonel in charge of the American base in Suffolk in 1980.

His report – in which he tells how a large red glow split into five white

'I felt it was under intelligent control'

objects that hovered for several hours in the skies near RAF Woodbridge – is already part of the National Archives.

Now he has revealed in greater detail how the suspected UFO resembled a "blinking eye" and fired "laser beams" right near his feet as he stood watching in amazement.

"I have no idea what we saw that night but I do know with great certainty that it was under intelligent control," said Halt, who had risen to be director of inspections for the US military in Britain when he retired in 1990.

He recalled being alerted to the phe-

AMAZING: An artist's impression of the craft described by Charles Halt, left

looked like a triangular shaped craft over Rendlesham Forest.

Two nights later he says he was interrupted at a family Christmas party and told: 'It's back.'

In the forest he and two assistants found three deep indentations in a triangular formation.

Suddenly, he saw a bright red and orange oval object with a black centre. "It reminded me of an eye and it appeared to be winking or blinking.

"It manoeuvred through the trees with an occasional vertical movement. When approached, it receded and

'It was gone in the blink of an eye'

silently broke into five white objects. They changed shape from elliptical to round and several other objects were seen to the south.

"It appeared at high speed and sent down strange beams at our feet before moving away.

"The whole time we had difficulty communicating with the base as our radio frequencies kept breaking up."

Another retired American service-

man, James Pennington, who was the senior security officer on the base at the time, said he saw the triangular craft in the forest on Boxing Day 1980.

He said it was covered in blue and yellow swirling lights.

"After 45 minutes, the lights intensified and it lifted off without any noise and manoeuvred through the trees and shot off at an unbelievable speed. It was gone in the blink of an eye."

He said 80 air force personnel saw the take-off. He took two rolls of photographs but was told by British defence chiefs that they were "over-exposed" and did not show anything.

The claims were posted on YouTube by the US Coalition for Freedom Information.

Aliens 'hit our nukes'

alleged alien autopsies that is said to have been covered up by US defence chiefs after a UFO crashed near a military base in New Mexico in 1947.

'UFO threat put our prisons on red alert'

THE mystery over the alleged UFO sightings in Rendlesham Forest 30 years ago has taken a fresh twist with the publication of a new book.

RICHARD SMITH reports on the author's conclusions.

THREE prison officers were placed on a red alert in December 1980 with the possibility all prisoners would have to be evacuated, claims Georgina Bruni in her book.

Just visiting: Did an alien craft visit RAF Bentwaters in Suffolk 30 years ago and interfere with nuclear weapons technology?

radio that aliens had landed inside the nuclear storage area, he said.

"I believe that the security services of both the United States and the United Kingdom have attempted – both then and now – to subvert the significance of what occurred at RAF Bentwaters by the use of well-practised methods of disinformation."

The six former U.S. Air Force officers and one former enlisted man, are to present declassified information which they claim backs up their

findings. They have witness testimony from 120 former or retired military personnel which points to alien intervention at nuclear sites in the US as recently as 2003.

They will urge the authorities to confirm that alien beings have long been visiting Earth.

A press conference today in Washington will also highlight testimony from retired U.S. Air Force Captain Bruce Fenstermacher, whose security team saw a cigar-shaped UFO hovering above F.E Warren nuclear

base in Wyoming in 1976. Researcher Robert Hastings, who last written on the subject, explained that so far the aliens appeared interested in "mere surveillance" but warned they seemed to have gone further in some instances.

"At long last, all of these witnesses are coming forward to say that, as unbelievable as it may seem to some, UFOs have long monitored and sometimes tampered with our nukes," he added.

They even landed at a Suffolk base, claim airmen

Daniel Bates

another site a week later There's a strong interest in our missiles by these objects, wherever they come from. I personally think they're not from planet Earth."

Colonel Charles Halt claims to have seen a UFO at RAF Bentwaters, near Ipswich, one of the few bases in the UK to hold nuclear weapons.

The sighting is said to have taken place 30 years ago. First he saw the object firing beams of light into the base then heard on the military

Friday, May 23, 2008 *The Coastal Advertiser* **NEWS 5**

www.coastaladvertiser.co.uk

UFO lights sighting 'missed opportunity'

SECRET Government files released for the first time have delivered a damning verdict on the famous alleged UFO sighting at a Suffolk air base – dubbed Britain's Roswell.

The files released yesterday from the National Archives show the Government's response to a UFO sighting at RAF Woodbridge in Rendlesham Forest in the early hours of Boxing Day in 1980.

Patrolmen based at the site from the United States Air Force (USAF) claimed they saw a small, triangular-shaped craft moving backwards through the woods before taking off.

A report written by the deputy base commander Lieutenant Colonel Charles Halt to the Ministry of Defence (MoD) said patrolmen saw an object with a "pulsing red light on top and a bank of blue lights underneath".

A release of the report a few years after the alleged incident led to worldwide headlines such as 'UFO Lands in Suffolk'.

The incident came at a time of Cold War tension at a site with nuclear weapons. But the new files indicate that because Lieutenant Colonel Halt only filed his report on January 13 – two weeks after the sighting – this prompted a lack of investigation by the British Government.

In a briefing document from the time, an MoD official wrote: "Overall, we believe that the fact that Col Halt did not report these occurrences to MoD for almost two weeks after the event, together with the relatively low-key manner in which he handled the matter (given resources available to him) are indicative of the degree of importance in defence terms which

HEADLINES: A cutting from the *News of the World* dated October 2, 1983, about the incident

should be attached to the incident.

"He himself took all investigative action which was required."

The briefing note added that because Lt Col Halt did not recommend any further investigation and because nothing was picked up on radar the MoD felt that "no additional action was required".

The papers were released following a long-running campaign led by investigative journalist and lecturer Dr David Clarke.

He said the briefing notes highlight a "total cock-up" by the Government into something which may have been of scientific interest. Dr Clarke said he believes that the patrolmen saw an aerial phenomenon rather than

"What we have finally got here from the documents are the real decision which were taken at the time," said Dr Clarke.

"It has got to be said that it was a total cock-up because if it was something serious the Government only got to know about it two weeks later.

"Why did the Americans not make a direct report of what happened to Whitehall and why did no-one from London get out from behind the desk and come to Suffolk and interview the American airmen who saw what they saw?

"It is a pity that the military made such a poor job about investigating it because

"It was the one they could have investigated at the time and done proper checks and we may now have the answers but instead they filed it away. It was a missed opportunity".

Leiston resident Brenda Butler, who wrote the first book, *Sky Crash*, on the UFO sighting, said the reason Lt Col Halt took two weeks to file his report was because he wanted the advice of the British base commander who was on a two-week holiday.

She added: "I do believe that the men did see something.

"Something must have happened because of all the secrecy and cover-ups. We went to the MoD offices

REPORT OF STRANGE LIGHTS: Studying the site of the alleged UFO sighting at Rendlesham in December 1980. Left, Brenda Butler and Dot Street at the alleged site of the Rendlesham UFO sighting. Photos: EADT

An MoD spokesman said: "UFO reports are examined by the Ministry of Defence solely to establish whether UK airspace may have been compromised by hostile or unauthorised military activity. If required, sighting reports are examined with the assistance of the department's air defence experts.

"Unless there is evidence of a potential threat, it is not an appropriate use of defence resources and no further work is undertaken to identify the nature of each sighting reported.

"The Ministry of Defence has no other interest or role regarding UFO

MoD's X-Files shed light on

By TOM POTTER
tom.potter@eveningstar.co.uk

House of Lords group raised disturbing issues about Britain's Roswell incident

IT'S regarded by those with a penchant for the paranormal to be one of the most significant UFO sightings of modern times.

The Rendlesham Forest incident, or Britain's Roswell as it has come to be known, has kept people guessing about the existence of little green men for nearly 30 years.

For the second time this year, the Ministry of Defence has disclosed previously classified files on sightings in the UK reported between 1981 and 1996.

In March we heard about boomerang-shaped objects seen from airport control towers and a woman's encounter with a Scandinavian-sounding "alien" in Norfolk.

Now, a new set of files may shed light on Britain's Roswell, as well as some other bizarre encounters.

The release is part of a three-year project between the MoD and The National Archives, aimed at opening up records to a worldwide audience.

The Rendlesham file reveals previously unseen letters between the MoD and members of the public and includes a memo from Lt Col Charles Halt (USAF deputy base commander), who was present during one of the sightings in December 1980.

File DEFE 24/1948 explores

STRANGE DAYS INDEED: Brenda Butler and Dot Street at the alleged site of the Rendlesham UFO sighting.

Fastfacts

More MoD revelations

■ Two men returning home from an evening out in Staffordshire were confronted by a lemon-headed alien who appeared from under a hovering UFO;

■ More than 30 sightings of bright lights were reported over central England in the space of just six hours in March 1993 – it was later discovered that most of the sightings were caused by a Russian rocket re-entering the earth's atmosphere;

■ The Belgian Air Force scrambled F-16 fighters to intercept UFOs reported by police officers and members of the public in March 1990 – the jets obtained "lock-ons" with their radars, but could not explain what caused the phenomena;

■ A young man returning home near Widnes ran off after seeing a UFO over a cemetery in July, 1996. He reported beams of light projecting on to the ground, a wailing noise and smoke rising from the ground.
Investigators discovered four smouldering railway sleepers at the scene - one with a hole burnt through it and still smouldering.

■ Dozens of sightings of a brightly illuminated oval object were reported over London in 1993 – the lights were actually caused by a Virgin airship.

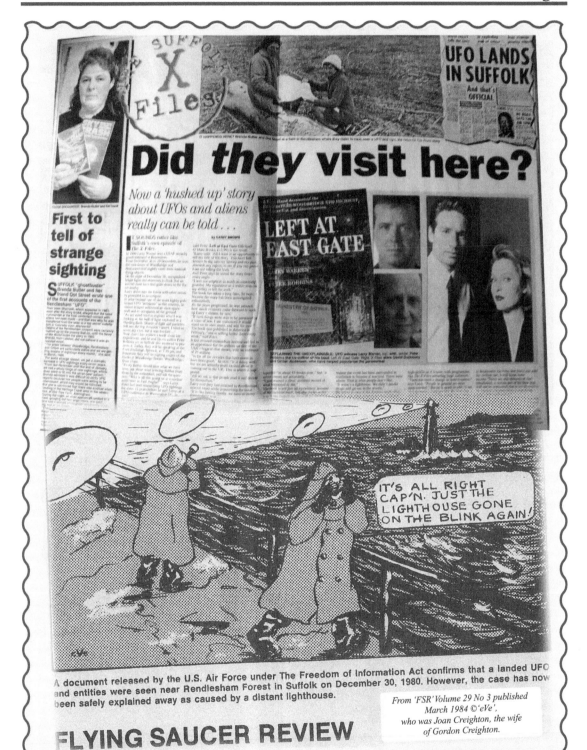

A document released by the U.S. Air Force under The Freedom of Information Act confirms that a landed UFO and entities were seen near Rendlesham Forest in Suffolk on December 30, 1980. However, the case has now been safely explained away as caused by a distant lighthouse.

From 'FSR' Volume 29 No 3 published March 1984 ©'eVe', who was Joan Creighton, the wife of Gordon Creighton.

FINDINGS BY PETER GEORGE PARISH

TREE,S AROUND WOODBRIDGE AND BENTWATERS STILL STANDING AFTER THE STORM 1987. SOME HAVE BEEN MARKED WITH SCRAPES AND BANGS WITH A HEAVY SHARP OBJECT, FROM GROUND TO THE TOPS, SIGNS OF TREE,S BEEN HEATED AS WELL SAP HAS BURST OUT OF THE BARK IN MANY PLACES.

I HAVE HAD, LOTS OF REMARKS. NAME A FEW
1. LIGHTNING. SOME ARE LIKE,
2. (DEER) WITH LONG LEGS
3. STORM, YES A FEW MIGHT BE
4. FORISTERY MARKS
5. PLANE CRASH
6. OR —

MARKS HIT INTO CLEAN WOOD 30FT OR MORE

SAP BURSLEY OUT

TREE SAP DRIPPING OFF. COULD BE WHAT HALY SAW

P.G.P.

P.G.P.

FOREST EYE PRODUCTIONS
PRESENTS

AN EVENING OF PRESENTATIONS & DISCUSSION PROMOTING
British UFO Free speech for All

Come along and have your say on all regional UFO
matters: sightings,experiences & information,which
can be added to existing data,and marked on a comprehensive incident map. Also featured will be a spe-
cially illustrated timeline of events that occurred over
the weekend of 26th – 28th December 1980 in Rendlesham Forest, for the purpose of removing confusion,
and establishing a definitive account to date. UFO
investigators will be in attendance to talk freely,or in
confidence,with anyone who has a story to tell,or
information to impart.
Guest speakers currently scheduled:
BRENDA BUTLER
LARRY WARREN
PETER ROBBINS

To Be Held On:
September 10th,2011
At
WOODBRIDGE COMMUNITY HALL   Ticket Price - £10 profits from
this event will be donated to the Martlesham RSPCA Rescue Centre.
6pm – 11pm

TICKET SALES:
        Please send stamped,self-addressed envelope to:
Mr G. GOODGER
108 Spring Road, Ipswich. IP4 2RR
        Cheques payable to G.Goodger.   Paypal orders
accepted via: paypal@spaceportuk.com. Please include a contact
phone number & address to send tickets. For further info: call 01473
423143 or 07811021230.   email: info@spaceportuk.com

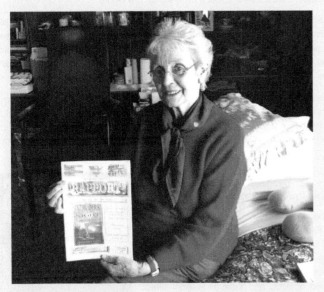

Elsie Oakensen

We discovered that Elsie Oakensen (her UFO was illustrated on the front cover of Volume 7) had passed away on 28th November 2012.

We interviewed Elsie about her UFO experiences, on a number of occasions, over the years, and found her to be an intelligent, truthful woman, who was kind enough to hand sign a number of her own books (despite a broken arm) which she gave to us free – not to make money, but to facilitate payment for future material obtained for us in *Haunted Skies*. Elsie was a tireless campaigner of the UFO subject and was always available to help people come to terms with their own UFO experiences, especially those who felt traumatised by what had taken place. She was a credit to the UFO cause and will be sadly missed.

Kath Smith

Somebody else who passed away within the last couple of years was Kath Smith, from the Isle of Wight UFO Society. We met her and her husband, Tom, some years ago, during a visit to the Isle of Wight. Kath gave us a large amount of personal letters and paperwork, collected over the years, as custodian of the group; they also included many of the original UFOLOG magazines. She was also a credit to the UFO cause and her commitment to preserving what is, after all, a slice of unique British UFO history is to be commended.

Volume 1 of *Haunted Skies* 1940-1959 *(Foreword by Tim Good)*

We present sightings from the Second Word War. They include many reports from allied pilots, who describe seeing unidentified flying objects, while on bombing missions over Germany. Some pilots we interviewed told of being ordered to intercept a UFO; one pilot was even ordered to open fire! In addition to these are reports of early close encounters, involving allegations of abduction experiences.

Another report tells of strange 'beings' seen outside an RAF Base. We also outline a spectacular sighting, in 1957, that took place in Bedfordshire, which appears identical to that seen over Oregon by employees of the Ames Research Laboratory, San Francisco. There are also numerous reports of 'saucer', 'diamond' and 'cigar-shaped' objects seen during these years.

Volume 2 of *Haunted Skies* 1960-1965 *(Foreword by Jenny Randles)*

We re-investigated what may well be one of the earliest events, involving mysterious crop circles discovered in June 1960, at Poplar Farm, Evenlode. A 'V'-shaped UFO over Gloucestershire, and an example of a early 'Flying Triangle' over Tyneside in early September 1960. This type of object attracted much media interest in the early 1980s, following attempts by the Belgium Air Force to intercept what became labelled as 'Triangular' UFOs. This book contains many reports of saucer-shaped objects, and their occasional effect on motor vehicles. We also, wherever possible, include numerous personal letters and interviews with some of the researchers. We should not forget the early magazines, such as UFOLOG, produced by members of the (now defunct) Isle of Wight UFO Society.

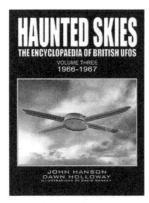

Volume 3 of *Haunted Skies* 1966-1967 *(Foreword by Nick Redfern)*

This was two years before manned landings took place on the Moon. In October 1967, there was a veritable 'wave' of UFO sightings which took place in the U.K, involving cross-shaped objects, reported from Northumberland to the South Coast, with additional reports from Ireland and the Channel islands. (The police in the USA also reported sightings of 'Flying Crosses'). The sightings took place at various times, mostly during the evening or early morning hours, and involved an object which was manoeuvrable, silent – and at times – apparently flying at a low altitude. Attempts were made by the police and various authorities to explain away the sightings as Venus, based on the fact that the planet was bright in the sky during this period, which is clearly, in the majority of sightings, not the answer.

Volume 4 of *Haunted Skies* 1968-1971 *(Foreword by Philip Mantle)*

This book begins with a personal reference to Budd Hopkins, by USA researcher – Peter Robbins.

We outline a close encounter from Crediton, in Devon, which was brought to the attention of the police. Further police sightings of UFOs have been tracked down from Derbyshire, and a police chase through Kent. Multiple UFO sightings occur over the Staffordshire area, which are brought to the attention of the MOD. UFO researchers – Tony Pace and Roger Stanway – travel to London to discuss the incidents with the MOD. Close encounters at Warminster are also covered. A domed object at Bristol and further UFO landings are covered. They include a chilling account from a schoolteacher, living near Stratford-upon-Avon, and a 'flying triangle' seen over Birmingham.

Volume 5 of *Haunted Skies* 1972-1975 *(Foreword by Matt Lyons, Chairman of BUFORA)*

Further examples of UFO activity at Warminster, involving classic 'sky watches' from such locations as Cradle Hill, was the focus of worldwide attention during this period. In addition to this are reports of mysterious footsteps heard. A visit from the 'Men in Black', and other amazing stories, form just a tiny part of some amazing material collected by us, over the years, during personal interviews with the people concerned. UFO fleets are seen over Reading, and a landed saucer-shaped object is seen at Lancashire.

A UFO, containing aliens, is seen at close range over Worcestershire. A local councillor also described seeing what he believes was an alien spaceship, with occupants. There is also an investigation into the famous Berwyn Mountain incident, when it was alleged, by some, that a 'craft' had landed.

Volume 6 of *Haunted Skies* 1976 1977 Jubilee edition *(Foreword by Kevin Goodman)*

Strange globes of light, seen moving in formations of three (often referred to as triangular in overall shape). Warminster, Wiltshire – reports of mysterious black shadows, flying globes of light and a triangular-shaped UFO seen over Cleeve Hill, near Cheltenham by police officers. There is also an investigation into a number of reported landings of alien craft around the Dyfed area, in February 1977. We present some original illustrations, drawn by children at the local school (which will be reproduced in colour, in a later edition of Haunted Skies). A triangular UFO is seen over Stoke-on-Trent. Comprehensive details were also obtained, regarding Winchester woman, Joyce Bowles – who was to report many encounters with UFOs and their alien occupants.

Volume 7 of *Haunted Skies* 1978 1979 *(Foreword by David Bryant)*

The famous debate into UFOs, held at the United Nations, is covered. A UFO landing at Rowley Regis, West Midlands – involving housewife Jean Hingley – labelled by the Press as the 'Mince Pie Martian' case. Many original sketches and additional information supporting her claims are offered. Another classic UFO sighting is re-investigated, following interviews held with Elsie Oakensen – a housewife from the Daventry area – who sighted a dumb-bell shaped UFO while on the way home from work. Thanks to Dan Goring, editor of EarthLink we were able to include a large number of previously unpublished sighting reports from Essex and London. We also include a close encounter from Didsbury, Manchester involving Lynda Jones, who is known personally to us.

Lightning Source UK Ltd.
Milton Keynes UK
UKOW06f0603020714

234360UK00005B/15/P

UNCOVERED

REVOLUTIONARY
MAGAZINE COVERS
THE INSIDE STORIES
TOLD BY THE PEOPLE
WHO MADE THEM

IAN BIRCH

CASSELL
ILLUSTRATED

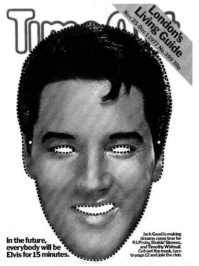

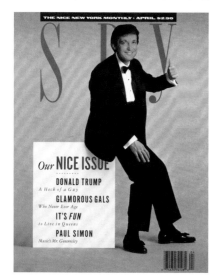

CONTENTS

FOREWORD

ANNE FULENWIDER

I first met Ian Birch while sitting in a cramped office on the 34th floor of the Hearst Tower in New York, when I was executive editor of *Marie Claire* under Joanna Coles (now chief content officer at Hearst), and a small group of us had been charged with improving the magazine's covers. Ian was brought in as a specialist, having launched several groundbreaking magazines in the UK – *Grazia*, *Red*, *Heat* and *Closer* – and was introduced, more or less, as the Irish cover-whisperer.

Typically, our covers had been worked on by three or four of us who crowded around our design director's desk, lobbing ideas for coverlines at the besieged creative director Suzanne Sykes, who was charged with translating our gibberish into something that both made sense and looked striking. These meetings were in stark contrast to my former place of employment, *Vanity Fair*, where Graydon Carter would gather ten or so of us in a wood-panelled conference room with that month's cover projected onto a large screen. The room was so grand that many of us were too intimidated to speak. The *Marie Claire* cover meetings were much more casual, spontaneous and conducive to creative thought, but still, we'd been stuck in the weeds. Ian's perspective, far as he was from our core audience of American women aged 21–35, was of an outsider, albeit with vast magazine experience. Which is why he was so effectively able to remind us of what we were there to do, no matter what our subject matter: create an immediate, emotional impact.

The great covers do this within the first milliseconds of eye contact. The image is arresting, the words complementary, but, most of all, a cultural moment is distilled to its essence. I remember exactly where I was, as I'm guessing many of us do, when I first saw the 1991 image of Demi Moore, naked and pregnant, and the 2015 reveal of Caitlyn Jenner's transgender identity, both on the covers of *Vanity Fair*. Yes, the impact of these covers can be deconstructed and explained, and their geneses were highly orchestrated – months of wooing a subject, of negotiations and collaboration between photographer, stylist, publicist and subject, hours of preparation on set to get just the right light, angle, and expression – and that's weeks before those gruelling hours of coverline brainstorms. A lot can go wrong. Which is why the perfect mix of elements is so elusive – and sometimes comes about accidentally. In the end the most successful covers give the illusion of having been produced by magic.

At my isolated boarding school in New Hampshire, far away from the buzzy world I longed to join, magazines were passed around like contraband in prison, and pored over for hours on end in our dorm rooms – missives from that impossibly glamorous world of New York City. Every page, every ad, every scent strip was analyzed for social codes and clues on how to be sophisticated. (To this day if I ever come across the scent of Giorgio Beverly Hills perfume I am immediately taken back to a freezing cold dorm room in the mid-1980s.)

I finally landed in New York, and gained a foothold in the world I had dreamed of. I've worked at four magazines, produced about 50 covers and led countless coverlines meetings, all in search of that magic alchemy. A lot has happened since I got here. When I landed at *Vanity Fair*, Madonna was on the cover, having given her first interview after the birth of Lourdes, and Bill Clinton's affair with Monica Lewinsky had just been outed by the Drudge Report. The internet had already begun its takeover of our attention spans. And yet, since then, as I'm reminded by Ian and his book, some of the most resonant cultural moments (as well as some of the just plain fun ones) have belonged to magazine covers. As Instagram takes over our lives and fake news spreads like wildfire across social media, I am forever grateful for magazines and their covers – beacons of culture, beaming light across the plains.

Anne Fulenwider is editor-in-chief of American *Marie Claire*

INTRODUCTION

IAN BIRCH

As a teenager in 1960s Belfast, I fell in love with magazines. They introduced me to a community outside of family and school. They taught me about words and pictures, how to structure and present an idea. They were seductive and aspirational. Especially potent was *The Sunday Times Magazine*, a weekly comet of colour and discovery. I remember seeing *Rolling Stone* for the first time in a Belfast boutique in 1968 while wondering if I could afford a Ben Sherman shirt. It was a revelation, a voice for a cultural shift which I only hazily understood but knew I wanted to be part of. I bought the magazine, not the shirt. Little did I realize that its co-founder, Jann Wenner, would be my boss 24 years later.

Like any business, a magazine's first job is to make money for the owner, and that's traditionally done through a combination of advertising and copy sales. The newsstand cover is obviously crucial here: it's the most important marketing tool. It follows that a successful cover is one that sells as many copies as it can to its intended audience. The publishing industry has spent millions over the decades on research, trying to find the magic cover formula. Some titles have come very close, like *People*, whose covers have been calibrated with forensic brilliance. But even *People* can trip up.

The received thinking goes something like this. A mainstream cover should be instantly recognizable under the 5/5 rule (we make our choice within five seconds from five feet away); it should have an attractive and accessible photograph with strong eye contact (we read the picture before the text and we prefer photography to illustration or pure type because it takes less time and effort to decode); it should have an easily digestible and relatable mix of cover lines that pepper the expected with the odd surprise (anything depressing like a tragedy should be wrapped up in empathy); it should have a tone of warm, light banter (somewhere between a pun and a punch line); and one of the dominant colours should be "buy-me" red. Don't get me wrong: to work within these commercial diktats and produce a cover that crackles *and* sells well is an enviable skill. Over the last 40 years, I have been lucky enough to work with designers and writers who have pulled this off.

But the covers here are different. I didn't choose them on the basis of sales – their newsstand numbers fluctuated between the dismal and the dynamic. I chose them because they broke boundaries and started conversations. They made a moment feel red-hot and meaningful. Some confronted taboos about race and sex. Some ridiculed hypocrisy. Some memorialized a catastrophic event. Some provided a voice that was absent from the mainstream. Some were rallying calls.

Some bordered on the crude. Some turned design conventions upside down. Some ended up hanging in galleries, such as George Lois's *Esquire* covers, exhibited in New York's MoMA in 2008.

They are social documents with unique backstories. I wanted to hear these stories from the creative mavericks behind them – the editor, the art director, the writer, the photographer, the photography director, the cartoonist, the stylist, the publisher and, occasionally, the celebrity or a relevant academic. That's why I start in the late 1950s; prior to this, key players are sadly either dead or unavailable. I end when covers were re-energized by the twin political thunderbolts of Brexit and Trump, and the warp speed of the political news cycle. These covers became more adversarial because they could and should.

As I write, there is an overwhelming sense that the post-World War II magazine era is ending. The internet has taken over as the engine of popular culture and, in the process, decimated the print business model. Revenues from advertising and circulation have been shrinking rapidly, and that has forced legacy companies to cut staff, close, combine or sell some titles and reduce the frequencies of others, invest – often belatedly and furiously – in digital, video and voice-enabled services, and search for other ways to monetize their still-sizeable subscriber files. It's a grim landscape, especially as platform monopolies like Google and Facebook suck up all the oxygen and most of the digital advertising money. And, like the entertainment and tech industries, publishing is facing an increasing number of sexual misconduct allegations, notably in high-end fashion photography. On the bright side, there has been a surge in the independent sector of handsomely designed niche titles, but as yet their commercial pulling power is limited. With technology, the barriers to producing magazines have never been lower, but the barriers to making them successful have never been higher.

And what of the future for magazines? Will they devolve further into marketing add-ons, stylish but supine? Like American public radio, will they ask their audiences for funding through a mix of subscription, membership fees and donation drives? Will they take a similar path to vinyl, which now enjoys a retro prestige? Kurt Andersen, astute social observer, former editor of *New York* and co-founder of *Spy*, hits the nail on the head: "Eventually, they'll become like sailboats," he said. "They don't need to exist anymore. But people will still love them, and make them and buy them."[1]

1 Quoted in Sydney Ember and Michael M Grynbaum, "The Not-So-Glossy Future of Magazines", *The New York Times*, 23 September 2017.

LATE
1950s

one

AUGUST 1958
FIFTY CENTS

THE HOMOSEXUAL VIEWPOINT

I am glad I am homo-sexual

D.F.

ONE

AUGUST 1958

Managing editor: Don Slater

Art director: Eve Elloree

Cover artist: Dawn Fredericks

Craig M Loftin is Lecturer in American
   Studies at California State University,
   Fullerton.[1]

In 1953, when McCarthyism raged, the United States' first openly gay magazine was launched on newsstands across the country.

CRAIG M LOFTIN:

Keep in mind that the Alfred Kinsey reports had come out. Everyone knew who Kinsey was. I mean he was on the cover of *Time* magazine. Kinsey's *Sexual Behavior in the Human Male*, in 1948, said that over a third of American men had had same-sex contacts. And he says, very bluntly, there is no reason to have laws against it. Now that's one of the big things that helped inspire the homophile movement. *One* came out of that political movement. This was not a magazine for leisure and fun. The underlying idea was to bring all gay people together as "one".

They were hoping that heterosexuals might pick up the magazine and flip through its contents and overcome their own prejudices. They would mail it to prominent judges, politicians and famous writers like Tennessee Williams, Gore Vidal and Norman Mailer.

Two-thirds of the magazine's 3,000–5,000 monthly readers preferred buying their copies at newsstands, largely because they were fearful of being on a subscription list that might get seized by police. Newsstand visibility, therefore, was an important factor in the magazine's national proliferation. *One*'s artists and editors had to fashion a visual style on the covers that would evoke gayness in a recognizable way, yet avoid inciting backlash from postal authorities, vice squads or censorship groups.[2]

Most of the illustrations were drawn by two women who were a couple. A commercial artist named Joan Corbin drew under the pseudonym Eve Elloree during the 1950s, and in the 1960s Dawn Fredericks took over most of Corbin's duties. This represented a rare example of female creative control within a male-dominated homophile organization.

There was a growing frustration from them and other women that they were not getting heard, and eventually a lot of them ended up leaving *One* and joining the Daughters of Bilitis, which was the first lesbian organization. They had their own magazine called *The Ladder* (*see* Figure 1), which started in 1956 and was modelled off of *One* basically.

Their illustrations were non-threatening, and non-threatening is a key concept here. These homophile organizations of the 1950s were very assimilationist organizations. They wanted to be accepted by society. Kind of like the black Civil Rights Movement in its earlier phases. You dress nice, you speak professionally, you win over the mainstream by showing them how patriotic and American and normal you are.

What's striking about this cover is how big the words are – huge letters proclaiming that in a shocking, daring way. But it's not some menacing image. I would describe it as a prideful stoicism that says, "I have a right to exist."

Figure 1 *The first issue of the United States' first national lesbian magazine,* The Ladder.

1 Craig M Loftin is the author of *Masked Voices: Gay Men and Lesbians in Cold War America* (SUNY Press, 2012) and *Letters to One: Gay and Lesbian Voices from the 1950s and 1960s* (SUNY Press, 2012).

2 C Loftin, "Drawing Attention: The Ambiguous Artwork of America's First Gay Magazine", paper presented at the Pacific Coast Branch of the American Historical Association Conference, San Diego 2012. Reproduced with kind permission of the author.

THE QUEEN

15 SEPTEMBER 1959

Editor-in-chief: Jocelyn Stevens

Editor: Beatrix Miller

Art editor: Mark Boxer

Associate editors: Quentin Crewe,
Drusilla Beyfus

Cover credit: "Photographed at the
Gargoyle by Desmond Russell."

Jocelyn Stevens bought *The Queen* for around £10,000 in 1957 as a 25th birthday present to himself. He immediately set about turning the genteel high-society fortnightly (launched in 1861) into a graphically innovative and sharper-tongued vehicle for the new generation of talent. He recruited Mark Boxer, his compatriot from Cambridge, as art director and Tony Armstrong-Jones, who would become Lord Snowden, as photographer. Stevens had such a volcanic temper that *Private Eye* nicknamed him "Piranha Teeth". Stories abounded of him tussling with staff in the office, firing people on a whim, throwing typewriters out of windows and terminating telephone calls by cutting the cord with a pair of scissors. He later told Sue Lawley on *Desert Island Discs*[1] that most of the stories were true.

This cover toasted the consumer "boom", the feature opening with "When did you last hear the word austerity? Nearly two thousand million pounds is pouring out of pockets and wallets and handbags and changing into air tickets and oysters, television sets and caviar, art treasures and vacuum cleaners, cigars and refrigerators."[2] Stevens later wrote: "It was our 'you've never had it so good'[3] issue and the Prime Minister liked the message. Reggie Maudling, who was Chancellor of the Exchequer, told me later that Harold Macmillan had arranged at the Cabinet meeting the following day for every Cabinet Minister to have a copy of the magazine in front of him. None of which stopped us attacking some of his Cabinet appointments following his election victory a month later."[4]

DRUSILLA BEYFUS:

The Queen was a class effort in every respect. The editorial mix was unlike anything else in its canon, combining sharp social observation, tiptop art direction and photography and pieces by literary stars.

Private jokes were allowed in print. A goat-footsure touch on the slippery slopes of social class distinction characterized the comment features, such as a witty survey of The Establishment[5] and a tilt at the machinations of newspaper gossip columnists. Literary lions counted. Among others, I recall pieces by James Thurber, Colin MacInnes, Penelope Gilliatt, Victoria Sackville-West, Clement Freud, Elizabeth Jane Howard.

We found a bifocal way of reflecting an upper-crust world, seeing things from the viewpoint of a bona fide paid-up member of the elite, and from a modern outsider's perspective.

The Boom cover is a great example of Mark Boxer's touch in combining images with cover-lines to put over the whole atmosphere of a story. The issue in every way represented a glamorous benchmark on the (temporary) end of national austerity.

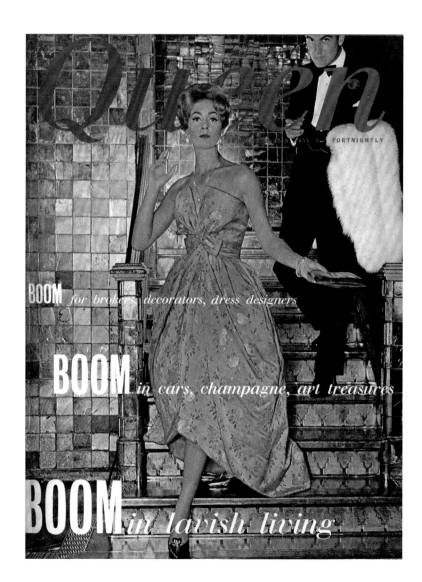

1   *Desert Island Discs*, first broadcast 8 March 1992.
2   Condensed from *The Queen*, 15 September 1959, p.29.
3   Harold Macmillan's famous soundbite from a speech he delivered at a Tory rally on 20 July 1957 in Bedford.
4   *The Sixties in Queen*, edited by Nicholas Coleridge and Stephen Quinn, Ebury Press, 1987, pp.10–11.
5   "The Establishment Chronicle", *The Queen*, August 1959.

TWEN

OCTOBER 1959 AND 20 APRIL 1960

Editor-in-chief: Adolf Theobald

Picture editing and layout: Willy Fleckhaus

DECEMBER 1964 AND JUNE 1966

Art director: Willy Fleckhaus

Assistant to art director: Christian Diener

Managing editor: Willi Herzog

Assistant art director (1964–6):
    Will Hopkins[1]

Anna von Munchhausen is content director
    at *Die Zeit* newspaper.

Germany had not seen a magazine like *Twen* before. Launched in Cologne in 1959, it spoke directly to the liberal post-war twentysomething generation (the name was an abbreviation of the English word "twenty"[2]). It championed pop culture, questioned society, looked outward to the United States and Britain and espoused sexuality in a big, sometimes profligate way. The design, by Willy Fleckhaus, introduced a radical 12-column grid together with a startling use of photography (contrasting large and small pictures) and typography (bold headlines with Brutalist-like slabs of text that cared more about design than meaning). Fleckhaus's influence was enormous.

Design critic Klaus Thomas Edelman believes that many of Fleckhaus's designs "express his continual attempts to make a fresh start for himself. A friend, Adolf Theobald, explains: 'Drafted by Hitler into the armed forces, and cheated out of his youth, Fleckhaus used graphics to relive the youth that he had been denied: protest, opposition, liberalism, sentimentality, pleasure – all these things were worked out, processed through the layout.'"[3]

ANNA VON MUNCHHAUSEN:

I fell in love with *Twen* in the mid-1960s as a boarding-school girl in Germany. Don't forget that it was a child of the late Adenauer[4] years: a chancellor over 80 years old led the country. Germany was busy forgetting Hitler and wanted to rebuild the nation – the *Wirtschaftswunder*[5] – without being told what role the Germans played from 1933 to 1945. The younger generation felt that under the surface there was much emotional repression in their parents' minds.

To read *Twen* meant you were a member of an urban young elite, enjoying life, enjoying free love and feeling optimistic about the future. It was a sort of guideline to what was hip. It invented a certain female role model: positive thinking, independent sexiness which was completely new to German women. Willy Fleckhaus invented the position of art director in Germany.

WILL HOPKINS:

When I first saw *Twen*, I loved it and decided that I was going to work for Fleckhaus. I'd say to people, the Lord told me I had to go to Germany. My wife

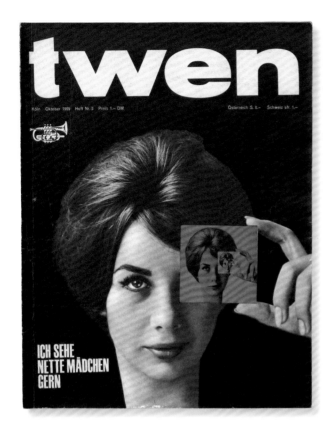

twen

Köln Oktober 1959 Heft Nr. 3 Preis 1.– DM   Österreich S. 8.– Schweiz sfr. 1.–

ICH SEHE
NETTE MÄDCHEN
GERN

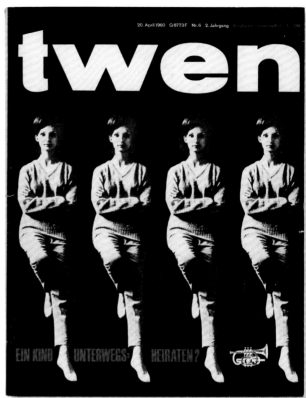

twen

20. April 1960 G 6773 F Nr. 6 2. Jahrgang

EIN KIND   UNTERWEGS: HEIRATEN?

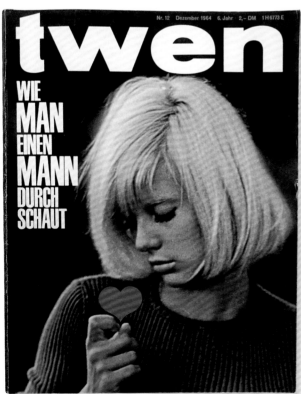

twen

Nr. 12 Dezember 1964 6. Jahr 2.– DM 1 H 6773 E

WIE
MAN
EINEN
MANN
DURCH
SCHAUT

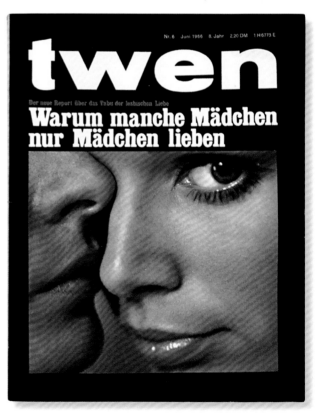

twen

Nr. 6 Juni 1966 8. Jahr 2.20 DM 1 H 6773 E

Der neue Report über das Tabu der lesbischen Liebe

Warum manche Mädchen
nur Mädchen lieben

and I were living in Chicago where I was working for Chess Records. Six months later, we were in Cologne.

I went to their office but Fleckhaus was on vacation. They said, give us your phone number, but I didn't have one so I went back every day and sat on their couch. One day, they got into trouble with a deadline so I started pasting up. I ended up spending two years there.

The cover would be arrived at very quickly. The black background, a picture of a beautiful woman, a provocative cover line and sometimes something a little ornamental by someone like Heinz Edelmann.[6] The trumpet was just an ornament.

Fleckhaus never had to justify what he was doing. Most of the time, when we did a cover, the editor was nowhere to be found. It was his magazine, not the editor's. He was very emotional about the way he chose pictures. We'd project slides on the wall and he'd say, take that out, take that out, take that out: very rapid, very intuitive.

One of my favourites is the Sylvie Vartan[7] cover [below left]. It was the first thing I saw Fleckhaus and Diener work on together. That cover expressed the German notion of romance and the sentimentality that they seemed to love.

1 Will Hopkins went on to art-direct magazines including
   Look, *GEO* and *American Photographer*.
2 Sourced from Steven Heller, "The Modern Master of
   Magazine Design", *Graphis* magazine, no. 249, vol. 43
   (May/June 1987), p.10.
3 Klaus Thomas Edelmann, "Paint It Black", *Eye* magazine,
   no. 3, vol. 1 (Spring 1991). Reproduced with the kind
   permission of *Eye*. Article available at: *http://www.
   eyemagazine.com/feature/article/paint-it-black*. Adolf
   Theobald was a co-founder of *Twen*.
4 Konrad Adenauer, first chancellor of the Federal Republic
   of Germany (West Germany), 1949–63.
5 The "Economic Miracle", also known as the "Miracle on
   the Rhein", describes the rapid reconstruction and
   development of the economies of West Germany and
   Austria after World War II.
6 Regular illustrator for *Twen* throughout the Sixties who
   also art-directed the Beatles' *Yellow Submarine* film.
7 December 1964. Vartan is a French singer who was at the
   forefront of the yé-yé pop sound in the 1960s.

1960s

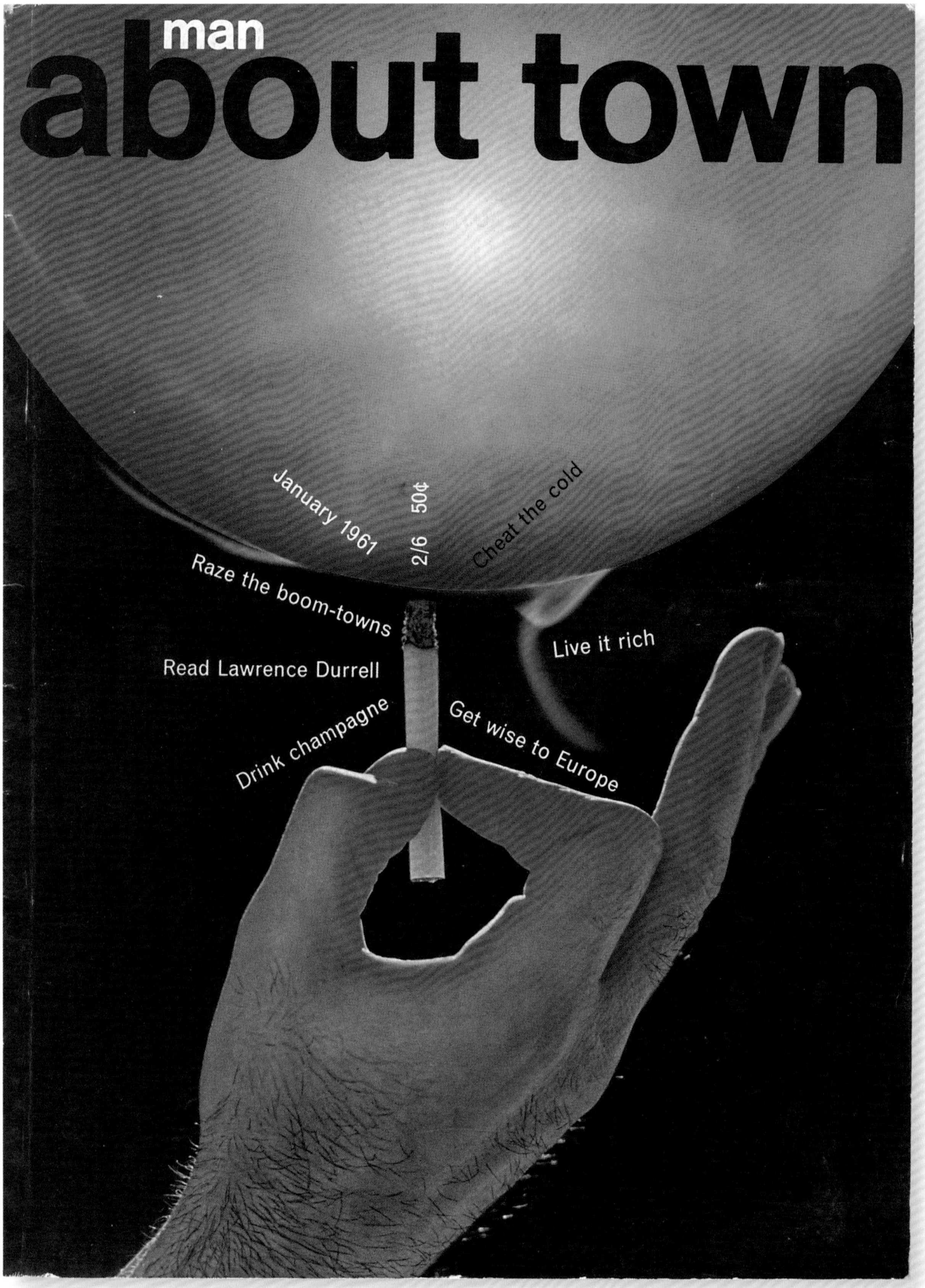

man
about town

January 1961   2/6   50¢   Cheat the cold

Raze the boom-towns

Live it rich

Read Lawrence Durrell

Drink champagne   Get wise to Europe

ABOUT TOWN

JANUARY 1961
SEPTEMBER 1961

Publishers: Clive Labovitch,
     Michael Heseltine
Editor: David Hughes
Art director: Thomas Wolsey
Photography for both covers:
     Terence Donovan
Art assistant: Jeanette Collins

Michael Heseltine and Clive Labovitch, freshly graduated from Oxford, set up Cornmarket Press[1] and bought their first magazine, the "undistinguished quarterly"[2] *Man About Town*, in 1959. They turned it into a sleek, sharp-witted and influential men's monthly, shortening the name to *About Town* in late January 1961 (and then *Town* in February 1962). As Heseltine later noted, Labovitch's "inspired decision was to recruit Tom Wolsey as art director"[3] from the prestigious Crawford's Advertising Agency.

JEANETTE COLLINS:

Tom was born in Germany and had a singular German accent that Peter Sellers learned for *Dr Strangelove*. He was slim, small and dapper with little hands – sort of perfect in every detail. He was like a little gremlin. I don't think I had a real conversation with him until years after I left *Town*. Everything was about work. He was amazing but at times impossible.

I remember one major fight which went on all day between Heseltine, Labovitch and the editor Nick Tomalin about where to crop the nipple on the fragmented mirrors cover.[4] As modest as that cover is, it caused absolute mayhem. Tom wanted the nipple in, and Michael said, "Over my dead body." Eventually, the nipple was cropped. *Town* had always distanced itself from any sort of soft porn-y covers and I would say here that Tom was putting a tentative toe into the permissive Sixties. When he lost, he went back to his office. Outside his door were the coat racks. He took down Nick Tomalin's coat, dropped it on the floor and jumped up and down on it. Then he picked it up very delicately, hung it back up and went, "Tee hee hee." That was the kind of relationship there was with editors.

The magic was done when you weren't there. Tom would come in late in the mornings and would go out early for a long lunch, returning at 4pm. He then shut himself in his office and worked late into the night. I would arrive in the morning to a pile of layouts to prepare for the printer.

I once wrote this about him: "Tom used typography as mortar to bond image and word. He did overprint a good deal, but far from destroying the image he often heightened its effect by using the type to echo angles within the picture, to emphasize a visual point, to create excitement or reinforce a mood."[5] One cover that sums this up is "The Balloon" where the type anticipates what the photograph couldn't – the balloon's explosion. And, by the way, that's Tom's hand – delicate and hairy.

Tom was always looking for "shock tactics", and the "new breed" of photographers such as David Bailey, John Bulmer, Donovan, Duffy and Don McCullin provided this. The "Anatomy of Anger" cover was a black-and-white photograph of Chita Rivera[6] by Donovan, but Tom gave it a graphic treatment to emphasize the mood with this hot-orange background, and the shocking-pink lightning flash at the bottom. The grainy effect was achieved at the developing and printmaking stage, and the artwork for the flash was supplied as an overlay. The result was a tightly designed explosion of anger.

1 According to Wikipedia, "The partners split in 1965, with Heseltine renaming his half of the business Haymarket Press to publish *Management Today*." https://en.wikipedia.org/wiki/Haymarket_Media_Group

2 Michael Heseltine quoted in "Haymarket 50 Years: 50 Glorious Moments", *Campaign*, 26 October 2007. http://www.campaignlive.co.uk/article/haymarket-50-years-50-glorious-moments-1-2/763156#z4uz4eeoFKzQ0Uqv.99

3 Ibid.

4 May 1962, "Facets of the Daily Mirror".

5 Jeanette Collins, "*Town* and Tom Wolsey", in *British Photography, 1955–1965: The Master Craftsmen in Print*, The Photographers' Gallery, London, 1983, p.10.

6 American actress who was starring in the smash-hit musical *Bye Bye Birdie* in London.

2/6 60¢   September 1961

about town

Anatomy of anger
Test match fever
Upheaval in politics
Lightning fighters
Shoot your own film

EROS

AUTUMN 1962

Editor and publisher: Ralph Ginzburg

Art director: Herb Lubalin

Associate editors: Warren Boroson,
    Susan Ginzburg

Cover photography: Bert Stern

Eros was a sumptuous half-book, half-magazine with a large format (13 × 10in), hardback covers and no advertising. The subject matter was the erotic, and Marilyn was the third cover, her last studio portraits which Bert Stern had taken six weeks before her death and published for the first time here, six weeks after it.

Ginzburg wrote an illuminating editor's note: "The scratches and orange crosses on many of the photographs on the cover and following pages are not defects. They were made by Marilyn Monroe herself, her own reactions to various shots that showed a strand of hair out of place or a pose she felt was somehow awkward. We thought her markings were so interesting that we decided to leave them in."[1]

SHOSHANA (FORMERLY SUSAN) GINZBURG:

Eros was entirely my idea. I was just a kid when we started that – 19 or 20. Ralph always wanted to publish a magazine, and I had just finished taking a course about Freud which called eros the life force. So I said to Ralph, "Everything is about sex so why don't we do a magazine about eros?" I didn't say, "Why don't we call it Eros." He said, "What would we put in there?" and I said, "Anything because everything is related to it. It gives us a lot of freedom while giving us a hook." The girly magazines like *Playboy*, *Dude* and *Nugget* were doing well then. Ours would be nothing like that: ours would be clean and classy, from day one. Full of joy and art.

Ralph knew Herb was the best designer in the world so we got him. The square format gave him so much more visual leeway that other magazines didn't have. We used a special printing method called flame set lithography which gave a vibrancy to the colour.

We knew Bert Stern. In those days, people had trouble getting anything published that showed nudity but wasn't trash. There was no handsome place to put that kind of art. That's why Bert wanted us because he knew what our attitude would be: honest and respectful. It was a collaboration between Bert and Herb, whose layouts made the pictures sing. Bert took such a loving view of Marilyn and even saved the negatives where she "x-ed" out the contact sheets. She did it in such a violent way like she was saying, "Make it gone." They looked too much like the way she thought she really was. Such self-hatred. She was a terrific actress but Marilyn isn't who she was. She was Norma Jean. We honoured her with this. It was our tribute.

1 *Eros*, Autumn 1962, p.5.

EROS

On June 21, 1962, Bert Stern took the last studio portraits of Marilyn Monroe. That was six weeks before her tragic death. A portfolio of these photographs begins on page three.

December 1963 Price One Dollar

Esquire

The magazine for Men

ESQUIRE

From 1962 to 1972, Madison Avenue art director George Lois and American *Esquire* editor Harold Hayes created some of the most original, ideas-rich, uncompromising and incendiary covers in magazine history. Lois often worked with photographer Carl Fischer, Lois creating the concept, drawing a tight sketch of each (Figures 2–5) and directing them, and then Fischer bringing it to life. "People would say to me, 'You got some balls doing those covers.' I would say, 'No, it's Harold who has the balls.' There's no editor in the world who would do that now – allow me to choose the article in the upcoming issue, and then accept each cover I created with appreciation and pleasure."[1]

DECEMBER 1963
Editor: Harold T P Hayes
Cover design: George Lois
Cover photography: Carl Fischer

Hayes asked Lois to do a "Christmassy" cover for December 1963. "Sonny Liston was perfect for the part," Lois later explained. "By now he was known by everyone as the meanest man in the world. He had served time for armed robbery and didn't give a damn about his image."[2] Lois didn't add Liston's name to the cover. It wasn't a story about the world-champion boxer, it was an image of a black Santa Claus.

GEORGE LOIS:
Harold understood that I was making a strong remark and it would be very controversial. A lot of liberals were pissed with the cover but he defended it big time. When Cassius Clay saw it, and he knew Liston was a convicted criminal, he said, "George, that's the last black motherfucker America wants to see coming down their chimney."

I couldn't go to Vegas for the shoot because I was directing TV spots in New York that week. I arranged for the photography of Liston by having Joe Louis, who was relegated to being a "greeter" at a casino, bring Liston into the room where Fischer was going to take the photographs. I knew Liston would cave in to Joe. Liston was a badass, but thought Joe Louis was a god. Louis told Liston that it would be fun to wear the Santa hat on a magazine cover.

Harold said that was the cover that really made *Esquire*, and he wasn't talking about the money or sales. Let me quote you what he wrote about it: "In the national climate of 1963, thick with racial fear, Lois's angry icon insisted on several things: the split in our culture was showing; the notion of racial equality was a bad joke; the felicitations of this season – goodwill to all men, etc – carried irony more than sentiment."[3]

There was a lot of hate mail but the culture understood it. *Time* magazine said it was "one of the greatest social statements of the plastic arts since Picasso's *Guernica*". Years later, there was an article in *Adweek* which talked about how that cover cost the magazine $750,000. They lost a lot of clients, all Southern accounts, a lot of Southern textile mills. Harold wasn't perturbed.

CARL FISCHER:

Sonny was living in Las Vegas at the time so I went out there with Christmas gear: the hat, the jacket. I set up something in the hotel room. He said, "Forget it. I'm not putting on any fucking Santa Claus hat."

By coincidence, and this was our good luck and not our wit, the hotel manager came by with his daughter, a cute little girl. Sonny liked her. The two of them started playing together, so I said, "Let's take a picture of her with the Santa Claus hat on." So I did and then I said, "Let's take a picture of the two of you together." He put his arm around her; she put her arm around him. I said, "That's great. Let's put the hat on you, Sonny, just for one shot." He said, "All right, goddammit." We had the picture.

I can never understand why people do these things. Sonny must have realized when he put on the hat and the little girl was pushed off camera but he didn't say anything. Maybe he was confused. Maybe he didn't realize. Maybe we did trick him. I don't know.

Figure 2 George Lois's preparatory sketch.

1 Interview with Ian Birch.
2 "The First Black Santa", in George Lois, *The Esquire Covers @MoMA*, Assouline, 2009, p. 56.
3 "Harold Hayes on George Lois and those Esquire Covers", ibid., p.25.

OCTOBER 1966

Editor: Harold T P Hayes

Cover design: George Lois

On 25 October 1965[1] John Sack, who had served in Korea and was then a writer and producer at CBS in New York, sent Harold Hayes a brilliant story idea. He wanted to tell "the true story" of a military unit as it moved from basic training in Fort Dix, New Jersey, to first combat in Vietnam. He wanted to portray the soldiers with all their doubts, fears and dreams as faithfully and comprehensively as he could. Sack was shaping the role of the embedded war reporter.

Hayes gave the go-ahead and the following January Sack was detailed to M company. He went with them to Saigon and soon "the incident happened". [2] A cavalryman, hearing voices from inside a bunker, told one of M company to throw a grenade into it. The grenade exploded and "ten or a dozen women and children came shrieking out in their crinkled pajamas; no blood, no apparent injuries, though...Then another soldier, 'a specialist', peered into the remains and cried 'Oh my God!' A second specialist shouted, 'What's the matter?' 'They hit a little girl' and in his muscular black arms the first specialist carried out a seven-year-old, long black hair and little earrings, staring eyes – eyes, her eyes are what froze themselves onto M's memory, it seemed there was no white to those eyes, nothing but black ellipses like black goldfish."[3]

A whopping 33,000 words, it's the longest story Esquire has ever published and has become a benchmark in the history of New Journalism and war reporting.

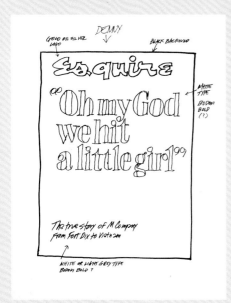

Figure 3 George Lois's preparatory sketch.

1 Sourced from Carol Polsgrove, *It Wasn't Pretty, Folks, But Didn't We Have Fun? Surviving the '60s with Esquire's Harold Hayes*, RDR Books, 2001, p.148.
2 John Sack, 'M', Esquire, October 1966.
3 Ibid.

GEORGE LOIS:

I had a cover about to go to press, and I swear I don't remember what it was. I usually didn't have the actual written piece in my hand on anything I worked on because I had to give them art two months ahead – beats me why. But when Hayes sent me John Sack's story, I perused through the pages and that quote punched me in the mouth. I called Hayes and said, "Kill the cover I did. I'll have a new one for you in three, four hours." I sent him it. He called me up and said, "Oh my God".

It was my chance to inform America that, similar to the Korean war, we were committing yet another act of genocide. The cover appeared when "only" 6,000 GIs had died. The stark design screamed to the world that something was wrong, terribly wrong. American boys, with mind-numbing hatred of the "gooks" – an insult used by most GIs in the Korean and Vietnam wars – were fighting in another brutally immoral, racist war.

Esquire

AUGUST 1966
PRICE 75c

THE MAGAZINE FOR MEN

"Oh my God –we hit a little girl."

The true story of M Company.
From Fort Dix to Vietnam.

APRIL 1968
PRICE $1

Esquire

THE MAGAZINE FOR MEN

The Passion of Muhammad Ali

APRIL 1968

Editor: Harold T P Hayes

Cover design: George Lois

Cover photography: Carl Fischer

In 1967 Cassius Clay, the world's heavyweight champion, converted to Islam under the tutelage of Elijah Muhammad, taking the name Muhammad Ali. "When Ali refused military service as a conscientious objector because of his new religion, a federal jury sentenced him to five years in jail for draft evasion," wrote Lois later. "Boxing commissions then stripped him of his title and denied him the right to fight."[1] Lois decided to pose Ali as a contemporary St Sebastian, after the 15th-century painting by Francesco Botticini in which the body is pierced by six arrows. St Sebastian was a martyr for his religious beliefs; so, argued Lois, was Ali.

Kurt Andersen calls this "the greatest cover ever created, making a political statement without being grim or stupid or predictable. It's not just a great idea, but visually elegant, economical, perfect."[2]

CARL FISCHER:

Ali arrived alone, as I remember. In those days, people were famous, but they were not unapproachable. They weren't surrounded by people taking care of them like today. I had the arrows made and practised with them. When you're doing a symbol, the only thing you really want to show is the symbol. You don't need a background. The focus was on the arrows. The design was the thing itself as so many good covers are: simple, direct statements.

GEORGE LOIS:

I told Ali to bring his pretty white shoes and trunks. I showed him a postcard photograph of St Sebastian. I chose it because it's one where the body is strong and simple and the head's in agony. I said, "Muhammad, I want you to pose like this." He said, "George, this cat's a Christian. I can't pose as a saint." Elijah Muhammad was in Chicago so we got him on the phone. Ali explained what we were going to do and then put me on. He wanted to know if I was a churchgoing Christian. I said, absolutely. Greek Orthodox, the mother church. Finally, he said he thought it would be a wonderful image. Phew ...

CARL FISCHER:

We had a technical problem: the arrows didn't stay horizontal when we pasted them on. They hung down, so even though it was a very simple idea, the solution was very complex. I hung a horizontal bar above Ali and from that we hung monofilament cables, fishing wire, very thin, very light, to keep the arrows in place. That forced Ali to stand still for a half an hour. Fortunately, he didn't play his celebrity, and it was fine. He was a very funny guy, very impressive and very gracious. He saw the problem that we had.

GEORGE LOIS:

When we had attached the arrows, Ali pointed to each one and said, "Hey George, Lyndon Johnson, General Westmoreland, Clark Clifford, Hubert Humphrey, Robert McNamara and Dean Rusk." I almost fainted. It was the best thing I ever heard.

When the cover came out, it was hated by everybody but the young people who were subject to the draft. When a man like him, who couldn't be more manly or more spiritual, can come out against the war, and risk going to jail for five years, it gave millions of young people courage. He went on a crazy college tour where he would do a kind of one-hour talk, telling funny stories. Not a militant speech but about being a black guy in a white world – where everything's white; where the snow is white; where it's "Snow White and the Seven Dwarves". He had this whole schtick. The kids would go crazy.

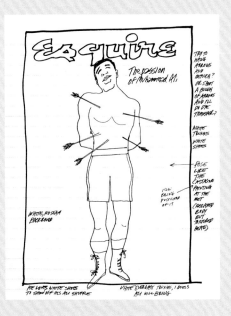

Figure 4 George Lois's preparatory sketch.

---

1 George Lois, "Proclaiming the Martyrdom of Muhammad Ali for Refusing to Fight in a Bad War", in *$ellebrity*, Phaidon, 2003.
2 Quoted by Lois on his website: http://www.georgelois. com/ali-as-st.-sebastian.html

MAY 1969

Editor: Harold T P Hayes

Cover design: George Lois

Cover photography: Carl Fischer

"An *Esquire* cover of me drowning in a can of Campbell's soup? I love it! But George, aren't you gonna have to build a giant can of soup?"[1]

So said Andy Warhol to George Lois when he heard the cover concept. Lois had already done multiple photomontage covers for *Esquire,* but this visual joke – part mocking, part homage – ranks as one of his finest. "You could look at it as just funny, or you look at it as how fame swallows people – the absurdity of fame," he later said. "But he really stood for something. Pop Art was ludicrous to me, but I could see why it was catching on."[2]

CARL FISCHER:

The basic shot was a soup can with the dirty lid open a certain amount so that we could get the logo in. I spent the day dropping children's marbles, one by one, into the soup. We did a million splashes and finally got one that made a nice hole to drop Andy into.

I photographed Warhol a lot. His mother and he lived up the block from me on Lexington. He would do anything to be on a cover of a magazine – and for no money. He ran an ad once in *The Village Voice* saying, "I'm available for endorsing products" for money. We had him come into the studio and said, "You're falling into the ocean, just about to drown and you're dying." We did a whole bunch of pictures of him with his arms up, his arms out, screaming, whatever. George sent it out to a retoucher and they put the two shoots together.

Figure 5 George Lois's preparatory sketch.

1 Quoted in George Lois, *The Esquire Covers @ MoMA*, Assouline, 2009, p.134.
2 Condensed from Alex Hoyt, "The Story Behind the Iconic Andy Warhol 'Esquire' Cover", the *Atlantic*, 7 June 2012.

MAY 1969
PRICE $1

Esquire

THE MAGAZINE FOR MEN

The final decline and total collapse of the American avant-garde.

PRIVATE EYE

5 FEBRUARY 1965
1963 ANNUAL

Editor: Richard Ingrams
Cover artist: Gerald Scarfe

Gerald Scarfe hit the spotlight in 1963 with a drawing inside *Private Eye* of Prime Minister Harold Macmillan, naked and bosomy on an Arne Jacobsen chair, in a wicked parody of Lewis Morley's famous photograph of Christine Keeler during the Profumo affair. The cartoon became the cover of the magazine's 1963 annual, which WH Smith promptly banned.

GERALD SCARFE:

In the early 1960s cartooning was incredibly bland. I worked for *Punch* where I'd done really typical cartoons of mothers-in-law behind the door with rolling pins waiting for the drunken son-in-law to come home and people on desert islands putting messages in bottles. Then along came *Private Eye* and the so-called satire boom. They just found me, and it was like a refreshing breath of air to be able to tell the truth after the crushingly dull and cloying 1950s.

I really did go for it. I knew when I was making a drawing that it had to be vicious. Richard Ingrams said, "You could always rely on Gerald to do something cutting or nasty." No more desert islands unless they had sharks in them. I realize that I do have this bitter side and it sort of enveloped me. But it seemed to be what I was meant to do.

I began to draw political figures. Macmillan was the first one. Strangely enough, there was an incredible reaction to it. Someone later said that no one since the 18th century had drawn politicians naked – not since Gillray. I was being continually likened to Hogarth, Gillray and Rowlandson[1] – whom, incidentally, I don't in any way draw parallels with or think of myself in the same ilk – but I can see why they said it because there is the same sort of *purpose* behind it. I'm giving my view on society and politics, which is what Gillray and Rowlandson did.

The Times sent me to draw Churchill because it was his last day in Parliament, 27 July 1964. The Sergeant at Arms had to give me special dispensation to draw in the House of Commons because you're not allowed to do that. In those days, we really didn't know what we know about personalities now, especially of that ilk. Churchill was still depicted in the newspapers, the *Daily Express* and so forth, as this bulldog figure, standing on the cliffs of Dover with a cigar defying the Hun with a bowler hat, and Vera Lynn singing in the background. Anyway, he was brought in by two helpers on either side. A shambling wreck of a man,

PRIVATE EYE

No. 82
Friday
5 February 65

1/6

obviously senile: it was an incredible shock. Poor old boy. He just sat there as an empty shell.

What was I supposed to draw? Was I supposed to draw the old bulldog or am I supposed to draw what I see? When I took it back to *The Times* they wouldn't publish it because they said, imagine what Clemmie, his wife, would feel if that came through the letterbox. I remember going to a *Private Eye* lunch that day and I told Peter Cook about it. "Oh, let's have it," he said. No such compunction at all there – bugger all that. So he stuffed it on the cover the week Churchill died and, ironically, it has been recently hanging in the House of Commons. That was a strange drawing for me: not really a caricature in my usual style.

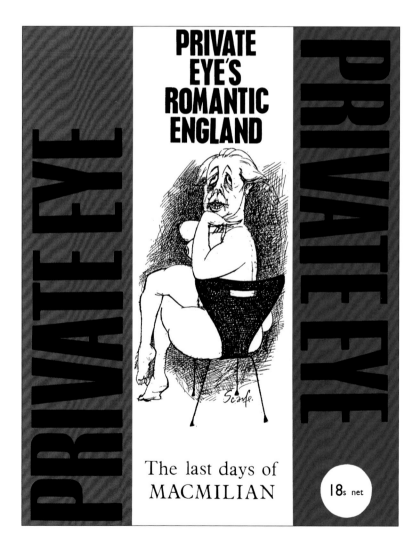

1 William Hogarth (1697–1764), James Gillray (c.1756–1815) and Thomas Rowlandson (1756–1827), pioneers of the satirical cartoon in the UK who made robust use of caricature.

FACT

SEPTEMBER/OCTOBER 1964

Editor and publisher: Ralph Ginzburg
Art director: Herb Lubalin
Contributing editor: Warren Boroson
Staff: Shoshana (formerly Susan) Ginzburg

In January 1964 Ralph Ginzburg launched *Fact*, a black-and-white quarterly he described as a "hell-raising, muckraking magazine of dissent that would try to improve society by bringing data to the fore that was not generally known".[1] Herb Lubalin's stark art direction perfectly framed this content.

The US presidential election would happen in November: Republican Senator Barry M Goldwater was running against incumbent Democrat Lyndon B Johnson. Alarmed by Goldwater's extreme conservative stance, and his advocacy of the use of nuclear weapons, *Fact* felt it had a duty to warn its audience.

It sent a questionnaire to the United States' 12,356 psychiatrists asking, "Do you believe Barry Goldwater is psychologically fit to serve as President of the United States?" Of this number, 2,417 psychiatrists responded and 1,189 said that he was not. The questionnaire left room for "Comments" and "over a quarter of a million words of professional opinion were received".[2]

The comments from the 1,189 pulled no punches about Goldwater's mental fitness and the risks he posed. Goldwater brought a libel action, seeking damages of $1,000,000. The court found against Ginzburg and Boroson. Goldwater was awarded $1.00 in compensatory damages and punitive damages of $75,000.

In response, the American Psychiatric Association issued the so-called "Goldwater rule" in 1973 which made it "unethical for a psychiatrist to offer a professional opinion unless he or she has conducted an examination and has been granted proper authorization for such a statement".[3] This is still in effect as I write in 2018, although some mental health professionals, who question President Trump's psychiatric state, believe that the rule should be revisited because it undermines their "duty to inform".

SHOSHANA GINZBURG:

I was married to Ralph and we were so worried that Goldwater would become president that we made plans to move to New Zealand. We knew he was out of his mind and were very afraid. We were shocked when he sued because he made it all the more public. The trial was amazing. We had a very good lawyer, Harris B Sternberg. He set up a huge blackboard in the courtroom with the article written on it. He went through it, sentence by sentence, and said, "Is this the sentence that offended you?" I was digging my fingernails into my palm not to laugh.

At one point, I was in the elevator alone with Goldwater and I said to him, "You might be surprised to know that you remind me of my dad." He looked at me as if I had stuck a pin in his finger. He didn't know what to do. I'm supposed to be his vile enemy and here am I saying something that might be taken as nice. If I have a chance to calm down an enemy, I'm going to do it.

We never thought there was a chance he would win. Never! We thought America was the land of free speech and it's absolutely basic that the public can question anything about a candidate running for president. We were so wrong. We were faced with huge fines and it eventually put *Fact* out of business.

How could that cover be more on point today?

1 Quoted in Philip B Meggs, "Two Magazines of the Turbulent '60s: A 'Perspective", *Print 48* (March–April 1994), pp.68–77.
2 Credited to Warren Boroson, "What Psychiatrists Say about Goldwater", *Fact*, vol. 1, issue 5 (September/October 1964), p.24.
3 Section 7.3 of the APA's *Principles of Medical Ethics*, p.9.

fact:

VOLUME ONE, ISSUE FIVE $1.25

1,189 Psychiatrists Say Goldwater Is Psychologically Unfit To Be President!

COSMOPOLITAN

JULY 1965

Editor: Helen Gurley Brown

Cover photographer: J Frederick Smith

Cover model: Renata Boeck

Senior editor (from 1968): Jeanette Wagner

Brooke Hauser is the author of *Enter Helen: The Invention of Helen Gurley Brown and the Rise of the Modern Single Woman*, Harper, 2016.

In 1962 Helen Gurley Brown created a publishing phenomenon with her lifestyle guide *Sex and the Single Girl* (Figure 6). With her husband David Brown, an executive at Twentieth Century Fox, she turned it into a franchise, with movie, record, newspaper and TV projects. Editing a woman's magazine was the logical next step. Hearst was looking for "a messiah"[1] to resuscitate its veteran but struggling title *Cosmopolitan*, and offered Helen the job. She became American *Cosmopolitan*'s first female editor since its launch in 1886. She started in March 1965, her first issue was July and it sold out. By December the third-quarter ad revenue was up 50 per cent and circulation was averaging a million copies an issue, almost 15 per cent above 1964.[2]

Two years later Brown summed up her audience: "My kind of swinger is a girl who just wants everything. She may have a career. She does have a love life. She may or may not have children. But she is really living. She is not living through a man, nor does she exploit men. She certainly is not a kept girl – she pays her own bills. She does not go out all night every night and sleep throughout the next day. When she is out late, she arrives at the office sharp at nine the following morning, even though she may be dropping on her feet. She has ideas. This is my credo for *Cosmopolitan* magazine."[3]

BROOKE HAUSER:

That July cover happened by accident. Helen loved the pin-up illustrations J. Frederick Smith had done for *Esquire* and he was assigned to do a story inside *Cosmo*. Most of the models then were kind of flat-chested and slim in the Twiggy mould. But when Helen saw his picture of the blonde busty model Renata Boeck she said, "That's the cover." Renata was German and one of what *Life* magazine had called the "Fraulein Fad"[4] models who were coming to America then. Helen was one of the first female editors to understand that women like to look at other beautiful women.

She was giving a voice to the working girl from a small town, as you can start to see in the cover lines. "When a working girl sees a psychiatrist" is pretty much the quintessential Helen Gurley Brown story. "The new pill" cover line is remembered as being one of the first major magazine stories about birth control. But if you read the article, it's not about what we think of as "the Pill".

JULY, 1965 ● 35¢

COSMOPOLITAN

The new pill that promises to make women more responsive

World's Greatest Lover— What it was like to be wooed by him! From the best-selling book, ALY

When a working girl sees a psychiatrist by Lucy Freeman
PLUS
You Think You're Neurotic by Oscar Levant

The Only Good Secretary— Complete Mystery Novel

Are you a Jax girl? See inside

It's about oestrogen therapy. The story goes that the original line was "the new pill that promises to make women more responsive to men". Hearst objected. Helen was distraught and called David who said, "Take off the last two words – to men." Because what else were they going to be responsive to?

David had been a managing editor at *Cosmopolitan* earlier in his career, and he helped her a lot. Practically every day, certainly for her first few months, she would call him up. He worked nearby, they would get in a cab and drive around Central Park, and she would ask him all of her urgent questions.

JEANETTE WAGNER:

Helen was a visionary. She was very, very focused on her audience which she knew well. She was narrow but deep, I guess I would say. She was not interested in anything particularly political. At one story conference, I suggested that we do an article on one of the women in the Black Panthers. She had no idea who the Black Panthers were. She didn't read *The New York Times* front pages. That was not her mission. Her mission was what she called the mouseburger that she tried to turn into a pussycat. The whole thrust of everything she did was to help that little mouseburger.

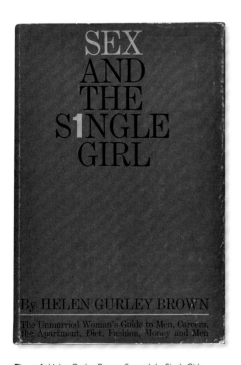

Figure 6 Helen Gurley Brown, *Sex and the Single Girl*, Bernard Geis Associates, 1962.

---

1 Terry Mansfield interview with Ian Birch.
2 Figures from Chris Welles, "Helen Gurley Brown Turns Editor", *Life*, 19 November 1965, p.66.
3 Quoted in "Helen Gurley Brown talks to Adelle Donen", *Queen* magazine, 10 May 1967.
4 "The Fraulein Fad: German Models are a Big Success in the U.S.", *Life*, 20 March 1964, p.95.

LIFE

25 MARCH 1966

Managing editor: George P Hunt

Los Angeles bureau correspondent:
 Gerald Moore

Cover & feature photographer:
 Lawrence Schiller

Art director: Bernard Quint

Cover credit: Lawrence Schiller –
 Bernard Quint

Launched in 1936, the photography-based news weekly *Life* reached two in five Americans by 1961.[1] One of its long-range assignments was "youth-watching"[2] and that included the rise of LSD. Still legal in 1966, the psychedelic drug was moving from the counterculture to suburbia; it was the perfect moment for the magazine to do a major investigation.

GERALD MOORE:

Larry Schiller had found some young people who were going to drop acid and had agreed to let him photograph them in a West LA apartment. We were there from eight in the evening until the next morning. Once in a while somebody would laugh or talk out loud or cry, but there wasn't a lot of emotion that you could *see*. Later, there was a lot of concern about being able to identify these people. We had their permission but the *Life* lawyers were still worried. It turned out that the young blonde woman in the pictures was the daughter of a General Electric vice-president. She had run away from home and nobody knew where she was.

At the same time that we were doing the LSD story, there was a discussion about a joint venture between Time Inc. and General Electric. The GE vice-president decided that we had identified this girl as his daughter and that we were going to print the photographs as a way of intimidating General Electric in the joint venture process. The lawyers had the art department make minor changes to her face so that a stranger looking at a picture of her and then looking at the pictures in *Life* wouldn't be able to say it was the same person.

Ken Kesey and the Merry Pranksters came to LA to put on an "Acid Test" dance. If there were a hundred people – they were not hippies but pretty conventional – I'd be surprised. It was in a dank old garage. There were two

THE EXPLODING THREAT
OF THE MIND DRUG
THAT GOT OUT
OF CONTROL

LSD

TURMOIL IN A CAPSULE

One dose of LSD is enough
to set off a mental riot
of vivid colors and insights
—or of terror and convulsions

MARCH 25 · 1966 ·   35¢

®

garbage cans, one smoking and one not, both filled with Kool-Aid. The one with the dry ice, the smoking one, had been laced with LSD. For a $2 admission fee you could drink as much Kool-Aid as you wanted. Most people drank some and then they basically stood around looking.

The Grateful Dead was supposed to play but something happened to their sound system. So they put recorded music on and had a strobe light. At some point, this guy started dancing and in a dark room with the strobe light going, it was probably the most active thing that happened all evening. I finally realized that these people didn't look like anything was going on but in their heads it was a massive experience.

Everybody convened in New York and agreed it should be a cover. I think Larry said, "Why don't you just put a bunch of LSD pills in somebody's hand and take a picture of it." I'm not sure that's really LSD in my hand. Bernie laid those colour slides on top, I guess, to indicate that there's something more to this than just pills.

We were not happy with that cover slug, "The Exploding Threat of the Mind Drug". It was meant to cover our asses with the social conservatives who were poised to say, "Oh, you're endorsing drugs now." *Life* could say it was reporting on a *threat*. It was a balancing act.

We convinced the editors that we needed to *not* skew the debate so badly that it resulted in the criminalization of LSD. It was criminalized anyway that fall but I don't think we contributed to that. No mainstream magazine had done this kind of comprehensive look at LSD before.

1   Quoted in David E Sumner, *The Magazine Century: American Magazines since 1900*, Peter Lang, 2010, p.90.
2   *Growing Up: The Best of Life*, Time-Life Books, Inc., 1973, p.251.

Automania

THE SUNDAY TIMES MAGAZINE

24 OCTOBER 1965
24 MARCH 1968
Editor, *The Sunday Times* & editor-in-chief,
    Times Newspapers: Denis Hamilton
    (1959–66)
Magazine editors: Mark Boxer (1962–5)
    & Godfrey Smith (1966–72)
Magazine art director: Michael Rand
Magazine art editor: David King
Magazine writer & film critic: George Perry
Illustrator on *The Sunday Times* newspaper
    and magazine: Roger Law

24 OCTOBER 1965
"Automania" editor: Derek Jewell
Illustrator: Alan Aldridge
Photographer: Denis Rolfe

1 Michael Rand interview with Ian Birch.
2 George Perry interview with Ian Birch.

British newspapers were strictly black and white until 4 February 1962, when *The Sunday Times* introduced a colour section, a 40-page magazine supplement. Heavily criticized at first, it soon added 100,000 sales and created the template for all UK newspaper supplements. Michael Rand's art direction was pivotal, developing "a rather uncomfortable mixture of grit and glamour that gives it tension and contrast".[1] It attracted lucrative new colour advertising and a new wave of brash, classless twenty-something talent; it mixed the high and lowbrow; it drove and defined 1960s culture. "The magazine's philosophy was never to give the public what they want, never to follow taste…No, we should lead taste."[2]

GODFREY SMITH:
I went to my old grammar school in Surbiton to do a talk for the boys. Instead of sitting still, they'd talk to each other and fart and generally be a nuisance. I did my best but, at the end of it, I said, "Look, chaps, what do you like to read about?" One voice said, "Cars." So we invented this word *Automania*, and then Mike started working on this Mini idea.

MICHAEL RAND:
Alan Aldridge, who was a junior in the promotions department at *The Sunday Times*, was also an illustrator. He showed us his portfolio, and we liked it. It reflected the Pop art of that period, so I thought it was a good idea to ask Alan to try a cover. My assistant, David Nathanson, had a Mini, so I dragooned him into lending it to us and, to his horror, getting Alan to paint it. The artwork was split down the middle of the car. One side was sporty with undertones of Bond and Superman, and on the other side was his wife or girlfriend, which reflected home, security and prettiness. Alan whitewashed the car and spent five days doing it. He used a hundred tubes of designers' gouache and six cans of Woolworth's silver spray. We were thrilled about it. Denis Rolfe then photographed it.

David was somewhat upset by the result. I suggested to David that he keep it because it would become a collector's piece and probably worth a lot of money but, no, he had to have it all washed off. I think he lost an opportunity there.

24 MARCH 1968
Photographer: Don McCullin

The cover announces Don McCullin's harrowing 12-page photo essay, "This Is How It Is". He photographed and wrote about the US Marines' bloody counteroffensive to take back the South Vietnamese city of Hue, which the North Vietnamese had captured in the Tet Offensive. The story won the coveted D&AD[1] Silver and Gold Awards in 1969.

MICHAEL RAND:
We decided to start a five-week series on America with this. It's one of his strongest Vietnam essays. Don became a sort of hero to the public at that time. He had an enormous effect on the quality of *The Sunday Times*.

GODFREY SMITH:
We didn't spare anyone's feelings when Don was in action. These pictures weren't news pictures: they were saying, "This is what war is like." Don is a very mild, rather gentle fellow who had this wonderful empathy with soldiers.

MICHAEL RAND:
Don used to shoot in black and white. We didn't impose on him to shoot in colour, but, in the end, he did and, somehow, he shot *harder* in colour. He didn't consciously shoot covers. I mean, he was shooting war. You couldn't actually ask a lot of photographers then to shoot a cover. I don't think many of them understood covers.

ROGER LAW:
It's a terrible thing to say but the adrenaline round the office was unbelievable when McCullin's stuff came in. Michael would discuss the presentation of the pictures with David who did that layout. David was a very important magazine designer at that time. *The Sunday Times* colour magazine was the newest thing since sliced bread and everybody wanted to work on it. Well, we did! David and I were very young and we had a really fucking irresponsible ball. Michael Rand was our mentor.

---

1 Design & Art Direction Awards – internationally prestigious awards in design and advertising.

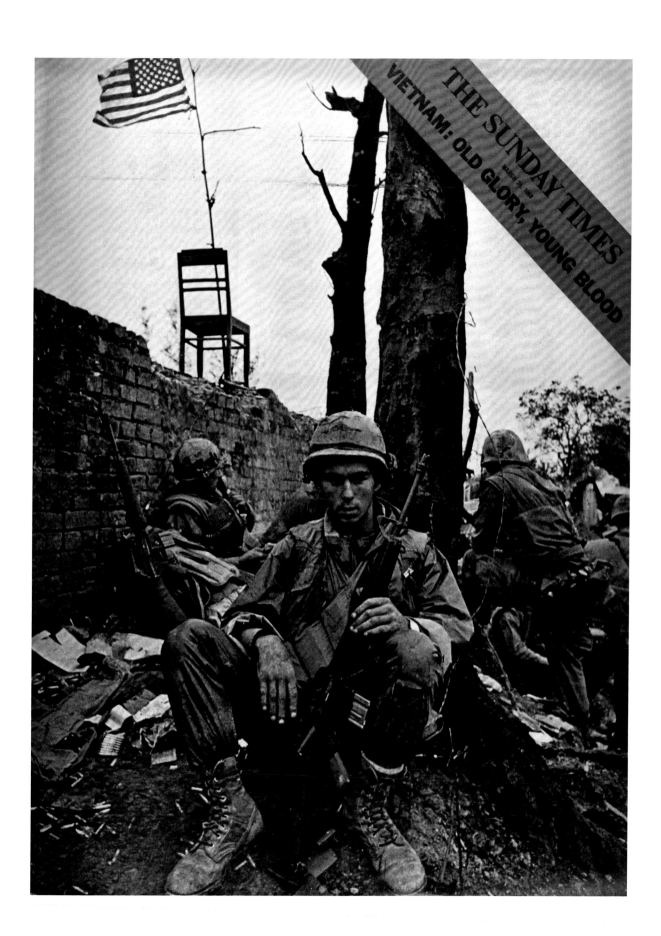

NOVA

JANUARY 1966

Editor: Dennis Hackett

Art director & cover photography:
   Harri Peccinotti

Cover star: Sonia Williams, aged four

Art director (1969–75): David Hillman

The *Nova* magic kicked in when Dennis Hackett joined in September 1965, a few months after launch. Harri Peccinotti's radical design and photography perfectly complemented Hackett's equally radical content.

HARRI PECCINOTTI:

It was one of those times when art directors at advertising agencies, like me, suddenly realized that magazines were freer and less restrictive, and were getting more adventurous. We were being impressed by *Town* and *Queen* and *Twen* and Henry Wolf at *Esquire* and *Show* and Herb Lubalin's *Eros*. There was incredible enthusiasm for magazine design.

Racialism in England was really bad in the mid-1960s. Almost still like "No Irish, no blacks, no dogs". There was an article about the problem, so Hackett and I thought of doing a cover. We decided that we would *not* put a sinister picture like a poverty-stricken area on the cover. That would have been the obvious thing to do. Instead, we thought we'd do a little girl like when she goes to church on a Sunday. Hackett wrote the title. I'm not sure I like it but he was very good at one-line titles. He wanted *Nova* to be provocative, that's for sure.

I took the photograph. It was just a little shot in my studio. The girl came with her mum and auntie. They dressed her up: we didn't do anything. We told them what sort of thing we wanted, but we didn't try to engineer it that way. I sometimes cringe a bit about it. Why? I don't know. It makes me uncomfortable probably because I'm one of the people the cover is aiming at. It's like being frightened to face up to what your country does or doesn't do.

CAROLINE BAKER:

Harri was a very political person, very into equal rights for everybody. He was horrified by the treatment of black people. He found black women really beautiful and always photographed them.

HARRI PECCINOTTI:

I don't remember any particularly bad reaction to the cover. I personally detest the idea of market research, asking people in the street what they think. I used to get into rows with Hackett and with those people who said, "What, you don't want to know what people think?" I never, ever paid attention to how many sold or who they sold to.

NOVA

JANUARY 1966 THREE SHILLINGS

YOU MAY THINK I LOOK CUTE
BUT WOULD YOU LIVE NEXT DOOR
TO MY MUMMY AND DADDY?

Start reading on page 14

VOGU

MARCH 1 1966 4/-

COLLECTIONS

VOGUE

MARCH 1966

Editor: Beatrix Miller
Photograph: David Bailey
Cover model: Donyale Luna

Born Peggy Ann Freeman in Detroit in 1945, Donyale Luna became fashion's first internationally celebrated African-American model. Her rise was meteoric: discovered by photographer David McCabe in 1964, she was on the cover of *Harper's Bazaar* by January 1965, though they used a drawing of her with an equivocally pinkish skin tone. In December she decamped to London, and three months later was the first woman of colour on the cover of British *Vogue* – eight years before American *Vogue* made a similar leap. "She happens to be a marvellous shape," editor Bea Miller told *Time*. "All sort of angular and immensely tall and strange. She has a kind of bite and personality."[1]

DAVID BAILEY:

There was a discussion with Bea about who we should use for the cover. There always was. Of course, she didn't give me a brief. I just do what I want. That's why I don't work with a lot of people because I can't do what they want. I'm great friends with Anna Wintour but I don't want to work with her. What she wants is nothing to do with what I do.

Donyale was a beautiful creature. An extraordinary-looking girl. She was a bit nervous. She had those flirty eyes. She was so skinny that she looked taller than she actually was. The hand? I used to do that a lot. It's a thing I got off Picasso who often showed one eye. Some people have said it was to hide she was black. That's the most stupid thing I've ever read.

I didn't care what colour she was. It didn't make a difference to me. We didn't do this thinking this was the first black cover. We did it because she was right for the job. It was at the right moment. There were more pictures of her inside with Moyra Swan and Peggy Moffitt.[2] Alexander Liberman, the creative head of *Vogue*, did say to me if you ever do pictures like that again, you won't work for Condé Nast. I thought it was because the pictures were lesbian-ish but, on reflection, I think it was because Donyale was black. I think he was trying to tell me not to mix pictures like that: this is just something I've thought of recently.

I'm sure *Vogue* got complaints. They got complaints all the time about Jean Shrimpton's legs. I pulled skirts up and sometimes *Vogue* would airbrush them down again. There seemed to be a lot of complaints from Scotland.

---

1 "Fashion: The Luna Year", *Time*, 1 April 1966.
2 Models Moyra Swan and Peggy Moffitt were both white.

DISC
and MUSIC ECHO 9d

JUNE 11, 1966   USA 25c

MERSEY UPROAR

after 'Whole Scene' attack

SEE PAGE 6

SANDIE
TV miming no CRIME!

Page 7

MERSEYS
jealous of the Hollies!

Page 8

CILLA
I just can't stop myself GIGGLING!

Page 8

BEATLES: WHAT A CARVE-UP!

BEATLES WEEK! They're back with a single, "Paperback Writer" and "Rain"—out tomorrow (Friday).

BUT WHAT'S THIS? The Beatles as butchers, draped with raw meat! Disc and Music Echo's world exclusive colour picture by Bob Whitaker is the most controversial shot ever of John, Paul, George and Ringo.

THE PLACE: A private studio in Chelsea, London. Whitaker is taking some new pictures of the Beatles, and decides that a new approach is needed.

"I wanted to do a real experiment — people will jump to wrong conclusions about it being sick," says Whitaker, "But the whole thing is based on simplicity — linking four very real people with something real.

"I got George to knock some nails into John's head, and took some sausages along to get some other pictures. Dressed them up in white smocks as butchers, and this is the result—the use of the camera as a means of creating situations."

PAUL'S comment after the session: "Very tasty meat."

GEORGE: "We won't come to any more of your sick picture sessions."

JOHN: "Oh, we don't mind doing anything."

RINGO: "We haven't done pictures like THIS before . . ."

Well, what's YOUR verdict? Sick—or super? Six LPs for the best six captions—of no more than 12 words—to the picture above. Send your entry to "Beatles Picture," Disc and Music Echo, 161 Fleet Street, London, E.C.4, before next Friday, June 17.

● PAUL in his own write—exclusive interview: Page 9.

DISC AND MUSIC ECHO

11 JUNE 1966

Editor: Ray Coleman

Photographer: Robert Whitaker

Disc and Music Echo was the first and only British pop music weekly to put an image from a new shoot the Beatles had done in March 1966 with Robert Whitaker on the cover. Whitaker's plan was to create a surreal triptych that sabotaged the popular perception of the Fab Four, but the project was never completed.

"I wanted to do a real experiment – people will jump to wrong conclusions about it being sick," Whitaker says on the front page. Controversy erupted a few days later when a second photograph from the set, with added toy dolls (Figure 7), was revealed as the cover of a new American LP, *The Beatles Yesterday and Today.* "I especially pushed for it to be an album cover,"[1] Lennon later admitted. Capitol Records, their American label, panicked, recalled the LP and then hit on the idea of pasting "a more generally acceptable"[2] photograph over the "Butcher"[3] sleeve. George Harrison thought the session was "gross"[4] and "stupid"[5] while Paul McCartney was more sanguine: "To us, this wasn't a big deal really because these kind of shocking things were part of the art scene"[6]. How the paper got this alternate shot and why it reversed the transparency remains unclear.

ROBERT WHITAKER:[7]

He [the Beatles' then PR, Tony Barrow] hated the session basically because he had six other journalists, all wanting to do interviews, and I was taking a long time. The Beatles were highly amused by what I was up to.

I'd got fed up with taking these Tony Barrow, squeaky-clean pictures of the Beatles, and I thought I'd revolutionize what pop idols are. They were all OK with it right up until the point where I started bringing trays of meat onto the set. Tony Barrow says the dolls were all dismembered. They weren't. They were exactly how I got them, in a box from the manufacturers. I asked for some dolls. I'd gone to Barley Mow Meadows where there was a doll factory, and they said, "Oh, we've only got bits."

They threw them in a box, which I emptied out in front of the Beatles. They then fiddled around with them – George has got an arm on his shoulder, Ringo's got a spare leg. John loved it. I shot them with eyes open, and eyes closed. George, because he was becoming a vegan, wasn't overly impressed. He said he'd never attend another of my photo sessions. I was rather amazed to see that Paul wrote rather favourably about it.[8] Ringo, being the sportsman that he is, I don't think was bothered either way.

According to Tony Barrow, Epstein wanted to burn the transparencies. But I don't know what to believe.

Figure 7 The original, recalled "Butcher" cover of The Beatles Yesterday and Today.

1 Quoted in *The Beatles: Eight Days A Week – The Touring Years* (dir. Ron Howard), Imagine Entertainment, Apple Corps, 2016.

2 Extracted from the letter to reviewers from Ron Tepper, Manager Press & Information Services, Capital Records Distribution Corp., 14 June 1966.

3 Called "Butcher" because of the white butcher coats and slabs of meat.

4 George Harrison in *The Beatles Anthology*, Cassell & Co, 2000, p.204.

5 Ibid.

6 Quoted in *The Beatles: Eight Days A Week – The Touring Years* (dir. Ron Howard), , Imagine Entertainment, Apple Corps, 2016.

7 Extracted from Jon Savage's interview with Robert Whitaker in April 1966, part of which he used for *1966: The Year the Decade Exploded*, Faber & Faber, 2015. Reproduced with the author's kind permission.

8 See The Beatles, *The Beatles Anthology*, Cassell & Co, 2000, p.204.

INTERNATIONAL TIMES

ISSUE 8, 13–26 FEBRUARY 1967

Editor: Tom McGrath

Explosions: John Hopkins

Art editor: Mike McInnerney

Operations: Peter Stansill

Front-page graphics: Mike McInnerney

ISSUE 52, 14–27 MARCH 1969

Editor and words: Peter Stansill

Art editor: Graham Keen

Images/layout: Graham Keen

Cover photography: Horace Ove[1]

The *International Times* (frequently abbreviated to *IT*) was Britain's first underground newspaper. Founded by the core team of John "Hoppy" Hopkins, (Barry) Miles, Jim Haynes and Jack Henry Moore, it was launched at London's Roundhouse on 15 October 1966 with a fund-raising "All Night Rave" which included live performances from Soft Machine and Pink Floyd. The rough-and-ready first issues "focused on avant garde art, music, happenings, theatre, film and literature, with occasional forays into censorship, personal freedom, the Vietnam war, student protests, and LSD and cannabis price trends in Notting Hill".[2]

MIKE MCINNERNEY:

The covers up until then had been mostly type – news items about alternative cultural activities and campaigning issues. I decided to make this one less like a newspaper and more like a periodical. It was my first full issue as art editor. I was trying to signal a kind of a new hippie universe with a counterculture mandala. The arabesque shapes have the symmetry of a mandala which is a balanced geometric composition that usually contains deities. But instead of deities I added the image of an exotically dressed female, a medieval woodcut of a mandrake figure and the *IT* girl[3] which had been established as our logo.

PETER STANSILL:

I became editor in 1968. Graham Keen, the art director, was there and that was it, basically. We had a whole crew of freelancers and it was like herding cats. Everybody was smoking dope and dropping acid. Everything was instant and unconsidered, often ill-considered, but the circulation just soared.

There was still that taboo about black/white interracial relationships. That's what we wanted to break. This might have been a provocative cover but not to us. I never asked anybody outside our readership what they thought about it. It was of no interest to me how it would be accepted, or not, in the wider world. The photograph was by the Trinidadian-British photographer Horace Ove who was documenting the emerging black consciousness in the UK. There are no cover lines. No accompanying story. It was, let's just send a visual message. We didn't need to comment on it. Horace's photograph is perfect.

---

1 Horace Ove started as a reportage photographer for *IT*, *Oz* and *Race Today* before becoming a distinguished filmmaker: his films include *Baldwin's Nigger* (1969), *Reggae* (1970) and *Pressure* (1975), the first full-length feature by a black director in Britain.

2 Peter Stansill, "The Life and Times of IT", 2016.

3 It was meant to be Clara Bow, the original Hollywood "It Girl", but a picture of Theda Bara was used by mistake.

The International Times   No 8   Feb 13-26 1967/1s

ginsberg • townshend (who) • snyder • mandrake root

it

SQUATTERS START TO RETAKE THE UNIVERSE

(See Centre Spread)

NO. 52, MARCH 14-27, 1969 UK 1/6

PRINTED AND PUBLISHED BY KNULLAR (PUBLISHING, PRINTING AND PROMOTIONS) LTD, 27 ENDELL ST., LONDON WC2

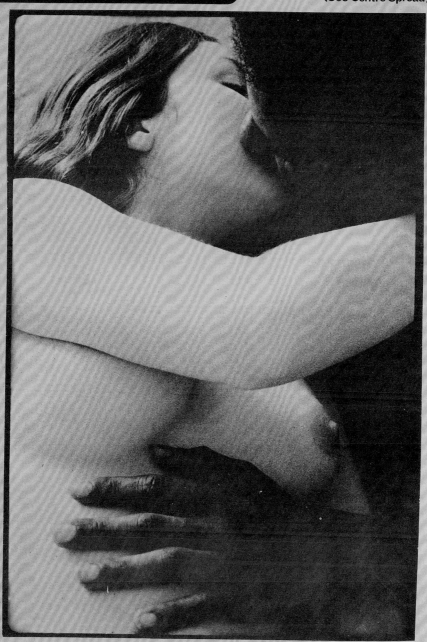

MANAGEMENT TODAY

FEBRUARY 1968

Editor: Robert Heller

Art director: Roland Schenk

In-house photographer (November 1971 – February 1972): Brian Griffin

Photographer (February 1968 issue): Lester Bookbinder

Roland Schenk has been called "a great unsung genius of British magazine design."[1] In the early 1960s he worked at *Du*, the uncompromisingly beautiful Swiss arts and culture magazine which was distributed in 60 countries. This experience was crucial when he became art director of *Management Today* in 1968. Owned by Haymarket Press, it delivered incisive business journalism in a large format and with glossy production values. Notoriously abrasive and demanding, Schenk soon became Haymarket's design director, creating an elegantly robust house style and setting new and exceptional design standards in the British periodical sector. Over the next 30 years he was involved in multiple Haymarket launches, including, notably, *Campaign,* which became the advertising industry's bible.

ROLAND SCHENK:

The ideal cover should transcend the trivial function of content indicator. It should provoke surprise and add an enigmatic dimension, inviting subconscious associations. It should be of artistic quality to prolong its exposure as an object. Cover lines were written later and were of no concern.

This was my first cover for *Management Today*. It satisfies the criteria defined above. The photograph is by Lester Bookbinder. An unusual aspect of the engine was considered. When visiting the Ford factory, Lester discovered this casting block, the mould into which the hot metal is poured, which made for a more surprising image.

BRIAN GRIFFIN:

Lester Bookbinder did the greatest covers that British magazines have ever seen. Incredible abstract still lifes. He is the most unheralded photographer this country has ever had.

ROLAND SCHENK:

I encouraged a non-trivial approach to the subject matter. In the case of *Management Today*, I made it happen due to the harmonious relationship with the editor, Robert Heller. In other cases, I had to resort to terror tactics like cutting short discussions and imposing my decisions in a fierce manner to quell further attempts at argumentation. This was necessitated by operational constraints and is quite contrary to my normal receptive manner.

BRIAN GRIFFIN:

Roland gave me my first break after I left college. I became the photographer for *Management Today* on a retainer of, I think, £25 a week. I began on 1 November 1972 and I left in February 1973, saying, "I'm just not going to work with you any more, I find you too difficult." And he said, "Well, I'm going to continue working with you." He imparted a kind of harsh, antagonistic brutalism which, in fact, shook me up and drove me to find a new way of seeing. It got me to the standard of photography I've now reached.

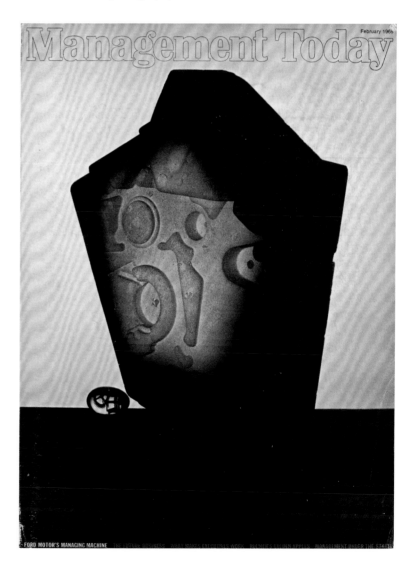

1   Lindsay Masters quoted in "Haymarket 50 Years: 50 Glorious Moments", *Campaign*, 26 October 2007.

1970s

THE BLACK PANTHER

21 FEBRUARY 1970

Staff: John Seale, Roberta Alexander,
   Brenda Pressley, Mumia Abu-Jamal
   (Wes Cook), Emory Douglas,
   Judi Douglas, Elbert "Big Man" Howard
Cover photography (21 February):
   Stephen Shames

Huey Newton and Bobby Seale formed the Black Panther Party for Self-Defense in October 1966 in Oakland, California, initially as a "civilian police patrol".[1] The following April they launched a weekly newspaper, *The Black Panther: Black Community News Service.*

On 28 October 1967 Newton and a friend were involved in a shoot-out with two officers from the Oakland Police Department. One of the officers, John Frey, was fatally wounded. Newton was arrested for Frey's killing, charged with first-degree murder, and on 8 September 1968 convicted of voluntary manslaughter and sentenced to two to fifteen years in prison. That night, two rogue policemen fired shots at the Panther headquarters, puncturing the iconic poster of Newton hanging in the office window. The following morning, Stephen Shames photographed the mutilated poster, which, sixteen months later, became the cover of a special issue. It was the second edition of *The Black Panther* that week and the sequence of the two covers was telling: the earlier celebrated Newton's 28th birthday on 17 February (Figure 8); the later gave "evidence and intimidation of fascist crimes by U.S.A."[2] In May 1970, Newton's sentence was overturned and a new trial was ordered. By August he was a free man.

THE BLACK PANTHER

Black Community News Service

25 cents

SATURDAY, FEBRUARY 21, 1970   VOL. IV NO. 12

PUBLISHED
WEEKLY   **THE BLACK PANTHER PARTY**

MINISTRY OF INFORMATION
BOX 2967, CUSTOM HOUSE
SAN FRANCISCO, CA 94126

SPECIAL EVIDENCE AND INTIMIDATION OF FASCIST CRIMES BY U.S.A. **ISSUE**

THE BLACK PANTHER 25 cents

Black Community News Service

THE BLACK PANTHER PARTY

HAPPY BIRTHDAY HUEY

Figure 8 The Tuesday 17 February cover, released to celebrate Newton's birthday.

1   Judy Juanita quoted in Lisa Hix, "Black Panther Women: The Unsung Activists Who Fed and Fought for Their Community", *Collectors Weekly*, 2 December 2016.
2   Cover story, 21 February 1970.
3   In its *Art as Activism: Graphic Art from the Merrill C. Berman Collection* exhibition (26 June 2015 – 13 September 2015) the New-York Historical Society states that this photograph is "attributed to Blair Stapp, Composition by Eldridge Cleaver, Huey Newton seated in wicker chair, 1967."

STEPHEN SHAMES:

I first came across Bobby at the San Francisco Peace March on April 15, 1967. It was an anti-Vietnam rally. Bobby was selling Mao's *Little Red Book*. I was a student at Berkeley and had a camera, and just out of the corner of my eye, I saw him, slowed down, and snapped one shot. There was a kind of very positive energy coming from him. We became friends and he became my mentor, like a father figure to me.

The Panthers were very, very media conscious. They knew that they needed images, and they liked my photography so we started working together. I saw myself as an artist for the movement. That's how I saw that I could contribute.

The Panthers made alliances with a lot of different groups. There were a lot of white people like me hanging out and working with them. Nowadays, people, especially white people, ask me, "How did you get in with the Panthers?" It's interesting. Black people don't ask that because the black community is open to everyone.

The police were all on alert the day of the verdict. They thought there was going to be a riot and they were ready to go in and kick ass. Bobby kept the Panthers off the streets. He's always been against riots, which he feels are just counterproductive. I mean, it's like a lot of people get killed, businesses get burned, people get arrested, and so what? It doesn't advance anything. Bobby's thing was always to organize, register people to vote, take over. A riot doesn't take over for you. A riot always gets put down. The police have more guns than the rioters.

It was very symbolic when the two police officers blasted that famous poster of Huey. It's like, here's the icon and, boom, they're attacking it. No Panther that I've talked to can remember who took that picture. There are conflicting versions.[3] Bobby says he choreographed the picture. Kathleen Cleaver says that Eldridge, who was her husband, choreographed the picture. At any rate, it was taken at the home of Beverly Axelrod, a white woman who was one of their lawyers and who was also, at that time, Eldridge Cleaver's lover. Someone had the idea to show both Huey's American and African roots. He has a rifle in one hand, a spear in the other and African shields in the background. He's African-American, after all, so why not?

LIFE

15 MAY 1970

Managing editor: Ralph Graves
Cover photography: Howard Ruffner

On 1 May 1970, American and South Vietnamese combat troops crossed into Cambodia. For the anti-war student movement, this extension of the Vietnam War was the last straw. Kent State University in Ohio held demonstrations and the National Guard was sent in. By noon on Monday 4 May, there were approximately 600 National Guardsmen on the campus commons, facing some 2,000 students. The students refused to disperse, the situation degenerated and a group of Guardsmen suddenly opened fire – 67 rounds in 13 seconds. Two men and two women, aged nineteen and twenty, were killed, and nine were wounded.

HOWARD RUFFNER:

I was a photographer for the student-run newspaper *The Daily Kent Stater*. On Monday morning, Bill Armstrong, the editor, received a call from *Life* magazine in Chicago. They were asking if there was anybody who had taken pictures over the weekend. Bill said, "Howard Ruffner, and he's right here." They asked me, "Would you mind covering what happens today?" Hey, it was exciting. I was going to be shooting for *Life*.

I walked down the hill, showed my press pass and crossed over behind the National Guard lines; the media all ended up there. Had I not been working for *Life*, I still question myself, would I have done that or would I have stayed on the side of the students and watched the Guard approach me, as opposed to following the Guard uphill as they approached the students?

LIFE

TRAGEDY AT KENT

Cambodia and Dissent:
The Crisis of
Presidential Leadership

A Kent State student
lies wounded

MAY 15 • 1970 • 50¢

The people who were really protesting were closest to the bottom of the hill. As you went up the hill, I would say 60 or 70 per cent were observers. Kent was a commuter campus and a lot of them had been away for the weekend. There was a mood of confusion and curiosity. What's going on here?

As soon as the last group of Guards reached the highest point, they turned, knelt down in unison and started firing. I thought they would either be shooting blanks or shooting over their heads. I started to hear screaming, "Oh my God, they're shooting real bullets." They were killing people. I took a few pictures of the student who was in front of me. He had been shot a couple of times in the abdomen and he was being attended to by a faculty member. I slowly turned to my left and saw John Cleary, who had also been hit. He was about 115 feet from the National Guard and I started taking pictures of him surrounded by several students attending to him. That's the one that went on the *Life* cover.[1] He was shot in the upper chest but he survived.

I got up and was approached by some students who said, "You gotta stop taking pictures." I said, "I have to take pictures." I was more in shock than scared. You could see the students were stunned, their eyes were glazed over. I felt like I was stealing something from them but I had to do it.

Later, the FBI came to my house: two men in dark suits. They wanted me to identify students in photos and I only told them what they already knew so it wasn't like I was giving them any secrets. But the FBI said, "Now your photographs, Mr Ruffner. Can you share those?" I said, "They're with *Life* magazine. I don't have anything to share with you." As they left, they said, "Well, if that's what you want to do with your blood money, Mr Ruffner..."

The pictures show the truth. I really believe that. I'm trying to get Kent State to put up a mural of all the photographs in as much chronological order as they can because it will show the truth.

---

[1] Most of the photographs for the cover story inside were by three Kent State students: Ruffner, John Filo and John Darnell.

OZ

MAY 1970

Editor: Jim Anderson

Cover credit: "This issue of OZ appears with
the help of Jim Anderson, Gary Brayley,
Felix Dennis, Bridget Murphy,
Richard Neville, Liz Watson and
David Wills."

The "school kids" included: Charles Shaar
Murray, Peter Popham, Deyan Sudjic,
Colin Thomas

Secretary: Marsha Rowe[1]

In 1970 *Oz* co-founder Richard Neville, about to hit 30, felt "old and boring" and invited readers under 18 to edit an issue. This became the infamous "*Oz* School Kids Issue". After the Obscene Publications Squad raided the *Oz* office, Neville and co-editors Jim Anderson and Felix Dennis were charged on two counts: obscenity and conspiracy to corrupt public morals. The trial began on 22 June 1971. The "*Oz* Three" were found not guilty on the conspiracy charge but guilty of two lesser offences. When the case went to appeal, the convictions were quashed.

JIM ANDERSON:

Richard had gone off to Ibiza and left me and Felix in charge. A fantastic set of kids had turned up. We looked at their material, and oh, my goodness, some of the cartoon illustrations ... there was the masturbating headmaster and particularly Vivian Berger's Rupert Bear collage.[2] Brilliant idea, just right for *Oz*.

Peter Ledeboer[3] had come back from Holland with this book *Dessins Erotiques* by the artist Bertrand.[4] It consisted entirely of drawings of this fantasy black woman in a series of erotic poses. There was only one which we and the kids all liked and I marked it for the centre spread. On the very last night, when the kids had all gone home, Felix insisted he wanted the centre spread for his Back Issue Bonanza. Our intended cover of the *Oz* secretary as a St Trinian's schoolgirl running bare-breasted through a playground with an Uzi was not working. That's when I had my fateful idea. "Oh, let's put the naked black ladies on the cover." It fitted perfectly across the front and the back. Felix and I scarcely looked at it because we were busy laying out the pages.

Then, at about two o'clock in the morning, we took a closer look. We were stoned. We were tired. We had to get the thing to the printer by eight. Felix said, "Hmm. We won't get away with the blow job." One woman was giving another a blow job. I had the idea of putting a photograph of one of the schoolboys, the one with the longest hair, over it. Problem solved. We didn't even notice the rat tail coming out of a vagina.

The shit soon hit the fan. We were busted within days and charged with publishing obscene material. Richard had been busted twice before in Sydney for the same thing and only been fined, so we decided not to take it too seriously.

That was it for a while. Then Mr Wilson got defeated in the election and Edward Heath came in. The new Conservative government took another look at

Oz, raised the stakes and dragged up this old common law conspiracy charge – to debauch and corrupt the morals of children and young persons within the Realm and to implant in their minds lustful and perverted desires. They assumed we had coerced the school kids into putting in the sexual material, that we had corrupted them. They saw this as a chance to deal the underground press a mortal blow.

Suddenly, it was all very serious. There were many signals that the 1960s were over, and one of them was the *Oz* trial.

DEYAN SUDJIC:[5]

1970 was my last year at school. It was in West London and very political so there was a hardcore of teenage Maoists. There were three of us: Peter Popham, who went on to become a foreign correspondent for the *Independent*, Colin Thomas, who is a photographer, and me. We saw the ad in *Oz* saying come and tell us what you would do with a school kids issue.

We thought, "that sounds interesting", so we applied. Richard Neville wrote back to say come and talk. We went along under the impression that we would be left to our own devices to do the magazine, and found ourselves in a Holland Park basement with a room of other young and ambitious careerists. It was a very masculine group that included Charles Shaar Murray and Viv Berger but not a lot of women.

It quickly became apparent that School Kids *Oz* was not so much about young people editing a magazine as the theme for an issue that was shaped by Richard, Felix and Jim. The cover came as a complete, and pretty unpleasant, surprise. None of us saw it before the issue came out on the newsstands. The response from my friends made me really understand for the first time that there was such a thing as feminism, and that it mattered.

MARSHA ROWE:

It's an appalling cover. I don't know what Jim and Felix were even thinking of. I mean, we had been for sexual freedom but then it became so that the only view of sexuality was through men's eyes. It was more and more objectifying. But, at that time, I didn't have that sort of analysis. I just thought, "Oh, men and their fantasies", really.

---

1 Rowe re-joined *Oz* after this issue, worked on their trial defence and later co-founded *Spare Rib* (*see* page 79).

2 Fifteen-year-old Vivian Berger did a cartoon strip inside which grafted a priapic Rupert Bear onto a story of sexual hijinks by Robert Crumb.

3 Ledeboer had recently quit *Oz*, where he was business manager, to start Big O Posters.

4 Bertrand (illustrator), *Dessins Erotiques*, Eric Losfield, 1969.

5 Deyan Sudjic is currently director of the Design Museum, London.

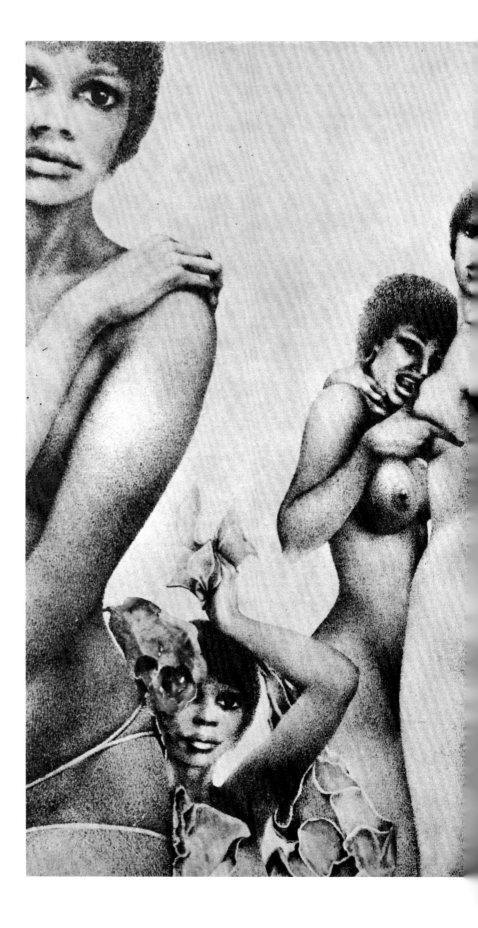

NOVA

SEPTEMBER 1971

Editor: Gillian Cooke

Art director: David Hillman

Fashion editor: Caroline Baker

Cover photography: Hans Feurer

Cap: 50p at Badges & Equipment

Nova's cover for its September 1971 issue has been credited with the invention of street style.

CAROLINE BAKER:

When I arrived at *Nova* in 1965 I was a little mouse who loved fashion and would run around looking like Twiggy. Then I met these really strong personalities like Harri Peccinotti and Hans Feurer who were very into women's lib and was influenced very much by them. *Nova* made me as revolutionary as *Nova* was, I think I could say.

Molly Parkin, the fashion editor, and Dennis Hackett had a major row – she and Dennis always used to row – and Molly left in 1967. Dennis called me in and said, "You look like you are interested in fashion. Do you want to give it a go?" I was like, "Oh, wow." So I became fashion editor. I had done no fashion at all and was suddenly thrown in the deep end. Dennis knew nothing about fashion, but he wanted me to be irreverent.

I had an obsession with dressing girls as boys. I thought men's clothing was so much more comfortable. It was shocking because in those days you didn't do that. In a way, it was what we were all wearing, the uniform of everybody who went on marches. Everybody would be wearing a flak jacket. The American army surplus was wonderful. It was such good cotton compared to the English, and a lot of it came from Laurence Corner.[1] Then it crept into woman's fashion. You could buy it for a few shillings, and be dead cool. This is when "street style" began to establish itself and a lot of fashion fanatics started following my work.

I did this story with Hans Feurer in Corsica. Photographers then were like artists in a way. Because it wasn't so commercial, you had total freedom to

NOVA

SEPTEMBER 1971

20p

ONE MAN'S MEAT IS
ANOTHER MAN'S
GLUCONO-D-LACTONE
DRESSED TO KILL
PETER WALKER,
CABINET SUPERSTAR
FIND THE
FACE THAT FITS YOU
MISSIONARIES
IN THE MELTING POT

interpret ideas that you had. The favourite models then were all Swedish, Dutch, Norwegian and German, who were quite free in their attitude. Those were the days before AIDS when you tended to have affairs with everybody. The pecking order was the photographer first, then the editors and assistants would shack up with the driver. Somehow, it wasn't dangerous. And we weren't settling down, were we, and having kids?

The cover is a close-up of the German model, Christiana, who was a very cool modern girl. I think the story was shocking in two ways: one, it portrayed war as a beautiful, fashionable subject, and, two, it showed women as these tough warriors. *M*A*S*H* was hugely popular at the time, and there was this famous nurse[2] in it. It was very linked to the women's movement and the way women were seeing themselves: "Why can't I be like a man, why can't I do this?"

I never realized how all these people like Calvin Klein and Kenzo were religiously buying *Nova* and would be inspired by what they saw in the magazine, and, a year later, you'd see it on the catwalk. Was I flattered? I was just really surprised.

1   Laurence Corner, at 62 Hampstead Road, London NW1, sold army and navy surplus clothes and accessories very inexpensively. A pair of camouflage trousers used in the shoot cost 63p.
2   Major Margaret J "Hot Lips" Houlihan (played by Loretta Swit).

SPARE RIB

LAUNCH ISSUE, JULY 1972
Editorial: Marsha Rowe and Rosie Boycott
Design: Kate Hepburn and Sally Doust
Cover photography: Angela Phillips

In November 1971 Marsha Rowe, who was working at *Oz* and its short-lived sister publication, *Ink*, invited all the women at *International Times*, *Time Out*, *Friends* and *Oz* to a meeting to discuss their lives in the underground press. It led to a second one in January 1972, when Rowe met Rosie Boycott, then at *Friends*, and suggested starting a magazine. *Spare Rib* launched six months later.

ROSIE BOYCOTT:

Those meetings were unbelievably exciting and completely revolutionary. Women would talk about sex, their mothers, their ambitions, about how they felt stifled by the work they did. What emerged so strongly was that, even though we all worked in "the underground", we were living absolutely traditional lives. We were still the typists, the tea-makers. There were no women editors of any underground papers.

MARSHA ROWE:

It changed lives, that meeting. It's so hard to describe how totally it was a man's world then. A man had to sign if you wanted to hire a television, buy a car or get a mortgage.

ROSIE BOYCOTT:

The underground was an incredibly good place for blokes because they got to take drugs, stay up all night, and, if women didn't want to sleep with them, they could say you're square. It was a very double-edged sword because if you didn't want to be promiscuous, you were a "straight".

MARSHA ROWE:

I thought of a magazine as your friend, your other intimate voice. We aimed to raise £7,000 but only managed £2,000 so we started with a minimal budget. I thought, "Well, obviously it's going to have all the things that a normal women's magazine would have but subverted." Instead of the women's page in the *Guardian*, we had a man's page.

ROSIE BOYCOTT:

Our fiction was by Margaret Drabble, Fay Weldon and Edna O'Brien, so it was amazing. George Best, of course, did not write that man's page – someone else wrote it for him. I don't think it was very good but we were smart enough to see this was a good cover line, and a huge surprise.

Our plan was absolutely not to do an underground magazine. In my head, I thought we could take over from *Woman* and *Woman's Own,* which between them sold about three-and-a-half to four million copies a week. The covers weren't fashion shots, they were more like Oxo Katie[1] shots. The faces on our first cover were something different – un-made up, youthful, friendly, energetic, and two women together. It was about sisterhood. The logo was done by Kate Hepburn who did a lot for Monty Python. Kate was a genius.

MARSHA ROWE:

I wanted a name like *Oz* which was meaningless but meaning could attach to it. I was in a relationship with Andrew Cockburn, the middle son of [the journalist] Claud Cockburn. One night we all went to a Chinese restaurant and Claud came out with this joke about spare ribs.

ROSIE BOYCOTT:

I mean, it's so corny but he picked up a spare rib and said, "That would be a very good title for your magazine." Both of us just said, "Of course." And then it could never be anything else.

ANGELA PHILLIPS:

Almost immediately, *Spare Rib* became controversial within the women's movement for being too traditional. Some of the more purist of the sisters felt that it was a bit of a sell-out. Not alternative enough. But I think that was its strength.

---

1   Long-running British TV commercial for Oxo gravy which started in 1958 and came to represent "Middle England".

spare Rib

the new women's magazine

JULY 17½p

The days Women
rocked the World
Georgie Best on Sex
Does the Government
care about Pensioners?
Richard Neville
on the Glossies
Growing up in the
Bosom Boom
8 page News Section
and lots more inside.

INTERVIEW

JULY 1972

Editors: Andy Warhol, Paul Morrissey,
    Fred Hughes
Managing editor & art director:
    Glenn O'Brien
Cover design: Richard Bernstein
Special contributing editor:
    Robert Colacello
Cover photo: Berry Berenson
Cover model: Pat Cleveland

In May 1972 Glenn O'Brien unveiled a new look for the monthly magazine *Interview*. The cover was in full colour for the first time with a bigger, "handwritten" logo that now included Warhol's name, following demands from its new financial backers.[1] This was primarily the work of artist Richard Bernstein and it remained the basic template for the next 15 years. "The overall effect was of an Andy Warhol portrait autographed by Andy Warhol – though Andy's hand had never touched the page," Bob Colacello later wrote.[2] Warhol confirmed this: "Sometimes people think I do the cover of *Interview*. Well, I don't. I haven't the time. But Richard Bernstein's faces are wonderful. They're so colorful and he makes everyone look so famous."[3]

July featured supermodel Pat Cleveland in rapture to a Sony TC-50 cassette recorder and microphone – a piece of technology that Warhol would often introduce to his interviewees as "My wife, Sony". *Interview* would become the insider handbook of "the disco decade".

PAT CLEVELAND:
Richard and Berry were kind of an item at the time. He always wore silk shirts, was very well dressed and had a soft heart. If Richard were a Disney character, he'd be Jiminy Cricket.

Berry was just beginning as a photographer, so Richard gave Berry her first cover job with *Interview*. Berry was the sister of Marisa Berenson, the actress and model, and they were the grandchildren of Schiaparelli. So I was photographed by the granddaughter of Schiaparelli![4] The cover is just the photograph. Richard didn't airbrush me.[5]

We had all been in Fire Island for the weekend and came back into the city in a limo to Berry's loft. She had this beautiful loft painted completely white – white walls, white floors – with lots of light. It was one of those shotgun, straight-through lofts on 2nd Avenue and 57th. At the time, only artists lived in those old buildings.

They transformed it into a studio. It was very amateurish. Berry had her Nikon and Richard guided her on how to get the composition right and set up the strobe lights. They decided to put some technology into the picture. Everybody had to have one of those Sony tape recorders then: it was like the first Walkman.[6] The microphone was a symbol of stardom. Everybody wants to have the mike. Everybody wants to speak into it.

This was the bright and brimming springtime of New York. It would be like if you were in Paris in the 1920s and were hanging out in the Café de Flore[7] where all the writers went. *Interview* was our answer to that.

1   Peter Brant and Joe Allen, sourced from Bob Colacello, *Holy Terror: Andy Warhol Close Up, An Insider's Portrait*, HarperCollins, 1990, p.106.
2   Ibid.
3   Andy Warhol quoted in *Richard Bernstein, Megastar*, Indigo Books, 1984, p.2.
4   Lauded Italian fashion designer at the height of her success between the two World Wars.
5   Bernstein often used collage and airbrush techniques to transform photographs into richly stylized portraits.
6   The first Sony Walkman went on sale on 1 July 1979.
7   Art Deco coffee house favoured by French writers and philosophers in the 1920s.

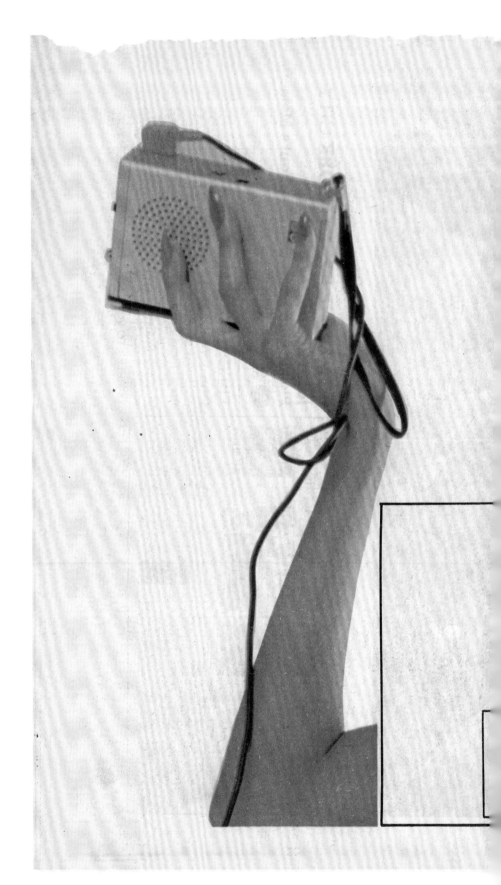

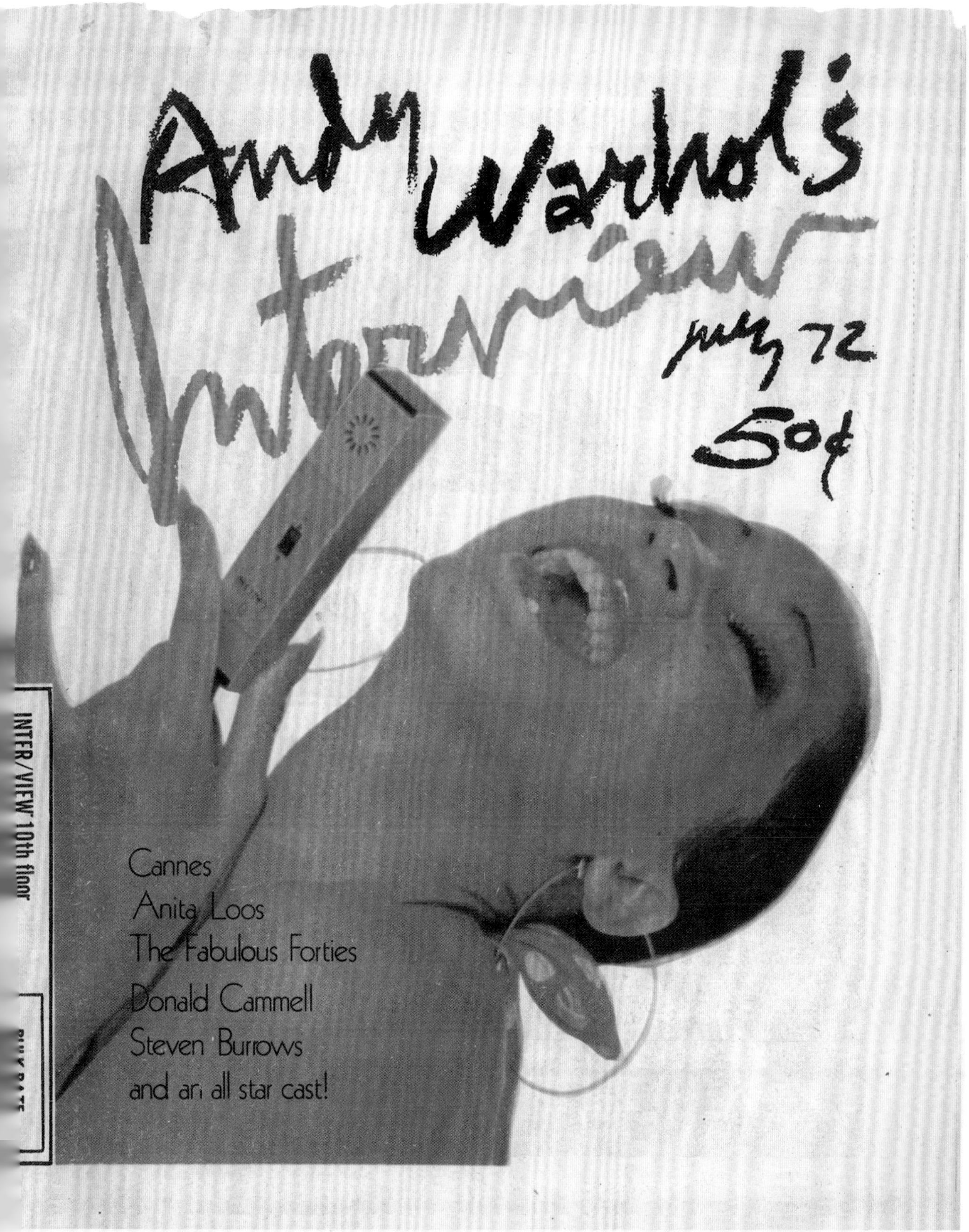

Andy Warhol's Interview

july 72

50¢

INTER/VIEW 10th floor

Cannes
Anita Loos
The Fabulous Forties
Donald Cammell
Steven Burrows
and an all star cast!

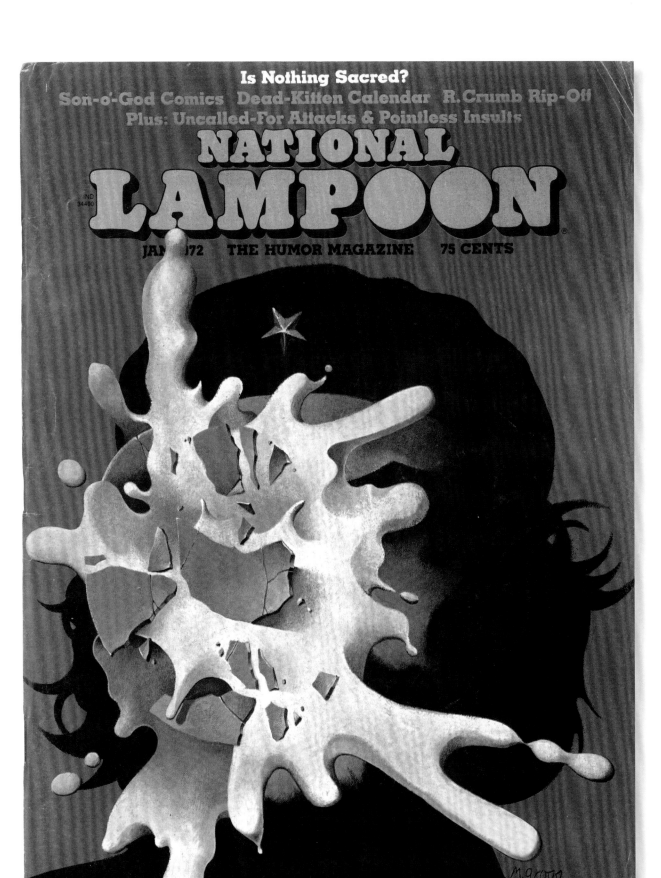

Is Nothing Sacred?

Son-o'-God Comics   Dead-Kitten Calendar   R. Crumb Rip-Off

Plus: Uncalled-For Attacks & Pointless Insults

NATIONAL LAMPOON

JAN. 1972   THE HUMOR MAGAZINE   75 CENTS

NATIONAL LAMPOON

JANUARY 1972
JANUARY 1973

Managing editor: Tony Hendra
Art director: Michael Gross
Contributing editor: Ed Bluestone
Cover photography: Ronald G Harris

In the early 1970s *National Lampoon*, the satirical monthly created by Harvard graduates Henry Beard, Doug Kenney and Rob Hoffman, was the incarnation of hip for its predominantly campus-based readership. Its notorious January 1973 cover began as a proposed subscription campaign: "If you don't subscribe, we'll kill this dog and, if that doesn't work, a cat, and the animal death toll will rise until you do." The campaign did not run but it was the perfect cover for the death-themed issue. "The shot was extremely hard to get; when the dog looked straight out at the reader he simply appeared victimized. Then someone had the notion of actually pulling the trigger. The dog reacted to the noise and this was the result."[1]

Without *National Lampoon*, there probably would not have been *Saturday Night Live*. It incubated talents like John Belushi, Bill Murray, Chevy Chase and Gilda Radner. British-born Tony Hendra was there from the start. He had come from the comedy duo Hendra and Ullett, regular performers on American TV variety shows in the 1960s.

TONY HENDRA:
The level of censorship on American television in the 1960s was acute. It basically meant that people of my generation could not mention or discuss any of the things that were on our minds, whether it was the sexual revolution, or liberation of any kind, and certainly not the Vietnam War. So it was a source

of explosive frustration. Going to the *Lampoon* was like walking out of a dark room into sunlight.

The Che cover with the cream pie was my first issue as managing editor, which was kind of a ridiculous term because there was no way to keep that bunch in any kind of management whatever.

I insisted that the title of the issue be "Is Nothing Sacred?" because that seemed to me to be a kind of modish, postmodern way of self-referencing, and so seemed to poke fun both at the people who were outraged and its actual target. I think it was me who said, "I don't think there's anything more sacred on campus at the moment than the Paul Davis Che poster." Everyone went, "Yeah, I guess so, and we fucking hate it." Nobody hated Paul Davis, but they thought the sanctification of that particular image was really obnoxious. I had originally wanted to take the poster and slam a cream pie onto it but Gross decided he wanted to show off his art skills, and do a parody of Paul Davis because he was an Ayn Rand fan. He did a lovely job.

The dog cover was Ed's idea. He was a wonderfully irreverent comedian who had a real hang-up about death. Casting was obviously crucial and the dog we eventually got was modelled on Freckles, my very sweet mutt who had a big patch on one eye. In a funny way, it was more moderate than a lot of the other covers we did around that period but it did nail the fact that what is really sacred for every American family is pets. So that was what gave it, if you'll excuse the expression, legs. Were people outraged by it? Absolutely. We certainly couldn't do that cover today without being shot, or banned for ever.

1 Tony Hendra, *Going Too Far*, Dolphin Doubleday, 1987, pp.244–5.

Death
The Adventures of Deadman Playdead Magazine
Last-Aid Kit Suicide Letters to Santa

NATIONAL LAMPOON

IND
34490

JAN. 1973, THE HUMOR MAGAZINE 75 CENTS

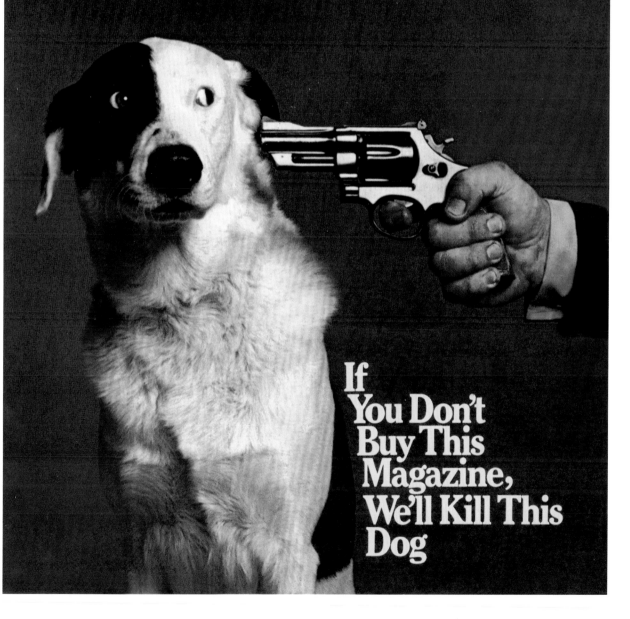

If
You Don't
Buy This
Magazine,
We'll Kill This
Dog

Time Out

London's Living Guide
October 12-18 1973 No.190 15p

Jealousy

You're liberated.
You're hip.
You don't mind.
Do you?

TIME OUT

12–18 OCTOBER 1973
25 NOVEMBER–1 DECEMBER 1977
5–11 MAY 1978
Publisher/sometime editor: Tony Elliott
Art director/cover design:
    Pearce Marchbank

Pearce Marchbank became art director of the pocket-sized fortnightly *Time Out* in early 1971. He introduced a radically new information architecture, lobbied to increase the format to the bigger A4 and make it a weekly, both of which happened with the 29 April 1971 issue. He soon left, but continued designing most of the covers on a consultancy basis until 1983. Lean, clean and witty, these set a benchmark in the evolution of the counterculture press through the 1970s.

PEARCE MARCHBANK:

I always assumed no one wants to buy the magazine so they've got to be given a kick up the bum to buy it. That's what I tried to do.

I redesigned the logo. I wasn't that pleased with it but the reaction was good, so we kept it. To tell you the truth, I didn't like the letter "T". It's a weak letter. There are very few swear words that start with a T and it hasn't got a flat left-hand side which is a pain for lining things up. The idea was that the logo was out of focus like a neon sign, which suggested entertainment, obviously, but it was transparent. The logo could be obliterated or partly readable or hover like a mark on a windowpane over the image. It gave you immense freedom.

I did win a fantastic battle with the money people in *Time Out* about the "Jealousy" cover because it sold out immediately. They said it was the worst cover they'd ever had but that shut them up. It was a very abstract piece about sexual jealousy: hence green with envy. It was before the days when people thought you had to put the contents of the magazine on the cover. *Cosmopolitan* was the start of the rot. Just have one thing on the cover and, if you really did have a special, put a flash in the corner.

There were open auditions for the *Elvis* musical at the Astoria Theatre in the West End, so anyone could go down and present themselves. I thought, would you get the part if you looked just like him? Let's do an Elvis mask you could stick on your face. It was nearly life-size. Unfortunately, Richard Williams, the editor at the time, changed the cover line. I wanted, "Put on the mask and go to the theatre at ten o'clock next Tuesday", or words to that effect. Richard changed it to "In the future, everybody will be Elvis for 15 minutes", a twist on the Andy Warhol saying, which doesn't have anything to do with the auditions.

My jokey ethos was the nearer to the Japanese flag you can get, the better the cover. The "red football" cover is the nearest I got. I remember we had nothing to go with. There were two football finals in one week,[1] so I asked Richard Williams if there was any combining factor about the teams, Arsenal and Liverpool. He said, "Yes, they're both red." I got a football sprayed red and stuck it on the cover. which was not really anything to do with anything but it led you into the piece.

TONY ELLIOTT:
The cover I always quote as being a classic is the "red football". We took it to a car spray place and had it sprayed Liverpool red. It's just so beautifully executed.

London's
Living Guide
Nov 25-Dec 1 1977 No. 399 30p

In the future,
everybody will be
Elvis for 15 minutes.

Jack Good is making
dreams come true for
P.J. Proby, Shakin' Stevens,
and Timothy Whitnall.
Cut-out the mask, turn
to page 12 and join the club.

1 Arsenal v Ipswich, FA Cup (6 May) and Liverpool v Bruges, European Cup (10 May).

Time Out

May 5-11 1978 No.422 30p

Red is the colour.

Clough's Forest having nicked Div. One and the League Cup, can Arsenal and Liverpool make it a
red flush in this week's FA and European cup finals? Inside, we talk to the men who make them tick.

NEW MUSICAL EXPRESS

19 JANUARY 1974

Editor: Nick Logan

Assistant editor: Ian MacDonald

Cover photography: Pennie Smith

Features: Charles Shaar Murray, Nick Kent

In early 1972 the new editor, Alan Smith, and his deputy, Nick Logan, were given 12 weeks to save a floundering *New Musical Express*. They did it in part by raiding the underground press for a younger, hipper editorial team, including Charles Shaar Murray, Nick Kent, Ian MacDonald and Pennie Smith. Sales soared from around 60,000 to 200,000 by the end of 1973, when Smith left and Logan, then 26, took over. He was faced almost immediately with a printers' strike in November, which kept the paper off the streets for nine weeks. This first post-strike issue introduced Logan's vision, which would turn the paper into Britain's most influential music weekly.

NICK KENT:

The strike was a very nervous time. We'd suddenly become really successful and then, boom, it was like an amputation for nine weeks. But Nick was able to plot.

NICK LOGAN:

I love this cover. In my opinion, it was the beginning of *NME*'s golden period. That's what makes it revolutionary, important.

I think it was the first time I introduced a full-page image on the front. I love the confidence and the Monty Python style of humour: taking the piss, basically. That wouldn't have happened without the strike, when there was also an enormous amount of bonding in the office. The issue looked so good and had such good content. It did feel like you'd released a dam of pent-up energy. Actually, at that time I thought, "This is going to be a hell of a ride." I wasn't sure

NEW MUSICAL EXPRESS

January 19, 1974   U.S. 50c/Canada 35c   8p

HELLO HELLO

WE'RE BACK AGAIN

EMERGENCY 3-DAY
CANDLELIGHT CRISIS
SHOCK SCANDAL ISSUE

**Jethro/Mott/Lennon
Sayer/Santana/ELP**

BYRON FERRARI: PRINCE OF SLEAZE

PAGE 18

what I was unleashing, and I thought, "Someone will get damaged here", and they did, and it was me[1] – and other people, of course.

PENNIE SMITH:

Nick left everybody to do what they enjoyed doing so he got the best from them. The photos were as important as the copy and they weren't cropped. I appreciated that because I shoot full frame, so luckily the front of the *NME* is more or less a 35mm frame. It was straight art, for want of a better word.

I think my advantage is that I didn't get involved with the music business, so I had a clean brain every time I did a shoot. I was interested in people and I shot them like they were my auntie. I have worked my whole life through innocence and in that way it's inadvertently come over as left field.

I had done some Roxy Music stuff before this. There was just Bryan, his PR chap, Dr Simon Puxley, and me walking along the beach at Bournemouth. Bryan was incredibly camera shy and I remember making a couple of rude jokes which made him laugh. Everything worked out a treat.

NICK KENT:

It was a great photograph. We were all works-in-progress as writers and photographers and the first fruition for many of us was that issue. You have to remember how fast things went then. Marc Bolan was a has-been at this point. David Bowie was still top dog but he was focused on America. That meant Roxy Music owned the British Isles. It was their fiefdom. Nick also viewed Ferry very highly.

PENNIE SMITH:

The cover looked like something new. It definitely felt classy and I don't think it's really dated. The *NME* was on such tosh paper, like orange wrapper paper, that I always printed my photos really hard so they looked very graphic on the page. Byron Ferrari? That used to get up Ferry's nose. He was referred to as something different every time[2] but I think it was done with affection.

---

1 Logan had a nervous breakdown in late 1976.
2 Ferry "misspellings" included Brain Fury, Biryani Ferret and Brawn Fairy.

PEOPLE WEEKLY

LAUNCH ISSUE, 14 MARCH 1974

Managing editor: Richard B ("Dick") Stolley

Cover photography: Steve Schapiro

People's mantra was ordinary people doing extraordinary things and extraordinary people doing ordinary things. Dick Stolley masterminded a mix of human interest stories that were told in a zesty, empathetic and scrupulously fact-checked way, and which he labelled "personality journalism" to separate it from pure "celebrity journalism". Parent company Time Inc. had poured an estimated $40 million into the launch and, astonishingly, within only 18 months it was making money and went on to become Time Inc.'s most profitable magazine – and a national institution. "This was the beginning of the 'Me Decade'," Stolley later said. "We found out that people in the news were quite willing to talk to us about themselves. They'd talk about a lot of personal things – their sex lives, their money, their families, religion. They'd talk about things that a few years earlier wouldn't even have been brought up."[1] He wrote "Stolley's Law of Covers",[2] which *People* still references today.

DICK STOLLEY:

I wince every time I look at that launch cover. We made several mistakes. First of all, no eye contact. And the timing was bad. The movie didn't open for three weeks.[3] We had too many cover lines down the side and they were all the same type size. We should have had two or three in large type and maybe one or two in small. The mistakes that we made were so monumental that it is a great tribute to the idea that it was good enough to overcome all of these blunders.

We decided that this would be a newsstand magazine. Time Inc. had not had a newsstand magazine since 1936 when *Life* started. Now, Time Inc. had no distribution system but we decided that we would promise a million sales every week. You just wonder what the hell was the thinking. That first issue, with all the publicity, sold nearly a million,[4] which was extraordinary, and then it went back down to about a half a million. After a few weeks it became apparent to our publisher, Richard J Durrell, a very smart guy, that we were going to have to spend a few million dollars to set up our own newsstand distribution system, which we did. Within a few weeks it worked.

The dumbest thing I did while editing *People* was not to put Elvis on the cover when he died. Time Inc. back then had a policy of never putting dead people on the cover. I should have been smart enough to ignore that strange tradition; I spent a weekend with Elvis once and I liked him, but he had gotten fat and sweaty, with smaller and smaller audiences, and I guess that's what convinced me. Anyway, I made the decision, nobody argued with me, and then, after we closed the magazine,[5] I went around to thank everybody because it was very late, two or three o'clock in the morning. They had radios turned on to Elvis songs and some were even crying. I thought, "Jesus Christ, did I screw up on this one?" To compensate, I put him on the cover five times in the next year. I quickly discovered that dead celebrities were among our bestselling covers, and still are.

---

1   Quoted in Curtis Prendergast (with Geoffrey Colvin), *The World of Time Inc.*, Atheneum, 1986, p.440.
2   Stolley's Law of Covers: "Young is better than old. / Pretty is better than ugly. / Rich is better than poor. / Television is better than movies. / Movies are better than music. / Music is better than sports. / Anything is better than politics. / And nothing is better than the celebrity dead."
3   *The Great Gatsby* (dir. Jack Clayton) was released 27 March 1974.
4   The launch issue sold very close to the target million – 978,000.
5   The cover, dated 29 August 1977, featured Ann-Margret and Marty Feldman. Elvis's death was covered by a 27-line item on the "Star Tracks" page.

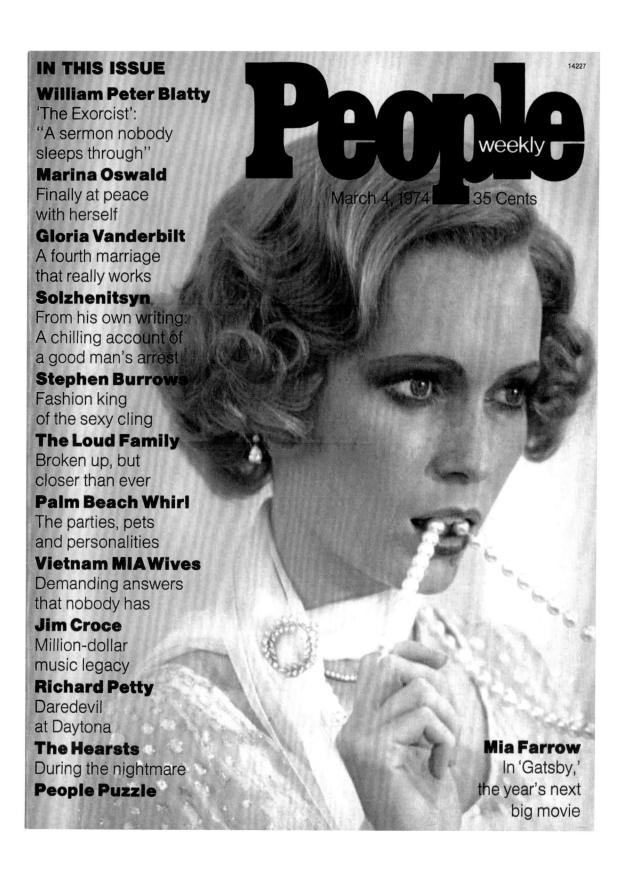

14227

People weekly

March 4, 1974   35 Cents

Mia Farrow
In 'Gatsby,'
the year's next
big movie

VOGUE

AUGUST 1974

Editor-in-chief: Grace Mirabella
Model: Beverly Johnson
Photographer: Francesco Scavullo
Fashion editor: Frances Stein

This was American *Vogue*'s first cover with a model of colour. It was so successful that Johnson was given a second the following June. *The New York Times* weighed the significance: "If, as some sociologists believe, fashion reflects social change, Beverly on the cover of *Vogue* is announcing that racial strife is in a cooling off period, that the Panthers have gone establishment in Oakland, and that the Black Muslims have deleted the expression 'white devil' from their vocabulary and are recruiting white members."[1] Grace Mirabella had a different take. In the same article she said, "We don't think of it as a milestone but I'm very proud to have had her there."

BEVERLY JOHNSON:

I had been working since 1971 and had done many covers of magazines like *Glamour*. But I now set my focus on *Vogue*. When I told my agent, Eileen Ford, that's what I wanted, she said, "Forget about it. You'll never be on the cover." I thought there is no reason to ask why. I knew she would never change her position. That's when I knew I had to leave the Ford Modeling Agency. So I left her – very nicely – and went to the Wilhelmina Agency, run by the Dutch model Wilhelmina Cooper. She said, "I can do it", and she did.

I didn't know it was going to be a cover: it was just a regular shoot. When it came out, the calls started. The first one was from Kenya. They asked me, "How does it feel to be the first woman of colour on *Vogue*?" I said, "What are you talking about? That's impossible. This is the Seventies. Didn't we do all the civil rights in the Sixties?"

In 1974 *Vogue*'s circulation tripled and they didn't attribute that to the fact that now black women were buying it. That's how in denial they were. Grace knew – everyone knew – but it was a secret they didn't want people to know.

What was interesting was the reaction from other models. I knew black models were always jealous, which I understood because I was the "token", right? But I wasn't prepared for the white models. I always worked on a white set – everyone was white apart from me – and they snubbed me. It was like, you can be on the cover of *Glamour* and all those other magazines, but not *Vogue*. Now, you've crossed the line. You're top in the coloured water fountain over there, but you can't be top of the white water fountain over here. I couldn't claim what I had accomplished. So it really was an awakening for me. I call myself the Jackie Robinson of the fashion industry.[2]

1 Ted Morgan, "I'm the biggest model, period", *The New York Times*, 17 August 1975.
2 African-American professional baseball player Jackie Robinson is credited with ending decades of segregation in the game when he played first base for the Brooklyn Dodgers in April 1947.

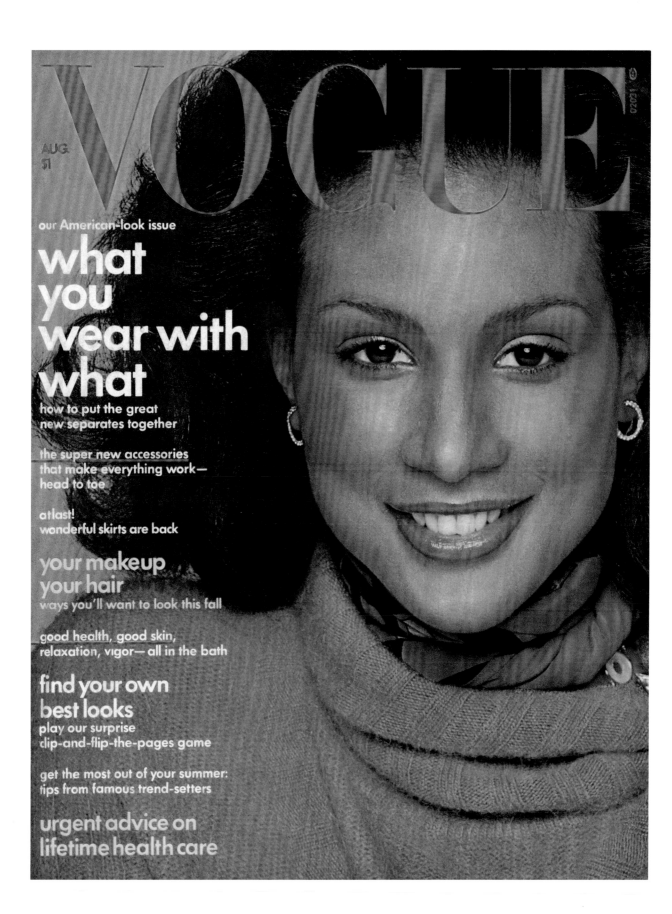

VOGUE

AUG.
51

02031

our American-look issue

what
you
wear with
what

**how to put the great
new separates together**

the super new accessories
that make everything work—
head to toe

atlast!
wonderful skirts are back

your makeup
your hair

ways you'll want to look this fall

good health, good skin,
relaxation, vigor— all in the bath

find your own
best looks

play our surprise
clip-and-flip-the-pages game

get the most out of your summer:
tips from famous trend-setters

urgent advice on
lifetime health care

PUNK

JANUARY 1976
Publisher: G E Dunn, Jr
Editor: John Holmstrom
Cover illustration and design:
   John Holmstrom
Resident punk: Eddy "Legs" McNeil
English correspondent: Mary Harron

Developed by G E Dunn, Jr, Eddy McNeil and John Holmstrom in autumn 1975, *Punk* – "a combination between Andy Warhol's *Interview* and *Mad* magazine"[1] – quickly came to embody the underground music scene coming out of New York's CBGB club. The catalyst was a Ramones gig there on 23 November. Lou Reed was in the audience.

JOHN HOLMSTROM:
I had seen the Ramones in the summer and loved them immediately. I felt like I had seen the Beatles at the Cavern Club. I thought they could be the first cover. Legs, Mary and I went to their CBGB gig.

MARY HARRON:
I always felt this excitement when I got near CBGB. You'd walk past boarded-up buildings, the Bowery bums, the welfare hotel that was next door. It was like our clubhouse. That was the funny thing: it was threatening yet friendly. It did provide this shelter from the storm. We always used to say everyone there was unpopular at high school. They had been the weirdos and outsiders.

JOHN HOLMSTROM:
There was no one there so we got the front-row table all to ourselves. After the show, we talked to the Ramones but they were horrible. Tommy and Johnny treated us like the enemy. That's why they didn't get the cover.

Legs was schmoozing their manager, Danny Fields, who said Lou Reed was in the audience. Would we like to interview him? Oh my God, yes! I was a big fan of Velvet Underground and Lou's *Metal Machine Music*, the ultimate punk rock statement, had just come out. I actually had it in quadraphonic, which impressed Lou. He didn't even have it himself. I asked him right off the bat about comic books. I think it disarmed him but it turned out he read EC Comics and knew the names of the artists like, Wally Wood and Will Elder.[2]

I had a lot of difficulty with the cover. I wanted to make Lou look like an insect. That's where the bug eyes came from. I tried antennae and butterfly wings but they didn't work, so I decided to make it look like an EC comic book as much as possible: to suggest horror, but not overstate it. The cult magazine *Famous Monsters of Filmland* was another big influence: all that cheesy Grade B stuff was grist for the mill. My inspiration for the logo and the lettering was the underground cartoonist Vaughn Bodē, who died right when *Punk* was starting. And a lot of fanzines then used a golf-ball typewriter but I hated that look. I was a cartoonist, so I figured I could hand-letter everything, and that became our style.

We brought out the perfect first issue and then it was a long slow slide downhill into oblivion. The punk movement only lasted a few years, but I guess it was only meant to.

---

1   Mary Harron to Ian Birch, 19 March 2017.
2   Both Wood and Elder had been founding cartoonists on
    Mad magazine when it launched in 1952.

NEW YORK

7 JUNE 1976

Editor: Clay Felker

Design director: Milton Glaser

Art director: Walter Bernard

Cover painting: "Ritual dances of the New
   Saturday Night", detail from a painting by
   James McMullan

In 1976, when entertainment mogul Robert Stigwood saw Nik Cohn's story about an emerging disco culture in working-class Bay Ridge, Brooklyn, he bought the film rights, thinking it would be an ideal project for John Travolta and the then-ailing Bee Gees, both of whom he had under contract. Vincent, the Italian-American teenager in Cohn's story, became Tony Manero (Travolta) in *Saturday Night Fever*, released the following year.

In December 1997 Cohn admitted in *New York* that Vincent had not existed; he was a composite of a gang member from Cohn's youth in Derry/Londonderry and a mod called Chris he had met in London's Shepherd's Bush in 1965. The club, 2001 Odyssey, was real but very different from Cohn's depiction. He confessed, "I knew nothing about this world. Quite literally, I didn't speak the language. So I faked it. There was no excuse for it … I knew the rules of magazine reporting, and I knew that I was breaking them."

JAMES MCMULLAN:

Nik and I were accompanied to Brooklyn by an African-American guy called "Toute Suite"[1] who had just won a big dance competition. At the time, I thought, "Nik has a thesis about these clubs, this music and he's got this black dancer who sees it from the inside," but as I spent time with them, they were not much more expert on what was happening than I was.

It was basically an Italian supper club and the owners had tried to turn it into this futuristic club on a very limited budget, so it was all about Christmas lights and pieces of Mylar on the walls. I had to use flash, so stuff that was hidden in the darkness got revealed in the photography. I did a painting of a young girl sitting alone in a booth and she was so obviously abandoned and feeling like that sort of social outcast we've all felt at some point. I decided to use the flatness that occurs with flash photography so it became the aesthetic of the paintings. I worked on them a long time. I felt I was doing something high level.

Clay said, "There's no drama here, no knife fights." I began to explain that I felt they were very emotional, and a real human record. Milton said, "Jim, just go outside for a minute and let me talk to Clay." Milton told him that they were not only great illustrations, but ground-breaking.

I finished the paintings but Nik was going through a writer's block about the story and still hadn't written it. I got so worried that the thing would never run that I wrote a story myself and showed it to Milton and Clay. I guess Clay then put a little more pressure on Nik and he finished it.

These were not illustrations in the usual sense because they did not illustrate Nik's story, which was quite different. *New York* ran a disclaimer, saying that my paintings were made up but that Nik's story was true.

It was Nik's story rather than a story of that disco. And it was a good story. He got a big payday: $500,000 which in those years was huge. I think he wrote a treatment for the movie, which they didn't use. I got nothing. I didn't press the issue, even though Nik told me that Stigwood was really impressed with the paintings and that he might not have read the article had it not been for them.

---

1 Sometimes written as "Tu Sweet".

Nigel Dempster, the World's Boldest Gossip
Governor Carey Hits Rock Bottom, by Ken Auletta
The Mid-Life Crises of 'Time' and 'Newsweek'

75 CENTS

JUNE 7, 1976

New York

Tribal Rites of the New Saturday Night
By Nik Cohn

VOGUE

FEB
60p

**the fresh taste
of spring**

racing green
how to wear it
and **what
to wear** with what
prettiest new
make-up
colours
tops and tunics
with more dash than cash
springboard to
health
new diets, new exercises,
new you
who's reading what?
the bedside reading guide

VOGUE

FEBRUARY 1977

Editor: Beatrix Miller

Art director: Terry Jones

Cover photography: Willie Christie

Fashion editor: Grace Coddington

Make-up: Barbara Daly

Cover credit: "Rowntree's jelly ... full of gelatine, a valuable source of protein and good for strengthening nails."

British *Vogue*'s art director Terry Jones loved to subvert. Here he breaks every rule for a fashion glossy: don't show food (and certainly never show someone eating it); don't use green (because it doesn't sell); and always have eye contact.

TERRY JONES:

I hated covers that were shot as covers. This was a beauty shot done for a colour promotion. Twice a year *Vogue* had colour promotions, and green was the colour this time. Grace had done the shot with Willie Christie, who she was married to at the time, and had put this as an inside shot. I thought, I'm going to push this and somehow Bea and the distributor agreed. We didn't run it past Liberman[1] but we did ask Bernie Leser, the UK managing director, who had only been in the job for six months. He said, "Go for it." But when it was on press Daniel Salem, the European president, saw it and screamed, "Get it off the press. It's not a *Vogue* cover." It was so far removed from anything that had been done before but it was too late. It went on sale and was the fastest-selling issue that year.

Bea gave me the support to do something different. To everyone else, she appeared fearsome but I never found her fearsome. I found her really good to work with. As creative director, you have to feed an editor ideas so the idea becomes theirs. The battle was always with the production department. They are the blockage between the creative and the printer. The printer will accept the challenge.

Figure 9 Christie's original polaroid.

WILLIE CHRISTIE:

All the props were green – a little green acrobatic airplane, a green table tennis bat, a green surfboard and the jelly. Marcie Hunt was the model and I shot a Polaroid of her in a green shirt and green baseball-type hat. Grace then said, "We're going to have her eating green jelly." We put it together but it just didn't work (*see* Figure 9). We didn't shoot any film of this version. I am sure you can see why! Then someone said, "Let's go in for a close-up." I had a 150 Hasselblad and went in tighter, tighter, tighter. We had no idea this would be a cover. When we saw the mock-up, we thought, "Bloody hell, that's amazing." The picture is like an abstract art piece, really.

---

1   Alexander Liberman, then editorial director of Condé Nast Publications, United States and Europe, based in New York.

RADIO TIMES

11–17 JUNE 1977
Editor: Geoffrey Cannon
Art director: David Driver
Cover drawing: Dennis Lillee by
    Ralph Steadman (16 March 1977)

By 1969 *Radio Times* had "degenerated into a publicity sheet for mass-market entertainment programmes".[1] The owners, BBC Publications, wanted change, and that came in September when Geoffrey Cannon and David Driver staged a virtual coup with their new editorial vision that lasted for over a decade. They created a hugely successful quality and inventively designed general interest magazine built around comprehensive TV and radio listings.

In March 1977 they sent artist Ralph Steadman to Melbourne to cover the Centenary Test between England and Australia. Australia won by 45 runs, the victory secured in large part by the magical relationship between bowler Dennis Lillee and wicket-keeper Rod Marsh. Steadman took a small sketchbook and camera. "I probably used my little Minox." Four years later, he recalled: "As he ran up to bowl, the people in the cheap stand were chanting 'Lillee, Lillee, Lillee': it was a sort of death ritual. There is always a stillness as the ball leaves the bowler's hand, people waiting, and then, if the ball is hit, the seagulls around the pitch take off like the souls of the dead in an Aztec sacrifice. That moment was the one I had to get, that moment of hushed violence. What I was drawing would probably cause me great trouble, because they were not sports drawings in the ordinary sense, they were pretty strong social comments."[2]

The cover brilliantly captured "that moment". It also announced the first Test match in the Ashes series at Lord's but Lillee was no longer in the Australian team.

GEOFFREY CANNON:
This is David's story. Choosing Ralph Steadman to cover cricket was an inspiration. The violence in modern cricket had never been portrayed like this. It was a revolutionary cover, no doubt, which I guess would be in anybody's top-ten *Radio Times* covers.

DAVID DRIVER:
I was told we couldn't afford to send him to Australia, but Ralph said, "I have a student card so I can get a cheap ticket. I really want to do it." Ralph didn't know

LONDON (BBC Radio London: page 54) 11-17 June 1977   Price 12p

RadioTimes

Fast and furious

There's no Lillee this time
so can England tame the Aussie
demon bowlers in the
Jubilee Test? Full coverage
from Thursday BBCtv
and Radio 3. Back feature:
Radio Times asks is
cricket a game—or war?

much about cricket so I gave him a full briefing. I knew he would just love the tone, the texture, the atmosphere. I knew he'd tear into it, and he did. He came back thrilled with the experience and did these wonderful drawings. Then the Australians came here three months later for the Jubilee Test. This was the Ashes and it was a real personality-packed confrontation between England and Australia. It was very aggressive, very bloody. The Australians loved Ralph's drawings and wanted to buy them, and I think many of them did.

RALPH STEADMAN:

Learning about cricket was the attraction. I first looked at WD Grace and the history of the game. I even went to the Oval to soak up the atmosphere. I got interested in the spectators, as I had at the Kentucky Derby.[3] The crowd is fascinating – the interaction between spectators and players.

[The English and Australians] were all intent on winning and therefore they expressed their inner determination, not in anger, but with more exertion than normal people. You are hurling a ball down at someone with a wooden bat; it's like a bullet. It's a bit alarming. I always hope someone catches it instead of being hit in the face. I played school cricket and you could be a slow-spin ball bowler so it would drop and bounce one way, and not the other, and confuse the batsman. It's an unknown quantity. The ball can do something surprising.

I was intrigued by the fact that people actually got so fascinated by it. I wanted to understand that obsession. I don't know how the readership reacted. No one told me that. They were far too frightened.

---

1   Geoffrey Cannon email interview with Ian Birch, August 2016.
2   Quoted from David Driver (ed.), *The Art of Radio Times: First Sixty Years*, BBC Publications, 1981, p.225. Interview by Peter Harle. Reproduced with kind permission from David Driver.
3   The legendary essay, "The Kentucky Derby is Decadent and Depraved, written under duress by Hunter S. Thompson, sketched with eyebrow pencil and lipstick by Ralph Steadman", *Scanlan's Monthly*, vol. 1, no. 4, June 1970.

SOUNDS

25 MARCH 1978

Editor: Alan Lewis

Features editor: Vivien Goldman

Cover feature: "It Can't Happen Here
Or Can It?" was the result of work by
Phil Sutcliffe, Caroline Coon,
Vivien Goldman, Jon Savage,
Pete Silverton, SOUNDS editorial
staff and Rock Against Racism.

By 1978 the grassroots movement Rock Against Racism (RAR) had become an important rallying point for countering the growing racial tension in Britain, and the neo-fascist National Front (NF), in particular. Vivien Goldman, a tireless champion of black music, decided *Sounds* had to take a stand. The cover and report inside were timely: RAR and the Anti-Nazi League were planning a London march culminating in an open-air music festival in Victoria Park on 30 April. Around 100,000 people would turn up.

CAROLINE COON:

"It Can't Happen Here" was a spontaneous demonstration: we felt a real sense of responsibility that we could make a difference. You can't be a rock and roll magazine and allow racism.

I said, "I'm going to interview Martin Webster." He was the National Activities Organizer for the National Front. I just rang him up. He'd heard of me and said, "Yes, come along". I did a lot of research and went with a stack of hard questions. Interviewing this racist was almost like a Monty Python sketch: it is so out of rational bounds that it becomes comedy.

I thought, I'm going to expose this bastard and deliver the best copy I can to Vivien. At one point I asked him, "If your policies are taken to their logical conclusion, 90 per cent of rock bands in this country will have to be repatriated to various parts of the world." "Yes, that's right," he replied, "And there they can amuse their own people." That drove the idea for the "Deported!" cover treatment. At the end of the interview, I could hardly bear what I'd heard.

I then had to take pictures of him. We were in the front room of his Victorian terrace in Connaught Road, Teddington, which was also the National Front office. I'd taken one picture but the light wasn't quite right. I stood him in another space, closed the door and saw this image of a very beautiful black youth on the back of the door, staring at me. Beside it was a picture of an older black musician who might have been Tapper Zukie – I can't remember. I knew I couldn't point that out to Webster so I quietly took the photograph. He had not wanted me to see it. The other side of the door had a Union Jack on it.

VIVIEN GOLDMAN:
I had the idea and masterminded it, but we wrote it like a commune. Caroline had a very pronounced sense of justice. Afterwards, the feeling was the paper had gone too far in that activist direction and they started to give space to Gary Bushell's Oi! bands that teetered on the edge of NF support. That's when I left *Sounds*. The struggle there was completely debilitating for me. But for a while we had a good run of being the activist face of punk in a much more unmediated way than *Melody Maker* or the *NME*, which were much bigger. We were the feisty, scrappy outsiders.

MARCH 25 1978 18p

TUBES, TELEVISION dates

sounds

PAUL SIMONON
(CLASH)

PHIL LYNOTT
(THIN LIZZY)

POLY STYRENE
(X-RAY SPEX)

CHARLIE TUMAHAI
(BEBOP DELUXE)

GEORGE CSAPO
(BETHNAL)

CARL LEVY
(CIMARONS)

ERROLL BROWN
(HOT CHOCOLATE)

ARRI UP
(SLITS)

FREDDY MERCURY
(QUEEN)

RAY LAKE
(REAL THING)

JEAN BURNEL
(STRANGLERS)

RITA RAY
(DARTS)

IS THIS THE FUTURE
OF ROCK 'N' ROLL ?

RACISM AND YOUR MUSIC — FACE TO FACE WITH THE FRONT

SPECIAL REPORT Pages 25-33

1980s

RAW

LAUNCH ISSUE, JULY 1980

Editors/publishers: Françoise Mouly
   & Art Spiegelman
Cover drawing: Art Spiegelman

By the late 1970s the underground comics scene was languishing: it was about to be re-energized by a new personal and professional partnership. Paris-born ex-architecture student and comics enthusiast Françoise Mouly had come to New York and met then unknown American cartoonist Art Spiegelman. Together they created *Raw*, a new "graphix magazine". *Raw* would champion visionary artists, showcase European comics and revolutionize the graphic novel when it introduced *Maus*, Spiegelman's Pulitzer Prize-winning work about surviving the Holocaust.

FRANÇOISE MOULY:

I wanted to bring together all that I discovered when I met Art. With me discovering American comics and Art discovering European comics, we wanted to put the two together. Furthermore, I had been shocked by the prejudices against comics in America: comics, it seemed, were for idiots. I didn't think that.

I had conversations with friends of Art's, such as Robert Crumb, who were adamant that the medium should remain the domain of throwaway and disposable publications on newsprint. I didn't want *Raw* to be thrown away. I wanted to find a middle ground between the expensive limited-edition art object and the throwaway underground comic. The first issue was intended to be a departure from everything else that was around at the time.

Art's inspiration in wanting to be a cartoonist was discovering the early *Mad* magazine – and that was true for many underground cartoonists – so a short, one-word name was important. *Raw* was meant in the sense of "uncooked", the

opposite of slick. I think Art chose the name because I couldn't pronounce it. It made him laugh to hear me say *Raw*.

I was pretty much able to do everything myself, so I didn't have to pay a staff. I was publisher. I put up the money. I got it printed. I did the distribution. I wanted a large-size format,[1] in part because in the independent bookstores at the time there were large-size magazines like *WET*, *Metropolis* and, later, *Émigré*. A lot of them were on newsprint, but I wanted good paper. So *Raw* was expensive compared to other comics: the first issue was $3.50 when other comics were a dollar.

When you launch a magazine, the one constant is the logo. We did the opposite. We changed the logo with every issue. It was designed by whoever did the cover. And we changed the subtitle every issue. The first issue is called *The Graphix Magazine of Postponed Suicides* with Art's drawing of someone jumping out of a window. It's from a quote by the philosopher E M Cioran[2] that Art and I liked very much: "A book is a postponed suicide."[3] It also functioned as our answer to many people who thought, "Oh, *Raw* is so depressing and dark."

I couldn't afford colour printing so I ran off a signature of colour panels of Art's drawing and we glued one to each cover, with Elmer's Glue. The quantities were manageable: the print run was 3,500 copies. It was very important to me that each issue remain a handmade product even though it was printed.

1   The first issue of *Raw* was 10½ inches × 14⅛ inches (27cm × 36cm).
2   Romanian philosopher who lived much of his life in Paris.
3   Quoted from "The Trouble with Being Born", *Raw*, vol. 1, issue 1 (July 1980), contents page.

i-D

LAUNCH ISSUE, AUGUST/SEPTEMBER 1980

Editors: Perry Haines, Terry Jones,
   Al McDowell

Special thanks to i-D photographer
   Steve Johnson, Ed Gillan, i-D stylist
   Caroline Baker, Anne Witchard and Trish.

Terry Jones launched *i-D* as a quarterly out of his house in north-west London a few months after the first issue of *The Face*. With a battle cry of "Fans, not critics", it championed street style both in its content (pared-down, head-to-toe portraits of "fans" with micro interviews that Jones called "Straight Up") and in its design (the landscape-shaped, handmade fanzine format). The logo was inspired, suggesting a winking eye and smiling face, and presaging the world of emoticons.

TERRY JONES:

Back in 1976 I had been discussing with Toscani[1] and Caroline Baker how the fashion world needed a new type of magazine. We were going to do something called *The Whole World Clothes Catalogue* but it never happened. The idea was that it would an international base for exchanging information – even as far as if you're going on holiday, you don't need a suitcase because you have found someone who is your size, and thinks like you, and you can use their wardrobe.

CAROLINE BAKER:

It was a bit of a clothes Airbnb but with no money involved. Toscani was very politically driven. So was Terry in a more subtle, visual way. Anti-bourgeoisie, into street style and the people.

TERRY JONES:

Right from the start, I wanted to create something that would become a collectable and not landfill. I wanted *i-D* to feel like a social document, so the

FASHION MAGAZINE Nº1 50p

street photography inside was about documenting that moment. "Straight up" is a Bristolian phrase. It's about asking a question and getting a straight answer, no messing.

The photographer was the journalist. Steve Johnson, who did the punk book[2] with me, was one of the key people to do the photos. He hated getting words from people, so invariably someone had to be there to take down the words. That was how Dylan Jones, Alex Sharkey and Caryn Franklin would start their careers.

There was also the idea that everyone's a star: the Warhol "15 minutes of fame" concept. It was democratizing and it was about style as opposed to fashion. Calling ourselves a "fashion magazine" was tongue-in-cheek: we had nothing to do with the business of fashion. It was about infiltrating the mainstream.

Every cover of *i-D* 1 and 2 was a unique piece because the fanzine printer, Better Badges, had never done a two-colour job like that before. So the chances of getting it in register were virtually zero. It went from fire engine red to rouge pink. It was meant to be fluoro pink but they would just tip the ink in. Knowing that you're not going to get a perfect result is what interests me.

I wanted to have it so there was no photographic image. It was about the concept of identity, your ID. And iD were the initials of my studio then, "informat Designer", always with a lowercase "i" because I was a fan of e e cummings.

The lowercase "i" for *i-D* created a face so, when you turned it around, it was a graphic of a winking eye and a smiling face. I could appropriate all the other things that the wink implies: seductive, in the know. There was also a hidden side: the closed eye. I wanted something as strong as the Playboy bunny.

---

1 The photographer Oliviero Toscani, *see Colors* (page 148)
2 Terry Jones and Isabelle Anscombe, *Not Another Punk Book*, Aurum Press, 1978.

ROLLING STONE

22 JANUARY 1981

Editor and publisher: Jann S Wenner

Chief photographer: Annie Leibovitz

Cover photograph: Annie Leibovitz, John Lennon and Yoko Ono in the "Morning Room" of their New York City apartment, early afternoon, 8 December 1980

Annie Leibovitz had memorably photographed John Lennon at the start of her career for a haunting cover in 1971.[1] Almost ten years later to the day, she walked into Lennon and Yoko Ono's seventh-floor apartment in the Dakota to do two sessions with them – on Wednesday 3 December, and Monday 8 December.

Leibovitz wanted to capture them in an embrace. Lennon was keen, Ono was not happy to lose her clothes, so Leibovitz suggested that she leave everything on, as a contrast. She took a Polaroid. When Lennon saw it, he said, "You've captured our relationship exactly."

He told Leibovitz how important it was for Yoko to be on the cover as well. "I promised John that this would be the cover. I looked him in the eye and we shook on it."[2] They planned to meet up later to review the transparencies. It didn't happen.

That Monday evening Lennon was shot by Mark Chapman outside The Dakota and pronounced dead at 11.07pm. Wenner was devastated. When he saw the pictures the next day, "My eye went right to it and John had said that's the one they wanted, too." Cover lines weren't necessary.

The issue was a remarkable memorial, sold a massive 1.45 million copies and helped shape Lennon's legacy. In 2005 the American Society of Magazine Editors voted it the number one magazine cover to appear since 1965.

MED 08675 · JANUARY 22ND, 1981 · $1.50 UK80p

RollingStone

JANN WENNER:

That image is just so resonant and rich with their own relationship and ideas and philosophy about life. Then the events of the day made it so incredibly powerful; it took on this other life on top of that. You see all the overtones of death and rebirth. It inadvertently portrayed the forthcoming moment. There's the art of it, and then there's the message of it, which is extraordinarily powerful, and then there is the prophetic nature of it.

I don't know where you find that combination of events: a great photographer, the moment, and all that stuff. I've never seen another cover of a magazine, ours or any other, quite as strong as that. The issue itself was done at the moment. It's right from the moment and, given who he was and who he was to us, it was one from the heart and I think that that heart is all over that issue. It's wounded, and it's bleeding, and it's in agony and it's full of love. You have the last official image of the two of them ever. It was both personal as well as professional. We had our job to do but we had our love to express.

John Lennon really helped get *Rolling Stone* off the ground in various ways. He was on the first cover, but more than that he gave us that kind of interview and that kind of access and that kind of news that built the magazine's reputation and name recognition again and again and again, whether it was the "Two Virgins" cover or the famous "Lennon Remembers" interview. He just opened up, whereas the Beatles had been so hermetically sealed off. We kind of became his official media spokesman for as long as he was alive.

1 *Rolling Stone*, 21 January 1971.
2 *Rolling Stone*, 22 January 1981, contents page.

THE FACE

MARCH 1985
Publisher/editor: Nick Logan
Art director: Neville Brody
Design: Neville Brody & Robin Derrick
Cover photography: Jamie Morgan
Styling: Ray Petri
Cover model: Felix Howard[1]

Eighties fashion saw the rise of the stylist, and Ray Petri led the charge. He invented the decade's young urban male uniform – MA1 jacket with orange lining, Levi's 501 jeans, white socks and Dr. Martens loafers. Petri's trademark "Buffalo" look was showcased in six influential shoots he did for *The Face* with photographer Jamie Morgan. This was one of them: Petri and Morgan lashed together classic tailoring with post-punk street style.

JAMIE MORGAN:

The word "Buffalo" was just right for us for many reasons. The rude-boy attitude was a big part of it, as was Bob Marley's song "Buffalo Soldier", talking about the black slaves taken to America. Also, the buffalo in Native American culture was honoured: it was used to clothe and feed a community. Then the white man destroys the culture and kills all the buffalo. To us, the American Indians and the buffalo represent the underdog, the cultural outsider. This was us. We all came from immigrant or mixed-race families. We kicked against the white establishment and the fashion industry – not in any heavy way – because we were not represented in establishment fashion magazines.

NICK LOGAN:

It was a golden day when Ray came through the door with Jamie. They had a couple of shots of Nick and Barry Kamen and it grew from that. We had a kind of ad hoc arrangement. As footballers will say, it's one game at a time. We'd just say yes to their next thing; we didn't need to talk about it.

THE FACE No. 59

GERMANY 5.80 DM

● MARCH 1985 85p US $2.75

THE FACE

KILLER

SAM SHEPARD AND JESSICA LANGE
HOLLYWOOD'S HOT COUPLE

Alison Moyet
Andy Warhol
Lovers rock
Pogues ◆ Brazil
Mel Smith

H A R D

Photo Jamie Morgan

JAMIE MORGAN:

The clothes were never our main concern. We always started with casting and a cultural or artistic point of view. We wanted to reclaim the idea that men are often far more flamboyant than women.

NICK LOGAN:

I needed persuading to run the "Killer" cover. I was a bit apprehensive about how it would be received, what it said about us, because Felix was only 12. And the word "killer", which was just torn out of a newspaper. But it looked fantastic and everybody in the office loved it. It's probably my favourite cover of *The Face*.

JAMIE MORGAN:

Felix was the son of a friend of Ray's. I just loved his face – that it was old and young, powerful and vulnerable, at the same time. This type of casting had no precedent and I wasn't sure people would get it.

We spent time in Jamaica partly because of the West London Jamaican community that we enjoyed so much and because we were working with reggae artists like Gregory Isaacs and Freddie McGregor. The words "killer", "hard" and "wicked" were all used in Jamaica and soon became part of London slang. I like to think we were part of the London cultural melting pot.

ROBIN DERRICK:

The magazine came out on Tuesday, and on Thursday I was in some nightclub, Do-Do's or The Wag, and people had newspaper headlines pinned to their clothes. It was extraordinary: it was that literal and that direct. Everyone knew where the idea came from. It was cool to copy *The Face*.

---

1   The following year Felix Howard appeared in Madonna's video for "Open Your Heart" and later he became a successful songwriter and music business executive.

NATIONAL GEOGRAPHIC

JUNE 1985

Editor: Bill Garrett

Cover subject: Sharbat Gula

Cover photography: Steve McCurry

In 1984 American photographer Steve McCurry was at the Afghanistan–Pakistan border, researching a story for *National Geographic* about the flood of refugees from Afghanistan, triggered by the Soviet invasion, when he spotted this 12-year-old orphan. She was deeply traumatized. Her village had been bombed and her parents killed; with her grandmother, brother and three sisters, she had walked for weeks in the middle of winter across the mountains to reach the camp. The photograph came to represent the complex emotions of the refugee – suffering, determination, defiance and dignity.

STEVE MCCURRY:

I was in the Nasir Bagh refugee camp outside of Peshawar and came across a tent that was being used as an elementary school for girls. I noticed this little girl with beautiful eyes in the corner of the tent, looking haunted. There was something unique and disturbing about her. This was a girl of simple means but she was holding her head high. I literally had a couple of minutes with her before she walked away, but everything worked – the light, her expression, the background, the shawl.

There's an authenticity to this picture. She's giving you exactly what is inside of her. I didn't speak Pashtun, her language; she didn't speak English and this was the first time she had been photographed. She wasn't sure what a portrait was. Who knows what was going through her mind and how much of that look was curiosity at me and the camera? She has an expression which is sort of neutral but with a hint of something positive.

There were two possible versions for the cover: one of her looking at the camera and one with her hand on her face. The picture editor at the time thought the one looking at the camera was too disturbing. He didn't want to show it to the editor, Bill Garrett. So we compromised: we'd show him both. Bill literally leapt to his feet when he saw the direct gaze and said, "There's our cover."

After 9/11, when the world's attention once again turned to Afghanistan, I wanted to go back again to find her. I never knew her name or any details about her. So in January 2002, I went with a team from *National Geographic* and we found her, living in the Tora Bora region. Her name was Sharbat Gula.

When I first saw her again, it was a bit of a shock. My reference was her at 12, not a woman around 30, married and a mother of three children.

We didn't embrace: it's just out of the question. But we did a second cover.[1] I photographed her in her burka holding the original picture.

That original picture has been reproduced millions of times as advertising for *National Geographic*. The ethics are clear: you don't want to be accused of exploiting an orphan who happens to be a refugee. Initially, compensation came from *National Geographic*,[2] but then I bought her a house. My sister Bonnie and I also started a non-profit called ImagineAsia.[3] We wanted to take some dramatic steps to make her life better.

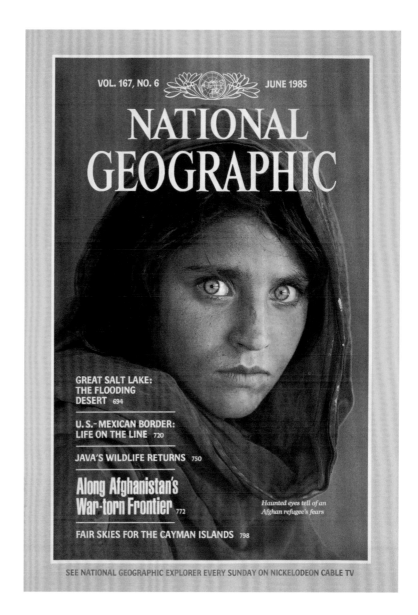

1 April 2002.
2 It established the Afghan Girls Fund in 2002 when the expulsion of the Taliban made it possible for girls to seek education, a right they had long been denied under Taliban rule. In 2008 it was extended to boys and given a new name, the Afghan Children's Fund.
3 ImagineAsia works in partnership with local community leaders and regional NGOs to help provide educational resources and opportunities to children in Afghanistan.

ELLE

OTTOBRE 1987

NUMERO
UNO
SPECIALE
L. 2000

SCOPRI
IL TUO
MODO DI
AMARE

VIAGGIO
A SUD
DI CAPO
NORD

IL RACCONTO
DI **ELLE**,
UN INEDITO
DI McINERNEY

QUALI SONO
LE NUOVE
VIRTÙ

IL PUNTO SULLO
STILE
90 PAGINE DI MODA

ITALIA L. 4000 FRANCIA F. 30 GERMANIA DM. 11 GRAN BRETAGNA LGS 2.80 SPAGNA PTAS 550 SVIZZERA FRS 7.80 SVIZZERA CANTON TICINO FRS 7.50 USA $ 4.50

ITALIAN ELLE

LAUNCH ISSUE, OCTOBER 1987
NOVEMBER 1987
DECEMBER 1987
JANUARY 1988 (PROPOSED COVER
IMAGE, NEVER PUBLISHED)
Editor-in-chief: Carla Sozzani
Managing editor: Eugenio Gallavotti
Art director: Robin Derrick

Italian *Elle*, published in a joint venture between Hachette and Rizzoli, was a departure from the brand's template. Carla Sozzani brought a level of experimentation that Hachette did not usually allow. But the big five Italian fashion houses grew seriously rattled when Sozzani didn't feature their product on the covers. Sozzani and art director Robin Derrick were fired after three issues.

ROBIN DERRICK:
Carla called me and said, "Will you do Italian *Elle*?" I was the art director of *The Face* and had just taken over from Neville [Brody] who was doing *Arena*.

I brought my kind of "cool" *Face* and *i-D* photographers who had yet to make their name like Nick Knight and Juergen Teller. Carla brought photographers from her *Vogue* background like Steven Meisel, Bruce Weber, Paolo Roversi. It was an amazing combination. Carla and I were really aligned. We laughed so much. Carla had this line, "*Ogni giorno una festa*" – every day's a party.

CARLA SOZZANI:
Nick Knight photographed the first cover. I wanted something that was purer in shape and look. The red turtleneck is Benetton and coat Montana. This collection was very clean and simple, almost severe – a little bit like my vision, super-minimal. We chose red, green and white because they were the colours of the Italian flag.

ROBIN DERRICK:
I loved the first cover but the difference between it and the weekly French *Elle* was too big. You could start to see the mismatch.

EUGENIO GALLAVOTTI:
The first issue sold out. We had more difficulties with the next issues.

CARLA SOZZANI:
Nick did the November cover as well and we had the Japanese model Maki Shibuya. For December, I asked Christian Lacroix if I could have a pattern for an evening dress from his last couture collection and put it in *Elle* so everyone

ELLE

NOVEMBRE

L. 4000

ESCLUSIVO
ELLE IN
RUSSIA
COSA STA
CAMBIANDO

**NUCLEARE
SI O NO**
DUE
SCIENZIATE A
CONFRONTO

LA MODA
DEGLI OPPOSTI
**MASCHILE
O FEMMINILE**

IL CORPO SOTTILE E
SENSUALE

ANNO I - N. 2 -
CANADA $ 5.95 FRANCIA F. 30 GERMANIA DM. 11 GRAN BRETAGNA LG̲ 650 SPAGNA PTAS 550 SVIZZERA FRS 7.80 SVIZZERA CANTON TICINO FRS 7.50 US

ELLE

DICEMBRE

L. 4000

GUIDA A UN GRANDE NATALE
LA MODA, I REGALI, LE RICETTE

IN **ESCLUSIVA**
PER LE LETTRICI
DI **ELLE** UNO
SPLENDIDO ABITO
DA SERA DI
ALTA MODA

CURARSI
CON IL
SONNO

SPECIALE
DENARO
COME E
QUANTO
INVESTIRE

INCHIESTA: CHE COS'È OGGI
L'AMORE

ANNO I - N. 3 - SPEDIZ. ABB. POST. GR. III/70

CANADA $ 5.95 FRANCIA F. 30 GERMANIA DM. 11 GRAN BRETAGNA LGS 2.80 GRECIA DRS 650 SPAGNA PTAS 550 SVIZZERA FRS 7.80 SVIZZERA CANTON TICINO FRS 7.50 USA N.Y.C. $ 4.50 OTHER $ 4.95

could make the dress. The model, Meg Grosswendt, is wearing the dress on the cover. Paolo Roversi took the photograph. I wanted to do another cover with him with a dress by Alaïa but they fired me before it came out.

They offered me an interesting amount of money to say I was leaving but I said, "Why? You are firing me. I am not ashamed, and anyway Diana Vreeland[1] had been fired from *Vogue*." They said, "Who is Diana Vreeland?" and I said, "There is one more reason for you to fire me. If you don't know who she is, we have no point of communication."

ROBIN DERRICK:

I knew I was being fired when the *fattorino* [office boy], who would come around with the post on a trolley, came into my office and started taking the magazine layouts down from the wall. The guy was deaf and dumb, so I couldn't talk to him.

My understanding is that they had received a telegram from the trading group for brands like Armani and Valentino. They said, unless the editorial direction of the magazine changed and featured more Italian clothes, they were going to withdraw their advertising – not just from *Elle* but from all the magazines in the Rizzoli Group. I was told at the time that that was $32 million worth of advertising. They fired Carla and me that day.

Our *Elle* was really up there, and beyond. We did three iconic issues: they were art pieces.

---

1   Fashion legend who was fashion editor at American *Harper's Bazaar* before becoming editor-in-chief of American *Vogue* in 1963. She was fired in 1971.

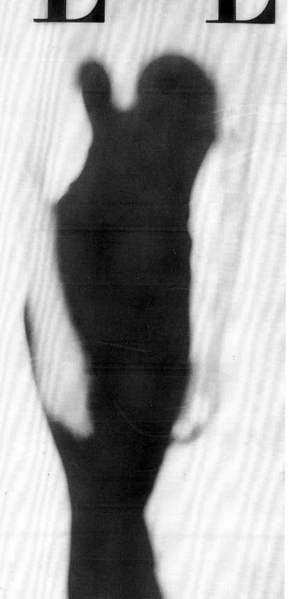

THE NICE NEW YORK MONTHLY ▸ APRIL $2.50

S P Y

Our NICE ISSUE

DONALD TRUMP
A Heck of a Guy

GLAMOROUS GALS
Who Never Ever Age

IT'S *FUN*
to Live in Queens

PAUL SIMON
Music's Mr. Generosity

SPY

**APRIL 1988
(COVER AND P.1)**

Editors: Graydon Carter & Kurt Anderson
Publisher: Thomas L Phillips Jr.
Executive editor: Susan Morrison
Art director: Alexander Isley
Photographs: Deborah Feingold (body) &
     Joe McNally/Wheeler Pictures (head)

Kurt Andersen and Graydon Carter hatched the idea for *Spy*[1] when they were working at *Time* in the mid-1980s. They wanted an exhaustively researched satirical monthly about "the great commercial machines"[2] that fuelled New York. Launched in October 1986, it was whip-smart, mischievous and sometimes merciless, but always happy to burn bridges as it skewered its privileged subjects. As Tina Brown noted, "It flatters media people by bothering to take them down."[3] *Spy* ridiculed Donald Trump from the first issue and coined the "short-fingered vulgarian" epithet that re-emerged in the rhetoric of the 2017 American presidential campaign. Trump has never forgiven them.

ALEXANDER ISLEY:
We wanted to do an April Fool's issue. *Spy* was getting the reputation of being the snarky bad boy, so, we thought, wouldn't it be fun to make it "Our Nice Issue" and, since Donald Trump had been the bête noire of *Spy* for a long time, do something *good* about him?

I had this idea of doing him with his signature thumbs-up, being "a heck of a guy". Then, when you opened it up, he'd have a red tail like the devil which went across the first spread. It was to telegraph to the world that it was "Our Nice Issue" – but not *really*. But the sales staff went and sold an ad on the spread, so the tail idea didn't work.

We thought, "Why not make it a magazine publishing joke and have the cover lines and barcode collapse instead?" It was Kurt's body, though he didn't want that to come out at the time. Throughout the shoot, Kurt was wise-cracking, saying Trump things like, "This is the best cover there's ever going to be." We had photos of Trump's head blown up and held them in front of Kurt, trying to match the angle and the pose and the light. The colour backgrounds are different on the two pages. It would have been an extra $400 to colour-correct the second image, but the publisher, Tom, said we couldn't do that.

SUSAN MORRISON:
I love that one. The colour palette is very playtime-y.

We didn't think too much then about Trump as a force of evil as much as a giant asshole. That does remind me of a cover we did later about the concept of people who had made Faustian bargains. I got Elvis Costello to be on the cover,[4] posing as the devil. We didn't want it to be someone in a sequined red outfit, so we dressed him in a very tailored suit like a Wall Street Master of the Universe with very subtle horns on his hairline. Costello was leaning forward like a businessman, handing out his card. In very tiny type on the bottom of the card is the phone number of Trump Tower. So, if you called that number, you got the reception of the Trump organization. I don't know if anyone called.

KURT ANDERSEN:

In an issue in 1988[5] we actually conducted a national poll of candidates including Donald Trump. He was at the time, ridiculously it seemed, flirting with the idea of running for president and we found that 4 per cent of Americans wished he were running. I never imagined that 30 years later this magazine, in this accidental, strange way, would have contemporary relevance. He wasn't the only thing we did but he was a major obsession.

1 The magazine's name was inspired by caricaturist Leslie Ward, who worked for Vanity Fair in the early 1900s under the pseudonym "Spy".

2 Graydon Carter, in Kurt Andersen, Graydon Carter and George Kalogerakis, *Spy: The Funny Years*, Miramax Books, 2006, p.5.

3 Tina Brown, *The Vanity Fair Diaries*, 1983–1992, Weidenfeld & Nicolson, 2017, p.346.

4 June 1989.

5 January–February 1988. Headlined "Nation to Trump: We Need You", the issue was part of *Spy*'s "Route 88 Campaign Manual".

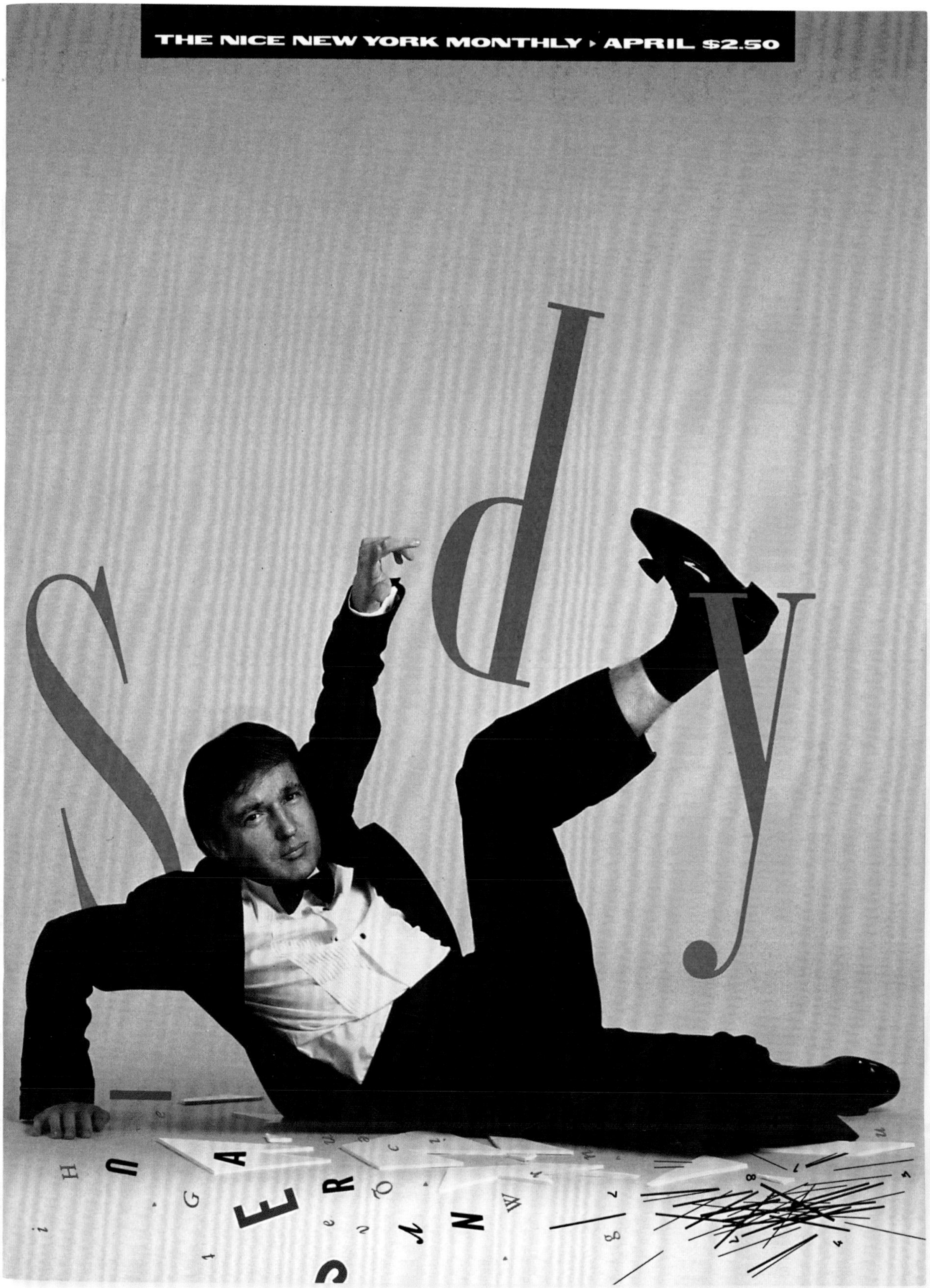
THE NICE NEW YORK MONTHLY › APRIL $2.50

1990s

THE FACE

No 22/JULY 1990 £1.50 • US $4.75

ITALY L5500 GERMANY 9.5DM SPAIN 435PTAS BELG. 105 BFR

THE 3RD SUMMER OF LOVE

Stone Roses on Spike Island, an A-Z of the new bands, Daisy Age fashion, Hendrix and psychedelia

'Kiss my butt!' Sandra on Madonna

Prince in Minneapolis: tour preview

Indian summer: photography Corinne Day

JOHN WATERS / MICKEY ROURKE / MARSHALL JEFFERSON / TIM ROTH

07

0 74470 72689 0

THE FACE

JULY 1990

Editor/publisher: Nick Logan

Assistant editor/features editor:
   Sheryl Garratt

Art director: Phil Bicker

Cover photographer: Corinne Day

Stylist: Melanie Ward at Z Agency

Model: Kate Moss at Storm

This was the cover that lit the fuse for Kate Moss.

PHIL BICKER:

I was trying to find a model who was the embodiment of *The Face*. It was the era of supermodels – Linda Evangelista, Cindy Crawford, Tatjana Patitz, Christy Turlington – but they all felt inaccessible and didn't have any real relationship to what *The Face* was doing. Photographer Corinne Day, who had been a model herself, came to see me with a fashion test shoot, half a dozen black-and-white prints and some contact sheets. Among the prints was an image of this young girl walking along the motorway in Ickenham, north-west London. As someone who'd grown up in the same London suburbs as Corinne, I connected with the setting of the photo and particularly to the model, Kate, who looked relatable, natural and authentic.

I think Corinne saw herself in Kate. Kate became her muse. I ran the single image in *The Face* a couple months later as part of a portfolio that featured the first published photos by Corinne, David Sims and Glen Luchford. Then Corinne and I started to work on ideas for a full Kate story.

Corinne went to Camber Sands[1] with stylist Melanie Ward and made a set of pictures with Kate. It was one of those stories where they went back to the location at least three times, an approach I would encourage with a lot of photographers at the time, as we worked to build stories together. The final images that ran captured Kate's teen spirit. But while it looked like she was wearing her own clothes, she's totally styled, actually wearing a lot of things Melanie and Corinne would wear at the time. They basically styled Kate as themselves: Birkenstock shoes, cheesecloth dresses, plus daisies around her neck. Kate wasn't a hippy-trippy chick. She was a streetwise Croydon girl who I'd see out at clubs. But even styled in this manner, her natural personality came through. The one really important thing relating to this was that there was very, very little fashion advertising in *The Face*. So we didn't have to adhere to that policy of putting certain clothing on somebody because there was an advertising page later in the magazine. We didn't have that restriction and that enabled people to feel more like themselves, which was great.

NICK LOGAN:

I remember liking the image, but it still wasn't that common for us to use a fashion image for a cover story. Sheryl said, "I've got these stories which I could pull together for the third summer of love." I said, "Brilliant, let's go with it." So it was pure accident, digging ourselves out of a hole.

SHERYL GARRATT:

Phil deserves the credit – not me. My memory was that we were hoping to get a shot from Spike Island[2] for the cover but couldn't get one, so we were casting about for something else. Phil came up with the shot of Kate. I didn't think it worked. Nick suggested we did Sandra Bernhardt who was a Q&A on the back page. We tried a Herb Ritts shot of her but it didn't work. It was too Eighties. Then Phil cut the feathers out from the headdress and put it over the masthead. Suddenly, it felt very forward-looking. It went from flat to cheeky, irreverent.

I didn't want any more of that pouting thing in fashion in the Eighties, that inaccessible perfection. I wanted more joy and colour because that's what was happening in dance and pop culture at the time. Everything had gone technicolour.

PHIL BICKER:

It had been a summer of festivals and ecstasy and it seemed that the Kate pictures had all those qualities without it being so literal. That was exactly what I wanted.

No one remembers it now, but we had done a Kate cover in May.[3] It was a World Cup cover and it was forgettable at best: it didn't feel like Kate at all. We'd only ever had a couple of people appear on the cover twice – one was Madonna – so why would we put this 16-year-old girl from Croydon on the cover two months later? There was a lot of kickback in the office about it.

I give credit to Nick for having his wits about him to see what was there. It wasn't an obvious cover but it was positive, spirited and natural. Its vibrancy was the opposite in a way to the stoic Felix on the "Killer" cover. It took the editors of *Vogue* another couple of years before they first worked with Kate: the quote was that they were waiting as "she hadn't grown into her features yet". That's what I was trying to beat.

We'd just been through Ray Petri and "Buffalo" which was very stylized fashion. Ray had died the previous year and we were looking for a new direction. Corinne and David Sims, in particular, brought that new kind of grunge, as it was later labelled, with Melanie's styling. Corinne's work with Kate was the beginning of that new look. It was very natural at first but it got dirtier as it went on. Heroin chic was born out of it, but this cover is the antithesis of that.

SHERYL GARRATT:
Corinne was exceptional. The way she shot was almost documentary. When she photographed musicians or actors she wasn't that bothered and would pose them, but when she photographed models she tried to show their personality. I think that was partly because every time she had modelled she felt her personality had been stolen from her.

---

1 Beach in East Sussex, UK.
2 Stone Roses' epic May Bank Holiday gig in Widnes, north-west England, 27 May 1990.
3 Photographed by Mark Lebon.

COLORS

LAUNCH ISSUE, AUTUMN/WINTER 1991

Co-founder of the Benetton group:
  Luciano Benetton
Editorial director: Oliviero Toscani
Editor-in-chief: Tibor Kalman
Cover by Oliviero Toscani & Tibor Kalman

ISSUE 2, SPRING/ SUMMER 1992

Cover credit (on p.2): "Albanians trying to
  flee their country swarm to ships in the
  port of Durres last August; 4,000
  attempted to board the freighter *Vlora*,
  bound for Italy. (We guess no one told
  them what a drag it is to visit Italy in
  August)."
Cover picture: Associated Press
Cover by Oliviero Toscani, Tibor Kalman,
  Karrie Jacobs, Lucy Shulte, Alice Albert

In 1982 Italian photographer Oliviero Toscani joined forces with global fashion brand Benetton to create the decade's most contentious advertising campaign. Called "United Colors of Benetton", it promoted the company's values over their clothes with provocative images that played with multiculturalism and the politics of difference. For their Autumn/Winter 1991 campaign, Toscani decided "to take a photograph that could not be censored. Something that would unite everyone, an untouchable image."[1] The image of a baby girl, Giusy, at the moment of birth, was widely attacked. It also became the launch cover of *Colors*, the new magazine Toscani then developed with trailblazing designer Tibor Kalman.

LUCIANO BENETTON:

A mutual friend, Elio Fiorucci, introduced me to Oliviero 36 years ago. I had been impressed by his Jesus Jeans campaign.[2] I was looking for someone with the ability to develop a non-traditional form of communication. Oliviero had all the right qualities.

Certainly it was a new philosophy, which instead of focusing on the product had elements of social commitment. As we were investing large sums of money it was worthwhile employing these funds for useful purposes. Our highly innovative approach and form of research surprised and, I think, wrong-footed many, including the advertising agencies.

The idea of *Colors* was financed by Benetton but did not address topics related to the company. Instead it was aimed at young creative people across the world – a magazine that thought outside the box, with extraordinary editors. As far as I was concerned, they had carte blanche. The essential point for me was to highlight different cultures and celebrate their diversities. We were aware it was not a magazine for everyone; it was for a very select audience.

Even for me, the photo of the newborn baby was a strong image, but I supported Tibor and Oliviero's decisions at all times. I have great affection for that first cover. It generated an extraordinary level of debate, with a clear division of public opinion. On one side, for example, the British had the billboards taken down the same day they were put up, while the maternity wards of British hospitals continued to request posters of the image for years afterwards.

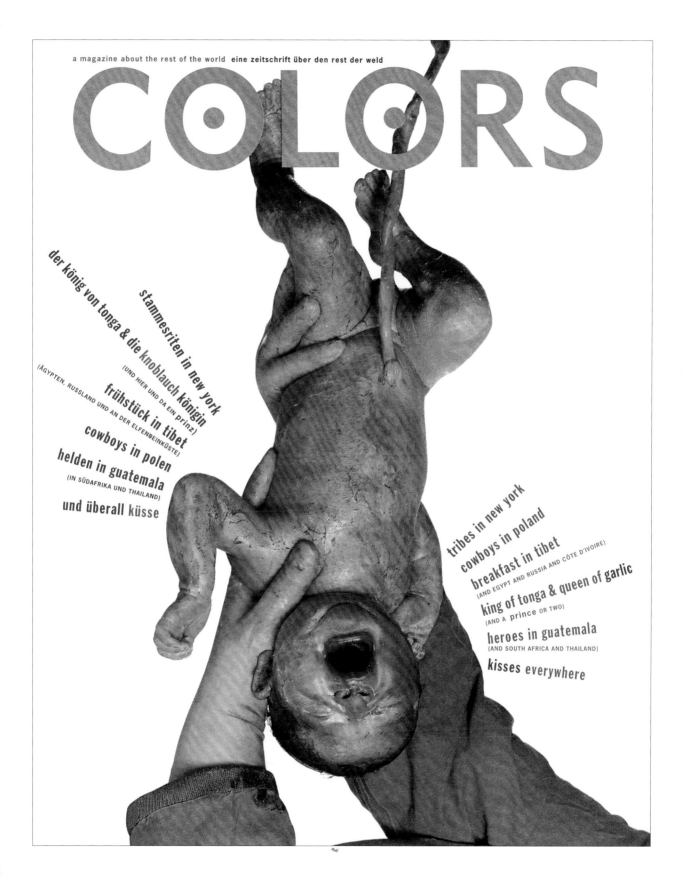

a magazine about the rest of the world **eine zeitschrift über den rest der weld**

COLORS

der könig von tonga & die knoblauch königin

stammesriten in new york

(UND HIER UND DA EIN PRINZ)

frühstück in tibet

(ÄGYPTEN, RUSSLAND UND AN DER ELFENBEINKÜSTE)

cowboys in polen

helden in guatemala

(IN SÜDAFRIKA UND THAILAND)

und überall küsse

tribes in new york

cowboys in poland

breakfast in tibet

(AND EGYPT AND RUSSIA AND CÔTE D'IVOIRE)

king of tonga & queen of garlic

(AND A prince OR TWO)

heroes in guatemala

(AND SOUTH AFRICA AND THAILAND)

kisses everywhere

BOTSWANA 0.50P CHINA 21Y ESP 430PTA FRANCE 22FF FRG 6,50DM HELLAS 750DR INDIA 75RE ITAL 5,000L JAPAN 900Y MACAO 32P NEDERL 8FL SWITZ 75FR UK £2.50 USA $4.00 UY 8400.00

COLORS

a magazine about the rest of the world no.2 spring summer 1992. ein Magazin über den Rest der Welt nr.2 frühjahr sommer 1992.

IMMIGRATION BRINGS... IMMIGRATION BRINGT...
new blood, neues blut, new food, neues
essen, new music, neue musik, new words,
neue wörter, new movies, neue filme, new
beliefs, neue weltanschauungen, new
romantic possibilities, neue romantische
möglichkeiten, and new excuses for
marching, und neue vorwände für paraden
...INTO AN OLD WORLD. ...IN EINE ALTE WELT.

Television (and other Aphrodisiacs)
Snacks (and other Garbage)
Fake Fat (and other Miracles)
Plus three (3!) Madonnas

Fernsehen (und andere Aphrodisiaka)
Knabberei (und anderer Abfall)
Fettersatz (und andere Wunder)
Plus drei (3!) Madonnen

MOSCOW GOES WILD...
Moskau wird wild...

and! the most beautiful chickens in the world
und! die schönsten Hühner der Welt

OLIVIERO TOSCANI:

A lot of the media were not accepting of the Colors campaign. They found it shocking. If you haven't got the balls to face the reality then you will say it is shocking. So I said to Luciano, let's do a magazine with the leftover money. But at the beginning it wasn't easy to sell it, not even to Luciano. As Machiavelli says, there is nothing more difficult and daring and complicated than something that starts a new path.

And, of course, you have to have people with you. After many interviews I chose Tibor. He worked for me. He was an arguer, he was a complainer. But what I really enjoyed about him was that he was intelligent. I always look for somebody who is on the other side of the wind. *Colors* was made with that idea.

I said, "Tibor, I want to do a magazine that doesn't exist, OK?" He was very fashion, very hip. He was working at *Interview* and he knew the places, he knew the people. I didn't want all that. First of all, everybody who comes and works at *Colors* should not have been a journalist before. It had to be their first experience so they will make great mistakes. Second, we had to make a magazine where the words are not serving the images and the images are not serving the words but they have to cross constantly. We have to make a magazine with no news and no celebrities. And more than that: it was in English always with another language. Normally, those two-language magazines are too boring. They look like company magazines but I didn't mind that. Actually, I had major discussions with Tibor about the first issue because he was afraid that *Colors* was too much of a corporate magazine and he didn't believe that a magazine without news and celebrities would work.

A cover has to provoke a reaction. Since marketing took over, provocation is a bad word. We have to eat everything soft, tasteless, chewable, digestible, and we get poison from that. When the first cover came out, the BBC interviewed me and I said, "Oh, of course, you British get upset to see a new-born baby. You wouldn't get shocked if it was a puppy."

The immigration cover is very modern, still today. It wasn't new at the time. That's an issue that goes on forever. There was a lot of immigration from Albania to Italy and suddenly Italy understood that we were a place where immigrants wanted to go. Normally, we were the country that wanted to go somewhere else. We pushed the fact that immigration is an incredibly positive thing. Look at what is written on the cover. Immigration brings new blood, new beliefs, new romantic possibilities – fantastic! You never put together those words. That was the copy I was looking for, to put together image and words to create a new meaning. That's typical *Colors*.

1 Quoted in Lorella Pagnucco Salvemini, *United Colors*, Scriptum Editions, 2002, p.50.
2 Controversial 1971 ad campaign by Toscani and Emanuele Pirella which superimposed Christ's pronouncement, "*Chi mi ama, mi segua*" ("If you love me, follow me") on a female bottom in denim mini-shorts.

VANITY FAIR

AUGUST 1991
Editor-in-chief: Tina Brown
Art and design director: Charles Churchward
Cover photographer: Annie Leibovitz
Stylist: Lori Goldstein
Features editor: Jane Sarkin

Tina Brown had been looking for a cover that "moved *Vanity Fair* decisively on from the 1980s, that made a statement of modernity, progressiveness, freshness, openness, after the heavy Trumpy glitz of that decade".[1] This was it.

During the session, Leibovitz had done a full-body nude shot privately for Moore, who was seven months pregnant with her second daughter, Scout LaRue. Moore recalls that during the shoot, "I commented that it would be great if they would use this for the cover, never giving it a second thought because I didn't imagine they'd be brave enough to use it."[2] Leibovitz agreed it would make a great cover: "Before then, if you were pregnant, you were supposed to hide in the corner and be heavily clothed."[3] After some lively debate at the magazine, Brown said a hugely enthusiastic yes and Moore also gave her approval. Condé Nast knew that there would be an uproar, so they warned the news trade in advance. Some refused to sell it; some demanded it be hidden in a wrapper like a pornographic magazine, making it even more tempting.

There was a media feeding frenzy. The arguments raged: it liberated pregnancy; it championed female empowerment; it was a powerful feminist statement; it screamed sexual objectification; it was high art; it was obscene. Brown added: "It seems we have broken the last taboo. And the perfection of it was that it was an unassailable platform for controversy. Who's ever managed to shock with family values before?"[4] Moore agreed, later commenting: "I did feel glamorous, beautiful and more free about my body. I don't know how much more family-oriented I could possibly have gotten."[5]

Sales went from 800,000 to well over a million. Its influence was enormous. Rival magazines plundered the idea.[6] It added further fuel to the tabloids' obsession with baby bumps and was even "held responsible for the rise of body-hugging maternity fashion".[7]

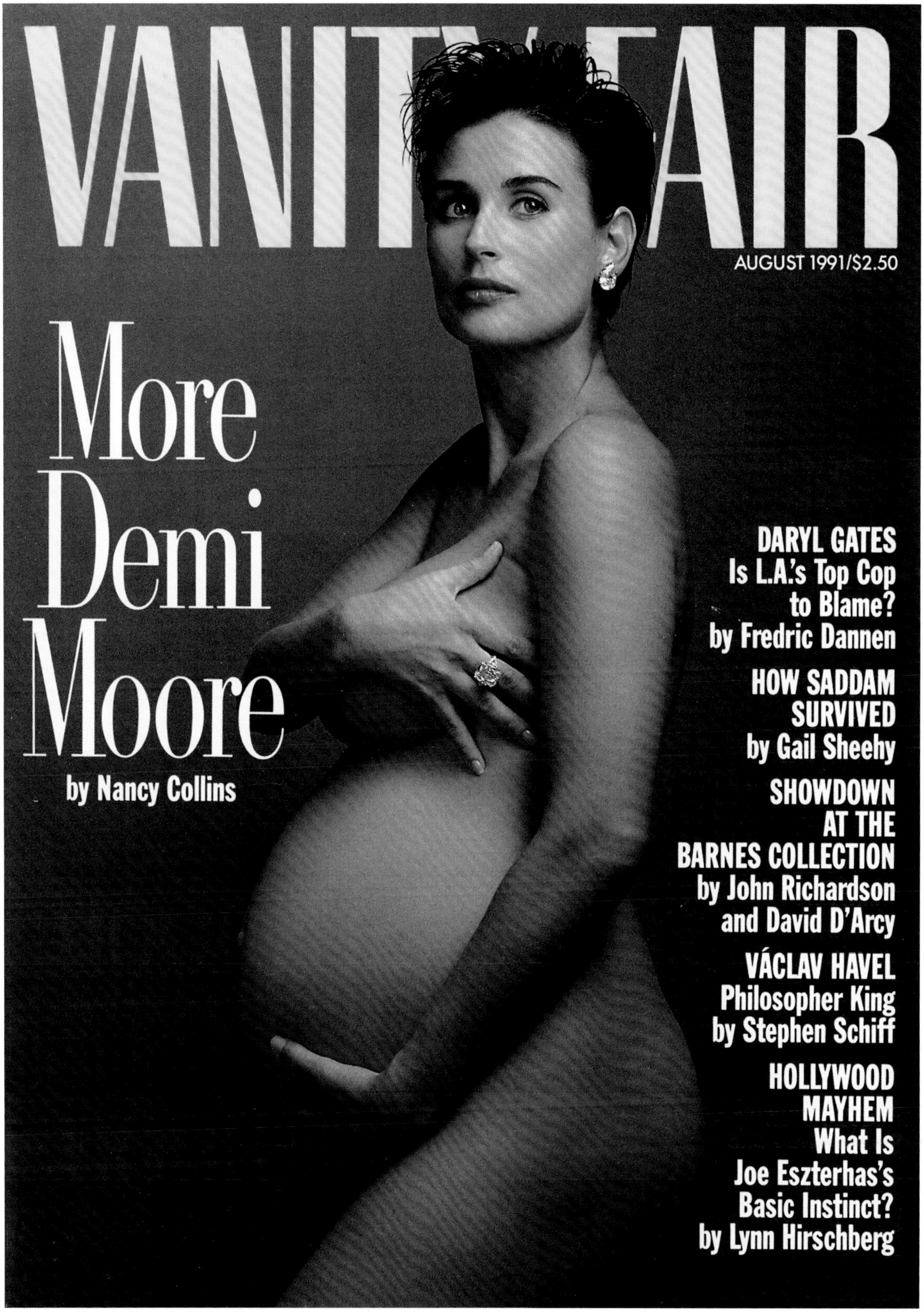

VANITY FAIR

AUGUST 1991/$2.50

More Demi Moore

by Nancy Collins

DARYL GATES
Is L.A.'s Top Cop
to Blame?
by Fredric Dannen

**HOW SADDAM
SURVIVED**
by Gail Sheehy

**SHOWDOWN
AT THE
BARNES COLLECTION**
by John Richardson
and David D'Arcy

VÁCLAV HAVEL
Philosopher King
by Stephen Schiff

**HOLLYWOOD
MAYHEM**
What Is
Joe Eszterhas's
Basic Instinct?
by Lynn Hirschberg

CHARLES CHURCHWARD:

We didn't know what we were going to get with someone that pregnant, but Annie knew Demi was one of those people you could collaborate with on extreme shots, something you didn't often find with actors at that time.

The naked shot wasn't specifically planned. The back-up was a close-up head portrait. Some clothes were sent out and I don't think we were even sure that we could use them. Lori Goldstein is important. She has that special talent of understanding what a photograph needs, how things can change in two seconds and you have to come up with a whole different outfit. The one difference between then and now – and it changed soon after this picture, really – is that fashion advertisers began insisting on their clothes being used, influencing covers. It became more difficult for stylists who brought what was best for the photo.

I believe Lori brought the green satin Isaac Mizrahi robe you see inside for the cover. It was for the colour and the fact you can do almost anything with it. Also, the diamond earrings[8] – in case nothing else works, at least you've got some shiny earrings.

The pictures came in and they caused quite a stir. The staff argued for days, back and forth. I laid out covers all different ways; one of them must have been the Mizrahi robe. The staff was fighting over the nude shot so much that it seemed like a good idea to put it on the cover. We knew something was there but we didn't know how much and what the reaction was going to be. From the first day, it became one of those covers that everybody was talking about, making magazine history.

1 Tina Brown, *The Vanity Fair Diaries, 1983–1992*, Weidenfeld & Nicolson, 2017, p.400.

2 Demi Moore in interview with Ian Birch.

3 Joanna Robinson, "Annie Leibovitz Speaks for the First Time About Her Historic Caitlyn Jenner Cover", *Vanity Fair*, 6 October 2015.

4 Tina Brown, *The Vanity Fair Diaries, 1983–1992*, Weidenfeld & Nicolson, 2017, p.400.

5 Quoted in Maxine Mesinger, "VF Dresses Demi in Paint", *Houston Chronicle*, 7 July 1992.

6 For example, *W*, *German Vogue*, American *Harper's Bazaar* and Australian *Marie Claire*.

7 Annie Liebovitz, *Annie Liebovitz At Work*, Jonathan Cape London, 2008, p.91.

8 The diamond jewellery was by Laykin et Cie.

ESQUIRE

FEBRUARY 1992
Editor-in-chief: Terry McDonell
Art director: Rhonda Rubinstein
Design consultant: Roger Black

This was the cover that brought back the bite that the American *Esquire* brand had in the 1960s.[1]

TERRY McDONELL:

I'd always thought that there was a wealth of telling imagery around white culture, but that few people noticed because they saw it all the time. In some cases it seemed grotesque to me, and in others sort of sweet.

We got these great pictures that were emblematic of white culture in America and ran them inside. One of my favorites was of a white breakfast at a Howard Johnson's,[2] exactly the kind of thing you pass over depending on how immersed you are in that culture. I'm talking about the white pancakes, the white placemat, the white milk. It was hilarious.

At the same time, I was working with Richard Ben Cramer on a story about the first Bush presidency called "George Bush's White Men". Richard was reporting for his seminal book *What It Takes: The Way to the White House*[3] and he had detail after detail that echoed the pictures with a subtext that asked "Is America really racist or not?"

To illustrate the piece, we used a photo of Bush in his living room in Kennebunkport, with lots of chintz and a horrible painting of children with big eyes by Margaret Keane. Bush is dressed casually and all his advisors are sitting around in white shirts. These are very, very white guys. Bush was unpopular at that time because of the Gulf War. It was a heightened political moment.

I wanted the cover to be as graphic as possible and that meant going with type. That would be surprising, and when you're surprising, readers pay attention. It was meant to be political, of course, and ironic because *Esquire* had a white readership. In that sense, the cover had a wonderful biting-the-hand-that-feeds-you feel to it.

RHONDA RUBINSTEIN:

The pictures we ran inside were ironic images by photographers such as Elliott Erwitt and Stephen Shore which poked fun at the lifestyles of gun-toting, flag-waving true believers — decades before the dubious achievement of "Make America Great Again". These documentary photos would not make for a great iconic cover, though we did try various comps.

The all-type cover emerged from Terry's fascination with the almost-imageless *Granta* cover on the family[4] and Roger Black's admiration of the Beatles' White Album. The simplicity and strength of the huge sans serif WHITE PEOPLE — filling the cover as large as possible, but still almost invisible – was further mocked by its 9-point small-cap subtitle. Due to the nuanced nature of this white-on-white design, execution was paramount. That happened during a long night on press when we enhanced the whiteness of WHITE PEOPLE by coating it with a clear glossy varnish.

TERRY MCDONELL:

Some people thought it was a mistake. There was a lot of "This is the one that's going to get you fired". Maybe it did. My editors thought it was very cool. Hearst management didn't quite understand it the same way, for obvious reasons.

All the best covers have an element of humour, and the humour here is the line at the bottom, "The Trouble with America". It's a kind of inside joke that the readership would get and identify with. It's tribal: we are smart together, we laugh at the same jokes. Like Bill Buford's cover of *Granta* about "The Family", which had a photograph of an idyllic *Father Knows Best*-like mom and dad and kids[5] with the line "They Fuck You Up". I thought it was wonderful, inspiring.

So I really wanted to do that White People cover. Did it sell? Not so much.

---

1 *See* page 27.
2 US hotel and restaurant chain.
3 Published by Random House in 1992, Richard Ben Cramer's book is regarded as a seminal account of the 1988 presidental election.
4 *Granta* 37, 1 October 1991.
5 A reference to a popular US radio and television sitcom of the 1950s.

esquire

THE MAGAZINE FOR MEN

FEBRUARY 1992·$2.50

WHITE PEOPLE

THE TROUBLE WITH AMERICA

ROLLING STONE

20 AUGUST 1992
Editor and publisher: Jann S Wenner
Art director: Fred Woodward
Photographer: Mark Seliger
Photography director: Laurie Kratochvil
Grooming: Lori Matsushima/Cloutier
Styling: Arianne Phillips/Visage
Cover story by Alan Light

In June 1992 a Texas Law Enforcement Association called CLEAT became aware of the words in "Cop Killer" by Ice-T's speed metal band, Body Count. They were outraged by lines like "I'm 'bout to bust some shots off / I'm 'bout to dust some cops off" and called for a boycott of Time Warner, the record's distributor. The controversy escalated, with high-profile figures such as President George Bush and Vice President Dan Quayle condemning the lyrics.

Ice-T, who wrote the words, defended it as a protest against police brutality: "It's a record about a character. I know the character, I've woken up feeling like this character."[1] All this was happening only two months after Los Angeles had witnessed six days of civil disturbance unleashed by the acquittal of four LAPD officers accused of using excessive force in the arrest of Rodney King.

Mark Seliger suggested putting him in full police uniform for the cover. Ice-T remembers Seliger saying, "This is the ultimate nightmare of a racist cop ... getting pulled over by you and having you have the billy club. It actually did what he said it was going to. It outraged a lot of people."[2] Fred Woodward brilliantly highlighted the tension in the fractured black-and-white typography.

ALAN LIGHT:
Mark and I had dinner the night before and he laid out the idea to me and we talked about whether Ice would go for it. I felt that he would get it, that he was savvy and brave enough to understand the kind of statement the uniform would make. It was provocative, no doubt, but that has always been Ice's game – and it was smart, it wasn't just provocative for its own sake.

MARK SELIGER:
I was working with Arianne, who is all about precision and accuracy.[3] Without her attention to detail – the baton, the cap, the badge, the carefully fitted shirt – the picture wouldn't have had the same kind of emotion.

We decided we wanted a very simple, stripped-out background. I didn't want there to be anything too distracting. We didn't tell Ice-T the idea until he got

Rolling Stone

ISSUE 637 · AUGUST 20TH, 1992 · $2.50 · CAN $2.95

SEARCHING FOR THE NEW NIRVANA

Ice-T Talks Back
(You Got a Problem With That?)

Greenmail in Rio: P.J. O'Rourke at the Earth Summit

ICE-T

there. He walked in and I said, "Want to have some fun?" He was a really warm, lovely guy, not an aloof artist, but very focused, and wanted to know your ideas.

I showed him the cop outfit and he goes, "I'm in," without any hesitation. When he stepped into the uniform, he became the character. He's also an actor, so it was a natural experience for him.

ARIANNE PHILLIPS:

He owned it. He understood the gravitas of how powerful the message would be on the cover of *Rolling Stone*.

MARK SELIGER:

I tried to create a kind of a poignant moment through the lighting. I wanted it to silhouette and the white background really helped that. We used a small light source to make everything drop off. I didn't want the gun to be a main focus. It's a movie gun, of course. We wouldn't bring a real gun to the set. The baton sold you on the idea that, even if they're not pointing a gun on you, they could beat you up.

It was important for me to have an understanding of what Ice-T was saying, so I asked him, "Do you really want to kill cops?" He said, "Look, do people question Bob Dylan when he writes a song about revolution or injustice or how the police and government mishandle power? No."

He likened it to writing a script for a John Ford movie. You don't see somebody going up to John Ford after a sheriff gets murdered in one of his Westerns and calling him a sheriff killer.

Once I'm done, I move on the next photograph. I typically don't follow what the reaction is, but Laurie sent me a handwritten note when she got the image, saying your pictures of Ice-T are absolutely amazing – make sure you duck when the shit hits the fan.

ALAN LIGHT:

Remember that Ice-T had already played a cop in the *New Jack City* movie. As he said in the "Cop Killer" interview, no one pinned a medal on him for presenting an upstanding cop, then they went crazy when he talked about a character wanting revenge on a bad cop.

No doubt the image upset a lot of people. But the thing about Ice-T is that he was up to any intellectual challenge and he knew (and we knew) that he could explain it, answer for it, back it up no matter what debate he might face. That was the secret weapon – he is so good that he didn't need to fear having to explain his decisions, and that's what people weren't ready for.

1   Ice-T to Alan Light, "The Rolling Stone Interview", *Rolling Stone*, 20 August 1992, p.31.
2   *Rolling Stone: Stories from the Edge*, documentary (dir. Alex Gibney and Blair Foster), Sky Arts, November 2017.
3   Arianne Philipps subsequently became a celebrated costume designer and Madonna's stylist for many years. She has been nominated for two Oscars.

HARPER'S BAZAAR

RELAUNCH ISSUE, SEPTEMBER 1992

Editor-in-chief: Elizabeth (Liz) Tilberis
Creative director: Fabien Baron
Cover model: Linda Evangelista
Cover photography: Patrick Demarchelier
Terry McDonell was editor-in-chief of
    Hearst's *Esquire* (1990–3).[1]

In 1992 Hearst lured Liz Tilberis away from British *Vogue* to American *Harper's Bazaar*. Her goal was to make *Bazaar* the most beautiful fashion magazine in the world. And, for a time, she did. She recruited a dream team including Fabien Baron, whose previous work at *New York Woman,* Italian *Vogue* under Franca Sozzani and *Interview* had marked him out as a major international talent. Baron transformed the tired title, reconnecting it to the ground-breaking art direction of Alexey Brodovitch between 1934 and 1958. This was the relaunch issue. *Vogue* took notice: it now had serious competition.

TERRY MCDONELL:

Vogue was going downtown, flirting with grunge. Liz went the opposite direction, cool but without any snobby chill. Fabien was the perfect collaborator. His typography was relentlessly innovative and sophisticated. Just look at the way he unbalanced the logo. Totally modern. By comparison, *Vogue*'s grunged-up models covered with type looked sloppy.

FABIEN BARON:

We felt the time was right for a radical change. We all wanted to do something really memorable, and Liz was ready to push for something new all the way to the cover. Magazine covers were quite busy in those days, covered in type, with complicated pictures, so I felt going simple and direct was the way to go. I liked the idea of a model playing with the logo, maybe tilt a letter to give the idea that *Bazaar* was changing.[2]

It was also her look – Linda's hair, attitude, and the fact that it was shot on a white background with just a single headline, and that Linda was the number-one model at the time. I said to Liz, "Let's make a statement, let's make it clear that it's new." It also came exactly at the time when the fashion message was shifting. Grunge and a new realness were starting, but we were also embracing elegance in a new way. That is what made *Bazaar* so special at the time – that mix of high and low, executed to the nth degree. Everything was controlled, perfected, and finished in a way other magazines had never gone before. You have to remember that when we took the magazine over, *Bazaar* was about "looking good at 40". This cover said, "to hell with all that stuff". It was a breath of fresh air and it became the magazine of reference for the fashion industry.

Bazaar became the perfect competition to *Vogue*. We didn't do it to give Anna [Wintour] a rough time; we just wanted to say something else and there was room to do that. Being more creative and forward was our goal, but that definitely created a war between Condé Nast and us at Hearst. Everybody out there thought we were doing the right thing though.

Liz was an amazing editor and the team visionary. We all loved her, and she understood how to work with people in a way that let them do what they did best.

---

1 McDonell had a pact with Tilberis: she would help him with *Esquire's* fashion; he would help her with "getting on in America".
2 It was also a reference to the December 1959 cover art directed by Henry Wolf featuring a Richard Avedon photograph of the American model Dovima climbing a ladder while carrying the letter "A".

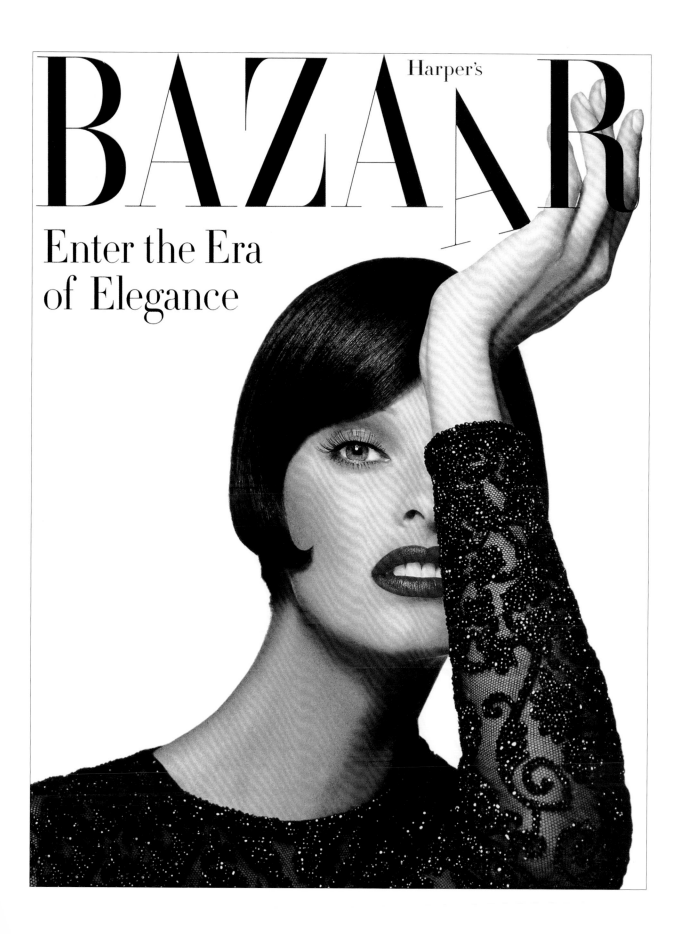

BAZAAR

Harper's

Enter the Era
of Elegance

WIRED

LAUNCH ISSUE, JANUARY 1993

President: Jane Metcalfe

Editor-in-chief/publisher: Louis Rossetto

Executive editor: Kevin Kelly

Creative directors:

John Plunkett & Barbara Kuhr

Cover photography: Neil Selkirk

Former novelist and tech evangelist Louis Rossetto wanted a new kind of magazine that fused 1960s hippie radicalism and libertarianism with his fervent belief in the power of the new digital technology to transform society for the better. He and his partner, Jane Metcalfe, teamed with designers John Plunkett and Barbara Kuhr in 1987 to develop a *Rolling Stone* for the digital age.

JOHN PLUNKETT:

We had high goals, philosophically and creatively. Louis and I had read two books: Stewart Brand's *The Media Lab: Inventing the Future at M.I.T.* and William Gibson's debut novel, *Neuromancer*. If you combine them, you can sort of see the germination of the magazine.

The design was not just me, but also my partner, Barbara Kuhr. When you're going from an old medium to a new one, you have a Catch-22. You have to use the old medium to announce the new one, so it's like the telegraph saying that the telephone is coming. Or ink on paper to announce electrons.

I wanted the cover and front sections to feel like lit-up screens, with text and images that flowed horizontally rather than up and down. I wanted it to look like you were walking into the middle of a conversation. That's what the dot-to-dot ellipsis design is meant to signify: "The Medium..." cover line. McLuhan was a big influence, so for the first issue we used his quote, which happens to be the first sentence of the first paragraph of *The Medium is the Massage*.[1] It's an amazing statement which is still becoming true, and somehow this man wrote it in 1967.

Louis made the great decision to put a writer, Bruce Sterling,[2] on the first cover. This brought up a whole host of challenges. We were trying to focus on the people who were doing extraordinary things. Not on the technology. But it turned out that most of these people were fairly ordinary looking. Bruce was a slightly overweight, mild-mannered, middle-aged white guy. He came in with a suit and tie, but we wanted to make him look as amazing as his work.

I had talked a lot with Neil, the photographer, prior to Bruce's arrival, about what can we do through technique to create an image that's not perfect, that is disjointed, just intermediated in some way. And Neil came up with a very simple device. It was literally some mirrored tiles that you would put on a bathroom wall. But if you fold those over a chair and then photograph someone's reflection in that, it creates the illusion of a "digitized" image.

NEIL SELKIRK:

They were one-inch-square mirrored tiles glued to a fabric so that they can follow a contour. Essentially, you just move the camera backwards and forwards until the person starts looking interesting. It also had the effect of looking pixellated. It was a considered solution to a problem rather than a piece of highly imaginative image making.

JOHN PLUNKETT:

It occurred to me, if we came in close on his eyes, we could say this guy had seen the future of warfare. It was a great story about cyber warfare.

Louis, Kevin and I really did see ourselves as a sort of pirate ship. We shared a belief that – and it differentiated us from most journalists – one should choose to be optimistic. It was a sort of militant optimism despite the best evidence. The magazine was an expression of that.

1   McLuhan's quote continues over the first five editorial pages with horizontal typography by Plunkett, and a "digitized" collage of images collected by him and illustrator Eric Adigard.

2   American science fiction writer whose work helped shape cyberpunk literature.

RAYGUN

JUNE/JULY 1994

Founder, editor-in-chief & publisher:
  Marvin Scott Jarrett
Founder & executive publisher:
  Jaclynn B Jarrett
Art direction & design: David Carson
Executive editor: Randy Bookasta
Cover: "Music and Animals" – three images
  combined in Photoshop and as collage
Photograph of Perry Farrell:
  Melodie McDaniel
Photograph of plane: Dan Conway
Photograph of dog: Jason Lamotte

Taking its name from David Bowie's song "Moonage Daydream",[1] the music monthly emerged in late 1992 at "the height of grunge, the early stages of electronica, and an important time in the development of indie rock", remembers Randy Bookasta.[2] The magazine's look was even more alt. David Carson, top-ranked surfer-turned-designer, unspooled one design convention after another, creating an interface of exuberant drift and decay, a sort of controlled chaos, in stark contrast to newsstand rivals *Spin* and *Rolling Stone*.

MARVIN SCOTT JARRETT:

My idea was to create an alternative music and design magazine that was as disruptive in the print world as MTV had been in television. I loved David Carson's work at *Beach Culture*[3] and thought by bringing him into a music magazine it could be revolutionary.

DAVID CARSON:

I tried never to repeat myself, and don't believe I did. You won't find two covers that look the same, in any respect. I hope all my work, as David Byrne described it, communicates "on a level beyond words ... and goes straight to the part that understands without thinking".[4] The Perry Farrell cover is largely me trying to experiment with layering and things that had become possible with Photoshop, even though I didn't myself use it. It combined some press photos with a portfolio piece someone had sent me. I was trying to use more colour than I normally did. I like the script font I would never have used, and haven't since. I think it kind of fits. I'm using the cover as my canvas, painting with shapes and letters and photos. I like that you can discover things in it and, in its own way, I think it fits the artist and music. What did Perry think of it? I never heard. I rarely did.

RANDY BOOKASTA:

This was a beautiful cover and a great example of David Carson's design taking multiple assets he was provided by our contributors to another level – the cover photo of Perry, illustrations, original fonts. One of our favourite photographers, Melodie McDaniel, took the image of Perry, and she also shot the photos of Trent Reznor inside. Carson actually intertwined both features inside the magazine to unique effect.

1 "Put your ray gun to my head".
2 Email interview with Ian Birch.
3 *Beach Culture* produced only six issues between 1989 and 1991 but won more than 150 design awards for Carson's art direction. In many ways, it was a spawning ground for *Raygun*.
4 David Byrne, 'Introduction', in Lewis Blackwell, *The End of Print: The Grafik Design of David Carson*, Laurence King, 2000.

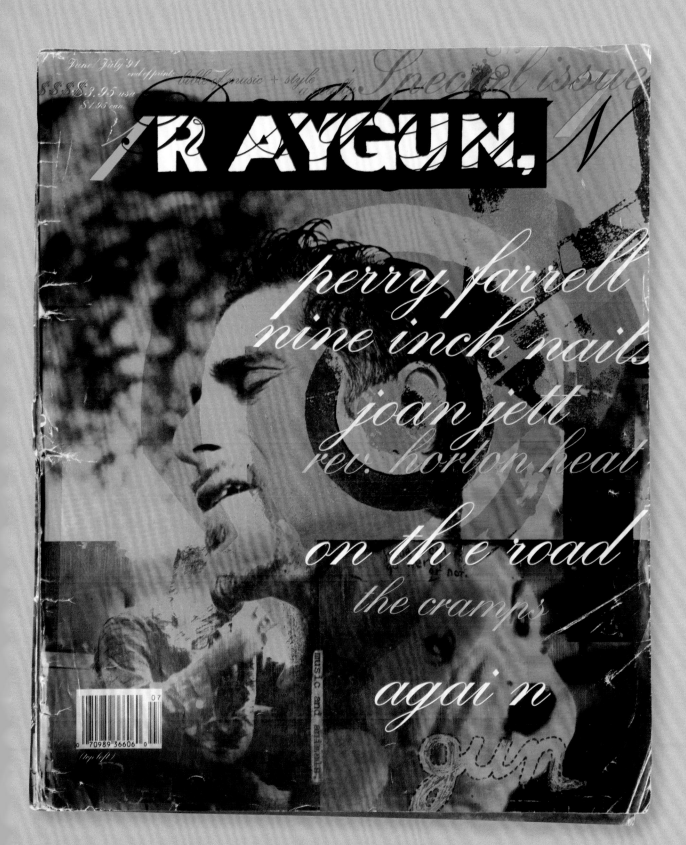

June/July '91 end of print
music + style *Special issue*

$3.95 usa
$4.95 can.

R AYGUN.

perry farrell
nine inch nails
joan jett
rev. horton heat

on th e road
the cramps

agai n

music and animals

0 70989 36606 0   07

(top left)

THE ECONOMIST

10–16 SEPTEMBER 1994

Editor-in-chief: Bill Emmott

Head of graphics: Penny Garrett

Head of picture desk: Celina Dunlop

The Economist has a long and noble history of irreverent covers: this image of "coital camels" was especially notorious. The cover story warned of the dangers lurking in the $210 billion worth of corporate mergers that had been announced so far that year.

BILL EMMOTT:

We may look as if we are part of the establishment, being a kind of high politics and business magazine read by relatively well-off people, but actually we like to stick two fingers up to the establishment on every possible relevant and appropriate occasion.

The camel cover was a strongly held and well-researched piece on the great temptation in business to "go for the deal" which makes the immediate bosses feel strong and proud, but which is not necessarily very good for the company, the shareholders or indeed the employees. I'm sure we could do the same thing now.

CELINA DUNLOP:

We were all sitting in Bill's office. The cover story had been agreed. We pretty quickly got the cover line. Honestly, a vision then just popped into my head, and that's quite troubling when you think it was animals mating.

We look for humour in everything. So it didn't feel like a sackable offence to say to Bill and everyone in the meeting, I see a rather ungainly coupling of ungainly animals – the idea that two companies would awkwardly approach each other and awkwardly merge. To my relief, everyone laughed.

Then it was about finding something that was acceptable because with some animals there's too much on show. We went through hundreds of pictures

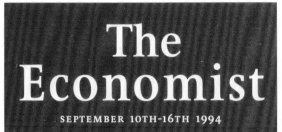

The Economist

SEPTEMBER 10TH–16TH 1994

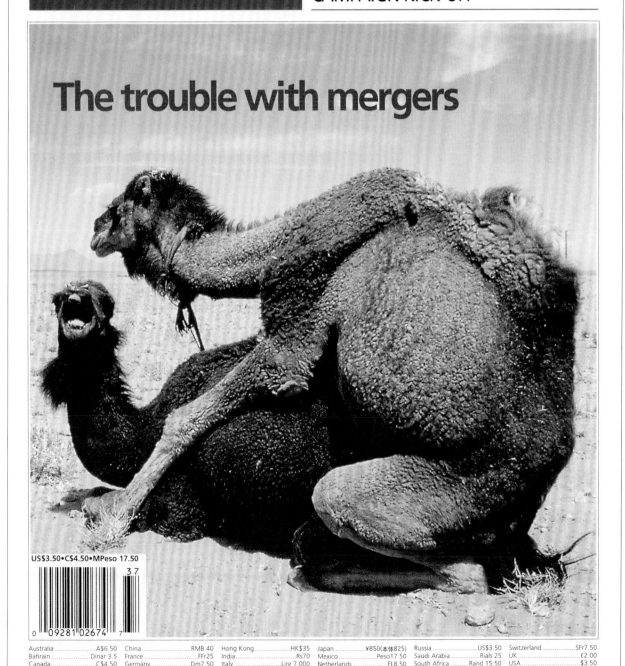

The trouble with mergers

US$3.50•C$4.50•MPeso 17.50

3 7

0   09281 02674   7

Australia ....A$6.50	China ....RMB 40	Hong Kong ....HK$35	Japan ....¥850(本体825)	Russia ....US$3.50	Switzerland...............SFr7.50
Bahrain ....Dinar 3.5	France FFr25	India Rs70	Mexico Peso17.50	Saudi Arabia...............Rials 25	UK £2.00
Canada ....C$4.50	Germany Dm7.50	Italy ....Lire 7,000	Netherlands FL8.50	South Africa ....Rand 15.50	USA $3.50

of animals copulating. We ended up with camels because they were nicely discreet. They could almost be hugging each other.

BILL EMMOTT:

It went out on the Thursday night and I must admit I suddenly thought, "I wonder how this will go down." Being the way time zones work, the first message I got came from Singapore. I remember thinking, "Uh-oh, Lee Kuan Yew[1] will be giving me a caning for this." But it was from a reader there saying it was the funniest thing that they'd seen in a long time. So I got an immediate lift from a surprising source.

As we went around the world, the most divided view we got was from America, where some people thought it was absolutely hilarious and others thought it was disgusting, blasphemous – well, not *blasphemous* but impure, if you like, and generally beneath the dignity of a supposedly serious magazine. A sort of "Outraged of Louisville, Kentucky".

CELINA DUNLOP:

We had a massive postbag. The response was completely 50/50. There were the "antis" who said, "I couldn't leave this out in front of my children or my clients." One of my favourites was, "The female camel is obviously in pain." The self-appointed feminists said, "How can you possibly depict this ravishment of a female camel?" I wrote back, "I'm not expert enough to know if that's a look of bliss or pain." On the other hand, other people said, "Can I have 14 copies because I want to give it to all my clients."

---

1 The first prime minister of Singapore. In 1994 he was "Senior Minister".

WALLPAPER*

**LAUNCH ISSUE, SEPTEMBER/
OCTOBER 1996**

Editor-in-chief: Tyler Brûlé
Art director: Herbert Winkler
Photographer: Stewart Shining
Fashion stylist: Anne-Marie Curtis
Prop stylist: Michael Reynolds
Tony Chambers joined Wallpaper* as creative
    director in 2003, editor-in-chief in 2007
    and then brand and content director in 2017.

In March 1994 Tyler Brûlé, a Canadian journalist based in the UK, was investigating a story in Afghanistan when he was shot in a sniper attack. While recovering from surgery back in London he hit on the idea for *Wallpaper** and launched it two years later. He gave voice to a style-savvy and entrepreneurial tribe he called "global nomads". *Wallpaper** became a gathering place for a new kind of cool that combined fashion, interiors and travel.

STEWART SHINING:

Tyler described [*Wallpaper**] as a kind of marriage between those independent British magazines like *The Face* and *i-D*, which we grew up on, and traditional American magazines like *Vogue* and *Bazaar*, which were the gold standard. Tom Ford had just come in with Gucci, and that was a big visual moment across the board, fashion-wise and design-wise.[1] That's why the models are in Gucci.

ANNE-MARIE CURTIS:

The dress was photographed without the belt because it didn't arrive. I am one of the few people who know that. I thought, "Is Gucci going to be upset?" but they loved it.

STEWART SHINING:

I, or my agent, asked what the budget was. In those days, that was less an issue. People just had lots of money. Tyler said, "Here's the hitch. We don't really have much money." So we had to do it on a nickel and a prayer. Tyler and Anne-Marie came to New York for the shoot. I'd never seen people so resourceful.

ANNE-MARIE CURTIS:

There was a lot of hustling behind the scenes. There definitely was this duality between how we were doing it and the world we were presenting.

TYLER BRÛLÉ:

When you look back at that cover, in a way it's provocative. We wanted to say this is a magazine that reflected the urbanization we were seeing. The 1970s and 1980s had been about this great flight to the suburbs and we saw the hollowing out of cities in Australia and Europe and North America. This was for people who wanted to be back in town. We wanted to say that in a way that was slick and modern and had a slight nod to the core audience who were born in the early 1970s. There was this world of shelter magazines out there, like *World of Interiors* and *Elle Decoration*, but this had to say fashion as well. And we wanted to speak to a dual audience. Guys should be included.

Culture went to some very dark places then, like heroin chic, but we always wanted to be that constant on the horizon which was sunny and positive and our own place.

TONY CHAMBERS:

It was a brilliant concept – the conflation of fashion and lifestyle, architecture and design. That's what made it sexy. It was ahead of its time then but now is completely mainstream.

1   Gucci, under new creative director Tom Ford, had seen a
    90 per cent sales increase between 1995 and 1996.

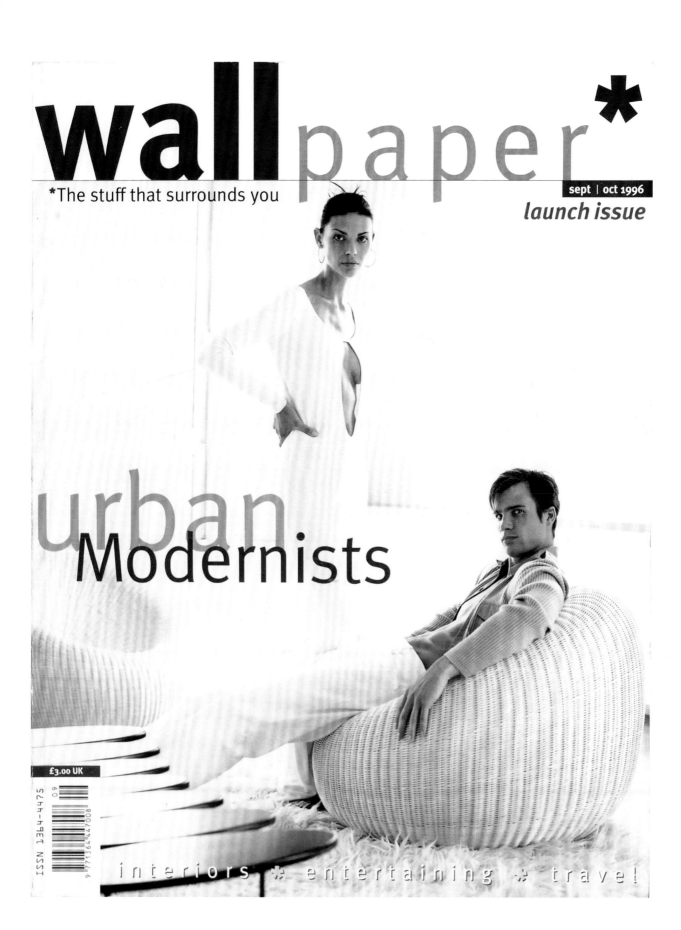

wallpaper*

*The stuff that surrounds you

sept | oct 1996
launch issue

urban
Modernists

£3.00 UK

ISSN 1364-4475

09

9 771364 447008

interiors ✳ entertaining ✳ travel

PRIVATE EYE

5 SEPTEMBER 1997

Editor: Ian Hislop

"The Diana cover was extremely controversial, to put it mildly."[1]

IAN HISLOP:

I wanted to suggest that there was an hypocrisy on the part of all of us in our attitude to her. We had consumed photographs, stories, information about her and, at the moment of her death, not only a lot of journalists but also a lot of the general public did an enormous volte-face and turned her into a saint. They started policing other people's levels of grief and were saying, "Well, how bad do you feel? You should feel much worse." They decided that the media were to blame again before they knew whether they were or not.

Then the issue was withdrawn. WH Smith decided they weren't going to sell it. It was in bad taste – which was not their call. Legal issues are bad enough but the magazine largely disappeared.[2] A lot of people just didn't want to sell it. We had to fight to get it back on sale.

We've never had such vitriol from people. They said, "You scumbags, why don't you crawl back under a rock and die?" "You should be strung up." "You are all utterly callous, emotionally crippled public-school twats." You know, fill in the description.

It was one of those periodic outbursts of hysteria, and it made no sense. Francis Wheen, who's the *Eye*'s most brilliant analyst, wrote a piece that morning called "The Mourning Papers" about what Fleet Street had been saying about Diana the week before. Things like "What is this woman doing? Nothing. Wasting her time in a bikini with some Arab playboy in the Mediterranean" and "Doesn't even look after her kids, they're at boarding school all of the time". A week later, she was Mother Teresa. It was a staggering bit of bullshit on the part of the media. They were either in symbiosis with the public or they were following the public, but we didn't join in.

Earl Spencer stood up and berated the surviving parent of two boys whose mother has just been killed saying, "The Windsors are unsuitable to look after you; blood is thicker, etc." He never looked after them at all and he was never going to. They both like their father, and they went and lived with him, unsurprisingly. It was rabble-rousing shite but he got a cheer from outside the funeral. I thought it was a really disgraceful performance by him. It was old-fashioned sort of Tudor aristocratic feuding. He's a shocker.

The royal family were in real trouble. They'd misjudged the mood to start with, they played it in the way they do, aloof and indifferent, trying to carry on as normal, and that wasn't working. But the funeral – the march – saved them because the most emotional part of the whole thing was two small boys in suits walking behind a coffin. Not weeping. Not singing "Candle in the Wind". But doing what we essentially sort of want upper-class British males to do, which is to survive.

Any regrets? Not at all. I didn't feel we traduced anyone or anyone's memory. Sometimes being the little boy who says "There aren't any clothes on" is quite uncomfortable. But, you know, it's the job.

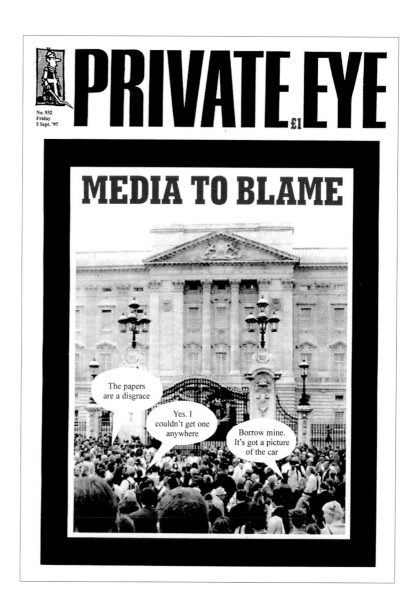

1 Ian Hislop in interview with Ian Birch.
2 Newsstand sales fell by a third.

BLUE

**LAUNCH ISSUE
OCTOBER 1997**

Publisher/Editor-in-chief: Amy Schrier
Design consultant: David Carson
Cover photography: Laura Levine

Founded in February 1996 by Amy Schrier, New York-based *blue*[1] was an independent lifestyle bi-monthly aimed at the growing interest in adventure travel, cultural exploration and action sports. "The name," says Schrier, "was intended to invoke the associations of blue sky, blue sea and blue planet."[2] Schrier was joined in July by designer David Carson, who had left *Raygun* in 1995 to start his own studio.

AMY SCHRIER:

Bringing David on as co-founder and creative director was probably the most important strategic move *blue* made because it highlighted how important design was going to be in the identity of the magazine. My attraction to his work was what he had done with surfing, snowboarding and skateboarding magazines[3] where his design conveyed the sense of freedom one experiences while doing the activities on the printed page. I wanted him to bring that sense of freedom to travel. We wanted *blue* to be as iconoclastic in the adventure travel field as *Raygun* was in music.

I interpreted the cover as jumping into the unknown, which is what we were doing and also what we imagined our readers were doing in their own travels. The cover image was actually part of a series. We ran three other Laura Levine images of people jumping in the water as full right-hand pages in the front of the magazine. That in itself was unique.

LAURA LEVINE:

My photograph on the cover as well as the three inside were all self-generated, personal fine art photographs conceived and created by me in 1984, years before I ever showed them to David Carson – or anyone else, for that matter. It was not an assignment, nor a collaboration, nor did the concept for the photo originate with an art director.

I happened to be at Jones Beach to shoot a Cyndi Lauper concert for *The New York Times* later that night. I arrived early to hang out by the pool. I was fascinated watching people of all ages, shapes, and sizes jumping off the diving board in a variety of styles and techniques. I visualized shooting a series of unconventional, surreal, minimalistic photographs capturing the divers/jumpers in flight; unusual compositions created in the camera by cropping out body parts in order to produce mysterious images depicting the subjects as

a journal for the new traveler

blue

premiere issue

72 >

0   71896 49430   3

$3.95 display until october 15, 1997

semi-abstract shapes frozen in mid-air against only sky, with no context or reference point as to up or down and no sense of where they were coming from or headed. Total freedom.

These were not professional athletes but regular New Yorkers. For each of them who dared take the leap, there was that one moment, frozen by my camera in mid-air, when they were flying, just like Superman or Supergirl. I achieved this by carefully composing each image in the viewfinder, anticipating each diver's trajectory, and most importantly, intentionally framing and cropping each airborne subject in the camera at the moment I clicked the shutter. I did not have a motor drive so I only took one frame per person. I took one roll of film – 37 images. I used black-and-white film simply because that's what I usually shot, printed and showed. After developing the film, I was pleased to see that practically every frame succeeded in conveying my artistic intent .

Several years later, while making portfolio rounds in LA, I included the contact sheet when showing my book to David Carson at *Beach Culture* in order to propose doing a swimwear fashion spread shot in a similar style. I showed him the contact sheet to give him an idea of what I had in mind, a template of sorts of my concept. He asked if he could hold on to the contact sheet, and that was that.

Several years after that, Carson asked me to print up several of the frames on the contact sheet as a possible cover for *blue*. The cover became one of my cropped-in-camera photos as a full bleed with minimal type and no manipulation. I was very pleased with it and his hands-off approach in running the image as is, respecting the original concept of the mysterious figure flying through the air and whose head I'd cropped out of the frame in that 250th of a second. He used a lovely simple font for the four letters: b l u e. It ran pretty much as I'd intended it to be seen when I first conceived of and shot it.

DAVID CARSON:

This is one of my all time favorite covers. Pretty gutsy for a new mag, but the photo did all that was needed.

LAURA LEVINE:

In 2005, it was named one of ASME's "Top Forty Magazine Covers of the Last Forty Years". Although I was not recognized for my role as the creator of the image, I'm pleased that the cover was honoured.

Figure 10 *Divers, Jones Beach, NY, 1984.* Photographed by and © Laura Levine.

1 This issue can be viewed online (along with the entire seven-year magazine archive) at www.bluemagazine.com.
2 Amy Schrier in interview with Ian Birch.
3 They were *Transworld Skateboarding, Beach Culture* and *Surfer*.

2000s

THE NEW YORK TIMES MAGAZINE

8 JUNE 2000

Editor: Adam Moss

Creative director: Janet Froelich

Director of photography: Kathy Ryan

Cover photography: Christopher Anderson

Cover story: Michael Finkel

In 2000 record numbers of Haitians tried to enter America illegally, usually by boat, first to the Bahamas, and from there to Florida. Writer Michael Finkel and photographer Christopher Anderson wanted to document the voyage and persuaded captain Gilbert Marko to take them on his inadequately equipped vessel. "Our trip, it appeared, had all the makings of a suicide mission."[1]

CHRISTOPHER ANDERSON:

I remember the moment Gilbert loaded up the boat. We were told there was going to be something like 25 people. We started counting and when we get to 46 people, we were like, "Wow …".

When we finally set sail, there was a ceremony on the top deck: songs, prayers and a chicken was sacrificed. Gilbert came down into the hold where we were hidden and sprinkled perfume water everywhere. There was a little locked cabinet in the hold, and every so often he would spray perfume in there too, say a couple of prayers, and then turn around and say, "Nobody go in there."

It was unbelievably hot in the hold. We were stacked literally on top of each other, knees to our chest. You think flying economy across the Atlantic is uncomfortable … Everything hurt: you felt nauseous from the smell and the dehydration. But the discomfort was far outweighed by the fear.

Up until this point, I really hadn't taken many pictures. I was trying to be very, very judicious about how and when I chose to make them. The act of photographing is a delicate intrusion. For the cover picture, it was the middle of the night and the water was coming up around our ankles. We realized we were sinking and felt this sheer terror that the end had come. David[2] said to me, "Chris, you better start taking pictures now because we're all going be dead in an hour." And so, sort of mechanically, without thinking about it, I made that picture.

The American Coast Guard picked us up before daybreak. They pulled a Zodiac boat up beside ours to transfer people off. They shouted to Mike and me, "Jump!" We had to know what was in that cabinet, so we dove back down into the boat which was now partially submerged and bust open the lock. Inside, we found a Vodou altar and flags. The Haitians have these embroidered Vodou flags of different spirits. They're quite beautiful. We grabbed them as souvenirs and then jumped down onto the Zodiac boat. I didn't get a picture of the inside of the cabinet. Man, I wish I had.

We were saved but I was in a sheer panic, thinking how can I go back to Kathy? I had only six rolls of film. One of them was the roll that I burned as the boat was sinking. It didn't dawn on me at the time that we didn't need 50 pictures. All we needed were the three pictures that they published.

I have thought about this for a long time: why did I make pictures of that moment when I assumed that we were all going to perish and my pictures would perish with me? There was probably a degree of doing something just to keep me occupied. But there was something more. The act of photographing was about my experience as much as the subject's experience. If there is a sense of terror communicated in that image, it's because that's what I was experiencing.

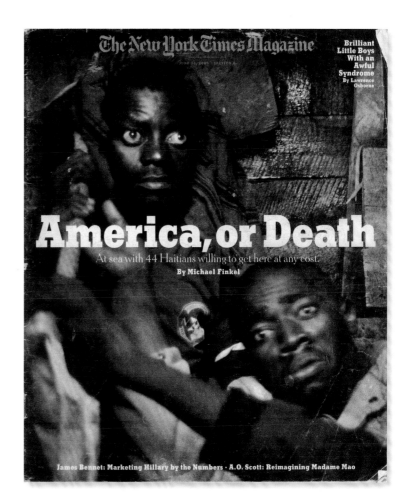

1 Michael Finkel, "Desperate Passage', *The New York Times Magazine*, 18 June 2000.
2 David, a Haitian migrant, acted as their guide and translator. He is bottom right on the cover.

9/11
THE NEW YORK TIMES MAGAZINE

23 SEPTEMBER 2001

Editor: Adam Moss

Art director: Janet Froelich

Photo editor: Kathy Ryan

Cover: "Phantom Towers", conceived by
Paul Myoda and Julian LaVerdiere; original
photograph by Fred R Conrad/The New
York Times; digital manipulation by *The
New York Times*

On the morning of 11 September 2001 Adam Moss realized that "this is not just an awful event, it's an historical awful event".[1] He asked the team to envision what readers would want to think about nearly two weeks later, when the next issue would come out. He suggested to Janet Froelich that she contact artists and architects for ideas for a memorial, "but most of them", *The New York Times Magazine* then art director remembers, "were too stunned to even consider it."[2] However, artists Paul Myoda and Julian LaVerdiere, who had already been working on an illuminated public sculpture[3] to mount atop the radio tower of World Trade Center 1, suggested "Phantom Towers", the concept that would evolve into the cover of the magazine, and subsequently New York City's annual memorial, "Tribute in Light".

JANET FROELICH:

When we arrived at the magazine that Tuesday morning we thought 30,000 people were dead. We were all grateful that it was one zero less. You had this almost physical pressure on you, the appalling grey dust cloud over Lower Manhattan. I think we all went into a kind of overdrive. You have to rise up out of your own horror and make sense of it on a wider cultural level.

Paul and Julian had been working on a project using beams projected off the top of the building like radio waves. When I went to see them about a memorial, they had this stunning idea of shining two beams up into the heavens from the spot where the Towers had been destroyed, and they sketched it for us (Figure 11).

PAUL MYODA AND JULIAN LAVERDIERE:

We initially did some brainstorming sketches with pencil and paper. We then found an online image of the towers from Jersey City [on the opposite side of the Hudson river], which had been taken after the buildings had come down, and made a version with Photoshop. We simply sculpted that horrific cloud of smoke, which was illuminated because of the rescue effort, into the shape of the Twin Towers. This is when we knew we had the image we wanted. It honestly frightened us because of its strange, ghostly power. At this time we came up with the title of Phantom Towers, because it reminded us of the phenomenon

The New York Times Magazine

SEPTEMBER 23, 2001 / SECTION 6

Remains of the Day By Richard Ford Colson Whitehead Richard Powers Robert Stone James Traub Stephen King Jennifer Egan
Roger Lowenstein Judith Shulevitz Randy Cohen William Safire Andrew Sullivan Jonathan Lethem Michael Lewis Margaret Talbot Charles McGrath
Walter Kirn Deborah Sontag Allan Gurganus Michael Ignatieff Kurt Andersen Jim Dwyer Michael Tolkin Matthew Klam Sandeep Jauhar Lauren Slater
Richard Rhodes Caleb Carr Fred R. Conrad Joju Yasuhide Angel Franco Joel Sternfeld Katie Murray Steve McCurry Carolina Salguero Lisa Kereszi
Jeff Mermelstein William Wendt Andres Serrano Richard Burbridge Paul Myoda Julian LaVerdiere Taryn Simon Kristine Larsen

of the phantom limb – something that is so obviously missing and absent, yet still feels so undeniably present.

JANET FROELICH:

Their project immediately felt like a potential cover. But we had to find a way to make it more than a manipulated skyline photograph. I wanted to convey the mournful quality of the light, the haunting power of the beams. I went through literally hundreds of images of the skyline, but most were lacking that ethereal quality. When I found the Fred Conrad photo (Figure 12), I knew we had the right image. Fred had been on a barge in the Hudson River shooting the wounded area of Lower Manhattan. There was a dust cloud and it was moving, as clouds do, horizontally across the skyline, illuminated perhaps by the moonlight in the cloudless sky.

We brought the image to Nucleus, a digital house we often used, and asked them to make that dust cloud vertical, and to add its reflection in the river. We worked with them for hours to get it right. As the image came together, I knew we had our cover. I phoned my editor, Adam Moss, and he came by to see it. He agreed.

PAUL MYODA AND JULIAN LAVERDIERE:

The image was first posted online, several days before the print version came out. During this time, we saw so many different responses, including many people who tried to politicize the image. Once it became public knowledge that we were working to transition the virtual image into an actual installation, Mayor Rudy Giuliani suggested we make the lights red, white and blue, to represent the firefighters, police and armed forces. We firmly stated we would never agree to this, for the politicization of the Tribute in Light was something we were always strongly against, and stated so publicly whenever we were given the chance. The artistic intent of the project was not to make an American gesture – people from over 90 countries were killed on that day – but rather, we wanted to create beacons of hope for the survivors and beacons of peace for those who perished.

JANET FROELICH:

The Municipal Art Society and Creative Time worked together to make this idea a reality. Every September in the night sky you see it – those twin beams of light shining into the sky from near Ground Zero. It is the most significant news story I was ever privileged to have been involved with.

Figure 11 Paul Myoda and Julian LaVerdiere, Proposal for "Phantom Towers".

Figure 12 Fred Conrad, View of the New York skyline from the Hudson River.

---

1 Kathy Ryan (ed.), *The New York Times Magazine Photographs*, Aperture Foundation, 2011, p.250.
2 Ibid.
3 It was called the *Bioluminescent Beacon*.

9/11
THE NEW YORKER

24 SEPTEMBER 2001

Editor: David Remnick

Art editor: Françoise Mouly

Cover credit: "9/11/2001" by
   Art Spiegelman & Françoise Mouly

"One of the realities of that day, for myself and for everybody I know, was the blue sky," recalls Françoise Mouly. "It was so difficult because it was such a beautiful day."[1] Mouly and Art Spiegelman had just left their SoHo apartment when they saw the first plane plough into the North Tower. Their immediate instinct was to grab their children from school. Their teenage daughter was at Stuyvesant High School, a few blocks from the Towers. After some difficulty, they found her "and the three of us watched the second tower fall in excruciating slow motion".[2] They turned uptown to get their younger son. Back home, David Remnick had called: he wanted a new cover. Mouly had overseen *The New Yorker*'s covers since 1993, but this one became a wife-and-husband collaboration. It "conveyed something about the abrupt tear in the fabric of reality",[3] she later wrote. It was a tear echoed on the cover, as the North Tower's antenna chops into the "W" of the logo.

FRANÇOISE MOULY:

I had to go into work to do the cover but I didn't want to leave my kids because we were in the part of the city that was quarantined. A friend of mine agreed to stay with them.

I was in complete despair. This was too vast. Nothing seemed adequate. It just seemed so impossible to try to respond to something that was so overwhelming. I said to David the only thing that will work is a black cover, just no cover. He was talking about using a photograph, which would, of course, have had news value because photographs weren't ever used on the cover. Art was not quite as desperate. He was making an image[4] which didn't work and which David hadn't expressed much interest in, but he wasn't giving up on it.

When I told Art that I was considering a black cover, he suggested adding in the two towers, black on black. That made sense to me because it was a double negative, the kind of image that would actually express its own negation. I remember the moment of drawing it and seeing it on the screen and going, "Oh my God, it works." It was difficult to explain why, because it was so subtle, so liminal. It was in between being there and not being there.

We heard on the grapevine that another magazine was considering doing a black cover so we weren't sure for a moment if we could go ahead with ours. But then it was back on.

I was extremely grateful that everybody was willing to go with something as fragile and borderline as this. I hoped readers would not rebel or say, "I don't get it." The image was signed by Art[5] and I remember one reader, who didn't see the black-on-black writing, wrote, "Does Art Spiegelman think he owns black?"

I worked very hard with the pre-press and production people. The guy I worked with a lot, Greg Captain, was stranded in Chicago and, because there were no flights, he had to drive back 14 hours to New York. I couldn't have explained what I was after by phone or email. I showed him the kind of effect I wanted – something that was the essence of fine art like Malevich's *White on White* or Ad Reinhardt's "black" paintings. Without catching up on his sleep, Greg then drove another 12 hours to the plant in Kentucky. They had to be the right blacks.

The image elicited an intense reaction from readers. Scores said they were touched and brought to tears. In many instances, they received the magazine as a subscription. They'd see the black cover, put it down, have breakfast, and, not right away but an hour or two later, the outline of the towers would jump out at them as they were seeing the magazine from a different angle. Then, it was like seeing a ghost.

I made a vow, and it wasn't true for my husband but it was for me and my children, that we wouldn't watch any of the footage on TV. It was breached a year later, on September 11 2002 when my daughter was in the same school and the teacher turned on the TV and made them watch the footage. I thought that was insensitive and cruel.

1 Interview with Ian Birch.
2 Françoise Mouly, *Blown Covers: New Yorker covers you were never meant to see*, Abrams, 2012, p.15.
3 Ibid.
4 Spiegelman's unused image "contrasted the lovely fall weather of that day with the horrible event that happened, with the towers covered in a Christo-like black shroud against a Magritte-style blue sky". Sourced from Jeet Heer, "The Uncredited Collaboration behind The New Yorker's Iconic 9/11 Cover", *The Atlantic*, 11 September 2013.
5 For personal and magazine policy reasons, the cover was originally credited only to Spiegelman. Jeet Heer tells the full story in his article for *The Atlantic* (*see* note 4).

PRICE $3.50

SEPT. 24, 2001

THE NEW YORKER

9/11
ARENA HOMME+

**WITHDRAWN COVER, AUTUMN/
WINTER 2001/2002
PUBLISHED COVER, AUTUMN/WINTER
2001/2002**

Editor-in-chief & design director:
　Fabien Baron
Fashion editor: Karl Templar
Cover photography: Steven Klein
Editorial director: Ashley Heath

The year 2001 was a big one for boy band *NSYNC, but its star attraction, Justin Timberlake, was itching to head in a more adult R&B direction. Repositioning his image began with the men's fashion bi-annual *Arena Homme+,* which Nick Logan had launched in 1994 as a competitor to *L'Uomo Vogue* and *Vogue Hommes Paris.*

FABIEN BARON:

Repackaging Justin Timberlake? Why not? Justin was at a turning point in his career, and probably at the time of the shoot, if you ask me, already thinking of leaving *NSYNC to go solo. We thought we needed to do something very different from the pretty boy Justin, something much cooler, more dangerous, less expected. At the time I was working a lot with Steven Klein so he was my first choice of photographer. We had already done a very successful shoot together with David Beckham,[1] so it felt like a natural choice and the vibe was a mix of American youth meets suburbia meets sexuality. Justin was really into it, he was very easy to work with.

　　After the shoot, when Steven and I looked at the pictures, I thought we should put an American flag in the logo. We were in The Hamptons, at Steven's place, looking at the prints and I said, "Should we burn them and see what happens?" Steven was into it, so we poured gasoline on the prints, set them on fire and quickly put out the flames when we thought it looked interesting. I remember Steven's assistant freaking out. He had spent so much time printing out these final prints we were destroying. We picked one we liked and I thought, "That's really decadent."

The magazine came out exactly on September 11, and that's when I realized the cover was in such poor taste. And the cover line, "Hit Me Baby One More Time", was so wrong. I got on the phone with the president at EMAP, and basically convinced him we should recall the magazine and do a new cover.

I look back at it now, and I still think it was a great cover. We were just unlucky with the timing. Justin was moving from one place to another and that's when the best covers happen.

ASHLEY HEATH:

Steven said to me that it was going to be the rebirth, destruction and resurrection of Justin. He wanted to do something fairly hardcore like a boxer who had been beaten up in the ring. Justin's management knew what they were getting, much as David Beckham's people knew when they came to us. We were very good at reinvention. Beckham was a wow cover at the time and it's almost become a formula now – "Let's take a footballer and make him look a bit homoerotic."

That was a really tough 48 hours. Steven immediately messaged me saying the magazine cannot come out. Fabien felt the same. There was resistance at first from our owners, EMAP, to reprint because of the cost. We didn't have any reserves of the beautiful German 120g gloss paper that we used. Fabien talked very convincingly with senior EMAP management, who said they would reprint. To EMAP's credit, they took the financial hit of at least £100,000. The order was to pulp all the issues. It was such a shame. It was almost like KLF torching £1 million except this was £100,000. I kept a few boxes of issues.

It was reprinted on different stock and the cover had a picture from the same session. It was a nice cover, but I always felt the replacement was like flipping a record and making the B-side the A-side. But the right decision was made.

1   The David Beckham in underpants cover, *Arena Homme+*, Autumn/Winter 2000.

HOMME
ARENA+

Justin Timberlake:
Hit Me Baby One More Time
Going Underground
2002 New Fashion Riot

£4.50

9 771353 197013

HOMME

ARENA+

Justin Timberlake
Streets Ahead of the Game
Going Underground
2002 New Fashion Spirit
380 Pages of Red Hot Style

£4.50

771353 197013

1 2>

ENTERTAINMENT WEEKLY

2 MAY 2003

Managing editor: Rick Tetzeli

Cover photographer: James White

Dixie Chicks (left to right): Emily Robison, Natalie Maines, Martie Maguire

Dixie Chicks publicist: Cindi Berger

On 10 March 2003 the Dixie Chicks kicked off their "Top of the World" tour at London's Shepherds Bush Empire. Singer Natalie Maines introduced their song "Travelin' Soldier" with these words: "Just so you know, we're on the good side with y'all. We do not want this war, this violence, and we're ashamed that the President of the United States is from Texas."

Betty Clarke reproduced part of this quote in her review of the concert,[1] which appeared in the *Guardian* two days later. American media outlets pounced and the backlash was ferocious. Right-wing commentators hurled slurs like "Traitors", "the Dixie Sluts" and "Saddam's Angels". The band received death threats. On 20 March 2003 the United States, Britain and several coalition allies invaded Iraq. Two months later Maguire told *Entertainment Weekly*, "We wanted to show the absurdity of the extreme names people have been calling us. How do you look at the three of us and think, those are Saddam's Angels?"[2]

Rick Tetzeli would later say: "At certain times, entertainment can speak to the culture at large, and this cover tapped into the widespread anger over George W Bush's disastrous Iraq adventure. After the Dixie Chicks stated their opposition to that war at a concert in Europe, they were vilified by many – including the US ambassador to Britain – as unpatriotic. The cover image was a ringing endorsement of their right to speak their minds, and in the end, of course, they were proved right: what their president had done was simply tragic."[3]

JAMES WHITE:

The shoot took place in a warehouse in Texas close to where they live and there was no paparazzi around. The first idea was that they would be nude, wrapped around an American flag. But as the shoot began to evolve in preproduction, they wanted to have bumper stickers of the slogans made and put them on their bodies. I thought, "This is not going to look good because they will get wrinkly, and you won't be able to read them clearly."

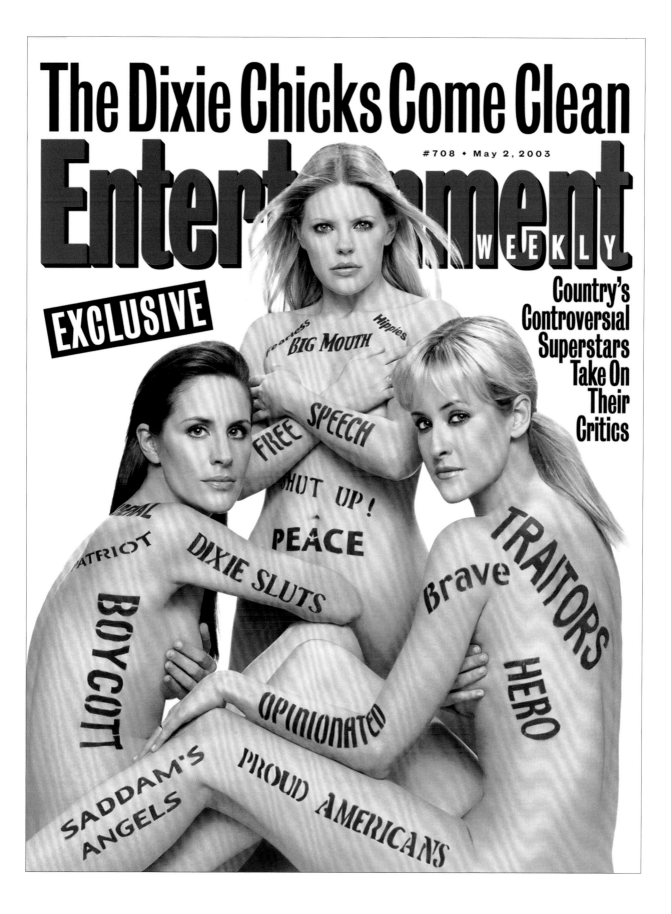

The Dixie Chicks Come Clean

#708 • May 2, 2003

Entertainment WEEKLY

EXCLUSIVE

Country's Controversial Superstars Take On Their Critics

I really pushed the idea of body paint,[4] which is a laborious process. It takes a long time and you have to figure out exactly where the words are going because there can only be one pose. So, everything had to be mapped out but we got it done really quickly. Within three or four hours everyone had their slogans on.

Cindi Berger, their publicist, was there and they had these intense conversations. The girls had been called a lot of vicious things, and they wanted to show that they weren't OK with this – at all. Every single word was taken seriously in terms of how it could be perceived and what was going to happen if they did write it. All three of them were equally as committed and passionate about doing this.

I definitely thought the cover was going to be controversial, for sure, but the one thing that caught me off guard was how much the photograph was imitated – most of it was tongue-in-cheek, which I like. It was a serious topic and to take it that step further and induce some humour is good.

1 Betty Clarke, "The Dixie Chicks", the *Guardian*, 12 March 2003.
2 Chris Willman, "The Dixie Chicks Take on Their Critics", *Entertainment Weekly*, 2 May 2003.
3 "EW's former editors share their favorite and least favorite covers over the years", *Entertainment Weekly*, 12 October 2015. Reproduced with the kind permission of Rick Tetzeli. http://ew.com/article/2015/10/12/ew-former-editors-favorite-least-favorite-covers/
4 Body painter Tara Meadows was on set as a back-up. Just as well as the shipment of bumper stickers didn't arrive.

THE NEW YORKER

21 JULY 2008

Editor: David Remnick

Art editor: Françoise Mouly

Cover illustration: "The Politics of Fear"
    by Barry Blitt

In the run-up to November 2008's presidential election, Barry Blitt's drawing for the cover for the 21 July issue of *The New Yorker* unleashed an inferno of protest from almost every constituency. Obama campaign spokesman Bill Burton dismissed it as "tasteless and offensive".[1] Republican John McCain thought it "totally inappropriate".[2] There were over 10,000 emails and letters of protest; conservative talk radio was apoplectic. David Remnick quickly responded: "The fact is, it's *not* a satire about Obama – it's a satire about the distortions and misconceptions and prejudices *about* Obama."[3]

Blitt's first sketch (Figure 13) also had Michelle Obama as a Muslim and showed conservative commentators Ann Coulter, Bill O'Reilly and Rush Limbaugh at a window looking horrified "at their 'worst nightmare'". "But it didn't seem correct to attribute the prejudices and hidden fears to only those three pundits, so I asked Barry to refine the image to its essence," Françoise Mouly later explained.[4] Blitt agreed: "It was a purer statement without them."[5]

BARRY BLITT:

I got a thousand emails right away, and that was very unpleasant. I sort of did have an idea that it would create a furore. I had the sketch at home, and a few people I showed it to thought I was crazy. I brought the artwork into *The New Yorker*'s office, which I don't always do, and I walked with Françoise over to the production people. You could see everybody was uncomfortable with it. It seemed like career suicide. David and Françoise were 100 per cent behind it. We all thought it would be immediately understood and that its intent was obvious. It was trying to depict all the innuendo that people were saying, to present how ridiculous it was.

The tide actually turned with *The Daily Show*'s coverage.[6] Before that, it was all hate mail I was getting, and after that I started to get a lot of good email. Either that or the haters got it out of their system right away. Obviously, all of those clips [on *The Daily Show*] were the point of the cover.

FRANÇOISE MOULY:

We were taken to task for not having a caption or a title on the cover to explain it. There was an outpouring of outrage from faithful readers who said, "I understand that you're being ironic. I am sophisticated enough to know that you mean it in jest, but I worry that others will lack that sophistication and will take it literally."

Satire has an object and the problem was that it was not shown here in an obvious way. Because the object of the satire is you, the reader. That's what made people so uncomfortable. Our lack of labelling made it hit home because it's asking, "Are you saying that this is what I am projecting?" The most threatening covers are those that are like mirrors of your prejudice. You see something you recognize.

I'm eternally grateful to David Remnick for having had the *noblesse* to stand up to the opprobrium. I mean, he was called a Nazi by Wolf Blitzer on television but he never offered a retraction or an apology, and now he can be very proud of that. But it wasn't easy at the time to stand by the image. I believe that part of the reason we have been able to publish images that stand the test of time is because they're offered without apologies. If we had to worry that we might have to retract an image, then you don't even try, you know?

Figure 13 Barry Blitt's first drawing for the cover of the 21 July 2008 issue of *The New Yorker*.

1 Sourced from http://www.nbcnews.com/id/25673296/ns/politics-decision_08/t/magazines-satirical-cover-stirs-controversy/#.Wbf1vYqQyuU

2 Ibid.

3 Rachel Sklar, "David Remnick on that New Yorker Cover: It's Satire, Meant to Target 'Distortions and Misconceptions and Prejudices' about Obama", *Huffington Post*, 21 July 2006.

4 Françoise Mouly, *Blown Covers: New Yorker Covers You Were Never Meant to See*, Abrams, 2012, p.57.

5 Interview with Ian Birch.

6 The satirical news show on Comedy Central hosted by Jon Stewart ran a collage of clips from Fox, ABC, CBS, NBC and CNN that clearly suggested Obama could be a Muslim.

PRICE $4.50   THE   JULY 21, 2008

THE NEW YORKER

2010s

TIME

9 AUGUST 2010

Managing editor: Rick Stengel
Pakistan/Afghanistan correspondent:
  Aryn Baker
Director of photography & visual enterprise:
  Kira Pollack
Cover photography: Jodi Bieber

"The Taliban pounded on the door just before midnight, demanding that Aisha, 18, be punished for running away from her husband's house. They dragged her to a mountain clearing near her village in the southern Afghan province of Uruzgan, ignoring her protests that her in-laws had been abusive, that she had no choice but to escape ... Her judge, a local Taliban commander, was unmoved ... The commander gave his verdict, and men moved in to deliver the punishment. Aisha's brother-in-law held her down while her husband pulled out a knife. First he sliced off her ears. Then he started on her nose. Aisha passed out from the pain but awoke soon after, choking on her own blood. The men had left her on the mountainside to die," wrote Aryn Baker in the opening paragraphs of her cover story. [1]

JODI BIEBER:

Aisha was in the "Women for Afghan Women" shelter. I had to photograph her there. Shay, my wonderful translator, and I arrived at ten in the morning. We went into a small room where a lot of young women slept. There was a red carpet with scattered cushions around the wall, a radio and one white fan. There was nothing to say, "This is Aisha's space."

I started photographing her but I didn't feel it coming together. I put my camera down and said to her, "Try to think of your inner beauty and your inner strength. I know you'll never forget what happened to you but I want you to try feel your power." She looked up, looked at me in that way, and I took the photo.

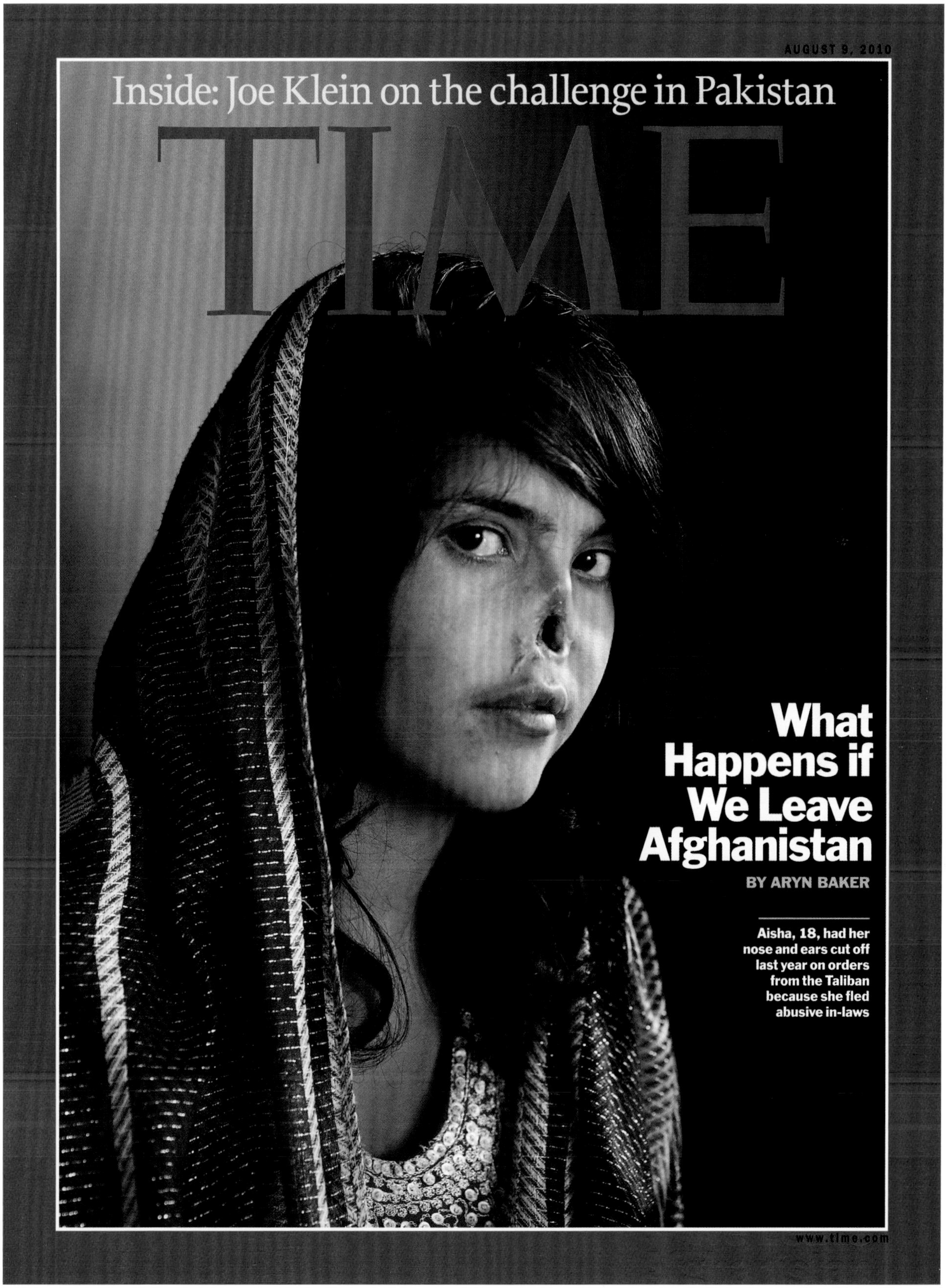
AUGUST 9, 2010
Inside: Joe Klein on the challenge in Pakistan
TIME
What Happens if We Leave Afghanistan
BY ARYN BAKER
Aisha, 18, had her nose and ears cut off last year on orders from the Taliban because she fled abusive in-laws
www.time.com

I thought I had failed because I didn't show her ears in the photograph. I didn't show her as vulnerable. I thought, *Time* isn't going to like the photograph. I was very worried.

KIRA POLLACK:

The picture came in, and I was blown away. I thought, "Wow, what would happen if it became the cover? I showed it to a few top editors, including Nancy Gibbs who was deputy editor at the time. Her feeling was: "What does this do to a child who sees it for the first time? This might be the most violent image a child has ever seen."

Each editor had a different point of view. A lot of people thought it was too much for the cover. Then we showed it to Rick. He was very thoughtful and silent. He did not say no. He brought it home for the weekend. He wanted to see what his wife and two sons, who were then nine and twelve, thought of it. On Monday he said, "I want to do this on the cover."

JODI BIEBER:

It didn't stop there. The headline, "What Happens if We Leave Afghanistan", caused a complete controversy.[2] I was on every TV station you could imagine. Even the Taliban wrote something denying that they were involved. An academic – I think she was from Cambridge – said, how could I objectify Aisha, that she had had her hair done and that I photographed her in a studio. It was so not the truth. People in the West said it was war pornography. And then it won the World Press Photo of the Year 2010.

But Aisha did get to America for a series of reconstructive surgeries at the Walter Reed Hospital in Washington. When you look at the photograph, I think you first see her beauty and then you see her nose. For me, it's about beauty and the beast, the darkness and the light. It's not a record of her; it's an interpretation of her and that could only have come from me. Aisha now lives with an Afghan-American family in the U.S.

---

1 Condensed from Aryn Baker, "What Happens If We Leave Afghanistan", *Time*, 9 August 2010.

2 The lack of a question mark added fuel to the fire of the controversy. As Rod Norland wrote in *The New York Times* on 4 August 2010: "Reaction to the *Time* cover has become something of an Internet litmus test about attitudes toward the war, and what America's responsibility is in Afghanistan. Critics of the American presence in Afghanistan call it 'emotional blackmail' and even 'war porn', while those who fear the consequences of abandoning Afghanistan see it as a powerful appeal to conscience."

VICE

MARCH 2012
Editor-in-chief: Rocco Castoro
Managing editor: Ellis Jones
Art director: Matt Schoen
Photo editor: Serena Pezzato
Cover photography: Maurizio Cattelan
   & Pierpaolo Ferrari

Launched in Montreal in 1994, the now-global free monthly *Vice* was a wildly renegade source of news for millennials. Cover images were extreme, defiant, outlandish. This trio of a toilet plunger, stapler and dildo was created by the Italian artist Maurizio Cattelan and photographer Pierpaolo Ferrari, who together had recently launched *Toiletpaper,* a surrealist bi-annual. For American distribution, *Vice* had to cover the dildo with a peel-off sticker. The UK published it untamed (Figure 14), while Australia, France, Spain and the Netherlands went with an alternative image of cigarette stubs in pink ice cream, also by Cattelan and Ferrari.

ELLIS JONES:

We called this one "The Holy Trinity" issue. Our photo editor then, Serena, helped bring it in for us.

SERENA PEZZATO:

I was a big fan of *Toiletpaper*, so I asked them if they would be interested in having some images published in *Vice*. They said they'd be happy to give us an exclusive preview of the forthcoming issue plus some outtakes. Everyone at *Vice* was super-excited. Maurizio felt very strongly about going with the dildo image because he and Pierpaolo knew that only *Vice* could pull it off. Not many other "regular" magazines could put something like that on the cover and not lose some of their advertisers and/or get criticized by readers and other media. It made sense to everyone at *Vice*, so we saw this as an opportunity to provoke – and to amuse – and to do it together with two incredible artists.

VICE

FREE
VOLUME 19 NUMBER 3

DILDO

FREE
VOLUME 10 NUMBER 3

The only concerns were about the shipping company potentially blocking the magazine deliveries to the subscribers because of the dildo, so we decided to cover it with a sticker. Matt designed the classic censor bar and it worked perfectly. I suggested to write the word "DILDO" on it to play a joke on the whole idea of censorship – rendering the bar a bit useless by saying what was underneath. Maurizio loved it.

I think we all felt like rascals carving a "dirty" drawing on the school desk. Personally, I liked the image because of its simplicity: in a way, it "equalizes" the three objects, so you are invited to forget about their functions and see them for what they are: inanimate material elements in different shapes. On the other hand, the dildo is placed there precisely to disrupt this abstraction and put your brain in a short circuit – a funny one.

MATT SCHOEN:

The sticker was one of those problem-solves that felt less like a compromise and actually helped the issue. When the magazine was distributed in New York, for about a month you would see dildo stickers on signs all over the city.

Figure 14 The cover without its censor bar sticker included.

TIME

21 MAY 2012

Managing editor: Rick Stengel
Design director: D W Pine III
Director of photography and visual
    enterprise: Kira Pollack
Cover photography: Martin Schoeller

This *Time* cover, for a story on attachment parenting, featured 26-year-old Jamie Lynne Grumet of Los Angeles and her son Aram, aged 3. It sparked a firestorm of comments, many of them negative: it was seen as offensive, exploitative, psychologically abusive, a shocking ploy to sell copies and a shameless attempt to stoke up the "mommy wars". Grumet's blog crashed with the weight of traffic. Seth Meyers on *Saturday Night Live* pointed out to *Time* that if they "wanted a great cover, you would have Photoshopped out the chair", which he did and showed the child hanging in mid-air. Seventy-three per cent of respondents to a Today.com poll said they didn't want to see the photograph in the first place.[1]

Managing editor Rick Stengel took to the media to defend the magazine. He told the *Washington Post*: "It's certainly an arresting image. It's an image to get people's attention about a serious subject. Judging by the reaction on Twitter this morning, some people think it's great, and some people are revolted by it."[2]

KIRA POLLACK:

It was a very hard shoot. There were so many awkward parts to the picture. It was a Sunday and the issue was going to close in two days.

MARTIN SCHOELLER:

I wasn't sure how to feel at first about photographing a woman breastfeeding, but it became more intriguing when I heard the child would be an almost

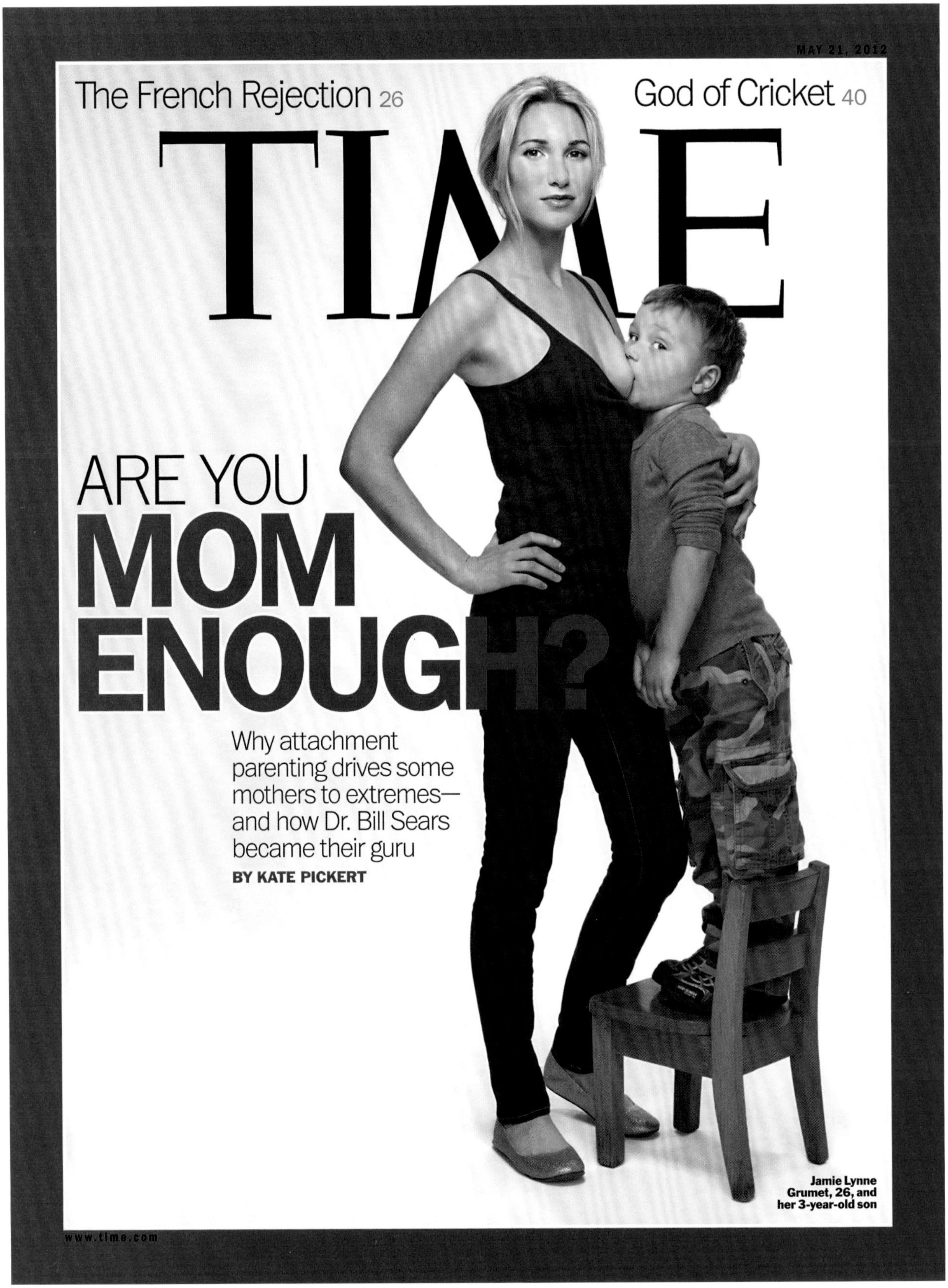
MAY 21, 2012

The French Rejection 26

God of Cricket 40

TIME

ARE YOU MOM ENOUGH?

Why attachment parenting drives some mothers to extremes—and how Dr. Bill Sears became their guru

BY KATE PICKERT

Jamie Lynne Grumet, 26, and her 3-year-old son

www.time.com

four-year-old boy. Especially considering my own son of the same age had not been breastfed for maybe three years by that point.

First I thought I'd do a Madonna breastfeeding kind of portrait, something with a spiritual feeling, but when I pictured how big this boy would look sitting on his mom's lap, I thought him standing would be the most amazing position to emphasize his age. I brought in my son's chair and he stood on that. The boy's dad was a Special Forces police officer, hence the camouflage pants. He was a full-grown kid, running around playing hunting bad guys with his dad in the backyard.

KIRA POLLACK:

Jamie's husband was very big, and she was very petite, and her son took after her husband. So, while he looks a lot older than he is, and he did the day he was born, that juxtaposition really worked well.

MARTIN SCHOELLER:

When I took the picture, it seemed so natural that he was breastfeeding. The mother and son were both happy to do it. Later it dawned on me how controversial this could be. Some people get more upset about breastfeeding than about gun violence. I was surprised by how vilely some people reacted. We all constantly see crazy, gratuitous violence in film and television, but somehow breastfeeding is off limits. That's terrible.

1 Quoted on https://thesocietypages.org/ socimages/2012/05/30/controversy-over-times-are- you-mom-enough-cover/

2 Quoted in Brian Braiker, "*Time* breastfeeding cover ignites debate around 'attachment parenting'", the *Guardian* US news blog, 10 May 2012. https://www. theguardian.com/world/us-news-blog/2012/may/10/ time-magazine-breastfeeding

THE GENTLEWOMAN

AUTUMN AND WINTER 2012

Editor-in-chief: Penny Martin
Art direction and design: Veronica Ditting
Cover photography: Terry Richardson

In 2010 independent Dutch publishers Gert Jonkers and Jop van Bennekom followed their influential bi-annual men's fashion magazine, *Fantastic Man*, with a bi-annual for women, recruiting Penny Martin to help them. This watershed cover paired two very different artists: the 46-year-old provocative fashion photographer Terry Richardson and 86-year-old acting royalty Angela Lansbury. Martin remembers the session as affectionate, funny and mutually respectful.

PENNY MARTIN:

We felt we had to be an antidote to what was out in the market at the time. There was a kind of pornography of femininity in women's magazines. You felt overly familiar with the look of women but you also felt that they were silenced. There was a sense of mediation by the agent, by the retoucher, by the photographer.

We wanted the cover to be a compliment to the sitter. Their personality was first and foremost. We didn't want them to be treated like a makeover where they feel like they're going to be made a fool of, put into clothes they'd never wear, and have their hair and make-up done so they don't look recognizable, and feel like a drag act. Angela was photographed at home in New York in her own clothing.

We needed warm, candid, funny. I'd seen a lot of photographs that Terry Richardson had taken of his mother,[1] and they were respectful and fun. I just felt that he would treat her like somebody who has a lot to say. Angela put on Terry's glasses. That happened on the spur of the moment, though it's a leitmotif that runs through many of his portraits and a kind of hallmark of Angela being

the gentlewoman

Fabulous women's magazine, issue n° 6
Autumn and Winter 2012

UK £6.00

USA $14.99

Angela Lansbury

in on the fun, not feeling like she's projected onto. Her glance says, "I know that you know that I know." It's a really complicit exchange. And she knows she looks fabulous. It's like, "I look hot, and you know it."

When an older woman is photographed in a woman's consumer title, it is often from the side, a bit like a Pietà. Suddenly, it's the really serious piece in the editorial well and it takes all the heat out of the shot. The girls get to be hot and carefree, and the older woman becomes the *grande dame*.

When the pictures came in, there was a kind of strange moment. I don't think it's happened before where we looked at them and started howling with laughter. People love that picture. It's a celebration of female role models, women of purpose. It's almost a political statement.

That cover changed everything. It summed up every ambition we had for *The Gentlewoman* in one shot. It sold like crazy and is one of our most reproduced images. I expected our commercial supporters to feel slightly quizzical about it. The big surprise was when I walked into showrooms in Italy, they'd go, "Ah, *la signora in giallo!*" – the Italian name for *Murder, She Wrote*.[2]

---

1 See *Mom/Dad*, Morel Books, 2010.
2 American crime drama TV series (1984–96) starring Angela Lansbury.

NEW YORK

12 NOVEMBER 2012

Editor: Adam Moss
Design director: Thomas Alberty
Photography director: Jody Quon
Cover photograph: "New York City, October 31" by Iwan Baan

Hurricane Sandy hit the New York region on Monday 29 October, causing a massive power outage. Tellingly, the Goldman Sachs Tower, and the immediate area around it in Lower Manhattan, continued to burn brightly. After 9/11, the finance company had invested in extensive protection against another possible catastrophe. For many, however, there was "nothing so richly symbolic as this display of literal power".[1]

ADAM MOSS:

It was during the last presidential election[2] where the haves and have-nots were a huge theme, and it occurred to us that the theme was also playing out, in a different way, in New York City, where half the city was enshrouded in darkness and half in the light. Jody, who's quite a genius, felt that there was an opportunity to actually capture that by helicopter.

JODY QUON:

On Wednesday morning I said, "We need to take the picture tonight." I didn't know when the power was going to go back on. I knew Iwan took pictures from the air. He's based in Amsterdam, but really he's like a vagabond. He happened to be in town to take pictures of the Parrish Art Museum in Eastern Long Island from the air for its architects, Herzog & de Meuron. He couldn't do it because the museum grounds were flooded. He said he'd love to do this. I said to him, "It'd be great to shoot it from the southernmost tip so that you can get a sense of the blackness, and then you get the lights."

I had not gone through a situation like this before. There were so many variables that I hadn't even thought about, but Iwan had. One was cash machines, which were no longer functioning. He had taken out a few thousand dollars, so he had the cash to charter a helicopter from a company out in Eastern Long Island that was still functioning.

Two, he had already reserved a rental car at the airport so he had wheels to get him out to Long Island. The trains were not functioning.

Is that unbelievable? It gets better. Normally, helicopters can only fly at a certain altitude because of all the planes from La Guardia, Newark and Kennedy. It's very dangerous. But the airports were closed so the pilot got special permission to go higher, so Iwan could get the right angle for the picture. Also, Canon had, by chance, loaned him the most sophisticated, state-of-the-art digital camera.

NEW YORK

The City and the Storm

Starting on p.17

$5.99 USA/CANADA

4 7

0 71658 01912 6

I remember looking at them with Adam the next morning. I was emotional, "Oh, my God, he made the picture."

IWAN BAAN:

The chances for this picture coming together were like one per cent.

When the power went out, I had this impulse to photograph the division in the city: those with power and light, next to those left powerless and in the dark. I've flown above New York countless times, so while on the ground, I knew exactly what I wanted to capture.

A heli-pilot who wasn't on a rescue mission agreed to take me up – if I could make my way to Long Island. While I was driving out there, Jody called me. In the short moment I had her on the phone before the line got disconnected I understood she had the same idea.

I had just acquired the Canon 1D X, which was at that time the most sensitive camera available. Until the 1D X, most cameras had an ISO of 1600 or 3200, but this one could go up to 51200 – meaning I could photograph in almost complete darkness from a vibrating and shaky helicopter.

My work revolves around the built environment: from the commissions I get from architects to the work I do on cities and how they grow, and how people adapt to many different environments. I try to remind people how fragile things can be, and how they can change in a moment. This was one of those unique moments we were able to capture.

ADAM MOSS:

It doesn't look like a magazine cover. It just looks like an amazing picture. When we faded out the logo and did the tiny little headline, it suddenly became a cover and told the story vividly. The response was huge. MoMA made a poster of it.[3]

1   Jessica Pressler, "Goldman Has the Power", *New York*,
     12 November 2012, p.26.
2   The 2012 election between Democrat Barack Obama
     and Republican Mitt Romney.
3   All proceeds from the poster were donated to the
     Mayor's Fund to Advance New York City to support
     Hurricane Sandy relief efforts.

BLOOMBERG BUSINESSWEEK

15–21 JULY 2013

Editor-in-chief: Josh Tyrangiel
Creative director: Richard Turley
Deputy photo editor: Emily Keegan
Features art director: Jaci Kessler

Hedge funders weren't happy with this conflation of high finance and low masculinity on the front cover of *Bloomberg Businessweek*. Josh Tyrangiel issued a statement: "The cover highlights the macho mythology of hedge fund managers, whose returns over the past decade have lagged behind the S&P 500. Yes, we're making them the butt of a joke; we're pretty sure they can take it."[1] There was another cover option – a story on Sears – but, as Turley later said, "It seemed very difficult to escape from this idea once it was hatched."[2]

In 2014 the magazine won a coveted Yellow Pencil at the D&AD (Design and Art Direction) Awards for a series of five covers in 2013 that included this one.

RICHARD TURLEY:

This wasn't just my cover. I did a drawing of a guy with a big penis based on an old *Rolling Stone* campaign, "Perception versus Reality".[3] Huge penis the perception; small penis the reality. Jaci and Emily then got involved.

JACI KESSLER:

I thought about a man standing in front of a chart that happened to have fever lines sprouting from the crotch area. It was clearly representative of penises but using totally mundane graphics.

I couldn't find the perfect guy, and we didn't have time to shoot a character model, so he's made of two stock images: one for his head and one for his body. I didn't want him to look macho or sexual at all, and he had to be fully clothed,

July 15 — July 21, 2013 | **businessweek.com**

Bloomberg Businessweek

Perception

The Hedge Fund Myth p8

Reality

slightly perplexed, unassuming. Although most people probably wouldn't think spending hours searching Getty Images for "man + middle-aged + collared shirt + profile view" is much fun, I loved it.

The arrows started off looking pretty standard – I was trying to have their placement tell the whole story. Richard kept pushing me to make the green one thicker and more rounded. Once that was decided, the red one got droopier and more pathetic-looking until we ended up with this. But I did want it to look pieced together, which is why I went with a flat, bold graphic for the arrows and a black-and-white halftone photo.

RICHARD TURLEY:

Everyone who saw it laughed, which is always a good thing. Josh wrote the cover lines. He had to have a couple of discussions with management but, in the end, they liked it too. There were only 2,000 hedge funders so we didn't care about their reaction.

JACI KESSLER:

I liked that a lot of people thought that we legitimately did not realize what we had done, which is ridiculous.

1 Seth Fiegerman, "'*Businessweek*' Cover May Excite Readers a Little Too Much", *Mashable*, 11 July 2013. http://mashable.com/2013/07/11/businessweek-hedge-fund-cover/#Oud6Yj4p4Gqu
2 "Bloomberg Creative Director Richard Turley dishes on 'The Hedge Fund Myth'" by Katie Myrick Parks, *Society for News Design*, 16 July 2013
3 Landmark advertising campaign created by Fallon in 1985.

ROLLING STONE

1 AUGUST 2013

Editor and publisher: Jann S Wenner
Managing editor: Will Dana
Design director: Joseph Hutchinson
Creative director: Jodi Peckman
Cover photo illustration: Sean McCabe
Cover story: Janet Reitman

On 15 April 2013, two homemade pressure cooker bombs exploded near the Boston Marathon's finishing line in Boylston Street. It was a scene of carnage: three people were killed and more than 250 injured. Police identified brothers Tamerlan and Dzhokhar Tsarnaev as suspects. Four days later, after a shootout which resulted in Tamerlan's death, 19-year-old Dzhokhar was captured, and formally charged on 22 April. *Rolling Stone* investigated. The magazine had a long and award-winning history of in-depth hard news stories. It published the cover online before the article which put the immediate focus on Dzhokar's picture – the same picture that *The New York Times*, for example, had run on its front page of 5 May 2013 with no backlash.

Rolling Stone faced a barrage of abuse and criticism: that it glamorized a suspected terrorist; that by cropping in on his tousled hair, brooding eyes and Armani Exchange T-shirt, it turned him into a kind of young Jim Morrison; that it endorsed Tsarnaev in the sense that a *Rolling Stone* cover denotes success and confers cultural importance. Some asked why the victims weren't on the cover. Others pointed out that Tsarnaev hadn't been convicted yet and that "The Bomber" cover line seemed to forget that a person is innocent until proven guilty. Boston Mayor Tom Menino suspected *Rolling Stone* had done it for publicity. CVS, the pharmacy chain, would not sell the issue "out of respect for the victims of the attack and their loved ones".

Rolling Stone issued a statement: "Our hearts go out to the victims of the Boston Marathon bombing, and our thoughts are always with them and their families. The cover story we are publishing this week falls within the traditions of journalism and *Rolling Stone*'s long-standing commitment to serious and thoughtful coverage of the most important political and cultural issues of our day. The fact that Dzhokhar Tsarnaev is young, and in the same age group as many of our readers, makes it all the more important for us to examine the complexities of this issue and gain a more complete understanding of how a tragedy like this happens." The issue doubled its newsstand sale.

JANN WENNER:

That was the news picture. It was an old photograph of that kid. I mean he looked so young and cute and innocent and that was the point of the story – the innocence of youth. It got us in an enormous amount of trouble because he looked so innocent.

I guess because he had long hair people say he looked like a pop star. If it had been on some other magazine other than *Rolling Stone* they wouldn't have said that. He's a kid who got caught in this turmoil, the system and lack of opportunity, and his brother's madness, and got torn apart.

JODI PECKMAN:

The image is from his Facebook page and was by no means something the entire world hadn't seen already. The decision to use it on the cover was simple. It was the only one that would have worked for clarity and instant recognizability. Not much else existed.

It wasn't meant to be the cover of that particular issue, but the story was huge. We had exclusive material and Janet Reitman, one of our best reporters, wrote it. So we went with this cover.

Sean didn't do much to the image, just enhanced it for clarity. It was a muddy image and he may have put a slight filter on it. We were blowing it up so big that some sharpening – for lack of a better word – was needed. There was no discussion about making him look better. It was more about trying to make it print better.

I had a hard time understanding the response. I mean, I understood the way people felt about this guy, but we didn't put him on the cover to make him look like a rock star. We put him on the cover because he was news, the same way we put Charles Manson on the cover back in the Seventies.[1] It's not like we liked the guy, for Chrissake.

1 *Rolling Stone* 61, 25 June 1970.

RollingStone

Issue 1188 >> August 1, 2013 >> $4.99
rollingstone.com

On the Bus With WILLIE NELSON

THE ARCTIC ICE MELT
REPORT FROM THE FRONT LINES OF CLIMATE CHANGE

JAY-Z's 'Magna Carta' Stumble

ROBIN THICKE
Pretty Fly for a White Guy

GARY CLARK Jr.
The Reluctant Guitar Hero

THE BOMBER

How a Popular, Promising Student Was Failed by His Family, Fell Into Radical Islam and Became a Monster

O

THE OPR

MAGAZI

AN O EXTRAVAGANZA!

Let's
Talk About
HAIR!

Everything You Need to Know to

- Grow It • Blow It • Awesomely 'Fro It
- Boost the Bounce • Beat the Frizz
- Handle the Gray and...

Have a Great Hair Day!

The
**Guilt-Free
Snack,**
pg. 114

**What's
Really Healthy**
Surprising News
From Dr. Oz

**Spread
Too Thin?**
Smart Advice
for the Seriously
Frazzled

**She Smokes,
She Smooches,
She Dances in
Bell-Bottoms!**
Behind the Scenes
of Oprah's New Movie

O, THE OPRAH MAGAZINE

SEPTEMBER 2013

Founder and editorial director:
    Oprah Winfrey

Editor-in-chief: Lucy Kaylin

Creative director: Adam Glassman

Cover photography: Ruven Afanador

A full afro had not been seen on the cover of a mainstream American women's magazine in a while. *O* was launched in April 2000 by Hearst and Oprah Winfrey, the entertainment mogul and philanthropist. This image of the magazine's founder hit a national nerve, prompted "Froprah" mania and clocked up over 337 million media impressions.[1] The issue won two National Magazine Awards in 2014.[2]

LUCY KAYLIN:

The topic of hair is often handled in a superficial way, despite its deeply personal, psychological and political implications. And every ethnicity has its own hair issues – something we wanted to explore for our very diverse readership. The idea was to start a big, fun, frank conversation about something that's on all of our minds.

As for the cover, we thought, "Let's see if Oprah would collaborate on a really bold hair moment". Adam Glassman, our cover magician, knew a wig maker, Kim Kimble, who'd no doubt come up with something cool. Andre Walker, Oprah's long-time hairstylist, was the "wig wrangler", and did an amazing job making it look natural on Oprah. Luckily, our cover model was very much into it. That was the secret sauce: Oprah's enthusiasm.

ADAM GLASSMAN:

We made it as big and curly as possible. It was like, "OK, I want to be liberated and wear my hair natural like it is when I come out of the shower." We'll do an exaggerated version of that. That conversation about wearing your hair more naturally really started after this cover.

The wig came in bubble wrap on a headstand in a special bright-pink travel box. It was like the unveiling of the crown jewels. We listened over and over again to the soundtrack of *The Lion King*. Oprah wanted that because she felt like this lioness with this mane of hair. I originally wanted it really stripped down, no jewellery at all, but Oprah is a jewellery person.

When we showed it to people before we went to press, they were very divided by it. Some asked if it was too much of a political statement. It really was not the intention.

LUCY KAYLIN:

That day on the set was just a blast. Oprah looked gorgeous when this 3lb wig landed on her head. She called it "wild thing". The wig was almost like another person. It required care and feeding.

This cover had the drama, the joy, the edge, the beauty that I wished for, and readers loved it. A lot of women of colour thought it was very liberating for this particular hairstyle to be celebrated in this manner because, of course, we all remember a time when to have a fully grown-out afro was a political decision. Along with a lot of other things from the 1960s and 1970s it was associated with racial strife. In the ensuing years, a lot of women of colour decided on their own or, in some cases, felt pressure to straighten their hair or subdue their curls, and that has a socio-political edge to it. This cover was "Yeah, this is beautiful."

Chris Rock really was an impetus for us. As he so smartly laid out in his documentary,[3] our hair is a deep and divisive and difficult issue. That's why this cover came across as this clarion call. It was celebrating the fact it's all good: you be you, have fun with whatever's growing out of your head.

1 Sourced from "Best Cover Contest 2014 Winners & Finalists", *ASME (American Society of Magazine Editors)* website. http://www.magazine.org/asme/magazine-cover-contest/past-winners-finalists/2014-winners-finalists
2 For "Leisure Interests" and "Best Cover Contest" in the Women's Service section.
3 *Good Hair* (dir. Jeff Stilson, 2009), narrated by Chris Rock.

THE BIG ISSUE

**"REMEMBRANCE DAY" SPECIAL,
3 NOVEMBER 2014**

Editor: Paul McNamee
Cover photograph: Bryan Adams
Cover subject: Sgt Rick Clement

Remembrance Day, which honours those in the armed forces who died in the line of duty, has a special resonance for *The Big Issue*. Between 8 and 10 per cent of its street vendors are ex-forces. The year 2014 was even more poignant, when the commemoration observed three major conflicts – the 100th anniversary of the start of World War I, the 70th anniversary of the D-Day landings, and the end of Britain's conflict in Afghanistan.

PAUL MCNAMEE:

I wanted something about the here and now, about men and women who had come back from serving with life-altering injuries. Not those who died serving, but those who have to live with incredible problems.

Through some weird links, I got to know Bryan Adams who had a book called *Wounded*.[1] He had spent time photographing the injuries of soldiers who had lost limbs – or much worse. I asked him if we could we use some of his imagery. He agreed and I settled on that particular image of Sgt Rick Clement, who lost his legs in Afghanistan in 2010 when he stepped on a Taliban roadside explosive device. He lost everything below the waist and died twice as docs fought to save him. His injuries were so severe that he shouldn't have been alive.

It's such a brilliant, arresting photograph. When you look at it first, you see a man in a dress uniform, sitting down. Then you realize he has no legs: his body is cut in half. I thought, that's the reality of what we're talking about. They go away as happy young boys and they come back with no limbs. It's classic-looking but at the same time shocking.

It was shortlisted for the PPA[2] Awards "British Cover of the Year", which is voted for by the public. We won. I think people reacted very honestly to it. They weren't looking at it professionally, saying things like "That's the right point size." So that was particularly good.

There was an incredibly emotional outpouring from everybody, a standing ovation, as Rick accepted the award with Bryan. Rick was delighted. He's quite deadpan. He said, "It's great to be in a room where there's more people legless than I am." I imagine that's a line he's used before but it's still a good line.

When he was in the rehabilitation hospital, he said he was determined to walk, and they said, "There's no chance, nothing exists for this." But they developed very expensive advanced prosthetics legs for him so he could actually stand up. He wanted to walk to the Cenotaph for the following Remembrance Sunday – and he did. That meant that the next year we could do a cover of him standing up. So the circle of the story was completed.

1 Bryan Adams, *Wounded: The Legacy of War. Photographs by Bryan Adams*, Steidl 2013.
2 Professional Publishers Association.

This is now.
We must not forget.

THE BIG ISSUE

EVERY MONDAY £2.50

SERGEANT RICK CLEMENT, 34

LONDON | November 3-9, 2014 No. 1127 | A HAND UP NOT A HANDOUT

ESSENCE

FEBRUARY 2015

Editor-in-chief: Vanessa K. De Luca
Creative director: Erika N Perry

#BLACKLIVESMATTER surfaced in 2013. The brainchild of Alicia Garza, Patrisse Cullors and Opal Tometi, it quickly became a rallying call for the black community to protest against racial inequality and police brutality. When 12-year-old Tamir Rice died from a gunshot wound in Cleveland in November 2014, *Essence*, the respected monthly for African American women, decided that it had to take a stand. They "invited activists, thought leaders and cultural figures to reflect on the meaning of this moment, and what we must do next".[1] It was their first celebrity-free, pure-type cover since their launch in 1970.

VANESSA K. DE LUCA:

One of our junior editors reached out to me and said, "How are we going to address this? We are all reeling from what it's doing to our community, what it's doing to our own psyches." I called the editors together and we started challenging each other about what we could do, what we should do. Could this be a cover? Can we do this under this corporate umbrella of Time Inc., quite honestly?

We couldn't agree, but that was a good thing because it meant that we're not all monolithic in how we see this BLACKLIVESMATTER idea. There were people who felt we should go all the way, radical. There were others who felt like no, there are ways to utilize this moment to drive change within existing social structures, within the justice system. It's like comparing the Black Panthers and Martin Luther King Jr. It's like two totally different parts of the spectrum.

We thought we have to try to find voices that represent all of those things. And it's up to the audience to decide where you land. It really was as if somebody pumped new life and breath into each one of us. We made our dream list of people. We had young people from the New York Justice League. We had the three young women who invented the hashtag. We had Reverend Al Sharpton for a different perspective as a civil rights leader and icon. We had Pulitzer Prize-winning author Isabel Wilkerson, who wrote a beautiful opening essay. We had Common and John Legend, who were extremely topical because of the movie *Selma*[2] and their song "Glory" that was up for an Oscar. It worked out well for us that February was Black History Month.

Erika and I finally decided on a pure-type cover. I thought, "As this is the first time we're doing this, let's go for broke," and it very easily became black and white with the hint of red. The treatment is graphic and spare in an issue that is just fraught with so much emotion. We wanted it to be in your face. Like you cannot turn away. This was not about selling anyone anything. It was about we want to do something – could this be a start?

We had over 41 million media impressions with people sharing the cover on Instagram, and black Twitter going crazy. Shonda Rhimes shot me an email and just said, "Yes." This is where our vision and our values came together quite clearly.

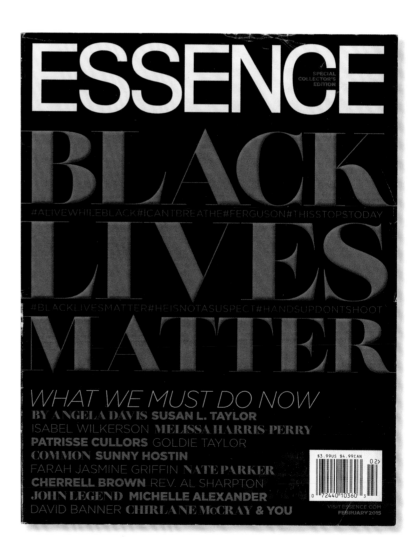

1 Introduction to the cover feature, "Black Lives Matter", February 2015, p.90.
2 *Selma* (dir. Ava DuVerney) was based on the voting rights marches from Selma to Montgomery in 1965. It was released in the USA on 9 January 2015.

ZEIT MAGAZIN

28 MAY 2015

Editor-in-chief: Christoph Amend

Creative director: Mirko Borsche

Art director: Jasmin Müller-Stoy

Designer: Mirko Merkel

Guest editor: Mohamed Amjahid

Cover caption: "Every day, people start out in the hope of a better life. We dedicate this issue to you. An especially large number of the refugees coming to Germany are from Arab countries /That's why ZEIT magazine appears in German and Arabic."

Weekly newspaper *Die Zeit* launched Germany's first magazine supplement in 1970. Christoph Amend, who became editor in May 2007, introduced a double cover, two consecutive photographs, illustrations or type treatments that make a pithy point. This was a special on refugees that Simon Kuper from the *Financial Times Weekend* read "open-mouthed" because it "presented refugees not as helpless mute victims on sinking boats but as grown-up humans with insights into their adopted country".[1]

CHRISTOPH AMEND:

I had the idea in the last days of 2014 when I read the first reports about refugees making their way to Central Europe. To edit, design and produce the issue was highly sensitive, so we hired Mohamed as a guest editor.

MOHAMED AMJAHID:

All the text had something to do with the new lives of refugees in Germany: learning a new language, fighting German bureaucracy, getting over homesickness and facing racism. The issue featured many new citizens, not only those from Arabic-speaking countries. However, *Zeit Magazin* decided to publish the texts in Arabic and German since most of the arriving people in 2015 spoke Arabic as their mother language.

JASMIN MÜLLER-STOY:

We split every page into two. Arabic type is read from right to left so it was difficult to lay out because our InDesign wasn't able to type the Arabic font in the right direction. We had to figure out how to turn the cover in one direction so you can read it as German, and turn it in the other direction to read it as Arabic.

MOHAMED AMJAHID:

I sometimes turned the monitors upside down because it was easier or I printed the pages out, putting them in the middle of the room and running in circles.

I am one of the few German journalists who speak Arabic as a mother language and I was the only one at the magazine who could read the issue. I felt a huge pressure. It was hard to translate the texts so they correspond and make sense at the same time.

JASMIN MÜLLER-STOY:

It was tricky to choose a colour for the cover. We first thought about green, but not all Arabian countries have green in their flag and we didn´t want anybody to feel excluded. So we decided to take a neutral colour. Yellow seemed to be perfect. Mohammed helped us find a font which looked modern.

We had this idea to use the first pictures that refugees took in Germany inside. The refugees really appreciated this gesture. We tried to do extra copies so they could get them. We took the magazine to several refugee camps in Germany.

MOHAMED AMJAHID:

Was there a message? Refugees welcome. Many German subscribers were amazed. Of course, some right-wing supporters complained that "their Germany will disappear now" because we had published in Arabic.

CHRISTOPH AMEND:

We never had so many requests from organizations and schools for extra copies. Friends from the magazine industry in New York wrote, saying, "We could never do that in America." It was quite a ride to publish half of a magazine that you can't read yourself.

---

1 *Financial Times Weekend*, 19 June 2015.

ZEIT MAGAZIN

Jeden Tag machen sich Menschen auf den Weg, in der Hoffnung auf ein besseres Leben. Ihnen widmen wir dieses Heft. Besonders viele Flüchtlinge kommen aus arabischen Ländern nach Deutschland

ZEIT MAGAZIN

ينطلقون كل يوم لأنهم يطمحون فـي حيـاة أفـضل. نـحن نهدي لــهــم هــذا العــدد. إن أكثرية اللاجئيــن في ألمانيا يتكلمون اللغة العربية

ZEIT  MAGAZIN

Nr. 22, 28. Mai 2015

Deshalb erscheint dieses ZEITmagazin
auf Deutsch und Arabisch

ܩܛܪܠ ܝܢܡܪܝܬ ܐܝܪܡܪܐ ܦ ܐܪܡ ܟܬܪܠ ܘ ܩܬܪܠܠܝ ܝܢܐ
ZEITmagazin ܝܢ ܚܡܪܐ ܐܝܗ ܚܐܦ ܩܝ ܡܐܝܢ ܚ ܐܢܡܪ ܡܦܝ ܩܝܡܪ

VANITY FAIR

"Call me Caitlyn"

by BUZZ BISSINGER *Photos by* ANNIE LEIBOVITZ

VANITY FAIR

JULY 2015

Editor: Graydon Carter
Features editor: Jane Sarkin
Fashion and style director: Jessica Diehl
Deputy editor: Dana Brown
Associate managing director: Ellen Kiell
Photograph of Caitlyn Jenner by
    Annie Leibovitz, styled by Jessica Diehl.

This was a milestone: the first cover with an openly transgender woman – Caitlyn Jenner. For the previous 65 years she had lived as Bruce Jenner, all-American hero, Olympic gold medallist and, most recently, reality TV star. To safeguard its exclusive, the magazine implemented a military-style level of planning and security. Only eight people knew about it and they could only use one computer, which was always offline, to work on the gigantic 11,000-word, 22-page feature. Condé Nast claims that more than 46 million people accessed content that related to the cover story on social media within the first 24 hours. The issue sold more than 430,000 on the newsstand, making it *Vanity Fair*'s best-selling issue for five years.

CAITLYN JENNER:

It was a very long decision with a lot of people, family, friends, relatives, God, my pastor. So many people who deal with gender dysphoria can sneak away, do what they have to do to live their life authentically, and then slowly work their way back into life, but because I was getting destroyed by the tabloids, I couldn't do that. It was so important that it was done right.

Vanity Fair was to be the first time that you learned my name and there would be the pictures. That couple of days of the shoot were the most fulfilling of my life. It was overwhelming. Annie was even crying at one point. My girl. I love Annie. The whole crew, the hair, the makeup, Jessica who did the styling, everybody really took it seriously because they knew the impact this could have on the marginalized trans world.

The cover was shot in my garage. We had to do everything in total secrecy. I had to put up walls around my house because the paparazzi were taking pictures from the surrounding mountains. We had security all over the mountains kicking people out.

I had this beautiful black off-the-shoulder Zac Posen dress that fit perfectly. Annie said, "Let's take a mirror and put it in behind the camera so you can see what we're trying to do here." I started crying. I had struggled for so long with identity, and that was the first time I looked in the mirror and liked what I saw. After it was over, the whole crew applauded.

The response was 99 per cent extraordinarily positive. And the article by Buzz Bissinger[1] was very important. He's a Pulitzer Prize-winning writer and was with me for three months writing that article. We did the book together.[2] The media kind of threw old Bruce under the bus, gone.

My biggest criticisms have been from the trans community. I got hammered for taking my appearance seriously. I get photographed every day, I try to dress properly. The trans community go: "What about all the people that can't do that, that don't have the money like this rich white girl to get things done that they need to get done? That's not representing our community." I think that, if you can present yourself in a positive manner where people are not uncomfortable around you, that helps everybody.

I am also criticized for being a conservative Republican. How can you be a conservative Republican and be trans? It's easy.

1   H G (Buzz) Bissinger, who wrote *Friday Night Lights* (Adison-Wesley, 1990), the story of a small town American football team, was chosen because he had a sports background and personal experience of cross-dressing.

2   Caitlyn Jenner, *The Secrets of My Life*, Trapeze, 2017.

ATTITUDE

JULY 2016

Editor: Matthew Todd
Art director: Peter Allison
Cover photographer: Leigh Kelly

A lifestyle monthly for gay men, British *Attitude* launched in 1994 and became famous for groundbreaking cover exclusives like David Beckham in 2002, when he was captain of England's national football team, and Tony Blair in 2005, the first time a serving British prime minister had spoken to a gay magazine. But this took it to another level. "The importance of a member of the royal family posing for the cover of a gay magazine for the first time cannot be overstated."[1]

MATTHEW TODD:

The cover has a lot to do with my experience of growing up as a gay man in the 1980s and feeling very alone. So to see Princess Diana then, even though she never explicitly said anything supportive of gay people, go to Mildmay Hospice, the HIV and AIDS hospice in London, and shake hands with people with AIDS was just incredible.

In 2012 I did a big feature on homophobic bullying and met quite a lot of parents of kids who'd been bullied. One young boy had killed himself. I did an interview with his father and, a few months later, he also took his own life.

I thought, "This is insane. Who could talk about this?" The royal family seemed like the obvious people. I wrote them a letter. These things take a long time but we started an ongoing discussion. Their Royal Highnesses are very keen not to be seen as celebrities. For them to engage with something, they have to have a genuine understanding of it.

In 2015 Prince William took part in a training session in Hammersmith about dealing with homophobic bullying as part of an initiative with the Diana Award. So, somewhere along the way, I like to think me writing to them may have provoked a genuine interest in the issue. Then, in early 2016, Kensington Palace agreed to the cover and invited us to bring some young LGBT people to tell Prince William what happened to them.

The focus of this cover and the feature inside was on LGBT mental health, because mental health is something that the Duke and Duchess are campaigning on. Their "Heads Together" campaign is something they're absolutely, totally, 100 per cent committed to. There are higher levels of addiction, anxiety, depression and suicide among LGBT people, so they wanted to engage with that.

We wanted to make sure that we had a really diverse mix of people, so we took a transgender person, a person who identifies as non-binary, two young gay black men, a young man who had an eating disorder, a lesbian woman who runs a youth project, a young Muslim man and Mena Houghton, the mother of a young gay man who died after years of homophobic bullying.

I've met prime ministers and superstars, but there's something very different about royalty. It might sound a bit crass but the only way to describe it is that it felt like there was a real sense of goodness about Prince William and an awareness of how he wanted to use his position. He genuinely wanted to help. Some of the young people were nervous so he was laughing and making jokes and telling us about how he'd been on the set of *Star Wars* to put us all at ease. He could not have been more charming. It was surreal.

It was my last issue as editor as well, so that was really great. I saw it as a very political cover. I was very aware that it would be seen all over the world, so we wanted to present a simple, stark message that would have impact. In the 1980s there was absolute savagery towards gay people; this is saying the opposite, that it's accepted and mainstream and that the highest figures in our society are supportive of it.

---

1 Matthew Todd, in interview with Ian Birch.

THE UK'S BEST-SELLING
& AWARD-WINNING
GAY MAGAZINE

ATTITUDE.CO.UK
JULY 2016 £4.85
@attitudemag

attitude

MAKING HISTORY

PRINCE WILLIAM MEETS ATTITUDE

"NO ONE SHOULD BE **BULLIED** FOR THEIR **SEXUALITY** OR ANY OTHER REASON"

07
9 771353 187045

NEW YORK

July 27–Aug. 9, 2015

Alleged assault: ca. 1960s   In 1967   In 1969   In 1969   In 1969   In 1969   In 1969   Ca. 1970   Ca. 1970   Ca. 1970

In 1971   In 1973   In 1975   In 1975   In 1976   In 1977   In 1978 and 1980   In 1979   Ca. 1979   In 1981

In 1982   In 1982   In 1984   Ca. mid-1980s   Ca. mid-1980s   In 1985–87   In 1986   In 1986   In 1987   Ca. 1987

Ca. late 1980s   Ca. late 1980s   In 1989   Ca. early 1990s   In 1996

Cosby:
The Women
An Unwelcome
Sisterhood

By Noreen Malone
A Portfolio by
Amanda Demme

NEW YORK

27 JULY–9 AUGUST 2015

Editor: Adam Moss
Design director: Thomas Alberty
Photography director: Jody Quon
Cover photographs: Amanda Demme
Cover story: Noreen Malone

In October 2014 a clip of stand-up comedian Hannibal Buress's routine in which he called Bill Cosby a rapist[1] went viral. This was not the first time "America's Dad"[2] had been accused of sexual misconduct. In 2005 ex-basketball star Andrea Constand made allegations against him, triggering a dozen women at the time to come forward with their own stories of assault.

The Buress clip galvanized more women to speak out; Cosby denied any wrongdoing. By the following July, there were 46 women, 35 of whom were willing to be photographed and interviewed for the magazine. In many ways, this cover presaged the "Me Too" movement that erupted two years later.

ADAM MOSS:

Jody felt very strongly that the Cosby accusers were not being taken seriously enough, and that there was an opportunity to gather as many of them as we could in one place, and to reframe the story in terms of the large numbers of people who had, one by one, come forward. She began against quite a bit of scepticism on my part that she'd be able to do this.

Very gradually, one person would say yes, and then another person, hearing that that person said yes, would do it. It took six months. There were a lot of reasons that they were reluctant to come forward. They were frightened. They weren't sure that they weren't somehow culpable. When we interviewed them, a lot of their feelings about their stories were quite the same.

JODY QUON:

I really couldn't believe it. I was a huge Cosby fan; I grew up with him. He was definitely a television role model. I went on the internet and made little dossiers of all the women who had come forward. I put them in chronological order by the year in which they said the incident happened. It went from the 1960s to basically the present. They were from all over the country and of every background and age. The list kept growing.

There was a little bit of resistance; no one could feel certain about how to evaluate the credibility of their stories. And this was also on the heels of the UVA *Rolling Stone* article.[3] I said, "Let me just cold call half a dozen of them." Six out of the six women that I found wanted their voices heard. They were so raw it was really moving.

Our strategy was to photograph the women in two different, unified colour schemes – black and white.[4] We didn't want the clothes to detract from who they were. Amanda, God bless her, came up with the idea to shoot them seated, feet on the ground, hands forward, ready. Almost like in a Western – "I'm ready for the duel."

AMANDA DEMME:

I wanted it to represent taking back power but in a very elegant way. It wouldn't have looked good in colour because every one of these ladies had a different tonality and the whole idea was that it had to look uniform. I am OCD. I have to have everything in straight lines, in grids. It's sort of military. I had everyone take off their jewellery, pretty much. And there was very little hair and make-up, and no mirrors so you could tszuj yourself. When they strip themselves of everything, they become super-powerful.

Most of them had never seen each other before and had never been in front of a professional photographer in their life. And they had a lot to say. They had been living with that secret for all those years. They felt so much anger but also hyper energy that they were finally going to be heard. I just said to them, look at me. You have to trust me. What I want everyone to see is your pain but not pity. You finally have your power.

In my presentation to the magazine, the empty chair was there just to show we had an uneven number and we needed one or three more people. But the magazine channelled my brain and turned that empty chair into an open seat. It was their time to have their voice and that's why it worked.

JODY QUON:

We didn't want any smiling for the whole portfolio. It was about empowerment. This was their moment, super-graphic. There was every emotion at every shoot

– crying, sadness, anger and then, at the end, exuberance. A sisterhood evolved. There was an incredible bonding, something we didn't even think to anticipate. Then the news broke of Andrea Constand in early July[5], and Adam decided to make it the cover.

ADAM MOSS:

"The Women" became the bold text and the word "Cosby" was done in this faint type, and was meant to very subtly give the ownership of the cover to the women. At sort of the last minute, we decided to do this chronologically and to insert the dates of the alleged assault. We had a chair that no one was in and the design director, Tom, just threw it on one version. We immediately understood the metaphor that it represented.

It became a hashtag, #theemptychair. Twelve thousand people participated (within the first 24 hours), and many of them described their own abuse stories, so it wasn't just about those people who had something to say about Bill Cosby. The empty chair became, in effect, what the whole story was about.

The impact was enormous. I've never seen a cover have as much of a public service role, per se. This was a piece of political activism. Ten more women came forward after this, and then it prompted various innovative legal strategies. Cosby didn't think he needed law enforcement at this point – because of the statute of limitations and various other things. Activist lawyers, newly enraged, devised new methods to bring some justice. The cover did, I think, reintroduce the case, and bring a kind of intensity to the consideration of it, and that's what I think a great cover can do. It can change a conversation.

1 Buress said: "He [Cosby] gets on TV, 'Pull your pants up black people, I was on TV in the 80s! I can talk down to you because I had a successful sitcom!' Yeah, but you rape women, Bill Cosby, so turn the crazy down a couple notches."

2 His role as Dr Cliff Huxtable in the 1980s hit sitcom *The Cosby Show* turned him into a cultural icon.

3 Sabrina Erdely, "A Rape on Campus", *Rolling Stone*, 12 November 2014. The magazine retracted the article, about an alleged group sexual assault by fraternity members at the University of Virginia (UVA), in April the following year.

4 These appear in the feature inside.

5 In 2005 Constand brought a civil case against Cosby, accusing him of drugging and molesting her. He defended himself in a deposition which was unsealed ten years later by a federal judge in Philadelphia on Monday 6 July 2015.

TIME

Meltdown.

TIME

22 AUGUST 2016
24 OCTOBER 2016

Managing editor: Nancy Gibbs
Design director: D W Pine III
Director of photography & visual enterprise:
  Kira Pollack
Cover illustrations: Edel Rodriguez

As soon as the July National Conventions were over, Donald Trump went on an extraordinary tear. He lashed out at the parents of a Muslim American soldier killed on duty in Iraq; he called President Barack Obama the "founder of ISIS". The Republican Party seemed in turmoil. *Time* responded with the "Meltdown" cover. Then, on 7 October, the *Washington Post* released a video showing Trump and TV host Billy Bush engaged in a crass conversation from 2005. *Time* responded with "Total Meltdown". As Mike Lupica commented: "You put those two covers together and it looks like he's the Wicked Witch of the West. He's shrinking and melting at the same time."[1] Rodriguez distils Trump into what he calls a "simple branding device" of lurid yellow hair, orange skin and braying mouth, which he has subsequently developed for more coruscating covers of *Time* and *Der Spiegel*. "He (Trump) loves *Time* magazine," Rodriguez later commented. "That's my main pleasure, knowing that these people are looking at it and it's ruining their day."[2] Many of Rodriguez's anti-Trump drawings appear on placards in street protests. He has made the artwork downloadable for this purpose.

EDEL RODRIGUEZ:

With the first Trump, everybody needed to vent. It had been a year of putting up with this nonsense, this awful human, and finally someone made an image. I just happened to be the person that delivered it. And it wasn't in an indie like the *Village Voice*. It was in *Time*. About 50 per cent of the problem is to get a big publication like *Time* to have the guts to publish something like that.

D W PINE III:

It was a Friday and Michael Scherer, our Washington bureau chief, was on the phone, talking about Trump. He said, "It seems like he's just melting down." I thought, "That's a visual." I talked to Edel over the weekend and he came back with a couple of versions.

On Monday our concern was, "Were we being fair? Was Meltdown too much?" On Tuesday there was another Trump blunder so we thought, "We're fine."

The challenge with the illustration was to make it look like Trump. Obviously, the orangey skin and those gold locks of hair help, but what did it for me was the simplicity of his mouth – open, and talking emphatically, no matter what, as the drips come down his face.

EDEL RODRIGUEZ:

That image is like a one-liner. If you're going to throw one-liners at me, I'm going to throw a one-liner at you. A good magazine cover should be able to take a complicated matter and communicate it directly to as many people as possible. I try to make something simple that speaks over a long term.

It's important to provoke a feeling, but if you just have a feeling without any intellectual backing, that's propaganda and I don't want to do that. I come from Cuba and grew up surrounded by meaningless political posters.

D W PINE III:

The Trump–Billy Bush incident enflamed everybody here. The focus of our story was how Trump was debasing his own party. I asked Edel if he wanted to take the GOP's elephant logo and do a similar kind of dripping treatment with it. Then, our story became more about how Trump was really going off the rails, especially when you compared him to a traditional candidate. But we don't live in traditional times. I said to Edel, "Why don't we have him completely melting down?" Within about a couple of hours, we came up with "Total Meltdown".

Trump never commented about these covers and yet he has on almost every other cover we have done. The "Total Meltdown" cover went on to win the ASME[3] cover of the year.

1   Mike Lupica on *Morning Joe*, MSNBC, 13 October 2016. Lupica is an author and columnist for the *New York Daily News* and an MSNBC contributor.
2   Katharine Schwab, "Meet The Preeminent Illustrator of the Trump Era", 16 January 2018. https://amp. fastcodesign.com/90157026/meet-the-preeminent-illustrator-of-the-trump-era?__twitter_impression=true
3   The American Society of Magazine Editors.

TIME

Total
Meltdown.

PRIVATE EYE

11–24 NOVEMBER 2016

Editor: Ian Hislop

Shortly after Gina Miller and Deir Dos Santos launched a legal challenge to the British government about triggering Article 50, which would start the countdown for the country to leave the European Union, *Private Eye* published this cover. There was an avalanche of frenzied complaints. One reader wanted to "shove our smug opinions so far up our asses that we choked our guts out – which was sort of charming in its way".[1] Another, a vicar, "told me it was time to accept the victory of the majority of the people and to stop complaining. Acceptance is a virtue, he said. I wrote back and told him this argument was a bit much coming from a church that had begun with a minority of twelve. Or you could say with a minority of one on Good Friday when all the others ran away."[2]

IAN HISLOP:

Nev Fountain and Tom Jamieson, two of our writers, came in with the bus fully formed. They had a yellow bus and I changed it to a decaying red bus just to match the pictures up. The bus was rusting in a field somewhere up in, I think, northern Scotland. It was a brilliant metaphor – the old music hall joke, the wheels have come off the bus, but done with the original Brexit bus with the big lie on the side. This is literally as the Brexit process runs into the sand.

It was a very, very striking cover, but it was a very, very annoying cover for a huge number of people who wrote in and said they thought we were attacking the Health Service or various things like that, but it was pretty clear what it was about. They were very cross indeed. I think there were certainly some people who've come to politics a bit late, or they've come to being passionate about politics a bit late, and usually with a single cause like Scottish nationalism – or they joined UKIP.[3] They're outraged that anyone disagrees with them, and outraged that anyone should laugh. Everything is so polarized and I think social media has made people ruder and less tolerant and less willing to argue the case, rather than just state an opinion or say, "It should be banned."

You can't just ban everyone you don't like. That's not really how it works. And, again, if you've won the election or you've won the referendum, that doesn't mean everyone has to shut up for ever. The argument goes on – that's the other bit of democracy.

1 Ian Hislop, "The Right to Dissent (and the Left Too)", George Orwell Lecture 2016, University College London, 15 November 2016.

2 Ibid.

3 The right-wing, populist UK Independence Party, which since its foundation in 1993 campaigned for UK withdrawal from the EU.

PRIVATE EYE

No. 1431
11 November –
24 Nov 2016
£1.80

BREXIT LATEST

THEN

NOW

INDEX

PICTURE CREDITS

10, 12 courtesy of ONE Archives at the USC Libraries; 14 courtesy Hearst Magazines; 16al courtesy Hans Döring, Munich; 16bl image courtesy Robin Benson; 20, 23 courtesy Haymarket Media Group Limited; 25 Marilyn Monroe photos by Bert Stern with permission of The Bert Stern Trust; 26, 30, 31, 35 courtesy Hearst Magazines and George Lois; 28, 29, 33, 34 courtesy George Lois; 37, 38 reproduced by kind permission of PRIVATE EYE magazine – www.private-eye.co.uk and Gerald Scarfe; 41 courtesy the Herb Lubalin Study Center; 43 courtesy Hearst Magazines; 46 LIFE logo and cover design © Time Inc. LIFE and the LIFE logo are registered trademarks of Time Inc used under license. Photo © Lawrence Schiller; 48 The Sunday Times / News Licensing; 51 The Sunday Times / News Licensing, photo © Don McCullin/Contact Press Images; 53 © TIME INC. (UK) Ltd; 54 David Bailey / Vogue © The Condé Nast Publications Ltd.; 58 Michael Ochs Archives/Getty Images; 60, 61 courtesy International Times Archive and http://internationaltimes.it/; 63 courtesy Haymarket Media Group Limited and Dave Dye; 67 Courtesy Dr Huey P. Newton Foundation, image: University of Virginia Library, Special Collections; 68 Courtesy Dr. Huey P. Newton Foundation, image: Alexander Street Press; 70 LIFE logo and cover design © Time Inc. LIFE and the LIFE logo arc registered trademarks of Time Inc. used under license.; 74–75 photo courtesy of the University of Wollongong Australia; 77 © TIME INC. (UK) Ltd.; 81 British Library, London / © British Library Board. All Rights Reserved / Bridgeman Images; 84–85 Courtesy of BMP Media Holdings, LLC.; 86, 89 Marty Dundics and National Lampoon, Inc.; 90, 92, 93 courtesy Time Out; 95 © Pennie Smith; 99 PEOPLE magazine © 1974 Time Inc. All rights reserved; 101 Francesco Scavullo/Vogue © Condé Nast; 102 © 2017, by John Holmstrom and PUNK Magazine, Inc; 107 courtesy New York Media, cover art by James McMullan; 108 Willie Christie / Vogue © The Condé Nast Publications Ltd; 109 © Willie Christie; 111 courtesy Radio Times and Ralph Steadman; 115 Bauer Consumer Media; 118 courtesy Françoise Mouly; 122 courtesy i-D; 125 © 1981 by Rolling Stone LLC. All Rights Reserved. Used by Permission; 129 courtesy Mix Mag Media; 131 Steve McCurry / National Geographic Creative; 132, 134, 135 courtesy Hearst Magazines; 137 courtesy Carla Sozzani; 138, 141 © Sussex Publishers LLC, courtesy Alexander Isley; 144 courtesy Mix Mag Media, photo © Corinne Day/Trunk Archive; 149, 150 courtesy Colors Magazine; 153 © Annie Leibovitz/Trunk Archive; 157 courtesy Hearst Magazines; 159 © 1992 by Rolling Stone LLC. All Rights Reserved. Used by Permission; 163 courtesy Hearst Magazines; 165 © Neil Selkirk; 167 courtesy Raygun Publishing LLC, image courtesy Jaap Biemans; 169 © The Economist Newspaper Limited, London (September 10th 1994); 173 © TIME INC. (UK) Ltd; 175 Reproduced by kind permission of PRIVATE EYE magazine – www.private-eye.co.uk; 177 Courtesy Amy Schrier; 179 © Laura Levine; 183 From The New York Times, 18 June 2000, © 2000 The New York Times. All Rights Reserved. Used by permission and protected by the Copyright Laws of the United States. The printing, copying, redistribution, or retransmission of this Content without express written permission is prohibited. Photo © Chris Anderson/Magnum; 185 From The New York Times, 23 September 2001, © 2001 The New York Times. All Rights Reserved. Used by permission and protected by the Copyright Laws of the United States. The printing, copying, redistribution, or retransmission of this Content without express written permission is prohibited. Courtesy Julian Laverdiere and Paul Myoda.; 186a courtesy Julian Laverdiere and Paul Myoda; 186b courtesy Fred Conrad; 189 Art Spiegelman/The New Yorker © Condé Nast; 192, 193 courtesy Ashley Heath, photo © Steven Klein/ArtPartner; 195 ENTERTAINMENT WEEKLY logo and cover design © Time Inc. ENTERTAINMENT WEEKLY and the ENTERTAINMENT WEEKLY logo are registered trademarks of Time Inc. used under license; 198 courtesy Barry Blitt; 199 Barry Blitt/The New Yorker © Condé Nast; 203 © 2010 Time Inc. All rights reserved. TIME and the TIME logo are registered trademarks of Time Inc. Used under license; 206-208 this cover, by Maurizio Cattelan and Pierpaolo Ferrari, first appeared in the March 2012 issue of VICE Magazine; 210 © 2012 Time Inc. All rights reserved. TIME and the TIME logo are registered trademarks of Time Inc. Used under license; 213 courtesy The Gentlewoman, Autumn and Winter 2012, photographed by Terry Richardson; 216 courtesy New York Media, photo Iwan Baan; 219 used with permission of Bloomberg LP © 2017. All rights reserved.; 223 © 2013 by Rolling Stone LLC. All Rights Reserved. Used by Permission; 224 Ruven Afanador / Harpo, Inc, courtesy Hearst Magazines; 229 courtesy The Big Issue, photo © Bryan Adams/Trunk Archive; 231 courtesy Essence; 234, 235 ZEIT MAGAZIN # 22/2015; 236 Annie Leibovitz/Vogue © Condé Nast; 241 courtesy Attitude Magazine, photo Leigh Keily; 242 courtesy New York Media, photo Amanda Demme; 246, 249 © 2016 Time Inc. All rights reserved. TIME and the TIME logo are registered trademarks of Time Inc. Used under license; 251 reproduced by kind permission of PRIVATE EYE magazine – www.private-eye.co.uk

Cover photo: davincidig/iStock

ACKNOWLEDGEMENTS

First, a big thank you to everybody I interviewed for your participation, enthusiasm and, of course, for letting me tell your stories.

Unless credited to other sources, all the quotes come from interviews I did throughout 2016 and 2017. With *One*, all the major protagonists had died so I talked to Craig M Loftin, Lecturer in American Studies at California State University, Fullerton, who has written widely about the period and the magazine.

For advice, support, insights, contacts and access to personal archives, a second big thank you to Jaap Biemans, Mark Blackwell, Marissa Bourke, Cath Caldwell, David Carey, Nicholas Coleridge, Ian Denning, Mark Ellen, Simon Esterson, Malcolm Garrett, Chris Heath, Suzanne Hodgart, Andrew Hussey, James Hyman, Richard Morton Jack, Jeremy Leslie, Mark Lewisohn, Shari Kaufman, Terry Mansfield, Terence Pepper, Jane Pluer, Marcus Rich, Kathy Ryan, Dave Rimmer, David Robson, Jon Savage, Jim Seymore, Peter Steinfels, Suzanne Sykes, Neil Tennant, Craig Tomashoff, Michael Watts, Fred Woodward and Wendy Wolf.

A third big thank you to my agent Juliet Pickering, Damian Horner who started the ball rolling, and the folks at Octopus: Pauline Bache, Joe Cottington, Sophie Hartley, Giulia Hetherington and Hannah Knowles.

The biggest thanks must go to my family – to my sons, William for his original thinking, and Matthew for his steady encouragement, but most of all to my wife, Markie, without whose support, understanding and copy skills this book would never have seen the light of day.

ABOUT THE AUTHOR

Ian Birch began his magazine career in the mid 1970s at *Time Out* in London before becoming a music journalist first at *Melody Maker* and then at *Smash Hits*.

He joined British *Elle* shortly after its launch, created *Sky* magazine and moved to New York in the Nineties to edit *Us* for Jann Wenner. He came back to the UK to become an editorial director at Emap where he helped launch *Red*, *Closer* and *Grazia*, and re-launch *Heat*.

In 2004 he returned to New York to edit *TV Guide*. He worked for Hearst on both sides of the Atlantic before becoming editorial director at Hearst UK where he oversaw such publications as *Cosmopolitan*, *Good Housekeeping*, *Esquire* and *Harper's Bazaar*. He received The Mark Boxer Award, awarded by the BSME (British Society of Magazine Editors), for outstanding services to the industry.

An Hachette UK Company
www.hachette.co.uk

First published in Great Britain in 2018 by Cassell, an imprint of Octopus Publishing Group Ltd
Carmelite House
50 Victoria Embankment
London EC4Y 0DZ
www.octopusbooks.co.uk

Text copyright © Ian Birch 2018
Design and layout copyright © Octopus Publishing Group 2018

ISBN 978-1-84403-904-3

A CIP catalogue record for this book is available from the British Library.

Printed and bound in China

10 9 8 7 6 5 4 3 2 1

Commissioning editors Hannah Knowles and Joe Cottington
Senior editor Pauline Bache
Senior designer Jaz Bahra
Picture research manager Giulia Hetherington
Picture researcher Sophie Hartley
Typesetter Ed Pickford
Copyeditor Robert Anderson
Production controller Dasha Miller